GOING ASTRAY

DICKENS AND LONDON

GOING ASTRAY

DICKENS AND LONDON

Jeremy Tambling

PEARSON

Longman

Harlow, England • London • New York • Boston • San Francisco • Toronto
Sydney • Tokyo • Singapore • Hong Kong • Seoul • Taipei • New Delhi
Cape Town • Madrid • Mexico City • Amsterdam • Munich • Paris • Milan

PEARSON EDUCATION LIMITED

Edinburgh Gate
Harlow CM20 2JE
United Kingdom
Tel: +44 (0)1279 623623
Fax: +44 (0)1279 431059
Website: www.pearsoned.co.uk

First edition published in Great Britain in 2009

The right of Jeremy Tambling to be identified as author of this work has been
asserted by him in accordance with the Copyright, Designs and Patents Act 1988.

ISBN: 978-1-4058–9987-1

British Library Cataloguing in Publication Data
A CIP catalogue record for this book can be obtained from the British Library

Library of Congress Cataloging in Publication Data

Tambling, Jeremy.
    Going astray: Dickens and London/Jeremy Tambling.
        p.   cm.
    Includes bibliographical references and index.
    ISBN 978-1-4058-9987-1
    1. Dickens, Charles, 1812-1870—Knowledge—London (England)   2. London (England)—In
literature.   3. City and town life in literature.   4. London (England)—Civilization—19h century.
I. Title.
    PR4592.L58T36 2008
    823′ .8—dc22

    2008028584

10   9   8   7   6   5   4   3   2   1
13   12   11   10   09

Set in 9.5/13 pt ITC Century Book by 35
Printed by Ashford Colour Press Ltd., Gosport

The Publisher's policy is to use paper manufactured from sustainable forests.

CONTENTS

LIST OF MAPS

PREFACE AND ACKNOWLEDGEMENTS

Going Astray: Dickens and London reflects an ongoing fascination with Dickens, which started abstractly enough by considering his relationship to Benthamite Utilitarianism and Romanticism. F.R. Leavis' analyses of Bentham in relation to Dickens were significant and influential here, of course, but it was a turn in my thinking when I read Michel Foucault on Bentham, in *Discipline and Punish*, and saw how the Panopticon, that fantasised prison-house which would do everything for society, worked by architecture, and this was, then, a way of creating how people think and behave: 'Morals reformed, health preserved, industry invigorated, instruction diffused, public burdens lightened, economy seated, as it were, upon a rock, the Gordian knot of the Poor Laws not cut but untied – all by a simple idea of Architecture!' (Bentham quoted Foucault, 207). From here it was a step to considering the city, as both architectural creation, and as necessarily, anti-architecture. I wrote about this in an essay which Stephen Wall generously accepted for *Essays in Criticism* (1986), and which became part of a monograph on Dickens, *Dickens, Violence and the Modern State: Dreams of the Scaffold* (1995), and continued to think about it through a book called *Henry James: Critical Issues* (2000) which involved discussion of James on New York's architecture, but which was intended to lead into a bigger project. This appeared with the title *Lost in the American City: Dickens, James, Kafka* (2002). It compared Dickens on the American scene with James, with much discussion of the American prison at Philadelphia, which both Dickens and James visited. How Kafka imagined the American urban, in *Der Verschollene*, i.e. 'The Man Who Was Never Heard of Again', which is better known by Max Brod's title, *Amerika*, was its third part. On completing this book, and coming upon a title, which of course quotes from Dickens' essay 'Gone Astray', I noticed a compulsion to repeat at work, because of course *Going Astray* echoes my American book's title. And since night thoughts are a form of going astray, it may be relevant that I also wrote about Blake's London in my monograph *Blake's Night Thoughts* (2004), and research for that leads into this present work on Dickens and London, which relies on that previous work, and draws on it.

This earlier writing happened while I was teaching in the University of Hong Kong, a locale allowing me to consider the colonial Asian city. T this appear in a book on the Chinese, ex-Portuguese colony of *Macao, Reading the Baroque* (2008), which I co-authored with took the photographs of the city which attempt to give a sense

– baroque spaces, folds and interleavings of different spaces – in a city which is, as great cities are, unrepresentable, impossible to capture. Louis Lo has also taken photographs for this book, so bringing interest in urban theory to the consideration of another, non-Asian city, and I am grateful for the insights that he has given: making the selection from over 2000 photographs was hard indeed. The difficulty with London is that it has been photographed and imaged endlessly: a library visit, or an internet search will quickly reveal images of everything that I discuss in this book; the task, then, has been to find images which will not seem like every other image, but which will show London in ways that de-centre the reader's expectations of the city.

My warmest thanks are due, then, to those who have helped with the book. They include those who have showed me London, or walked it with me, some over many years; in particular the late Graham Martin, and Colin Davies, giving the comments of a scientist. I must thank Chris Barlow and Malcolm Andrews; they both read a draft of the text, making very helpful comments. I thank also Pam Morris, always inspirational on Dickens, for reading the chapters, though I have not stolen her suggestion, which I am sure is right, that Bradley Headstone and Eugene Wrayburn are two sides of Dickens in different moments of his career, in conflict with each other. Brian Worthington, who taught me *Little Dorrit* at 'A' Level, also helpfully read the chapter on that novel. Chapter three was first read in draft at a *Dickens Quarterly* conference at Edinburgh in 2004; and I am glad to have met Dickens scholars there who have been a source of encouragement, such as David Paroissien. And Malcolm Andrews has been wonderfully supportive throughout, as has Michael Hollington. At the University of Manchester, colleagues who have helped with discussion and information include Malcolm Hicks, Roger Holdsworth, Jeremy Gregory. I must also thank Jan Piqqott, for clarifying some points of detail. Also I thank Philip Langeskov for being such an ideal publisher, especially in his vision for the book and desire to make it a reality, and for marshalling six readers whose clarity of comments have been in inverse ratio to my ability to work out their identity. Thanks are due to Colin Reed for the layout of the book. I must thank Pablo Tsui and Ian Fong who both helped as research assistants in Hong Kong, and the staff of the University Library there, and in Manchester, Rose Goodier and the John Rylands library of Manchester. And thanks to Paul Fung, for assistance in preparation of the manuscript. I am grateful to John Fisher, Jeremy Smith, Michael Melia and Jason Burch at the Guildhall Library in the City of London, Jo Wisdom at St Paul's Cathedral, and the Image and Design Department at London Metropolitan Archives for help in providing me with the maps which appear in the book. (The Collage image database of the Guildhall will supply many other images and maps for the interested.) I am grateful to the museum of the Royal Bethlem Hospital in Beckenham, South London, for their guardianship of the Cibber statues of melancholy and madness which have so much motivated the thinking in this book. Paragraphs of material on *Sketches by Boz* appear in different forms in a chapter on the prison in Dickens and Charles Reade, in a book edited by Jan Alber, *Stones of Law: Bricks of Shame*, to be published by Toronto University Press (2008). Members of my immediate family have supported and encouraged me in many ways: Pauline, to whom the book is dedicated, with everything, and much more besides, Kirsten with her own enthusiasms which entailed us looking at Samuel Richardson's London, Felix for walking the city and photographing, and developing his own extensive knowledge of London.

Publisher's acknowledgements

The publishers are grateful to the Guildhall Library, City of London, for permission to reproduce the maps of London in the plate section.

NOTE ON TEXTS

The citations of Dickens below are taken from the new Penguin editions, both for convenience of reference, because they have good notes and accurate texts, and because in the case of Cruikshank and Phiz, they both use the full range of illustrations. Other Dickens texts which do not appear in the Penguin have been cited below, with the abbreviations used in the book. Further editions of Dickens which have been used, usually because they have excellent notes or introduction, appear in the Bibliography. Throughout the text, a reference is first cited in the text with a full endnote citation; after that a short reference appears either in the text or the endnote, and the reader is referred to the Bibliography for full details.

AN	*American Notes*, ed. Patricia Ingham, 2000.
BR	*Barnaby Rudge*, ed. Gordon W. Spence, 2003.
BH	*Bleak House*, ed. Nicola Bradbury, 2003.
CB	*Christmas Books* 2 vols, ed. Michael Slater, 1971.
DC	*David Copperfield*, ed. Jeremy Tambling, 2004.
DS	*Dombey and Son*, ed. Andrew Sanders, 2002.
ED	*The Mystery of Edwin Drood*, ed. David Paroissien, 2002.
GE	*Great Expectations*, ed. David Trotter and Charlotte Mitchell, 2003.
HT	*Hard Times*, ed. Kate Flint, 2003.
LD	*Little Dorrit*, ed. Stephen Wall and Helen Small, 2003.
MC	*Martin Chuzzlewit*, ed. Patricia Ingham, 1999.
NN	*Nicholas Nickleby*, ed. Mark Ford, 1999.
OCS	*The Old Curiosity Shop*, ed. Norman Page, 2001.
OT	*Oliver Twist*, ed. Philip Horne, 2003.
OMF	*Our Mutual Friend*, ed. Adrian Poole, 1997.
PP	*The Pickwick Papers*, ed. Mark Wormald, 2000.
PI	*Pictures from Italy*, ed. Kate Flint, 1998.
SSF	*Selected Short Fiction*, ed. Deborah A. Thomas, 1976.
SB	*Sketches by Boz*, ed. Dennis Walder, 1995.
TTC	*A Tale of Two Cities*, ed. Richard Maxwell, 2003.
CS	*Christmas Stories*, ed. Margaret Lane (Oxford: Oxford University Press 1956).
HR	*Holiday Romance and Other Writings for Children*, ed. Gillian Avery (London: Everyman 1995).
J1	*Sketches by Boz and Other Early Papers, 1833–39*, ed. Michael Slater.

J2	*The Amusements of the People – Reports, Essays and Reviews, 1834–5*, ed. Michael Slater.
J3	*Gone Astray and Other Papers from Household Words, 1851–59*, ed. Michael Slater.
J4	*Dickens' Journalism: The Uncommercial Traveller and Other Papers 1859–1870*, ed. Michael Slater, and John Drew.
Letters	*Letters of Charles Dickens*, ed. Madeline House and Graham Storey, 1965–2002 12 vols (Oxford: Oxford University Press).
Life	*The Life of Charles Dickens*, by John Forster (1872–74), ed. J.W. T Ley (London: Cecil Palmer 1928).
MHC	*Master Humphrey's Clock and Other Stories*, ed. Peter Mudford (London: Everyman 1997).
MP	*Miscellaneous Papers* 2 vols (London: Chapman and Hall) (Gadshill Edition of the Works of Charles Dickens, 1906–08); reprinted with an introduction by P.J.M. Scott (Millwood, NY: Kraus-Thomson 1983).
Speeches	*The Speeches by Charles Dickens*, ed. K.J. Fielding (Oxford: Oxford University Press 1970).
UT	*The Uncommercial Traveller and Reprinted Pieces*, ed. Leslie C. Staples (Oxford: Oxford University Press 1958).

INTRODUCTION
Going Astray: Dickens and London

Dickens' daily walks were less of rule than of enjoyment and necessity. In the midst of his writing they were indispensable, and especially, as it has often been shown, at night. Mr Sala is an authority on London streets, and [. . .] has described himself encountering Dickens in the oddest places and most inclement weather, in Ratcliffe-highway, on Haverstock-hill, on Camberwell-green, in Gray's-inn-lane, in the Wandsworth-road, at Hammersmith Broadway, in Norton Folgate, and at Kensal New Town. 'A hansom whirled you by the Bell and Horns at Brompton, and there he was, striding out, as with seven-league boots, seemingly in the direction of North-end, Fulham. The Metropolitan Railway sent you forth at Lisson-grove, and you met him plodding speedily towards the Yorkshire Stingo. He was to be met rapidly skirting the grim brick wall of the prison in Coldbath-fields, or trudging along the Seven Sisters-road at Holloway, or bearing under a steady press of sail underneath Highgate Archway, or pursuing the even tenor of his way up to the Vauxhall-bridge road'. But he was equally at home in the intricate byways of narrow streets as in the lengthy thoroughfares. Wherever there was 'matter to be heard and learned', in backstreets behind Holborn, in Borough courts and passages, in City wharfs and alleys, about the poorer lodging-houses, in prisons, workhouses, ragged-schools, police-courts, rag-shops, chandlers' shops, and all sorts of markets for the poor, he carried his keen observation and untiring study. 'I was among the Italian boys from 12 to 2 this morning', says one of the letters. 'I am going out to-night in their boat with the Thames Police', says another. '[. . .] For several consecutive years I accompanied him every Christmas Eve to see the marketings for Christmas down the road from Aldgate to Bow; and he had a surprising fondness for wandering about in poor neighbourhooods on Christmas-day, pass the areas of shabby genteel houses in Somers or Kentish Towns, and watching the dinners preparing or coming in'.

Life 11.3.836–37

I

London. London's streets, its people, its crowds, its buildings. It is Dickens' constant subject, from his early journalism, *Sketches by boz*, to *The Uncommercial Traveller*, from his first novel, *Pickwick Papers*, to the unfinished *The Mystery of Edwin Drood*. The range of the London his writing absorbs can be gauged from his biographer, John Forster (1812–76), quoting Sala. It shows that the novelist not only knew and used London, but that it was an obsession for him. And, it seems from Sala, *walking* London, not using the new Underground system, which, opening in 1863, ran between Paddington and Farringdon Road.

And, because this is Dickens, he is not simply walking but *writing* 'London', which means he is writing *about* London, and, by writing, creating London. As

Whistler said about painting Brussels, that its inhabitants had no idea of its beauty, 'I will have to invent their town for them as I did the Thames for the Londoners'.[1] The same could be said of Dickens. And 'writing London' is a pun: London also writes, constructing Dickens.[2]

London in cliché has become 'Dickensian': OED dates the word from 1881, ten years after his death. The journalist Walter Bagehot (1826–77) noted the special relationship:

> Mr Dickens' genius is especially suited to the delineation of city life. London is like a newspaper. Everything is there, and everything is disconnected. There is every kind of person in some houses, but there is no more connection between the houses than between the neighbours in the lists of 'births, marriages and deaths'. As we change from the broad leader to the squalid police-report, we pass a corner and we are in a changed world. This is advantageous to Mr Dickens' genius. His memory is full of instances of old buildings and curious people, and he does not care to piece them together. On the contrary, each scene, to his mind, is a separate alertness of observation that is observable in those who live by it. He describes London like a special correspondent for Posterity.[3]

Bagehot is right, while underestimating how much Dickens *does* affirm connections. But London is not just explicitly Dickens' subject, nor his content, it is the origin of his art, producing its poetry, writing Dickens. But however much of 'heritage' interest there may be in Dickens, in films and in television, there is no immediate approach for us to that source; we can only return to the clichés of what London looks like. In Huysmans' novel, *A Rebours* (1884), Des Esseintes decides, on a whim, to visit London. But he wanders into an English bar in Paris for a drink:

> He drifted into a daydream, calling to mind some of Dickens' characters, who were so partial to the rich red port he saw in glasses all around him, and peopling the cellar in fancy with a new set of customers – imagining here Mr Wickfield's white hair and ruddy complexion, there the sharp, expressionless features and unfeeling eyes of Mr Tulkinghorn, the grim lawyer of *Bleak House*. [. . .] The Londoner's home as described by the novelist – well lighted, well heated and well appointed, with bottles being slowly filled by Little Dorrit, Dora Copperfield or Tom Pinch's sister Ruth – appeared to him in the guise of a cosy ark sailing snugly through a deluge of soot and mire. He settled down comfortably in this London of the imagination, happy to be indoors, and believing for a moment that the dismal hootings of the tugs behind the Tuileries were coming from boats on the Thames.[4]

Even though this representation of 'the Dickens world' does not include Dickens' working-classes and people on the verge of ruin, it suggests how early ...ble image of Dickens as the novelist of middle-class London has ...ders. Present-day London offers little access to that Dickens and ...tes that Dickens records may be there still by accident, but their ... gone, like many of the specific buildings which are discussed. ...r Huysmans' gentle Dickensian parody, Henry James (1843–1916) noted the historical break between Dickens and then contemporary London, writing about Christmas week in 1888, 'when the country houses are crowded at the expense of the capital', 'then it is that I am most haunted with the London of Dickens, feel most as if it were still recoverable, still exhaling its queerness in patches perceptible to the appreciative'.[5] Apart from the modernisations of London at the end of the nineteenth century, which eliminated many places Dickens wrote about specifically, no attempt to revisit Dickens' sources can get beyond the Blitz of 1940. Not can it penetrate the destruction wrought by post-war urban planning, pulling down markers of nineteenth-century London: the Euston arch (1837), James Bunstone Bunning's Coal Exchange (1849) and Blake's birthplace in Soho being small examples.[6]

One novel, *Hard Times* (1854), varies the rule that Dickens writes exclusively about London. Intensely urban, it is set in 'Coketown', an anonymous Lancashire mill-town, Manchester or Preston. But that is like a colony of London: Mr Gradgrind, its capitalist, becomes a Member of Parliament, so he moves up from Coketown, while Mr Harthouse patronises it as a London snob. Otherwise, overwhelmingly, Dickens responded to London, not statically, but as it altered during his writing years. Many novels give a pre-railway London of the 1820s and 1830s. *Pickwick Papers* (1836–38) is set in 1827. *Bleak House* (1852–53) is of the 1830s. *Little Dorrit* (1855–57) is specifically of 1825. The year 1824 was memorialised in *David Copperfield* chapter 11, when Dickens was twelve and worked in the blacking-factory. That is also the period of *Great Expectations* (1860–61). In contrast, *Our Mutual Friend* (1864–65) and *The Mystery of Edwin Drood* (1869–70) both use the railway, even more than *Dombey and Son* (1846–48), but its existence is implicit from *Pickwick Papers*, when it turns Shakespeare's 'The course of true love never did run smooth' (*A Midsummer Night's Dream* 1.1.134) into chapter 8's title, 'Strongly illustrative of the Position, that the Course of True Love is not a Railway'. Dickensian London was disappearing before the novels appeared: the Preface to *Little Dorrit* knows that, noting how the Marshalsea had completely vanished. Today, whoever tries to find Dickens' London on the ground, will find it substantially gone: fragments only remain, as suggested by the photographs included here to help invent that vanished London.

The topic, then, is Dickens and London, and for the next two sections of the Introduction I will give reasons for thinking it significant. The final section gives specific hints on how the book should be read, and used.

II

Why should we, living in the twenty-first century, in a multi-ethnic – indeed, post-colonial – London, driven mainly by finance and business services, be interested in the configuration of Dickens' London? Is it not nostalgia? Nostalgia means looking back on something that never existed, and refusing to live in the present: the danger is that looking at Dickens' London produces an eccentric disregard of the historical processes that have shaped the city, and makes for a readership who simplifies Dickens along with the city, which is looked at only for its Dickensian past. And is not the idea that there can be some access back to a London of the past 'essentialist', meaning by that word that it presupposes some ahistorical quality to 'London' which survives through all changes, and which can cause it to be described as a unity? Has there ever been a single London? What continuity is there between the Strand of 1827 – the year of Blake's death, the fictional year of the *Pickwick Papers* and known to us only through historical representations – and the Strand today?

Perhaps being able to think about the London that has been called Dickensian acts as a critique of the present London as a world city. It suggests that the old city, with its problems, can critique the new. London now, with huge inequalities of wealth (top directors paid 113 times more than the average UK worker), which are more massive than anywhere else inside the country of which it is the capital, is part of two divisions: one North–South, and the other capital versus provincial, and part of a geography of inequality, which has produced the danger of making all other places in Britain seem irrelevant in comparison to it. And disparities between London and the regions are more than matched by increasing inequalities inside London's boroughs. Indeed, they have exacerbated them. London has the highest incidence of child poverty, a wider gender pay gap, more homelessness and overcrowding, and more disparities in life chances than any other region. Women in Kensington and Chelsea live nearly six years longer than women in Newham, men from these first two areas six years longer than men from Southwark. The success of London as a 'global city' rests on these inequalities.[7] These reflections on the present-day city, as overlarge, and cannibalistic on the rest of the country on which it nonetheless depends, make it quite different from the Victorian city, which was never so monolithic in comparison to Birmingham, or Manchester, or Liverpool, but there are also continuities. Mr Wemmick's reflection that he was new to London once (*GE* 21.111) – his father came from Liverpool – suggests how the city has pulled people towards it not just because of its attraction (as for Pip), but because it has created poverty outside it: the Irish after the Famine drawn to London's slums in *Bleak House* indicate that.

In *Our Mutual Friend*, Mr Podsnap's question to the foreigner 'How Do You Like London?', saying that it is 'Very Large' and 'Very Rich', suggests the tie-up between government laissez-faire (present-day neoliberalisation) and London's wealth. Podsnap asks: 'And Do You Find, Sir ... Many Evidences that Strike You, of our British Constitution in the Streets of the World's Metropolis, London, Londres, London?' His question is quite empirical, like one part of this book, because the inquiry is related to the streets, not to anything theoretical or abstract: 'I Was Inquiring ... Whether You Have Observed in our Streets as We should say Upon our Pavy as You would say, any Tokens –'. The word 'tokens' he glosses, for the foreigner, as 'Signs', 'Appearances', and 'Traces' (*OMF* 1.11.135–36). Taking the hint from Mr Podsnap, this suggests that the streets can be read for *signs*, i.e. for indications of what cannot be seen, perhaps because it has been repressed. Also, they are to be read for what is on the surface, for its *appearances*, for what can be seen. Third, the streets can be read for their *traces*, as the foreigner has done, when he has found obvious evidences of horses having been in them. The alliance of horse-dung, or dung of any kind, with money is not merely a key to *Our Mutual Friend*, but shows what the Constitution is worth, in its promotion of London as having its streets paved with gold. So Mr Dorrit thinks of 'the golden street of the Lombards' (*LD* 2.16.645). Mr Podsnap can see that is the way the conversation is going, so he does not pursue his question: he specialises in not knowing what he does not want to know about.

The word 'traces' leads also, by association, to what the philosopher Jacques Derrida (1930–2004) calls 'the trace', an idea alluded to with the corpse of Nemo, in *Bleak House*, found dead in chapter 10 of the novel, and, as a victim of London's poverty, never seen by the reader while he was alive:

> And, all that night, the coffin stands ready by the old portmanteau; and the lonely figure on the bed, whose path in life has lain through five-and-forty years, lies there, with no more track behind him, that any one can trace, than a deserted infant. (*BH* 11.173)

'Track' and 'trace' are, of course, etymologically linked. There are traces associated with Nemo, however, which, once discovered, in the form of love-letters, will lead to the threat of blackmail that runs through this text. The 'trace' means, as it does in Derrida, the pre-existence of writing which has inscribed the street, the human body, and the city alike. All these have the signs of writing upon them, the markers of history; the city is textual throughout, not accidental, not just there, but culturally produced, and to read the streets is the aim of urban analysis. With Dickens, it is not possible to read his streets literally, but his novels show the trace, invisible markers of how the city has been culturally constructed, the memory of history, much of it repressed.

Streets are the sphere of interest of the sociologist Henri Lefebvre (1901–91), whose work on 'everyday life' appeared in a book on urban space, *The Production of Space*, which insists on the idea that space (including in that term what we understand by places, zones and areas) is not pre-given; we do not start with it; it comes into existence as a result of social forces which produce it. Space cannot be thought of either abstractly, or geometrically (having natural perspectives), but as what is inhabited in ways where borders define it, and dictate social relationships and subjectivity. Lefebvre discusses three conceptual modes for thinking about space: (a) spatial practice, (b) representations of space, and (c) representational spaces, which might be better called spaces of representation. 'Spatial practice' means how people make sense of space in their everday lives, how people perceive and use their space. Representations of space refer to how people conceive space, for example by mapping it. Spaces of representation means how space is lived, and imagined, 'changed and appropriated'.[8] This book will give many examples of people's use of space, for instance, in the habitual journeys they take between office and home. Space is mapped throughout; the city is seen as complete, as when Wemmick names the six bridges of London 'as high as Chelsea Reach' (*GE* 2.17.291). And people appropriate space, even the prison, or, with the garden at the top of the offices in St Mary Axe (*OMF* 2.5.276).

Going Astray: Dickens and London explores how Dickens' texts perceive the space of London, how they map it, aware of its contrasts, and how they imagine space as comprising areas characterised by different moods which create character. But not all spaces are representable, or mappable. Some are so incomprehensible that they cannot be made sense of: the point applies to Mrs Todgers' servant Tamaroo in *Martin Chuzzlewit* whose general 'total lack of comprehension' makes her 'a perfect Tomb for messages and small parcels; and when dispatched to the Post-Office with letters, had been frequently seen endeavouring to insinuate them into casual chinks in private doors, under the delusion that any door with a hole in it would answer the purpose' (*MC* 32.479). These letters provide a classic case, in London, of 'going astray'. The significance of space – which creates the necessity for letters and indeed for the Post-Office – has been neither realised, nor mapped. Tamaroo does not live within urban space; she has been overwhelmed by it.

While Lefebvre requires noting how people can represent space to themselves, *Martin Chuzzlewit*'s sense of people living in urban space tests the sociologist's divisions, as with Mrs Gamp's description of how to reach the mythical Mrs Harris: 'Mrs Harris through the square and up the steps a turnin round by the tobacker shop' (*MC* 40.588). This creation of spatial relationships which she believes in indexes Mrs Gamp's mind as not single but split. As there is no way to find Mrs Harris, there is no way to map Mrs Gamp's mind. Though she thinks in terms of spatial relationships, there is still an *aporia* in her thinking, i.e. a gap, a space which cannot be bridged or crossed to reach Mrs Harris: her directions are not complete. Architects think of spaces with no aporias between them, as do town planners, as Dickens' illustrator Phiz shows in the American section of *Martin Chuzzlewit*, picturing, on a map, 'The thriving town of Eden, as it appeared on paper' (*MC* 21.339). (The town, of course, has not yet been built.) Space in *Martin Chuzzlewit*, 'chuzzles' the wit, whatever that means – perhaps a stronger form of 'puzzles' – by being both vertiginous and labyrinthine, so it must be appropriated, tamed. Architecture is a means of expressing dominance over it, like the splendid offices of the Anglo-Bengalee Disinterested Loan and Life Insurance Company, with its main offices with massive blocks of marble in the chimney-pieces, and a parapet on the top of the house (*MC* 27.410–11).[9] Dickens' novels define space, map it, and attempt to change it, but they include at their centre awareness of the aporia: i.e. that all systems of thought, all maps, all narratives, can only be constructed by ignoring an uncanny space inside them. Reading Dickens in and on London, then, must respond to a double demand. One sees the space created in the novels as responding to London as a pre-given, social reality which, however intimidating, must be faced. The other is intrigued by the possibility of finding other spaces, not mappable, in that given space of the city.

III

Cities have increasingly come to the forefront in arguments about post-modernism, post-colonialism, and globalisation. They may be industrial, or capital, or new and planned, or old, 'colonial city', or 'world city', or 'global city', or 'post-colonial city', marked by modernity and by an ancient past. They may be unknowable, or construct specific forms of mood and subjectivity; they both break down communities or create the conditions for multi-culturalism; they are marked by a distinctive architecture which they nonetheless exceed, and they produce specific spaces. Anyone embarking on a study of London must consider both the texts which deal with cities in these contexts, to say nothing of a massive literature on London itself. One dominant and essential discussion of the city is that of Walter Benjamin (1892–1941) in his work on nineteenth-century Paris, the *Arcades Project*. The writing was interrupted by the Second World War, and by the occupation of Paris by the Nazis; Benjamin, before committing suicide, rather than fall into the hands of the Nazis, left the manuscript with the librarian of the Bibliothèque Nationale, Georges Bataille. And hence it reached publication in its unfinished form. I draw on the *Arcades Project* in this study, to compare Paris and London, and to conceptualise the city.[10] Benjamin's work takes the form of a mass of quotations, put together as if in a montage; in this way he broaches the Paris arcades, fashion, prostitution and gambling, the streets of Paris, the panorama, modes of lighting the streets, and photography. Every stray detail locatable about Paris was drawn on; no piece of information was to be left out from the various folders he compiled as irrelevant; even if its relevance was not discernible at the time, it was collected for further use.

Benjamin called Paris 'the capital of the nineteenth century', which must be seen as a major challenge to a conceptualisation of Dickens' London: for why was London, despite being greater in size, not the 'capital'? Why does it take second place, as in Des Esseintes' sense of it in *A Rebours* as a combination of fog and middle-class comfort? The question haunts this book, and several answers will be attempted to it. Benjamin, who refers only a few times to Dickens, noted how much he needed London: needed it in ways which this book explores. Benjamin wrote when criticism, as opposed to appreciation of Dickens was still comparatively new, relying on G.K. Chesterton, who discussed

Dickens in 1906.[11] The insights accumulate, and suggest some pointers for this book. They occur within the sections on the *flâneur*, the stroller, the distinctive Parisian type created by the newly built Arcades, the observer of the market-place.[12] Benjamin quotes from the German Marxist Franz Mehring:

> Dickens. In his letters he complains repeatedly when travelling, even in the mountains of Switzerland . . . about the lack of street noise, which was indispensable to him for his writing. 'I can't express how much I want these [streets]', he wrote in 1846 from Lausanne, where he was working on one of his greatest novels, *Dombey and Son*. 'It seems as if they supplied something to my brain, which it cannot bear, when busy, to lose. For a week or a fortnight I can write prodigiously in a retired place . . . and a day in London sets me up again and starts me. But the toil and labour of writing, day after day, without that magic lantern, is immense . . .' (*Arcades* 426: for the letter to Forster, see *Letters* 4.612)

While 'noise' and 'retired' contrast with each other, suggesting that Dickens missed London noise, the letter indicates more the need of London streets and crowds, 'numbers of figures'. Benjamin meditates on the 'magic lantern', quoting Chesterton, that Dickens' 'tales always started from some splendid hint in the streets' (57). Dickens bears this out: a letter to Forster from Genoa (8 October 1844) discusses his difficulties in starting to write: 'Put me down on Waterloo-bridge at eight o'clock in the evening with leave to roam about as long as I like, and I would come home, as you know, panting to go on' (*Letters* 4.200). Another extract, including a quotation from Dickens' fragment of autobiography, reprinted by Forster in his *Life of Charles Dickens*, Benjamin calls: 'On the allegorical element':

> Dickens . . . mentions, among the coffee shops into which he crept in those wretched days [when he was working at the blacking-factory at the age of twelve] one in St Martin's Lane, 'of which I only recollect that it stood near the church, and that in the door there was an oval glass plate with COFFEE ROOM painted on it, addressed towards the street. If I ever find myself in a very different kind of coffee room now but where there is such an inscription on glass, and read it backwards on the wrong side, MOOR EEFFOC (as I often used to do then in a dismal reverie), a shock goes through my blood'. That wild word, 'Moor Eeffoc' is the motto of all effectual realism (233) [the coffee-shops were in Maiden-lane; 'one in a court (non-existent now) close to Hungerford-market, and one in St Martin's-lane' (*DC* 897–98)].[13]

What does it mean to think of Dickens in 'allegorical' terms, even when he is being autobiographical? It obviously means seeing the world in reverse. And as disconnected, and yet organised (with those double letters: OO, EE and FF). Why the MOOR? Another Chesterton passage follows immediately, 'Dickens and stenography', which has to do with 'arbitrary characters', i.e. ones which cannot be read, letters lacking a recognisable physiognomy:

> He describes how, after he had learnt the whole exact alphabet, 'there then appeared a procession of new horrors, called arbitrary characters – the most despotic characters I have ever known; who insisted, for instance, that a thing like the beginning

of a cobweb meant "expectation", and that a pen-and-ink skyrocket stood for "disadvantageous"'. He concludes, 'It was almost heartbreaking'. But it is significant that somebody else, a colleague of his, concluded, 'There never *was* such a short-hand writer'. (*Arcades* 233–34)

The passage has the potential to make the city a text, with a system and a defiance of any system of reading built into it. While compelling reading to become allegorical, seeing that which is 'other', it makes the writer produce a script from which he is alienated. We shall not understand Dickens if we do not see his writing London as writing short-hand. It all has the suggestiveness and baffling nature of MOOR EEFFOC, which looks like a code to be deciphered.

Benjamin quotes Chesterton: Dickens has 'the key to the street' (437). The phrase seems technical; meaning that the door is closed to someone. Mr Lowten tells Job Trotter, who should be in the Fleet prison, but has been locked out when the prison closed for the night: 'you can't get in tonight; you've got the key of the street, my friend' (*PP* 46.621). Uriah Heep points out that, however 'umble his origins were, he never was 'in the streets', unlike David Copperfield (*DC* 52.754). *Pickwick Papers* uses the conceit of the prisoner locked out of the prison; *Little Dorrit* the free man locked inside the prison, and later, Amy Dorrit locked out of the jail which is her home, and spending the night in the streets. These are suggestive, but Chesterton's insight is, as picked up by Benjamin, potentially deeper: 'He could open the inmost door of his house – the door that leads into that secret passage which is lined with houses and roofed with stars' (438). The street here becomes the most secret inner chamber, an interior. It leads into the next citation headed 'Dickens as a child', which combines looking and thinking as something allegorical, never looking at the thing itself, but at something other, and that in a virtually traumatised state:

> Whenever he had done drudging, he had no other resource but drifting, and he drifted over half London. He was a dreamy child, thinking mostly of his own dreary prospects . . . He did not go in for 'observation', a priggish habit; he did not look at Charing Cross to improve his mind or count the lampposts in Holborn to improve his arithmetic. But unconsciously he made all these places the scenes of the monstrous drama in his miserable little soul. He walked in darkness under the lamps of Holborn, and was crucified at Charing Cross. So for him ever afterwards these places had the beauty that only belongs to battlefields. (*Arcades* 438)

The pun on 'cross' reads place-names allegorically. The passage suggests the next, called 'On the psychology of the flâneur':

> The undying scenes we can all see if we shut our eyes are not the scenes that we have stared at under the direction of guide-books; the scenes we see are the scenes at which we did not look at all – the scenes in which we walked when we were thinking about something else [. . .] We can see the background now because we did not see it then. So Dickens did not stamp these places on his mind; he stamped his mind on those places. (*Arcades* 438)

The first half of this quotation suggests allegorical vision: seeing is not beholding what is in front of the eyes, but seeing differently, other; the mind is made of what has not been consciously viewed. The last sentence suggests that there is no agency here; the mind and places change places, the mind is full of places which the memory cannot necessarily remember seeing, and places meet the subject with memories of earlier looking: the disconnection between mind and memory means that places intrude with traumatic force, as memories of battlefields. Nor are places deserted, as the next entry from Chesterton shows:

> In May of 1846 he ran over to Switzerland and tried to write *Dombey and Son* at Lausanne . . . He could not get on. He attributed this especially to his love of London and his loss of it, 'the absence of streets and numbers of figures . . . *My* figures seem disposed to stagnate without crowds about them'. (*Arcades* 438)

If the history of the nineteenth century can be written through its addictions, London was Dickens' drug, his 'magic lantern', even if 'London looks very dull and is dark, and dreary enough after the bright sea side' [i.e. Broadstairs] (*Letters* 5.628). Streets, figures and crowds, they generate, for Dickens as *flâneur* his own 'figures': figures of speech, fictional characters, and a 'figural', that is to say, allegorical, sense of reality.[14]

IV

How should the reader use this book? Any way that is wanted, of course, though the ideal reader will go through it from start to finish. It is for those interested in London, and therefore in Dickens, and equally for those primarily interested in Dickens, at whatever level. I discuss the novels and the journalism cumulatively, but despite its Gazetteer at the end, the book is not encyclopaedic, and there are some London places that Dickens mentions, for instance in his journalism, which are not included, nor are the photographs representative of London, even, necessarily, of Dickens' London.

I have taken the novels chronologically; though I do not specifically discuss *Martin Chuzzlewit*, because I have already done so in *Lost in the American City*; nor *Hard Times*, nor *A Tale of Two Cities*, whose historical London I read through *Barnaby Rudge*. ('Two cities', however, suggests that the city in Dickens is a metonymy for a civilisation, so putting two ways of life under comparison; unless, that is, the 'two cities' are Paris before and during the Revolution.) Lastly, material on *The Mystery of Edwin Drood* is combined with *Our Mutual Friend*. For the novels I have discussed, each chapter has a desire to relate the texts to London, another, to see how foregrounding London locales shapes a reading, and an interest in critical theory. The city can be seen empirically, but every reading must have a theoretical aspect; much of what needs to be said cannot be seen empirically. The critical theory derives from the three 'masters of suspicion', as Paul Ricoeur called them, who write about urban modernity: Marx, Nietzsche and Freud. The city is present for each of them, and each has created traditions of critical theory, some German, some French and some British and American, all of which intersect interestingly with each other. Each leads to new ways of reading, whose validity I test here in the accounts given of the novels.

A second way to take the book is as giving an approach to reading the nineteenth-century city: London, but not just London. A third will see it as a contribution to critical writing about cities. However the reader approaches it, the book combines several things. It is empirical about places on the ground, some of which can still be visited, and which for some readers still contain their ghosts of Dickens. While remembering that Dickens' London is perceived allegorically, it also tries to be specific about sites, their histories and their differences, remembering Disraeli's advice to himself as novelist: 'One should generally mention localities, because very often they indicate character'.[15] So localities are in here, and the gradations between them are discussed, and as many pieces of information are included about them, which attempt, however loosely, to relate them to Dickens. The book uses knowledge of localities and refers, especially in endnotes, to then contemporary pictures. The photographs here are not reprints from the past, but contemporary; working from images which were available in Dickens' time, and not yet lost. This empiricist approach is not separate from the attempt to be theoretical both about Dickens and about the city. Though the subject of Dickens and London has been tried before, in scholarly work I have been glad to use, I do not think it has yet found its decisive discussion, because that would have to respond both to urban cultural studies and to Dickens; it would have to both know London and conceptualise the nineteenth-century city.

The reader may need to follow discussion of the novels with the Dickens text. Ideally, for some of the chapters, an A to Z of London will help, supplementing the older maps of London which have been reproduced. And the book was written in part from the basis of specific itineraries made following routes specified in Dickens' texts, and these itineraries, given here, may be followed, as with a guide-book. Chapter three, on *Oliver Twist*, suggests some routes that may be walked; so does chapter five, which looks specifically at Camden Town (for *Dombey and Son*) and chapter six, which looks at the Strand for *David Copperfield*. Chapter seven looks at Holborn, for *Bleak House*. Chapter eight has a section on Southwark, for *Little Dorrit*. Chapter eleven discusses the Thames, and some specific waterside sites there, such as Limehouse. The ideal reader will follow some of the itineraries proposed, either mentally or on foot, while responding to the modern photographs of London.

The photographs were taken over seven days, travelling on foot, by bus, underground and occasionally car, looking for fragments of that London which existed for Dickens, while knowing that London then was no more than a fragment, or a ruin, not a whole world which has now been lost. At no time was there the intention to illustrate the novels, or even to suggest that they could be better understood by photographs. As in Dickens' time, there were revealed the same juxtapositions of wealth and poverty (a quarter of a mile's walk out of Bishopsgate, past Norton Folgate into Shoreditch will show that); poor areas had remained poor, though some poor areas now looked gentrified, like the Wilton Square in Hoxton which Gissing discusses, which is surrounded by impoverished twentieth-century buildings. Looking for London by night, it was striking to see that modern street and flood lighting now made Dickens' night-scenes brighter than day-time photographs. The night is now not 'other' to the day, but has become the day in a more kitsch-like form. Baudelaire said that the ghost haunts Paris in broad day; and it can hardly now do so in the City and Westminster at night-time, where there are no longer any shadows to give differences. Men sleeping in boxes under the arches at the viaduct of Cannon Street station, site of the medieval Steelyard for the merchants of the Hanseatic league, were in brightly lit, floor-lit passages; a difference from the experience of the lost that the Uncommercial Traveller has in 'Night Walks'. The photograph in each case works from an image that was part of pre-1870 visual culture, but obviously includes modern buildings, and, often, signs of a new consumer-culture replacing an earlier Victorian consumerism. But this seems justifiable, because the city shows at any moment different chronologies, details which were then and are now anachronistic; it has its emergent and disappearing forms of life and architecture at all times. It makes the point that the London Dickens looked at was both objective and contemporary, but also non-contemporary; looking both at cultural forms which were subordinate and vanishing, and also invoking a London not yet but perhaps about to come into being: the city is not just the subject of representation, but of a creation, which is of itself at different moments. The photographs, aware of these different folds of time within them, invert chronology: some new things seem old, or repeat the old, some old seem new.

The book contains, apart from the endnotes, historical maps and a gazetteer, to give a sense of different spaces, and to identify places, and to see what can be said about them, without thinking that such information can cover their personal memories of which the texts are a record. The last map will be most recognisable today: the Crutchley Ordnance Survey Map of 1863, which shows the state of the railways then; it gives the largest overview of London and the new suburbia. In contrast, the first is that of the Dutch Johannes de Ram, who mapped London in the 1690s; it shows the city as it was being rebuilt after the Fire: it should be looked at in conjunction with chapter one, which decribes how London extended itself through the eighteenth century. The next group of nine are from the Greenwood map of London, published in 1827, relating to a London that Dickens knew at the age of fifteen. No. 10 is the Cruchley map of 1846, which gives an overview of the city, with details of the West End and

East End following. I deliberately chose to work with old maps, which the reader is urged to follow with a magnifying-glass and to make comparisons with the A to Z, because I wanted to give the texture of London as it was represented then, which modern maps could not do. The Gazetteer has dictionary entries for parts of London, districts, streets, and specific sites, that Dickens names, or which are associated so closely with his work that they cannot be excluded. It does no more than supplement the main text, acting like snapshots of London in contrast to the photographs; if readers look at it independently, they must consult the index to see where the place appears in the text. Omissions in the Gazetteer are usually because all I have to say about the site already appears in the main text.

CHAPTER ONE

THE *EIDOMETROPOLIS*:
A VIEW OF LONDON

The passengers change as often in the course of one journey as the figures in a kaleidoscope.
Sketches by Boz, 'Omnibuses', 167

My father thought you . . . might like to take a walk about London. I am sure I shall be very happy to show London to you.
Great Expectations 2.2.175

I · EIGHTEENTH-CENTURY LONDON

London life, including its omnibuses, makes life into a kaleidoscope, and produces thoughts which are kaleidoscopic in character. But to start with some fixed points. If we want to map nineteenth-century London, it would be good to go back a century before, and to start with the London which was built in brick, not, as before, predominantly in wood, after the Great Fire of 1666. An early map of London, such as that of de Ram (map 1), made after the Fire and the rebuilding of the City, would put all the emphasis on that quarter or enclave called the City. This book spells it with the capital C, to differentiate it from everything else. The river Thames, approaching London from the west, comes up in an almost due north direction, and makes an almost ninety-degree turn, to flow south-east. The medieval city of Westminster is on the left-hand side of that northwards progress. Waterloo Bridge, built in stone, and renamed from being the Strand Bridge because of Wellington's success on the battle-field at Waterloo in 1815, and opened two years to the day after the battle, is almost exactly on the point of this turn. The Roman City of London is virtually at right angles to Westminster and downstream of it, north of the river. London Bridge, crossing the river into the City, is therefore at the centre. A road comes straight up to it from the south towards it. Since the 1920s, this road has been designated the A3: it originates in Portsmouth, where Dickens was born, in 1812, and it turns right towards London after reaching Kingston-upon-Thames in Surrey.

This road, the A3, if we now consider it as coming south from London Bridge, goes through the Borough and Southwark, and then splits. The A2, as the Dover Road, goes out through south London as the Old Kent Road: it is the path taken by David Copperfield in chapter 13 of that novel. The A3 goes off towards Kingston south of Kennington Common, while the southwards-bound present A23 continues towards Brighton via Brixton and Streatham. In the eighteenth century, Southwark was fairly built up, but not Lambeth Marshes to the west, nor anywhere much to the east of the Tower of London. The latter, north of the river, marks the City's eastern limit.

Going north, having crossed London Bridge, the road continues as Gracechurch Street, and Bishopsgate, becoming the Roman road that led to the north of England (the present A10). A road from the West comes into London as Oxford Street. Once inside, it crosses eastwards as Holborn, goes over what used to be the Fleet River, becomes Newgate Street and runs into a street named successively Cheapside, Poultry and Cornhill. Having crossed Gracechurch Street, it becomes Leadenhall Street, leaving the City at Aldgate. From further south in Gracechurch Street, a right-hand turn, Fenchurch Street, runs up to Aldgate. The Whitechapel Road, going east from there, through the East End, becomes the A12, going out to Colchester and up to Yarmouth, another progress familiar from *David Copperfield*.

The City is about one square mile in size, with Roman walls and gates. From east to west, these are: Aldgate, Bishopsgate, Moorgate, Cripplegate, Aldersgate (immediately to the north of St Paul's Cathedral, and the beginning of the A1), Newgate and Ludgate. Not till the second half of the eighteenth century did development progress other than east and west, hugging the shores of the river. Extensive development north and south, into suburbs, came in the nineteenth century, especially with the railways. Before that, the biggest area of development was north of the city, as far as Old Road. This goes east to meet the A10 at Shoreditch church, an area within fields. Westwards, Old Road meets the present A1, which as it goes north out of Aldersgate Street, becomes Goswell Road, where Pickwick lived. West of that, Clerkenwell, reaching to the Fleet River, was also built up in the eighteenth century. West of the City had less development. The Strand, following a shallow curve turning round the north of the river, leads out of Charing Cross (Dr Johnson: 'the full tide of human existence is at Charing Cross') into Fleet Street. 'Char' as in Charing, may come from a word meaning 'turn'. Fleet Street, beginning with Temple Bar, crosses the Fleet, becoming Ludgate Hill. This area belonged to the City, being called Farringdon Ward Without (i.e. outside the walls), a ward added to the City in 1393 to make twenty-five wards altogether inside the City. The road ascends to St Paul's, which Christopher Wren (1632–1723) completed in 1710.

Legal London, north of Fleet Street, and one of London's three nodes, along-side Westminster and the City, was centred on Lincoln's Inn Fields, designed by Inigo Jones in 1631, and the largest square in London, at twelve acres. Two roads from Holborn descend to the Strand and Fleet Street: Chancery Lane on the east, Drury Lane on the west. They virtually frame Lincoln's Inn Fields. At the west end of the Strand, the road runs down, as Whitehall, towards West-minster Hall. Development beyond Westminster ran out, in the eighteenth cen-tury, at Tothill Fields. Development north of St James' Park, originally grounds for the medieval St James' hospital, on the site of which Henry the Eighth built

St James' Palace, stopped at Oxford Street, then called Tiburn Road. St James' Park was first laid out as a formal garden in Stuart times.

In 1694, when the Bank of England was founded, London, with 500,000 inhabitants, had overtaken Paris, and was double Amsterdam's population. Rebuilding after the Fire – an event which exists as a far-off memory in Dickens' London – had adhered to the plan of the medieval streets, using brick and stone, not timber. By 1750, with a population of 675,000, London was Europe's largest city. That was the year of the opening of Westminster Bridge (replaced in 1862), which joined Westminster to Lambeth, and so to Southwark, so guaranteeing the opening up of the south of the Thames. That development was expanded with Blackfriars Bridge in 1769, making a second connection between the south and the City. In 1757, the New Road (Marylebone Road, Euston Road and Pentonville Road), opened as a ring-road north of Oxford Street, from Paddington to Islington. Its existence guaranteed future building both south and north of it.

By then, the West End, north of Whitehall, had developed. The seventeenth century had seen the laying out of Lincoln's Inn Fields, then squares: Bloomsbury, Soho, Golden, Red Lion, St James', and Leicester. The latter was called Leicester Fields, being south of Leicester House (built in the 1630s on what is now Lisle Street, and pulled down in 1791). Eighteenth-century developments were part of a westwards development. Squares such as Hanover, Berkeley and Grosvenor, south of Oxford Street, and Cavendish Square north of it became more fashionable, though the future George the Second lived at Leicester House for ten years before his succession in 1727, like his son, Frederick, who died there in 1751. Each square presumed a whole development of streets radiating out of it. The second half of the eighteenth century saw the laying out of Portland Place, Portman Square and Manchester Square, north of Oxford Street. The exception was Bloomsbury's Bedford Square (1776).

Disraeli, whose London homes were in Mayfair – he died in Curzon Street, near where Lord Steyne attempts to seduce Becky Sharp in *Vanity Fair* – comments on this development in his novel *Tancred* (1847) chapter 10. He discusses London's 'vastness' – in comparison with Paris and Constantinople – and monotony. 'Pancras is like Mary-le-bone, Mary-le-bone is like Paddington; all the streets resemble each other; you must read the names of the squares before you venture to knock at a door'. Disraeli refers to 'Gloucester Place, and Baker Street and Harley Street, and Wimpole Street, and all those flat, dull, spiritless streets, resembling each other like a large family of plain children, with Portland Place and Portman Square for their respectable parents'. The analysis is borne out with Dombey's house in *Dombey and Son*. For Disraeli, 'the Inns of Court, and the quarters in the vicinity of the port, Thames Street, Tower Hill, Billingsgate, Wapping, Rotherhithe, are the best parts of London;

Interior, St George's, Hanover Square, John James, 1725. As with Wren and Hawksmoor, and in contrast to Inigo Jones' St Paul's, Covent Garden, the presence of galleries brings the congregation nearer to the pulpit; the church being considered a machine to preach in. A fashionable church, Mrs Nickleby expects her daughter to marry Sir Mulberry Hawk here. (Photographs: Louis Lo)

they are full of character; the buildings bear a nearer relation to what the people are doing than in the more polished quarters'.

> The old merchants of the times of the first Georges were a fine race. They knew their position and built up to it. While the territorial aristocracy, pulling down their family hotels, were raising vulgar streets and squares upon their sites, and occupying themselves one of the new tenements, the old merchants filled the straggling lanes which connected the Royal Exchange with the Port of London, with mansions which, if not exactly equal to the palaces of stately Venice, might at least vie with many of the hotels of old Paris. Some of these, though the great majority have been broken up into chambers and counting houses, still remain intact. (*Tancred*, 155)

One of these mansions is the house of Clennam, in *Little Dorrit*. Hogarth (1697–1764), whose art is so much centred on London, had not shared Disraeli's enthusiasm for the City. Born near Smithfield, he moved west to Soho (1724), then to Covent Garden, and ran an academy in St Martin's Lane, and died at Chiswick, his country home since 1748. He satirised the pride of the Alderman in *Marriage à la Mode* (1745); his meanly-kept house overlooking London Bridge, with his coat of arms cut into the window, is seen in plate 8: Hogarth similarly satirises City gormandising in plate 8 of *Industry and Idleness* (1747), perhaps in the hall of one of the City Livery companies, the Fishmongers, in King William Street, belonging to the time when the Industrious Apprentice has become rich and Sheriff of London.

By 1801, London's million population was double that of Paris. But the City's population was no more than a sixth of the whole metropolis. England's second city was no longer Norwich but Liverpool, but London was ten times greater. Manchester had 75,000, Birmingham 71,000. By 1851, London had reached three million. Liverpool was then just under 400,000, Manchester 250,000, Birmingham 232,000, Leeds 172,000. London's population was six and a half million by 1901; Manchester and Birmingham both half a million. A brief list of artistic productions will show a certain pride in London's distinctiveness. *London Magazine* started in 1820, *Punch: Or the London Charivari* in 1841, the *Illustrated London News*, run by Herbert Ingram, Henry Vizetelly, Frederick Bayley and John Timbs, in 1842. It was the first time London had an illustrated weekly paper. In opposition to this last, the *Graphic* began as a weekly magazine in 1869, edited by William Luson Thomas (1830–1900), with an attempt to show ordinary life in London. The artist Thomas Shotter Boys (1803–74), brought out his Canaletto-like *Original Views of London as It Is* (1842). John Tallis brought out *London Street Views 1838–1840*, revised in 1847; it displayed maps and the elevations of buildings in the main streets. Thomas Hosmer Shepherd brought out *Metropolitan Improvements* (1827), *London and its Environs* (1829), and *Mighty London* (1855). Timbs wrote *Curiosities of London* (1855), recording antiquarian details of the old city. Mid-century London from Fulham to Poplar extended nine miles; from Camberwell to Highbury, seven miles. The London docks, digging for which began in 1800 (with the West India Docks, on the Isle of Dogs) employed 20,000 people; in 1824, over 23,000 ships were using the docks.[1]

Late eighteenth-century visitors commented on fogs, and later, on gas-lamps (Pall Mall was so lighted from 1807, all London by 1842), on expensive shops, displaying women's silks, chintzes or muslins, or confectionery, or fashion goods, the pastrycook shops.[2] The Pietist Carl Philip Moritz described London and England in 1782, in letters to a Berlin friend. Moritz came up the Thames, and landed at Dartford on the south side of the river (in Kent), and went by post-chaise from there through Greenwich to Westminster. His ship would come up more slowly through the Thames, negotiating the numerous vessels. Moritz comments on St James' Park, the Strand, influenza, the food, including bad coffee and toast, walking from his lodging at the Adelphi to the Royal Exchange – the length of Berlin – going to the Custom House to find his luggage, the pleasure-gardens – Vauxhall Gardens, and Ranelagh – London squares, the New Road, the British Museum, the Haymarket theatre, St Paul's and its Whispering Gallery, and on Westminster Abbey, before going to visit other parts of England, travelling from the Strand to Richmond by stage-coach.[3]

II · WORDSWORTH'S LONDON

Another mapping of London comes through the poetry of William Wordsworth, who died in 1850, aged eighty. His widow then brought out his autobiographical poem *The Prelude*, which he had been revising since completing a first version in 1805. (The history of the text is more complex than that, but I quote below from the 1805 version.) Wordsworth seems to have visited London first in 1788, when at Cambridge.[4] In *The Prelude* Book 7, there is a survey of London on the basis of several visits, including one of 1802, when Charles Lamb (1775–1834) had shown him round, especially in Smithfield, and at Bartholomew Fair (see chapter nine).[5] Wordsworth on late eighteenth-century London complements Moritz, and, as a conscious outsider to the city, he contrasts with Dickens.

The Prelude says he had heard of London before, from a schoolfriend who had visited there, and wondered:

> how men lived
> Even next-door neighbours, as we say, yet still
> Strangers, nor knowing the other's name (7.116–18)[6]

Like Moritz, Wordsworth mentions Vauxhall, and Ranelagh. The first are described by Dickens ('Vauxhall Gardens by Day', October 1836, reprinted in *Sketches by Boz*), and by Thackeray (*Vanity Fair* chapter 6). Ranelagh Gardens, now part of Chelsea Hospital gardens, were laid out in 1742, with a famous centre-piece comprising a rotunda; it closed in 1805. Other tourist-sights follow:

> The River proudly bridged; the dizzy top
> And Whispering Gallery of St Paul's, the tombs
> Of Westminster; the Giants of Guildhall;
> Bedlam, and those carved maniacs at the gates,
> Perpetually recumbent; Statues – man,
> And the horse under him – in gilded pomp
> Adorning flowery gardens, 'mid vast squares;
> The Monument, and that Chamber of the Tower
> Where England's sovereigns sit in long array,
> Their steeds bestriding . . . (7.129–38)

This quotation juxtaposes St Paul's and Westminster Abbey, and the giants Gog and Magog, the object of the visit into the City in 'Gone Astray'. These giants were also displayed at St Dunstan's Church in Fleet Street, where they are viewed by David Copperfield and his aunt (*David Copperfield* 23.357). The other statues, Michelangelesque male nudes of Melancholy and Raving Madness, the latter enchained, rested above the gateway outside Bethlem Hospital (Bedlam) when it stood in Moorfields (1676–1815).

That building had been to the design of the Surveyor Robert Hooke. The statues travelled with the 122 patients who were taken by hackney coaches to Lambeth Marsh in 1815. It was designed by James Lewis, with two wings and a central block; the dome was added in 1844 by Sydney Smirke. The statues

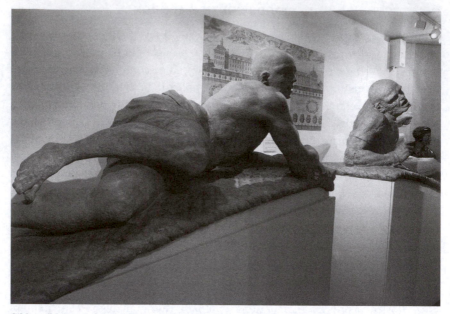

Cibber: 'Melancholy' and 'Raving Madness': statues made for Bedlam at Moorfields, and displayed when Bedlam moved to Lambeth Marsh: now in Royal Bethlem Hospital Museum, Beckenham.

were by the Dutch artist Caius Gabriel Cibber (1630–1700).[7] Madness in Chains is invoked in Hogarth's portrayal of madness at the end of *The Rake's Progress* (1735). Wren's Monument (1677), commemorating the Fire of London (1666), had an allegorical scene in bas-relief on the west side of its base, also designed by Cibber, showing Charles the Second, in Roman costume, and his brother the Duke of York (later James the Second) visiting the afflicted in the City after the Fire. Wordsworth's last reference is to the Armoury in the Tower of London, where the armour of medieval and Tudor knights are yet on display; monuments of greatness or of greatness gone mad. By Wordsworth's time, the Tower could be visited, as the country's first public museum. Its menagerie lasted from the end of the seventeenth century until 1834 when it moved to Regent's Park. Its Public Records only moved to Chancery Lane in the 1850s. Its Armoury, with the Line of Kings, which Rowlandson illustrated in 1809, had been organised as a display in the 1680s, along with the Spanish Armoury (dedicated to the Armada), and the Grand Storehouse, of historic and captured trophies, and cannon. After the Restoration, even the Crown Jewels were displayed.[8]

From this monumental and public London, Wordsworth passes to people in the streets, for example, 'a travelling cripple, by the trunk cut short/And stumping on his arms' (7.203–204). His identity is explained by one of Lamb's *Essays of Elia*. 'A Complaint of the Decay of Beggars in the Metropolis', which discusses the hypocrisy which was then sweeping the streets clean of beggars.

Lamb shows that this particular person had been brought low during the Gordon Riots of 1780 (see *Barnaby Rudge*, discussed in chapter four).

Here we reach the new subject that the city posed: how to read it, and how to think about it. Describing it even is imposible. That problem makes Wordsworth notice allegorical forms, as though allegory – describing one thing in terms of another – was both urban and suited writing about the city. Nature and natural forms might fit with symbolism – finding the 'right' image to express an idea – but allegory seems deliberately arbitrary, in its way of picturing what is in and of the city, and as a combination of picture, or image, and words.[9] Hence the personifications in noting London crowds:

> Face after face; the string of dazzling wares,
> Shop after shop, with symbols, blazoned names,
> And all the tradesman's honours, overhead:
> Here, fronts of houses, like a title-page,
> With letters huge inscribed from top to toe;
> Stationed above the door, like guardian saints,
> *There*, allegoric shapes, female or male,
> Or physiognomies of real men,
> Land-warriors, kings, or admirals of the sea,
> Boyle, Shakespeare, Newton, or the attractive head
> Of some quack doctor, famous in his day. (7.157–67)

Human faces, to be 'read', not just looked at, take their place with other forms of writing, such as 'symbols', and the 'blazoning' of heraldry, and 'honours' (visual markers). Shop-fronts are the elaborate title-pages of books, with, above them, human figures (like Cibber's Melancholy and Madness). Moritz had noticed the same:

Especially in the Strand, where one shop jostles another, and people of very different trades often live in the same house, it is surprising to see how from bottom to top the various houses often display large signboards with painted letters. Everyone who lives and works in the house sports his signboard over the door; indeed there is not a cobbler whose name and trade is not to be read in large golden characters. (33)

Wordsworth notices that the faces of real people have been pressed into allegorical service in these signs. They represent something beyond themselves. The last lines suggest that symbolic and allegorical significances may have faded, like the guardian saints and the blazoned names. Even faces of 'real men' no longer relate; they are anachronisms: Shakespeare is in the same context as some doctor now shown to be a quack.

The 'allegoric shapes' are 'physiognomies', the subject of the Zurich Zwinglian minister Johann Caspar Lavater (1741–1801). For him, the face (which is the 'physiognomy') is something more than merely physical: it is an allegorical image by which the person's character may be read. Physiognomy becomes a 'talent' for interpreting faces.[10] The physiognomy is both objective, describing what there is in the face to be seen, and it is subjective interpretation, and it is impossible to know which of these it is, and whether any face can be known, or not. To see the physiognomy is to see what may, or may not be, interpretable. Appropriately, then, Dickens' major illustrator, Hablot Browne, called himself 'Phiz' (for 'physiognomy'). It means that he (a) gives people faces, (b) interprets faces, (c) creates faces. Those faces are allegories, and Phiz corresponds to Dickens, allegorist and physiognomist of London, giving London a face as much as the novels give an 'eidometropolis': i.e. an image (Greek *eidos*: form, type, idea) or a representation of the metropolis.

Wordsworth continues with what may be seen in different spots, with the 'throng'. Going homeward, he notes a multi-cultural collection of peoples, including those who are selling: 'the Italian', 'the Jew' and 'slow moving Turk/ With freight of slippers piled beneath his arm!' (7.214, 217–18). Then another inventory:

> The Swede, the Russian; from the genial south,
> The Frenchman and the Spaniard; from remote
> America, the Hunter-Indian; Moors,
> Malays, Lascars, the Tartar, the Chinese,
> And Negro Ladies in white muslin gowns. (7.224–28)

He continues with 'spectacles within doors': with animals and plants on exhibition, and to artworks, and begins by saying that what he will describe is not authentic art, not 'subtlest craft,/By means refined attaining purest ends', but rather, 'imitations' (7.236–38):

> Whether the Painter, whose ambitious skill
> Submits to nothing less than taking in
> A whole horizon's circuit, do with power
> Like that of angels or commissioned spirits,
> Fix us upon some lofty pinnacle,
> Or, as a ship on waters, with a world
> Of life, and life-like mockery beneath,
> Above, behind, far stretching and before;
> Or more mechanic artist represent
> By scale exact, in model, wood or clay,
> From blended colours also borrowing help,
> Some miniature of famous spots or things, –
> St Peter's Church, or, more aspiring aim,
> In miscroscopic vision, Rome itself . . .
> All that the traveller sees when he is there. (7.240–54, 259)

This passage refers to the 'Panorama', as developed and patented in 1787 by Robert Barker (1739–1806), with a panoramic picture of Edinburgh. He exhibited 'London from the Roof of the Albion Mills' (flour mills, opened in 1783) in 1791, just before the mills were burned down. In 1793, the Panorama moved to a brick-built rotunda, where Cranbourn Street meets Leicester Square.[11]

Similarly, Wordsworth's reference implies a Panorama like the *Eidometropolis* of the Bankside-born landscape painter and water-colourist Thomas Girtin (1775–1802), about whom Turner, two months younger, was supposed to have said, 'If Tom Girtin had lived, I should have starved'. The *Eidometropolis*, Girtin's now lost view of London, spread over 1,944 square feet of canvas, had been painted from the roof of the British Plate Glass Manufacturing Company on the south side of Blackfriars Bridge. It was a variant on the *Eidophusikon*, developed by the scene-painter Philip de Loutherbourg (1740–1812) in the 1780s, an early version of what would become the 'magic lantern' (we have already referred to this), showing movable representations of various natural effects, such as a storm at sea. Barker, continuing from de Loutherbourg, developed an approach to perspective which would give the appearance of all-round vision on a curved surface. Girtin's *Eidometropolis* was exhibited at the Lyceum. Wigley's Great Room, Spring Gardens was another site for Panoramas, as was the rotunda in Leicester Square. The Panorama becomes part of what must be looked at: so David Copperfield and Steerforth visit a Panorama (*DC* 20.300).[12] From Paris, in 1847, Dickens writes of:

> wandering into Hospitals, Prisons, Dead-Houses, Operas, Theatres, Concert Rooms, Burial-grounds, Palaces, and Wine Shops. In my unoccupied fortnight of each month, every description of gaudy and ghastly sight has been passing before me in a rapid Panorama. (*Letters* 5: 19)

The successor to the Panorama was the Diorama – huge, illuminated paintings on translucent material. This, invented by Louis-Jacques Mandé Daguerre (1787–1851), was displayed in Paris in 1822: the first London Diorama, in Regent's Park, followed in 1823: one chapter for *Pictures from Italy* is called 'A Moving Diorama'. The comprehensive view of things is suggested by Cruikshank's title-page for the monthly parts of *Sketches by Boz*, showing Dickens and Cruikshank in an air-balloon above the crowds. Artist and illustrator of the *Sketches* view all things comprehensively, and bring their readership into line with what they see.

Wordsworth describes the pantomime, popular theatre, and Jack the Giant-killer:

> He dons his coat of darkness; on the stage
> Walks, and achieves his wonders from the eye
> Of living Mortal covert, as the moon
> Hid in her 'vacant interlunar cave'.
> Delusion bold! And how can it be wrought?
> The garb he wears is black as death, the word
> *Invisible* flames forth upon his chest. (7.281–87)

Delight in the theatre – even in 'the very gilding, lamps and painted scrolls' (7.408) passes into seeing the law-courts as theatrical, like the oratory of Pitt and Burke in Parliament.

III · DICKENS IN LONDON

Dickens was born in Portsmouth (1 Mile End Terrace, now 393 Old Commercial Road) ten years after Wordsworth's survey of London. We can map his biography onto London places. The family moved to London, when he was three, for a brief moment, on account of John Dickens' work at the Navy Pay Office at Somerset House.[13] They stayed at 10 Norfolk Street (22 Cleveland Street), from January 1815 to 1817. The road leads up from Oxford Street, still virtually London's northern limit, towards what *Nicholas Nickleby* calls 'the dowager barrenness and frigidity of Fitzroy Square' (*NN* 37.446), laid out by Robert Adam in the 1790s, south of the New Road (Euston Road). John Dickens was then posted to Chatham (2 Ordnance Terrace) but in 1822 the family returned to London, to 16 Bayham Street, Camden Town, a row of houses built ten years earlier, reflecting new housing developments begun on the northern side of the Euston Road, and visible in Map 3.

The family had London connections: a godfather, Charles Huffam, a boat-rigger, lived at Church Row (now Newell Street, which still possesses eighteenth-century houses), in Limehouse 'in a substantial, handsome sort of way, and was kind to his godchild' (Forster, 1.1.12). An uncle, Thomas Barrow, lived at Gerrard Street in Soho, and something of that may appear in the description of Mr Jaggers' house in *Great Expectations*. His grandmother lived in

22 Cleveland Street: where the Dickens family lived in 1815; an area of small shops; this part was then Norfolk Street. Note the bowed window, and the area in front of the house, to the right, with railings (compare *BH* 4.51).

Oxford Street. His sister, Fanny, became a music student in Hanover Square. A *Household Words* article, 'New Year's Day', describes being taken to the Bazaar in Soho Square (nos 4–6), in the angle between present-day Charing Cross Road and Oxford Street.[14] This belonged to John Trotter, an army contractor, who, after the Napoleonic Wars, turned his warehouse into a bazaar for the wives and daughters of army officers to sell their handiwork. It continued till the end of the 1880s. Soho Square, with a statue of Charles the Second by Cibber, was in place by 1681, but the area south of Oxford Street and present-day New Oxford Street was now poor: *Nicholas Nickleby* refers to the 'labyrinth of streets which lies between Seven Dials and Soho' (*NN* 765), where Nicholas and Kate wander, lost, for half an hour. Two of the *Sketches by Boz*, 'Seven Dials' (September 1835), and 'Meditations in Monmouth Street' (September 1836) discuss the St Giles area: in 'Gin-Shops' (February 1835), Boz goes away from Seven Dials:

> we will make for Drury Lane, through the narrow streets and dirty courts which divide it from Oxford-street, and that classical spot adjoining the brewery at the bottom of Tottenham-court-road best known to the world as the 'Rookery'. (*SB* 217)

OED gives 1792 for the first use of 'rookery', meaning a cluster of mean tenements (i.e. houses where the rooms were occupied by separate families) occupied by the poorest people. Forster confirms that the child Dickens had 'a profound attraction of repulsion to St Giles. If he could only induce whomsoever took him out to take him through Seven-dials, he was supremely happy. "Good Heaven!" he would exclaim, "what wild visions of prodigies of wickedness, want and beggary, arose in my mind out of that place!"' (*Life* 1.1.11).

This area opens 'Gone Astray' (*Household Words* 13 August 1853, *J3* 155–65), written as the autobiography of 'a very small boy indeed', a little boy lost. Unsigned, like all *Household Words* pieces, it fictionalises childhood and connects disparate childhood memories, while giving a progress through London. The boy – perhaps Dickens between 1822 and 1824, though he dates himself as eight or nine – has been taken by an adult to see St Giles' Church exterior, where beggars and gypsies used to congregate, including, famously, one character, Bamfylde Moore Carew (1693–1759). His *Life and Adventures* as a 'noted Devonshire stroller and dogstealer' appeared in 1745. Adult and child then proceed to Northumberland House in the Strand. At that point, the 'I' of the narrative loses his guide, and wanders down the Strand to see the statues of Gog and Magog at Guildhall, passing Temple Bar, and St Dunstan's, with its own Gog and Magog, into Fleet Street. This area is perhaps the centre of Dickens' London, as it was for Charles Lamb (1775–1834), writing in 1802:

> I was born under the shadow of Saint Dunstan's steeple, just where the conflux of the eastern and western inhabitants of this twofold city meet and justle in friendly opposition at Temple-bar.[15]

Giants and the clock outside
St Dunstan's in the West: a
shadow of the spirits of the
chimes pictured by Daniel
Maclise and Richard Doyle,
where they use the church's
tower (built 1831, John Shaw)
(*CB* 1.144, 149).

Lamb had been born in the Temple, at no. 2 Crown Office Row, the son of a servant to Samuel Salt, an MP and lawyer, who rented the chambers there in which the Lambs lived.[16] Described in Thackeray's *Pendennis* (1850) chapter 29, recalling his own experiences living there in 1831, as the centre for anachronistic living, it is the area central to *Bleak House*, and it concludes Dickens' last completed novel, where Mr Twenlow 'fares to the Temple, gaily' (*OMF* 4, Chapter the Last, 797). The boy of 'Gone Astray' has reached Fleet Street when he sees the giants at St Dunstan's: for Lamb, with his passion for crowds, 'the man must have a rare recipe for melancholy, who can be dull in Fleet-street. I am naturally inclined to hypochondria, but in London, it vanishes, like all other ills' (Lamb, 1.39). The boy sees St Paul's in the distance with its cross of gold which lures him on. After reaching Guildhall, he searches the City, which is defined by the names of banking-houses in Lombard Street: Smith, Payne and Smith, Glyn and Fairfax, Baring, and Rothschild.

He wanders northwards, looking in courts and yards and little squares, including the 'court of the South Sea house' 'where Threadneedle-street abuts upon Bishopsgate' (Lamb 2.1). Lamb had worked there in 1791, and described it in 'The South-Sea House' (*Essays of Elia*), detailing the clerks, noting that they were all bachelors, 'for the establishment did not admit of superfluous salaries'. The company closed in 1853, the year of 'Going Astray'.

The boy continues to Austin Friars, wondering 'how the Friars used to like it'. He finds himself on 'Change, i.e. the Stock Exchange, situated between Throgmorton and Threadneedle Streets, in Capel Court, off Bartholomew Lane, which connects the streets. He saw 'the shabby people sitting under the placards about ships, I settled that they were Misers who had embarked all their wealth to go and buy gold-dust . . . and were waiting for their respective captains to come and tell them that they were ready to set sail. I observed that they all munched dry biscuits, and I thought it was to keep off sea-sickness'. He comes southwards to the Mansion House, the Lord Mayor's official residence (George Dance, 1752). He follows with the India House in Leadenhall Street (*DS* 4. 46), saying that Sir James Weir-Hogg (1790–1876), lawyer and conservative politician, and twice Chairman of the East India Company, would have been proud of him.

Later, he ventures east, into the theatre at Goodman's Fields, Whitechapel. The first theatre which opened, in 1729, in Leman Street, Whitechapel, saw the first production of Fielding's *The Temple Beau* (1730). Another followed, where David Garrick (1717–79) started out as Richard the Third, in 1741, but this theatre was gone by the beginning of the nineteenth century. Dickens writes about seeing a playbill for 'a scene in a play then performing at a theatre in that neighbourhood which is no longer in existence', and describes going into a theatre with GR (George Rex) painted on the front. Perhaps it was the Royalty theatre, in Wellclose Square, off the Ratcliff Highway, which, opening in 1787, was called in 1813 the East London theatre, until 1826 when it was burned down. Reopening in 1828, it failed and closed three days later.[17] Or perhaps visiting the theatre is a fantasy of 'going astray', of attempting to lose the self within the eighteenth century.

The passage ends with the boy finding a watchman who took him to a 'watchhouse', the booth for the nightwatchmen. 'When I think of us in the rain, I recollect that we must have made a composition, like a vignette of Infancy leading Age'. The visual image recalls Blake's illustration for 'London' in *Songs of Experience*: we will return to it in chapter four. He sleeps, waking to find his father looking at him. 'This is literally and exactly how I went astray. They used to say I was an odd child, and I suppose I was. I am an odd man perhaps'. Oddness comes from the desire to be lost, which therefore unconsciously uncouples the self from the older guide, doubling the self through the fantasy of the self as the boy unable to read the streets as the man, the conscious, self-aware subject can; 'Gone Astray' is the desire to have disappeared in the streets, or to be what Clennam, in *Little Dorrit*, calls 'a waif and stray everywhere' (*LD* 1.2.35). It is the desire which Dickens expressed to 'represent London – or Paris – in the new light of being actually unknown to all the people in the story, and only taking the colour of their fears and fancies and opinions. So getting a new aspect and being unlike itself. An *odd* unlikeness of itself' (*Life* 9.7.751). Boy and man are odd; the writing wishes to 'odd' the city.

The writing, of the child lost in London and spending what money he has on food, and being persecuted by older boys, while comic, recalls *Oliver Twist*, and the child who has 'lost her road' in *The Old Curiosity Shop* (1.11) who complements the old man walking the night streets, and *Dombey and Son* when Florence gets lost, and specifically *David Copperfield* chapter 11, describing the boy working in the factory. Loneliness and lostness are seen as having no beginning; life has always 'gone astray'; London produces straying as it produces narratives.

However fictionalised, this account confirms how the child Dickens possessed parts of London. In other senses, the family possessed little, if anything. They moved in 1823 to 4 Gower Street North, north of the New Road and the Gower Street running from Bedford Square to Euston, laid out in 1790 and more fashionable.[18] All street-roaming free ended when John Dickens was taken to prison for debt at the Marshalsea (February to May 1824). The boy, now working at Warren's blacking-factory, moved from lodging with a Mrs Roylance in Little College Street in Camden Town (now College Place – but the house no longer exists) to Lant Street in Southwark.

The episode, crucial to *Dombey and Son*, *David Copperfield* and *Little Dorrit*, will be discussed in chapters relating to these novels, but, since the episode of 'Gone Astray', written after *David Copperfield*, is presumably presented as happening *before* 1824 and the novel's experience of the factory, it affirms a desire to be lost pre-dating that lost state, which therefore repeats going astray. It implies that there was never another state than being astray, or 'odd'.

When John Dickens was released, the family moved first to North End, Hampstead, which would have given John Dickens and Charles Dickens, both travelling from Hampstead down to the Strand, a round ten miles commute each day. The following move, at the end of 1824, was to 29 Johnson Street, Somers Town, an area associated with Mr Skimpole (*BH* chapter 43). Somers Town had been divided from Bloomsbury by the opening of the New Road. The aristocratic Somers family leased it out in 1784 for the building of a suburb, including the Polygon development (destroyed in the 1890s, on the site of Polygon Road and Oakshott Court), while Johnson Street, the most northerly one in the development, and looking towards Camden Town, was created around 1796. Mr Skimpole lives in the Polygon, on the north side of Clarendon Square. It had been home for William Godwin, and of Mary Wollestonecraft in the 1790s. Placing Harold Skimpole in Somers Town, the novel becomes autobiographical; John Dickens ghosts Skimpole, even if the latter escaped the debtors' prison.

When Charles Dickens left working in the blacking-factory (Michael Allen assumes this was in spring 1825), he attended school at Wellington House Academy in Hampstead Road, an area gone under the railway associated with Euston Station. By March 1827, he was working as a clerk for Ellis and Blackmore at no. 1 South Square (before, Holborn Court) and at Charles Molloy's, a

Royal College Street: the plaque over the central house records that Rimbaud and Verlaine lived here in 1873: the poverty associates them with Micawber and the Dickens family in 1824.

solicitor in Symonds' Inn, Holborn. In 1827, the family was evicted for non-payment of rent, and moved into the Polygon as lodgers. By 1831 – on the evidence of the autographs on the readers' slips in the British Museum, for which Dickens acquired a reader's ticket in 1830 – they were living again at Norfolk Street. Later homes, in 1832 and 1834, were at North End, Hampstead, when the family was split up, and John Dickens stayed there with Mrs Davis, a laundress, while the others were at 21 George Street, Adelphi (*Letters* 1.5, 47n); another was 18 Bentinck Street, off Marylebone Lane, perhaps as lodgers only.

By 1834, by when Dickens' writings had begun appearing as the 'sketches' of *Sketches by Boz*, he was living at Furnival's Inn in Holborn, in which he changed lodgings in 1836; by 1837, married, he was living at 48 Doughty Street. His marriage was solemnised at James Savage's Gothic-built St Luke's (1824), in Sydney Street in Chelsea (see p. 273; opposite the Royal Brompton Hospital, which came in the 1840s). Brompton was a village; Catherine Hogarth's parents lived at York Place in the Fulham Road (now gone), Dickens moved to Selwood

Terrace in the Fulham Road before his wedding. In *Nicholas Nickleby*, Kate works for Mrs Wititterly in Cadogan Place, off Sloane Street, called:

> [the] connecting link between the aristocratic pavements of Belgrave Square and the barbarism of Chelsea. It is in Sloane Street, but not of it. The people in Cadogan Place look down upon Sloane Street, and think Brompton low. They affect fashion too and wonder where the New Road is. (21.260)

(Sir Hans Sloane's daughter married the Baron Cadogan of Oakley in 1717, hence the various site-names for the estate, when it was built on: Sloane Square, for instance, in 1771.) It seems possible to see Dickens reminding himself of his own past.

By 1839, the Dickens family were living at 1 Devonshire Place, opposite York Gate, one of the entrances into Regent's Park. The house was more bourgeois than the Doughty Street town-house, with a brick-walled garden standing between it and the New Road. By 1851, he had moved to Tavistock House in Tavistock Square, laid out in the 1820s by Thomas Cubitt. In 1856 he bought Gad's Hill, near Rochester in Kent, and in 1860, he moved there permanently, and died there, in 1870. Catherine Dickens died in 1878 at Gloucester Crescent, between Primrose Hill and Camden Town. As editor of *All the Year Round*, the journal which succeeded *Household Words*, Dickens maintained, as well as other London properties, lodgings in Covent Garden's Wellington Street.[19] This provides the context of much of *The Uncommercial Traveller*. In that way, he never left London. In the 1860s, as a bachelor figure, father of a family, and associated with Ellen Ternan, he had simultaneous plural uses for London, which in turn allowed him to be a figure who could be defined in different ways, depending on the occasion: not a single subject, not one 'Dickens'.

This movement through London addresses may be compared with another, perhaps more middle-class artist, with a more developed double life than Dickens: William Powell Frith (1819–1909), who in 1859 painted Dickens in his study at Tavistock House. Frith came from Yorkshire to London to study art, first in Charlotte Street, which was part of an artists' colony, staying with his family at 11 Osnaburgh Street, Regent's Park from 1839 onwards. Dickens lived in that street for a short time in 1844. On marriage, Frith stayed in lodgings in Charlotte Street (1845), moving in 1847 into a first house, 13 Park Village West, where there was gas-lighting, and then into a larger house at no. 12 with its own Italianate octagonal tower; this colony of cottages, which represented the picturesque in London, had been designed by Nash, and continued by James Pennethorne. Frith's next house was in 1852, Pembridge Villas, Bayswater, a new suburb created by the opening of the Great Western Railway at Paddington, a painting of which he exhibited in 1862; houses reached by steps, with porticos, and with bathrooms and water-closets. Frith's mistress, Mary Alford, lived at 14 Duke Street, St James, and after 1862, at 12 Oxford Terrace (now Sussex Gardens); she lived with an older friend, Sophia Dolby, and both worked

19 Curzon Street, Mayfair, where Disraeli died 1881; see also *Vanity Fair* chapters 36 and 37. Beau Brummell, the dandy (1778–1840), had lived in the street.

as lodging-house keepers. After his wife's death, Frith married Mary in 1881, moving with her in 1888 to a suburban address, near the Crystal Palace, to Ashenhurst, 7 Sydenham Rise in South London (1888). After her death he moved to 114 Clifton Hill, St John's Wood in 1896; now there were not five servants, as in 1881, but a cook, a housemaid, and a nurse.[20]

Dickens' London is dissimilar to this, nor is it Thackeray's, nor Trollope's. Neither Thackeray nor Trollope make the city part of a personal history which is partially clear, partially opaque to the person who writes about it. Thackeray's London place-names are often fictionalised, but a Dickens scene can usually be identified, at least in terms of area. Usually, where a site remains unspecified (e.g. where Mr Gride lives in *Nicholas Nickleby*), it registers a slackness which ignores social relationships as constructed spatially. Thackeray's London tends more to the club-land existence of the West End. Dickens' London is more working-class, centred more on areas east of Charing Cross, and more suburban. Thackeray, who moved from Great Coram Street, near the Foundling Hospital, to Young Street, off Kensington High Street, and died in Palace Gardens, was more interested in the aristocracy than Dickens: so was Trollope, who lived in Montagu Square.[21] So Kensington plays little part in what follows in this book; it is more the sphere of James' London novels; in an essay entitled 'London' (1888), James regrets not having time to write about it, 'having sacrificed Kensington, the once-delightful, the Thackerayan, with its literary vestiges,

1820s houses on Park Lane, with Hyde Park beyond the cobbled lane: Disraeli lived at the last house on the right in the row, 1839–72.

its quiet pompous red palace, its square of Queen Anne, its house of Lady Castlewood, its Greyhound tavern, where Henry Esmond lodged' (*Collected Travel Writings* 43).[22] Kensington Palace was a Jacobean house redesigned by Wren and Hawksmoor for William and Mary in 1689.

Dickens and Thackeray intersect, with Mayfair in particular, but Disraeli, Thackeray and Trollope work differently from Dickens by using different locales to point up class-differences, tiny rises and falls in the social scale; it is part of the 'silver fork' tradition out of which the first two of these novelists emerge, which is both critical of and conniving with minute social distinctions.[23] 'Silver fork' novels were associated with the tradition of Robert Plummer Ward's novel of 1825, *Tremaine, Or, the Man of Refinement*, Disraeli, Bulwer, and Mrs Gore (1799–1861) and the 'Dandyism' associated with Alfred Count D'Orsay (1801–52), and centred at Gore House, site of the present Albert Hall, home of Lady Marguerite, Countess of Blessington (1789–1849).

IV · READING THE CITY

The city induces a kaleidoscopic vision: the kaleidoscope, an optical instrument, producing numerous coloured reflections ('beautiful forms'), constantly altered by rotating the instrument, was patented in 1817, and belongs to the new visual culture of the urban nineteenth century, along with the eidometropolis, and the Panorama and the Diorama, and the magic lantern.[24] Wordsworth is both alienated and fascinated by these changing 'shapes', which defy any secure knowledge, including biographical or autobiographical:

> How oft, amid those over flowing streets,
> Have I gone forward with the crowd, and said
> Unto myself, 'The face of every one
> That passes by me is a mystery!'
> Thus have I looked, nor ceased to look, oppressed
> By thoughts of what and whither, when and how,
> Until the shapes before my eyes became
> A second-sight procession, such as glides
> Over still mountains, or appears in dreams;
> And once, far-travelled in such mood, beyond
> The reach of common indication, lost
> Amid the moving pageant, I was smitten
> Abruptly, with the view (a sight not rare)
> Of a blind Beggar, who, with upright face,
> Stood, propped against a wall, upon his chest
> Wearing a written paper, to explain
> His story, whence he came, and who he was.
> Caught by the spectacle my mind turned round
> As with the might of waters; an apt type
> This label seemed of the utmost we can know,
> Both of ourselves and of the universe;
> And, on the shape of that unmoving man,
> His steadfast face and sightless eyes, I gazed,
> As if admonished from another world. (*The Prelude* 7.626–649 (259–61))

We can compare this passage on 'the crowd' with others. First Dickens:

A wonderful fact to reflect upon, that every human creature is constituted to be that profound secret and mystery to every other. A solemn consideration, when I enter a great city by night, that every one of those darkly clustered houses encloses its own secret, that every room in every one of them encloses its own secret; that every beating heart in the hundreds of thousands of breasts there, is, in some of its imaginings, a secret to the heart nearest it! Something of the awfulness, even of death itself, is referable to this. No more can I turn the leaves of this dear book that I loved, and vainly hope in time to read it all. No more can I look into the depths of this unfathomable water, wherein, as momentary lights glanced into it, I have had glimpses of buried treasure and other things submerged. It was appointed that the book should shut with a spring, for ever and ever, when I had read but a page. It was appointed that the water should be locked in an eternal frost, when the light was playing on its surface, and I stood in ignorance on the shore. My friend is dead, my neighbour is dead, my love, the darling of my soul, is dead; it is the inexorable consolidation and perpetuation of the secret that was always in that individuality, and which I shall carry in mine to my life's end. In any of the burial-places of this city through which I pass, is there a sleeper more inscrutable than its busy inhabitants are, in their innermost personality, to me, or than I am to them? (*A Tale of Two Cities* 1.3.14–15)

The 'great city by night', with its 'darkly clustered' houses, which themselves form a crowd, comprises hundred of thousands of individual secrets. The crowd, which so pleased Lamb, and which is the theme of 'The Man of the Crowd', a short story which is the prototype of a detective mystery, written by Edgar Allan Poe (1840), has become the new reality. Dickens writes in 1846, 'I don't seem to be able to get rid of my spectres unless I can lose them in crowds' (*Letters* 4.622).

Poe's sense of the man, who refuses to be alone and seeks out crowds, and who is potentially criminal because unknowable, and unreadable, is discussed by Walter Benjamin, comparing Poe with Bulwer (1803–73), the English novelist, whose *Eugene Aram* (1832) has as subject the 'great criminal' (*Arcades* 440). Writing on the *flâneur*, Benjamin cites part of this passage from Bulwer:

> Through this crowd, self-absorbed as usual – with them, not one of them – Eugene Aram slowly wound his uncompanioned way. What an incalculable field of dread and sombre contemplation is opened to every man who, with his heart disengaged from himself and his eyes accustomed to the sharp observance of his tribe, walks through the streets of a great city! What a world of dark and troubled secrets in the breast of every one who hurries by you! Goethe has said somewhere, that each of us, the best as the worst, hides within him something – some feeling, some remembrance, that, if known, would make you hate him. (4.5)[25]

In Bulwer and Dickens, the city produces the crowd, and the anonymous man of the crowd, who haunts the crowd. But, as the city produces people who live within the context of other people, so it also makes them more private, like Nadgett in *Martin Chuzzlewit*, who 'belonged to a class, a race peculiar to the city; who are secrets as profound to one another as they are to the rest of mankind' (*MC* 27.426). So Georg Simmel, in 'The Metropolis and Mental Life', argues that in the city, people shield themselves against the shock that impacts upon them from too much nearness to other people in street-life: this produces a new psychology, a new, more intense, mental life.[26] Nadgett is a *flâneur*, and, as a man 'in possession of his incognito', as Benjamin quotes Baudelaire (*Baudelaire* 40), he is a detective, like Inspector Bucket; the latter appears as a *flâneur* when he watches Tulkinghorn's funeral (*BH* 53.804–805).

How city-people interact is discussed by Friedrich Engels (1820–94), in *The Condition of the Working Class in England* (1845). He calls London the 'great commercial capital of the world', discussing what is necessary for people to live in such contiguity with each other, in a city where 'Londoners have been forced to sacrifice the best qualities of their human nature to bring to pass all the marvels of civilization'. What follows is also quoted by Benjamin as specially true of London,

And still they crowd by one another as though they had nothing in common, nothing to do with one another, and their only agreement is the tacit one – that each keep to his own side of the pavement, so as not to delay the opposing streams of the crowd – while no man thinks to honour another with so much as a glance. The brutal indifference, the unfeeling isolation of each in his private interest becomes the more repellent and offensive, the more these individuals are crowded together within a limited space. (*Arcades* 427–28)[27]

A self-imposed discipline here maintains privacy; but, for Engels, who notes how the city produces a new type of behaviour and tacit agreement between people not to talk, it is the very condition of alienation. Comparing Dickens with Engels: the division that has been created in the city is as complete as death; each 'darkly clustered house' is the burial place of a secret, where families are divided from each other. For Dickens, this makes the city the incentive and challenge to produce narrative, from the sense that coincidence, for instance, will unfold secrets.

Wordsworth sees the crowd but also the beggar in a sudden, chance moment, which shocks him out of the sense that the crowd is all there is, all that can be known being individual faces, each hiding a mystery. This makes the scene spectral; the subject is absent from what he sees. An epiphany comes from the beggar. The text of his life, which he cannot read, and which therefore is severed from what he is, typifies, or emblemises something central in Dickens: the self's inherent lack of knowledge of the self. The beggar is a split subject, separate from his story.

In *A Tale of Two Cities* the city known by night cancels out previously held knowledge, and becomes a form of death. If it keeps its mystery, like death, it becomes 'other' even to the self who is in it. Writing about it, or about the self formed by it, is like describing death, the unknowable. Writing the city becomes a form of 'going astray', taking the writer from his knowledge. For the modernist French writer, Maurice Blanchot (1907–2003), 'writing' is that which loses the author: 'to write means to consign oneself to the interminable, the writer . . . loses the power to say "I"'. Writing, not revealing the self, as autobiography is supposed to do, goes astray, suspends the self which thinks it is directing the writing in a state of worklessness (*desoeuvrement*). It is the state of what Blanchot calls 'solitude'.[28] In this state, the writer is divided from his writing.

One example, from all those Dickens speakers whose language goes astray – Jingle, Pecksniff, Mrs Gamp, Chadband, Skimpole, Flora Finching: Mr Micawber. His subject is London:

'Under the impression,' said Mr Micawber, 'that your peregrinations in this metropolis have not as yet been extensive, and that you might have some difficulty in penetrating the arcana of the Modern Babylon in the direction of the City Road – in short,' said Mr Micawber, in another burst of confidence, 'that you might lose yourself – I shall be happy to call this evening, and install you in the knowledge of the nearest way.' (*DC* 11.167)

'Arcana' means 'secret'. Mr Micawber goes astray in a sentence about a boy going astray; he fears that David Copperfield both will not know the secret of the city, and will be caught by its secret, its reserve, whose quality takes away certainty. Negotiating the city and writing are both risky activities, and the only person to guide is the one whose poetry of speech least ensures knowledge of the 'nearest way' (a phrase from *Macbeth*). Micawber's language is the spirit of Dickens' art, which if it knows it is astray knows there is no 'proper' way, and is led as language leads it. As Wordsworth pauses, 'as if admonished from another world', he is rebuked for his sense that he should be able to know something of the faces he sees. This 'other world' is that of the blind beggar. In Dickens, the other world is London, and venturing into it, being in it, writing it, is to be held by fascination, held by a secret that cannot be read (but which all the novels attempt solutions for) and to feel that describing the most familiar is going astray.

CHAPTER TWO

STREET-SCENES
Sketches by Boz, with *Pickwick Papers* and *Nicholas Nickleby*

We have a most extraordinary partiality for lounging about the streets. When-ever we have an hour or two to spare, there is nothing we enjoy more than a little amateur vagrancy – walking up one street and down another, and staring into shop windows, and gazing about, as if, instead of being on intimate terms with every shop and house in Holborn, the Strand, Fleet-street and Cheapside, the whole were an unknown region to our wandering mind. We revel in a crowd of any kind – a street 'row' is our delight – even a woman in a fit is by no means to be despised, especially in a fourth-rate street, where all the female inhabitants run out of their houses and discharge large jugs of cold water over the patient, as if she were dying of spontaneous combustion, and wanted putting out. Then a drunken man – what can be more charming than a regular drunken man[?] . . . And what, we ask, can be expected but popular discontent, when Temperance Societies interfere with the Amusements of the People?[1]

There seemed to be not much to add to our knowledge of London until his books came upon us, but each in this respect outstripped the other in its marvels. In *Nickleby* the old city appears under every aspect . . . it is our privilege to see and feel it as it absolutely is. Its interior hidden life becomes familiar as its commonest outward forms, and we discover that we hardly knew anything of the places we supposed we knew the best.   *Life* 2.4.123

I · STREET-LIFE: *SKETCHES BY BOZ*

Dickens began publication in December 1833 with essays and sketches appear-ing in magazines, which in book form, and with George Cruikshank's illustra-tions, became *Sketches by Boz* (1836). This chapter looks at these, and at their London, and that in novels which succeeded them, *Pickwick Papers* and *Nicholas Nickleby*. Discussion of *Oliver Twist*, the text in between these last two, is held over for the next chapter. As arranged thematically by Dickens for an edition of 1839, the fascination of *Sketches by Boz* is evidently with street-life. Boz, who is 'lounging', is a *flâneur*; unlike Wordsworth, who was no *flâneur*, no loiterer. 'Our Next Door Neighbours' (March 1836) opens:

> We are very fond of speculating as we walk through a street, on the character and pursuits of the people who inhabit it; and nothing so materially assists us in these speculations as the appearance of the house doors. The various expressions of the human countenance afford a beautiful and interesting study; but there is something in the physiognomy of street-door knockers, almost as characteristic and nearly as

infallible. When we visit a man for the first time, we contemplate the features of his knocker with the greatest curiosity, for we well know, that between the man and his knocker, there will inevitably be a greater or less degree of resemblance and sympathy. (*SB* 58)

Dickens restates Wordsworth's interest in 'physiognomies', and the passage discusses door-knockers, and the solecism of replacing them by bells in the new buildings of Eaton Square. Similarly, the chambers where Scrooge lives, perhaps in the City, possess a door-knocker which transforms into Marley's face as Scrooge approaches it (*A Christmas Carol, CB1* 54); the idea allowed Thackeray in *The Rose and the Ring* (chapter 4) some fun with the porter Gruffanuff whose unpleasantness at the door means he is magicked into a door-knocker.[2] Dickens' sketch about neighbours concludes with the account of a mother and boy who have come to London out of the country. The boy is dying of disease, presumably consumption; he says: 'bury me in the open fields – any where but in these dreadful streets. I should like to be where you can see my grave, but not in these close crowded streets; they have killed me' (*SB* 66).

But the next section of *Sketches by Boz*, called 'Scenes', and beginning with 'The Streets – Morning' (July 1835) and 'The Streets – Night' (January 1836) has, unlike the boy, no alienation from London streets, which are rather explored as though the city 'were an unknown region to our wandering mind', and as if shops had no familiar things in them, only unfamiliar. London is experienced at different times, night and day. In book-form, 'The Streets – Morning' and 'The Streets – Night' are succeeded by 'Shops and their Tenants' (October 1834), and 'Scotland-yard' (October 1836). Each of these five pieces begin with comments on London streets. The cancelled opening for 'Scotland-yard' runs:

> If our recollection serves us, we have more than once hinted, confidentially, to our readers that we entertain a strong partiality for the queer little old streets which yet remain in some parts of London, and that we infinitely prefer them to the modern innovations, the wide streets with broad pavements, which are every day springing up around us.[3]

Sketches by Boz has a sense of achievement in evoking what has disappeared, as though Dickensian London was gone before it started in Dickens. The coal-heavers in their public-house in 'Scotland-yard' (October 1836) are of the 1820s and long before that, since they can remember back to before 1798, when the Patent Shot Manufactory was built in Waterloo (demolished 1950). The sketch mentions a forgotten 'landmark': Pedlar's Acre (*SB* 88). This was a part of Lambeth on the south bank of the Thames, between Westminster and Waterloo Bridges, still remembered in a window in the frequently rebuilt medieval church of St Mary at Lambeth: in the sixteenth century the pedlar donated the land to the church if he and his dog could be remembered by it.

While streets are the source of wonder, they do not allow for a single, unified London; significantly, the 'Morning' and 'Night' articles were not written

Nicholas Hawksmoor's St George's, Bloomsbury, scene of 'The Bloomsbury Christenings' in *Sketches by Boz*. The church has a Corinthian portico, derived from St George, Hanover Square, with a double set of columns, and the tower is virtually independent of this, being placed on the north side, ritually speaking, and ascending from 'solid base to fanciful spire' (Pevsner). Note the lion and the unicorn.

in symmetry with each other. What is evident, however, is the commitment to London. Dickens' first published piece, and short story (December 1833), 'A Dinner at Poplar Walk' (which became 'Mr Minns and his Cousin') describes a bachelor working at Somerset House, with lodgings in Tavistock Street, Covent Garden. He contrasts with John Dickens, who had also worked there. It is a cosy arrangement: he need only walk across the Strand to get to his work; but it effectively isolates him. The bachelor plagued by relations returns in 'The Bloomsbury Christening' (April 1834). He lives in Pentonville, while his nephew has taken a house in Great Russell Street, which he says is near Bedford Square, but which his uncle identifies with Tottenham Court Road (*SB* 538). This nephew wants his son christened at St George's, Hawskmoor's church in Bloomsbury Way, completed in 1731, and more fashionable than St Giles in the Fields, since that was surrounded by a rookery.

Another Example: the young, exploitative law student in 'The Steam Excursion' (October 1834) notes a 'street breakfast' at the corner of a bye-street, near Temple Bar: Dickens' description of this gave material for Cruikshank's illustration of 'The Streets. Morning' (*SB* 68).

> The coffee was boiling over a charcoal fire, and large slices of bread and butter were piled one upon the other, like deals in a timber-yard. The company were seated on a form, which, with a view both to serenity and comfort, was placed against a neighbouring wall. Two young men, whose uproarious mirth and disordered dress bespoke the conviviality of the preceding evening, were treating three 'ladies' and an Irish

labourer. A little sweep was standing at a short distance, casting a longing eye at the tempting delicacies; and a policeman was watching the group from the opposite side of the street. The wan looks, and gaudery finery of the wretched thinly-clad females, contrasted as strangely with the gay sun-light, as did their forced merriment with the boisterous hilarity of the two young men, who now and then varied their amusements by 'bonneting' the proprietor of the itinerant coffee-house. (447–48)

The details of the 'sketch' of London life here, its tableau presentation Hogarthian, develops from Pierce Egan (1772–1849), author of *Life in London, or The Day and Night Scenes of Jerry Hawthorn Esq. and his Elegant Friend Corinthian Tom* (1821), dedicated to George the Fourth, and illustrated by Cruikshank and his brother Robert. Corinthian Tom, Regency buck, shows London to Jerry Hawthorn, his country cousin; the other character is Bob Logic, the Oxonian.[4] The two rakes in Dickens' sketch are seen more realistically than in Egan, in their raffishness, and low-level cruelty, so are the three prostitutes; while the Irish labourer, the sweep and the policeman – legislated into being in 1829 – are significant, symbolic presences, who define space (the policeman is in a position of surveillance, whereby he reads the space of the others), and are defined by it.[5]

Not only streets, Boz observes city-types. 'Shabby-Genteel People' (November 1834) picks out male attempts at respectability, distinguishing the shabby-genteel type from others with whom he is not to be confused: further, he observes, quasi-autobiographically, where such a one lives: 'in a damp back parlour in a new row of houses at Camden-town, half street, half brickfield, somewhere near the [Regent's] canal'. This would be near the New North Road, created in 1812. This is the 'miserably poor man who feels his poverty and vainly strives to conceal it' (307): not working class, but holding on to appearances of being 'genteel'. The phrase 'shabby-genteel' returns in *Pickwick Papers*, describing the court for insolvent debtors, set up in 1813, which met in Portugal Street, in Lincoln's Inn Fields. The Court's fate is:

> to be somehow or other held and understood by the general consent of all the destitute shabby-genteel people in London, as their common resort, and places of daily refuge. It is always full. The steams of beer and spirits perpetually ascend to the ceiling, and being condensed by the heat, roll down the walls like rain: there are more old suits of clothes in it at one time, than will be offered for sale in all Houndsditch in a twelvemonth; and more unwashed skins and grizzly beards than all the pumps and shaving-shops between Tyburn and Whitechapel could render decent between sunrise and sunset. (*PP* 42.571)

The passage defines London east and west, and by the people who most proliferate in it; those defined by the second-hand, and the need to keep themselves genteel.

'Thoughts about People' (April 1835), develops shabby-gentility by considering London's loneliness, through the figure of the person who has moved into it for work from the country. A shabby-genteel, friendless clerk is seen for a moment on a Bank Holiday Monday in St James' Park, and then imagined working in a 'back office' in the City, and dining solitary every evening at five 'somewhere near Bucklersbury' (252). He eats a small plateful of 'roast beef, with greens, and half-a-pint of porter. He has a small plate today because greens are a penny more than potatoes, and he had "two breads" yesterday, with the additional enormity of "a cheese" the day before'. After returning to the office for a last half hour, he goes home to his 'little back room in Islington' (253). Cruikshank shows him eating in the restaurant with the hat on the peg behind him, as it goes on the peg in the office; the restaurant and its routines are equivalent to the office. Sometimes he must take a letter to his employer, 'a wealthy man of business' in a house in Russell Square. This glimpse is succeeded by the study of the old misanthropical type who at death bequeaths property to a Bible Society, 'and the Institution erects a tablet to his memory expressive of their admiration of his Christian conduct in this world' (254). He is followed by a view of 'particular friends, hackney coachmen cabmen and cads' and 'London apprentices' who are compared favourably with 'the precious puppyism of the Quadrant [i.e. Regent Street, completed around 1820], 'the whiskered dandyism of Regent-street and Pall Mall, or gallantry in its dotage any where' (255). 'Dandyism', a topic of *Bleak House* (12.189), evokes Carlyle and defines this prose against such texts praising dandies: Disraeli's *Vivian Grey* (1826) and Bulwer's *Pelham* (1828), novels of the 'silver fork' school.

Moments of pessimism and identification with poverty and separateness in the sketch appear in 'Brokers' and Marine Shops' (December 1834), 'Gin Shops' (February 1835), and 'The Pawnbroker's Shop' (June 1835). 'London Recreations' (March 1835) notes the 'small gentility' within the middle-class, and discusses middle-class family lives, in contrast to those of bachelor clerks: 'the regular City man, who leaves Lloyd's at five o'clock, and drives home to Hackney, Clapton, Stamford-Hill or elsewhere' (117).[6] It comments on his pleasure in his garden, and compares it with the retired man who lives with his wife 'say in the Hampstead-road, or the Kilburn-road, or any road where the houses are small and neat, and have little slips of back garden' (118). The interest in town-houses (Russell Square) and in suburban private houses suggests something characteristic of London which Sharon Marcus discusses: whereas in Paris, there was at this time a vigorous building of apartment-blocks, so that the Parisian defined himself as urban, and as living contiguously with other urban types, in London, apartments were identified with cheap lodging-houses, and the ideal was the individualised house (hence the emphasis on the garden, as a marker of individuality) within the suburb.[7]

Boz observes the peculiarities of places, as in 'Shops and their Tenants' (October 1834), based 'on the Surrey side of the water – a little distance beyond the Marsh-gate'. Until 1844, the Marsh Gate was a turnpike, at the junction of Lower Marsh and the Westminster Bridge Road. The sketch discusses a house which has got into Chancery (the *Bleak House* world begins here), where everything has been ruined: however many times the shop is opened, it fails. Then there is 'Astley's' theatre (May 1835). The area between 'the Marsh-gate and the Victoria Theatre' appears in 'The Streets – Night'.

Boz has no alienation from anything in London, not from habitual drunkenness, nor from prisoners seen leaving Bow Street, as in 'The Prisoner's Van' (November 1835). Here two child prostitutes, Emily and Bella, sixteen and fourteen, are off to the treadmill at Cold Bath Fields Prison, Clerkenwell, with other prisoners, 'boys of ten' and 'a houseless vagrant going joyfully to prison as a place of food and shelter, handcuffed to a man whose prospects were ruined, character lost, and family rendered destitute by his first offence' (317). The conjunction of these types of prisoner points up the absurdity of the penal system. Bow Street is where the magistrates commit the Artful Dodger to prison (*OT* 3.6.366–69). The girls are only glad they are not going to the 'stone jug', i.e. Newgate. This prison, which is at the heart of Dickens (see *Oliver Twist*, *Barnaby Rudge* and *Great Expectations*), is the subject of 'Criminal Courts' (October 1834), and 'A Visit to Newgate'. The latter was written for *Sketches by Boz* when it appeared in volume form in 1836, and records a visit made on 5 November 1835 with John Black, who edited the *Morning Chronicle*, which published so many of the original *Sketches*. Dickens visited Newgate for a second time, 27 June 1837, with Forster, Macready and Hablot K. Browne, so shaping *Oliver Twist*.

Rebuilt in 1782, to designs by George Dance the younger, Clerk of the City Works, this Newgate replaced the prison that *Barnaby Rudge* describes being burned in the Gordon Riots. Until 1813, it held debtors as well as convicted criminals. 'A Visit to Newgate' culminates in a description of three condemned men. They have been identified: as Robert Swan, aged thirty-two, a soldier in the foot guards convicted of robbery with menaces, who had hope of a reprieve (which happened), and John Smith and John Pratt, convicted for homosexual offences with each other and hanged on 27 November 1835.[8] To record these last names is to remember the injustice: they were the last to be hanged in England for homosexuality. Dickens' text notes the first man's stillness, but then, when he is seen again, he is walking up and down. Of the two others, one is leaning against the fireplace, with his back to the visitors, while the other looks out of the window. Though it would seem that neither's face can be seen, the text specifies that one man is melancholic; the other, with 'pale haggard face and disordered hair', a 'ghastly' appearance and with 'eyes wildly staring before him' is maniacal, like one of Cibber's allegorical statues, a representation of despair. Both, 'motionless as statues', are as if already dead (*SB* 245).

Smith and Pratt had been committed for trial by the magistrate Hesney Wedgwood at the police-court at Union Hall in Southwark. Wedgwood said that they had been found in a room in a lodging house. 'The detection of these degraded creatures was entirely due to their poverty, [for] they were unable to pay for privacy, and the room was so poor that what was going on inside was easily visible from without.'[9] Though all three men Boz sees were poor, there seems to be an implicit class difference; these homosexual men had not only infringed the law, but were in dire poverty (so Wedgwood's word 'degraded' has a double meaning). Hangings for sodomy, however this was defined, usually as 'indecent assault', had ended in practice in continental Europe in 1803, but in England continued till 1835, though the death penalty was only ended by the Offences Against the Person Act in 1861 (transportation, or ten-year terms in prison served instead). An attempt at legislation in 1841 had been unsuccessful. There were 46 people hanged for the 'crime' between 1810 and 1835, 32 were reprieved, 713 received the sentence of the pillory (discontinued after 1816) or were imprisoned. These figures need to be contextualised by the point that legislation in 1828 reduced the evidence required in trials of sodomy.[10] Boz makes no comment on the offence; perhaps the melancholia and madness represents his construction of it. It puts the men beyond Robert Swan's self-control, and within an eighteenth-century literary and artistic code for describing, imagining and constructing men in despair. The sketch ends with an attempt at imagining a man's last night alive. This condemned man is a married Bill Sikes, so that there is a construction of masculinity in the sketch, which moves from noting the dignified, even 'jaunty' soldier to the two homosexuals, figures of passivity, to the man whose 'vice', wife-beating, indexes his other crimes. And the impossibility of representing adequately Smith and Pratt does not imply anything other than fascination with them: for Dickens and male homosexuality, there are such figures as Steerforth and Heep, who imply something like it, to be considered, and Bradley Headstone; for lesbianism, there is Miss Wade.

From the prison, we turn to another oppressed part of London. The 'rookery' which was around St Giles in the Fields – 'adjoining the brewery at the bottom of Tottenham-court-road' has already been mentioned; it appears in 'Gin-shops':

> The filthy and miserable appearance of this part of London can hardly be imagined by those (and there are many such) who have not witnessed it. Wretched houses with broken windows patched with rags and paper: every room let out to a different family and in many instances to two or even three; fruit and 'sweet-stuff' manufacturers in the cellars, barbers and red-herring venders in the front parlours, and cobblers in the back; a bird-fancier in the first floor, three families on the second, starvation in the attics, Irishmen in the passage; a 'musician' in the front kitchen, and a charwoman and five hungry children in the back one – filth every where – a gutter before the houses and a drain behind them – clothes drying and slops emptying from the windows: girls of fourteen or fifteen with matted hair walking about barefooted, and in white great-coats, almost their only covering; boys of all ages, in coats of all sizes and no coats at all; men and women, in every variety of scanty and dirty apparel, lounging, scolding, drinking, smoking, squabbling, fighting, and swearing. (217)

This examines one house from the cellar upwards to the ground floor, the first floor, the second, and the attic, place of most poverty; then descends again, to show that the passages have other tenants than those in the rooms (the Irish), as do the kitchens. The gutter and the drain isolate each house by the filth of what is thrown into them front and back, and the piece ends by noting girls, boys, and men and women. The passage continues to say 'You turn the corner, what a change!' and the 'splendid gin-shop' is described; it seems a contrast to the rookery, but is not, because the people in there are from it, and will return 'to beat their wives for complaining and kick the children for daring to be hungry' (220).

The rookery, which recalls 'Gone Astray', is depicted in Hogarth's *Gin Lane* (1751), and it influences Dickens, not only for the piece's title, or the area. Hogarth puts, in the distance, the steeple of St George's, Bloomsbury; the pyramidal structure based on Pliny's descriptions of one of the seven wonders of the world, the Mausoleum at Halicarnassus. It is surmounted by a statue of George the First and pictures the pomposity of power and the remoteness of religion. Houses are falling, a theme in the description of 'Tom-All-Alone's' in *Bleak House*, chapter 16, as much as for *Little Dorrit*, and, as an ironic sign of a cross above the church, there is a prominent sign for a pawnshop; as there is in Cruikshank's picture of 'The Pawnbroker's Shop', and as there is in the picture of Mr Brownlow being robbed in *Oliver Twist* (*OT* 75). The multiple coffins in *Gin Lane* find analogues in *Oliver Twist*, with the boy sleeping among them, and Nancy's obsession with them (*OT* 3.8.384). Dickens knew Lamb's commentary on *Gin Lane*: for Lamb, every detail '*tells*':

> Every part is full of 'strange images of death' . . . Not only the two prominent figures, the woman and the half-dead man . . . but everything else in the print contributes to bewilder and stupefy – the very houses . . . tumbling all about in various directions, seem drunk, seem absolutely reeling from the effect of that diabolical spirit of phrenzy which goes forth over the whole composition . . . Not content with the dying and dead figures . . . he shows you what (of a kindred nature) is passing beyond [the action]. Close by the shell, in which, by the direction of the parish beadle, a man is depositing his wife, is an old wall, which, partaking of the universal decay around it, is tumbling to pieces. Through a gap in this wall are seen three figures, which appear to make a part in some funeral procession which is passing by on the other side of the wall, out of the sphere of the composition.[11]

Dickens, reviewing Cruikshank's picture-series 'The Drunkard's Children', in *The Examiner* (8 July 1848) referred back to *Gin Lane* for comparison, and showed that he knew exactly where the area was: 'a most neglected, wretched neighbourhood (the same that is only just now being cleared away for the extension of Oxford Street), and an unwholesome, indecent, abject way of life':

> We have always been inclined to think the purpose of this piece not adequately stated, even by Charles Lamb. 'The very houses seem reeling', it is true, but they quite as powerfully indicate some of the more prominent causes of intoxication among the neglected orders of society, as any of its effects. There is no evidence that any of the actors in the dreary scene have ever been much better off than we find them. The best

are pawning the commonest necessaries, and tools of their trades, and the worst are homeless vagrants who give us no clue to their having been otherwise in bygone days. All are living and dying miserably. Nobody is interfering for prevention or for cure ... The beadle (the only sober man in the composition except for the pawnbroker), is mightily indifferent to the orphan-child crying beside its parent's coffin ... The church is very prominent and handsome, but coldly surveys these things in progress underneath the shadow of its tower ... (*J2* 105)

Lamb describes, in a partly formalist manner, how the picture works, and how Hogarth makes 'a part stand for the whole', so that the picture implies more than it shows; Dickens' critique, more historical, emphasises the *laissez-faire* attitude of church and state. The correction of Lamb does not take away from the dominant sense of ruin: London as the ruin, in Hogarth's time and in Lamb's and Dickens'. In these 'strange images of death' (*Macbeth* 1.3.95), lifeless houses are alive and reeling, while the woman who has been breast-feeding her baby, who is falling to its death, is dead.

II · PICKWICK PAPERS

Mr Weller's knowledge of London was extensive and peculiar. *Pickwick Papers* 266

Sam Weller and Mr Pickwick are the Sancho and the Quixote of Londoners, and as little likely to pass away as the old city itself. (Forster, *Life* 2.1.92)

As *Sketches by Boz* included Newgate, so the *The Pickwick Papers* tends inevitably towards the Fleet prison, while there are also references made to the Whitecross prison as wholly unacceptable for Pickwick to consider going to.[12] The Fleet prison, on the east side of the Fleet River, north of present-day Ludgate Circus, was a medieval prison burned in the Peasants' Revolt, in the Fire of London, and in the Gordon Riots, and ending its prison-life in 1842. This novel makes it a figure of London.

The circumstances which produced *The Posthumous Papers of the Pickwick Club* (April 1837 to November 1837) have been often discussed, and how a novel intended to be 'illustrative of manners and life in the country' became, after three splendid instalments, in its fourth a London-based text, through the appearance of Sam Weller, a particular 'specimen of London life' (*Letters* 1.154), at the White Hart Inn in one of 'the obscurer quarters of the town'; namely, in the Borough (10.129).[13] The inn, pulled down in 1889, had been Jack Cade's headquarters in 1450.

At this point the novel almost begins again, with a possible hint, in 'philosophers are only men in armour' (10.142) that Pickwick may be like Cervantes' Don Quixote. The hiring of Samuel Weller follows in chapter 12. The pattern even repeats *Don Quixote* (1605), whose hero makes his first expedition without Sancho Panza, and returns to start again with him, in Part 1, Chapter 7. The connection between Don Quixote and Pickwick was made during the course of the novel's serialisation (see Kinsley, lvii), as well as by Forster, and

The George, Borough High Street: seventeenth-century coaching inn, with balconies surviving, mentioned in *Little Dorrit* chapter 22; Sam Weller is met at the White Hart Inn, an equivalent to this one. If Dickens knew the association of Elizabethan drama with such inns, there may be a suggestion of an alliance between Sam Weller and Elizabethan comic drama.

of course, it is Dostoyevsky's theme, when he brings together Cervantes' hero, and Dickens', and his own holy fool, Prince Myshkin in *The Idiot*, as three instances of Christ-like goodness, where goodness has to be seen as complete folly.

> The main idea of the novel is to depict the positively good man [. . .] Of all the good figures in Christian literature, Don Quixote is the most complete. But he is good only because he is at the same time ridiculous. Dickens' Pickwick (an infinitely weaker conception than Don Quixote, but still immense) is also comic and succeeds because of this. Sympathy is aroused for the good man who is ridiculed and who does not know his own worth, and this sympathy is aroused in the reader too. This arousing of sympathy is the secret of humour.[14]

That Pickwick is mad is Sam Weller's own suspicion, as when he tells Pickwick that 'you rather want someone to look arter you Sir, ven your judgement goes out a wisitin'' (22.305). If Christ belongs to what Michel Foucault would call the history of madness, which is also the history of folly, Pickwick, and perhaps Sam too, are also involved in that history, as is Myshkin: madness as innocence. Madness is a dominant strain in the interpolated tales within *The Pickwick Papers*, as if these carry the burden of thinking of melancholy-madness, as the alternative to Pickwick and Sam's comic madness.[15] Such a state is sexless, though the relationship is perhaps unconsciously homoerotic (less unconscious with the analogous, mirroring, cases of Jingle and Trotter, who go together to the West Indies). Put into the context of the novel, there is the implication that to be abroad in London is either to be paranoid-mad, or requires an alternative form of madness, a folly which is innocent, but which, according to Forster, may be what London generates, as much as it produces the suicidal madnesses that come out of paranoia. To find the city inducing madness is Dickensian, and will be marked throughout several novels, and Dostoyevskian: Svidrigaylov tells Raskolnikov when he expounds to him the nature of St Petersburg, a city, it seems, like London:

> I'm convinced there are lots of people in Petersburg who talk to themselves while they walk. It's a city of semi-lunatics. If we had been a scientific nation, our doctors, lawyers, and philosophers could have made valuable investigations, each in his own field, in Petersburg. You won't often find a place like Petersburg where so many strange, harsh and gloomy things exert an influence on a man's mind. Think what the influence of the climate alone is worth. And in addition, it is the administrative centre of Russia, and its character must be reflected in everything.[16]

It is easy to minimise the organisation of *Pickwick Papers*, though it introduces the lawyer Perker in chapter 10, in the same moment as Sam appears, and has the misunderstanding between Pickwick and Mrs Bardell in chapter 12, and the law-suit commenced by Dodson and Fogg in chapter 18, and Pickwick and Dodson and Fogg meeting in chapter 20. The first half of the book, to chapter 25, pursued Jingle and Trotter, who reappear in the Fleet Prison in chapter 42, but the action which brings Pickwick to the Fleet has been set going, kept before the reader in chapters 26, and 31, and 34, which gives the trial, in instalment 12. The experience of the prison continues through instalments 14 to 16. In a way anticipating *Bleak House*, the novel's keynote is the law, and in chapter seven, where *Bleak House* is discussed, the law's locales and specificities will receive fuller discussion. With this novel, it is specific-ally the law versus innocence; almost everything Pickwick does falls foul of the law in some way. He is literally impounded in chapter 19, with Captain Boldwig saying that he is being 'bullied' by Pickwick (the lawyers, Dodson and Fogg, accuse Ramsey, a hapless bankrupt from Camberwell of 'bullying' them in chapter 20 (260)). He is arrested in chapters 24 and 25, appearing before the magistrate Mr Nupkins, before being imprisoned in chapter 40.

   Chapter 31, 'Which is all about the Law, and sundry Great Authorities learned therein', directs consistent irony against the law, as embodying London, almost, as it had, autobiographically, for Dickens. It begins with discussion of clerks around the area of the Temple, including the articled clerk who 'knows a family in Gower Street and another in Tavistock Square'. There is the salaried clerk who 'repairs to the Adelphi at least three times a week, dissipates majes-tically at the cider cellars afterwards, and is a dirty caricature of the fashion, which expired six months ago'. (These locales will be discussed in relation to *David Copperfield*.) Lowest in the scale, after the middle-aged copying clerk, are 'the office lads in their first surtouts, who feel a befitting contempt for boys at day-schools, club as they go home at night, for saveloys and porter, and think there is nothing like "life" '(402). The passage develops the satire directed against Dodson and Fogg's clerks mentioned in chapter 20, the man in the brown coat (Wicks), who lives in Somers Town (20.260), the man mixing a Seidlitz powder, presumably for a hangover, and Jackson. Jackson reappears in chapter 31, collecting subpoenas from the Temple, and then, instead of returning to Dodson and Fogg's offices at Freeman Court, Cornhill, forcing his way into Pickwick and Sam's presence at the George and Vulture, off Lombard Street, where he makes them take subpoenas. Pickwick and Weller in response progress down Cheapside and up Newgate-street (the association gives Pickwick pause and makes him walk on in silence) towards Gray's Inn Square, to Perker's chambers. The journey is spent listening to Sam's narrative of the pork-shop which they pass, and of its ex-owner, a man who, perhaps 'in a fit of temporary insanity' converted himself into sausages. In Perker's chambers, Lowten is getting rid of Mr Watty, a bankrupt who has been in Chancery for four years; he is described as 'a rustily clad, miserable looking man, in boots without toes and gloves without fingers. There were traces of privation and suffering – almost of despair – in his lank and care-worn countenance' (31.408). Madness is not far off here. The action proceeds to Lincoln's Inn Old Square, to see Sergeant Snubbin and Mr Phunky, Snubbin's junior in the case.

This narrative gives a virtual definition of the London it constructs for this novel; legal London with its insolence of office, and the law's delays: the clerks at the beginning of the chapter are matched by the privileged lawyers at the end. A precision about locales and the precise relationship of the narrative to them gives the sense of one London, which is always oppressively there, imposing action on the inhabitants. The narrative that Sam tells suggests another London, timeless and mad, and impossible to know in terms of time or place.

The Chancery suitor as a theme is resumed in chapter 44, where the cobbler who has been in the Fleet for twelve years for contempt of court dies there, and it produces Pickwick's protest on hearing that the man was ill for half a year: 'has this man been slowly murdered by the law for six months?' (44.593). Don Quixote goes out to deal with injustice wherever he finds it, but misreads each situation, even if such misreadings may also give an unexpected access to truth, and significance. Parson Adams, in Fielding's *Joseph Andrews* (1742), derives from Don Quixote, with an innocence which is stressed, and which invariably means that he is trapped by every situation he is in. Pickwick is different from either of these in having unwitting confrontations with the law, and in being victimised by it, and it is this he responds to, by setting himself against it, in what Sam Weller calls a display of 'Pickvick and principle' (25.332). The point is amplified in chapter 44, when Sam, who has put himself into prison, in order to be near Pickwick, says 'I takes my determination on principle' and then proceeds to explain in a story how principle can lead to suicide, as it does with the clerk from the government office, from Kensington.[17] Sam's narrative of what he has done and what the clerk did (44.584–85) is dialogical, in Mikhail Bakhtin's sense; that is, in Sam's 'shiftings and changings of the discourse', 'principle' is articulated both in the language of the self and the language of the other. It is seen as both supreme dignity and obstinacy, productive of working fellow-diners in the clerk's regular restaurant to the 'wery confines of desperation and insanity'. It is part of the activity of *Pickwick Papers* to question the status of innocence, and whether it can associate with principle, which may be itself a form of madness. So it is with Boythorn in *Bleak House*, who stands upon 'principle', and has entered into a lawsuit against the Dedlocks. He argues with Skimpole, who as 'a mere child' disavows its necessity or its power of command (*BH* 18.294). And Pickwick's readiness to go to prison rather than pay Dodson and Fogg will be rethought in Arthur Clennam's masochistic attraction towards the Marshalsea.

What becomes evident is the antagonism of law to innocence, as that which is, perhaps by definition, outside its authority, not recognising it. In so far as London is the embodiment of this law, as well as its defiance, it is significant that by the end of the novel everyone has moved out of it, to Dulwich Village (Pickwick and Sam, and Mr and Mrs Wilkins), to Dingley Dell (Mr and Mrs Snodgrass), to Richmond (Mr Tupman), to Shooter's Hill (Mr Weller senior), to the West Indies (Jingle and Trotter) and to Bengal with the East India Company (Bob Sawyer and Benjamin Allen). The city proves to be the source of possibility, and impossible at the same time.

Pickwick can know so much of this London, but once in, he resists knowing the Fleet in all its enormity (45.610). There is no involvement in trauma here, a contrast with Prince Myshkin in *The Idiot*; Pickwick coming out of the prison is not scarred by it; this is not the case with later Dickens texts. So, too, the full awareness of London is kept at a distance: knowledge about London streets comes to him, as much as he can take, from Sam who tells him about sleeping under the dry arches of Waterloo Bridge (16.212), and, when going through Whitechapel, of how poverty and oysters go together, while his father adds the detail about poverty associating with pickled salmon (22.294–95). Two miles beyond Mile End, which would be going towards Epping, the setting for the early scenes of *Barnaby Rudge*, which contain their own misanthropes, Mr Weller explains how turnpike men are solitaries with a desire to take revenge on mankind: 'if they was gen'lm'n you'd call 'em misanthropes, but as it is, they only takes to pike-keeping' (22.295). The misanthrope is Dickens' subject throughout: in this narrative he appears as Gabriel Grub the sexton (chapter 29). Weller gives a rich throwaway comment on life and *ressentiment* as present at the margins of London. Mr Weller and Sam speak as knowing the city's every gradation: as when Weller senior says that he never knew a respectable coachman who wrote poetry, except for one who made a copy of verses the night before he was hung for a highway robbery, 'and *he* wos only a Cambervell man, so even that's no rule' (32.437). What is it about Camberwell, which has now been mentioned twice?

III · *NICHOLAS NICKLEBY*

They rattled on through the noisy, bustling, crowded streets of London, now display-ing long double rows of brightly-burning lamps, dotted here and there with the chemists' glaring light, and illuminated besides with the brilliant flood that streamed from the windows of the shops, where sparkling jewellery, silks and velvets of the richest colours, the most inviting delicacies, and most sumptuous articles of luxuri-ous ornament, succeeded each other in rich and glittering profusion . . .

As they dashed by the quickly-changing and ever-varying objects, it was curious to observe in what a strange procession they passed before the eye. Emporiums of splendid dresses, the materials brought from every quarter of the world; tempting stores of everything to stimulate and pamper the sated appetite and give new relish to the oft-repeated feast; vessels of burnished gold and silver, wrought into every exquisite form of vase, and dish, and goblet; guns, swords, pistols and patent engines of destruction; screws and irons for the crooked, clothes for the newly-born, drugs for the sick, coffins for the dead, and churchyards for the buried – all these jumbled each with the other and flocking side by side, seemed to flit by in motley dance like the fantastic groups of the old Dutch painter, and with the same stern moral for the unheeding restless crowd . . . Life and death went hand in hand . . . (*Nicholas Nickleby* 32.390–91)

Dickens' London emerges seamlessly out of journalism; its writing responds to hard, empirical observation, though we must always mark the trace in his writing which indicates that seeing always sees what has been given to vision through previous texts. What is seen relates to how the city has already been created in writing. But, that said, 'London' now becomes something else: 'an unknown region to our wandering mind', which is a mind 'going astray', becom-ing what the text creates it. *Nicholas Nickleby* (March 1838–September 1839) seems effortlessly all-encompassing about London, even more than *Sketches by Boz*, *Pickwick Papers*, or *Oliver Twist*. And its interests are dual. While it goes east to the City and beyond that to Bow, south to Southwark and Lambeth, it includes 'the West End' (10.126). It knows Hyde Park, and Mayfair, 'between Park Lane and Bond Street' (32.392–93). Kate Nickleby works for Madame Mantalini, milliner and dress-maker, in a street near Cavendish Square, north of Oxford Street and so north of Mayfair. It is perhaps in Wigmore Street (10.127). All of this, including the Sir Mulberry Hawke theme, associates with satire con-ducted against the 'silver fork' school of novels, a fictitious extract from one of which, *Lady Flabella*, Kate reads to Mrs Wititterly in Cadogan Place (28.345).

Another sphere of action is Soho, which takes in Golden Square, Ralph Nickleby's house, and Newman Noggs' former home 'at the sign of the Crown, in Silver Street [now Beak Street] Golden Square. It is at the corner of Silver Street and James Street, with a bar door both ways' (7.93). Nearby is Miss Knag's brother, 'an ornamental stationer and small circulating library keeper, in a

(*left*) Allegorical statue of George the Second, Roman Emperor-style by John Van Nost (1753), Golden Square, Soho (see *NN* 2.22).
(*Right*) Meard Street, Soho: early eighteenth-century shopfronts and houses; the blocked windows represent the power of the window-tax (1696–1851).

(*below*) The present Old Vic Theatre in the Waterloo Road, Lambeth, opened in 1818 as a local theatre for melodrama, and called The Royal Coburg (see *NN*.30.373); renamed the Royal Victoria in 1833, reopened after a period of closure in 1880 by Emma Cons as a temperance amusement hall, run by her niece Lilian Baylis from 1912 to 1937.

by-street off Tottenham Court Road' (18.218), not far from Norfolk Street, where Dickens had lived. As 'Gin Shops' in *Sketches by Boz* describes a house in the rookery, so *Nicholas Nickleby* has a parallel passage, discussing a slum near Golden Square; 'slum' being a then new word. 'Back slums' meaning the low, unfrequented parts of town, appeared in Pierce Egan's *Life in London*, and the expression was used by Dickens in a letter of 20 November 1840, 'I mean to take a great, London, back-slums kind of walk tonight' (*Letters* 2.152), while, with the sense of 'bad housing', 'slums' was used by *The Times* in 1845.[18] *Nicholas Nickleby* makes the house an allegory of the stages, or phases, of poverty. Whereas Hogarth presented his narrative sequences of 'Stages' or 'Progresses' in different pictures, Dickens makes the house the image of grada- tions of poverty (note, in the quotation following, the word 'progressive'), from the genteel Kenwigs family on the first floor, to Newman Noggs on the top.[19] The last includes Dickens' own secret insignia of shame, the blacking-bottles:

> To judge from the size of the houses, they have been at one time tenanted by persons of better condition than their present occupants, but they are now let off by the week in floors or rooms, and every door has almost as many plates or bell-handles as there are apartments within . . .
>
> In the parlour of one of these houses, which was perhaps a thought dirtier than any of its neighbours, which exhibited more bell-handles, children and porter pots, and caught in its freshness the first gust of the thick black smoke that poured forth night and day from a large brewery hard by, hung a bill announcing that there was yet one room to let within its walls . . .
>
> The common stairs of this mansion were bare and carpetless; but a curious visitor who had to climb his way to the top, might have observed that there were not want- ing indications of the progressive poverty of the inmates, although their rooms were shut. Thus the first-floor lodgers, being flush of furniture, kept an old mahogany table – real mahogany – on the landing-place outside, which was only taken in when occa- sion required. On the second storey the spare furniture dwindled down to a couple of old deal chairs, of which one, belonging to the back room, was shorn of a leg and bottomless. The storey above boasted no greater excess than a worm-eaten wash-tub: and the garret landing-place displayed no costlier articles than two crippled pitchers, and some broken blacking-bottles. (*NN* 14.163–64)

As the rooms always to let are like the second-hand clothes evoked in 'Monmouth Street', and in *Pickwick Papers*'s reference to Houndsditch, objects represent people in their broken-down state and ruin; the legless chair leads towards the words 'crippled' and 'broken'. That is part of London, as much as the pleasure that can be gained from looking at its shops at night from the coach rattling by at speed (the condition in which the modern city is experienced).

To see London in a state of ruin, a topic already touched on in this chapter, will lead into a consideration of Walter Benjamin on the city, and on seeing it in an allegorical mode. Benjamin began the *Arcades Project* in 1927, after a study of allegory and of melancholy, called *The Origin of German Tragic*

Drama. This takes as its models baroque tragedies, German 'mourning plays' (*Trauerspiel*) of the seventeenth century. These plays are not familiar to most readers, but Benjamin does also help with examples from *Hamlet*. *The Origin of German Tragic Drama* is fundamental for understanding the *Arcades Project*, and for understanding Dickens. To consider this, we should go back to the idea of London as the magic-lantern show, which, as pioneered in 1802, was called a 'phantasmagoria'. Here, reality comes and goes in the form of optical illusions, as with this quotation from *The Old Curiosity Shop*, where Quilp is trying to frighten Kit:

> Quilp said not a word in reply, but walking so close to Kit as to bring his eyes within two or three inches of his face, looked fixedly at him, retreated a little distance without averting his gaze, approached again, again withdrew, and so on for half-a-dozen times, like a head in a phantasmagoria. (*OCS* 48.368)

London was Dickens' phantasmagoria, an optical wonder, as well as optical illusion, only capable of being partially read. Benjamin, who saw London as Dickens' phantasmagoria, implies that the city cannot be seen single, empirically. It is worth noting that the phrase *trompe l'oeil* appears first in French in 1803. It implies the power of the optical illusion, as with the Panorama, which was intended to deceive the eye into thinking that it was looking not at a framed and signed picture, but at reality. *Trompe l'oeil* recalls the point that Wordsworth called the Panorama's 'imitations' (*The Prelude* 7.238). London's visual culture comprises *trompe l'oeil*: it tricks the eye. But the word 'phantasmagoria' also implies something more meretricious. It has a precise sense within Marx, for *Capital* begins by arguing that people's relationship to the commodities on sale in shops (such as those described in the passage from chapter 32 of *Nicholas Nickleby*) are distorted:

> The existence of . . . things *qua* commodities, and the value relation between the products of labour which stamps them as commodities, have absolutely no connection with their physical properties and with the material relations arising therefrom. There it is a definite social relation between men, that assumes, in their eyes, the fantastic [phantasmagorical – *phantasmagorische*] form of a relation between things. In order to find an analogy, we must have recourse to the mist-enveloped regions of the religious world. In that world, the productions of the human brain appear as independent beings endowed with life, and entering into relation with one another and the human race. So it is in the world of commodities with the products of men's hands. This I call the Fetishism which attaches itself to the products of labour, so soon as they are produced as commodities, and which is therefore inseparable from the production of commodities.[20]

In modern capitalist, urban society, the commodity becomes a thing in itself, endowed with life, or with spirit. Inanimate, it is unconsciously treated as animate. The point that the products are the work of factory-labour is forgotten; the only relationships which function in this society give place to

All Souls', Langham Place: Upper Regent Street: Nash's *trompe l'oeil* effect supplementing the shape of the church to complete a vista looking up Upper Regent Street, place of commodity-culture, at the point where the street veers left as the body of the church projects right, out of the picture.

the commodity above the person. Commodities, part of London, 'that great emporium' (*The Prelude* 8.594), full of commodities, therefore exist as 'fetishes'. Marx borrows the word from colonialists bringing back objects from Africa, which they imagine have a special animistic function.[21]

In *Nicholas Nickleby* chapter 14, even objects in the passageways outside the rooms of the lodgers are, however reduced and broken-down, part of the commodity-world. For Marx, whom Benjamin quotes, fascination with the commodity means being held by the phantasmagoria (*Arcades* 18). Something of the phantasmagoria appeared in 'Gin Shops' in *Sketches by Boz*, which notes the fashion for plate-glass, gilding and gas-lights in linen-drapers and haberdashers' shops, continues with chemists' shops suddenly evincing a 'rage for mahogany, varnish and expensive floor-cloth', the same with hosiers, then with 'keepers of wine-vaults', and finishing with the bright exterior and interior of the gin-shop. This specious glitter contrasts with the conditions of the rookery. The 'highly coloured' Valentine's Day card that Sam Weller buys at the print-seller's window near Leadenhall Market demonstrates the power of the new factory-made commodified version of love, where Cupid shepherds lovers towards the genteel, Nash-built (1824), spire of All Souls', Langham Place:

> The whole [design] formed a 'valentine' of which, as a written inscription in the window testified, there was a large assortment within, which the shopkeeper pledged himself to dispose of to his countrymen generally, at the reduced rate of one and sixpence each. (*PP* 33.431)

That the text must explain what a Valentine is tells its own story of a new commercial drive in luxury goods which produces bourgeois marriage as the commodity.

Fascination with the phantasmagoria emphasises something strange about the commodity. It will be remembered that Benjamin finds an allegorical element in Dickens (*Arcades* 233). That interest is apparent from the passage in *Nicholas Nickleby* chapter 32, which shows Dickens' interest in the Dance of Death motifs of the late medieval period. These were depicted as woodcuts by many artists, but particularly Holbein (1497–1543), in a sequence of 1538. In *Pickwick Papers*, the 'stroller' who tells his tale speaks of the clown dressed for the pantomime:

> The spectral figures in the Dance of Death, the most frightful shapes that the ablest painter ever portrayed on canvas, never presented a picture half so ghastly. (*PP* 3.50)

It is a frequent figure in Dickens: *Little Dorrit*'s Miss Wade calls Henry Gowan:

> the dressed-up Death in the Dutch series; whatever figure he took upon his arm, whether it was youth or age, beauty or ugliness, whether he danced with it, sang with it, played with it, or prayed with it, he made it ghastly. (*LD* 2.21.700)

The ghastly is ghostly. The Dance of Death is allegorical, but allegory works in another sense, relating to Benjamin saying in *The Origin of German Tragic Drama* that in seventeenth century drama 'the corpse becomes quite simply the pre-eminent emblematic property'.[22] It may be compared with Hamlet's fascination with the skull of Yorick, where this is both an allegorical emblem (Death) and the ruin of the body. Dickens' fascination is with the corpse. Discussing the Paris Morgue, in 'Railway Dreaming' (*Household Words* 10 May 1856), he says that in it:

> the bodies lie on inclined planes within a great glass window, as though Holbein should represent Death, in his grim Dance, keeping a shop, and displaying his goods like a Regent Street or Boulevard linen-draper. (*J3* 375)

If the corpse is the perfect allegorical emblem, Dickens makes exactly Benjamin's move, in identifying this object with the nineteenth-century commodity behind plate-glass in a London fashion-house.

For Benjamin, Baudelaire's poetry shows 'the gaze of the allegorist . . . of the alienated man' (*Arcades* 10). So, in part with Dickens: he has the look of a melancholic, like the appalled look of John Harmon when he sees the corpse of his *alter ego* in the morgue in Limehouse (*OMF* 1.3.33). Harmon looking at George Radfoot killed, in the place of himself, is a survivor looking at the self as dead: enabled to see itself as if allegorically, as if under the sign of death. Benjamin quotes the line from Baudelaire's 'Le Cygne' ('The Swan' 1859), 'Everything becomes an allegory for me' (*Arcades* 10). Baudelaire's preoccupation was the modernisation of Paris then being carried out by Baron Haussmann (1809–91), Prefect of the Seine under Napoleon the Third. Benjamin considers Haussmann's boulevards as exhibitions of Napoleonic imperialism, designed to make barricades, such as those used in 1848, impossible, so that there could be no more revolution in Paris (*Arcades* 11–12). Here is the relevant stanza of Baudelaire:

> Paris change ! Mais rien dans ma mélancolie
> N'a bougé ! Palais neufs, échaufaudages, blocs,
> Vieux faubourgs, tout pour moi devient allégorie,
> Et mes chers souvenirs sont plus lourds que des rocs.
>
> (Paris changes ! But nothing in my melancholy
> has changed ! New palaces, scaffoldings, blocks [of stone],
> old neighbourhoods, everything for me becomes allegory,
> and my dear memories are heavier than rocks.)[23]

Whatever changes have happened, the city is seen allegorically, as if one change suggested that Paris that had gone. Calling Baudelaire the *flâneur*, he says that he stands 'on the threshold', as not yet wholly the wholly desolate big-city dweller. 'He seeks refuge in the crowd. [...] The crowd is the veil through which the familiar city beckons to the *flâneur* as phantasmagoria' (*Arcades* 10). The *flâneur* retains some objectivity, but identifies with crowds as increasing the sense of the city as phantasmagoric, both a source of pleasure and as dead, making a vision of the city split, divided.

For Benjamin, calling Dickens an allegorist means that objects tend to become allegorical, and a ruin, testifying to the deadness of the commodity-world. Dickens as *flâneur* knows both the commodity and the ruin, as can be seen from one of the *Sketches by Boz*: 'Brokers' and Marine-store Shops'. The piece starts with the mock-pastoral of 'that street at the back of Long-acre' composed of brokers' shops, 'where you wander through groves of deceitful, showy-looking furniture' (*SB* 209). After satirising the gentility implied in that, he passes the brokers' shops in some poor neighbourhood; here is a jumble of things, including 'street door knockers' (211). They allegorise how human life has been turned into the ruined object. Illustrating how the goods in the brokers' shops often reflect the character of the neighbourhood, he passes to Drury Lane and Covent Garden, which, because it is 'essentially a theatrical neighbourhood' (212), means that all the goods acquire a double allegorical significance; they are emblematic, props and costumes used for plays, and they allegorise the neighbourhood, their unsorted, ruinous state images what the area is, and enables a partial reading of it.

The third area is Ratcliff Highway, in the East End. Here everything for sale is nautical; the sailor ends up pawning or selling all that he has before he has been long ashore and 'it is an even chance that he afterwards unconsciously repurchases the same things at a higher price than he gave for them at first' (213). A round dance is performed with goods, almost like a dance of death. Last come the shops in Southwark, 'near the King's Bench and in "the Rules"'. *Nicholas Nickleby* says that partly because of fear of the plague, the King's Bench prison, like the Fleet, had licensed the existence of 'the rules' for prisoners, and it explains these:

> The Rules are a certain liberty adjoining the prison, and comprising some dozen streets in which debtors who can raise money to pay large fees, from which their creditors do *not* derive any benefit, are permitted to reside by the wise provisions of the same enlightened laws which leave the debtor who can raise no money to starve in jail'. (*NN* 46.570)

Mr Bray, whose house Nickleby visits to see Madeline Bray, lives within the 'rules' while being technically imprisoned.

'Brokers' and Marine-store Shops' finishes in those parts of Southwark where prisoners for debt might reside. These places for pawning make up curiosity shops as well:

> Light articles of clothing, first of the ruined man, then of his wife, and at last of their children, even of the youngest, have been parted with piecemeal. There they are, thrown carelessly together until a purchaser presents himself – old and patched and repaired, it is true, but the make and materials tell of better days and the older they are, the greater the misery and destitution of those whom they once adorned. (213)

The descent from the West End to the prison tells its own story of ruin; Dickens reads London allegorically, as the home of the commodity, which contains the signs of its own collapse.

But there is a difference between Baudelaire looking at Paris changing under the direction of the centrally driven, imperialistic urges of Napoleon the Third, aiming to make Paris resemble an imperial capital, and Dickens looking at London. And Dickens is not wholly a *flâneur* since it is only half the truth that he is alienated from London. Objects in Dickens' London are unreal, like the Valentine, but London is not T.S. Eliot's 'unreal city' (*The Waste Land*). There are too many objects here from which there can be no separation. In this chapter, such objects have included: coal, door-knockers, coffee, bread and butter, timber, beer, spirits, beef, greens, potatoes, cheese, surtouts, saveloys and porter, cider, Seidlitz powder, millinery, stationery, oysters, pickled salmon, pork sausages, mahogany and marine stores. Dickens' London comprises these, as part of the popular culture becoming commodified culture that it observes. It knows something of the condition in which the hats and dresses are pro-duced, but does not withdraw from these things into a desire to de-realise the city. For that reason, discussion of London can only work through looking at specific detail. The city must be seen as both alienated, dead, and as full of the remembrances of a popular culture now marked by signs of their degradation.

Baudelaire's *flâneur* knows that he is also part of commodity-culture (*Arcades* 10), but Dickens, it will become apparent in future chapters, is both aware of that, and unaware, more ready to take London as having no alienation from it, while also reacting violently from it. It is a different, non-Parisian view. Its weakness is that it is less critical of the city of capital than is Baudelaire and less aware of its own position in the market-place; its strengths are obvious, though they remain, as this book shows, a challenge to describe.

CHAPTER THREE

NEWGATE LONDON
Oliver Twist

Near to the spot on which Snow Hill and Holborn Hill meet, there opens, upon the right hand as you come out of the city, a narrow and dismal alley leading to Saffron Hill. In its filthy shops are exposed for sale huge bunches of second-hand silk hand-kerchiefs of all sizes and patterns – for here reside the traders who purchase them from pickpockets. Hundreds of these handkerchiefs hang dangling from pegs out-side the windows, or flaunting from the door-posts, and the shelves within are piled with them. Confined as the limits of Field Lane are, it has its barber, its coffee-shop, its beer-shop, and its fried-fish warehouse. It is a commercial colony of itself, the emporium of petty larceny, visited at early morning and setting-in of dusk by silent merchants, who traffic in dark back-parlours, and go as strangely as they come. Here the clothesman, the shoe-vamper, and the rag-merchant display their goods as sign-boards to the petty thief; and stores of old iron and bones, and heaps of mildewy fragments of woollen-stuff and linen, rust and rot in the grimy cellars.

Oliver Twist 2.4.204

I · HANGING CLOTHES

In *Oliver Twist*, everything tends towards the presentation of hanging, how-ever indirectly. In the above quotation, Dickens follows Fagin travelling from Whitechapel, through the City, towards the den where he was first found. Fagin hurries through the City, not wanting to be recognised, but falls into 'his usual shuffling pace' when he reaches 'his proper element'. He crosses the Fleet valley at Snow Hill, which issued out of Newgate, on the City side. Snow Hill, where Bunyan died, now goes down to West Smithfield (then called Chick Lane, or West Street) but in the 1830s, it turned to run south of that, past Field Lane into Holborn.

The address to the reader – 'you' – indicates the investigative journalism that this piece is, as it shows one secret London folded inside another London, including an alternative economy, which runs on the recirculation of stolen goods, particularly clothes. The writing recalls passages from *Sketches by Boz*: 'Seven Dials', 'Meditations in Monmouth Street', and 'The Pawnbroker's Shop', set off Drury Lane. In the nineteenth century, the second-hand clothes trade was often Jewish-owned: in George Cruikshank's picture of Monmouth Street, the name 'Moses Levy', which does not appear in the text, may be seen, along-side such a jokey name as 'P. Patch'. The narrator writes with contempt about Holywell Street's second-hand clothiers: 'the red-headed and red-whiskered Jews who forcibly haul you into their squalid houses, and thrust you into a suit

Roads coming in to Seven Dials; compare Cruikshank's illustration for Seven Dials, *Sketches by Boz*. The pub is of the 1830s.

of clothes, whether you will or not, we detest' (*SB* 96).[1] The trade was moving from Monmouth Street in Seven Dials to Whitechapel, and was run by Jews, especially in Houndsditch, and Cutler Lane and Petticoat Lane. Fagin is associated with Field Lane, Holborn, and Whitechapel.

Items of second-hand clothing have several significations. They provide for the wearer a ready-made range of fashions and styles from which he must model his behaviour and into which he must fit. They are traces of former modes of life, former lives: being in second-hand clothes means knowing that someone has been there before you, just as, with the city, there is no first entry into it; it has been inhabited before; it cannot have newness. Being in and of the city, and inhabiting second-hand clothes relate to each other: in going through Dickens, we return again and again to places evoked earlier, and come to such sites as to second-hand clothes. And second-hand clothes emphasise the theatrical nature of social existence: all is display. Made of fabric, they show that all lives are fabrications. And ironically, the predominant article for sale in Field Lane is the handkerchief, which holds opposite meanings. It is an item of fashion on display, therefore to be stolen, and it is also the means of execution, as Master Bates shows to Oliver when he demonstrates to him, with the aid of a handkerchief, that the Artful Dodger will be hanged (1.18.150). Clothes and hanging are paired: hanging clothes are a sign of death. Fagin in the condemned cell remembers how the hanged 'changed from strong and vigorous men to dangling heaps of clothes' (3.14.445). Clothes hang out from the surrounding houses in Cruikshank's picture of Sikes on the roof, a rope round his neck.

Cruikshank's illustration to Master Bates demonstrating hanging (1.18.147) shows a claustrophobic, prisonous setting: the back of the room has a prominent door, but it is shown locked. Hanging is often implied in these pictures, and not in the insouciant way of the *Pickwick Papers* where no. 27 in the Fleet prison is indicated by 'the likeness of a man being hung, and smoking a pipe the while, chalked outside the door' (*PP* 42.560). Cruikshank shows three men hanged, in a tiny billboard to the left of Fagin in 'Oliver is Introduced to the Respectable Old Gentleman' (1.8.65). 'The Last Chance' (1.12.427) shows the noose, and 'Fagin in the Condemned Cell', a development from *Sketches by Boz* combines with the terror of being hanged, claustrophobia, which is often indicated by people or things pushed towards the corners of rooms, or the corners of buildings, and, in this case, by the thickness of Newgate walls. Their massiveness is shown by the shadows of the grating from the sun coming in from the outside (the bars are set into the middle of the wall). Above Fagin's head is writing, where the words 'Ordered By the Sheriffs Death' can just be seen. The office of Sheriff, founded in 1132, with responsibility for both the City and, until 1888, the county of Middlesex, would have been an alderman of the City of London, a deputy to the Mayor; he evokes the power of the City.

Field Lane's entertainment takes place at the Three Cripples on Saffron Hill, or simply the Cripples (1.15.116, 2.4.206). The word 'cripples' has resonances throughout Dickens, whose fascination is always with the cripple, whether Tiny Tim or Silas Wegg, just as it is with the body as something puppet-like, dangling on string. As is suggested by Cripplegate, the old City gate at the end of Wood Street, giving on to St Giles Cripplegate (St Giles being patron saint of cripples), cripples gathered round the outside of the walls, begging. Perhaps the pub's title draws on the carnivalesque tradition of Breugel, who in a picture of 1568 shows five cripples, necessarily beggars, dressed in holiday gear, with paper hats, one with a mitre.[2] In which case, the name of the public house suggests something other in London than the modern busy commercial capital. It contrasts with the travels taking place throughout this novel, many of them on roads towards hanging. This chapter examines four such journeys.

Oliver Twist, or, The Parish Boy's Progress, was written in twenty-four monthly instalments, appearing in *Bentley's Miscellany*, beginning in February 1837 and running through to April 1839 – though it was published, complete, in book-form, in November 1838. When Dickens began, he was half-way through *Pickwick Papers*, so he was writing the two novels together. In April 1838, he began serialisation of *Nicholas Nickleby*, so that though *Pickwick Papers* had finished, he was still writing two novels together. (And at the same time, from November 1837, to June 1839, the completed version of *Sketches by Boz* was also being serialised.) A first point to be made might be to compare the energy of Dickens' criminals, walking through and around London, with the energy in writing. The word 'progress' recalls John Bunyan's *The Pilgrim's Progress* (1678–84) and Hogarth's series, *The Harlot's Progress* and *The Rake's Progress* (both 1732). And journeying plays on the genre of the picaresque novel, which had dominated *Pickwick Papers* and was to continue with *Nicholas Nickleby*; the idea of moving characters from place to place, and so creating separate episodic adventures for them. In *Oliver Twist*, people are given gruelling journeys. 'Oliver walked twenty miles that day' (1.8.58) is one intimation of distances people will cover.

Since these passages are about journeys, note the confidence in mapping London, not just its well-known places, since all these descriptions are of unknown or unacknowledged parts of London and argue an intense know-ledge of areas and street-names. The investigative sense claims the ability to speak about areas off limits to bourgeois society. The movements within London, passing through different areas, are those made by criminals, so that their omnipresence is contrasted with the ignorance of polite society, but they do not move with ease, which recalls the oddness within the name 'Cripples'.

II · ISLINGTON TO FIELD LANE

As John Dawkins objected to their entering London before nightfall, it was nearly eleven o'clock when they reached the turnpike at Islington. They crossed from the Angel into St John's-road, struck down the small street which terminates at Sadler's Wells' theatre, through Exmouth-Street and Coppice-row, down the little court by the side of the workhouse, across the classic ground which once bore the name of Hockley-in-the-hole, thence into Little Saffron-hill, and so into Saffron-hill the Great, along which, the Dodger scudded at a rapid pace, directing Oliver to follow close at his heels . . .

Oliver was just wondering whether he hadn't better run away, when they reached the bottom of the hill: his conductor, catching him by the arm, pushed open the door of a house near Field-lane, and drawing him into the passage, closed it behind them. (1.8.63)

That is the first London journey. By chapter 8, Oliver Twist has left the town where he was a workhouse boy, seventy miles from London (1.8.57). But where is the town? In *Bentley's Miscellany*, where the novel first appeared, it was named at the start as Mudfog, following on from an article written by Dickens for the first instalment of *Bentley's Miscellany* in January 1837: 'Public Life of Mr Tulrumble, Once Mayor of Mudfog'. Signed 'Boz', it ends by saying that 'at some future period, we may venture to open the chronicles of Mudfog'.[3] It is usually assumed that Mudfog equals Chatham, where Dickens lived from 1817 to 1822. Mudfog reappeared in Dickens' article 'Full Report of the First Meeting of the Mudfog Association For the Advancement of Everything' (*Bentley's Miscellany* October 1837), but Chatham is wrongly positioned for

Oliver Twist to walk down the Great North Road and appear at Barnet, Hertfordshire, ten miles north of London, and a coaching-station for the Great North Road. Dickens may have a town outside London in mind for Mudfog, but it seems possible that the town of chapters 1 to 8 is London in another form, and in another mode of writing, where there is no attention paid to topography, another part of the wood, as it were. It makes more sense of the point that Mr Bumble must go to Clerkenwell (1.17.137). The 'manufactory' in which Monks meets Mr and Mrs Bumble, and under which the river runs also might be argued to recall Dickens' experiences in the blacking-factory on the water's edge in London (3.1.307). In 1835, Dickens had published, out of twenty pieces called 'Sketches of London', six sketches, with the generic title 'Our Parish', where the parish is specified to be 'suburban' (*SB* 26). And the parish is the target of *Oliver Twist*'s first chapters.

At Barnet, Oliver is picked up by Jack Dawkins, the Artful Dodger. The two have walked on through Finchley towards Islington, and to the Angel. Later, the route is followed by Noah Claypole and Charlotte, who pass through Highgate archway (3.5.349), two miles out from the lights of London. They then reach the Angel at Islington, where Noah 'wisely judged, from the crowd of passengers and number of vehicles, that London began in earnest'. Their route parallels the boys', since they cross into St John's Road, and are soon 'deep in the obscurity of the intricate and dirty ways which, lying between Gray's Inn Road and Smithfield, render that part of the town one of the lowest and worst that improvement has left in the midst of London' (3.5.351). 'Improvement' is ironic. Noah and Charlotte end up at The Three Cripples.

The Angel Inn is met from the north by Upper Street, part of the present A1, the Great North Road. Upper Street has passed over the Regent's Canal (1820), which at this point runs underground. At the Angel, Pentonville Road, where Mr Brownlow lives, goes west, and City Road goes east. The road running south, towards the centre, takes three forks: one to the west is Roseberry Avenue, directly south is St John's Street, and another south-east road is Goswell Street ('God's well'). Jack Dawkins and Oliver Twist reach Sadler's Wells theatre – what Wordsworth called 'half rural Sadler's Wells' (*The Prelude* 7.267). Roseberry Avenue (1889–92), has replaced the little streets by which the boys reach Exmouth Street and Exmouth Market. But to give the area some context, if, instead of going south-west, they had gone the other way up present-day Exmouth Market to the east, they would have run into Spa Fields, scene of mass meetings of November and December 1816, where Arthur Thistlewood intended a riot to capture the Tower of London and the Bank of England. Here the entertainer Mr Maunders was said to have had a cottage (*OCS* 19.151).

Late Victorian Roseberry Avenue is bisected by Farringdon Road, which was begun in the 1840s, as Victoria Street, and renamed in 1863. A Victorian improvement, a reminder that *Oliver Twist* began as pre-Victorian, it cut down from above Mount Pleasant, following the Fleet, to join the older (1737) Farringdon Street. On the other, and north side of the Roseberry Avenue/ Farringdon Road intersection is Mount Pleasant, the 'ill favoured and ill savoured' district of Grandfather Smallweed (*BH* chapter 21). The Post Office Sorting Office there replaces Cold Bath Fields Prison, built in 1794, closed in 1877 and demolished with the building of Roseberry Avenue.[4] Coldbath Square is immediately on the other side of the Avenue. Coppice Row, its name faintly remembered in 'the stump of an old forest tree' in the little narrow street where the Smallweeds lived, significantly in the vicinity of the prison, ran down where Farringdon Road was built. Going down that road, on the right is Baker's Row, which skirts the site of the Clerkenwell workhouse on its left. That was built in 1727 for the parishes of St James and St John in Clerkenwell, near the Coldbath (a well of cold water, 'discovered' in 1697). On the other side of the workhouse, demolished in 1883, is Crawford Passage. Below Baker's Row, on the left, is Bowling Green Lane. Baker's Row and Crawford Passage continue into Ray Street (Rag Street, until 1774) and Back Hill, on the site of Hockley-in-the-Hole, which had a Bear Garden. Addison refers to Hockley-in-the-Hole in *The Spectator* no. 31 (5 April 1711), while in *The Beggar's Opera* (1728), Mrs Peachum says to Filch, 'You must go to Hockley-in-the-Hole, and to Marybone, child, to learn valour'.[5] The valour was to be learned as much from the tortured animals as anything else, at these two open spaces (Marylebone Gardens opened in 1650 and closed in 1778).

In giving the journey, Dickens is writing as an antiquarian, drawing on the eighteenth-century name of the area, as if establishing a difference between then and 'now'. He continued the practice, in the Introduction to the Third Edition of *Oliver Twist* (1841), defending it against the provocation caused by Ainsworth's 'Newgate novel' *Jack Sheppard*, which, illustrated by Cruikshank, began serialisation in *Bentley's Miscellany* in 1839. In Ainsworth's novel, Jack Sheppard (1702–24), hanged at Tyburn, having been shopped by the informer Jonathan Wild (c.1682–1725), who was to be executed six months later, was made the nobly-born hero. His nobility justified crime. Dickens' Introduction therefore referred back to Gay, and noted that there 'the thieves are represented as leading a life which is rather to be envied than otherwise' (457), and that only Hogarth showed the 'miserable reality' of the lives of thieves. In contrast, he considers his own descriptions of 'the cold, wet, shelterless midnight streets of London; the foul and frowsy dens, where vice is closely packed and lacks the room to turn; the haunts of hunger and disease, the shabby rags that scarcely hold together' and asks, 'where are the attractions of these things?' (458). His models, he says, are Fielding, Defoe and Hogarth, who 'brought upon the scene the very scum and refuse of the land' (459). The phrase reappears in *Barnaby Rudge* (49.407).[6]

If, in going down these 'midnight streets', a phrase which consciously or unconsciously quotes Blake's poem 'London', and which is not merely metaphorical in this context, given the hour, the boys had turned left from Hockley-in-the-Hole, they would reach Clerkenwell Green: 'clerk's well', another of the springs and wells associated with the Fleet River. Instead, keeping almost due south, past Herbal Hill, they reach Saffron Hill, which runs out as it approaches Charterhouse Street. Beyond, was Field Lane. The rural nature of the area still appears in place-names. Saffron Hill was formerly a part of Ely-gardens, getting its name from its saffron. Vine Hill and Vine Bridge get their name from the Vineyard attached to old Ely House. This is the area which is later defined as 'between Gray's Inn Road and Smithfield'. When Farringdon Road was built, it abolished many slum areas that have been described, areas which are noted as full of 'the lowest orders of Irish' (1.8.63), and it redefined the Fleet valley, which had had Saffron Hill as its westwards slope. And the valley was bridged by the Holborn Viaduct, completed in 1869, which put an end to the meeting of Snow Hill (on the City side) and Holborn Hill at a narrow bridge.

Victorian improvements minimise the point that as Doughty Street, where Dickens wrote *Oliver Twist*, is only two streets to the west from Gray's Inn Road, so the areas of London described in *Oliver Twist* are interconnected. Clerkenwell Green, where Mr Brownlow is robbed (1.10.74) was reprieved from the destruction caused by building Clerkenwell Road in the 1870s, and is to its north, after it crosses Farringdon Road going east. It is no distance from Field Lane (it is visible from the top of Saffron Hill); simply a matter of crossing Farringdon Road.

St James', Clerkenwell Green, once part of a Benedictine nunnery; rebuilt by James Carr, 1792, the steeple rebuilt 1849; seen from near Saffron Hill, across the Fleet valley.

Clerkenwell Green, south of St James' Church (designed in 1792 by James Carr), had, by the end of the eighteenth century, no green, and had became associated with both poverty and with radicalism, and Chartist demonstrations in the 1830s and 1840s. Its oppositional character was accentuated by the presence, on its west side, of the Middlesex Sessions House, built in 1782, enlarged in 1860, closed in 1920.[7] Oliver Twist is taken to the magistrate Mr Fang in Hatton Garden (nos 52–53); this is the road parallel to Saffron Hill, running from present-day Holborn Circus to Clerkenwell Road. Fang and Fagin are almost literally neighbours, a point reinforced by their names. Mutton Hill which is referred to (1.11.79) is now non-existent. Further, when Mr Brownlow takes Oliver Twist home, the chapter begins: 'the coach rattled away down Mount Pleasant and up Exmouth-street, over nearly the same ground as that which Oliver had traversed when he first entered London in company with the Dodger, – and turning a different way when it reached the Angel at Islington, stopped at length before a neat house in a quiet shady street near Pentonville' (1.12.86). It is as if the original dipping south that Oliver has made from the allegorical Angel, in going to Fagin's must be reversed in a deliberate symmetry. There is something suggestive in the repeated 'down' of the first paragraph of this section, and 'the bottom of the hill' in the other; London's topography suggests a downward progression.

III · BETHNAL GREEN TO CHERTSEY

By the time they had turned into the Bethnal Green road the day had fairly begun to break. Many of the lamps were already extinguished, a few country wagons were slowly toiling on towards London, and now and then a stage-coach, covered with mud, rattled briskly by, the driver bestowing, as he passed, an admonitory lash upon the heavy waggoner, who, by keeping on the wrong side of the road, had endangered his arriving at the office a quarter of a minute after his time. The public-houses, with gas-lights burning inside, were already open. By degrees other shops began to be unclosed, and a few scattered people were met with. Then came straggling groups of labourers going to their work; then men and women with fish-baskets on their heads, donkey-carts laden with vegetables, chaise-carts filled with live-stock or whole carcasses of meat, milkwomen with pails, and an unbroken concourse of people trudging out with various supplies to the eastern suburbs of the town. As they approached the City, the noise and traffic gradually increased; and when they threaded the streets between Shoreditch and Smithfield, it had swelled into a roar of sound and bustle. It was as light as it was likely to be till night set in again, and the busy morning of half the London population had begun.

Turning down Sun-street and Crown-street, and crossing Finsbury-square, Mr Sikes struck, by way of Chiswell-street, into Barbican, thence into Long-lane, and so into Smithfield, from which latter place arose a tumult of discordant sounds that filled Oliver Twist with surprise and amazement. (1.21.170–71)

When Oliver Twist is caught again, walking through Clerkenwell (1.15.120), he is returned to Fagin at another place, 'the other ken' (1.13.104). The progress to Fagin goes east across Smithfield market (which will be discussed in chapter nine), 'although it might have been Grosvenor Square, for anything Oliver knew to the contrary' (1.16.124). The choice is between two huge open spaces: Grosvenor Square, which, symbolising Augustan England, is indifferent to what Oliver Twist represents. Sikes, Nancy and Oliver cross Smithfield at eight in the evening, making Nancy think of prisoners who are to be hanged at eight the next morning. The text's attention, as far as the thieves is concerned, is moving away, subtly, from Fagin towards Sikes and Nancy: Sikes recalls that when he was captured at 'Bartlemy time', he could hear everything from Newgate prison, where, of course, the prisoners are kept.

Sikes, Nancy and Oliver turn into a 'very filthy narrow street, nearly full of old-clothes shops' (1.16.127), and entering a house, in Whitechapel, go down a flight of stairs. 'They crossed an empty kitchen, and open[ed] the door of a low earthy-smelling room, which seemed to have been built in a small back-yard' (1.16.128). Captured, Oliver is able to wander round the house, which is 'a very dirty place; but the rooms up stairs had great high wooden mantel-pieces and large doors, with paneled walls and cornices to the ceilings, which though they were black with neglect and dust, were ornamented in various ways' which makes Oliver think it has once seen better days (1.18.145).

The following chapter, Fagin leaves the house at Whitechapel, going north towards Spitalfields, and on to Bethnal Green to find Sikes. Brick Lane, connecting these areas, was laid out in the seventeenth century, and was for making and firing bricks for the Spitalfield area;[8] Commercial Street, joining Whitechapel High Street to Spitalfields was built in 1845, continuing to Shoreditch High Street in 1858. Fagin takes backroads and alleys, and as he 'glides' along, from Whitechapel to Spitalfields and Bethnal Green, 'creeping' – the word recalls the etymology of 'cripple' – becomes a 'loathsome reptile' (1.19.153). The text is alienated from him as it is not from Sikes, and certainly not from Nancy. Bethnal Green, its centre at what is now called Bethnal Green Gardens, had developed with the silk-weaving industry associated with Spitalfields and the Huguenots throughout the seventeenth century. Bethnal Green accommodated the journeymen workers for the industry at Spitalfields, which Hogarth depicts with the *Industrious and Idle Apprentices at their Looms* (1747). It became a separate parish from Stepney in 1746, and like Spitalfields, became more and more crowded and poorer in the early nineteenth century. Bethnal Green Road, meeting Shoreditch High Street (the A10, the Roman north road) came into being in 1879, as a result of improvements by the Metropolitan Board of Works; but how poor the area was is suggested in Arthur Morrison's *A Child of the Jago*, set in Old Nichol Street, two blocks north of Bethnal Green Road, east of Shoreditch.[9] It would not be a bad guess that placed Sikes' lodging in Old Nichol Street. Fagin and Sikes discuss a housebreaking that Sikes plans at Chertsey in Surrey, and for which Oliver's help is needed. It becomes apparent that Fagin is trying to corrupt Oliver into a life of crime. Returned to Whitechapel, he gives him to read:

> a history of the lives and trials of great criminals, and the pages were soiled and thumbed with use. Here, he read of dreadful crimes that made the blood run cold; of secret murders that had been committed by the lonely wayside, and bodies hidden from the eye of man in deep pits and wells, which would not keep them down . . . but had yielded them up at last, after many years, and so maddened the murderers with the sight, that in their horror they had confessed their guilt, and yelled for the gibbet to end their agony. Here, too, he read of men who, lying in their beds at dead of night, had been tempted and led on by their own bad thoughts to such dreadful bloodshed . . . (1.20.164)

The most popular collection of tales was *The Newgate Calendar, or Malefactor's Bloody Register*, which first appeared in 1728 and reappeared in four volumes between 1824 and 1828. Charley Bates fears that the Artful Dodger will not make it into the Newgate Calendar (3.6.363), because his fate is to be transported to Australia. But *Oliver Twist* is firmly in Newgate-historical mode, and when Fagin tells Oliver on their first meeting that the Artful Dodger will be a 'great man', he thinks back to Jonathan Wild in Newgate, and of Fielding's version of him (1743).[10]

Spital Yard, Spitalfields, Norton Folgate, night-time. In the house in this yard Susanna Annesley, mother of John Wesley, was born in 1696.

St Leonard's, Shoreditch High
Street, viewed from Old Street;
George Dance (1740) built over
the older church where James
and Richard Burbage, architects
of the first theatres in
Shoreditch, are buried.

Oliver is taken to Sikes at Shoreditch to go with him to Chertsey. The second itinerary, already quoted, follows their westwards route 'between Shoreditch and Smithfield' and out of London towards Chertsey. They start out on the Bethnal Green road; the huge numbers coming in from the country are explained when it is seen that they cross the Cambridge (A10) road. That, and the Cambridge Heath Road, to the east, running into Mile End Road, the Old Ford Road, from Essex to Cambridge Heath Road, and the Whitechapel Road (the A11 to Newmarket, and the road to Colchester), would have been filled with cattle brought in, east–west, from Essex, Suffolk and Cambridge-shire, going to Smithfield. The Hackney Road, Bethnal Green Road and the Whitechapel Road would have been filled with cattle and drovers.

Sikes and Oliver must cross Shoreditch High Street, and across into Holywell Street, site of a Priory for Augustinian nuns outside the City boundary, and then into Curtain Road which as it goes south eventually connects with Sun Street. The route becomes allegorical: they are going towards the place of mass slaughter (Smithfield), and the place where they start, Shoreditch (perhaps 'sewer ditch'), only evokes Folly Ditch, in Jacob's Island, where Sikes will die.[11] In Sun Street, Sikes and Oliver enter the old boundaries of the City of London, and out of them again with Crown Street (no longer there, though Crown Place still intersects Sun Street, marking where Crown Street started). They are north of the City as they cross Finsbury Square, designed between 1777 and 1791, by George Dance the Younger (1740–1825), who took over from his father (1695–1768) the function of city architect and surveyor. He designed Newgate (1770) and built out from the single square mile that comprised the City; Finsbury Square being one such development. They cross over the City Road, on the west side of the Square, and into Chiswell Street, where Dance lived, and past the Whitbread brewery on its far left (1750). This gets them to Barbican (an outer fortification of the city walls, pulled down by Henry the Third). They turn down Aldersgate, and into Long Lane on the right, and so, for Oliver's second time, into Smithfield on market-day.

They cut down to the south of Smithfield, to Hosier Lane, which they follow to the west, towards Holborn: at that point Sikes sees the clock of St Andrew's, Holborn, a church designed to be visible from the Fleet valley. It is seven: the pair have walked for one and a half hours (1.20.169). St Andrew's was rebuilt after the Fire by Wren (1687) and again in 1960 after the War. From this point on, as they leave the city, the route is not specified, since they are passing through the fashionable part of the town, and where the rich live is not of interest to this text. The next place named is Hyde Park Corner, with its tollgate for entrance to traffic coming into London from the west, and then Kensington, which, in the census of 1801, was a country parish of less than 10,000 people, with farms and market gardens.

Sikes and Oliver take a lift on a cart going to Hounslow, and pass different mile-stones: Kensington, Hammersmith, which had the first suspension bridge in London (1827: renewed by Bazalgette in the 1880s), Chiswick, six miles west of Hyde Park Corner, and still rural (the railway arrived in 1849), Kew Bridge (built in 1759, and rebuilt in stone in 1784–89; the present bridge is of 1903), and Brentford. The last place is where Betty Higden walks from in *Our Mutual Friend* going to her death upriver, and is the route taken by Riderhood when going to Plashwater Weir Lock, and later still, by Headstone. *Our Mutual Friend* returns to *Oliver Twist* in its interest in criminals going upstream, and by its interest in the river.

They have reached Isleworth, and go on to Hampton. Another lift takes them through Sunbury; it is seven in the evening, twelve hours from Holborn. There is a reference to the ferry-house, with the water beyond, and that sense of the unknown is counterpoised by a brief description of a graveyard. They are dropped at Lower Halliford, home for forty years of Thomas Love Peacock (1785–1866), who, while working for the East India Company (1819 to 1856) lived there at weekends, staying in London during the week; it was also, later (1849–58), home to his son-in-law, George Meredith. From there they walk to Shepperton, pass that and come to Chertsey Bridge (1785), crossing that to a deserted house; then they return over the bridge to Chertsey, this time with Barney and Toby Crackit. Chertsey is virtually on the M25, which gives some idea of the north–south distance Oliver has travelled throughout London. The robbery begins after half past one in the morning, after over twenty hours of travel.[12] The contrast between the detailed street-by-street account of walking through London and the lesser importance attributed to the little Thames towns outside London is strong; yet even the sense of the journey through these towns is amazingly circumstantial. Just as the Bow Street Runners can talk about a robbery at Edmonton in Middlesex (2.8.249), and associate that with thieves from Battlebridge, London is seen to invade the pastoral retreat of Chertsey, as appears in the waking dream that Oliver has when he thinks that he is in Fagin's old home again, and wakes to find that he is under the eye of both Monks and the Jew at the window (2.11.282–84): Monks recognised as he was seen earlier at the market town where Oliver went to send off a letter (2.10.269–70). Monks' appearance suggests another form of criminality within the text, in addition to Fagin; and that the latter is seen, or if Oliver is only dreaming, apparently seen, suggests something hypnotic about London, for Chertsey is far out of Fagin's orbit. Fagin's London, or London's Fagin, inescapably invades consciousness, causing the person who leaves it to return to it.

IV · NORTH LONDON

He went through Islington; strode up the hill at Highgate, on which stands the stone in honour of Whittington; turned down to Highgate Hill, unsteady of purpose, and uncertain where to go; struck off to the right again almost as soon as he began to descend it, and taking the footpath across the fields, skirted Caen Wood, and so came out on Hampstead Heath. Traversing the hollow by the Vale of Health, he mounted the opposite bank, and crossing the road which joins the villages of Hampstead and Highgate, made along the remaining portion of the heath to the fields at North End, in one of which he laid himself down under a hedge and slept. (3.10.398)

The third journey described is again Sikes', but he is alone, after Nancy's murder. In Book 3 chapter 3, she took an hour at night to cross two miles of London, from Spitalfields to the Mayfair part of Hyde Park, in order to find Rose Maylie (3.3.330). The amount of time suggests something of the absence of roads through the city, and the absence of connection between the two parts: the City and the West End, with the Holborn area being particularly bad for crossing over. It makes all London disconnected, all of it, therefore, islands of separation, and potentially criminal. Nancy arranges to meet Rose Maylie and Mr Brownlow again on London Bridge between eleven and twelve on a Sunday night, while she walks from the Middlesex to the Surrey shore; the mist that hangs on the river is said to make visible only 'the tower of old Saint Saviour's church and the spire of Saint Magnus, so long the giant-warders of the ancient bridge' (3.8.381). Presumably the bridge is the new one of 1831, not the ancient one; however, the description does not contradict that. The Southwark church is St Saviour's, later Southwark Cathedral (1905). Wren's church, St Magnus the Martyr, in Lower Thames Street, in the City, was completed in 1687; it is the church which in *The Waste Land* holds 'inexplicable splendour of Ionian white and gold', and it stood alongside the approach to the old bridge in a virtually exact alignment with it. These two churches, whose names anticipate Nancy's fate as martyrdom, and the saving of Oliver, are like the fantasies of Gog and Magog, to be discussed further in chapter four; as 'giant warders', they protect the bridge, as a liminal, non-claustral space between the City and Southwark.

The three talk on steps descending from the bridge towards St Saviour's, and are overheard by Noah Claypole. This results in Nancy's murder at Sikes' house, 'down Spitalfields way' (3.10.401). Sikes crosses from Field Lane to find her, 'looking straight before him with savage resolution, his teeth so tightly compressed that the strained jaw seemed starting through his skin', and holding on his 'headlong course' (3.9.395). The adjective anticipates the name Bradley Headstone, and his murderousness. Murder happens in 'a mean and badly-furnished apartment of very limited size, lighted only by one small window in the shelving roof and abutting on a close and dirty lane' (3.2.317). Sikes goes on the run. His journey begins by repeating in reverse that of Oliver and the Artful Dodger. Getting to Islington means going west and north, up the City Road, from Old Street. Going up City Road would bring him back to the Angel, but since he is heading towards Highgate, a modern Bill Sikes would leave it before then for the New North Road, which goes up through Canonbury Road to join the present Holloway Road. This would bring him to Highgate Hill. The Whittington Stone, which stands in ironic contrast to this refugee from the city, and which as good as tells him to turn again too – which he will do, under the power of what Freud calls the 'compulsion to repeat' – had been placed at the foot of Highgate Hill on the west side of the road, in 1821, the third of three successive stones on the site. *Barnaby Rudge* (4.30) says that in the eighteenth century there were 'no long rows of streets connecting Highgate with Whitechapel, no assemblages of palaces in the swampy levels, nor little cities in the open fields'. Connection between the 'high' (Highgate) and the low (Whitechapel, Spitalfields) fascinates Dickens; like Bill Sikes, Joe Willett walks from Islington to Highgate (*BR* 31.260), and the text records, with scepticism, the experience of Dick Whittington, with the bells sounding and attracting him back to London.

Sikes turns to Highgate Hill, 'unsteady of purpose and unsure where to go', leaves the road, and by doing so, passes Caen Wood (Kenwood House), and gets onto Hampstead Heath, down to the Vale of Health and back to North End. But the paragraph which begins with him striding, ends with him sleeping under the hedge, and then becoming indecisive, unable to do any one thing. He makes back for London; returns to the Heath; sets off for Hendon, a mile north-west of Hampstead, but on getting there, returns to the Heath, without having got what he wanted; then sets off for Hatfield, nineteen miles out of central London. Arrived there, he sets off from Hatfield towards St Albans, the place where Bleak House is situated. At last he returns to London, determined

Spaniards Inn, and tollhouse, between Highgate and Hampstead; called Tea-gardens in *Pickwick Papers* chapter 46.

to enter 'the metropolis' at dusk 'by a circuitous route' (*OT* 3.10.406). The contrast with the itinerary to Chertsey is striking.

The passage begins something new: a study of the criminal's thought-processes. Until now, Sikes has been viewed externally, though that is not entirely true of the writing of the second journey, but there is a perceptible shift with his impossible attempt to escape, which simply brings him back in a circle to London. The paragraph which begins: 'Where could he go, that was near and not too public, to get some meat and drink? Hendon. That was a good place' (3.10.399) shows a new introspection where the voice of the narrator becomes that of Sikes questioning. The passage notes how he runs, then, 'with a strange perversity' loiters. The text constructs him now as burdened by consciousness, which becomes self-consciousness as people 'seem' to view him with suspicion. Guilt is not mentioned, but evidently, he feels he is under the eye of the other. Hence the repetition-compulsion, the inability to go in a linear direction, to take the step beyond. Hence, too, when he has arrived at Hatfield, which takes him beyond the bounds of the present M25, on its northern stretch, and when he is a 'stranger' in the pub, he gives himself away in the company of the 'antic fellow, half pedlar and half mountebank' (3.10.399), who, like Autolycus in *The Winter's Tale*, is selling a quack remedy to 'country-folk'. The antique (old), antic (mad) and antic (acting) figure unexpectedly exposes the bloodstain on Sikes' hat. Noticeably, the text changes from calling him a 'robber' (3.12.399) as it has done up till now, and for the first time calls him a 'murderer' (3.10.401): the change suggesting that he has now deepened his self-awareness, he has become something else. The same 'perversity of feeling' and 'irresolution' hangs over him as the coach from London passes through and he hears for the first time the news of the murder, and then he resolves to go on further, to St Albans, six miles further north. He is fearful of what is before him, and has the additional sense of 'that morning's ghastly figure following him at his heels', which he cannot shake off.

At that point the text generalises: 'Let no man talk of murderers escaping justice, and hint that Providence must sleep. There were twenty score of violent deaths in one long minute of that agony of fear' (3.10.402). The text's interest has changed from Oliver Twist's innocence, or consideration of Fagin, to the idea of guilt, and to the thought of a man possessed. He is pursued by a look: by the eyes of Nancy, which follow him everywhere, and which have more hallucinatory power than Whittington's bells. Though he involves himself in putting out a fire on a farm, in which, like Macbeth 'he bore a charmed life' (3.10.404), he has no rest. And the Shakespeare allusion only indicates how central Sikes has become to the text's interest. He resolves to return to London, which has, it seems, been acting as the magnet to him all day, however unconscious: he cannot bear being in the countryside. London draws everyone to it in this text. Though he has plans to escape to France, it is London the criminal needs, and he resolves to return to it, unable to bear the countryside. In the picture 'Sikes Attempting to Destroy his Dog' (3.19.405), Cruikshank shows the dome of St Paul's on the horizon, as if implying a symbolism which will be further exploited by the novelist, for example in *The Old Curiosity Shop* chapter 15, and in *Great Expectations* 2.1, of the church as remote and aloof, or as a source of salvation that cannot be laid hold of.[13] St Paul's symbolises one London which is not for Sikes, but which nonetheless claims him, as he returns there under the power of a death-drive.[14]

In the 1841 Introduction, Dickens defended the absence of any 'redeeming trait' in Sikes, by thinking there may be natures 'utterly and irredeemably bad' but he then adds that 'there are such men as Sikes, who, being closely followed through the same space of time, and through the same current of circumstances, would not give, by one look or action of a moment, the faintest indication of a better nature' (460). Yet this, as a bourgeois attitude which calls the criminals 'the very dregs of life' (456) and 'scum', is barely sustained by the text which in this chapter has created Sikes as a solitary, and as held by guilt which has extraordinary somatic effects upon him, energising him and making him pull in resolution. It is inconsistent too, since Philip Collins (*Dickens and Crime*, 267) notes that Dickens, in his public readings of the murder of Nancy by Sikes, identified with Sikes, as murdering Nancy, even writing that 'I have a vague sensation of being "wanted" as I walk about the streets'.

Modern view, including St Paul's, seen coming down from Archway Road from the Great North Road, to the east of Highgate Hill, going towards the Holloway Road; suggesting the attraction of London for Bill Sikes trying to leave it.

V · JACOB'S ISLAND

Near that part of the Thames on which the church at Rotherhithe abuts, where the buildings on the banks are dirtiest and the vessels on the river blackest with the dust of colliers and the smoke of close-built low-roofed houses, there exists, at the present day, the filthiest, the strangest, the most extraordinary of the many localities that are hidden in London, wholly unknown, even by name, to the great mass of its inhabitants . . .

In such a neighbourhood, beyond Dockhead in the Borough of Southwark, stands Jacob's Island, surrounded by a muddy ditch, six or eight feet deep, and fifteen or twenty wide when the tide is in, once called Mill Pond, but known in these days as Folly Ditch. It is a creek or inlet from the Thames, and can always be filled at high water by opening the sluices at the Lead Mills from which it took its old name. At such times, a stranger looking from one of the wooden bridges thrown across it at Mill-lane, will see the inhabitants of the houses on either side lowering from their back doors and windows, buckets . . . in which to haul the water up; . . . Crazy wooden galleries common to the backs of half-a-dozen houses, with holes from which to look upon the slime beneath; windows broken and patched . . . rooms so small, so filthy, so confined . . . wooden chambers thrusting themselves out above the mud and threatening to fall into it . . . dirt-besmeared walls and decaying foundations, every repulsive lineament of poverty, every loathsome indication of filth, rot, and garbage; – all these ornament the banks of Folly Ditch. (3.12.417)

The fourth itinerary requires the greatest imaginative distance for the bourgeois reader, who is taken by the novelist to a locality south of the river, in Bermondsey, in Rotherhithe. The first two paragraphs of the chapter discuss Rotherhithe, and then specify part of the general neighbourhood: Jacob's Island, which is not so far downstream as the church (St Mary's (1715), whose architect was John James). It is nearer the present Tower Bridge, downstream of where the road Shad Thames (St John at Thames – the name recalls the landholdings of the Templars, the Knights of St John) runs to meet the river. At that point, St Saviour's Dock is the outlet for the Neckinger River, which is one of London's partially underground rivers, rising in St George's Fields, and supposedly so called because of the word 'neckerchief', suggesting the hangman's noose for pirates who were executed here. Certainly an appropriate location for what happens to Sikes. The area seems to have been a miniature Venice of waterways which low tide left as mere mud. The three streets, Bermondsey Walk, Jacob Street and Wolseley Street (then London Street) formed its eastward limits, as did Dockhead. These streets run into Mill Street, where there was a water-mill, built by the monks of Bermondsey Abbey. Mill Pond is now called Folly Ditch, and is where water came in from the Thames to power the mills. The view described is from outside, looking in, and the appeal is to the stranger coming into the area, to get the view from the bridge. The passage continues with an anticipation of Tom-All-Alone's and *Bleak House*: 'Thirty or forty years ago, before losses and chancery suits came upon it, it was a thriving place, but now it is a desolate island indeed' (3.12.418). Jacob's Island images Britain and London.

The chapter brings together 'flash' Toby Cratchit, who has a hideaway here, Tom Chitling, who was first seen when released from a house of correction (1.18.151), and a robber of fifty called Kags who has returned from transportation. Three cripples, perhaps. They comment on the great events that have happened: Fagin's arrest, and Bet's hysteria, and Charley Bates' escape, before Bill Sikes arrives, preceded by his now lame dog: it is Tuesday, two days after the Sunday night when Nancy met Brownlow. She was killed early on Monday morning: Fagin is hung exactly a week later, Monday being the day for hanging, as the condemned colonel says to Wemmick, 'I think I shall be out of this on Monday, sir' (*GE* 2.13.262). But the man who arrives 'was the very ghost of Sikes' (3.12.421): as if he has died already, and his living on means nothing. He gets to the roof, pursued by the crowd, and aims to jump for it into the dry ditch 'at the risk of being stifled' (3.12.426). It anticipates Bradley Headstone dying in the mud: both men seem attracted to the river; Headstone, always, as under the power of a death-drive, which he acknowledges in himself (*OMF* 4.15.781).

In the room, Sikes is called 'the murderer' as he shows the full force of his violence against Charley Bates, but in the last episode, on the roof, he is only called 'the criminal' and 'the man', until the moment when he turns and sees the eyes of Nancy upon him, and reacts with terror, when he is called 'the murderer', and falling with the rope around his neck, hangs himself. If a fixed identity is death, identity is confirmed by death, for he is called 'the murderer' again as he swings lifeless against the wall. Cruikshank drew pictures of Sikes in the condemned cell at Newgate, as though this was one possibility for how he might have ended. He is sketched sitting with his arms folded, as opposed to Fagin, who appears in what Cruikshank finally drew, with his right hand to his mouth, in a frenetic gesture of biting, and his left hand drawn across his body.[15] The text decides that state execution is left for Fagin, as more passive throughout, and only caught because of Noah Claypole turning informer. This choice of which person to have hanged at Newgate turns attention to Sikes as the active figure brought into passivity. His death is accident, but it is also virtual suicide; he is driven to his hanging by fantasies of the feminine which, driving him back to London, simultaneously make him, like Macbeth, 'try the last', yet let him down, destroy his masculine identity, as he falls for 'five-and-thirty feet'. 'There was a sudden jerk, a terrific convulsion of the limbs, and there he hung, with the open knife clenched in his stiffening hand' (3.12.428). The sense of masculinity which has collapsed in a horrifying orgasmic moment is followed up by: 'The old chimney quivered with the shock, but stood it bravely': an image of phallicism holding up in contrast. Even the distance he falls confirms the sense of great distances crossed throughout, in this novel (thirty-five is half the number of miles Oliver walks to London). The number of feet corresponds to Sikes' age, which was revised down from forty-five years (1.13.98) to thirty-five. The coincidence of numbers implies that his whole course of life has been a process of self-destruction, or preparedness for death, while he dies, 'nel mezzo del cammin di nostra vita' – in the middle of the journey of our life (Dante's *Inferno* 1.1); cut off half-way before reaching the biblical age of seventy.

Dickens did not think that the scene could be illustrated: the action was 'so very complicated, with such a multitude of figures, such violent actions and torch-light to boot, that a small plate could not take in the slightest idea of it' (*Letters* 1.440).[16] The text makes Sikes undone by his vision of Nancy's eyes. In Cruikshank, however, he is shown driven to the very corner of the building, up against the low parapet wall, under broken chimney-pots, and looked at by his dog, which was also seen in the previous picture, 'Sikes Attempting to Destroy his Dog' (*OT* 3.19.405). It has been suggested that Nietzsche makes the dog the image of the ego.[17] The idea fits here. Dickens stresses the feminine force that kills Sikes, and does not mention the presence on the roof of the dog – which has preceded Sikes and presumably given the clue to the chasers where Sikes is – until after Sikes has died. Cruikshank masculinises the scene, as with the tensions shown in the man's body (in his legs and his left arm particularly), and he makes the dog both the expression of what he is, and Sikes' onlooker, rather than Nancy's spectre.

Jacob's Island, 'improved' after the cholera of 1849, became the subject again of the Preface to the Cheap Edition of Dickens' novels (1850), when he made fun of Sir Peter Laurie (1778–1861), Lord Mayor of London in 1832, and a commercial success as a saddler. Laurie was parodied before in *The Chimes* (1844) as Alderman Cute (*CB1*, 166–74) who advertises himself as a practical man, intending to 'put down' everything that the poor do. If Laurie says that Jacob's Island does not exist, because it was only part of a work of fiction, Dickens says that since Laurie appeared in his fiction, he must be a fiction too. This ironises that Utilitarian spirit which does not read novels, and it is written in the context of Dickens speaking for the Metropolitan Sanitary Association, formed in 1849; the argument is that nothing can be done for 'the poor' until 'their dwelling-places are made decent and wholesome' (*Speeches* 461). Yet there is a trap: 'decent' is the word whereby Dickens' text mocks Bradley Headstone; the word which is used to picture the conditions in which the poor should live returns to suggest that being 'decent' is the ultimate condemnation: the person who struggles from pauperdom to mere 'decency' will experience such schizoid reactions to this genteel poverty as to make him criminal.

In a letter to Angela Burdett-Coutts of 7 January 1853 about conditions in Bermondsey, Dickens discusses Hickman's Folly, a line of houses in Dockhead, noting the wooden houses, and that there was 'no more road than in an American swamp'. He describes a 'wan child looking over at a starved old white horse who was making a meal out of oyster-shells. The sun was going down and flaming out like an angry fire at the child'. He adds, 'the child, and I and the pale horse [pale to suggest death: see Revelation 6.8] stared at one another in silence for some five minutes, as if we were so many figures in a dismal allegory' (*Letters* 7.2–3). The same letter notes changes in Jacob's Island. It is interesting that Dickens allegorises Bermondsey; though he obviously knew Jacob's Island, he also allegorises that; it is all London, the city as a trap. It is 'hidden' London (*OT* 3.12.416), the place for those who have 'powerful motives for a secret residence', or who are 'reduced to a destitute condition indeed' (3.12.418). As hidden, it compares with what is obscene: in journalism, Dickens refers to 'obscene Field Lane' (*J2* 50). The more destitute, the more the need to hide: such are the constraints that bourgeois society – symbolised by Sir Peter Laurie – imposes on the down and out.[18] All *Oliver Twist* means to show what has been hidden, but in another way, the novel shows that all London is hidden, though it is also visible. Dickens' journalism has led him to that point: to reveal what is repressed knowledge. The fascination with that double sense of London, seen and not seen, constitutes London as an allegory of itself, as well as necessitating an allegorical reading of it. If allegory means 'speaking other', it suggests that London speaks other than the way it seems, and it requires seeing what cannot be seen, what is not meant to be seen.

CHAPTER FOUR

LONDON AS RUIN
Tales from *Master Humphrey's Clock*

London is a vile place, I sincerely believe. I have never taken kindly to it since I lived abroad. Whenever I come back from the Country, now, and see that great heavy canopy lowering over the housetops, I wonder what on earth I do there, except on obligation.   *Letters*, 10 February 1851 6: 287

I · ANTIQUARIAN HISTORY

The texts of this chapter, those appearing in Dickens' weekly *Master Humphrey's Clock*, including *The Old Curiosity Shop* and *Barnaby Rudge*, are fascinated by history: by public events, such as the Gordon Riots, which are the backbone of *Barnaby Rudge*, and by antiquarian details about forgotten London. Both interests came from the historical novels of Scott (1771–1832).[1] From the beginning, Dickens had wanted to write an historical novel, and had signed a contract with John Macrone in May 1836 to produce 'Gabriel Vardon, Locksmith of London'. Half the completed *Sketches by Boz* had appeared in volume form, as *Sketches by Boz: First Series* (February 1836), and *Pickwick Papers* had begun serialisation (April 1836), but the project was to complete 'Gabriel Vardon' as a book by the end of 1836. In the event, *Oliver Twist* (1837–38) succeeded as a serial-novel, so did *Nicholas Nickleby* (1838–39).

Dickens' antiquarian details are not just for anecdotal interest, nor signs of nostalgia. For Nietzsche, the antiquarian impulse 'knows only how to *preserve* life, not how to engender it; it always undervalues that which is becoming because it has no instinct for divining it'. In that way Nietzsche sees antiquarianism as a paralysing form of history.[2] But Dickens' interest in the past, in these texts, is not in it for its inherent, nor for its curiosity value, nor for its chronology, but as containing other histories neglected but inherent within modernity. Showing how things get left behind, but also that the city contains several time-scales in it, some given more attention than others, Dickens identifies with the residual, and what modernity sets aside. Walter Benjamin in his work on allegory thinks of a history which records 'the untimely, the sorrowful, the unsuccessful'. He sets this against history as the triumphant record of progress or improvement.[3] In Dickens, too, narrative history has been replaced by something else: an interest in allegorical details, which impels the sense that history may be seen differently from realist, narrative terms.

II · *MASTER HUMPHREY'S CLOCK*

On 4 April 1840, Dickens began *Master Humphrey's Clock*, the short-lived weekly with stories inserted, which was to be written by him in its entirety. *The Old Curiosity Shop* began as no. 4 (25 April 1840), continued in nos 7, 8, 9, 10 and 11, and then, from no. 12 on, occupied the whole journal until 6 February 1841. It began as one of the 'Personal Adventures of Master Humphrey' (*MHC* 133), as a novel set in contemporary London, but moving away from it. *Barnaby Rudge: A Tale of the Riots of 'Eighty*, the fulfilment of 'Garbriel Vardon', began the week after the end of *The Old Curiosity Shop* (13 February 1841), running till 27 November 1841. Novel and journal, with 88 issues, concluded together, the last, double, issue giving Master Humphrey's death. *Barnaby Rudge* was the first of two historical novels by Dickens, *A Tale of Two Cities* being the other; and as that was about revolution in the capital city, so this first historical novel took, as subject, rioting, the anti-Catholic pogrom led by Lord George Gordon in London in June 1780.[4]

In *Master Humphrey's Clock* and its stories and novels, Dickens' form of antiquarianism is demonstrable from the illustrations by George Cattermole (1800–68), watercolourist and book illustrator, who had been a pupil of the architectural draughtsman John Britton (1771–1857), and had worked on his *Cathedral Antiquities of England* (1814–35). Britton's project combined antiquarianism and topography, where Gothic architecture was seen as an authentically 'English' style. He went on to propose, in 1837, a Society for the Preservation of Ancient Monuments.[5] Cattermole's first painting for the Royal Academy was a view of Peterborough Cathedral. In addition to the combination of the Gothic and grotesque that Cattermole offered, additional pictures came from Phiz. It is not difficult to see the division of labour in *Master Humphrey's Clock*: six woodcuts by Cattermole plus the frontispiece pick out historical details, while the thirteen by Phiz are more energetic and grotesque, though there is something more nostalgic in the last two. '*Barnaby Rudge* in Master Humphrey's Imagination', shows the power of reverie, as the figures from *Barnaby Rudge* appear in dream with a flag which announces the title of the novel, and the characters from *The Old Curiosity Shop* disappear to the right, some of them up the chimney. The last, 'Master Humphrey's Room Deserted', comes after the death of Master Humphrey. The frontispiece, by Cattermole, has medieval halberds going up the sides as a frame, and forming at the top a gothic arch. Vignettes from *The Old Curiosity Shop* go up and down the sides, and two scenes from *Master Humphrey's Clock* appear in the middle. One is the circle of men gathered round Master Humphrey's table, the other an illustration for 'Mr Weller's Watch' (*MHC* no. 9). Phiz and Cattermole also worked woodcuts into the text of *The Old Curiosity Shop*, seventy-five in all.[6] They were joined by Samuel Williams and Daniel Maclise; *Barnaby Rudge* had seventy-six woodcuts, mainly by Phiz, though Cattermole provided seventeen.

Gatehouse and medieval wall in Charterhouse Square, with buildings behind; the Carthusian Priory (1371), Thomas Sutton's Charterhouse School (1611 until 1872), and still home for Charterhouse pensioners.

These texts and their illustrations lead us to Dickens, antiquarian London, and allegory. Master Humphrey speaks of himself as a 'mis-shapen, deformed, old man' (31), and recounts how 'the truth burst upon me for the first time' – perhaps on his birthday – 'how keenly [his mother] felt for her poor crippled boy' (31–32). His friendship with the deaf gentleman, whose name he does not know (33), is of a piece with this sense of personal privation. He enlarges on that friendship and that with Jack Redburn and Owen Miles (60–66), as if stressing that the knowledge of London that the four have, comes from damaged lives. The dominant sense of that pervades *Master Humphrey's Clock*, and *The Old Curiosity Shop* (as with Maclise's picture of the Sexton who walks with a crutch (55.417)), and it is parodied in the figure of Quilp the dwarf. In *Barnaby Rudge*, a sense of privation, of trauma which has formed the personality, exists with the titular figure, who was born an idiot immediately after the double murder committed by his father. Barnaby Rudge's friends are a raven, Grip, and Hugh, who is illegitimate and outcast, a 'handsome satyr' (21.176), called a 'centaur' and 'animal', and rendered animal-like, especially in Phiz's woodcut (*BR* 11.99). This associates with what John Willet says, that Hugh is to be treated as an animal (11.100).

Master Humphrey, melancholic, and potentially misanthropic, introduces himself, in the first week, as living:

> in a venerable suburb of London, in an old house, which in bygone days was a famous resort for merry roysterers and peerless ladies, long since departed. It is a silent, shady place, with a paved court-yard . . . full of echoes' (28)

It is a part of London unaffected by the Great Fire. It has 'worm-eaten doors, and low ceilings crossed by clumsy beams . . . walls of wainscot, dark stairs, and gaping closets'. Later comes the description of the clock, Master Humphrey's memories of which go back some sixty years (32) – to 1780, the date of the principal action of *Barnaby Rudge* (see *BR* chapter 33), and the year of the burning of Newgate by the rioting crowd, and its subsequent rebuilding. Going back sixty years recalls Scott's initial novel: *Waverley; Or, 'Tis Sixty Years Since* (1814). Cattermole's room is Tudor in date, and in his picture of the room, Phiz adds the date 1581, to the cartouche above the fireplace, so making the house virtually 300 years older than the events of *Barnaby Rudge*, and 360 years older than the ending of the narrative of *Master Humphrey's Clock*. We have come round a full circle. It is that London that *Master Humphrey's Clock* engages with.

The narratives to be told come out of the clock, where they have been placed; they 'beguile time [from ten at night to two in the morning, once a week] from the heart of time itself' (34). The clock, then, speaks of 'time itself', as its image; it is echoed in *The Mystery of Edwin Drood*, whose Gothicism repeats something of the three Cattermole-illustrated texts discussed here, when Mr Grewgious looks in through the western door of the Cathedral of Cloisterham: ' "Dear me . . . it's like looking down the throat of Old Time" ' (*ED* 9.94). Time devours its children. Yet the idea of 'beguiling time' is not simple. While it includes suspending its onward motion, or even staying in the past, as much in *Master Humphrey's Clock* does (as with the introduction of Pickwick and Weller into the circle, while Mr Pickwick's tale (nos 5 and 6), by being of the time of James the First is also of the past), it also includes staving off death. And that can only be done by time itself. The force of death keeps off death. Being beguiled by time produces a self-deceptive thought, as in *Edwin Drood*:

> A drowsy city, Cloisterham, whose inhabitants seem to suppose, with an inconsistency more strange than rare, that all its changes lie behind it, and that there are no more to come. A queer moral to derive from antiquity, yet older than any traceable antiquity. (*ED* 3.23)

But letting time beguile time is not to be held by an inconsistency that disbelieves in change and that therefore refuses to acknowledge time. Nor is it to evade the linear movement of time; it is more complex, implying a doubling of perception of time, where it is both allowing time to go on and also denying the pastness of the past, claiming that the past is not over, not simply consumed.

The first inset narrative of *Master Humphrey's Clock*, introduced in no. 1, tells how Jo Toddyhigh falls asleep in the music-gallery of the Guildhall of London and sees the giants Gog and Magog, sitting on the ledge of the stained-glass window, with, in the illustration by Phiz, a clock below them, so associating them with Master Humphrey. The statues of Gog and Magog, familiar from 'Gone Astray', are also seen in *Dombey and Son* 4.46. Their association with clock-time is noted in a reference to them in *Barnaby Rudge* (40.319), in the context of the existence of these giants also on the clock of St Dunstan-in-the-West in Fleet Street (see *DC* 23.357). In 1841, that was an antiquarian detail, since the church had been demolished in 1828, and was rebuilt by John Shaw in 1831 without the clock. As in *Nicholas Nickleby* (11.135), where Gog is 'the guardian genius of London', Gog and Magog in Guildhall are called 'guardian genii of the City' (*MHC* 41) – not of London, but more specifically, the 'ancient city' (*MHC* 43), the City of London, a detail which only emphasises the antiquarianism of the text, since the City of London, as opposed to London in *Nicholas Nickleby*, is a confined area, with limited capacity for growth, so an area more definable by its past than by what would happen to it in the future.[7]

Dickens elevates the giants more than W.H. Ainsworth, whose *The Tower of London* (1840) made Gog and Magog two of three gigantic warders who claim

Gog, one of the giants carved by Richard Evans in 1953, for the West Gallery of the Guildhall, replacing the giants of Richard Saunders (1708), destroyed in the Blitz; compare Phiz's illustration of these older giants in *Master Humphrey's Clock*.

descent from Henry the Eighth; the third being Og, and their companion Xit, a dwarf.[8] In Jo Toddyhigh's dream, the giants recall their compact, that, as Magog explains, they should:

> entertain each other with stories of our past experience; with tales of the past, the present, and the future; with legends of London and her sturdy citizens from the old simple times. That every night at midnight when Saint Paul's bell tolls out one and we may move and speak, we thus discourse, nor leave such themes till the first grey gleams of day shall strike us dumb. (44)

These giants, who think of old simple times, provide one draft title for the text: 'The Relaxations of Gog and Magog' divided 'into portions like the Arabian Nights'. They survey London from above, panoramically. Walter Benjamin cites G.K. Chesterton on this passage:

> Dickens: 'There floated before him a vision of a monstrous magazine, entirely written by himself . . . One characteristic thing he wished to have in the periodical. He suggested an Arabian Nights of London, in which Gog and Magog, the giants of the city, should give forth chronicles as enormous as themselves' . . . Dickens had numerous projects for serials. (*Arcades* 535)

A continuous, unfolding serial, an always starting, never completed chronicle, told by figures who see all: it is the dream of the panorama, and a collector's dream, to be able to go on gathering stories, never ceasing: Master Humphrey's dream. It is a dream which refuses to think of the inanimate as such; wooden giants have an alternative life, nothing is entirely lost in the past, where objects still have the night-time power of speech till they are struck dumb.

The giants mirror the men who gather round Master Humphrey: their dumbness is paralleled by the deafness of the particular story-teller who has written this story. The anachronism within the writing appears in contrast to the onward ticking of time, except that the clock is 'quaint' and 'queer' and 'old', like the 'queer' house. These are expressions used by Dickens in a letter to Forster (13 January 1840, *Letters* 2.6), about the 'old file' who lives in the house. The clock's time seems to be anachronistic; it does not survive Master Humphrey.

The first narrative, told by Magog, which spreads over issue no. 2, is of Elizabethan London, the period that Ainsworth writes of in *The Tower of London* (1840). No. 3 opens with Master Humphrey speaking at midnight, and introducing the deaf gentleman, Jack Redburn, and Mr Miles, before giving the second narrative, which is set in the reign of Charles the Second, and is confessional in character. This prepares for the fourth instalment, where Master Humphrey begins telling *The Old Curiosity Shop*. After its conclusion, the text returns to Master Humphrey's circle. Twelve is heard from both the clock and, distantly, from St Paul's, and Master Humphrey doubles the clock-theme by narrating his recent experience of seeing the clock of St Paul's, which:

did not mark the flight of every moment with a gentle second stroke as though
it would check old Time, and have him stay his pace in pity, but measured it with
one sledge-hammer beat, as if its business were to crush the seconds as they came
trooping on. (*MHC* 135)

This negativity suggests an ambivalence about time as destructive; so time must
be 'beguiled by time', which makes time not a unitary concept, but as marked
by what Derrida calls *differance*, something inside it as a concept which
means that it is not just ongoing and destructive, but that it keeps something
else inside it, like the fantasy of Gog and Magog. In terms of negativity, clock-
time and the city are inseparable; however nostalgic *Master Humphrey's
Clock*, it is absolutely urban, because the city enforces punctuality, and time-
keeping: the men of Master Humphrey's circle keep time in their punctual
meetings. St Paul's, as the centre of London, keeps time in a sadistic mode.
To find another time within London, which is not that of being crushed, or
beaten by a sledge-hammer (as Orlick tries to kill Pip in *Great Expectations*),
becomes the motivation for writing, and is a form of thinking historically.

Master Humphrey develops the 'fancy ... that this was London's Heart,
and that when it should cease to beat, the City would be no more'. That is
mechanical time, and it echoes in Estella in *Great Expectations* at her coldest,
saying, 'I have no heart' only one that 'if it ceased to beat, I should cease to be'
(*GE* 2.10.237). Estella may be the image of the mechanical city of London,
whose centre is St Paul's. In Master Humphrey's thought, 'the great heart of
London throbs in its Giant Breast' – i.e. in St Paul's. The language of giants
makes St Paul's the analogue of those apocalyptic figures Gog and Magog
(Revelation 20.8), but the writing emphasises the inexorability of life within
the city in relation to the same 'indomitable working' of the clock (135–37).
And here, the impassive working of time negates change:

> Wealth and beggary, vice and virtue, guilt and innocence, repletion and the direst
> hunger, all treading on each other and crowding together, are gathered round [St
> Paul's.] Draw but a little circle above the clustering house-tops, and you shall have
> within its space, everything with its opposite extreme and contradiction, close
> beside. (135–36)

The passage affirms the separated nature of the 'thousand worlds' which
coexist in the city, all subject to the same deadening time. The 'Heart of London'
is uninfluenced by the lives within the city; the image contrasts with the end of
Wordsworth's *Sonnet upon Westminster Bridge* (1802): 'Dear God! The very
houses seem asleep/And all that mighty heart is lying still'. In Wordsworth,
London is the heart, with no need for any other. Master Humphrey's text puts
the life of London into relationship with something of emptiness or deadness
at the centre. Life in the text and in the city is infected by something mechanical and abstract.

At the end of *Barnaby Rudge*, the writing turns again to some last thoughts
of Master Humphrey and then to the account of how his friends found him

dead the day after the readings finished for good: 'the chimney-corner has grown cold, and MASTER HUMPHREY'S CLOCK has stopped for ever' (147). Clock and owner figure each other; Master Humphrey is allegorised in his clock. He speaks as perhaps a clock would: he is the mask for the clock, and he is fearful that what may be true of St Paul's clock – that life revolves round dead mechanism – may be true of himself and his circle, and his heart. Time is at the centre of London. If 'time' must be found to beguile the time of St Paul's, London cannot be seen as static, but must be put into a narrative which both finds alternative times, and which accepts that city-structure is in, and is of, time. In a development from the fear expressed here of mechanical time, Miss Havisham, in *Great Expectations*, a fully misanthropic and a more reclusive Master Humphrey, stops the clocks. She allows herself no alternative to the sledge-hammer motions of time, but cannot thereby obliterate time: she knows when it is her birthday. Because, here, the stories come out of the clock, as manuscripts which have been deposited there, the clock is an archive of dead London; it produces in the manuscripts that which is other, ghostly, and different from the hegemonic sense of time as destructive in its progression. And so the novel-length narratives that come from it speak of what is 'old', and also give an historical novel which is unusual in the extent to which it is the record of the untimely, the sorrowful and unsuccessful.

III · THE OLD CURIOSITY SHOP

The Old Curiosity Shop begins with Master Humphrey meeting Nell and her grandfather. If, as in a cancelled passage in the first chapter, Nell is supposed to be selling diamonds, that might place the beginning of the action around Hatton Gardens, but the suburb where Master Humphrey lives is not specified, nor the locale of the curiosity shop in the first chapter, whose opening initial letter shows a scene from Pump Court, one of the courtyards of the Temple.[9] The third paragraph of the novel refers to a sick man in St Martin's Court, which before the building of Charing Cross Road, ran from Leicester Square, across the now gone Castle Road, to St Martin's Lane; this setting would fit a prevalent idea that the curiosity shop was at the corner of Green Street and Castle Road.[10] It seems to be situated in a long and straight street (41.309–10), but as rendered by Cattermole in the first illustration, 'The Shop', seems to be a double of Master Humphrey's chamber and to be a figure for old London. As such, it has disappeared: Kit shows his children the place at the end, but 'new improvements had altered it so much, it was not like the same. The old house had been long ago pulled down, and a fine broad road was in its place'. Kit cannot remember where it was, saying, 'that these alterations were confusing' (65.556). There is no placing the shop: it is a figure for London, and for thinking about history as dead relics, which, when considered allegorically, may still have the power to speak.

The route out of London that Nell and her grandfather take is also un-specified, though areas are clearly separated, and mapped in terms of rings around the city. They go out from 'long deserted streets' (15.121), which imply the centre of town, through 'the labyrinth of men's abodes which yet lay between them and the outskirts', then through 'haunts of commerce and great traffic', then into the poor parts, into a 'straggling neighbourhood' full of brickfields, then into 'small garden patches bordering the road':

> Then came the public-house, freshly painted in green and white, with tea-gardens and a bowling-green, spurning its old neighbour with the horse-trough where the wagons stopped; then fields; and then some houses, one by one, of goodly size with lawns, some even with a lodge where dwelt a porter and his wife. Then came a turnpike; then fields again with trees and haystacks; then a hill; and on top of that the traveller might stop, and – looking back at old Saint Paul's looming through the smoke, its cross peering above the cloud (if the day were clear) and glittering in the sun; and casting his eye upon the Babel out of which it grew until he traced it down to the furthest out-posts of the invading army of bricks and mortar whose station lay for the present nearly at his feet – might feel at last that he was clear of London. (15.122)

Cattermole has already illustrated Nell and her grandfather going out of town, at the end of chapter 12 (104), in an image which recalls Blake's for his poem 'London'. But in Blake, the boy leads the old man who is on crutches, and is solicitous for him, both figures being necessary for a representation of what London is. (The figure of Quilp as the dwarf, as if child and man at once, condenses these figures into a parody of the doubleness within London.) Cattermole, in contrast to Dickens' text, shows the old man leading, and the girl looking back, as if more attached to the curiosity shop which is behind them. The picture brings out the enclosing sense of London; the figures are surrounded by buildings, invading bricks and mortar. In the last sentence of the quotation there seems a possible reference to an alternative form of going out of town in George Cruikshank's etching 'London going out of Town – or The March of Bricks and Mortar' (1829). Here, bricks are being shot out of mortar kilns into the countryside round London. Robert Patten explains that this picture, for the second series of *Scraps and Sketches* (1829), was because:

> the lord of the manor at Hampstead [Sir Thomas Maryon Wilson (1800–69)] had just introduced a bill authorizing the enclosure of the Heath; two years previously, Eton College had received permission to build on its lands at Primrose Hill . . . Cruikshank uses the traditional device of a creature composed of nonhuman parts . . . to create an army of builders' automatons marching on spade and pick legs, with chimney-pot bodies and hod or cowl heads. These troops attack nature, 'mortarly' wounding trees, discharging cannonades of hot bricks to fire the hay ricks, shooting rubbish onto the fields.[11]

If any such allusion to Cruikshank is there, it might suggest the setting of the picture as Hampstead. Cattermole shows a distant prospect of London, separated from the travellers who sit under a tree which encloses their space; cattle are seen at a river bank a little way beyond. Yet the narrative refuses to specify Hampstead, and the phrase 'the traveller' separates the passage from the specificity of Nell and her grandfather's actual journey; it is as if London is leaving London.

In contrast, other locales are designated. Quilp lives on Tower Hill and has 'Quilp's Wharf' on the Surrey side of the river, opposite the Tower: he possesses both sides of the Thames. His wharf (there seems to be an unspoken pun on dwarf and wharf) is tiny and its only inhabitant is an 'amphibious boy', who with Quilp parodies the old curiosity shop, as peopled by the old man and the girl. Quilp lives off the rents of 'whole colonies of filthy streets and alleys by the waterside', has shares in the ventures of East Indiamen, and smokes smuggled cigars (which suggests the West India docks) 'under the very nose of the Custom House' and makes appointments on Change (4.35). The warehouse retreat, which Cattermole illustrated, is called the Wilderness (21.168, 23.177). Dick Swiveller lives in the neighbourhood of Drury Lane (7.60). Mr and Mrs Garland live in Finchley (21.165), north of Hampstead, on the Great North Road; their cottage is old-fashioned Gothic 'with a thatched roof and little spires at the gable-ends, and pieces of stained glass in some of the windows, almost as large as pocket-books' (22.174): fitting for people whose lack of relationship with the modern world is figured in the father's and the son's club-feet (14.116, 118), which aligns them to Master Humphrey. Solomon Brass, and his sister Sally, live at Bevis Marks, close to 'the wearing apparel exposed for sale in Duke's Place and Houndsditch' (33.255), and near enough for Sally Brass to buy a second-hand stool for Dick Swiveller in Whitechapel, in the open street opposite the London hospital (35.265). The Brasses end up in the poverty of St Giles. These elements define another half of this text, where London is not left behind.

The title *The Old Curiosity Shop* may be related to Hazlitt in 1818, writing on Crabbe's poetry, that it is 'like a museum or curiosity-shop: every thing has the same posthumous appearance, the same inanimateness and identity of character'.[12] This anticipates Richard Altick's point that museums were junk shops, 'descendants of the antiquarian shops that served eighteenth century collectors – George Humphrey's, for example, whose accumulated stock was pretentiously named "Humphrey's Grand Museum" . . . when it was established in St Martin's Lane in 1778–9, prior to sale by auction' (Altick, *The Shows of London* 428). Clocks and curiosities unite as witnesses to time. Altick discusses rarities being landed at Thames wharves in the eighteenth century. Private museums were existing by the time of Queen Anne. The purchase of curios for cabinets went back to the founding of the Royal Society in 1662 (Altick, *The Shows of London* 12–13). Wordsworth evokes the museum for a comparison, when thinking about the 'delight' he experiences from moment to moment while at Cambridge:

                      Carelessly
I gaz'd, roving as through a Cabinet
Or wide museum (throng'd with fishes, gems,
Birds, crocodiles, shells) where little can be seen
Well understood, or naturally endear'd,
Yet still does every step bring something forth
That quickens, pleases, stings; and here and there
A casual rarity is singled out,
And has its brief perusal, then gives way
To others, all supplanted in their turn. (*The Prelude* 3.651–60)

In Dickens, the old curiosity shop, or warehouse contains 'old and curious things which seem to crouch in odd corners of this town . . . suits of mail standing like ghosts in armour . . . fantastic carvings brought from monkish cloisters, rusty weapons . . . distorted figures in china and wood and iron and ivory; tapestry and strange furniture which might have been designed in dreams' (*OCS* 1.13). 'The Shop' shows three suits of armour framing the figures of the girl, Master Humphrey and the old man, who holds a candle high. The figures in armour are like Gog and Magog as silent watchers (they could even, unknowingly, suggest *The Prelude* 7.131–38, on the association of the giants with the figures in armour in the Tower of London). They are ambiguous presences, like everything of the past, matching the old man, Nell's grandfather, who 'might have groped among old churches and tombs and deserted houses and gathered all the spoils with his own hands' (*OCS* 1.13). He reads as if he was an antiquarian, in a time when a professional historian criticised antiquarianism: 'Unless it . . . goes on to their high value as forms part of a greater whole, antiquarian study is a mere matter of curiosity'.[13] But it is also the case that the warehouse is a shop, and its curiosities are also commodities. Walter Benjamin quotes G.K. Chesterton, 'every shop . . . was to [Dickens] the door of romance' (*Arcades* 57). The title 'the old curiosity shop' invites in the person who sees it; the curio or commodity fascinates the collector, because it has been taken out of chronological time; its value is that its context has changed. An image of the past in the present, it leads to thinking how the past exists in the present, both as the emblems of London which indicate that it is no more than the ruin, or as containing something which is 'other' within its ruins, retrievable within the present.

IV · *THE OLD CURIOSITY SHOP* AND ALLEGORY

The novel's first chapter closes with a woodcut by Samuel Williams (1788–1853). He had been asked by Chapman, Dickens' publisher to produce a picture of Nell asleep surrounded by the curios from the curiosity dealer's warehouse: the accumulation of detail is suggestive of Oldbuck's 'den' as described in Scott's *The Antiquary*, where, among the 'wreck of ancient books and utensils, with a gravity equal to Marius among the ruins of Carthage' a black cat sits: 'the floor, as well as the table and chairs, was overflowed by the same *mare magnum* of miscellaneous trumpery, where it would have been impossible to find any individual article wanted, as to put it to any use when discovered' (*The Antiquary* 3.22). The recurrence of this image as it is applied, in *Dombey and Son*, to Mr Brogley, a 'Caius Marius who sits upon the ruins of other people's Carthages' (*DS* 9.134), associates him, as broker and second-hand dealer, with Dickens as the collector of the out of date and out of place.

At first, the last paragraph of the chapter ended with Master Humphrey back with his clock, whose ticking contrasts with the scene that has been left behind:

> But all that night, waking or in my sleep, the same thoughts recurred, and the same images retained possession of my brain. I had before me the old dark murky rooms – the gaunt suits of mail with their ghostly silent air – the faces all awry, grinning from wood and stone – the dust and rust, and worm that lives in wood – and alone in the midst of all this lumber and decay, and ugly age, the beautiful child in her gentle slumber, smiling through her light and sunny dreams. (1.22)

The image of Nell asleep was discussed by Thomas Hood (1799–1845) in the *Athenaeum* (7 November 1840), who wrote:

> . . . we do not know where we have met, in fiction, with a more striking and pic-turesque combination of images than is presented by the simple, childish figure of little Nelly, amidst a chaos of such obsolete, grotesque, old-world commodities as form the stock in trade of the Old Curiosity Shop. Look at the Artist's picture of the Child, asleep in her little bed, surrounded, or rather mobbed, by ancient armour and arms, antique furniture, and relics sacred or profane, hideous or grotesque: – it is like an Allegory of the peace and innocence of Childhood in the midst of Violence, Superstition, and all the hateful or hurtful Passions of the world. How sweet and fresh the youthful figure! How much sweeter and fresher for the rusty, musty, fusty atmosphere of such accessories and their associations! How soothing the moral, that Gentleness, Purity, and Truth, sometimes dormant but never dead, have survived, and will outlive Fraud and Force, though backed by gold and encased in steel.[14]

This prompted Dickens, his gratitude to the by now deceased Hood noted in the Preface to 1848 edition, to add four paragraphs before the last:

> I sat down in my easy-chair; and falling back upon its ample cushions, pictured to myself the child in her bed: alone, unwatched, uncared for (save for angels), yet sleeping peacefully. So very young, spiritual, so slight and fairy-like a creature pass-ing the long dull nights in such an uncongenial place – I could not dismiss it from my thoughts.
>
> We are so much in the habit of allowing impressions to be made upon us by exter-nal objects, which should be produced by reflection alone, but which, without such visible aids, often escape us; that I am not sure I should have been so thoroughly pos-sessed by this one subject, but for the heaps of fantastic things I had seen huddled together in the *curiosity*-dealer's warehouse. These, crowding upon my mind, in con-nexion with the child, and gathering round her, as it were, brought her condition

palpably before me. I had her image, without any effort of imagination, surrounded and beset by everything that was foreign to its nature, and furthest removed from the sympathies of her sex and age . . . She seemed to exist in a kind of allegory; and having these shapes about her, claimed my interest so strongly, that (as I have remarked) I could not dismiss her from my recollection, do what I could.

'It would be a *curious* speculation', said I, after some restless turns across and across the room, 'to imagine her in her future life, holding her solitary way among a crowd of wild grotesque companions; the only pure fresh youthful object in the throng. It would be *curious* to find . . .'.

I checked myself there, for the theme was carrying me along with it at a great pace, and I already saw before me a region on which I was little disposed to enter. I agreed with myself that this was idle musing, and resolved to go to bed and court forgetfulness. (1.20–22, my emphases)

Here, deriving from Hood, 'allegory' seems anachronistic, as though not of the nineteenth century, but the Elizabethan world when the shop's relics might have had meaning. Forster, in *The Examiner* (4 December 1841, compare *Life* 2.7.152) wrote that 'from the image of little Nell asleep amid the quaint grotesque figures of the old curiosity warehouse, to that other final sleep she takes among the grim forms and carvings of the old church aisle; the main purpose is never put aside . . . It was out of the more hideous lumber and rottenness that had surrounded the child in her grandfather's home, that Quilp and his filthy gang had taken life . . .' Forster glosses Hood, and what Dickens will write about the speculations of Master Humphrey. Both Quilp – a Richard the Third-like figure, more deformed than Master Humphrey, a nightmare version of him – and his gang are of the history piled into the curiosity shop, which they occupy in chapter 11. They are figures of the grotesque past of the London that Nell must escape, leaving not just modern, capitalist London, but that which in its past has produced that capitalist spirit, which Dickens, defying normal chronologies, identifies with the anachronistic figure of Quilp. In chapter 27, Nelly arrives at an old town, which still has a gothic-arched town-gate, which includes an empty niche missing its statue. At that moment, coincidentally, she sees Quilp, 'like some monstrous image that had come down from its niche' (*OCS* 27.212). The Gothic spirit is alive in the spirit of capitalism: this is different from Ruskin's 'nature of Gothic' as expounded in *The Stones of Venice*.

Cattermole illustrated the other picture which Forster referred to, in chapter 72 (546). It shows the tombs of a Gothic church, the old man seated on one, and in front of him, in the foreground, a tombstone with the word 'Here' written upon it. The rest of the tomb is not seen, being cropped by the lower edge of the picture. The previous picture (71.539) showed the child lying dead in a room with a Gothic embrasure, in a bed with religious motifs on the bedhead, and an hourglass near the bed: a Renaissance allegorical detail. The allegorical nature of *The Old Curiosity Shop* is signalled in the reference to *The Pilgrim's Progress* (15.123) but there is more. Master Humphrey gives reasons for liking to wander London at night; he thinks of the constant pacing up and down of feet, and of the sick person in such a narrow confine as St Martin's Court, hearing the pacing of feet all the time, made to think:

> of the hum and noise being always present to his sense, and of the stream of life that will not stop, pouring on, on, on, through all his restless dreams, as if he were condemned to lie dead but conscious, in a noisy churchyard, and had no hope of rest for centuries to come. (1.9)

The equivalence of death and sleep, which, running through the text, makes Steven Marcus say that 'the England of this novel is nothing less than a vast necropolis',[15] affects the portrayal of Nell asleep. Her situation at the end of the chapter, alive and sleeping amongst inanimate, dead things, is an allegory of the other situation, at the beginning of the chapter, of the dead being dead, yet conscious, whilst live things are going on all around. As Hood describes her as asleep and alive with everything that is dead and inanimate around her, it is apparent that she is death-marked in the text, or already dead yet conscious. Her sleep allegorises her death, in the first two of Cattermole's final three illustrations, while her state throughout is one of death, yet still compelled to participate in life. She is a reverse, or an allegory, of the Dance of Death, where the skeleton dances with the live person, and dances them into the grave; for she is as if already dead, part of the old curiosity shop, which is another name for death.

Medieval relics in the curiosity shop recall the allegorical woodcut by Dürer, 'Melencolia 1' (1513). Here, the angel-like woman sits in a position of melancholy with her head in her hand, and with objects lying around her on the floor in an unused state. Similarly, there is no relationship between Nell and the objects of the warehouse: it is an alienated state, indicative of her death. The old man sitting in his easy chair and meditating on Nell asleep in her bed, becomes a repetition of her and her unconscious melancholia and echoes Dürer's woodcut. As he thinks of her 'holding her solitary way among a crowd of wild grotesque companions' (1.22), this, which is prompted by Williams' picture and Hood's review, becomes Dickens' own reading of what creates Quilp. He, like an animated grotesque from among medieval curios, enters the shop in chapter 3, at the end of which Master Humphrey leaves the text.

Discussion of allegory can go further via Theodor Adorno, who commented on Dickens, and through Walter Benjamin, his friend, who discusses Dürer's picture in *The Origin of German Tragic Drama* (1927), arguing that props in Baroque tragic drama are obvious stage properties, artificial and temporary, and as if gathered together by chance (like the objects of the old curiosity shop). Melancholy, for Benjamin, is the state of mind that knows that there is no coherence within personal subjectivity, nor coherence between that subjectivity in ruins and the object world. Benjamin sees the objects lying on the floor in Dürer's work as emblems whose meaning has been lost: 'the utensils of active life are lying around unused on the floor, as objects of contemplation'. This follows a description of the setting for a Baroque drama, where it is said that 'a whole collection of stage properties are lying scattered about the floor'. The object appears to be 'a symbol of some enigmatic wisdom because it lacks any natural, creative relationship to us' (*The Origin of German Tragic Drama*, 132, 124, 139). But meaning is declared lost, fragmented. It seems that Benjamin would back the importance of the antiquarian against the historian, because the antiquarian makes less pretence of getting collected objects to compose themselves into a whole. There is no single history or symbolic meaning to be read from the relics in the room (and there can be no single history that can be read from London either). Dickens in seeing the girl living in 'a kind of allegory' follows Hood, but is not confined to Hood's meaning; Nell becomes part of the incongruity of objects within Williams' illustration.

Adorno, influenced by Benjamin's cultural criticism, and by *The Origin of German Tragic Drama*, discusses *The Old Curiosity Shop* in 1931, finding in it traces of baroque allegory (363): in the old curiosity shop, in the marionette theatre, in the waxworks and in the churchyard. He quotes 'she seemed to exist in a kind of allegory' – words which Walter Benjamin cites in the *Arcades Project*. He first quotes Dickens' entire paragraph containing the statement, and then Adorno, on the 'useless' object which is not redeemed:

> Nell's death is decided in the sentence that reads, 'There were some trifles there – poor useless things – that she would have liked to take away, but that was impossible' [*OCS* 12.102]. Yet Dickens recognised that the possibility of transition and dialectical rescue was inherent in this world of things, this lost, rejected world; and he expressed it, better than Romantic nature-worship was ever able to do, in the powerful allegory of money with which the depiction of the industrial world ends: 'two old, battered, smoke-encrusted penny pieces. Who knows but they shone as brightly in the eyes of angels, as golden gifts that have been chronicled on tombs?' [*OCS* 44.338–39.] (*Arcades*, 208)

In the first quotation, the child is identified with the curios, which are to be swept away by the forces of modernisation, which are also the forces of Quilp. In the second, the penny pieces have the signs of the industrial city on them, but they are also bright, as if like the angels' eyes which look at them. (The contrast is chapter 30.235, where the old man stands, 'his white face pinched and sharpened by the greediness which made his eyes unnaturally bright, counting the money of which his hands had robbed her'). The coins' random, forgotten quality contrasts with official history, but even that is what has 'been chronicled on tombs': so it has been forgotten, lost, like the objects of the descriptions written in gold, not copper as the coins. As curios themselves, these coins contest public history, indicating another history which cannot be absorbed into a history of progress, or of modernisation.

Curios and coins question the distinction between the animate and the inanimate. Adorno is fascinated by those textual objects whose 'useless' existence is between the animate and inanimate, just as, in *Master Humphrey's Clock*, London's life has the clock as its centre, and the fantasy of Gog and Magog. Adorno finds the characters in the novel not presented as free-standing individuals (364), which comments on their destruction at the hands of bourgeois society, as represented by Quilp. Nell and her grandfather come across itinerant showmen, exhibitors of Punch, sitting among the tombs:

> Perched cross-legged upon a tombstone behind them, was the figure of that hero himself, his nose and chin as hooked and his face as beaming as usual. . . . In part scattered upon the ground at the feet of the two men, and in part jumbled together in a long flat box, were the other persons of the Drama. (16.129)

The characters – Judy, the child, the hobby-horse, the doctor, the foreign gentleman who can only say 'Shallabalah', the neighbour who will not admit that a tin bell is an organ, the executioner and the Devil are all present, as allegorical figures whose reality tests the question of what it means to be alive or dead. The illustration counterpoises Punch with the word 'SACRED' on an adjoining tombstone; and the puppets appear as lifeless as the bodies under the stones. There is a similar questioning of life and death with Mrs Jarley's waxworks, about which Benjamin notes their 'unchanging air of coldness and gentility' (Benjamin 532, quoting *OCS* 27.208). These words are spoken by Mrs Jarley, approvingly. The description fuses death and life (in the pose of gentility), it comments on gentility as coldness, indicating how much that passes for life is death. At the end of the chapter, Nell sees Quilp, and then in dream associates him with the waxworks; with Mrs Jarley, the figure who desires classical deadness and gentility; and with the mechanism of a barrel-organ (27.214): Quilp is alive and dead together (he is indeed 'amphibious', like his boy).

A later moment questioning the distinction between human and machine is in the steel-mill at Birmingham, where the men work to the time imposed by the furnaces, and Nell talks to a man (he gives her the coins), who sits and looks at the fire, 'keeping so very still that he did not even seem to breathe' (44.335): Phiz illustrated this inertia, with the man cupping his chin in his hands, like Dürer's Melencolia.

The allegorical presentation in this novel, which makes Quilp both medieval and capitalist, dissolves a single time-frame; Dickens responds to the idea of the city as set in time by a beguiling of time by the heart of time, discovering the past in the present, the present in the past. Fascination with pre-bourgeois modes of existence becomes a way of dissolving the bourgeois world. This fascination Master Humphrey's antiquarianism also participates in, though he meets something more allegorical than his own dealings with time when he encounters Nell in the old curiosity shop.

V · TOWARDS *BARNABY RUDGE*

In Nell, lost in London at the beginning, the assemblage of emblematic objects in the curiosity warehouse never amounts to anything, except the fragmentation of meaning which is all that the collector knows. Benjamin compares the allegorist with the collector, whose spirit activates the old curiosity shop, which includes Nell. The collector-spirit is also in Master Humphrey, who passes from thinking about the curiosity shop to thinking it would be 'curious' to see Nell and the grotesques in relation to each other. Old London is but a collection of relics, curios, ruins of previous times, like 'old Saint Paul's' in chapter 15; a museum, since museums house ruins. If the fascination in these texts is with the old-fashioned, that associates with Cattermole's artistry, which includes the Tudor Maypole Inn in *Barnaby Rudge*. Indeed, the opening pictures of *Master Humphrey's Clock*, *The Old Curiosity Shop* and *Barnaby Rudge*, all by Cattermole, show old-fashioned interiors or exteriors, complementing Dickens' opening description in *Barnaby Rudge* of the Maypole Inn in 1775, which is like the ambiance of *Master Humphrey's Clock*:

> Its windows were old diamond pane lattices, its floors were sunken and uneven, its ceilings blackened by the hand of time and heavy with massive beams. Over the doorway was an ancient porch, quaintly and grotesquely carved. (*BR* 1.7)

This is in Epping Forest, near Chigwell, twelve miles from London, and near the Warren, the great house described in chapter 13. The name relates to a different, personal and traumatic past: Dickens' blacking-factory, and since murder was committed in the Warren, it possesses an allegorical status suggesting a perpetuating violence from the past. A 'warren' is also labyrinthine, like the past, like London – *Barnaby Rudge* begins with Gabriel Varden's night-time approach to London's 'labyrinths of public ways and shops, and swarms of busy people' (3.33) – as if London contains its record of failure within it, which the novel, by writing an episode of London history, wants to confront, or eliminate. Historical change is noted, as when describing London streets at night: 'it would be difficult for the beholder to recognise his most familiar walks' in the London of that time (16.137). This preludes discussion of the dangers of the city and the progress to be hanged at Tyburn (16.140) – which ceased after the Gordon Riots. Chapter 16 shows Barnaby Rudge's father prowling in the metropolis, and crossing from Clerkenwell over London Bridge to Southwark, then, having returned, wandering the 'back ways, lanes and courts, between Cornhill and Smithfield' (18.154). The text aligns criminality and rootlessness in the city, and putting the father into the atmosphere of Southwark, aligns him as pariah with Dickens' father. The writing is modern, noting that Rudge feels 'nothing in common with the slumbering world around . . . [he endures] a kind of suffering, on which the rivers of great cities close full many a time, and which the solitude in crowds alone awakens' (18.150).

VI · *BARNABY RUDGE* AND LONDON

Barnaby Rudge has been read as a response to Chartism.[16] The Cato Street conspiracy of 1820, which ended with six men, including the leader, Arthur Thistlewood (1774–1820), being hanged and beheaded at Newgate, produced a decade of working-class and radical agitation which continued into the next decade with the 'Captain Swing' agricultural riots of the autumn of 1830,[17] protests over the Poor Law Amendment Act (1834), Richard Oastler's Ten Hour movement to limit child-labour and hours of work, and the campaigns of Feargus O'Connor (1794–1855), in setting up the Marylebone Radical Association (1835). This London radicalism was followed by William Lovett and Francis Place's setting up of the London Working Men's Association (1836): Lovett (1800–77), with Henry Hetherington (1792–1849), had already set up the National Union of the Working Classes, in 1831. Place (1771–1854), born in Drury Lane, had belonged to the radical London Corresponding Society (1792–99) which assembled at the Bell Tavern in the Strand. He was instrumental in the 1824 repeal of the Combination Acts of 1799 and 1800, which had outlawed trades unions.

The East London Democratic Association began on 29 January 1837, and, associated with the Spitalfields silk-weavers, became the London Democratic Association.[18] Outside London, 1837 also saw the Glasgow Cotton Spinners' strike. Meetings in Birmingham in 1838 initiated Chartism, and, in 1839, the Anti-Corn Law League. The Charter, asking principally for universal male suffrage, was presented to Parliament on 14 June 1839. Its decisive rejection produced riots and mass meetings, the most significant being the Newport uprising of 4 November 1839, killing twenty-four. In December, Carlyle produced *Chartism*, analysing 'the Condition-of-England Question', and commenting on 'Chartist torch-meetings'.[19] A second petition was presented and rejected on 2 May 1842. On 6 March 1848, the Chartists were part of a demonstration against income tax in Trafalgar Square, and they demonstrated on 10 April on Kennington Common. On that occasion, the Duke of Wellington masterminded the military defences of London, making much of being able to put bridges between the demonstration and the militia.[20]

Chartism seems to have been less active in London than in the provinces. E.P. Thompson notes that the demonstrations of the National Union of the Working Classes, however impressive in size, 'compare poorly with the even greater demonstrations at Birmingham, drawn from a smaller population'.[21] He sees a gulf fixed between the 'shopkeepers and superior artisans' who comprised the demonstration and the mass of London labourers. A London paper, *The Chartist* (30 June 1839) noted London's weakness:

> The fact is, that, be it from listlessness, ignorance, want of thought, incapacity to reason as to political causes and effects, or satisfaction with things as they are, the great majority of the working men of the metropolis are altogether indifferent as to

representation. They feel certain evils, and they complain of them, but they do not apply themselves to consider whence they proceed . . . In the metropolis, where the lead should have been taken, there is nothing doing, and unless the metropolis be set working, all agitation elsewhere is useless. It is here that the seat of Government is. A demonstration in the streets of London comes before the very eyes of those who make the laws.[22]

Reading London, then, must include noting that it could not be 'the capital of the nineteenth century', unlike Paris, because, whereas in 1789, 1830, 1848, and 1871 Paris lived through revolutions which had the potentiality to change everything, no such revolutionary lead could come from London, which was impoverished in this even with regard to Manchester or Birmingham. *The Old Curiosity Shop* evokes Birmingham and 'bands of unemployed labourers' who 'paraded in the roads, or clustered by torchlight round their leaders, who told them in stern language of their wrongs, and urged them on to frightful cries and threats' (*OCS* 45.341): the scene is illustrated by Phiz as one of inciting to violence. The mood connects *The Old Curiosity Shop* and *Barnaby Rudge*, and if Dickens treats the reactionary violence there against Catholics as analogous to Chartist demonstrations, commentary must also notice the ambiguity in the presentation, how London resists revolution, as the Chartists knew.

In *Barnaby Rudge* chapter 35, Lord George Gordon , the anti-Catholic fanatic, and melancholic, arrives at the Maypole, with John Grueby and Mr Gashford, his unscrupulous secretary, who will die as a suicide, 'a wan old man, diseased and miserably poor . . . in his bed at an obscure inn in the Borough' (683). In chapter 37 Gordon goes up to London from Chigwell, along 'the whole length of Whitechapel, Leadenhall Street, and Cheapside, and into Saint Paul's churchyard . . . along the Strand, up Swallow-street, into the Oxford-road, and thence to his house in Welbeck-street, near Cavendish-square' (37.309). This names public, monumental London, not the half-forgotten streets, or lost landmarks of *Sketches by Boz*, or the unknown ones of *The Old Curiosity Shop*; this fashionable, West-End, governmental London is comparatively rare in Dickens.

In chapter 44, Gashford follows Hugh, and Dennis, the Hangman, 'up Parliament Street, past Saint Martin's church, and away by Saint Giles' to Tottenham Court Road, at the back of which, upon the western side, was then a place called Green Lanes', the earlier name given to Norfolk (Cleveland) Street, where Dickens' family lodged in 1815:

a retired spot, not of the choicest kind, leading into the fields. Great heaps of ashes, stagnant pools, overgrown with rank grass and duckweed; broken turnstiles; and the upright posts of palings long since carried off for firewood, which menaced all heedless walkers with their jagged and rusty nails; were the leading features of the landscape, while here and there a donkey, or a ragged horse, tethered to a stake and cropping off a wretched meal from the coarse stunted turf, were quite in keeping with the scene, and would have suggested (if the houses had not done so sufficiently of

St Giles in the Fields; architect
Henry Flitcroft (1733), following
the style of James Gibbs'
St Martin-in-the-Fields (1726).

themselves) how very poor the people were who lived in the crazy huts adjacent, and
how foolhardy it might prove for one who carried money, or wore decent clothes, to
walk that way alone, unless by daylight. (44.366–67)

This margin of the city is the home of Hugh and Dennis. *Barnaby Rudge* maps
the city like *The Old Curiosity Shop* chapter 15. Each locale has something
distinctive within it, such as St Giles – or the Fleet market, described again in
antiquarian terms – 'at that time' (*BR* 8.80, 60.501). Moorfields and Mile-end,
mentioned because of 'a catholic gentleman of small means', trying to get
out of London (61.506), are places for Irish immigrants, while Whitechapel is
Jewish. The riots open up London, destroy its secret spots. They start from
St George's Fields which 'were really fields at that time' (48.401). St George's
Fields, named after the church of St George the Martyr, was where Londoners
campaigned for 'Wilkes and Liberty' in 1768, while he was held at the King's
Bench prison, itself in St George's Fields. It was the prison for Smollett in 1759,
and where Smart died in 1770. In 1768, the Riot Act was read and some sixteen
people were killed by the army.[23] At the same time, the common rights to graze
animals on St George's Fields were taken away, and the fields were enclosed.
The result was new building on the land which transformed it utterly. The
rioters cross into Westminster and the City by the three bridges (Westminster,
Blackfriars – Hugh breaks open its Tollhouses (67.560) – and London Bridge),
attacking Catholic homes.

Chapters 64 and 65 reach the attack on Newgate, 'then a new building' (61.509). Dickens wrote to Forster: 'I have just burnt into Newgate, and am going in the next number to tear the prisoners out by the hair of their heads', and then, 'I have let all the prisoners out of Newgate, burnt down Lord Mansfield's, and played the very devil. Another number will finish the fires . . . I feel quite smoky when I am at work' (*Letters* 1.377, 385).[24] Dickens refers to the rioters burning the Bloomsbury Square house of William Murray, a hanging Lord Chief Justice and the Earl of Mansfield (1705–93). They attempt the same for his 'country seat' at Caen Wood (where Bill Sikes flees) 'between Highgate and Hampstead, bent upon destroying that house likewise, and lighting up a great fire there, which from that height should be seen all over London' (66.552). Chapter 66 concludes with the release of the prisoners in the New Jail at Clerkenwell, which had been built to house an overflow of prisoners from Newgate. Again, Dickens' enthusiasm is not separate from that anarchism.

Riots are succeeded by reaction which criss-crosses London:

At the Lord President's in Piccadilly, at Lambeth Palace, at the Lord Chancellor's in Great Ormond Street, in the Royal Exchange, the Bank, the Guildhall, the Inns of Court, the Courts of Law, and every chamber fronting the streets near Westminster Hall and the Houses of Parliament, parties of soldiers were posted before daylight. A body of Horse-Guards paraded Palace-yard, an encampment was formed in the Park . . . the Tower was fortified . . . a numerous detachment of soldiers were stationed to keep guard at the New-River Head, which the people had threatened to attack, and where, it was said, they meant to cut off the mainpipes, so that there might be no water for the extinction of the flames. In the Poultry, and on Cornhill . . . iron chains were drawn across the street; parties of soldiers were distributed in some of the old city churches while it was yet dark; and in several private houses (among them Lord Rockingham's in Grosvenor Square) . . . (67.555)[25]

The first sentence here involves at least nine separate areas, or bodies of power which must be protected. The area of chaining off implies the barricading of an arterial straight road through the city, and the protection of the City's centre.

Institutions are threatened: prisons, the Bank – an earlier building than Soane's (1788) – the Mint, the Arsenal at Woolwich, and the Royal Palaces, including the Queen's palace (Buckingham Palace: more important to the nineteenth than the eighteenth century). Bedlam is threatened with being opened, and prisons burned: the Borough Clink in Tooley Street, the King's Bench, the Fleet, and the New Bridewell.[26] City places are named where firing happened, the Poultry and Cheapside, with bodies being dumped in St Mildred's, a church rebuilt after the Fire and closed after 1872. The naming in its orderliness contrasts with the crowd's anarchy, which 'drove many sane men nearly mad themselves' (67.557). The crowd, 'composed for the most part of the very scum and refuse of London, whose growth was fostered by bad criminal laws,

The Mansion House, the official residence of the Lord Mayor.

bad prison regulations and the worst possible police' (49.407) is set against this monumental London, and the tone is ambiguous, as 'scum' suggests. E.P. Thompson quotes Edward Gibbon Wakefield (1796–1862) on the danger of the demonstrators of 1831 drawing on the 'helots of society', the 'costermongers, drovers, slaughterers of cattle, knackers, dealers in dead bodies and dogs' meat, cads, brick-makers, chimney-sweepers, nightmen, scavengers, etc' (*The Making of the English Working Class* 894–95). This happens here, and the ambiguity of the tone is because despite hatred of the power of the police (in terms of prison and the death-sentence), the language sides with authoritarianism. As with *Oliver Twist*, there is fascination with the crowd, as ambiguous, placeless, and as produced by the city: 'a mob is usually a creature of a very mysterious existence, particularly in a large city. Where it comes from or whither it goes, few men can tell . . . it is as difficult to follow to its sources as the sea itself' (52.429). This is the crowd that devastates 'Romish chapels' in 'Duke Street, Lincoln's Inn Fields, and Warwick Street, Golden Square' (50.418). A similar crowd reaches Moorfields, 'where there was a rich chapel, and in which neighbourhood several Catholic families were known to reside' (52.434).[27] The crowd firing Newgate comprehended 'the most desperate and utterly abandoned villains in London' (63.522). The greater the anarchy, the more noting place-names acts as an armature, becomes a way of guaranteeing London's solid, authoritarian qualities.

Chapter 77, full of references to the ongoing of clock-time, shows the night-time building of the scaffold and the gibbet outside Newgate for Hugh and Dennis; Dickens supplements hangings from *Oliver Twist* and *Nicholas Nickleby* in this, what Patrick Brantlinger calls Dickens' 'second Newgate novel' (*The Spirit of Reform* 95). It stands:

> with its black paint blistering, and its nooses dangling in the light like loathsome garlands. It was better in the solitude and gloom of midnight . . . than in the freshness and the stir of morning: the centre of an eager crowd [like St Paul's clock in *Master Humphrey's Clock*]. It was better haunting the street like a spectre, when men were in their beds; and influencing perchance the city's dreams; than braving the broad day, and thrusting its obscene presence upon their waking senses. (77.640)

The chapter closes with 'two cripples – both mere boys – one with a leg of wood, one who dragged his twisted limbs along by the help of a crutch'. They are hanged in Bloomsbury Square. The narrator notes the sadism of the authorities – 'their misery was protracted' – on account of their defiance. Nor is this the end: 'another boy was hanged in Bow Street; other young lads in various quarters of the town. Four wretched women, too, were put to death'. There is a last tableau of a young man hanged in Bishopsgate Street, whose mourning father – a contrast to the oppressive fathers of this novel – has not the money to receive his body (77.648–49). The hangings parallel the riots in their extensiveness throughout London. To memorialise their violence is part of Dickens' history-writing, noting 'the sorrowful, the unsuccessful'.

Hugh, who is hanged, calls the gallows 'that black tree of which I am the ripened fruit' (77.646), so punningly equating it with his father, Sir John Chester. He had encountered Chester earlier, when he woke from a dream to find him standing over him. That waking moment, developing from Oliver Twist's dream of Fagin and Monks, makes Hugh say that he was dreaming of him, and of a place, saying, 'We're not where I thought we were. That's a comfort'. The text adds, 'He looked round him as he spoke, and in particular looked above his head, as though he half expected to be standing under some object which had had existence in his dream' (28.235). This 'object' suggests the gallows: his dreams are of the scaffold, but it seems as if the scaffold and the father come together. (And Chester has sent Hugh's mother to the scaffold, as appears from *BR* 11.100, 75.628–69.) Patriarchy aligns itself with the gallows, and the gallows are literal and, as chapter 77 indicates, are that which influences the city's dreams.

In Dostoyevsky's *Notes from Underground* (1864), the Underground Man says that 'cities can be intentional or unintentional'. The city's 'intention' seems to be to create paranoid dreams, to make people feel that they are always standing under an object existing in their dreams. They dream of being on the scaffold. The city constructs paranoia, while the word 'obscene', as used about the gallows, makes them phallic in dream-life, and, when exhibited in daytime, the embodiment of patriarchy and the city together. The other obscene thing Dickens' texts note, Jacob's Island, remains hidden; but it contrasts with this obscenity – the gallows – which is allowed to be brought into the open (and which helps to create Jacob's Island, as a refuge for criminals). No attempt by Dickens to rein in the crowd as a destructive force can overturn that point, that 'London, fiercely animated, proves [to be] the cruel antagonist',[28] like Quilp, one of its avatars, in relation to Nell. Not surprisingly, Barnaby, escaped from the gallows, and unable ever to 'separate his condemnation and escape from the idea of a terrific dream', as if everything that had happened had been a kind of allegory, can never be tempted back into London (*BR*, Chapter the Last 687–88).

Master Humphrey's circle in its retreat, shows its emotional agreement with him. Its mode of existence turns out to be the only way of negotiating city-existence, though it is drawn back to that old London as though under the power of having been traumatised by it. Gog and Magog have wanted to tell 'legends of London and her sturdy citizens from the old simple times', but history does not allow that; it produces, rather, the narrative of London being smashed by its citizens, and smashing them in its turn, in *Barnaby Rudge*.

CHAPTER FIVE

CAMDEN TOWN
Dombey and Son

The first shock of a great earthquake had, just at that period, rent the whole neighbourhood [of Camden Town] to its centre. Traces of its course were visible on
every side. Houses were knocked down; streets broken through and stopped; deep
pits and trenches dug in the ground; enormous heaps of earth and clay thrown up;
buildings that were undermined and shaking, propped up by great beams of wood.
Here, a chaos of carts, overthrown and jumbled together, lay topsy-turvy at the
bottom of a steep unnatural hill; there, confused treasures of iron soaked and rusted
in something that had accidentally become a pond. Everywhere were bridges that
led nowhere; thoroughfares that were wholly impassable; Babel towers of chimneys, wanting half their height; temporary wooden huts and enclosures, in the
most unlikely situations; carcases of ragged tenements, and fragments of unfinished
walls and arches, and piles of scaffolding, and wildernesses of bricks, and giant
forms of cranes, and tripods straddling above nothing. There were a hundred
thousand shapes and substances of incompleteness, wildly mingled out of their
places, upside down, burrowing in the earth, aspiring in the air, mouldering in the
water, and unintelligible as any dream. Hot springs and fiery eruptions, the usual
attendants upon earthquakes, lent their contributions of confusion to the scene.
Boiling water hissed and heaved within dilapidated walls; whence, also, the glare
and roar of flames came issuing forth; and mounds of ashes blocked up rights of
way, and wholly changed the law and custom of the neighbourhood.

In short, the yet unfinished and unopened Railroad was in progress; and from the
very core of all this dire disorder, trailed smoothly away, upon its mighty course of
civilization and improvement.   *Dombey and Son* 6.78–79

I · THE RAILWAY WORLD

*Dealings with the Firm of Dombey and Son, Wholesale, Retail and for
Exportation* narrates the fortunes of a great City merchant and his family.
The title refers not principally to people but to a City-based family firm trading
abroad, for instance with the West Indies, and on good terms with the East India
Company.[1] It is unusual amongst Dickens' novels in being set in its own time;
the passage about the railway was written in the very years of a second 'railway mania' (1845–47); the first boom and collapse having happened between
1835 and 1837. In the period of railway mania, there was an explosion of shares
in joint-stock companies, and the vertiginousness of all this gambling, as it was
called, is conveyed in the passage quoted, with its sense of building as 'aspiring
in the air', building over nothing.[2] The major example of railway speculation was
George Hudson (1800–71) who by 1848 owned 1,450 of 5,000 miles of railway

in Britain, and was chairman of various railway companies centred on York. Through various swindles, discovered in 1849, he stayed safe, while shares collapsed in value.

Throughout the nineteenth century, walking was the dominant and compulsory form of transport for most people. Dickens' thirty-mile walk to Rochester was not exceptional.[3] Long journeys prior to the railway were made by four-horse-drawn stage-coach (as portrayed in the picture by Phiz, 'My First Fall in Life', *David Copperfield* 293, and as described in 'Early Coaches' in *Sketches by Boz* chapter 15). Inside town they were made by post-coach (as Estella goes the ten miles from Eastcheap to Richmond in *Great Expectations*, 2.14.233) or by private carriage or by Hackney-coach ('Hackney-coach Stands' (*SB* chapter 7)) or by the two-wheeler cabriolet. The last was introduced from Paris in the 1820s (as Pickwick travels from St Martin-le-Grand to the Golden Cross, in *Pickwick Papers* 2.21, and as Cruikshank shows in 'The Last Cabdriver' (*SB* 176). Paris also supplied the horse-drawn omnibus, which started by going from Paddington to the City, in 1829. The omnibus (see *SB* chapter 15) expanded in importance after the hackney-coach lost its monopoly in 1832. The hansom cab came in 1834; horse-drawn trams appeared at the end of the 1860s, carrying people far into the suburbs; electrification of trams followed at the end of the century.

Alongside these transformations, the railway added something new: the sensation of speed.[4] George Stephenson (1781–1848) pioneered the Stockton to Darlington Railway (1825) and the Liverpool to Manchester Railway (1830), but the first railroad in London – apart from the Surrey Iron Railway, a horse-drawn train from Wandsworth to Croydon (1803–46), connecting the Thames and the Surrey canal – was that from London to Greenwich. This rail route had nothing to do with a pre-existent waterway. It opened at Spa Road, Bermondsey, 8 February 1836, running on a viaduct to Deptford.[5] It was extended to London Bridge on 14 December 1836, and to Greenwich on 24 December 1838: London Bridge became London's first terminus.

The 'earthquake' of the opening quotation from *Dombey and Son* characterises the effective turning upside-down caused by building the railway in Camden Town ('Camberling Town' to the inhabitants of Staggs' Gardens, which is in the middle of it). The passage, which gives the 'shock' of the 'unnatural', and the creation of new 'wildernesses', describes the cutting for the London to Birmingham railway, for 'the great working town of Birmingham' (*PP* 50.667), with a population of 150,000, had been granted two MPs in the Reform Bill of 1832, and became a municipal borough in 1838.

Construction of this railway happened in two stages, beginning in 1834, with the son of the pioneer, Robert Stephenson (1803–59), in charge. By 1837, trains were running out of a depot at Chalk Farm, to Harrow and Watford and Boxmoor. The second stage extended from Chalk Farm: it took trains to Euston Square, which was opened on 17 September 1838. Until 1844, trains left

Euston Station by being pulled on ropes for a mile up to the depot; then the engine was put onto the front, for the journey to Birmingham. The London and Birmingham line amalgamated with the Grand Junction Railway (Birmingham to Manchester, 1837) and the Liverpool and Manchester Railway, becoming the London and North Western Railway. For Euston Station, Philip Hardwick (1792–1870) built a Doric arch in 1839, inscribed 'London and Birmingham Railway'; it was destroyed in 1963. For Michael Freeman, this arch had neither a functional nor social message but a hieratic one:

> Here railway magnates sought to represent themselves as part of a new leadership breed, the Victorian capitalist class. The most powerful evocation of this role came in the use of groups of classical columns, as colonnades or as porches. Most stunning of these was the free-standing portico, as at Euston. Here the eye was drawn not to the station complex itself [enlarged in 1849 by the addition of a Great Hall] but to the screen front of seven stone blocks linked by iron railings, the main block (or propyleum) forming the central 'incident'.[6]

A series of thirty-four lithographs plus frontispiece by John Crooke Bourne (1814–96), with a text by John Britton, illustrate the situation as it existed in 1839.[7] Bourne shows the Doric arch, and then the railway going underneath the Hampstead Road Bridge, preparations for which destroyed Dickens' school, Wellington Academy. The third picture shows workmen – hundreds of them, tiny figures in contrast to the titanic structures being built – constructing the retaining wall on the sides of the cutting that took the train from Euston as far as the bridge over the Regent's Canal. The view is from the north, looking south towards London, and the bridge is to carry the old Park Street, connecting with Regent's Park. The next picture shows the iron suspension bridge that carried the railway over the Regent's Canal; its view is from the west looking east, so that the Camden Road bridge can also be seen through its arch. Three following drawings show the Stationary Engine House at Camden Town, and the depot, where heavy goods and livestock coming into London were unloaded (the Round House, as part of this depot, was to be built in 1847). The area occupied over thirty acres. The next picture is the entrance to the mile-long Primrose Hill tunnel.

Euston, then, was London's second terminus. Elsewhere, the London to Blackwall railway (closed in 1926) ran its three and a half miles from the Minories (outside the City) to Blackwall in 1840, for those who wanted to go on passenger steamers. Fenchurch Street Station opened the following year, as the first City terminus. Rebuilt, it was to be used by the London, Tilbury and Southend Railway. (It was rebuilt in 1935.) Victoria travelled by train from Slough to London in 1842 on a line which opened in 1838. In 1843, Turner painted *Rain, Steam and Speed: The Great Western Railway*, showing the train hurtling over the bridge at Maidenhead, and Paddington, a collaboration between Brunel and the architect Matthew Digby Wyatt, opened to serve the

Railway tunnel for trains through Primrose Hill, London to Birmingham Line; classical style, like a Greek temple, or entry to a tomb. There are six carved heads above the central arch.

Railway line towards Euston and central London: the Round House, in Camden Town, can be seen on the skyline on the left.

Great Western Railway in 1854. William Powell Frith (1819–1909) began painting the scene at Paddington in 1860: *The Railway Station*, which shows a crowd under two vistas of rounded arches of wrought iron and glass, running down towards the end of the shed, was first displayed at Flatow's Gallery in the Haymarket in 1862. Frith recalls Hogarth in the sense of giving a series of narratives in the painting. On the right are seen two top-hatted, bourgeois-looking detectives from the City of London police (formed in 1839), Michael Haydon, holding handcuffs, and James Brett. They are arresting a fraudster about to board the train; his wife is standing in the open carriage.[8] Trains and detectives are both parts of Victorian urban modernity.

Building Euston was part of the first phase of railway building, the second being the years of 'railway mania'. In 1846, Parliament legislated that no termini should be built inside the Marylebone Road, the City Road, Finsbury Square, and Bishopsgate Street. Waterloo, serving the London and South West Railway, opened in 1848, to be further developed (1853, and 1864), and rebuilt (1900 to 1922). King's Cross, designed by Lewis Cubitt (1799–1883), brother of the builder Thomas Cubitt, opened in 1852 for the Great Northern Railway. Victoria, for the London, Brighton and South Coast Railway, opened its new station in 1860 (enlarged in 1908), taking trains across the Thames on the new Grosvenor Bridge. The Grosvenor hotel accompanied the station. Charing Cross opened in 1864. In the same year, the London, Chatham and Dover Railway pushed its way through to Ludgate Hill, and in the following year, extended itself to join the new Metropolitan underground (Paddington to Farringdon Street, 1863) at Farringdon Street. (Ludgate Hill Station closed in 1929.) Broad Street opened in 1865, closed in 1984. Cannon Street (South Eastern Railway) opened in 1866, W.H. Barlow's St Pancras opened in 1867, its hotel (Gilbert Scott), 1872.

A financial crisis, occasioned by the fall of the Overend Gurney bank in May 1866, which had become too speculative in trading overseas, and in developing railroads, diminished the pace of construction after 1870. Liverpool Street, bringing in trains which, since 1840, had previously stopped at Shoreditch, opened in 1874, for the Great Eastern Railway. Holborn Viaduct as a separate terminus for the London, Chatham and Dover Railway opened in 1874 (and was replaced in 1990 by the Thameslink line). Blackfriars, called St Paul's Station until 1937, opened in 1886, using a new Blackfriars Railway Bridge. Marylebone, for the Great Central Railway, was the last (1899). Such expansion, however, hardly describes the numbers of suburban stations opened within London, nor the development of new underground railways, the District line beginning in 1869, and the Circle begun in 1868 and completed in 1884, the Northern line beginning in 1890, with electrification of the lines following at the end of the century.

II · DOMBEY'S LONDON

Camden Town, north of the Euston Road, is north of the geography of much of *Dombey and Son*. Mr Dombey lives in Marylebone, a 'tall dark, dreadfully genteel street in the region between Portland-place and Bryanstone-square' (3.34), south of Dickens' home in Devonshire Terrace. Brystanston Square was laid out in 1812, and, like Blandford Street, took its name from the Portman home in Dorset (Sir William Portman had been Lord Chief Justice in 1553). Portland Place was laid out by the Adam brothers in 1778, and named for the Duke, William Bentinck. In the first chapter, Mr Dombey's wife dies in child-birth, and Dombey needs a wet-nurse for Paul. The choice is Polly Toodles, from Staggs' Gardens; her husband is at present a navvy, 'mostly underground', but expecting to work from the completed Euston Station. Miss Tox has got the recommendation for Polly Toodle from the Queen Charlotte's Royal Married Females maternity hospital, which was founded in 1739 in Lisson Grove, to the west and north of the Marylebone Road. Mr Dombey works in the City, so he travels eastwards every day; his office being 'just round the corner' from the East India Company's house in Leadenhall Street, where Lamb had worked from 1792 to 1825. A little timber midshipman marks the site of Sol Gills' shop, which is the home of Walter Gay, who works across the road at Mr Dombey's. The midshipman reappears in 'Wapping Workhouse' (*UT*): the Uncommercial, stepping eastwards, says, 'I had got past the India House, thinking in my idle manner of Tippoo-Shahib [Sultan of Mysore, who died at Seringapatam, fighting Wellington] and Charles Lamb, and had got past my little wooden midshipman, after affectionately patting him on one leg of his knee-shorts for old acquaintance sake' (*J4* 43). The East India Company had warehouses in Fenchurch Street. East India House was in Leadenhall Street; its latest buildings, of 1799, designed with a classical frontage by Richard Jupp (1728–99).[9]

In chapter 6, Susan Nipper and Polly Toodle and Florence go on their illicit visit to Staggs' Gardens. Instead of coming home by going westwards, they head for the Pentonville Road, since they mean to get to City Road where Rob, the Charitable Grinder, goes to school. He is on his way back, and under attack from a party of boys and 'a ferocious young butcher'. As the women set off for him, an alarm of 'Mad Bull' is raised: it is market-day (6.84, 85). Rob is like cattle for the slaughter, while the presence of cattle in the streets suggests how two time-scales operate in London: the modern and the yet unmodern. Florence Dombey is lost and kidnapped by Mrs Brown. She is presumably taken down to somewhere near Moorgate, and made to find her way to her father's office, but ends up on Thames Street, where Walter finds her. The result of this episode, and the discovery that Polly Toodle and Susan Nipper have taken Paul and his sister Florence to see Staggs' Gardens, is that Polly is sacked. The passage presages the moment where Florence will once again be on the streets, and abandoned by her father (chapter 48).

Sol Gills, in debt, like John Dickens, and Mr Micawber, loses his goods to Mr Brogley, who lives in Bishopsgate Street Without. Walter must go further east to find Captain Cuttle, who lodges in Brig Place, with Mrs MacStinger, 'on the brink of a canal near the India Docks, where there was a swivel bridge which opened now and then to let some wandering monster of a ship come roaming up the street like a stranded leviathan' (9.136). Presumably, these are the West India Docks, but the text is non-specific, because of the place given in the text to both the Indies. Later Captain Cuttle escorts Susan Nipper and Florence to Ratcliffe, one of the poorest parts of the docks region. And again later, he wanders round Limehouse Hole, 'his old neighbourhood, down among the mast, oar, and block makers, ship-biscuit bakers, coal-whippers, pitch-kettles, sailors, canals, docks, swing-bridges, and other soothing objects' (60.921). The tone may be nostalgic, like much of the writing centring on Gills and Cuttle and even Walter Gay, but the geography makes London a world centre; even beyond the firm of Dombey and Son, the novel is fascinated with speed, with trade and London docks, with ships going out, with India and China.

Dombey and Son contrasts the West End, including Mrs Skewton in Brook Street (30.463), and Cousin Feenix being shaved at Long's hotel in [New] Bond Street (31.479), with this East End. It stresses the mean living-conditions of people in the West End (Miss Tox in her 'dullest of No-Thoroughfares' in Princess' Place, in chapter 7). The church associated with Paul Dombey's christening and burial is in the West End, perhaps Nash's All Souls', Langham Place (1824); Florence, however, is married in an unnamed City church (chapters 56, 57). There are other locales: Mr Morfin lives in Islington (13.194), Mr Feeder is going to observe the mysteries of London from the vantage point of staying with two old maiden ladies at Peckham (14.212): Peckham being where Walter Gay went to school (4.52), as Goldsmith taught in a school in Peckham on first coming to London in 1756. Sir Barnet and Lady Skettles live at Fulham (24.375), Briggs' family are associated with Bayswater (14.206). The text speaks sympathetically of Battlebridge, and of Ball's Pond in Islington (31.478). Toots goes up to Finchley to get some chickweed for Florence (32.503). Chapter 33, 'Contrasts', moves between Norwood, where Carker lives, in the south-east of London, also used in *David Copperfield* for the childhood home of Dora Spenlow, and a suburb near the Great North Road, presumably Finchley, where Harriet Carker and her disgraced brother live:

> The neighbourhood . . . is neither of the town nor country, The former . . . has made a stride and passed it, and has set his brick-and-mortar heel a long way in advance; but the intermediate space . . . as yet, is only blighted country, and not town; and here, among a few tall chimneys belching smoke all day and night, and among the brickfields and the lanes where turf is cut, and where the fences tumble down, and where the dusty nettles grow, and where a scrap or two of hedge may yet be seen, and where the bird-catcher still comes, occasionally, though he swears every time to come no more – this second home is to be found. (33.514–15)

The place, which has had no 'improvement' (that which the railway gives) is an allegory for Carker's 'outcast' brother and sister, while the chapter adds another outcast: Mrs Brown's daughter, returned from transportation and now going on to London.[10] It contrasts with the Bank Director's country retreat in Kingston-upon-Thames (36.555).

III · DICKENS AND RUSKIN

When Paul is ill, Susan Nipper and Walter Gay go by hackney-coach to try to find Polly Toodles at Staggs' Gardens, but are confronted by Euston Station:

> There was no such place as Staggs's Gardens . . . Where the old rotten summer-houses once had stood, palaces now reared their heads, and granite columns of gigantic girth opened a vista to the Railway world beyond. The miserable waste ground, where the refuse-matter had been heaped of yore, was swallowed up and gone; and in its frowsy stead were tiers of warehouses, crammed with rich goods and costly merchandise. The old by-streets now swarmed with passengers and vehicles of every kind; the new streets that had stopped disheartened in the mud and waggon-ruts, formed towns within themselves, originating wholesome comforts and conveniences belonging to themselves, and never tried or thought of until they sprung into existence. Bridges that had led to nothing, led to villas, gardens, churches, healthy public walks. The carcases of houses, and beginnings of new thoroughfares, had started off upon the line at steam's own speed, and shot away into the country in a monster train.
>   . . . Wonderful Members of Parliament, who little more than twenty years before, had made themselves merry with the wild railroad theories of engineers . . . went down into the north with their watches in their hands, and sent on messages before by the electric telegraph, to say they were coming. Night and day the conquering engines rumbled at their distant work, or, advancing smoothly to their journey's end, and gliding like tame dragons into the allotted corners grooved out to the inch for

their reception, stood bubbling and trembling there, making the walls quake, as if they were dilating with the secret knowledge of great powers yet unsuspected in them, and strong purposes not yet achieved.

But Staggs's Gardens had been cut up root and branch. Oh woe the day! When 'not a rood of English ground' – laid out in Staggs's Gardens – is secure! (15.244–45)

Though there are potentialities in this passage to suggest the railways as oppressive, it nonetheless reads more like unambiguous praise of them, and of the electric telegraph system, which, patented in 1837, developed as something inseparable from the smooth running of the railway, in order to give warning of the train, and enforcing a standard time throughout the country.[11] Dickens concludes by combining Wordsworth's 'On the Projected Kendal and Windermere railway' (1844):

Is then no nook of English ground secure
From rash assault?

with Goldsmith's *The Deserted Village* (1770):

A time there was, ere England's griefs began,
When every rood of ground maintained its man (58–59)

Yet there is nothing here of Ruskin's hatred of speed, or of the changes that the railway makes: nothing of Letter 5 of *Fors Clavigera* (1 May 1861) on the loss of the rocky valley between Buxton and Bakewell (both in Derbyshire), 'divine as the Vale of Tempe':

You cared neither for Gods nor grass, but for cash (which you did not know the way to get); you thought you could get it by what the *Times* calls 'Railroad Enterprise'. You Enterprised a Railroad through the valley – you blasted its rocks away, heaped thousands of tons of shale into its lovely stream. The valley is gone, and the Gods with it, and now, every fool in Buxton can be in Bakewell in half an hour, and every fool in Bakewell at Buxton; which you think a lucrative process of exchange . . .

Praise of the railways in *Dombey and Son* is symptomatic of passages which produced John Ruskin's criticism, that Dickens was 'a pure modernist – a leader of the steam-whistle party *par excellence* – and he had no understanding of any power of antiquity . . . his hero is essentially the ironmaster' (referring to *Bleak House*: to the generic industrialist from the north, who was behind so much railway expansion).[12]

Ruskin's critique of Dickens is not ignorable, but three points should be noted, first that Dickens' later fiction does include the sense of how the railway has produced in its turn as much desolation and urban squalor and blackening of the city as it has destroyed previous slum conditions. *Our Mutual Friend* 2.1 brings out the destruction of neighbourhoods under the railways, as they impoverished huge areas by climbing over them in the form of viaducts, and, as areas were destroyed to build termini, pushing people out and creating, by the cheap trains that were finally enforced by Parliament in 1883, working-class areas outside London which became the base for people to travel into the city every day. And second, Staggs' Gardens was not rural, like the valley between Bakewell and Buxton, or the Lake District, nor was it a traditional site, or one of 'antiquity'. Camden Town, north of the Marylebone Road, was not an old neighbourhood, being land that had been passed on by Charles Pratt (Baron Camden in 1765), for building 1,400 houses, in the first instance, in 1791. As Camden became Viscount Bayham, and as his wife's name was Jeffrey and his son Baron Brecknock, Bayham, Pratt, Jeffrey, and Brecknock all became street-names in Camden Town, which, getting its parish church in 1824 (see p. 218), became separate from St Pancras (which had gained a new parish church, designed by Inwoods, father and son in 1822: both churches were expressions of the Greek Revival). Camden Road, striking out towards Holloway, came in 1825. A statue to Cobden was put in Camden High Street in 1868. In 1873, Rimbaud and Verlaine lived at 8 Great (now Royal) College Street.

Third, and crucially, Staggs' Gardens evokes Dickens' autobiography: clearing the way suggests the desire to forget a background very unlike Ruskin's. Dickens came from Chatham to live at 16 Bayham Street, Camden Town in 1822, in a now destroyed house on the east side of the road near the junction with Greenland Road, like the four-roomed house in Camden Town, which, in *A Christmas Carol*, the Bob Cratchit family inhabit. For Forster:

> Bayham-street was about the poorest part of the London suburbs then, and the house was a mean small tenement, with a wretched little back-garden abutting on a squalid court . . . A washerwoman lived next door, and a Bow-street officer lived over the way. (*DC* 887)

Forster concludes, 'thus [Dickens] took, from the very beginning of this Bayham-street life, his first impression of that struggling poverty which is nowhere more vividly shown than in the commoner streets of the London suburb' (887). He recalls:

> there were at the top of Bayham-street some almshouses, and were still when [Dickens] revisited it with me nearly twenty-seven years ago, and to go to this spot, he told me, and look from it over the dust-heaps and dock-leaves and fields (no longer there when we saw it together) at the cupola of St Paul's looming through the smoke was a treat that served him for hours of vague reflection afterwards. (889)

The family moved south, to Gower Street North, in Somers Town, but Dickens' next lodging returned him to Camden Town, to 37 Little College Street. The woman who looked after Dickens, Mrs Roylance, who had previously looked after children at Brighton, became the original for Mrs Pipchin in *Dombey and Son* chapter 8 (*DC* 897).[13] After that it was Lant Street in Southwark for Dickens, and a return to Little College Street, and then back to Somers Town, and Wellington Academy. In 'Our School' (*Household Words* 11 October 1851), the Railway has 'cut it up, root and branch'. Dickens' writing may be seen to annihilate Wellington Academy three times: first by implying its destruction in *Dombey and Son*, as part of the ground of 'Staggs's Gardens', then by writing about its headmaster as Mr Creakle in *David Copperfield*, then by pronouncing it dead in 'Our School'. In 'An Unsettled Neighbourhood' (*Household Words* 11 November 1854) there is a passage of autobiographical writing descriptive of Bayham Street, saying that everything has been changed by the raiload, which has replaced one form of squalor by a new state, which is called 'unsettled, dissipated, wandering . . . nomadic' (*J3* 245). Out of one state into another, much more modern. The old goes with few regrets, uprooted first by the power of the railway, second by the power of a new writing, which may itself be 'nomadic' – going astray – and called 'modernist' in only a slightly different sense from Ruskin, and which will be commented on more in relation to *David Copperfield*.

As nightmarish as the associations with Camden Town and Southwark is what happens to Florence. Her going astray somewhere around the Pentonville Road, which turns her into a pauper-child (like Oliver Twist, who is also stripped of smart clothing and given pauper garments) suggests that Dickens is thinking of Agar Town, between the Euston Road and the Regent's Canal, which, leased by William Agar in 1810, rapidly became a slum, covering green fields north of the Marylebone Road, land now occupied by St Pancras Station and its environs.[14] The Midland Railway acquired the land in 1866, demolished the shanty-town within two months, and opened St Pancras Station. Agar Town was east of Somers Town, which included the space of the existing British Library, and which Lord Somers leased out in 1784 for building. It too became a slum, and, being where the Dickens family lived after 1824, is also comprehended in Staggs' Gardens. Somers Town, an area of 'several mean streets which the appearance of the houses and the bad state of the road denoted to have been recently built', is the home of Mr Snawley in *Nicholas Nickleby*: Smike is abducted to a house on 'the extreme borders of some new settlements adjoining Somers Town' (*NN* 38.474). Smike and Florence, abducted in nearly the same place (and still later 'on the streets', like David Copperfield), awaken fearful memories, which the railway must erase, so making the novel to be of the present. But the erasure means that there is something ambivalent about modernity; hence some readers find a sense of loss in the disappearance of 'Staggs's Gardens'. This sense of ambiguity about the new, which is as it were innocent and experienced at the same time, is paralleled by the portrait of Paul Dombey, who has a 'strange, old-fashioned, thoughtful way' (8.109) with him, as well as being both 'imperious' (so becoming like his father) and 'childish and sportive'. He has the character of the 'odd child', who is potentially a man, and the likelihood of becoming (if he lived) the 'odd man' from the essay 'Gone Astray'. The novel's title is given full weight when Mr Dombey and his son are seen together, as:

the strangest pair . . . that ever firelight shone upon. Mr Dombey so erect and solemn, gazing at the blaze; his little image, with an old, old face, peering into the red perspective with the fixed and rapt attention of a sage. Mr Dombey entertaining complicated worldly schemes and plans; the little image entertaining Heaven knows what wild fancies, half-formed thoughts, and wandering speculations. Mr Dombey stiff with starch and arrogance; the little image by inheritance and in unconscious imitation. The two very much alike, and yet so monstrously contrasted. (8.109–10)

Man and boy together confuse chronologies which make childhood grow into harmonious adulthood, as does the monstrous character of Quilp (Paul is compared to a goblin). Similarly, the new railway is new and as if old, at the same time. It belongs to a new time which displaces old privileges, and which gets directly to the point, like the railway: the question Paul Dombey asks, 'Papa! What's money after all?' is absolutely analogous in the way it cuts through issues, and redefines ground. Railway and child, both new, both seem more developed than what they relate to, or what they replace: hence, as a marker of the new, Paul Dombey's oddness.

IV · TRAINS AND TRAUMA

Those who study the physical sciences, and bring them to bear upon the health of Man, tell us that if the noxious particles that rise from vitiated air, were palpable to the sight, we should see them lowering in a dense black cloud above such haunts, and rolling on to corrupt the better parts of a town . . .

Oh for a good spirit who would take the house-tops off, with a more potent and benignant hand than the lame demon in the tale, and show a Christian people what dark shapes issue from amidst their homes, to swell the retinue of the Destroying Angel as he moves forth among them! For only one night's view of the pale phantoms rising from the scenes of our too-long neglect; and from the thick and sullen air where Vice and Fever propagate together, raining the tremendous social retributions which are ever pouring down, and ever coming thicker! (47.701–2)[15]

Dickens' 'modernism' appears in this passage of self-reflexive writing, which turns on the city, and begins with a passage asking what 'Nature' is, and how 'men work to change her' so that it becomes 'natural to be unnatural' (47.700). Perhaps it may be said that if it has to be Mr Squeers who praises up Nature in the words 'she's a rum 'un, is Natur' (*NN* 45.556), then there is no concept of Nature in Dickens. Rather, there is the sense that the conditions of the city make it impossible to think in such terms, and that as an agent of change, the railway is certainly not an agent of nature. It is now 'natural to be unnatural'. That fits Paul Dombey; the child who seems odd, who of himself – quite apart from his disastrous education – contradicts, in his short life, ideas of natural growth. *Dombey and Son*, on the basis of chapter 47, attempts to see the city as a whole, bringing into focus 'the unnatural outcasts of society', and showing 'odious sights' 'at the lightest mention of which humanity revolts, and dainty delicacy living in the next street stops her ears, and lisps, "I don't

MAPS OF LONDON, 1690 and 1827

1. The Johannes de Ram map of London, c.1690, made for the accession of William and Mary (1688) whose portraits appear above the schematic view of the Thames. The map, which makes the Thames prominent, is virtually bisected by London Bridge. The river is here a busy thoroughfare (in 1700, London was the port for 80% of England's imports, 65% of its exports). A few details: south of London Bridge, there are, to the east roads towards Kent; that to Bermondsey passes the then newly rebuilt St Mary Magdalen (1680), on the site of Bermondsey Abbey; the Neckinger River flows past, coming out at the Thames by St Saviour's Dock (east of which is Jacob's Island). In the Westminster area, left, and north of the river, note the distance from the City. Scotland Yard can be seen, and the then arrangement of Charing Cross and the Mews, with Leicester Fields (laid out in the 1670s) and St James' Fields (1660s).

2. Christopher and John Greenwood's map of London, eight miles to the inch, made between 1824 and 1826, succeeding those of John Rocque (1746) and Richard Horwood (1799). The old and new London Bridges appear together, the new being under construction.

3. Camden (Greenwood 1827, detail): a decade before the opening of Euston Station. Euston Square is centre-right. Regent's Park has the Regent's Canal wrapped round its north side, north of that note Chalk Farm. West of Regent's Park is the Edgware Road (the A5), a Roman road leading ultimately towards Wales (part of Watling Street). All the housing development in Camden Town is east of Arlington Road, extending towards St Pancras, whose church and workhouse can be seen. The area is bisected by the Fleet River.

4. Soho (Greenwood 1827, detail): the area between Regent's Street and St Martin's Lane, and north of Charing Cross, as far as Fitzroy Square (top left).

5. Westminster (Greenwood 1827, detail): the map gives a sense of the area from Whitehall to Charing Cross, with the Strand to the east, and with a sense of how little development there was beyond Westminster. Lambeth on the south side of the river possessed Lambeth Palace, a riverside palace, approached by water; south of that see Vauxhall Gardens.

6. Clerkenwell (Greenwood 1827, detail): the area for the first route in the chapter on *Oliver Twist*; from the Angel to Holborn Hill, which runs down to the covered-over Fleet River, and Farringdon Street. The area, which is south of the Regent's Canal, contains the City Road, and Goswell Street, which has the Charterhouse to its west, and runs down towards Holborn. Gray's Inn Road runs down to Holborn on the west, and Doughty Street is two blocks to the west of that; Calthorpe Street runs east off Gray's Inn Road towards Cold Bath Fields prison; it is in this area that Flora Finching lives (*Little Dorrit*).

7. East End (Greenwood 1827, detail): the space to the east of the City, Whitechapel to Mile End, and out towards Stratford; close to the City, Whitechapel is succeeded northwards by Spitalfields and Bethnal Green and Shoreditch (top right and top left); further out to the north is Hackney. South of the Whitechapel Road is the hinterland for the docks, with Ratcliff and Shadwell.

8. City (Greenwood 1827, detail): the map emphasises how packed together this area is: the City is one square mile, extending without as far as Holborn. It is, however, for Dickens, an area in decline. The waterside is much changed since the map. Blackfriars Bridge, with open spaces both north and south, seems to be on a straight north–south axis (the same evidence of planning is true of the other bridges).

9. The Borough (Greenwood 1827, detail): the area most associated with Dickens' childhood, and, like Camden Town, a place of origin for both Dickens and his novels.

10. South of the river (Greenwood 1827, detail): Bermondsey, including Jacob's Island east of St Saviour's Dock, going towards Rotherhithe and Deptford. North of the river is Wapping and the area towards Limehouse in the east.

(Captions continued at the end of the plate section)

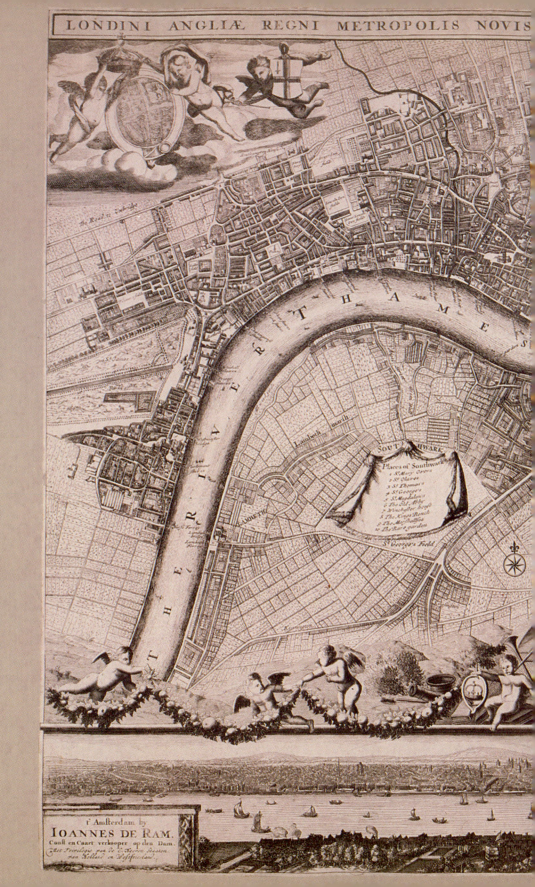

THE RIVER THAMES

SOUTHWARK

Places of Southwark
1 S.t Mary Overies
2 S.t Olaves
3 S.t Thomas's
4 S.t George's
5 S.t Magdalens
6 The old Abbe
7 Winchester house
8 The Kings Bench
9 The Marshalsea
10 The Bare garden

St George's Field

t' Amsterdam by
IOANNES DE RAM.
Const en Caart verkooper op den Dam.
Met Privilegie van de E. Hooghe Staten
van Holland en Westfriesland.

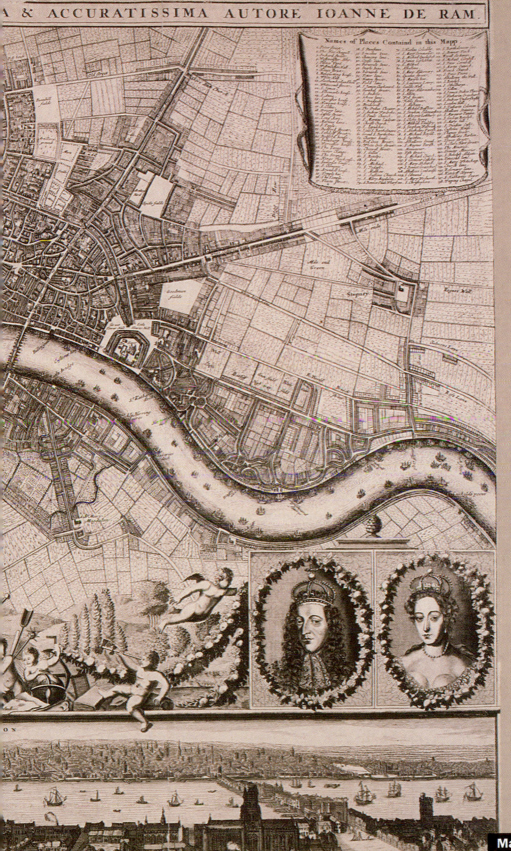

Names of Places Contaiñd in this Mapp.

Map 1

Explanation

Public Buildings.
Park or Pleasure Grounds.
Woods or Plantations.
Field.
Garden.
Walks or Nursery Grounds.
Wastelands.

MAP of LONDON, FROM An Actual Survey made in the Years 1824, 1825 & 1826

C. and J. GREENWOOD.

Published by the Proprietors
GREENWOOD, PRINGLE and Co.
13, REGENT STREET, PALL MALL
London.

Map 3 Camden

Map 4 Soho

Map 5 Westminster

Map 6 Clerkenwell

Map 7 East End

Map 8 City

Map 9 The Borough

ONDON DOCK

Garden

Map 10 Bermondsey

CRUCHLEY'S New Plan

LONDON and its ENVIRONS.

Map 11

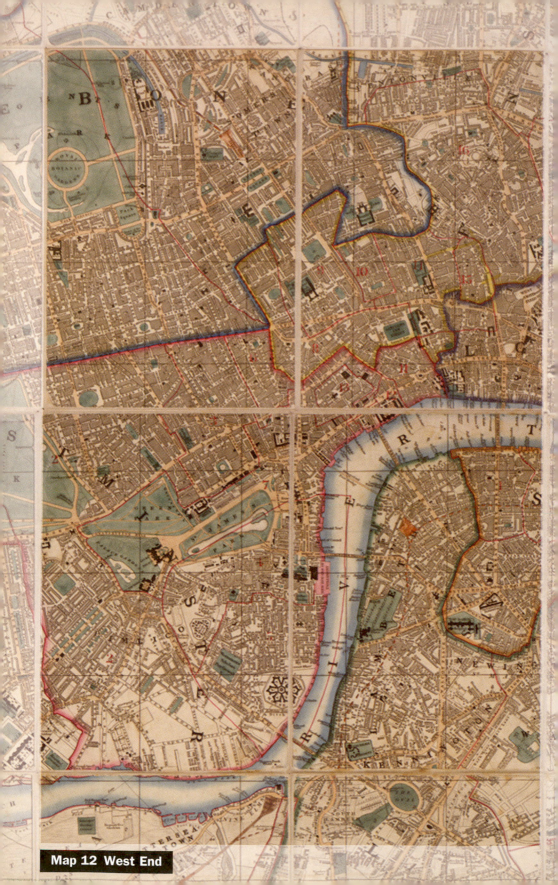

Map 12 West End

Map 13 Tower Hamlets

ORDNANCE MAP OF THE

NTRY round LONDON.

Map 14

MAPS OF LONDON, 1846 and 1863

11. The Cruchley map of London and its environs, January 1846. George Cruchley (1796–1880) first produced a map of London in 1827; the 1846 version goes from Hammersmith in the West to the River Lea, on the east side of the Isle of Dogs. South, it includes Wimbledon, and Dulwich: not the Crystal Palace, which has not yet arrived at Sydenham. North, it extends from Hendon in the west, through Hampstead and Caen Wood to Highgate and towards Hackney and Stoke Newington; the part of Essex that it shows (Walthamstow) is not yet built up, like, in the south, the area south of Deptford, Lewisham, which is watered by the Ravensbourne river. The boundaries shown are those of the City (in blue), Westminster (pink), Southwark (ochre), and county boundaries and parish boundaries. Note the attention to railways: those completed, in progress or planned. Unlike Greenwood, Cruchley extends London much further, and the value of this shows in the attention to railways. It brings out the scale of Dickens' London.

12. West End (Cruchley 1846, detail): this includes from left to right, north of the river, Regent's Park, Euston Square (bisected by the present Marylebone Road), Somers Town, St Pancras, and Pentonville including the Angel. Below, still north of the river, are Marylebone, the line of Regent's Street, Soho and Lincoln's Inn Fields. Far right, beyond Holborn and Farringdon Street, is Smithfield. In the Pimlico area may be seen Millbank Penitentiary. The Vauxhall, Westminster, Waterloo and Blackfriars Bridges are visible; south of the river may be seen Battersea, Vauxhall Gardens, the Archbishop's palace and gardens, a black pattern indicating Bedlam, and the obelisk south of Blackfriars Bridge.

13. Tower Hamlets (Cruchley 1846, detail): this shows the City Road coming south, with the Artillery Ground (1641) to its west; the oval shape of Finsbury Circus is just inside the jurisdiction of the City. The area, enclosed to the north by the Regent's Canal, which, on the east side, comes down to the Thames with Bow Common east of it, includes Hoxton and Hackney. South is Bethnal Green. South of that is the Whitechapel Road, and the highly industrialised area down to the London Docks and the Thames: to the right, Limehouse is visible, and St Anne's church, south of Commercial Road. Left, and just north of the river is the Tower of London; a little downstream, south of the Thames is the creek of St Saviour's Dock.

14. The Ordnance Map of the Country round London, dated 1 April 1863, is also from Cruchley, and includes much of the area ringed by the present M25: note Esher in the southwest, and Hounslow, and Barnet, and in the north-east, how Essex has become more developed: Epping Forest is visible, and the Thames has north of it West Ham and the then still underdeveloped East Ham, Dagenham and Hornchurch, and Dartford in the south. The map's interest, making the river much less significant, is its display of railways, engendered by many rival companies. Victoria, Waterloo (and Nine Elms Station at Vauxhall, 1838, which preceded Waterloo as a terminus), and London Bridge are shown, with a dotted line indicating the then present building of the extension to Charing Cross. Paddington is seen, like Euston, next to Regent's Park; King's Cross is visible, as is Fenchurch Street. North of that is Bishopsgate Station, at the intersection of Shoreditch High Street and Bethnal Green Road (1846); this made way for Liverpool Street Station. South, Elephant and Castle Station was of 1863; the line was to be carried north to Southwark's Blackfriars Bridge Station (1864); the then railway bridge (1864) over the Thames still has stanchions upright in the river. The line was to continue to Blackfriars (1886), Ludgate Hill (1865), and Holborn Viaduct (an extension of Farringdon Street). East of Blackfriars is the site of Cannon Street (1866). East of the Elephant and Castle is the Bricklayer's Arms station (1844). Also shown is the new terminus at Farringdon Street (1863), which linked, via the Metropolitan underground railway, with Paddington.

believe it!'" (47.701). The 'unnatural outcasts', and those who pretend, out of their class superiority, that the 'unnatural' does not exist, are equally cultivated products of the city, and 'most unnatural, and yet most natural in being so' (47.700).

The accuracy of perception of violent juxtapositions between outcast and respectable London, both equally natural or unnatural, but co-existing with each other in 'the next street', was a feature of *Oliver Twist*. It suggests the desire to see London whole, making it 'palpable to the sight'. This drive has been commented on by Raymond Williams, and it finds its expression throughout *Dombey and Son*, creating its 'realism', which may be defined as the attempt to see society as a 'totality'. The title of the nearly central chapter 33, 'Contrasts', indicates one intention that animates the entire novel: as a paradigm of the book, it gives contrasts of location – south and north London, prosperous and miserable suburb, and contrasts of relations, and of fortunes. Yet it affirms that, despite contrasts, there are underlying connections which cannot be denied, and which the novel-form must show, reading London in order to do this. The railway, as unnatural as 'Staggs's Gardens', the slum it replaces, becomes a force to show how these different Londons (fail to) cohere with each other. Though, as Freeman suggests (*Railways and the Victorian Imagination* 109–14), the train reinforced class distinctions, by creating different carriages, First Class, and Second Class and Third, it simultaneously produced the 'levelling sentiments' (Freeman, 5) which are so disapproved of by Mr Dombey. Freeman quotes from Thomas Arnold, who said, on seeing the train pass through the Rugby countryside, that feudality had gone for ever (Freeman, 29). Dombey must be driven in the train by Mr Toodles, whose proximity cannot be shaken off. Dombey takes his mourning and loss and anger at Toodles into the train with him and projects these onto what he sees, so that:

> tortured by these thoughts, he carried monotony with him, through the rushing land-scape, and hurried headlong, not through a rich and varied country, but a wilderness of blighted plans and gnawing jealousies. (20.311)[16]

The train travels, for him, like the triumphant, and remorseless, and indomitable, monster, Death. (All three adjectives appear in the account of the journey.) And what can be seen is only a wilderness, replacing the wilderness that there had been when the railway was under construction. This description of Dombey's impressions in the train slips between being subjective and realist: the train is death, to Dombey, in threatening to break down his isolated subjectivity, in bringing his way of life to a close, but the writing becomes simultaneously more realist, and apocalyptic:

> Louder and louder yet, it shrieks and cries as it comes tearing on resistless to the goal: and now its way, still like the way of Death, is strewn with ashes thickly. Everything around is blackened. There are dark pools of water, muddy lanes, and miserable habitations far below. There are jagged walls and falling houses close at hand, and

through the battered roofs and broken windows, wretched rooms are seen, where want and fever hide themselves in many wretched shapes, while smoke, and crowded gables, and distorted chimneys, and deformity of brick and mortar penning up deformity of mind and body, choke the murky distance. As Mr Dombey looks out of his carriage window, it is never in his thoughts that the monster who has brought him there has let the light of day in on these things: not caused them. (20.312)

The novel and the train act analogously to each other in letting the light of day in: battered roofs and broken windows are exposed, brought into visibility by the train, which is thus like the good spirit which takes off the housetops, and which is monstrous in that it questions the distinction between the natural and the unnatural and implies, perhaps, that there never has been anything natural. The passage, because it demonstrates that to see something means viewing it with a particular subjective gaze, shows that realism itself is subjective, even if unacknowledged as such, and this means that Dickens cannot simply be a 'realist' writer; there is no standpoint from which to read London which is outside it. This affects the expressed desire to remove the housetops, so that it can be seen better how corruption rises and spreads through the city. The reference is, in part, to cholera epidemics, present in London in 1832 (and again in 1848 and in 1854). There is expressed here the desire to see the impossible, to reveal 'pale phantoms' which are only detectable by taking off the roofs of houses, by representing the unrepresentable by causing upheavals equivalent to those of the 'earthquake' occasioned by the train.

The novelistic desire associates with the railways, which have 'the secret knowledge of great powers yet unsuspected in them': which knowledge gives them indeed the power of death. This appears most powerfully in chapter 55, when Carker is killed by the train. Pursued by Dombey from Dijon, he has arrived at Dover, and boarded a train which would stop at a station where he could divert to another town. It has been assumed that this was Paddock Wood in Kent, which acquired its name in 1844, when a branch line ran from it to Maidstone. A station on the London to Dover line was installed here, in 1842.[17] Paddock Wood is now virtually within London's orbit. But Carker never makes Maidstone (the place where John Jasper was to be hanged).

The chapter, giving Carker's flight out of France, anticipates his death:

Some other terror came upon him quite removed from this of being pursued, suddenly, like an electric shock, as he was creeping through the streets. Some visionary horror, unintelligible and inexplicable, associated with a trembling of the ground – a rush and sweep of something through the air, like Death upon the wing. He shrunk, as if to let the thing go by. It was not gone, it never had been there, yet what a startling horror it had left behind. (55.829)

The train traumatises before it is seen, and the sensation of it keeps returning throughout chapter 55, before Carker is killed by the oncoming express at the station. Repetition precedes the event, which it brings on; it is an instance of what Derrida calls 'the trace', which precedes experience of it. The sensation is that of 'shock', the word that was earlier applied to the building of the railway, and implying that the course of city life will now never run smooth (like a railway), but as a series of traumas. Part of the writing of *Dombey and Son* entails learning that; these new powers diminish the people within the text, dwarfing even Mr Dombey, and perhaps it may be said that this accounts for some of its nostalgia, as with Gills and Captain Cuttle, and even with elements of Walter Gay.

On Friday, 9 June 1865, nearly twenty years after starting *Dombey and Son*, and over forty years since the blacking-factory, Dickens survived a railway accident at Staplehurst in Kent, itself sufficiently near Paddock Wood. On Thursday, 9 June 1870, he died, after twenty-four hours' unconsciousness: a coincidence of date noted since Forster's time. The train, the tidal express, had left Paris on its way to Charing Cross in London at 7 that morning, and Folkestone at 2; the accident took place at 3, when the train left the rails on the bridge over the river Beult in Kent. The foreman of the platelayers on the line had loosened the plates, mistaking the time that the train would come. Of the hundred passengers, ten died, fourteen were injured.

Details of the crash appear in Dickens' letters. On Saturday 10 June he wrote to F.C. Beard that he was 'in the carriage that did not go down but hung in the air over the side of the broken bridge. I was not touched – scarcely shaken' – but the postscript adds, 'I can't sign my flourish today' (49). The same letter uses a phrase that he 'worked for hours among the dying and dead', which reappears, with slight variants, in further letters written over the next two days to William Day, Forster, Charles Lever, Frederic Ouvry, Miss Coutts and Mrs Brown, and Catherine Dickens and T.J. Arnold, Thomas Headland, Lever again, and Macready. On 10 June, to Lever, he cannot sign his flourish, 'being nervously shaken', though to Ouvry he says that he is 'scarcely shaken'. By 11 June he admits to being shaken, and in a formulation which keeps returning, but appears first in his letter to his wife (11 June), he is shaken, not by the shock, but by the work among the dead and the dying. With variations, that appears in the letter to Arnold, to Headland, to Lever, to Macready, to the station-master at Charing Cross, where the train was bound, to Henry Austin's wife, to J.B. Buckstone, John de Gex, and Frederick Dickens. The 'not by . . . but by' enlarges more and more on what did *not* shake him – the 'beating and dragging of the carriage' (to Mrs Henry Austin) while it also emphasises the 'work' involved in taking out the dying and the dead. On Tuesday, 13 June, he writes from Gad's Hill a letter to Thomas Mitton telling him about the accident, about the two ladies who were his companions (Ellen Ternan and her mother) and about the work among the dead and dying, and about the manuscript for *Our Mutual Friend* (no. 16) that he had with him. 'But in writing these scanty words of recollection, I feel the shake and am obliged to stop' (57). Similar letters continue: to George Russell (13 June), to Mrs Sartoris (14 June), to Mrs Winter (14 June), to Geraldine Jewsbury (15 June), to Augustus Tracey

(15 June), to H.M. Merridew (17 June) where he speaks of an incapacity to bear much noise, and to Mrs Hulkes (18 June) where the word 'shaken' is repeated in relation to a passenger: 'in the course of going over the viaduct, the whole of his pockets were shaken empty' (61). On 29 June, he says that he has got his voice back – 'I most unaccountably brought somebody else's out of that terrible scene' (65). The nature of trauma is to attack the self's identity.

As the letters progress, it becomes evident that he has been shaken, not just by the experience of working among the dead and dying, but by the accident. There has been a short period of incubation; what Freud calls a 'latency period' and he is found thinking about his death, as when he tells J.T. Fields that he may change before he can come to America 'and establish a Castle in the other world' (*Letters* 11.256). On 15 February 1867 he writes from Liverpool that, 'I am not quite right within, but believe it to be an effect of the Railway shaking. There is no doubt of the fact that, after the Staplehurst experience, it tells more and more, instead of (as one might have expected) less and less' (11.314). Here, it is the railway which is said to shake rather than Dickens, who is shaking because he has no autonomy, as if he is caught within the machine. Forster, practical about the point that Dickens was driving himself to death with his public readings, finds this last sentence an instance of his self-deception, 'to justify him in his professed belief that these continued excesses of labour and excitement were really doing him no harm' (Forster, 8.7.705). If so, it is one or both of two things: a drive towards death, and an instance of Dickens' desire to read the accident as a trauma which could not be escaped from – which would, then, perhaps accentuate the death-drive. On 29 July 1868, Dickens comments again on 'that horrible Staplehurst day', saying that his watch, '(a special Chronometer) has never gone quite correctly since' (12.161). The memory also contributed to him saying, 'I am haunted by the dreadful accident to the Irish Mail' (25 August 1868, 12.173), which had killed thirty-three people. A day later he writes:

> My escape in the great Staplehurst accident of 3 years ago is not to be obliterated from my nervous system. To this hour I have sudden vague rushes of terror, even when riding in a Hansom Cab, which are perfectly unreasonable, but quite insur-mountable. I used to make nothing of driving a pair of horses habitually though the most crowded parts of London. I cannot now drive, with comfort to myself, on the country roads here; and I doubt if I could ride at all in the saddle. My Reading-Secretary and companion know so well when one of these odd momentary seizures comes upon me in a Railway Carriage, that he instantly produces a dram of brandy, which rallies the blood to my heart and generally prevails . . . (*Letters* 12.175)

Carker's experience travelling across France has become Dickens'. On 16 April 1869 he tells Mark Lemon that the phrase 'Railway Accident' 'has had a dread-ful significance to me, ever since the Staplehurst occasion' (12.335). In a letter to Forster on 22 April 1869, after enduring a breakdown during his readings, he said that he had told F.C. Beard 'a year after the Staplehurst accident, that I was certain that my heart had been fluttered' (12.341). In 'A Fly-Leaf in a Life' (22 May 1869, *All the Year Round*, and only in 1897 included in *The Uncommercial Traveller*), the narrator describes, in a life filled with activity and 'constant railway travelling', a pause for rest recommended by his doctor. He comments on exhaustion and on having been unable to achieve what he calls 'the constantly recurring task'. I 'began to feel (for the first time in my life), giddy, jarred, shaken, faint, uncertain of voice and sight and tread and touch, and dull of spirit' (*J4* 387–88).

It seems as if Dickens begins with one trauma, the poverty which produced the blacking-factory, and thinks of the railways as a modernisation erasing that period. But 'An Unsettled Neighbourhood', whatever its humour, registers a new sense of disturbance, and by 1865, Dickens has found himself in another traumatic situation, activated by the very forces intended to destroy the first. Freud describes two stages in trauma:

> It may happen that a man who has experienced some frightful accident – a railway collision, for instance – leaves the scene of the event apparently uninjured. In the course of the next few weeks, however, he develops a number of severe psychical and motor symptoms which can only be traced to his shock, the concussion or whatever it was. He now has a 'traumatic neurosis.' It is a quite unintelligible – that is to say, a new – fact. The time that has passed between the accident and the first appearance of the symptoms is described as the 'incubation period,' in a clear allusion to the pathology of infectious diseases.[18]

Dickens came out of the accident 'apparently uninjured', so that the damage that was done psychically, which accounts for the shaking, the loss of voice, the inability to sign his name, the compulsion to narrate the incident and to enlarge on it more and more, the anxiety to say what has not shaken him and what has, implies what has been called, in regard to such things, 'an inherent latency within the experience itself'.[19] But which latency period, and for which trauma are we speaking? One in and after the blacking-factory episode of 1824, or in and after the railway accident of 1865?

The accident did not inaugurate a period of trauma ending only with Dickens' death. For Freud, '*Nachträglichkeit*', i.e. delayed reaction, or deferred action, suggests that an experience may awaken previous powerful impressions which have been working in the subject but which are aroused at a later stage.[20] Dickens' death on the anniversary of the accident may have been a case of *Nachträglichkeit*, or, the railway accident may even have included in it its own *Nachträglichkeit*, taking hold because arousing in Dickens sensations felt earlier. Pip, in *Great Expectations*, has the sense in his delirium of being a steel beam of a vast engine, and 'wanting to have the engine stopped and my part in it hammered off' (*GE* 3.18.462), five years before the accident.

Perhaps the second event reactivated the first, which makes *Dombey and Son* and *David Copperfield* reactions to the first, and *Dombey and Son*, with its strange identification of the train as death, preparing the way for another, even drawing it on. If the trauma is put into the terms of Jacques Lacan, who follows Freud, it is the 'unassimilable', the missed encounter, the sense that something has been there, and been missed, has eluded perception.[21] The missed encounter is with what Lacan calls 'the real', which may be defined here as that which is outside symbolisation, outside all the grids that language imposes on experience, but glimpsed at in traumatic moments of 'nameless shock', as *Dombey and Son* expresses it; while the knowledge that the experience has been missed is also traumatic.[22]

The railway as a threat to life appears in a short story written after the Staplehurst accident: 'No.1 Branch Line: The Signalman', the short story which forms the last chapter of 'Mugby Junction' (December 1866). The narrator encounters a signalman working in his box by the side of the railway, and arranges to meet with him a second night-time. The signalman tells him the second time that he mistook him, on seeing him the first time, for another figure, warning, and waving his right hand across his face, while shielding his eyes with his left arm. He tells him that he has been witness to two sets of death on the line. Both times, a spectral figure appeared beforehand, as if to give warning. The narrator arranges for them to meet once more, but this time, it is only to find that the signalman has been killed by a train coming out of the tunnel.

The text is structured by very detailed sets of repetitions, and the railway is related to three occasions of deaths.[23] The spectral figure, his left hand over his eyes and his right hand waving, an intimation of accidental death, of shock and of terrified warning, becomes the driver trying to give warning, but, in the event, still killing the signalman in an accident which seems to be destined to happen, and necessary to complete the narrative. And the accident seems not purely personal in character. It surpasses the fears of the signalman, who seems to be expecting death, because the narrator, who is a stranger to the railway-line, seems also caught up in the process when he utters the words that the driver will shout as he waves his arm: 'For God's sake clear the way' (*CS* 530), and feels a 'nameless horror' (535) – the sense that Lacan gives to trauma – before realising that the signalman has died. The person who tells, and the narrator inside the tale, the signalman, who tells of his fears, are both figures of trauma, carried by something impersonal, machine-like in its power of repetition.

If the train 'clears the way' in Camden, so it does in 'The Signalman' to devastating effect, and it is associated with the power of modern urbanisation. Dickens' London allows the traumatised self a constant repetition of painful and unavoidable experiences, and it may be said that the desire in *Dombey and Son* is to sweep those away, while half-knowing that what replaces those parts of London is also potentially traumatic: 'not a rood of English ground' is secure. It is a marker of what makes Dickens so significant: that the writing after *Dombey and Son* does not flinch from the implications of such trauma.

CHAPTER SIX

MODERNISING LONDON
David Copperfield

I am not sure that it was before this time [of Dickens' father leaving prison] that the blacking warehouse was removed to Chandos-street, Covent-garden. It is no matter. Next to the shop at the corner of Bedford-street in Chandos-street, are two rather old-fashioned houses and shops adjoining one another. They were one then, or thrown into one, for the blacking-business; and had been a butter-shop. Opposite to them was, and is, a public-house, where I got my ale, under these new circumstances. The stones in the street may be smoothed by my small feet going across to it at dinner-time, and back again [. . .] We worked, for the light's sake, near the second window as you come from Bedford-street; and we were so brisk at it, that the people used to stop and look in. Sometimes there would be quite a little crowd there. I saw my father coming in at the door one day when we were very busy, and I wondered how he could bear it.

Now, I generally had my dinner in the warehouse. Sometimes I brought it from home, so I was better off. I see myself coming across Russell-square from Somers-town, one morning, with some cold hotch-potch in a small basin tied up in a handkerchief. I had the same wanderings about the streets as I used to have, and was just as solitary and self-dependent as before . . . (903)

Until old Hungerford-market was pulled down, until old Hungerford-stairs were destroyed, and the very nature of the ground changed, I never had the courage to go back to the place where my servitude began. I never saw it. I could not endure to go near it. For many years, when I came near to Robert Warren's in the Strand, I crossed over to the opposite side of the way, to avoid a certain smell of the cement they put upon the blacking-corks, which reminded me of what I was once. It was a very long time before I liked to go up Chandos-street. My old way home by the Borough made me cry, after my eldest child could speak.

In my walks at night, I have walked there often, since then, and by degrees, I have come to write this. *David Copperfield* 904

I · WARREN'S BLACKING-FACTORY

The London so fearful to Dickens was Camden Town, discussed with *Dombey and Son*, the Strand, particularly around Charing Cross, and, to a lesser extent, the Borough, which is subject both of *David Copperfield* (1849–50) and *Little Dorrit*.[1] *David Copperfield* returns, particularly, to the Strand area. Although the London of the novel is of the 1820s, twenty years earlier than *Dombey and Son*, it is under the power of modernisation, as it certainly was by the time of writing both the autobiographical fragment of the late 1840s (quoted above) and the novel itself. London was becoming more of an apparent single entity.

Up to the 1850s, there was no readily available definition of London's limits: *The Times* could say in 1855, even, that there is 'no such place as London after all'.[2] This was partly because of problems of local government, and the lack of a sense of the place as a single 'metropolis': not till 1889 would London become single, with the formation of the London County Council. Up till then, the city's various Podsnaps could denounce 'centralisation' as 'not British', or as French (*OMF* 1.11.144).

Part of the effect of *David Copperfield* for its readership is the sense of the creation of a single city supported by its suburbs – picking out certain areas: Highgate (residence of the Steerforths, Dr Strong, and the place of David Copperfield's first marriage), Norwood (Mr Spenlow), Putney (Mr Spenlow's sisters), Hornsey, where Betsey Trotwood's husband is buried (chapter 54) in a churchyard which would be the resting-place of Samuel Rogers, in 1855. Nearer places returned to repeatedly are the Borough, Westminster from the Strand through to Fleet Street, and around St Paul's churchyard (for Doctors' Commons). St Paul's has already been given a symbolic significance, before it is seen: its picture, its dome pink, appears on Peggotty's work-box (2.28).

David Copperfield's leading character, called, henceforth, DC (CD in reverse, like MOOR EEFFOC), arrives in London on three separate occasions, each initiatory. The first, in chapter 5, is when he comes up from Blunderstone in Suffolk, having spent time at Great Yarmouth, in Norfolk, 120 miles away from London. Great Yarmouth is perhaps to be considered as like Chatham in Kent, Dickens' home between 1815 and 1823. It was the first place to erect a memorial (designed by William Wilkins and completed in 1820) to the Norfolk-born Nelson. When Dickens wrote *David Copperfield*, Nelson's column, planned in 1838, had been completed in Trafalgar Square (1843), one of the principal sites in London which was to impose a way of seeing the city as monumental, and mapping everything in relation to it, imposing what Lefebvre would call a dominant 'representation of space' on Londoners. But there is no mention of Trafalgar Square in this text.[3] DC has been sent by his step-father, Mr Murdstone, to school at Salem House at Blackheath, as a way of separating him from his mother. He arrives at the Blue Bull, or the Blue Boar, in Whitechapel, where he is met by Mr Mell, who takes him the six miles there.[4] Teacher and pupil cross London Bridge by stage-coach, and stop at an almshouse, presumably in Southwark. Here Mr Mell, whose name, Charley, makes him, like DC, potentially autobiographical, plays the flute to his mother. Mr Creakle, the headmaster at Salem House, also comes from Southwark, and had in earlier life been a hop-dealer (6.97), associated with the brewing industry in the Borough, which used hops brought up from Kent. Tungay, the wooden-legged assistant, also worked with him in the hop-business. The link between *Dombey and Son* and *David Copperfield* as both fictional autobiographies appears here; Paul Dombey goes to the deadening Dr Blimber's school; DC suffers at Salem House.

The second initiation into London implies the Borough, but gets closer to sites near the Strand. In chapter 11, DC has been sent back to London by Mr Murdstone, forced to work in the wine-warehouses of Murdstone and Grinby, down at the river's edge, near Blackfriars. The house where he works, in age and waterside position, is re-evoked with Mrs Clennam's house in *Little Dorrit*. Bringing the warehouse into the City, away from where Dickens actually worked, as a twelve-year-old, on a site now covered by Charing Cross Station, Dickens associates DC's experience with the City. So too, Mr Micawber's house is in the City Road (Islington). Micawber escorts DC across 'the arcana of the Modern Babylon' in the direction of the City Road, to Windsor Terrace, shabby, but attempting to be genteel. So its name, with out-of-London and regal associations, suggests; perhaps, if Dickens recalls *The Merry Wives of Windsor*, he suggests that Micawber may be a version of Falstaff. Mrs Micawber has a notice at the door, advertising the place as a boarding establishment for young ladies, as Dickens' mother had done, but no-one comes. Their servant, the 'Orfling', comes from St Luke's work-house, 'in the neighbourhood': built originally in 1782, it was on the City Road between Shepherdess' Walk to the south, place of the Eagle Tavern. Develop-ing from a previous pleasure garden called the Shepherd and Shepherdess, Thomas Rouse opened the Eagle in 1824. The workhouse was adapted as a hospital in 1871, and the surviving parts have been converted as flats. From the autobiographical fragment that Dickens wrote, it seems that the 'Orfling' had come to London with Dickens' parents from Chatham workhouse, which is the one we may presume that Oliver Twist came from (if, of course, we accept the identification of Mudfog with Chatham). The orphan from Chatham workhouse is cited by Forster as a source for the Marchioness in *The Old Curiosity Shop* (899), which implies a sense in which Oliver, the Marchioness and the 'Orfling' are figures within Dickens' autobiography: not relating to Dickens' actual life, but to the results of his myriad representa-tions of it.[5]

Yet the text refuses to speak about the place where Dickens worked: at no. 30 Hungerford Stairs, near Hungerford Bridge, off the Strand, on the east side of Craven Street, in a position which has entirely disappeared, owing to the remodelling of Hungerford Market, and the building of the Embankment.[6] The evasion allows a continual return to the place in an unacknowledged way. DC follows the autobiographical account Dickens wrote preceding beginning *David Copperfield*, of his own experience of working in the blacking-factory, and which Forster used. DC begins by saying that 'modern improvements have altered the place: but it was the last house at the bottom of a narrow street, curving down hill to the river, with some stairs at the end, where people took boat'. The differences in the autobiographical version, which is fuller, more bitter, less anxious about keeping a readership, have been italicised. They make most significant the rats which 'rise up' (literally, and as ghosts, and as sickening memories, with the power to make the person vomit, and as elements of what must be repressed from social existence):

> It was a crazy [*tumble-down*] old house with a wharf of its own, abutting on the water when the tide was in, and on the mud when the tide was out, and literally over-run with rats [after house: *abutting of course on the river, and literally overrun with rats*]. Its panelled [*wainscoted*] rooms, [*and its rotten floors and staircase*], discoloured with the dirt and smoke of a hundred years, I dare say; its decayed floors and staircase; the squeaking and scuffling of the old grey rats down in the cellars, and the dirt and rottenness of the place; are things, not of many years ago, in my mind, but of the present instance. [After staircase: *and the old grey rats down in the cellars, and the sound of their squeaking and scuffling coming up the stairs at all times, and the dirt and decay of the place, rise up visibly before me as if I were there again. The counting-house was on the first floor, looking over the coal-barges and the river.*] (11.165, 895)

The warehouse, whose description evokes Jacob's Island, is part of Stuart London, that which was being destroyed in the years after Waterloo. For the factory to move from it to Chandos Street (see the epigraph for the chapter) is a faint sign of 'improvement'. But in the narrative, things get no better. After Mr Micawber has gone to prison and been freed from it, and departed from London to Plymouth, another naval town, like Dickens' Portsmouth or Chatham, DC sets out to find his aunt in Dover. He walks towards Greenwich, sleeps at Blackheath, by Salem House, walks to Rochester and Chatham and arrives at Dover.

The third time DC arrives in London is as a young man. The coach from Canterbury comes in past Blackheath, and stops at the Golden Cross at Charing Cross, where Pickwick begins his adventures (*PP* 2.21). But Charing Cross is adjacent to Hungerford Market. DC stays at the Golden Cross, sees *Julius Caesar* at Covent Garden, and re-meets Steerforth. The two see London sights, and take a stage-coach to Highgate, where DC stays for some days. It is an unconsciously erotic initiation into London, in terms of his attraction to Steerforth, which resumes in chapter 24, 'My First Dissipation', when he drinks with Steerforth and his friends, and revisits the theatre, this time drunk, where he sees Agnes, who, pointedly, asks him with whom he has fallen in love (25.375–76). London has been returned to from chapter 23 on when DC meets his aunt in Lincoln's Inn Fields, goes to St Paul's churchyard to become a Proctor, lodges at Buckingham Street in the Adelphi, attends the party given by the Waterbrooks at Ely Place, entertains Uriah Heep at Buckingham Street, putting him up for the night when it is too late for him to return to his lodgings at the New River Head, Islington (the passage contrasts with the re-meeting with Steerforth in chapter 24), and falls in love with Dora Spenlow at Norwood. Mr Spenlow's partner, Mr Jorkins, lives near Montagu Square (35.513).

This is polite London, its settings integral to the narrative of the rise of the bourgeois hero, but chapter 27 changes, when DC finds Tommy Traddles, a friend at Salem House. He lodges 'in a little street near the Veterinary College' at Camden Town (Little College Street, now College Place), but:

> I found that the street was not as desirable a one as I could have wished it to be, for the sake of Traddles. The inhabitants appeared to have a propensity to throw any little trifles they were not in want of, into the road: which not only made it rank and sloppy, but untidy too, on account of the cabbage-leaves. The refuse was not wholly vegetable either, for I saw a shoe, a doubled-up saucepan, a black bonnet, and an umbrella, in various stages of decomposition, as I was looking out for the number I wanted.
>
> The general air of the place reminded me forcibly of the days when I lived with Mr and Mrs Micawber. An indescribable character of faded gentility that attached to the house I sought, and made it unlike all the other houses in the street – though they were all built on one monotonous pattern, and looked like the early copies of a blundering boy who had not yet got out of his cramped crick and mortar pothooks – reminded me still more of Mr and Mrs Micawber. Happening to arrive at the door as it was opened to the afternoon milkman, I was reminded of Mr and Mrs Micawber more forcibly yet. (27.408)

The house is occupied by the Micawbers. The incidents of Windsor Terrace – the relations with the tradesmen – are repeated. DC is, effectively, returning to Dickens' childhood with Little College Street, where Dickens lodged twice. The initiation repeats an earlier one. The road is described in 'The Old Man's Tale about the Queer Client' in *Pickwick Papers*; Heyling completes his revenge on his father-in-law by going to his 'wretched lodging' from 'that corner of the old Pancras Road, at which stands the parish workhouse' – roughly, where the present-day underground station for Camden Town is – and walking from there across the top of Bayham Street:

> proceeding by the dead wall in front of the Veterinary Hospital, they entered a small bye-street, which is, or was at that time, called Little College Street, and which, whatever it may be now, was in those days a desolate place enough, surrounded by little else than fields and ditches (*PP* 21.287–88).

Mr Micawber tells DC that a washerwoman who exposes hard-bake for sale in her parlour window lives next door, and a Bow Street Officer lives opposite: this particular dates the action to the 1820s, and recalls Dickens living at the top of Bayham Street (*DC* 887). Little College Street stands in for Bayham Street, as well as having its own memories of Mrs Roylance. Later in the novel, Micawber, living in lodgings at the top of Gray's Inn Road, leaves London for Canterbury (*DC* 36.535), as if following DC's itinerary. His impoverished lodgings are also close to Little College Street: a secret reminder of that other London, associated with the blacking-factory and the prison.

II · THE STRAND

An early nineteenth-century map of the Strand, three-quarters of a mile long, Disraeli's 'finest street in Europe, blending the architecture of many periods',

King Charles the First on horseback (the wreath was laid on 30 January, the work of the Royal Stuart Society; this photograph was taken on 3 February 2008).

with 'river ways a peculiar feature and rich with associations' and with 'Fleet Street, with its Temple . . . not unworthy of being contiguous to [it]' is almost unrecognisable from the standpoint of the present.[7] Its most major changes are at the two ends. At the western edge, Whitehall came up to Charing Cross, where stands, surrounded by bollards with William the Fourth's insignia on them, Hubert Le Sueur's statue of 'King Charles on horseback, surrounded by a maze of hackney-coaches' (*DC* 21.299).

It was placed there in 1675, after the 1647 demolition of Charing Cross (1291), one of twelve marking the funeral cortège of Edward the First's wife, Eleanor of Castile, moving southwards from Nottinghamshire. A replica was placed outside Charing Cross Station in 1865. Like other London public spaces, Charing Cross was used for punishment, particularly the pillory. (The stocks were used up till 1830, in, for instance, Portugal Street, the pillory the same year, at the Old Bailey.[8]) After 1831, distances in Britain were to be measured from the statue of Charles, making it the centre of both the metropolis, and of a novel where King Charles' head intrudes into Mr Dick's text (the two-hundredth anniversary of Charles' execution (30 January 1649) intersected with the novel's writing).

Running into Charing Cross from the west was Pall Mall, becoming Cockspur Street. Warwick Street, named for the house of a Royalist writer, Sir Philip Warwick, demolished in 1827, comes into Cockspur Street on the south, while south of Cockspur Street, behind Whitehall on the west, was Spring Gardens, site of a pre-Civil War pleasure-ground, and revived with the Restoration. Nash's Suffolk Street comes into Cockspur Street on the north; here Earls of Suffolk once had stables; here Richard Dadd (1817–86), possible origin for Mr Dick, murdered his father in 1843. East of Suffolk Street is Whitcomb Street (which, becoming Wardour Street, is the only street to run through Soho, and connecting with Oxford Street). Next to that was the King's Mews: the Dunghill Mews, the Great Mews, and the Green Mews. 'Mews' records the point that birds had been kept there; now it was stables, and so 'mews' comes to apply to streets for horses. Entrance to the Mews from the north was down Castle Street. Adjacent to these Mews, designed by William Kent in 1732, was the Golden Cross Inn, its centre where Nelson's column stands, and next to it were further houses and shops.[9]

Nash's Regency design for London included preparations for laying out Trafalgar Square, regretting that a vista down Pall Mall could not quite be completed by St Martin-in-the-Fields, which was not quite in alignment with it. The Mews were pulled down, replaced by the National Gallery of William Wilkins (1778–1839), architect of University College, London: the Gallery, which opened in 1838 on the north side of Trafalgar Square, used columns from the recently demolished (1826) Carlton House, and was designed to be seen best from Pall Mall.

St Martin's was east and north of the Golden Cross, and St Martin's Lane continued south to the Strand; that continuation was destroyed by laying out Trafalgar Square. When it reached the Strand, Northumberland House was opposite, object of attention in 'Gone Astray'. Running into the Strand from the south, directly east of Northumberland House, was Northumberland Street. (Northumberland Avenue, connecting Trafalgar Square with the Victoria Embankment, was built in 1876: the Embankment between 1864 and 1870.) East of Northumberland Street, Craven Street survives (redeveloped in the 1730s). In *Oliver Twist* chapter 41 Mr Brownlow lives there after returning from the Caribbean; he has moved from Pentonville, and assumed a more central address to become guardian of the twelve-years-old Oliver Twist (the same age as Dickens in 1824, when he was working without a father on a site immediately adjacent to this street). In terms of spatial practices, Pentonville suited Brownlow the bookish bachelor, Craven Street the patriarch.

East of Craven Street was Hungerford Market, built for Sir Edward Hungerford on the site of his house, burned down in 1669. The market was rebuilt in 1833 by Charles Fowler (1792–1867) who had completed designing Covent Garden market, with which Hungerford had similarities. Hungerford Market was demolished to make way for Charing Cross Station, in 1860. Brunel built a suspension bridge from the South Bank to Hungerford Market in 1845, the two together explain *Little Dorrit*'s reference to the 'hanging bridge' next to the 'fish-market' (*LD* 2.9.556). Brunel's bridge, its chains used for the Clifton supension bridge, was replaced by Sir John Hawkshaw's railway

Arcading, Covent Garden market, 1830.

bridge (1864). The redesigning of Hungerford Market is the modernisation Dickens refers to in the initial quotation heading this chapter.

East of Hungerford Market is present-day Villiers Street, at the bottom of which is the water-gate designed by either Inigo Jones, or Balthasar Gerbier, for York House, so called because Mary gave the house, first built in the thirteenth century, to the Achbishop of York. York Watergate indicates how far out the Thames has been pushed by the Embankment. Villiers Street was built in the 1670s by the property speculator Nicholas Barbon on the site of York House, which had belonged to James the First's favourite George Villiers, Duke of Buckingham (1592–1628), and which passed to his son at the Restoration. Barbon's streets reflected the second Duke's names; hence Buckingham Street, where Dickens himself lodged for a short while, around 1831 (possibly at no. 15, the corner house on the east side), and which is the home of David Copperfield when he lodges with Mrs Crupp (23.362). Peggotty spends time in London, and in chapter 32.472, takes a lodging in Hungerford Market, only two streets west of Buckingham Street (35.505). But it was 'a very different place in those days' – i.e. the old Hungerford Market, which Dickens could not bear to revisit.

Adjacent to Villiers Street, on the east side of the Strand, on the south, was the development called the Adelphi, designed by Robert, James, and William Adam, for some fifty houses. It was built between 1768 and 1775 on four main streets: present-day Adelphi Terrace (then Royal Street) to the south, John Adam Street to the north, Robert Street to the west, and Adam Street to the east.[10] The south front of Adelphi Terrace dropped down to the Thames, and was mounted on a row of fifteen arches, which provided an arcade and gave access to six underground roads, leading to storage vaults. Another access to these vaults was from York Buildings, and from Durham Street: the latter name a reminder that the site had previously been the town house for the Bishops of Durham. It was pulled down after the Civil War. The Osborne hotel, mentioned in *Pickwick Papers* 54.714, seems to have been on the corner of John Adam Street and Adam Street. DC calls the Adelphi a place of escape:

> I was fond of wandering about the Adelphi, because it was a mysterious place, with those dark arches. I see myself emerging from some of these arches, on a little public-house close to the river, with an open space before it, where some coal-heavers were dancing, to look at whom, I sat down upon a bench. I wonder what they thought of me! (11.171)

If the coal-heavers suggest 'Scotland-yard' (*SB*), this suggests how Dickens might have come to know about them. The area was near Scotland-yard itself. The public house was the Fox-under-the-hill (*DC* 901); *Pickwick Papers* (42.560) mentions it as the site of a brawl between a butcher and a coal-heaver. Augustus Egg's triptych, 'Past and Present' (1858), shows the suicidal wife underneath the arches of the Adelphi, looking towards the Surrey shore. In 'Mrs Lirriper's Lodging', the Christmas Story for *All the Year Round* 1863, the abandoned wife, Mrs Edson, tries to commit suicide here; she is rescued by Mrs Lirriper, whose lodging-house is in Norfolk Street, off the Strand, and who was married at St Clement Danes. The Adelphi's riverside position was altered by the Victoria Embankment, and the complex was partially demolished in 1936. The Adelphi is what Michel Foucault calls a 'heterotopic' space, an other space, which modifies the way it was intended to be used and perceived.[11] So, in *Little Dorrit*, when Clennam walking down the Strand (in 1825) is halted by a 'stoppage on the pavement, caused by a train of coal-waggons toiling up from the wharves at the river-side'. He notices Rigaud and Tattycoram, and follows them into the Adelphi where there is 'a sudden pause . . . to the roar of the great thoroughfare', and onto the terrace there (*LD* 2.9.555). The text notes how much outside the great world of movement the Adelphi was; as a space allowing for secrecy, privacy, and lounging.

Beyond the Adelphi, and Ivybridge Lane, where the medieval part of Westminster ended, was the precinct, a liberty, distinct from either the City or Westminster, called the Savoy, comprising lands and houses given by Henry the Third to Peter, Count of Savoy, uncle of Henry's Queen (Eleanor of Provence) in 1246. It became the property of the house of Lancaster, and the home of John of Gaunt, who rebuilt it. With Henry the Eighth, it became a hospital, then a prison for deserters (until 1820), and had chapels, and barracks, and was effectively a separate parish; it was destroyed in 1811 when work began on the Strand (Waterloo) Bridge, and the approach to it.[12] Before

Savoy Buildings, south side of the Strand: though early twentieth century, the inscriptions here mark the presence of Fountain Court, where Blake died: the inscription on the right notes that Fountain Court derived from the Fountain Tavern on this site. The inscription on the left says that in this tavern the political opponents of Sir Robert Walpole met (if this is the Kit Kat club, it was pro-Whig, and Walpole), and that the Coal Hole was here, meeting place of the Wolf Club, of which, in 1826, the actor Edmund Kean (1787–1833) was a leading member.

that, the Savoy had extended as far as Somerset House. Within its complex was Fountain Court, where Blake died in 1827.[13]

The Strand is completed by Somerset House, and King's College Gateway (designed by Sir Robert Smirke, in 1828), and Strand Lane, with its Roman bath, where DC bathes (*DC* 35.511), the old Strand Theatre, which contained Barker's Panorama, and Arundel House, in medieval times the town-house of the Bishop of Bath and Wells, then given to Henry Fitz-Alan, Earl of Arundel (1549), and destroyed in 1678. What lies beyond is St Clement Danes, and Temple Bar, and Fleet Street, where DC goes when hungry to stare at a venison shop (11.171). Present-day Surrey and Arundel Street recall Arundel House. Essex Street, where Magwitch lodges (*GE* 3.1.335), is the far end of the Strand, its name recalling the house of Robert Devereux, Earl of Essex. Magwitch's lodgings look out, at the back, onto the Temple.

Returning towards Charing Cross, on the north side of the Strand, means going away from the Aldwych, a development completed in 1905. Before, Drury Lane ran into the Strand (and another branch into Wych Street). The 'famous alamode beef-house' was 'near Drury Lane': here DC 'ordered a "small plate"' of that delicacy to eat with the bread which he had brought from home (i.e. from the Micawbers). 'What the waiter thought of such a strange little apparition coming in all alone, I don't know; but I can see him now, staring at me as I ate my dinner, and bringing up the other waiter to look. I gave him a halfpenny for himself, and I wish he hadn't taken it' (11.171). The incident, as so often in this novel, recalls a previous episode; David Copperfield and the friendly waiter in chapter 5. The autobiographical fragment (896), says that the alamode beef-house was Johnson's, in Clare Court. This led out of Drury Lane into Clare Market, now covered by Kingsway (opened 1905). Poll Green, one of the boys who worked with Dickens in the factory, had as father a fireman, who worked at Drury Lane theatre, while 'another relation of Poll's, I think his little sister, did imps in the pantomime' (896: the equivalent passage in *DC* 11.166 says that he worked 'in one of the large theatres'). Between Catherine Street and Wellington Street, was Sydney Smirke's Exeter Arcade (1842), torn down in 1863.[14]

Going west, past Wellington Street, the sixteenth-century Exeter House was destroyed in 1670 and replaced by Burleigh Street and Exeter Street. Between them was Exeter Hall, built in 1829 by Gandy-Deering for religious meetings, and demolished in 1907. It replaced Exeter Change, which had been a bazaar including a menagerie; this latter went afterwards, for a short time, to the King's Mews at Charing Cross. The menagerie included, from 1809 to 1826, an elephant. Another bazaar was planned – glass-roofed, and with two rows of shops – but Exeter Hall was built instead (Geist, 327–28), monument to a new serious middle-class Evangelicalism. Behind these streets was Covent Garden, where David Copperfield stared at pineapples (11.171). The Adelphi theatre (*PP* 31.402), began in 1806 as the Sans Pareil, for a merchant to show off the talents of Miss Scott, his daughter, and it reopened in 1819 with its present name, but has been rebuilt several times since. The clerks in *Pickwick Papers* who get in half-price do so halfway through the triple bill that the theatre characteristically puts on.

The Strand continues east past Southampton Street, Bedford Street and Agar Street, past the house where Miss La Creevy works as a miniature painter (*NN* 3.33) till it reaches the area which was 'rebuilt' (*DC* 11.171). Dickens' autobiographical fragment describes the boy being unable to resist the stale pastry put out in 'Tottenham-Court-Road' on his way to Hungerford Stairs from 'Little-College-Street', and continues:

> there were two pudding shops between which I was divided, according to my finances. One was in a court close to St Martin's Church (at the back of the church), which is now removed altogether. The pudding at that shop was made with currants, and was rather a special pudding, but was dear: two penn'orth not being larger than a penn'orth of more ordinary pudding. A good shop for the latter was in the Strand, somewhere near where the Lowther Arcade is now [somewhere in that part which has been rebuilt since – *DC*.11.171]. It was a stout, hale pudding, heavy and flabby; with great raisins in it, stuck in whole, at great distances apart. It came up hot, at about noon every day; and many and many a day did I dine off it.

The Lowther Arcade was part of new developments behind St Martin's, planned by Nash, and initiated between 1829 and 1831 (Geist, 328–36). North of St Martin's was William the Fourth Street. South of it was the new Duncannon

Street, named for Lord Duncannon, who in 1832 became Chief Commissioner of the Office of Woods, Forests, Land Revenues, Works, and Public Buildings. It cut across the old churchyard of St Martin's, and signs of the tombs are still visible. Behind was Adelaide Street, named for William's wife, Adelaide of Saxe-Meiningen (1792–1849). The Lowther Arcade, famous for toys, ran parallel to William the Fourth Street through the block beyond to reach 'West Strand', an area Nash's followers built up as four-storied, with stucco and uninterrupted shop-fronts on the street level. The attempt was to bring commercial success to this part of London, to complement Piccadilly. Coutts moved in 1904 from further down the Strand into Nash's block, with its cupolas at each corner. Chandos Street, built in 1725, and named for James Brydges, the Duke of Chandos, and including Chandos House, built by Robert and James Adam for the third Duke, leads out of William the Fourth Street, running parallel with the Strand. Reaching Bedford Street, it becomes Maiden Lane, birthplace of Turner in 1775 over his father's barber shop. At Bedford Street, it becomes the second site of Warren's blacking-factory. The route has returned to Charing Cross, and to another reference, the boy visiting a public-house:

> one evening, when I had been somewhere for my father, and was going back to the Borough over Westminster-bridge, that I went into a public-house in Parliament-street, which is still there, though altered, at the corner of the short street leading into Cannon-row. (901)

Derby Gardens leads out of Parliament Street, and meets Cannon Row, which runs into Bridge Street. The incident, though not the area, is in the novel (11.171). It is, perhaps, the fifth time that Dickens is seen making the place more general in the novel than in the fragment, and drawing attention to modernisation, as if keeping up the sense that the place was actually at Blackfriars, and making London more anonymous.

St Martin-in-the-Fields reappears in chapter 40, when DC returns from working at Highgate, and comes down St Martin's Lane. 'Now, the church which gives its name to the lane, stood in a less free situation at that time, there being no open space before it, and the lane winding down to the Strand' (40.587). He sees Martha, the prostitute who came to London from Yarmouth (chapter 22). He also sees Peggotty, looking for Emily. The action pauses, as they go through a door existing 'in those days' (40.588) into the Golden Cross. DC notes the association: the last time he was in that Inn was with Steerforth, who seduced Peggotty's niece. A double process works here: connecting incidents and linking them with places, while simultaneously emphasising that the places have changed; as if repressing the past by saying it has been swept away. The text of *David Copperfield* has not allowed this area of the Strand around Charing Cross to have traumatic memories; it rather chose to situate the blacking-factory in Blackfriars. This, however, is a repressed move;

it means that Steerforth, who is remembered in the humiliation of the factory, and is contrasted with the boys working there (11.160), is associated with the actual scene, in a way that the text has avoided showing. And Traddles is mentioned in chapter 11 alongside Steerforth, but the text associates him with DC's early life, through the moment in chapter 27, when he is seen to be lodging with Micawber, as a virtual replacement for DC and, indeed, Dickens. Traddles is linked with DC's degradation and no threat to it, Steerforth is separated from it. Yet the Golden Cross marks the spot where Steerforth's existence intersects with DC's other life, the one he will not own to, especially to Steerforth. The degradation of the factory is counterposed by the sense of Steerforth as the symbol of everything that is sexually magnetic; it allows for the reading that the twelve-years-old CD feels a sexual degradation in the factory work which, while unacknowledged in the case of the ten-years-old DC, is nonetheless part of the shame felt. Hence the area must be revisited, and changed, to become the place where DC can be successful.

The emigrants for Australia leave from Hungerford Stairs to join a ship at Gravesend, from where their final departure is made. The Micawbers were 'lodged in a little, dirty, tumble-down public house, which in those days was close to the stairs, and whose protruding wooden rooms overhung the river' (57.809). The description evokes the factory in which Dickens worked, and its fictional substitute, as this was described in chapter 11; indeed, the historic public house, the White Swan, was next to the factory and appears in chapter 11: DC bought 'a plate of bread and cheese and a glass of beer, from a miserable old public house opposite our place of business, called the Lion, or the Lion and something else that I have forgotten' (11.171). Had he forgotten? Perhaps, but the text is disingenuous in the way the public house is brought back; DC is bold enough to create the fiction of saying that 'although my association of them [the Micawbers] with the tumble-down public-house and wooden stairs, dated only from last night, both seemed dreary and deserted, now that they were gone' (57.817). The text plays with its own repression; DC says he knew *only from last night*! The reader is being fooled, while the author, CD or DC, disavows his own past and memories. In the phrase 'in those days', already quoted from chapter 57, the text shows that it is on the side of modernity. It is creating a 'representation of space' which has erased the painful past, while at the same time deliberately playing with that other space, which, in psychic terms, has certainly not been erased. Throughout, there is an emphasis on how the environment has changed, so that there can be a consideration of London as a space which once held Dickens' past. The new representation of space, in so far as this takes place in the novel – and it is not consistent – serves the Freudian function of enabling a repression of painful memories at the moment when they are awakened, but it is crucial to note how the text has wanted, as if masochistically, to recall the memories in order to repress them.

III · THE BOROUGH

The Borough was seen as the scene of poverty, in the account of Mr Mell and his mother, and this continues with the scene of Mr Micawber's imprisonment, to which he returns, with 'a sentimental expression', as if idealising the scenes of his youth, in chapter 49.711. In another textual displacement, like that of the factory at Hungerford Stairs being relocated to the area round Blackfriars, Micawber is not sent to the Marshalsea, but, as if differentiating him from John Dickens, to the King's Bench prison. This was also in the Borough (the word applies to both the area, and to the High Street), so that the action 'over the water' stays within Southwark. The King's Bench prison was initially between two other prisons in the Borough High Street, the White Lion (south) and the Marshalsea (north). Pulled down in 1775, it was relocated further south, at the meeting of the Borough High Street and Newington Causeway, on the west. Sold off and demolished after 1879, it had 224 rooms and 500 prisoners.

Pickwick in the Fleet leads towards Micawber, who in his turn suggests Skimpole, never imprisoned, Dorrit in the Marshalsea, and Magwitch in Newgate. In *David Copperfield* there is the desire to bring together the oppression of the child and of the man. DC moves to Southwark, and hires a room, which, if the autobiographical fragment is followed, is to be thought of as in Lant Street. 'A back-attic was found for me at the house of an insolvent-court agent, who lived in Lant Street in the Borough. Where Bob Sawyer lodged many years afterwards . . . the little window had a pleasant prospect of a timber-yard' (899). Dickens comments on the landlord, his wife and son; Forster adds that they become the Garland family in *The Old Curiosity Shop* (899). In *David Copperfield*, the room is 'a quiet back-garret with a sloping roof, commanding a pleasant prospect of a timber-yard' (11.178). The Orfling moves south of the river too, and the two spend time on old London Bridge, sitting in the old stone recesses, and looking at the sun lighting up the golden flame on the top of the Monument; in such playful and idyllic moments, the space of representation undergoes a change, modified by the imagination of the child.

When DC runs away to Dover, he walks from Blackfriars Bridge to the Obelisk at the end of the Blackfriars Road, which had been set up in 1771 at St George's Circus, in honour of Mayor Brass Crosby, a radical who supported Wilkes, and who had commissioned it, two years after the completion of Blackfriars Bridge, and the Blackfriars Road.

The Waterloo Road, Blackfriars, the Borough Road, the London Road going south to the Elephant and Castle, the Lambeth Road, and Westminster Bridge Road converge at this spot, and the 1771 inscriptions on the Obelisk mark out distances: One Mile Thirty-five feet from Fleet Street (for access from Blackfriars Bridge), One Mile Forty feet from London Bridge (from the Borough), and One Mile from Palace Yard Westminster (from Westminster Bridge). Southwark and Waterloo Bridges added to the urbanising of this part

Obelisk at St George's Circus,
St George's Fields.

of Southwark, and the expression 'South London' appeared in the 1820s, the time of this novel. DC wants to go by coach, from the Borough High Street, but his box and money are stolen, and he must go on down the Old Kent Road on foot, past St Thomas' watering-place, which had been used for executions. He leaves London, but is always sure of his way, because he possesses London. And as with so much in the book, DC's journey is repeated: chapter 40, called 'The Wanderer', already discussed, ends with Mr Peggotty going across West-minster Bridge to find lodgings on the Dover Road; he echoes DC's journey of chapter 12.

In chapter 46, DC calls on Mr Peggotty at Hungerford Market, and they go out, looking for Martha. They go down the Strand, through Temple Bar, to Blackfriars Bridge, and see her walking in the opposite direction, near where DC used to work. They reverse direction, and follow her, towards Westminster, past Westminster Abbey, down towards Millbank, to an old deserted ferry-house, which DC says was still there when he writes. The passage evokes:

> [a] melancholy waste of road near the great blank Prison. A sluggish ditch desposited its mud at the prison walls. Coarse grass and rank weeds straggled over all the marshy land in the vicinity. In one part, carcases of houses, inauspiciously begun and never finished, rotted away. In another, the ground was cumbered with rusty iron monsters of steam-boilers, wheels, cranks, pipes, furnaces, paddles, anchors, diving-bells, windmill-sails and I know not what strange objects, accumulated by some speculator, and grovelling in the dust, underneath which . . . they had the appearance of trying to

hide themselves. The clash and glare of sundry fiery Works upon the river-side, arose by night to disturb everything except the heavy and unbroken smoke that poured out of their chimneys. (47.685–86)

Martha seems part of this refuse, which includes within it, however, its own fiery passion, as she contemplates, and is rescued from, suicide. This part of London is separated from both 'the lighted and populous streets' (47.693) and from Highgate from where the bell of St Paul's can still be heard, as a unifying force. Millbank answers to Blackfriars area in its poverty and humiliation, as is apparent when it is realised that Dickens has deliberately created this journey for Martha from one riverside situation to another. In the terms of Lefebvre, it shows her own 'spatial practice', the way she uses the city. In this mapping of the city, Blackfriars and Millbank become the sites of female sexual degradation, while the Strand around Charing Cross is the centre for DC's humiliation, first as a boy, then as a young man (chapters 11–12, 19–21). If Steerforth is associated with the Golden Cross, Emily is found in the also allegorically named Golden Square, place of the suicide of Ralph Nickleby, when Martha takes DC there, and into the surrounding 'sombre streets . . . where the houses were once fair dwellings in the occupation of single families, but have, and had, long since degenerated into poor lodgings let off in rooms' (50.721). But that women are mapped onto such poor areas of London, or kept in the suburbs, like Rosa Dartle, indicates a reason why it could not be the capital of the nineteenth century. Balzac called Paris 'cette grande courtisane', but to characterise the city as a woman could hardly be true of representations of London.[15] Dickens wrote in 1855, 'in a great city, Prostitution *will be some-where*' (*Letters* 7.691), but that admission disavows the power of eroticism by diminishing it, while knowing what is true of the 'great city'.

IV · THE MODERN BABYLON

I landed in London on a wintry autumn evening. It was dark and raining, and I saw more fog and mud in a minute than I had seen in a year. I walked from the Custom House to the Monument before I found a coach; and although the very house-fronts, looking on the swollen gutters, were like old friends to me, I could not but admit that they were very dingy friends.

I have often remarked – I suppose everybody has – that one's going away from a familiar place, would seem to be the signal for change in it. As I looked out of the coach-window, and observed that an old house on Fish-street Hill, which had stood untouched by painter, carpenter, or bricklayer, had been pulled down in my absence, and that a neighbouring street, of time-honoured insalubrity and inconvenience, was being drained and widened; I half expected to find St Paul's Cathedral looking older. (59.825)[16]

Here, DC records his fourth initiation into London; and the novel seems on the brink of becoming the opening of *Bleak House*. Putting these novels together, and thinking of what follows *Bleak House*, it may be possible to register a change in Dickens' sense of London: modernisations are necessary, and continue intensely throughout the 1860s, but they make for less of the exuberance that had been associated with earlier writing about the streets, and may even have diminished something in Dickens' writing in his last decade. The alterations here are those associated with rebuilding London Bridge. Fish Street Hill went down directly to old London Bridge, losing its importance when the new Bridge was built upstream, requiring the new King William Street (1835), to link the Bridge with Cornhill. The discussion of change, putting London into the past, like painful experience, is ambiguous, indicative of something happening throughout the book. A new London is being called into being, and its character is expressed in Pentonville Prison, which, not named as such in the novel, but newly built in 1842, is the subject of a visit made in chapter 61. Dickens was intensely aware of Pentonville (*Letters* 5.57, 257). Space is produced in this modern prison to give each prisoner their own cell, separate from each other, creating spaces of isolation, producing in each a sense of their single individuality. Intended to offer training to prisoners who were destined for transportation, Pentonville reflected, to some measure, the representation of space that Bentham wanted in the Panopticon, space that would teach the prisoner his own solitude. The journalist William Hepworth Dixon, in *The London Prisons* (1850), which Dickens knew, criticised Pentonville, emphasising that the isolation was 'all a dream'. The point emerges in chapter 61, where

Queen Anne's Gate: no. 40, Bentham's home, rented to James Mill, from 1814–31; he lived there with John Stuart Mill.

it seems Uriah Heep and Littimer are in communication with each other. The intended representation of space fails as the prisoners create, to a certain extent, an alternative space of representation for themselves, but Dixon makes another interesting point when he says that the Pentonville prisoners had become 'half idiotic' on the journey out to Australia (*Letters* 5.686 n.). The idea of independent sturdy single individuality which was to be produced through disciplining and punishing – which is close to what DC, if not the novel, stands for – fails altogether, producing versions of Mr Dick.

Chapter 59 suggests that while London is 'familiar', and has been made so in the novel, it is a source of melancholy that it must always be in change. A double desire is at work, to write London as lessening its corners of repression, as modernisation changes sites and the representation of things. But the book's interest in memory, which gives sites a significance which may be personal, and if so can only be guessed at, announces another desire, to stay with the other, repressed, areas of London. This duality suggests that despite the fascination with which it is described, London cannot quite be at the centre of *David Copperfield*, for this novel sides, ultimately, with the desire to make London a site for the successful individual, one of its most important differentiations from the later 'autobiographical' novel, *Great Expectations*. It is significant that the traumatic and affective episode to which the book leads – the drowning of Ham and Steerforth (chapter 55) – happens outside London.[17] Of course, it exceeds in scope the comic undoing of Uriah Heep in another out-of-London setting, at Canterbury (chapter 52).

On a strange compulsion, DC is drawn out of his Covent Garden lodgings, back to Yarmouth to encounter this trauma of the 'tempest'. But Yarmouth does not end things; DC must return Steerforth's body to London. The private tragedy of his relationship with the hero he has worshipped is brought into the very centre of his triumph as a novelist, in the respectable suburb of Highgate, the place of the earlier death of Dora (chapter 53), which is outclassed by the affective relationship with Steerforth, whose life and death frames Dora's. The aftermath of Dora's death is passed over; but there must be two farewells for Steerforth, one at Yarmouth sands, and the other when he is laid on the bed at Highgate. London does not have the signifying power of the seductive woman, but rather of the seductive male, which differentiates it from Paris, and gives to the Golden Cross, at Charing Cross, a different power of affect.

CHAPTER SEVEN

LONDON BEFORE THE LAW
Bleak House

I · LONDON AS ARCHIVE

Chapter 1: In Chancery

LONDON. Michaelmas Term lately over and the Lord Chancellor sitting in Lincoln's Inn Hall. Implacable November weather. As much mud in the streets, as if the waters had but newly retired from the face of the earth, and it would not be wonderful to meet a Megalosaurus, forty feet long or so, waddling like an elephantine lizard up Holborn-hill. Smoke lowering down from chimney-pots, making a soft black drizzle, with flakes of soot in it as big as full-grown snow flakes – gone into mourning, one might imagine, for the death of the sun. Dogs, undistinguishable in mire. Horses, scarcely better; splashed to their very blinkers. Foot passengers, jostling one another's umbrellas in a general infection of ill-temper, and losing their foot-hold at street corners, where tens of thousands of other foot passengers have been slipping and sliding since the day broke (if this day ever broke), adding new deposits to the crust upon crust of mud, sticking at those points tenaciously to the pavement, and accumu-lating at compound interest.

Fog everywhere. Fog up the river, where it flows among green aits and meadows; fog down the river, where it rolls defiled among the tiers of shipping, and the water-side pollutions of a great (and dirty) city. Fog on the Essex marshes, fog on the Kentish heights. Fog creeping into the cabooses of collier-brigs; fog lying out on the yards, and hovering in the rigging of great ships; fog drooping on the gunwales of barges and small boats. Fog in the eyes and throats of ancient Greenwich pensioners, wheezing by the firesides of their wards; fog in the stem and bowl of the afternoon pipe of the wrathful skipper, down in his close cabin; fog cruelly pinching the toes and fingers of his shivering little 'prentice boy on deck. Chance people on the bridges peeping over the parapets into a nether sky of fog, with fog all around them, as if they were up in a balloon, and hanging in the misty clouds.

Gas looming through the fog in divers places in the streets, much as the sun may, from the spongey fields, be seen to loom by husbandman and ploughboy. Most of the shops lighted before their time – as the gas seems to know, for it has a haggard and unwilling look.

The raw afternoon is rawest, and the dense fog is densest, and the muddy streets are muddiest, near that leaden-headed old obstruction, appropriate ornament for the threshold of a leaden-headed old corporation: Temple Bar. And hard by Temple Bar, in Lincoln's Inn Hall, at the very heart of the fog, sits the Lord High Chancellor in his High Court of Chancery.

So begins *Bleak House* (1852–53).[1] It puts 'London' at its head, like a dateline for a reporter (the unknown person who writes half of *Bleak House* in the present tense), or an address for a letter, or a stage-direction; it makes London the margin or border, from where action starts; but there will be no movement from the margin. The other half comes from Esther Summerson, where Dickens writes as a woman. Her past-tense narrative speaks of 'the unknown friend to whom I write' (67.985). In *Bleak House*, where London has a detective police-force, the 'great (and dirty) city' has its own fog, what Guppy calls a 'London particular' (OED gives only this citation for this phrase).[2] The novel, with its nine deaths (so Ruskin), makes London the centre for the law.[3] But that is imaged in Mr Krook's rag and bottle warehouse just off Chancery Lane, by Lincoln's Inn Hall, which takes in bones, kitchen-stuff, old iron, waste-paper, ladies and gentlemen's wardrobes. 'Everything seemed to be bought and nothing to be sold there' (5.67). London as waste. The action opens with the bored Lady Dedlock noticing the handwriting on a legal document (part of the interminable case of Jarndyce versus Jarndyce), and asking, 'impulsively; "who copied that?" ' (2.26). The solicitor, Mr Tulkinghorn, noting her animation, finds out who did; discovering it was the law-writer Nemo (no-one), whose name is an alias for Captain Hawdon, the soldier whom Lady Dedlock loved and had a child by (Esther Summerson) and then left. He lodges upstairs in the rag and bottle shop. But the solicitor finds him too late: the room has 'the bitter, vapid taste of opium', and the 'discoloured shutters are drawn together, and through the two gaunt holes pierced in them, famine might be staring down – the Banshee of the man upon the bed' (151). 'Banshee' suggests a reference to the Irish famine of 1846–52; starving Irish labourers being at the margins, here, as brick-makers, as inhabitants of the slum, Tom-All-Alone's.[4] What 'stares' is like a death's head. Death outside looks at the death inside; while the solicitor, later to be murdered, looks on, and will be stared at, in his turn, by the pointing allegorical Roman pictured in the ceiling above. Holborn suggests the hollow bone, the skull. Nemo's body furthers the sense of formlessness and lifelessness implicit in the novel's opening, including the landscape seen in rain in chapter 2. Old letters in Nemo's room, and so in the rag and bottle shop, which came from Lady Dedlock to him, indicate that he was her lover. The letters, when purloined, as happens after chapter 32, gone astray, give opportunity for blackmail, and drive Lady Dedlock to her death.

The novel is concerned with wasted places. Phiz's illustrations include the Frontispiece, showing Bleak House, 'The Ghost's Walk' at Chesney Wold, 'Tom-All-Alone's', and 'The Mausoleum at Chesney Wold'. Other pictures emphasise places not people: for example, 'A New Meaning in the Roman', where the dead body of Mr Tulkinghorn has been removed, and the picture shows his room. Draft titles for the novel evoke spoiled places. They were: *Tom-All-Alone's* (the first title; as a possibility it persisted for nine of the ten pages), and *The Ruined House*. A new page gave *Tom-All-Alone's* and *The Solitary House That Never Knew Happiness*, with the subtitle changed to *That Was Always Shut Up*. Then *Bleak House Academy* (the word 'academy' returns in the novel), then *The East Wind* are indicative. On page three of sheets of paper giving draft titles, *Tom-All-Alone's* was followed by *Building* followed by *Factory* followed by *Mill*, then came *The Ruined House that Got into Chancery and Never Got Out*. This is the first mention of Chancery. Page five tried the title *The Solitary House That was Always Shut Up* followed by *Never Lighted*, page 6: *The Ruined Mill that Got into Chancery and Never Got Out*, page seven: *The Solitary House Where the Wind Howled*. (This title suggests *Wuthering Heights* (1847).) Page eight gave the same as page six, but 'Mill' was crossed out and replaced by 'House'. Page nine gave the title – crossed out, but providing the heading for chapter 1 – *In Chancery*, following with the same title as for page eight. The last page dropped *Tom-All-Alone's*, and became *Bleak House and the East Wind: How they Both Got into Chancery and Never Got Out*, and then, *Bleak House*.

Where places are so much a crux, they are more to be marked. We note the presence of Tom-All-Alone's, and Chancery, become a place, not just a metaphor. The words 'building', 'factory' and 'mill' are suggestive, because they apply to a house – whether this is called 'Tom-All-Alone's' (inside London) or 'Bleak House' (outside London, at St Albans) – and to Chancery. Perhaps 'Alone' and 'London' link, London creating loneliness. The house has got into Chancery, like the East Wind, which blows from London's East End, is associated with industrial smells and disease. In these ideas of a house which gets into Chancery, the idea from 'Shops and their Tenants' (*SB*) is replayed of the shop that always fails. Chancery becomes the building, the factory and the mill, the ruined house or mill, as 'Bleak House' becomes a place to learn, an academy. Behind these titles is the image of a house which may be anywhere, but which is Chancery, building, factory and mill all together, and ruined, 'where the grass grew'. Because everything has got 'into Chancery' (note the distinction between 'in' and 'into'), everything is locked into a state of chance (the first page's 'chance people'), or of imprisonment (they have 'never got out'), so that Chancery is London, like Bleak House: the literal house may be outside London, but the literal is less important than its kinship with Tom-All-Alone's, inside.[5]

As the threshold to the novel, place-names that will be significant later in the text are here or implied. Though this novel obscures places and landmarks, because of the mud and the fog (which we discuss later), the opening of the book, already quoted, invokes Lincoln's Inn Hall, Holborn Hill, the river, Greenwich, and Temple Bar before circling back to its starting-point, Lincoln's Inn Hall, and the centre, Holborn.[6] In a novel whose argument turns on the power of the past, on things of 'precedent and usage', and on people who would turn back the clock, it is significant that these buildings record London's medieval existence. And the old, retired and disabled seamen at Greenwich Hospital, in prison-like 'wards', are also part of London's past and foreign wars; they also comprise London.

    Lincoln's Inn begins everything. A fourteenth-century foundation, its records go back to 1422, when it rented land belonging to the Bishop of Chichester (hence Chichester Rents in Chancery Lane), while its Hall was built in 1490 in Gothic style, and added to around 1624, with workmanship by Inigo Jones. Illustrated by Thomas Rowlandson, it was ornamented by Hogarth's painting: *Paul before Felix*, placed behind the Lord Chancellor's seat, commissioned by the Lord Mansfield of *Barnaby Rudge*. Hogarth used as text: 'And as [Paul] reasoned of righteousness, temperance, and judgement to come, Felix trembled' (Acts 24.25), and Ronald Paulson says the picture, rather than 'illustrating the biblical text, is about a bad lawyer, Tertullus [in the picture], and a bad judge, Felix, who can only be made to "tremble" by the words of the defendant himself'.[7] Because of the geographical placing of that 'leaden-headed old obstruction', another of the Inns of Court is alluded to in 'Temple Bar', which includes a punning reference to the 'bar': the law as exclusive, and excluding. Behind Lincoln's Inn Hall is Lincoln's Inn Fields, second of the first two London squares laid out by Inigo Jones, Covent Garden the first.[8]

    Bleak House begins with the Lord Chancellor having moved from Westminster Hall, where he sat for Michaelmas term, which began on 29 September, and lasted for a few weeks. He is now holding court in Lincoln's Inn Hall (now Old Hall): a practice which began in the eighteenth century. As if making the

New Hall, Lincoln's Inn Fields, 1845, designed by Philip Hardwick, replacing the Old Hall, where *Bleak House* opens.

action more ironically apocalyptic, the novel concludes the lawsuit in Westminster Hall (chapter 65), finishing inside term, not outside, as at the beginning. Westminster Hall, improved by Sir Charles Barry in his rebuilding of the
Houses of Parliament, is the only part of the Palace of Westminster which survived the fire of 1834.[9] It was begun by William the Second (1099) and altered
by Henry Yevele for Richard the Second (1399). Until 1882, when the Royal
Courts of Justice opened in the Strand, it housed the Law Courts, that is: the
Court of Chancery, which since the Judicature Act of 1873 had become a
division of the High Court of Justice; the Court of the King's Bench; the Court
of Common Pleas and the Court of the Exchequer. Chancery had been the
highest court of judicature next to the House of Lords. It was a court of common law, and a court of equity. The first issued writs, the other proceeded on
the basis of conscience, giving relief in cases where there was no remedy in
common-law courts. The first was a court of record, for archives.[10]

Archives, and their burning, are at the heart of *Bleak House*. At the end of
the first chapter, the papers are cleared away and the court locked up:

> If all the injustice it has committed, and all the misery it has caused, could only be
> locked up with it, and the whole burnt away in a great funeral pyre, – why, so much
> the better for other parties than the parties in Jarndyce and Jarndyce! (1.19)

The court could burn up, but this would not eliminate Jarndyce and Jarndyce,
because the files and papers have been removed, leaving an empty court.
There is a tendency towards self-destruction within the building, archive of
so much miserable history. Susan Shatto quotes Dickens' speech to the
Administrative Reform Society in 1855, drawing on the burning of the old
Houses of Parliament in 1834:

> I think we may reasonably observe, in conclusion, that all obstinate adherence to rub-
> bish which time has long outlived, is certain to have in the soul of it more or less that
> is pernicious and destructive; more or less that will some day set fire to something or
> other; more or less, which freely given to the winds would have been harmless, which
> persistently retained, is ruinous. (*Speeches* 206, quoted Shatto 34)[11]

Dickens anticipates the theme of Jacques Derrida in *Archive Fever*: that there
is something within an 'archive' – the place for official histories – that has a
tendency to destroy itself, something Derrida calls 'anarchivic' (against the
archive, or anarchic), or 'archiviolithic' (violating the archive from the beginning).[12] The death-drive, discussed in Freud's *Beyond the Pleasure Principle*,
on which Derrida draws, has a 'silent vocation' 'to burn the archive and to
incite amnesia' (*Archive Fever*, 12). That is *'le mal d'archive'*, the evil in the
archive. *Bleak House*'s London comprises an archive, which is self-combustible:
Mr Krook's shop becomes the symbol of the archive, and Krook's spontaneous
combustion (chapter 32) is the death-drive, 'archive fever', entropic, destructive.
In Phiz's illustration 'A New Meaning in the Roman', the finger of the allegorical
figure in the ceiling points down, not at Tulkinghorn, but at a stain, all that is

Example of restored Elizabethan buildings up Holborn Hill, with Staple Inn behind it. The griffin marks the City's westward limits. The later nineteenth century emphasised the black of the timbers: earlier photographs make no such stress on colour.

visible: everything disappears into mud, or the stain, or the dust (22.352), like houses falling (16.257). At the end, everything of Jarndyce versus Jarndyce has disappeared in costs: Miss Flite's birds, which her archiving has named, have been released, and presumably killed.

II · LEGAL LONDON

Bleak House's second place-name is 'Holborn Hill', which, parallel to Fleet Street and to the north of it, climbs up from the Fleet River. Walter Besant says of it that 'before the building of the Viaduct in 1869, there was a steep and toilsome descent up and down the valley of the Fleet. This was sometimes called "the Heavy Hill" . . . in consequence of the melancholy processions which frequently passed from Newgate bound Tyburn-wards, "riding in a cart up the Heavy Hill" became a euphemism for being hanged. From Farringdon Street to Fetter Lane was Holborn Hill, and Holborn proper extended from Fetter-Lane to Brook Street'.[13] The Megalosaurus, if coming westwards, uphill from the Fleet, would have passed sites of former Inns of Chancery, which from medieval times, served for the clerks working in the Chancery, and later for other attorneys and solicitors; some ten of them by 1470. Thavies Inn, seen in the second of Hogarth's 'Stages of Cruelty' (1750), and Barnard's Inn were on the south side, then Staple Inn, opposite the entrance of Gray's Inn Road. On the northern side was Furnival's Inn. Further west, left of Gray's Inn Road, is South Court, then Holborn Court, where Dickens worked from 1827 to 1828 as a clerk at the law-firm of Ellis and Blackmore: here Traddles lives as a lawyer (*DC* 59). Dickens' second workplace was for a few months at the law-firm of Charles Molloy at 8 New Square, Lincoln's Inn. His third was also associated with the law: it was as a freelance reporter for Doctors' Commons, so bridging the gap between law and journalism.

These Inns reappear throughout Dickens. In *Sketches by Boz*, 'The Steamboat Excursion' (October 1834), shows the law-student Percy Noakes, and his laundress. He makes up a committee with Mrs Taunton and her daughters – they live in the upper half of a house in Great Marlborough Street, south of Oxford Street (*SB* 441) – to arrange a steam excursion down the Thames. His base is Furnival's Inn, where Dickens was then living. Pickwick goes to Raymond Building in Gray's Inn to find Mr Perker, who has offices there (*PP* 10.138). He is diverted to the Magpie and Stump, in the vicinity of Clare Market, next to Lincoln's Inn Fields, 'closely approximating to the back of New Inn' (20.271). Clare Market, with its slums, was cleared for the building of Kingsway (1905); it had been established in the seventeenth century on land belonging to John Holles, Earl of Clare. It survives as a street-name (like

Crypt of St Mary-le-Bow, Cheapside; medieval London under Wren's church: showing a nave with two rows of columns with single-scallop capitals (Pevsner); still used for ecclesiastical trials; old home of the Archbishop of Canterbury's Court of Arches, until this moved to Doctors' Commons.

Entry to gatehouse of Clifford's
Inn, Fleet Street; appears in
Our Mutual Friend 1.8, when
John Harmon takes Mr Boffin
into the passage to speak to him.

New Inn and Clement's Inn). Sitting in the Magpie and Stump, Pickwick says,
"'Curious little nooks in a great place, like London, these old Inns are'" (20.273),
so drawing out old Jack Bamber's stories, about madness and suicide amongst
the law-students in these Inns, including one about Clifford's Inn (chapter 22).
They take the reader back to the beginning of the nineteenth century, and
donate to the Inns a history of madness and decay, dating back to their origins.

Thavies Inn appears as a street-name in *Bleak House* chapter 4, where
Mr Guppy takes Ada, Richard and Esther to it from Lincoln's Inn: "'We just twist
up Chancery Lane, and cut along Holborn, and there we are in four minutes'
time, as near as a toucher"'. The street, 'under an archway', is 'narrow . . . of
high houses, like an oblong cistern to hold the fog'. The Jellybys' untidiness
and squalor is associated with Chancery. After Mr Jellyby's bankruptcy, they
move to furnished lodgings in Hatton Garden (30.474); from the south side of
Holborn to the north. Barnard's Inn, named after a lawyer, and where Pip
lodges (*GE* 2.2), also belonged to Lincoln's Inn. Pip and Mr Wemmick walk
there from Little Britain. Barnard's Inn is reached through a wicket gate into
'an introductory passage into a melancholy little square that looked to me like
a flat burying-ground' containing half-a-dozen or so houses:

> I thought the windows of the sets of chambers into which these houses were divided,
> were in every stage of dilapidated blind and curtain, crippled flower-pot, cracked
> glass, dusty decay and miserable make-shift, while To Let To Let To Let, glared at me
> from empty rooms, as if no new wretches ever came there, and the vengeance of the

soul of Barnard were being slowly appeased by the gradual suicide of the present occupants and their unholy interment under the gravel. A frouzy mourning of soot and smoke attired this forlorn creation of Barnard, and it had strewn ashes on its head, and was undergoing penance and humiliation as a mere dust-hole. Thus far my sense of sight; while dry rot and wet rot and all the silent rots that rot in neglected roof and cellar – rot of rat and mouse and bug and coaching-stables near at hand besides – addressed themselves faintly to my sense of smell, and moaned, 'Try Barnard's Mixture'. (*GE* 21.173)

This decay recalls Satis House. One of the windows from Barnard's Inn, its sashes rotten, almost succeeds in guillotining Pip when he raises it: a more genteel, nineteenth-century replay of the disaster in *Tristram Shandy* (5.17) when the window comes down upon Tristram Shandy, with consequences for his masculinity. There is the same sense of impotence in these Inns.

Staple Inn exists behind a façade of sixteenth century shops, 'certain gabled houses some centuries of age' (*The Mystery of Edwin Drood* – which adds that they are 'as if disconsolately looking for the Old Bourne that has long run dry'). In 1792, Wordsworth stayed at Staple Inn, and three years later at Lincoln's Inn, noting 'the privileged regions and inviolate':

> Where from their airy lodges studious lawyers
> Look out on waters, walks, and gardens green. (*The Prelude* 7.187–88)

Dickens pairs Holborn with Cloisterham for nostalgic age.

Staple Inn is the chambers (offices and bedroom) of Mr Grewgious, who lives in a corner house in the inner quadrangle, with, over the 'ugly portal', the inscription 'PJT 1747':

> a little nook composed of two irregular quadrangles, called Staple Inn. It is one of those nooks, the turning into which out of the clashing street, imparts to the relieved pedestrian the sensation of having put cloth into his ears, and velvet soles on his boots. It is one of those nooks where a few smoky sparrows twitter in smoky trees, as though they called to one another, 'Let us play at country', and where a few feet of garden mould and a few feet of gravel enable them to do that refreshing violence to their understandings. Moreover, it is one of those nooks which are legal nooks, and it contains a little Hall, with a little lantern in its roof, to what obstructive purposes devoted, and at whose expense, this history knoweth not.
>
> In the days when Cloisterham took offence at the existence of a railroad afar off . . . in those days no neighbouring architecture of lofty proportions had arisen to overshadow Staple Inn. (*ED* 11.112–13)[14]

Furnival's Inn, an Inn of Chancery, ceased belonging to Lincoln's Inn in 1817. Dickens lived in its new buildings from 1834 to 1837. John Westbrook has lodgings there (*MC* 37). It included Woods hotel, where Mr Grewgious eats dinner. Staple Inn also houses Neville Landless (chapter 17) and Mr Tartar. When Rosebud flees to London from Jasper, he lodges her at Furnival's (chapter 20), before taking her to Mrs Billickin's lodgings in Southampton Street, Bloomsbury Square.

'Chambers' (*All the Year Round*, 18 August 1860; *The Uncommercial Traveller*), resumes the preoccupations of the narratives of Jack Bamber in *Pickwick Papers* chapter 21; the histories are instances of solitude. Gray's Inn is a 'strong hold of Melancholy' (*J4* 159), 'one of the most depressing institutions in brick and mortar known to the children of men'. Its 'arid Square, Sahara Desert of the law' evokes *Our Mutual Friend* on the space between Battle Bridge and Holloway – 'a tract of suburban Sahara' (*OMF* 4.42). Like the windows in Barnard's Inn, the staircases are rotten and falling in. 'Chambers' describes Mr Parkle living in dust in Gray's Inn Square, perhaps in Field Court, with the laundress, Mrs Miggot, whose squalor recalls the laundress in *Pickwick Papers* (20.270). Another narrative describes another bachelor, neighbour to Parkle. He finds four faults with life: 'firstly, that it obliged a man to be always winding up his watch, secondly, that London was too small; thirdly that it therefore wanted variety, fourthly that there was too much dust in it'. One evening the man tells Parkle that he is going out of town, for:

> What is a man to do? London is so small! If you go West, you come to Hounslow. If you go East, you come to Bow. If you go South, there's Brixton, or Norwood. If you go North, you can't get rid of Barnet. Then, the monotony of all the streets, streets, streets – and of all the roads, roads, roads – and the dust, dust, dust! (*J4* 164)

Before going he hands Parkle his watch. He returns to his room and hangs himself, and a suicide note asks that his body should be cut down by Parkle.

Before commenting on this, other episodes in 'Chambers' should be noted: the man who lives in 'a corner of the Temple', has a fit, and dies, on Christmas Eve, alone, while those in the chambers above assume that he is playing blind-man's buff, since he is making such a noise; and the officer from a South American regiment, who is in hiding in Lyon's Inn, on account of debts, and who tells a tale of the previous occupant, who had borrowed furniture from a disused cellar in Lyon's Inn, and was strangely accosted one night by the owner of the furniture, who thereafter disappeared. 'Chambers' concludes discussing laundresses' larcenous practices.

The words 'going out of town', a euphemism for suicide, make London equivalent to life; Hounslow, Bow, Brixton or Norwood, and Barnet are each Hamlet's 'bourne from which no traveller returns'. *Bar*net is, like Temple Bar, a barrier. Beyond it lies Bleak House (*BH* 6). London being so 'small', it resembles a prison, or a chamber in an Inn of Court or Chancery, which, thereby, become identified with London, and so with life. It repeats Mr Tulkinghorn's 'one bachelor friend' in *Bleak House*:

> a man of the same mould and a lawyer too, who lived the same kind of life until he was seventy-five years old [this man is fifty-five], and then suddenly conceiving (as it is supposed) an impression that it was too monotonous [the same word appears with Parkle's friend], gave his gold watch to his hair-dresser one summer evening, and walked leisurely home to the Temple, and hanged himself. (22.353)

The pun on 'mould' and the idea of suicide in 'the temple' are crucial. Parkle's and Tulkinghorn's friends show the desire to be free of clock-time, for London is measured by the clock, and winding the watch (a circular, mechanical motion, which takes over the character of these lawyers) illustrates city-existence as marked out by the divisions of clock-time. London suggests solitude, suicide, and, since all characters mentioned here are bachelors, sexlessness. These Chambers' attributes are 'Solitude, Closeness, and Darkness' (*J4* 169), and lack of imagination, apart from the 'whisper' heard about Clement's, 'how the black creature who holds the sun-dial there was a negro who slew his master and built the dismal pile out of the contents of the strong-box' (169).[15] The buildings seem to come out of one act of primal violence, repeating another (the enslaving of a man), and their suicidal tendencies – their archive fever – are therefore inbuilt.

Temple Bar is the last place in *Bleak House*'s opening. Removed to Hertfordshire (1878) and now sited north of St Paul's cathedral, it was built to Wren's design after 1670.[16] Like Holborn Bars, surviving as two stone obelisks, one at the corner of Gray's Inn Road, the other near Staple Inn's entrance, Temple Bar showed how the City of London in the thirteenth century had received legal authority to extend its control beyond the Roman City's bounds. It is a 'leaden-headed old obstruction, appropriate ornament for the threshold of a leaden-headed old corporation', that corporation being the City of London. 'Leaden-headed' evokes Leadenhall Street as central to the City. Temple Bar acts as threshold into both Holborn and *Bleak House* and Chancery, which, when described, produces the warning, 'Suffer any wrong that can be done you, rather than come here': Dickens' version of 'Lasciate ogni speranza, voi ch'entrate' – 'Leave all hope, you who here enter' – the inscription over Hell Gates in Dante's *Inferno* (canto 3 line 9).

Description of Holborn by the first narrator returns in chapter 10, several locales being distinguished. Mr Krook's rag and bottle shop, where Miss Flite and Nemo lodge, is thought to be in Star Yard, off Carey Street, which turns off to the left going up Chancery Lane from Fleet Street. Mr Snagsby's Law Stationery shop is in Cook's Court, i.e. Took's Court, off Cursitor Street, on the right. A cursitor was an officer of the court of Chancery; the post was abolished in 1835. The right side contained Serjeant's Inn, the Rolls Chapel, the Cursitor's office and Symonds' Inn, which contains the offices of Mr Vholes (39.620), while Richard Carstone moves in from Queen Square, Bloomsbury (18.283) to next door (51.780). Symonds' Inn, north of the Rolls Chapel, functioned as an inn between 1468 and 1540, but its buildings were pulled down only in 1873, 'and until that time the Inn housed a variety of offices, including those of the masters and registrar in Chancery, and the Affidavit Office, precursor to the Chancery Chambers Registry of today'.[17] Mr Snagsby likes walking in Staple Inn, behind Took's Court, and in the Rolls Yard, immediately south of Cursitor Street, which contained the Chancery Writ Office, supervised by the Master of the Rolls, the deputy to the Chancellor.[18] Antiquarian and local historian, he speculates on the presumed stone coffins under the Rolls Chapel.

The Snagsbys' servant, Guster (this novel's successor to the Orfling), was farmed out, as an orphan, to an asylum at Surrey Hall, Tooting, five miles south-west of Charing Cross.[19] Surrey Hall had been bought as a school in 1804, and sold, in 1825, to Peter and Richard Drouet. As with *Oliver Twist* 1.2, where orphans are farmed out, Peter Drouet contacted the Poor Law guardians of various London parishes, including Holborn, who sent children there from their workhouses, paying four shillings and sixpence per week, which Drouet pocketed. The children remained, officially, in the care of their Board of Guardians. The asylum held some 1,400 children, 200 of whom died through cholera between December 1848 and January 1849: their deaths were also blamed on the low-lying nature of Tooting, and the inadequacy of clothing and solid food for the children. After a coroner's jury returned a verdict of manslaughter, Drouet was tried but acquitted. Guster would have come from the Holborn workhouse, in the Gray's Inn Road, south of Elm Street.

Guster can see into 'Coavinses' the sheriff's officer's backyard', in Cursitor Street. The officer who arrests Skimpole for debt in chapter 6 threatens him with 'jail' or 'Coavinses', 'a 'ouse', a 'sponging house' where people arrested for debt were kept for twenty-four hours, while their property was gone over by the bailiffs.[20] In chapter 15, 'Bell Yard', Skimpole says that Coavinses is dead, and Jarndyce takes Ada and Esther to see his children. The house belonged to someone called Coavins, his officer, or 'follower', was Neckett, who lived in Bell Yard (running from Fleet Street to Carey Street). As Dickens had rented offices at 5 Bell Yard when working as a shorthand reporter at Doctors' Commons, the name suggests autobiography: on one side of Chancery Lane is the place of debt, and imprisonment; on the other, the place of work, for Charley (Charlotte) maintains her younger siblings (Tom and Emma) by being a washer-girl; and her name, if not her gender, is Dickens', who rescued his father from the 'ouse. Jarndyce and the others climb three flights of stairs to the top of the house, past Gridley who also lives there, his room 'covered with a litter of papers'. Two sides of the law come together: its concern for prop-erty and its power to hold those it possesses by making them write endless memorials, like Mr Dick's in *David Copperfield*.

Mr Snagsby tells his apprentices how he has heard that a brook 'clear as crystal' 'once ran down the middle of Holborn, when Turnstile really was a turnstile, leading slap away into the meadows'.[21] The language is apocalyptic: 'And he showed me a pure river of water of life, clear as crystal, proceeding out of the throne of God and of the Lamb. In the midst of the street of it, and on either side of the river was there the tree of life . . .' (Revelation 22.1, 2). Holborn becomes a City of God, new Jerusalem, or it makes the valley of the covered-over Fleet River an ironic, subterranean, river of life. The two approaches to Lincoln's Inn Fields from Holborn are Little and Great Turnstile, and, like Temple Bar, they were a means of preventing access to Lincoln's Inn Fields (called Fields, not meadows); it is as if Mr Snagsby is imagining that to the north of the turnstile were meadows, as if the area as far north as the turnstile is prisonous. The stream was either the Fleet, the bourne in the hollow, or a tributary of the Fleet, running down the street and into the Fleet (and referred to in *Edwin Drood*). In Snagsby, Dickens indicates the significance of seeing present-day London as the effect of the past. Thinking of the countryside reconciles Snagsby to his prison.

Higher up on the left of Chancery Lane is Old Square, where Kenge and Carboy have their offices. Esther arrives there from the coach from Reading which drops her at the White Horse Cellar in Piccadilly, at the corner of Down Street, which runs into Piccadilly from Mayfair. She is taken via 'the dirtiest and darkest streets that ever were seen' (presumably St Giles' Rookery, i.e. Tom-All-Alone's) to 'an old gateway' (in Chancery Lane itself) 'and drove on through a silent square [Old Square] until we came to an old nook in a corner, where there was an entrance up a steep broad flight of stairs, like the entrance to a church. And there really was a churchyard outside, under some cloisters, for I saw the gravestones from the staircase window' (3.42–3). Esther is delivered over several thresholds into Chancery, and sees an alliance between the law and the church: the law claiming a sacral character. In the same way, the psychoanalytic critic Norman O. Brown says 'the first city was a cathedral city' – so giving the city always, tendentially, a sacral character.[22] The alliance of the cathedral city with age appears with Cloisterham in *The Mystery of Edwin Drood*, while the cathedral's alliance with the law is the subject of Kafka's *The Trial*, especially the chapter, 'In the Cathedral'; here the priest's affinity with the law is obvious: he is the prison chaplain. In the same way, Mr Bucket is associated with the Temple by a pun: in the context of Mr Bucket using his forefinger, 'the Augurs of the Detective Temple invariably predict that when Mr Bucket and his forefinger are much in conference, a terrible avenger will be heard of before long' (53.803). The Augurs of Roman temples foretold the future. The detective force is called 'the Detective Temple', associating them with sacredness, with Holborn, with the authority of religion, and with mystique.[23]

Esther is escorted to Kenge and Carboy by the lawyer's clerk, William Guppy, whose upward mobility appears when in chapter 9 he proposes to Esther, saying he earns two pounds a week. He lodges at Penton Place, Pentonville (the area had gone down since Mr Brownlow's time); he goes home down Gray's Inn Road, and then right, up Pentonville Road. This continues past the Angel, where the road divides: Mr Micawber's City Road going east, Pickwick's Goswell Road right. Old Street turns left out of Goswell Road; there, Mr Guppy eats lobster and lettuce with his mother (20.316), and Esther and Caddy visit in chapter 38. By the end, Guppy has been admitted on the roll of attorneys, and rented a house in Walcot Square, Lambeth. Having six rooms, plus kitchen, he anticipates Jobling and his mother living in the house as well. The other clerk in Kenge and Carboy is Bart Smallweed, who lives at Mount Pleasant (21.332). Guppy's assistant, Jobling, seen in chapter 7 visiting Chesney Wold as a tourist with Guppy, comes from market gardens down by Deptford (20.317).[24] He lodges under the name of Weevle at Krook's, and, revealing the power of fashion to dictate popular visual culture, fills the room with reproductions of female beauties taken from 'The Divinities of Albion, or Galaxy Gallery of British Beauty'.

Tulkinghorn lives in the more spacious Lincoln's Inn Fields: perhaps Dickens draws on Forster's house, where he lived from 1834 to 1856, and on the adjacent Inigo Jones design: certainly, the house is Baroque:

> formerly a house of state . . . let off in sets of chambers now; and in these shrunken fragments of its greatness, lawyers lie like maggots in nuts. But its roomy staircases, passages, and ante-chambers still remain, and even its painted ceilings, where Allegory, in Roman helmet and celestial linen, sprawls among balustrades and pillars, flowers, clouds, and big-legged boys, and makes the head ache – as would seem to be Allegory's object always, more or less. (10.158)

Lincoln's Inn Fields; John Forster lived at no. 58, architect Henry Joynes (1730). Dickens read *The Chimes* there (1844) and drew on it for Tulkinghorn's house; no. 59, Lindsey House, now divided, was by Inigo Jones.

When seen in his apartment, his house and office, with one middle-aged man sitting outside in the hall in a pew (law and religion associated again), and no clerks, Tulkinghorn works out a problem, by moving about the round top of an inkstand and two broken bits of sealing-wax. He is creating, however unconsciously, a 'space of representation', as Lefebvre would say, like an architect in control. But actual spaces, in London, indicate an interconnectedness which is denied by the class-bound and socially constructed lives of people, which produce for each their own social space and limits of privacy. Tulkinghorn tells no-one anything: 'the middle-aged man in the Pew, knows scarcely more of the affairs of the Peerage, than any crossing-sweeper in Holborn'.

This is the text's first, indirect, reference to Jo, turned away as a witness at the inquest on Nemo, which was held at the Sol's Arms ('Sol' for the sun, and 'solicitor'). (Perhaps this was the Old Ship Tavern in Chichester Rents.) In chapter 16, Jo shows Lady Dedlock where Nemo is buried, with 'houses looking on it every side, save where a reeking little tunnel of a court gives access to the iron gates'. On 4 April 1868, Dickens wrote to a Boston philanthropist, Sarah Hammond Palfrey:

> Convey yourself back to London . . . and walk through the centre avenue of Covent Garden market from West to East: that is to say, with your back towards the church, and your face towards Drury Lane Theatre. Keep straight on along the side of the Theatre, and about half-way down, on the left side of the way, behind the houses, is a closely hemmed-in grave yard – happily long disused and closed by the Law. I do not remember that the grave-yard is accessible now, but when I was a boy it was to be got at by a low covered passage under a house, and was guarded by a rusty iron gate. In that churchyard I long afterwards buried the 'Nemo' of 'Bleak House'. (*Letters* 12.91)

The road out of Covent Garden is Russell Street, which meets Drury Lane past the theatre; the editors of the *Letters* say that this graveyard was that of St Martin-in-the-Fields. But the church must be St Mary-le-Strand, though the burial ground was technically in the parish of St Martin-in-the-Fields. The burial ground was closed in 1853.[25] Dickens makes the scene a memory of himself as a boy, as if identifying with Jo.

Before discussing this particular sacral, forbidden site, other London locations should be noted. Jarndyce, Ada and Esther take lodgings near Oxford Street 'over an upholsterer's shop' (13.202). Newman Street, then an artists' colony (see *The Newcomes* chapter 39; Benjamin West, Thomas Stodhard and John Russell had all lived here), runs north out of Oxford Street. Here, Prince Turveydrop, engaged to Caddy Jellyby, runs the Academy for teaching Deportment, which belongs to his father. When the son goes to teach at another school in Kensington, his father eats at the 'French house, in the Opera Colonnade', situated in Haymarket. That shows Mr Turveydrop's adherence to the Regency and dandy world of George the Fourth, whom he may even represent. *Nicholas Nickleby* calls it the resort of foreigners who live near Golden Square: the

Newman Passage, between
Newman Street (1746), north
of Oxford Street, and leading
into Rathbone Street, also early
eighteenth century: both streets
were artists' colonies, and
had been since the time of
Benjamin West (1738–1820),
who settled in London in 1763.

'dark-complexioned men who wear large rings, and heavy watch-guards and
bushy whiskers, and who congregate under the Opera colonnade, and about
the box-office in the season, when Mr Seguin gives away the orders' (*NN* 2.22).
Arthur Seguin sang in Italian opera until he emigrated to America in 1838: the
'orders' were free tickets.

Mr George likes south London: in chapter 21, he crosses Waterloo Bridge,
going to Philip Astley's theatre in Westminster Bridge Road. And in chapter 27,
passing the 'cloisterly' Temple, and Whitefriars, and Blackfriars Bridge, and
Blackfriars Road, he gets into the Elephant and Castle area, where Mr and
Mrs Bagnet have a musical-instrument shop. The area is about to lose its status
as at the meeting point of roads from Surrey and Kent and from the bridges of
London, to the train, the 'iron monster': a form of modernisation more intense
than Nash's rebuilding of the West End (27.438, compare 53.839). After enjoying
Astley's, Mr George recrosses the Thames, returning to the region around the
Haymarket and Leicester Square:

> which is a centre of attraction to indifferent foreign hotels and indifferent foreigners,
> racket-courts, fighting-men, swordsmen, footguards, old china, gaming-houses, exhib-
> itions, and a large medley of shabbiness and shrinking out of sight.

He arrives 'by a court and a long whitewashed passage at a great brick building composed of bare walls, floor, roof-rafters, and skylights, on the front of

Royal Opera Arcade, the work
of John Nash, parallel to the
Haymarket: home of dandyism,
but after Beau Brummell
(1778–1840), who left
England in 1816.

which, if it can be said to have any front, is painted GEORGE'S SHOOTING
GALLERY ETC' (21.350).

Perhaps Dickens remembered Green's Shooting Gallery, in Savile House,
a seventeenth-century mansion which went through various tenants. Around
1840 it housed Miss Linwood (1755–1845)'s exhibition of embroideries of
famous paintings, and a shooting gallery where Edward Oxford practised
before trying to shoot Victoria on Constitution Hill in 1840 (he was sent to
Bedlam, and later Australia).[26] *Bleak House* chapter 26 returns to a description
of Leicester Square on a wintry morning, and its 'tributary channels', and its
foreign population, 'a colony of brigands', exiles from various countries who
parade themselves as gentlemen. Flora Tristan (1803–44), whose *London
Journal*, written after visiting Britain in 1839, appeared as *Promenades dans
Londres* (1842), discusses the habit of the French in London, playing on the
English 'mania for titles', so styling themselves as barons, counts and mar-
quises; 'many are suspected of being in the pay of the French government and
the police are said to keep an eye on the movements of republican refugees
in London. The rest of them are fashionable society gentlemen trying quite
simply to make a living'.[27]

Leicester Square shares a name with Sir Leicester, a gentleman, established,
old and, though very English, a Paris habitué. These figures, Flora Tristan's
'foreigners who possess no capital or credit, no profession or trade' (Tristan 30),
question Sir Leicester's separateness, while Leicester Square indicates a part

of London that is the antithesis of him. Chesney Wold and Leicester Square, however contrasted, are linked by Mr George, born at one, living in the other. Mr George describes his countryside origins to Phil Squod, who has never seen the country, but recalls, aged eight, meeting a tinker at Clerkenwell, and becoming one himself in locations which recall *Oliver Twist*: Saffron Hill, Hatton Garden, and 'Smiffeld' (21.420). The shooting gallery is for men practising in the dying days of duelling; but the only shot fired comes from a foreign woman, Mlle Hortense, antithesis of Sir Leicester and the Leicester Square types. She focuses the possibility of revolution, which Sir Leicester dreads as he recalls Wat Tyler (2.26); revolution is not forgotten when, with reference to Mr Skimpole, who lives in the Polygon in Somers Town, so ghosting the Dickens family, Esther notes that the area has poor Spanish refugees staying there (43.672). They arrived after 1823, when Ferdinand VII's victory in the Battle of Trocadero made him revoke Spain's liberal constitution, and assert absolute rule. The name of Piccadilly Circus' restaurant, the Trocadero (1896), often rebuilt, suggests how cities adopt place-names which abolish the separateness of places, for the London Trocadero adopted its name from the Paris Trocadero, so perpetuating the memory of revolution's defeat.

III · CONSECRATED GROUND

In chapter 16, the narrator describes Tom-All-Alone's. It is where Jo lives, and, as St Giles' Rookery, was discussed when looking at *Sketches by Boz*. Jo emerges from it in the morning, to eat his breakfast on the doorstep of the Society for the Propagation of the Gospel in Foreign Parts. This had been founded in 1701, and until 1835, when it moved to Pall Mall, had its headquarters at 77 Great Queen Street, which, though now divided by Kingsway from Lincoln's Inn Fields, then led into it from the north-west corner. Its other end leads into Drury Lane. In chapter 10, the areas of Cook's Court and Lincoln's Inn Fields were connected by reference to a crow flying; chapter 16 also unites separate areas. It opens with Sir Leicester Dedlock pained with gout at Chesney Wold in Lincolnshire, looking at the portrait of Lady Dedlock, who has 'flitted away' to stay at the London town-house. The question is asked:

> What connexion can there be, between the place in Leicestershire, the house in town, the Mercury in powder [the servant at the town-house, with powdered hair], and the whereabouts of Jo the outlaw [note the pun: outside legal London] with the broom, who had that distant ray of light upon him when he swept the churchyard step? What connexion can there have been between many people in the innumerable histories of this world who, from opposite sides of great gulfs, have, nevertheless, been very curiously brought together! (16.256)

Dombey and Son chapter 47 indicated how Dickens' novels are fascinated by establishing connections. *David Copperfield* cannot quite connect; Steerforth and Heep, as two alternative forces in DC's life, never meet, and Dora is separate from both. But *Bleak House* starts with disconnection (two narratives, including one autobiography, from a Dame Trot whose name continues from Trotwood Copperfield) and enforces connections through London, and the contiguity of its streets. Tom-All-Alone's is near Lincoln's Inn, separated by less than the distance of Queen Street, and not separated in any other sense, since the property of Tom-All-Alone's is in Chancery, and part of the Jarndyce case. On the other side of Holborn Hill lies Smithfield, alluded to through reference to blinded oxen being brought in on market-day. The rookery, legal London and the meat-market are contiguous. Chapter 16 passes over the day, and moves to Tulkinghorn in his chambers, a little south of Jo. He is meditating on a writ against Gridley. Allegory above him (it contrasts with the Mercury in powder at the Dedlock town-house, whose classical and allegorical name makes him a messenger of death) seems to indicate 'with the arm of Samson' – another allegorical, biblical, figure – that Tulkinghorn should look out of the window. A lady, Lady Dedlock disguised as Hortense, is looking for Jo, to ask him about Nemo, and to get him to take her, as if he was the Mercury, to the sites associated with Nemo. They visit Cook's Court, Krook's house, the public house, and then take 'a longer walk' to the pauper graveyard.

Phiz's picture, 'Consecrated Ground', shows how the graveyard level has reached to half-way up the window of a house, as indicated by the height of the man who is seen through the house window. The half-legible word 'MINCING' under the picture of a mincing-machine, and a bullock in another picture suggest the carnivorous state of things here; a death's head on one of the tombstones, a visual emblem or allegory, looks towards the reader. If the word on the tombstone on the left is MEMO, that may pun on NEMO, implying how much this novel concerns remembering, which is what Esther's autobiography does. The lady disappears, and the chapter ends with two paragraphs. The first, in the style of the newspapers' 'fashionable intelligence' announces that 'The Mercury in powder is in no want of society to-night, for my Lady goes to a grand dinner, and to three or four balls'. The last returns to Sir Leicester at Chesney Wold, and to Mrs Roucewell's comments to Rose on the ghostly step upon the Ghost's Walk.

The Mercury in powder, in permanent disguise (eighteenth-century costume) is outdone by Lady Dedlock in disguise, by Jo, another Mercury, and Allegory, as attendant upon Tulkinghorn, himself another allegory of death. Allegory gives warning, like the footsteps on the Ghost's Walk, but the lawyer cannot see it; his destiny being not to see the woman in time, as later (chapter 48, immediately after Jo's death) he fails to see the woman who shoots him (his meeting with her in chapter 42 anticipates that). Jo leading Lady Dedlock through London is another form of allegory, pointing forwards: in Phiz's picture, pointing towards the grave. (And he does point forward: Jo, his death hinted at in this chapter, dies before Lady Dedlock does.) Dickens' number-plan for instalment no. 5 ends: 'Jo. *Shadowing forth of Lady Dedlock at the churchyard.*

Pointing hand of Allegory – consecrated ground "Is it Blessed?"'. The 'shadowing forth' makes Phiz's 'Consecrated Ground' an anticipation, or a figuring forth of when Lady Dedlock is found dead at the entrance to the churchyard. 'Pointing hand of Allegory' makes Allegory and the boy both allegorical, and suggests that not only is this churchyard 'consecrated ground', sacral, but so is all the area covered in the chapter; even if 'blessed' (Lady Dedlock's word) also means 'cursed', or 't'othered' (Jo's word). The ghost's walk of the end of the chapter recalls the language of how Nemo is buried 'to be an avenging ghost at many a sick bedside, a shameful testimony ... how civilization and barbarism walked this boastful island together' (11.180). It draws on the death of Lady Dedlock, which Phiz shows in 'The Morning', accompanying chapter 59.

The differences between 'Consecrated Ground' and 'The Morning' are several. In the first, the view is from the inside of the churchyard looking out, showing Lady Dedlock and Jo on the threshold of this consecrated place, but barred, as this novel is full of thresholds which bar. In the other, the view is from the exterior, looking towards the gateway, and showing the woman dead upon the steps, emphasising her exclusion from what she wants, identification with the dead lover. The gate's bars separate her from the sacred place, like Temple Bar; but her right arm extends through them, pointing towards the grave the finger showed before. In both pictures, the lamp above the gate is shown, but in the earlier, the light comes not from it but behind the two living figures who are looking in, as if the light points the way to the unseen tomb. Below the boy's finger a tombstone can be seen with the word 'sacred' upon it; indicating not just the irony of the poverty and the degradation, but that sacredness and waste must be seen as identifiable. London, its people and locales, has been 'connected' through the writing, and through these pointing fingers, to which may be added the finger of Mr Bucket, 'comparing fore-fingers' with Allegory (53.803) when searching Tulkinghorn's chambers. The policeman also makes connections, but the difference between his finger and the others is that his mode is accusatory, and objectifying, reducing the person to whom he points to the position of death.

IV · 'MUDFOG'

Bleak House compares with Kafka's novel, *The Trial* (*Der Process*), which is not so much the record of a single instance, or event, but the ongoing 'process' continuing throughout that text, and which, it seems, Josef K., arrested by the Court, pulls towards its conclusion: his own death. In 1916, Kafka published a short story, 'Before the Law', included in *The Trial*'s 'In the Cathedral' chapter. Here a man comes up from the country, and requests admittance to the law. Admission is never gained, but always delayed, deferred. The man is at the threshold of the law all his life, just as *Bleak House* is the novel of the threshold.[28]

Kafka may have taken the idea of the man from the country from *Bleak House* chapter 1, where the man from Shropshire (Mr Gridley) is seen trying to get access to Chancery. Since the men in *Bleak House* and *The Trial* have been drawn to the city for law, law becomes associated with the urban, as outside the sphere of nature, but instead, the place of money-making, of accumulation.

'Before the Law' is a parable in and of *The Trial*. In the novel, the story is continued by commentaries by the Priest and Josef K. on the various existing commentaries on it. It seems that interpretation, which is subsequent to the narrative, is part of it. Or, carrying that statement over to consider the process whereby the law establishes its meaning, as the Priest says about the trial, 'the judgment isn't simply delivered at some point; the proceedings gradually merge into the judgment'.[29] Perhaps there is no conclusion to be reached because the text cannot be, finally, interpreted. As the priest tells Josef K., 'the text is immutable, and the opinions are often only an expression of despair over it' (220). There is a symbiotic relationship between text and commentary, whereby the one becomes the other, or, to put it in other terms, the event becomes its representation. So a trial and literature duplicate each other, for the process of law and of literature involves a glossing of earlier documents, and the meaning of the text is never complete, but always in process, always commented on. And the same applies to London, a text never completed, but always in change; there is never an authentic London, nor can it provide a beginning for a text.

The law, as text, may be immutable, but its existence is not the less impossible. Literature cannot begin from a position of authority, any more than *The Trial* can, since it starts: 'Someone must have slandered Josef K., for one morning, without having done anything truly wrong, he was arrested' (3). No authority: the beginning of literature seems to be someone – name not disclosed – telling lies about Josef K. – name not fully disclosed. Secrecy and the absence of authority, absence of legitimation, for which the law substitutes, begins narrative.

Similarly, *Bleak House* begins with 'London', but the appearance of an originating authority that that might give, of a stable, enduring place, is erased by the rest of that paragraph. London is only mud, indescribable, formless waste, reaching up to the blinkers of the horses. Perhaps 'mud' evokes 'muddle' and so the tangle of texts and papers that must be interpreted: as Krook says about himself and the Lord Chancellor, 'we both grub on in a muddle' (5.70). But 'mud', while implying 'papers' is also real, as if it is consequent on the waters of some primeval flood retiring, where the landscape now only supports the Megalosaurus, an animal named in 1824 (OED credits Richard Owen (1804–92) in 1841 for 'dinosaur'). Dinosaur models were made by Benjamin Waterhouse Hawkins (1807–89), sculptor and natural history artist, who worked at the Hyde Park Great Exhibition of the Works of all Nations in 1851, the first of those world fairs which Benjamin, thinking of the equivalent Paris Exhibition

Dinosaurs, Crystal Palace Park, Sydenham.

of 1855 calls 'places of pilgrimage to the commodity fetish' (*Arcades* 17). When Joseph Paxton's Crystal Palace moved to Sydenham Hill, South London, reopening in 1854, Hawkins contributed thirty-three dinosaurs for its exhibition space.[30] But dinosaurs in *Bleak House* are in their proper sphere. The pre-human flood has smoke 'lowering down', making a 'soft black drizzle', in the place of rain, supplemented by flakes of soot, replacing snowflakes. These, in another conceit, have 'gone into mourning, one might imagine, for the death of the sun'. This apocalyptic event which, like a flood, ends humanity, locates the action of *Bleak House* in an impossible time, post-catastrophe, outside time, after an undescribed term which is 'lately over', where nothing happened. In this London, where there is rain, as implied by umbrellas (another form of black shading, and another form of mourning), and where a 'general infection' also implies the imminent apocalyptic, the paragraph ends with myriads of indistinguishable 'foot passengers *losing* their foot-*hold* . . . adding new *deposits* to the crust upon crust of mud ['crust' returns to the language of geology], sticking at those points tenaciously to the pavement, and *accumulating* at *compound interest*'. The italicisations reveal the invisible presence of money in the paragraph, and in London, and identify money with excremental mud. Increments (compound interest) and excrements (the people identified with the street's waste) seem identical.

Glossing that, we should return to Norman O. Brown discussing the city as the place of bourgeois capital, where the accumulation of money denies a relationship or responsibility to the other (the opposite of gift-giving), which is expressed in how sexuality is sublimated (diverted) into accumulation:

> The city is a deposit of accumulated sublimation, [the evasion of the sexual] and by the same token a deposit of accumulated guilt. The process of expiation . . . has been reified and passes into piles of stone and gold and many things besides. Hence a city is itself, like money, *crystallised guilt* . . . But guilt is time: 'In the city time becomes visible' says [Lewis] Mumford. In monumental form, as money or as the city itself, each generation inherits the ascetic achievements of its ancestors . . . as a bet to be paid by further accumulation of monuments . . . every city has a history and a rate of interest. (Brown 248, my emphasis)

Alienation in the city includes the point that it puts a price on time, measuring time out, making it part of acquisitiveness; hence the suicides we have mentioned hand back their watches. Alienation creates the 'general infection of ill temper', expressed in the first paragraph by the sense of people dominated by the city which has turned into its ruin, into mud; sliding around in what the mud, and the city, both allegorise: money. London is no place for people. An archive of 'crystallised guilt', London is burnt out, like the sun. In the second paragraph it has disappeared through 'fog everywhere', encompassing London (Essex, Kent); up the river where it 'flows' (both river and fog flow) to corrupt green 'aits and meadows', such as Brentford Ait, or Isleworth Ait, islands in the Thames, and 'down the river where it rolls defiled among the tiers of shipping, and the waterside pollutions of a great (and dirty) city'. The ambiguity of 'it' identifies the river with the fog, and makes the river stain the fog, defile it, as the fog defiles what it touches. The contrast between 'flows' and 'rolls' makes the fog, like the Thames, flowing where the river is not tidal, above Teddington Lock, rolling where it is. Such connection between river and fog makes London inseparable from its fog, which is its non-representable being. And 'at the very heart of the fog sits the Lord High Chancellor in his high Court of Chancery'. The sentence is ambiguous. The Lord Chancellor is there, certainly. But the heart of the fog is, definitionally, nothing; the more it is penetrated, the more its being is nothing, only dirt that stains, like the non-body of the allegorical Lord Chancellor, Krook, or the stain on Tulkinghorn's floor. Law and fog are expressions of each other, and the introduction ends with extending the fog's universality to the law:

> This is the Court of Chancery; which has its decaying houses and its blighted lands in every shire; which has its worn-out lunatic in every madhouse, and its dead in every churchyard, which has its ruined suitor, with his slipshod heels and threadbare dress, borrowing and begging through the round of every man's acquaintance. (1.13)

What has no authority, or reality, other than that of fog, has disastrous effects. The law's omnipresence extends to *The Trial*, when Josef K. is told by the painter Titorelli that his attic, his studio, is part of the law court: 'there are law court offices in practically every attic' (164).

Why does Dickens move from a London that has vanished in mud and fog, to the law, so that to be before the law – as we are, in the first three paragraphs – is to be in the fog? In *The Trial*, the law works to secure guilt, but while it creates guilt, it looks out for it: as Willem, the warder who has come to arrest Josef K., says at the beginning, 'our department, as far as I know, and I know only the lowest level, doesn't seek out guilt among the general population, but, as the Law states, is attracted by guilt, and has to send us guards out' (8–9). So Tulkinghorn and Bucket do not go after crime, but after guilt, which law is drawn to, and which it finds appealing, including, doubtless, sexually appealing. Perhaps that accounts for the new 'indefinable freedom in Tulkinghorn's manner' (48.744) in seeing Lady Dedlock for what he does not know will be the last time, when he knows her secret.

Guilt, for Freud, is 'the most important problem in the development of civilisation'.[31] Yet, if law is attracted into being by guilt, guilt cannot arise without the law causing it. Norman O. Brown calls the city the place of guilt which is not acknowledged because it is the place of those who admit no responsibility – no connection – to the other; yet, following Kafka, guilt attracts the law. Lady Dedlock, who has denied her relationship to Hawdon, 'so long accustomed to suppress emotion, and keep down reality, so long schooled . . . in that destructive school which shuts up the natural feelings of the heart, like flies in amber' (55.851), becomes 'before the law' as its subject, drawn into it. Like all the innocents of *Bleak House*, Esther Summerson feels 'guilty yet innocent' (3.31). Illegitimate, she is alone, having no relative 'in law', though she has in actuality. With no name of the father to appeal to, she is 'before the law', outside it. She is as much 'Nemo' as her father, even if she does not bear his name legally, nor know she bears it allegorically. But she is also 'before the law', like John Jarndyce, saying, 'we can't get out of the suit on any terms, for we are made parties to it, and *must* be parties to it, whether we like it or not' (7.119). Or, as Miss Flite, 'the little mad old woman' who constantly comes 'before the law', trying, literally, to look into it (1.15) says about the court: 'there's a cruel attraction in the place. You *can't* leave it. And you *must* expect' (35.566). Derrida would name this being '*en mal d'archive*: in need of archives'. That implies 'burning with a passion. It is never to rest, interminably, from searching for the archive right where it slips away. It is to run after the archive, even if there's too much of it, right where something in it anarchives itself' (*Archive Fever* 91). Desire for the archive is for memory, narrative, that which will affirm an identity for the nameless; the irony is that the archive burns itself up, like the one who needs it.

The law is attracted to guilt, Miss Flite is attracted to law, as if to the archive. She says what she does because she wants a judgment, which would, legally, establish guilt, or, in novelistic terms, secure an ending. But desiring a judgment implies being *en mal d'archive*, possessing an unattributable guilt which is felt as unease. Miss Flite has been caught by the lure of the law, which is attracted to her type. Legal London, consecrated ground, is attracted to the guilt it blights.[32] It cannot be moved away from; to be before the law is to be before London, possessed by it. The 'it' in law and in London, which causes and desires guilt, is non-substantial, like fog. Dickens' texts are structured by characters' compulsion to come to London, or leave, yet return, or inability to leave, or need to stay within calling-distance. Compulsion towards an absent centre, whose existence nevertheless devastates the subject, is part of London's fascination.

(*Left*) Seventeenth-century stone gateway on College Hill, City, adjacent to Dick Whittington's mansion and the church (St Michael Paternoster) where he founded a college (1423). (*Right*) Queen Anne (1702) houses, St Laurence Pountney Hill; the style is that for the Clennam house (*LD* 1.3.45).

(*Below*) Originally two late seventeenth-century brick houses, much altered, facing away from the river; the one on the left has a shopfront to its side, not visible here: a possible inspiration for the Clennam house in *Little Dorrit*, photographed from St Laurence Pountney churchyard: fourteenth-century church destroyed in 1666.

CHAPTER EIGHT

LONDON AND TABOO
Little Dorrit

It was a Sunday evening in London, gloomy, close and stale. Maddening church bells of all degrees of dissonance, sharp and flat, cracked and clear, fast and slow, made the brick-and-mortar echoes hideous. Melancholy streets in a penitential garb of soot, steeped the souls of the people who were condemned to look at them out of windows, in dire despondency. In every thoroughfare, up almost every alley, and down almost every turning, some doleful bell was throbbing, jerking, tolling, as if the Plague were in the city and the deadcarts were going around. Everything was bolted and barred that could by possibility furnish relief to an overworked people. No pictures, no unfamiliar animals, no rare plants or flowers, no natural or artificial wonders of the ancient world – all *taboo* with that enlightened strictness, that the ugly South Sea gods in the British Museum might have supposed themselves at home again. Nothing to see but streets, streets, streets. Nothing to breathe but streets, streets, streets. Nothing to change the brooding mind, or raise it up. Nothing for the spent toiler to do but to compare the monotony of his seventh day with the monotony of his six days, think what a weary life he led, and make the best of it – or the worst, according to the probabilities.

At such a happy time, so propitious to the interests of religion and morality, Mr Arthur Clennam, newly arrived from Marseilles by way of Dover and by Dover coach the Blue-eyed Maid, sat in the window of a coffee-house on Ludgate Hill. Ten thousand responsible houses surrounded him, frowning heavily on the streets they composed [. . .] What secular want could the million or so human beings whose daily labour, six days in the week, lay among these Arcadian objects, from the sweet sameness of which they had no escape between the cradle and the grave – what secular want could they possibly have upon their seventh day? Clearly they could want nothing but a stringent policeman.

Mr Arthur Clennam took up his hat and buttoned his coat, and walked out [. . .]

He crossed by St Paul's, and went down, at a long angle, almost to the water's edge, through some of the crooked and descending streets which lie (and lay more crookedly and closely then) between the river and Cheapside. Passing, now the mouldy hall of some obsolete Worshipful Company, now the illuminated windows of a Congregationless Church that seemed to be waiting for some adventurous Belzoni to dig it out, and discover its history; passing silent warehouses and wharves, and here and there a narrow alley leading to the river, where a wretched little bill, FOUND DROWNED, was weeping on the wet wall, he came at last to the house he sought. An old brick house, so dingy as to be all but black, standing by itself within a gateway. Before it, a square court-yard, where a shrub or two and a patch of grass were as rank (which is saying much) as the iron railings enclosing them were rusty; behind it, a jumble of roots. It was a double house, with long, narrow, heavily-framed windows. Many years ago, it had had it in its mind to slide down sideways; it had been propped up, however, and was leaning on some half-dozen gigantic crutches . . .

He went up to the door, which had a projecting canopy in carved work, of festooned jack-towels and children's heads with water on the brain, designed after a once-popular monumental pattern; and knocked. (1.3.43–47)

I · THE CITY

Little Dorrit (1855–57) is Dickens' only novel named after a woman.[1] A geography can be constructed from a strong collection of women in the novel, who divide up London between them. Little Dorrit and her sister Fanny in Southwark, and Maggy as well, Mrs Clennam in the City and even Affery, Mrs Plornish, Flora Finching and Mr F.'s Aunt in Holborn, Mrs Merdle in Harley Street, Cavendish Square in Marylebone, Miss Wade and Tattycoram in Mayfair, and Mrs Gowan in Hampton Court, the *ultima Thule* of this London: these women give images to help read the city, and added reason for noting the text's dominant emotions. From the passage quoted above, these are: melancholy, mourning, depression and despair, or what Mr Plornish calls 'melancholy madness' (1.12.157), which may be anger, sometimes suppressed. This is the novel where Miss Wade writes autobiographically about not being a fool, about having an unhappy temper, and where she acknowledges her love-affair with

Harley Street, north of Cavendish Square.

Henry Gowan (like Rosa Dartle with Steerforth) which leaves her wanting revenge. Flora Finching's talk recalls the Mrs Nickleby-type comedy of speech in free-association; it amalgamates Dickens' mother (as seen in Mrs Nickleby) and Maria Beadnell, Dickens' early love, but provokes consideration of Flora as one whose life was ruined by her father, and her husband. Flora's talk's madness shields from worse madness, like that of Mr F.'s Aunt. Mrs Clennam, self-imprisoned, self-torturing, justifies herself in telling her story, and her confession temporarily makes her regain use of her limbs.

These angry and repressed emotions relate to the description of London on Sunday evening, riddled by images of its prisonous nature, which laments the absence of nature and art in the city, all 'taboo'.[2] 'Taboo' is credited by OED to Captain Cook (1728–79) for its first use in English in 1777, and said then to mean 'that a thing is forbidden'; OED associates it with a word used in the Tonga islands, making it Polynesian, like the South Sea gods.[3] In *David Copperfield*, Mr Micawber says he 'has been under a Taboo' in Uriah Heep's service: a state of enforced self-repression (*DC* 49.717). Freud's *Totem and Taboo* (1913) associates the taboo with such words as 'sacred', 'consecrated', 'uncanny', 'dangerous', 'forbidden' and 'unclean'.[4] 'Totem', which associates with the American Indian tribes, is of similar date for first appearing in English (OED: between 1760 and 1776). For the European imagination, South Sea gods would be totemic objects. A totem is tabooed, and its existence creates a taboo, but a taboo, as an agent of law, creates the idea of a totem, something sacral, untouchable. It is not possible to establish primacy here; without a taboo, there cannot be a totem, without a totem, no taboo. Totem and taboo are similar concepts, even if Freud constructs a narrative of how the totem (representing the father, and patriarchal authority) comes into being.[5]

Dickens' word 'ugly' to describe these gods is an unfortunate part of a nearly-inevitable Eurocentric aspect to the text, even though the word is implicitly saying that it is London which is really facially ugly. But 'ugly' invokes these gods as tabooed figures, untouchable, sources of 'strictness' (the manuscript reading is 'rigidity', a word associating with Mrs Clennam). The taboo is apparent in everything being 'bolted and barred'. A series of prisons are contained in a prison, and the law watches over it. *Little Dorrit* calls the lawyer Bar, a contraction of Temple Bar, which Mr Dorrit passes under going to Mrs Clennam (2.17.652). Bar also suggests Barnacle, who as a member of the ruling class, is, as Bar says, talking to him, 'in the innermost sanctuary of the temple' (2.12.585). Temples and Bars come together, interchangeable. In chapter 3, London as prison is associated with the British Museum, which was also closed on Sundays (it began Sunday opening in 1896).[6] The prison is also associated with religion, through the gods in the museum – like a temple – who issue the taboos. Taboos extend over ordinary people who can do nothing on the seventh day for relief from previous days, and they make the prison the place of the taboo: it has a religious force, so that those inside are set apart, made sacred, consecrated by their confinement. Being in prison means being under a taboo, while the existence of prisons secures the power of the taboo, reifies it, makes it visible. The city is the taboo place as much as its prisons are. People must make the 'best of things', or 'the worst', presumably suicide, itself tabooed. This writing permits no engagement with people, who are, rather, treated as separate objects. Clennam is called 'Mr Arthur Clennam' three times during the passage, as though he had never been introduced before. Alienation in the city means being under a taboo.

Arthur goes to his mother's house, in present-day Upper Thames Street (that part of Thames Street west of London Bridge), perhaps by Botolph Lane (named after St Botolph Billingsgate, one of fourteen churches not rebuilt after the Fire). The house is, essentially, opposite the Marshalsea, on the Thames south bank. Rain falls: indeed this novel associates London with rain (see chapters 9, 14, 17, 29), adding poignancy to the posters with FOUND DROWNED 'weeping' on the walls, a notice proleptic for the female suicide, the prostitute, seen by Amy and Maggy wandering London (1.14.191), and disappearing with a 'strange wild cry' like a Dantean damned soul.[7] 'Weeping' suits London in black, mourning, like the snow melting slowly on the Clennam house: 'you should see [snow] there for weeks, long after it had changed from yellow to black, slowly weeping away its grimy life' (1.15.194–95). Mourning and melancholia combine.

Clennam crosses the City from its west (Ludgate Hill) towards its southern limit. He approaches his mother's house from Cheapside, passing signs of the City, which, being called 'Worshipful', are given a religious sanction. As churches only waiting 'for some adventurous Belzoni', they are like the pyramids at Giza which Belzoni (1778–1823) excavated; his drawings and models of Thebes were exhibited in 1821 at the Egyptian Hall, at no. 22 Piccadilly (William Bullock's private museum, built in 1812, and pulled down in 1905. The hall also contained South Sea island figures, which Cook had brought back). The image of Belzoni excavating, used before in Boz's description of Seven Dials (SB 92), adds point to the repeated going 'down', and makes all the buildings mausoleums, like the British Museum. Later, in Rome, Little Dorrit hunts out the ruins of Rome, as images of 'the ruins of the old Marshalsea' (2.15.639). The Marshalsea had closed by the time Dickens wrote, so the novel is excavating a way of life associated with it: old Rome images the old Marshalsea, which images London as a virtual ruin, as Walter Benjamin suggests that we may see in the modern city 'the monuments of the bourgeosie as ruins before they have crumbled' (Arcades 13). So the Clennam House is already a ruin, before it crumbles (2.31.827): to reclaim the city of Dickens is to revisit what was then ruined.

The Clennam house is anticipated in Nicholas Nickleby when Newman Noggs takes Mrs Nickleby and Kate 'into the City, turning down by the riverside', stopping 'in front of a large old dingy house in Thames Street, the door and windows of which were so bespattered with mud that it would appear to have been uninhabited for years . . . Old and gloomy and black in truth it was, and sullen and dark were the rooms once so bustling with life and enterprise. There was a wharf behind, opening on the Thames' (*NN* 11.136–37). Mrs Nickleby comes from there to Golden Square to see Ralph Nickleby, saying that it is a mile from her house to the Old Bailey – adjacent to Ludgate Hill. She then reverses the direction, going from the Old Bailey to her home: 'All down Newgate Street, all down Cheapside, all up Lombard Street, down Gracechurch Street, and along Thames Street, as far as Spigwiffin's Wharf' (*NN* 26.327). Her route is more northerly than Clennam's. The façade of the Clennam house has a projecting canopy with ornamental swagging around putti, 'designed after a once popular monumental pattern'. Everything seems out of time and out of place. Phiz pictures it twice, in 'Mr Flintwinch has a mild attack of irritability' (369) and 'Damocles' (820). These pictures show variants of the door. In the first, the projecting canopy is supported by caryatids, and there is a broken pediment, from which a child's head, in the gap, looks down. In the second, the arch is complete and there is no child, but the semicircular space is filled by ornamental swagging, and it is perhaps not possible to see if there are figures in it. The canopy protrudes less. The first arch is more baroque, with its ironically allegorical Cupid, giving the illusion of the child dominating in the house, that which has never happened. The canopy is still emphasised in the second arch, and there are decorations set into a cartouche in the wall above the door but the child's absence, and replacement by Rigaud, usurping a place by lounging in the first floor window above, indicates a house left desolate. Figures are allegorical in this novel, as when Clennam sees in 'Mr Chivery . . . quite an Allegory of Silence, as he stood with his key on his lips' (1.22.274). Historically, it may be that the canopy dates the house as late seventeenth or early eighteenth century, rather than the Palladian style associated with Georgian architecture, which made façades flatter.[8]

Another view of the Clennam house/'House of Clennam' appears when the neighbourhood seems 'under some tinge of its dark shadow':

> the dim streets . . . seemed all despositories of oppressive secrets. The deserted counting houses, with their secrets of books and papers locked up in chests and safes [note the pun on 'chests']; the banking-houses, with their secrets of strong rooms and wells, the keys of which were in a very few secret pockets and a very few secret breasts; the secrets of all the dispersed grinders in the vast mill . . . he could have fancied that these things, in hiding, imparted a heaviness to the air [implying melancholia] . . . He thought of the secrets of the lonely church-vaults [not bank-vaults], where the people who had hoarded and secreted in iron coffers were in their turn similarly hoarded, nor yet at rest from doing harm; and then of the secrets of the river as it rolled its turbid tide between two frowning wildernesses of secrets . . . (2.10.567)

The passage anticipates the passage on secrecy opening *A Tale of Two Cities* 1.3. 'Secret' becomes a keynote in *Little Dorrit*.[9] The house typifies the

City-spirit; it frowns (a word used of the houses in 1.3.44), like the prison on the opposite bank, and like Mrs Clennam (1.5.62). Frowning, announcing the taboo, comes from repression, even though Mr Flintwinch, a partner in the House of Clennam, trades with other counting-houses and wharves and docks, and the Custom House, and the Royal Exchange, and coffee-houses, such as Garraway's and Jerusalem.

II · MARSEILLES/MARSHALSEA

The opening two chapters of *Little Dorrit* are set in Marseilles, 'thirty years ago', so, 1825. Marseilles was the access-point for France for a journey from the Middle East, Egypt, or further, from China, like Clennam. In Marseilles, the travellers have to be quarantined, which puts them into a virtual prison. Arthur Clennam, now forty, is coming back to his home after twenty years in Canton (Guangzhou) in southern China, and after the death of his father, in business there. His arrival back in London is where chapter 3 opens. He has come from Dover on the Blue-eyed Maid, so called because of the coaching inn in Borough High Street (the name still exists), where the coach arrived. The inn is virtually next door to the Marshalsea Prison. But Arthur goes on to Ludgate Hill, in the City, by St Paul's, delaying visiting his mother.

Chapters 3 to 5 show him with Mrs Clennam, invalided, paralysed, wheelchair-bound. In chapter 3, it emerges that he has decided to leave the family business, and he notices in the corner, a girl working, whom Affery calls 'Little Dorrit'. Wondering whether his parents have done something wrong that needs 'reparation', Clennam examines the house, and sees his father's portrait, 'earnestly speechless on the wall, with the eyes intently looking at his son as they had looked when life departed from them', like the 'paralysed dumb witness' that is Allegory in *Bleak House* (48.752). Wondering who Little Dorrit can be, he resolves to watch her.

Chapter 6 echoes the novel's opening:

> Thirty years ago there stood, a few doors short of the church of Saint George, in the borough of Southwark, on the left-hand side of the way going southward, the Marshalsea Prison. It had stood there many years before, and it remained there some years afterwards, but it is gone now, and the world is none the worse without it. (1.6.72)

There is a second start to the novel, recalling the first, and not just by the pun on names. The Marshalsea, where John Dickens went, was a medieval prison, attacked by Wat Tyler's men in 1381; its name came from a court held by the Steward and Marshal of the King's household. The prison that Dickens describes was the version rebuilt in the 1780s. As Jack Bamber, telling Mr Pickwick about the 'queer client', says, it was 'the smallest of our debtors' prisons' (*PP* 21.279). Bamber talks about the squalor in the 'crowded alleys' around the prison, as if making the two spaces, inside and outside, inter-changeable, both prisonous. The Marshalsea had closed finally by 1849, so necessitating the novel's opening in 1825, but that makes it unclear how much the action is of the 1820s and not of the 1850s. The Marshalsea comprised a debtors' prison and a smugglers' prison, the latter for offenders against the revenue laws, and defaulters to excise and customs. The two cell blocks are described, as supposed to be separated by an iron-plated door, though not in practice. The details follow of how twenty years before, Mr William Dorrit was brought to prison, his family accompanying him, and how Amy Dorrit was born in prison, like Oliver Twist in a workhouse.

Chapter 8 connects the two parts of the narrative. Arthur Clennam has followed Little Dorrit back to the Marshalsea. By a coincidence, he finds himself locked in the prison overnight, which gives him the irrational feeling that his mother's self-imprisonment may be linked to Dorrit's imprisonment for debt, that perhaps she may be saying that she has paid the penalty for this man's suffering by her wheelchair existence. In the next chapter, he is in the midst of Southwark, as an alternative space to the London seen before. It is symbolised by the Marshalsea, with St George's church next to it (pictured in its aloofness in 'Little Dorrit's Party' (193)). Prison and church make an ironic combination, one encouraging a false sense of dignity. Mr Dorrit's brother, Frederick, not in the Marshalsea, plays a clarinet as dirty as himself (he is nicknamed 'Dirty Dick') in a small theatre orchestra (presumably the Surrey theatre). He is symbolised by the overall shabbiness of the area; seen at its worst outside the prison, of worse quality than ever seen in Rag Fair. The text notes how the people coming to the prison have no identities, everything in them being made up from cast-off or borrowed clothes. Arthur is taken by a 'nondescript' to a coffee-shop in the High Street, and then to Frederick Dorrit's lodging, which, though not identified, may be in Lant Street, where Dickens lodged while his father was in the Marshalsea. Lant Street, whose 'dulness is soothing', recalls Bob Sawyer and Mrs Raddle.[10] In *Little Dorrit*, it contains 'Mr Cripples' Academy'; the name echoes the Three Cripples in *Oliver Twist*, and compares with the Clennam house being said to be on crutches. Frederick Dorrit escorts Clennam upstairs, where 'the little staircase windows looked in at the back windows of other houses as unwholesome as itself, with poles and lines thrust out of them, on which unsightly linen hung'. Dorrit lives in the back garret, 'a sickly room with a turn-up bedstead in it' (1.9.107).[11] Talking to Amy takes Clennam out of Lant Street to Southwark Bridge Road, and onto Southwark Bridge, the Iron Bridge, which provides a liminal space for talking. Southwark, indeed, seems to be the part of London the text wants to endorse the most, despite its poverty. Its most respectable image is Mrs Chivery's shop in Horsemonger Lane – near another prison. This is distinguished by an attempt at gentility, being 'Chivery and Co. Tobacconists, Importers of pure Havana Cigars, Bengal Cheroots, and fine-flavoured Cubas, Dealers in Fancy

Snuffs etc., etc.' (1.22.274). These place-names imply the colonial exotic within this urban squalor. Since John Chivery is the Romantic lover, the shop and the prison together produce the melancholia that allows him to practise writing his tombstone, as an autobiographical record. And it is significant that the novel ends at Southwark, with Flora Finching and Little Dorrit in the pie-shop, before her marriage.

III · MRS CLENNAM'S SECRET

Egypt, first evoked with the Meagles 'staring' at the Sphinx at Giza (1.2.35), is reinvoked when its Biblical Plagues are pictured in Mrs Clennam's house (1.3.48), and it recurs in chapter 5 when Arthur Clennam tentatively attempts to break some taboos. He begins by saying that all three of them – 'Yourself, myself, my dead father' – have something to settle – upon which she 'sat looking at the fire with the impenetrability of an old Egyptian sculpture'. He then says she directed his father; that her will obtained over him, and made him go to China. This, of course, is a taboo topic, in reversing the order of patriarchy. Egypt returns when Mrs Clennam looks at the fire 'with the frown fixed above [her eyes] as if the sculptor of old Egypt had indented it in the hard granite face, to frown for ages' (1.5.62). Remembering the last words of his father, and the watch sent back from China to Mrs Clennam, Arthur asks whether his father 'had any secret remembrance which caused him trouble of mind – remorse . . . is it possible, mother, that he had unhappily wronged any one and made no reparation?' (1.5.62). This is the second breaking of a taboo, imputing blame to the father, excavating his buried secret life. The third breaking implicates the mother. 'You were the moving power of all this machinery before my birth; your stronger spirit has been infused into all my father's dealings, for more than two score years' (1.5.63). He virtually blames the mother for any fault that the father committed. As an Oedipus figure ('I want to know' [1.10.128]), the taboos he breaks uncover the private lives of his father, and of his mother. In so doing, he does what the child attempts to do, according to Freud: he tries, unconsciously, to break into the mystery of the 'primal scene'. He does not know he is doing that; he thinks that financial 'reparation' is needed. When he says 'reparation', the word is echoed by the mother, saying she has been making reparation for her sins 'in prison and in bonds here'. As if proving her power to repress herself, she refuses to eat the oysters brought to her: they become tabooed objects. But what Clennam does not know, the secret he has not probed, but which Freud on the primal scene could tell him, is that what he wants to know has to do with the sexual, and it is this which has triggered off the financial scandal.

At this point, we need to recall the secret, unfolded in Book the Second chapter 30 by Mrs Clennam, under blackmail by Rigaud (in a blackmailing opposite from the one that threatens Lady Dedlock). Clennam's father was brought up by old Gilbert Clennam, his uncle, who gave him to be married to Mrs Clennam, presumably for business-reasons which are masked as religious. Mrs Clennam discovers after the marriage that her husband has gone through a form of marriage with a singing girl, whose child by him is Arthur Clennam. Mrs Clennam has discovered the singing girl through a letter found with the watch, whose letters, DNF, 'Do Not Forget', constitute a love-message (the meaning of the acronym is expounded in 2.30.808). She has blackmailed the singing girl and taken Arthur from her, so that, as Mrs Clennam says – she is determined to tell her story, and not have it told by Rigaud – 'the presence of Arthur was a daily reproach to his father' and 'the absence of Arthur was a daily agony to his mother'. She also indicates that her marriage has been sexless: 'Arthur's father and I lived no further apart with half the globe between us, than when we were together in this house' (2.30.810). She says that when the watch came back to her from her dead husband, she read DNF as meaning not to forget the insult to her. Her anger with the other woman and her husband is sexual jealousy, unconsciously evidenced when, as she says this, she gains freedom in her paralysed wrist; her body is activated as she thinks about the wrong done to it, a wrong wherein, however, she remains collusive. Her anxiety is to be thought of as Clennam's mother; tabooing any reference to the point that she is not (with 2.30.807, compare 1.15.197, where her interruption of Flintwinch ironically puts emphasis onto the point that she is 'not' something, i.e. not Arthur's mother; that she is a negation).

Rigaud, however, will not let her get away with her interpretation of DNF. He says that she has suppressed the codicil to the will that Gilbert Clennam drew up, and which she wrote for him. She suppressed a thousand guineas which Gilbert Clennam in remorse wanted to give to 'the beauty' that 'she hunted to death' (2.30.812). Another detail about that emerges later: the woman, confined in a madhouse kept by Ephraim Flintwinch, the twin brother of Jeremiah Flintwinch, died when Arthur Clennam went to China. He was sent there to keep him deprived of a mother, and her of a son. Mrs Clennam also suppressed a thousand guineas that should have gone to the family of Frederick Dorrit as the patron of the singing girl, either to his daughter or, if he had none, to the youngest daughter of his brother, i.e. Amy Dorrit, as daughter of William Dorrit. This act of suppression took place with the knowledge, though not the agreement, of Clennam's father, whose sending the watch back with DNF on it meant that Mrs Clennam was not to forget the wrong she had done. She justifies the act by saying that the girl, and Mr Clennam, had gone astray, led by 'those accursed snares which are called the Arts' (2.30.812). The codicil which she kept, she handed to Flintwinch to get rid of, on the night that Arthur Clennam came back. Flintwinch gave it to his twin brother Ephraim who was waiting in the house for the tide to take him to Antwerp: here, one of the importances of the location of the Clennam house appears; it is associated with London as a port-city; its 'others' include Antwerp, Marseilles, and Canton. Ephraim has had charge of Arthur's mother since he ran on a criminal basis a private lunatic asylum, where she was confined, and from where she wrote confessional letters to Mrs Clennam, begging forgiveness, driven mad by her imprisonment. Ephraim has had handed to him all these papers, by Jeremiah Flintwinch (Book the First, chapter 4), but they went from him at his house amongst the wharves at Antwerp, into the hands of Rigaud, who is now using them to blackmail Mrs Clennam. If Rigaud is not paid, Arthur Clennam, a prisoner himself, a repetition of his literal mother before him in her different prison, will open a copy of the papers.

The shock of this threat, or the threat of this shock, means that Mrs Clennam frees herself from her self-imposed paralysis, leaves the house, and crosses London Bridge to the Marshalsea prison to reclaim the papers before it is too late. As she crosses, in her hysteria (well over a mile), people say that she is mad, as they did to Nancy, crossing London to reach Rose Maylie (*OT* 3.3.330). Perhaps she is mad. Affery Flintwinch believes that the other woman, Arthur's mad mother, has been kept in the house, and that she haunts it. The sounds Affery hears are of the house becoming more and more rotten, and collapsing – as happens in the chapter 'Closed', burying Rigaud as it falls. Amy and Mrs Clennam witness its collapse. Affery has been right in her facts, wrong in the theories deduced from them, but she has been more right than she knows. The other woman *has* ghosted the house through Little Dorrit working there. Houses in Dickens – it is part of his sense of London's strangeness – acquire 'odd impressions', a phrase which comes when Mr Meagles says there is 'one of those odd impressions in my house, which do mysteriously get into houses sometimes, which nobody seems to have picked up in a distinct form from anybody and yet which everybody seems to have got hold of loosely from somebody' (1.27.344). The echo in that strange speech of the 'nobody' of Dickens' draft title 'Nobody's Fault' will be noticed: that the house falls is nobody's fault, and Mrs Clennam getting out of her wheelchair indicates the power of agencies working throughout which are nobody's responsibility, not consciously controlled by the ego.

Arthur's mother and Amy Dorrit, her ghost, almost, who marries Arthur, unconsciously double each other, both cheated out of money, parallels in their relation to the two Dorrit brothers. In the way they relate to different generations, they seem, implicitly, mother and daughter. Amy – Little Mother, Little Dorrit – the reverse of Maggy, the woman who is no more than a child, resembles Paul Dombey as strangely combining two ages, woman and child together, allowed to be neither child nor woman. The prostitute on London Bridge in the scene already mentioned, when Amy and Maggy have 'the key of the street', would like to think of Amy as an innocent child, but on discovering she is a woman, cannot, as Hillis Miller says, finding this the most poignant scene in Dickens, 'gain . . . a moment's peace and innocence for herself by kissing her' (1.14.192).[12] This woman destined for suicide, a shadow of Arthur's

mother, cannot accept that the city could produce innocence out of experience. Arthur's mother's madness, suggestive of how the nineteenth century
constructed hysterical women, and Amy's submissiveness in the prison, are
reverse images of each other. Mrs Clennam, her paralysis what Freud would
call an hysterical symptom, and her enforced sexlessness a repression of her
womanhood connived at by the patriarchy of Gilbert Clennam, ghosts both
these women. Arthur's mother has haunted the house symbolising a wrong
perpetuated by it, and when reparation becomes an open issue, the house, as
holding a secret, as a taboo in itself, has come crashing down, its totemic force
lost. So it is appropriate that, for whatever reason it happened, Phiz's picture
of the house in 'Damocles' should show no child. The secret is out, there was
neither child nor marriage: as Mrs Clennam said to the woman: 'You have a
child; I have none' (2.30.809).

The taboo the text must break is complex, relating to the revelation of the
character of Gilbert Clennam, to the fault of Arthur's father (which does not
wholly negate the idea of 'Nobody's Fault'), in relation to the two women and
to his son, and the double fault of Mrs Clennam, in (a) engineering the virtual
death of Arthur's mother, which is inseparable from the cruelty to Arthur, and
the cruelty to her husband, and (b) suppressing the money that should have
come to Amy. She has been motivated by revenge. The Clennams have been
intensely Christian, and Dickens' text, with its appeal to a varying readership,
is ambiguous about whether the fault of the desire for revenge is inherent in
Christianity, or in their particular Evangelical brand of it. But the text sees
a two-way process taking place. An older generation projects onto the next
a guilt-feeling, such as the one Arthur feels throughout. The biblical idea
that 'the transgressions of the parents are visited on their offspring', which
Mrs Clennam supplements with 'there was an angry mark upon [Arthur] at his
birth' (2.31.824), so making him like Cain – an image Dickens appropriated for
himself (*DC* 897) – becomes one generation's guilt pushed onto another. The
next generation is structured by guilt.

Here we can turn to Nietzsche, who reverses that drift in *Thus Spoke
Zarathustra*, in discussing the desire for revenge. Redemption, for Zarathustra,
means attainment of freedom from thinking about revenge. The requirements
of 'justice', however, are what sanction talk of 'revenge' – 'Revenge we will
practise, and defamation of all who are not the same as us'; so Zarathustra
characterises the 'tarantula-hearts' in their vows to themselves. These tarantulas are the very agents of justice. And what is revenge taken against? It is
against otherness, difference, against the point that people are not the same as
each other, something that 'the tarantulas' cannot abide:

> You preachers of equality, the tyrants' madness of impotence cries out of you thus
> for 'equality': your most secret tyrants' desires disguise themselves in words of virtue!
> Soured arrogance, repressed envy, perhaps the arrogance and envy of your
> fathers: they burst out from you as flames and the madness of revenge. What the

father kept silent, that comes in the son to be spoken, and often I found the son to be the father's unveiled secret.[13]

The argument is that this desire which works against others is a secret envy, which feeds talk about justice with revenge. Nietzsche argues that the present generation may be fed by a particular anger and envy but that this has built up from the previous generation. Instead of a mode of thought which says that the father's generation was fine, and that the problem has to do with the younger generation, this argument intuits that the failure was inherent in the previous generation. It is this which Arthur realises, but probing it breaks family taboos. The knowledge produces in him a reaction which is not vengeful, but the guilt passed on to him makes him masochistic. The passing on of his parents' 'transgressions' to him has this self-destructive impulse that systematically leads him towards the Marshalsea as if it had a strange attraction, to work out his 'fault' or his 'crime' as he calls it through 'reparation' (2.26.747).[14]

Nietzsche's *The Genealogy of Morals* (2.4) links the German for guilt, *Schuld*, to the word for debt, *Schulden*.[15] Creation of guilt means nothing other than the creation of someone who feels responsible to pay his debts. *Little Dorrit* places at its centre, and at London's centre, a debtor's prison as a factory turning out a sense of guilt, of worthlessness. All the evasions Mr Dorrit and his family practise, and their patronage of Old Nandy (1.31) must be understood in the light of their awareness, conscious and unconscious, of this. Further, there is a symmetry between the house and the Marshalsea on either sides of the river. In Mrs Clennam's prison-house, debts have not been paid, and guilt has been repressed. The Marshalsea prison is a state-machine for producing guilt. In the house, while guilt has not been acknowledged, Mrs Clennam has become paralytic, as a way of denying the denied body, and punishing the self while repressing knowledge of guilt. In the prison, the guiltless – the debtor – was constructed as guilty, with fatal consequences for his ability henceforth to face the world. He cannot acknowledge ever being in prison. Both Mrs Clennam and Mr Dorrit are constructed as split subjects, both knowing something and not knowing it at the same time. And the confined woman has, Arthur deduces, a sense of responsibility for Dorrit in his confinement, so that she sees herself as striking a balance (1.8.104). This balancing means that her payment of a debt is not reparation but self-justification. Her paralysis means escape into disavowal: 'I am shut up from the knowledge of some things that I may prefer to avoid knowing' (1.15.200).

Production of guilt relates to a feeling of inadequacy in relation to the past. Nietzsche speculates that:

> the living generation always recognizes a juridical obligation towards the earlier generation, and particularly towards the earliest generation, which founded the race . . . Here the conviction prevails that the race only *exists* by virtue of the sacrifice and achievements of the forefathers – and that one is obliged to *repay* them through sacrifice and achievements: a *debt* is recognized, which gnaws incessantly by virtue

of the fact that these forefathers, in their continued existence as powerful spirits [this is what Freud would see as their totemic character] never cease to grant the race new advantages and advances in strength. (*Genealogy* 2.19, 69)

In other words, guilt as indebtedness is always felt towards an irrecoverable past, and towards having a sense of inferiority in comparison to the previous generation. Hence Dorrit's children cannot tell their father that they work (1.12.154). And Clennam feels personally guilty for his parents' fault.

Guilt engrained in Mr Dorrit appears in Book the Second, when the prison, which he has left, is the tabooed subject. He then shows even more the shades of his prison-house, that he cannot leave it, because a man who cannot speak of his past is imprisoned by it. He can only speak of what is 'perfectly proper, placid, and pleasant' (2.5.501), as Mrs General – whom he is in danger of marrying, to confirm this repressed state – advises. For she 'was not to be told of anything shocking' (2.2.475). Her name associates militarism with having nothing to say; as if recalling Blake: 'to generalize is to be an idiot'.[16] As the widow of a 'stiff commissariat officer' (2.2.471), she associates with Mrs Merdle, widow of a colonel (1.21.266), and embodiment of society's power to repress its knowledge of the past, when she remeets the newly enriched Fanny (2.1.460). Mrs Merdle consorts with Mrs Gowan, the widow of a Civil Servant functionary – parallel to the military – a colonial 'Commissioner of nothing particular somewhere or other [who] had died with his drawn salary in his hand' (1.17.234). Happy to marry her son off, Mrs Gowan cuts the Meagles, with Mrs Merdle's collusion (1.33.415–16). Two things come together: how guilt is constructed so that it cannot speak of the past, that it accepts the taboos which are laid upon it, and how readily people use repression, which hides their own guilt.

IV · BLEEDING HEART YARD

Apart from the City, and Southwark, London is extensively referred to in *Little Dorrit*. Bleeding Heart Yard, where the Plornishes live (Mrs Plornish's father is in the workhouse at Marylebone), and where Doyce has his factory, is east of the west end of London, going up Theobald's Road, once 'an old rustic road towards a suburb of note, where in the days of William Shakespeare, author and stage-player, there were Royal hunting seats' (1.12.150). The road continues as Clerkenwell Road. Hatton Garden, which contains Bleeding Heart Yard, comes up to meet it from the south, and it is adjacent to Saffron Hill and the squalor of Field Lane. The text describes Bleeding Heart Yard in terms of an almost vanished 'ancient greatness', and reads the changes allegorically:

as if the aspiring city had become puffed up in the very ground on which it stood, the ground had so risen about Bleeding Heart Yard that you got into it down a flight of steps which formed no part of the original approach, and got out of it by a low gateway into a maze of shabby streets, which went about and about, tortuously ascending to the level again. (1.12.150)

Bleeding Heart Yard, between
Hatton Garden and Saffron Hill;
a nineteenth-century space for
small factories.

'Shabby', applied to Southwark-people, and now to the streets, as though they
wore clothes, should be noted, as should the sense that archaeology is required
to trace Bleeding Heart Yard. Antiquarianism returns too, in considering the
remote sources of Bleeding Heart Yard's name, whether it had to do with
murder or love, while faded gentility hangs over the area in the poetry of 'a
tambour worker, a spinster and romantic, still lodging in the yard' (1.12.150).
This area is owned by Mr Casby, whose rent-collector is Mr Pancks.

Casby, loosely based on George Beadnell, the banker living in Lombard
Street who made his daughter, Maria Beadnell, unavailable to Dickens, lives
in 'a street in the Gray's Inn Road, which had set off from that thoroughfare
with the intention of running down at one heat into the [Fleet] valley, and up
again to the top of Pentonville Hill'. This refers to abortive building speculation going north-west somewhere near the present Calthorpe Road; the house
where Casby lived looked, till new improvements occurred, 'with a baulked
countenance at the wilderness patched [again the clothes image] with unfruit-
ful gardens and pimpled with eruptive summer-houses, that it had meant to
run over in no time' (1.13.159). There is a disappointment associated with
remeeting Casby and Flora Finching and Mr F.'s Aunt, but Flora's endless
conversation shows one possibility of breaking taboos, since she says much
spontaneously which shows up the power of patriarchal repression, both from
her father, and from Mr F., a businessman in the wine-trade. When she lets drop
that 'Romance was fled with the early days of Arthur Clennam, our parents

tore us asunder we became marble and stern reality usurped the throne, Mr F. said very much to his credit that he was perfectly aware of it and even preferred that state of things' (1.24.302), the 'statue bride' (1.24.304) indicates that her marriage was sexless – like the Clennams and Flintwinches. Mr F.'s Aunt, whose every angry remark is implicitly accusatory, guilt-inducing, may indicate as a proxy what Flora has suffered (not least from her) and what she could say if she chose, but her oppressive madness is also part of the past that Flora cannot escape. Flora finishes the meeting with Clennam by telling him that she walks in the afternoons in Gray's Inn Gardens, where she hopes to see him. The woman's space is carefully defined for her, and she is hobbled all the time by Mr F.'s Aunt as chaperone, a more terrifying Mrs General, because unlike Mrs General, there is indicated a reality and history that has been repressed in what she says.

Clennam, leaving, goes on a walk which may be followed. Pancks says he is going 'Citywards', so Clennam goes with him, though it is apparent that this is not his direction. The men walk back towards the City with Pancks expounding 'the Whole Duty of Man in a commercial country' (1.13.176) and leaving Clennam on the other side of Smithfield, at Barbican. (They would have gone down to the end of Gray's Inn Road, down Holborn, up Charterhouse Street and to Aldersgate). Pancks lives at Pentonville (1.25.315), so his route takes him up Aldersgate towards Islington. Clennam then goes down Aldersgate towards St Paul's, 'purposing to come into one of the great thoroughfares for the sake of their light and life' (1.13.177); he needs the phantasmagoria to live in London. He is returning towards where he was in chapter 3, but sees the injured Cavalletto being taken to St Bartholomew's hospital, having been knocked down by the 'Mail' coaches coming out of Lad Lane (part of Gresham Street) or Wood Street. Having helped Cavalletto, Clennam goes in the opposite direction from the City, back towards Covent Garden, via Snow Hill and Holborn, to his lodging where he sits and looks at the 'blackened forest of chimneys' (1.13.180): the phrase repeats his looking out of the window at his mother's house (1.3.53, 56).

Another place may be considered here, since it adjoins Gray's Inn Road: the Foundling Hospital, where Mr and Mrs Meagles have gone to hear the music in the chapel, which had an altar-piece by Benjamin West. They take a maid for their daughter, Pet, the orphan Tattycoram, the last part of the name being a tribute to the philanthropist who established the hospital, Captain Thomas Coram (1668–1751), merchant, ship-builder, master of a ship trading with the American colonies, and trustee of colonies in Georgia in the United States and Nova Scotia. Hogarth painted him in 1740, and like Handel, was a governor of the Foundling Hospital (which received its Royal Charter in 1739). Mr Meagles refers for comparison to the Paris Hôpital des Enfants-Trouvés, founded in the seventeenth century, as one of many such in French and Italian towns. Tattycoram's name has changed from Harriet Beadle – this implies an official

Nineteenth-century statues in the old school room, now Parish Hall, for St Botolph without Bishopsgate: Charity girl (*left*) and Charity boy (*right*).

who has imposed the name, as happens with Oliver Twist – to another which associates her both with the shabbiness of second-hand clothes, and the name of the patriarch who established the hospital.

'Coram' is only slightly less offensive than 'Beadle', but just as certainly advertises Harriet's origins. Miss Wade, who represents both political passion, a certain feminism and lesbianism, can tell Mr Meagles, 'What your broken plaything is as to birth, I am. She has no name, I have no name' (1.27.351). 'Broken' is suggestive: who, or what has broken her?

V · MRS MERDLE'S PARROT

The Meagles have a cottage-residence in Twickenham, which Clennam reaches via Fulham and Putney Bridge, and Putney Heath and a ferry at Richmond. The cottage is full of commodities, souvenirs or 'spoils' from different parts of the world, and the first time it is seen, it shows how Pet Meagles (as 'Pet' she also, virtually, 'has no name') is reduced to being an object amongst objects. Tattycoram says she has seen Miss Wade, and Pet immediately says, 'Oh Tatty . . . take your hands away. I feel as if someone else was touching me'. It is almost subliminal, this introduction of the caressing touch of the other woman, the sense of a sanctioned touch and a tabooed one. The sexual nature of Tattycoram cannot be admitted, though in response Tattycoram 'set her full red lips together, and crossed her arms upon her bosom' (1.16.214).

The cottage contrasts with three other houses: the first in Harley Street, Cavendish Square, where Mrs Merdle lives. This is artificial in another sense from the Meagles, showing art trying to be nature (hence the parrot in the cage), while being as theatrical as Fanny's profession is: Mrs Merdle emerges from behind a curtain (1.20.257).[17] The opposing rows of houses in the street set themselves against each other, and people in the houses are 'staring at the other side of the street with the dullness of the houses' (1.21.264). 'Staring', which animates the houses and de-animates their inhabitants, recalls its use on the novel's first page: 'Everything in Marseilles, and about Marseilles, had stared at the fervid sky, and been stared at in return, until a staring habit had become universal there' (1.1.15). Dull staring suggests the universal condition of prisoners. De-animation extends to Mrs Merdle in whom Merdle acquired 'a capital bosom to hang jewels upon'. This commodification of the woman, and her self-commodification, anticipates Veblen's *Theory of the Leisure Class* on conspicuous consumption by nearly fifty years.[18] And the word 'capital' contains several puns. It means 'excellent', it makes the woman the embodiment of capitalism, it makes her bosom architecture, and makes her allegorise that London that Harley Street represents: London as the capital, the bosom to hang jewels on.

The second contrast with the Meagles is Mrs Gowan's grace-and-favour apartment at Hampton Court, home of snobbery, social falsity and gentility, parallel to the Marshalsea (Gowan says his mother lives in a 'dreary red-brick dungeon at Hampton Court' [1.26.330]). Hampton Court had ceased being a royal residence after George the Second's death; George the Third let it out as grace-and-favour lodgings, rent-free for those who had rendered some service to the crown, and Victoria opened it to the public. Dickens says that the inhabitants disapprove of this, especially on Sundays. And because the residents are described as camping in Hampton Court, they are sarcastically called 'Bohemians' (1.26.331), a word which evokes Thackeray's *Vanity Fair*, chapter 64, which OED gives as the first use of the word in English. But that Bohemians are really on the side of the establishment is Dickens' (and Marx's) sense, not Thackeray's. The premises are tiny, and the inhabitants live in an atmosphere of social falsity, with 'affectations of no-thoroughfares, which were evidently doors to little kitchens' (1.26.331).

A last house to be discussed is where Miss Wade lives temporarily 'in one of the dull bye-streets in the Grosvenor region, near Park Lane' (2.27.344). When Tattycoram flees to Miss Wade, Mr Meagles and Clennam go searching for her house, riding up to the top of Oxford Street and then walking among the great and little streets, which are 'equally melancholy' and of which 'there is a labyrinth around Park Lane':

> Wildernesses of corner-houses, with barbarous old porticoes and appurtenances . . .
> Parasite little tenements with the cramp in their whole frame, from the dwarf hall-
> door on the giant model of His Grace's in the Square, to the squeezed window of the
> boudoir commanding the dunghills in the Mews, made the evening doleful. Ricketty
> dwellings of undoubted fashion, but of a capacity to hold nothing comfortably except

Onslow Square, South Kensington: Thackeray's home from 1854 to 1862, when he moved to 2 Palace Green, Kensington. Built as stuccoed houses by C.J. Freake c.1846.

a dismal smell, looked like the last result of the great mansions' breeding in-and-in; and where their little supplementary bows and balconies were supported on thin iron columns, seemed to be scrofulously resting upon crutches. Here and there a Hatchment, with the whole science of Heraldry in it, loomed down upon the street, like an Archbishop discoursing on Vanity. The shops, few in number, made no show; for popular opinion was as nothing to them. The pastry-cook knew who was on his books, and in that knowledge could be calm, with a few glass cylinders of dowager peppermint-drops in his window, and half-a-dozen ancient specimens of currant jelly ... Everybody in those streets seemed ... to have gone out to dinner, and nobody seemed to be giving the dinners they had gone to. On the door-steps there were loung-ing, footmen with bright parti-coloured plumage and white polls, like an extinct race of monstrous birds ... The roll of carriages in the Park was done for the day; the street lamps were lighting; and wicked little grooms in the tightest fitting garments, with twists in their legs answering to the twists in their minds, hung about in pairs, chewing straw and exchanging fraudulent secrets. (1.27.345)

Much here recalls the description given in 1.3: as is the City, so is the West End. Much recalls Mrs Clennam's house; for example the architectural decorations that do not compensate for the monotony of the streets, and the crutches. Most monotonous are the corner houses, which, as in American cities, turn the gaze either way, without offering anything new. The hatchment is part of the allegorical message of the street, where everything speaks simultaneously of emptiness (Vanity) and pride: the area is nearly the same as the Vanity Fair, or Mayfair, of Becky Sharp and Rawdon Crawley, who settle to 'live well on nothing a year' (chapter 36) in Curzon Street, Mayfair. Clennam and Meagles find themselves in 'one of the parasite streets, long, regular, narrow, dull, and gloomy; like a brick and mortar funeral'. 'Parasite' recalls the world of the grace-and-favour apartments. The men inquire at 'several little area gates, where a dejected youth stood spiking his chin on the summit of a precipitous little shoot of wooden steps'. Eventually, they find a 'dingy house, apparently empty, with bills in the windows, announcing that it was to let. The bills, as a variety in the funeral procession, almost amounted to a decoration'. This is where Miss Wade lives, as well as Tattycoram; and they are admitted by an old woman into an upstairs room. Here, where everything seems temporary, the reverse of the bourgeois interior of the Meagles, there is a disdain of the values of the street outside, a sense of how façadal it is, how little it knows. Tattycoram repudiates Meagles with 'passionate defiance' and 'stubborn defiance', and says that rather than return with him, 'I'd be torn to pieces first. I'd tear myself to pieces first'. Meagles' last speech to Miss Wade sets her against the bourgeois world: 'you were a mystery to all of us, and had nothing in common with any of us', as if she were to be excluded; and adds:

> you don't hide, can't hide, what a dark spirit you have within you. If it should happen that you are a woman who, from whatever cause, has a perverted delight in making a sister-woman as wretched as she is (I am old enough to have heard of such), I warn her against you, and I warn you against yourself. (1.23.351)

There are too many taboos for Mr Meagles to consider here. He knows, and he does not know, Miss Wade's character. For Walter Benjamin:

> The figure of the lesbian woman belongs among Baudelaire's heroic exemplars . . . The nineteenth century began openly and without reserve to include the woman in the process of commodity production. The theoreticians were united in their opinion that her specific femininity was thereby endangered; masculine traits must necessarily manifest themselves in women after a while. Baudelaire affirms these traits. At the same time, however, he seeks to free them from the domination of the economy . . . The paradigm of the lesbian woman bespeaks the ambivalent position of 'modernity'. (*Arcades* 318)

Miss Wade is the lesbian as modern, with her 'dark spirit', and resisting modernity, in disdaining the commodity-values which are represented by the street. Her significance here is to be located in this 'empty London house' (2.20.690) which, in the heart of Mayfair, declares its unreal character. She is near the Barnacles, who in 'Mews Street, Grosvenor Square' are controllers of the Circumlocution Office: another tabooed space, since 'you mustn't come into the place saying you want to know, you know', as Barnacle Junior says (1.10.128). She affronts that space, and nearby Brook Street, where Mr Dorrit will reside (2.16.641), near where Fanny and Edmund Sparkler will live, their house introduced with its perpetual smell of 'yesterday's soup and coach-horses '(2.24.724). That insight appears in the chapter, 'The Evening of a Long Day', being the Sunday of Merdle's suicide. That chapter, where 'the bells of the churches had done their worst in the way of clanging among the unmelodious echoes of the streets' (2.24.724), again recalls the melancholy of chapter 3.

Miss Wade is the touch of difference in this context. She has an astonishing rule-breaking separate chapter of narrative in the text: Forster did not like it (perhaps it brought out the Podsnap in him). She writes her confession to Clennam, as if, despite herself, she must speak to someone else. 'The History of a Self-Tormentor' (2.21) cannot be fitted into the text, but must remain outside, heterogeneous to it. It discusses Gowan. The argument that he represents Dickens' critique of Thackeray has often been advanced, and is suggestive; but something anti-Thackerayan appears not just in Gowan, but in Dickens' response to Mayfair, the sphere of *Vanity Fair*. Miss Wade is rebellious in a way that Becky Sharp, born in Greek Street, Soho, is not, and her account of Gowan finishing their affair – 'we were both people of the world, that we both understood mankind, that we both knew there was no such thing as romance, that we were both prepared for going different ways to seek our fortunes like people of sense' (2.21.701) comments on the values of that world which presumes to make Miss Wade the tabooed figure. If Miss Wade is a 'self-tormentor', she resembles Mrs Clennam on the other side of London.

VI · THE WARM BATHS

When Mr Dorrit leaves the Marshalsea, Amy asks Clennam whether he will pay his debts, and comments that it is 'hard that he should pay in life and money both' (1.35.444). Clennam thinks of this as the only 'taint' of the prison on her: if so, the taint may be the spirit of anger, or rebellion at what imprisonment means and is obviously produced by the prison. Amy has the mildest version of Miss Wade's spirit: 'If I had been shut up in any place to pine and suffer, I should always hate that place and wish to burn it down, or raze it to the ground' (1.2.37). Clennam disagrees with Amy, perhaps because he is tempted towards the prison, unconsciously in 1.8. when he has to stay there (if Dickens had 'the key of the street', Arthur has 'the key of the prison') and then in 2.26, when he insists on going to the Marshalsea, to pay in life and money both. He is a 'self-tormentor' in wanting the prison. Pickwick goes to prison because his innocence will not recognise the law, but Clennam, the man with no will (1.2.35), whose death-drive makes him think of 'flowing away monotonously, like the river' (1.16.218), enters the prison-house with another prison taint: a belief that he should be there. The term 'self-tormentor', said either by or about Miss Wade (depending on who is supposed to have written the chapter-title 'The History of a Self-Tormentor'), anticipates the word 'masochist' (OED: first citation 1892). It recalls how Tattycoram speaks of tearing herself in pieces, becoming a 'broken plaything'. Clennam seeing Miss Wade and Tattycoram together feels that 'each of the two natures must be constantly tearing the other to pieces' (2.20.691). Sexual relations are masochistic: if this novel only allows that to be true of lesbians, that does not negate the relevance of the insight. In Clennam, the negation of the sexual 'will', which feminises him, is his masochism. Hence he has created the situation where he can be tortured by his mother (2.28.786).

Miss Wade's rage against the prison is also masochistic, since anger against it is like Tattycoram 'plucking at her lips with an unsparing hand' (1.2.40), sexual rage directed against the body as itself the prison; suggesting that sexual anger works both sadistically and masochistically at once, depending on whether the prison is seen as outside, controlling, repressing, or inside, creating a desire to destroy itself. The novel integrates women and London because it sees women's passion as locked up within the city; repression that produces the prison being, as with Mrs Clennam, sexually based. Her attitude to the 'suppliant' or 'defaulter' appears in her religion:

> Forgive us our debts as we forgive our debtors, was a prayer too poor in spirit for her. Smite thou my debtors, Lord, wither them, crush them . . . this was the impious tower of stone she built up to scale Heaven. (1.5.61)

Working with the interchangeability of being in debt and feeling guilty, she wants guilt-feelings to be increased. Yet the draft title *Nobody's Fault* suggests that there can never be anything but a normative 'default'. Faults cannot be attributed singly: it is not possible to assign guilt. The attitude which runs debt and guilt together is the City-spirit. Clennam says that he is the child of parents 'who weighed, measured, and priced everything: for whom what could not be weighed, measured and priced, had no existence' (1.2.35). The expression implies a spirit that can *only* weigh literal indebtedness, enforcing it through imposition of guilt, aligning the Protestant ethic and the spirit of capitalism. It certainly cannot respond to the 'other'. But 'guilt' is *not* a matter of money. Though Clennam thinks that his parents' wrong was financial, he never learns that the financial injury came from a sexual fault. Nietzsche connects what he would call Mrs Clennam's *ressentiment* with an adherence to 'the ascetic ideal', which includes a hatred of the body. That appears in the unconscious of her words to Arthur: 'Only touch me, for my hand is tender' (1.3.51). Tender, so *noli mi tangere (the language of John 20.17)*? Tender, so only touch me (do not come nearer)? Please touch me, because I am tender? The tenderness is her self-torment, never healed, which makes her not forget, but insist on the wrong done her: 'to lead a life as monotonous as mine has been during many years, is not the way to forget. To lead a life of self-correction, is not the way to forget' (1.30.378). She is her own Panopticon, correcting herself. The self-corrector is the self-tormentor. Dickens' London is full of them. Do not touch me, do not forget.

What about self-torment in a man: for example, Merdle?[19] Having got where he has by bribes, he is the debtor about to default, as his body-language shows: 'with his hands crossed under his uneasy coat-cuffs, clasping his wrists as if he were taking himself into custody' (1.33.417). He is uneasy in civilisation, personified by Mrs Merdle's parrot, uneasy with his body. Uneasiness links him with Miss Wade, who is not 'easy' with other people, especially 'great people' (2.21.697).[20] Such lack of ease makes her project onto those others the accusatory feelings that she has as a divided subject herself. For Freud, the ego allows the superego to torture it, to ensure that the self remains under self-correction, and the price is lack of ease, *Unbehagen* (discontents), as Freud calls it in *Civilization and its Discontents*.[21] Merdle's unease means that he must make his own self-divided body have and be his own 'stringent police-man' (1.3.44) (Latin: *stringere*, 'to draw together, bind tight'). He is hesitant and incoherent before Dorrit, admiring of Fanny (2.16.642–43), one reason, perhaps, why she is the last person he talks to, borrowing a lady's penknife from her, and possessed by awareness of Dorrit's death, as he shows in a chance remark to Fanny:

> 'I was speaking of poor papa when you came in, sir'.
> 'Aye? Quite a coincidence', said Mr Merdle. (2.24.731)

As he walks down the streets to his death, Fanny through tears of vexation and boredom seems to see him 'appear to leap, and waltz, and gyrate, as if he were possessed by several Devils' (2.24.734). The insight is Dostoyevskian. Dickens' London gives double vision. Mr Merdle is both self-correcting, acting as the 'gentleman' that his Chief Butler denies him to be (2.25.740) and full of devils which he cannot arrest in himself. And he is also impelled by the 'infernal powers' of the West End, as he complains before (1.33.418). What he does is for them, but the text brings out the emptiness of that for which the self corrects itself. Merdle will next be seen a naked body in the warm baths somewhere in Mayfair. His suicide combines memories of Roman baths (the baths are marble), so enforcing the comparison with Mr Dorrit, who has died in Rome; it includes baptismal associations. Merdle evades 'Tyburn Tree' (2.12.586) by laudanum and a penknife. Public baths had been legislated for in the Public Bath and Washhouse Bill of 1846, which allowed parishes to set up provisions for the poor to wash themselves and launder clothes; the first to be opened in London was in St Martin's parish, in Orange Street, Leicester Square, next to the National Gallery; a second followed in Goulston Street, running north out of Whitechapel Road. In a revision of the Bill in 1847, improved facilities were offered for small tradesmen.[22] If it is one of these, Merdle has lost class, in wanting anonymity. 'Mr Merdle has destroyed himself' says Physician, in a phrase which compares with 'self-correction' and 'self-tormentor'. The Chief Butler calls that 'an ungentlemanly act' (2.5.740). As smooth as Henry Gowan, he speaks for the London which has the power of torment.

CHAPTER NINE

TRAUMATIC LONDON
Great Expectations

When I told the clerk I would take a turn in the air while I waited, he advised me to go round the corner and I should come to Smithfield. So, I came to Smithfield, and the shameful place, being all asmear with filth and fat and blood and foam, seemed to stick to me. So, I rubbed it off with all possible speed by turning into a street where I saw the great black dome of Saint Paul's bulging at me behind a grim stone building which a bystander said was Newgate Prison. Following the wall of the jail, I found the roadway covered with straw to deaden the noise of passing vehicles; and from this, and from the quantity of people standing about, smelling strongly of spirits and beer, I inferred that the trials were on.

While I looked about me here, an exceedingly dirty and partially drunk minister of justice asked me if I would like to step in and hear a trial or so: informing me that he could give me a front place for half-a-crown, whence I could command a full view of the Lord Chief Justice in his wig and robes – mentioning that awful personage like waxwork, and presently offering him at the reduced price of eighteen-pence. As I declined the proposal on the plea of an appointment, he was so good as to take me into a yard and show me where the gallows was kept, and also where people were publicly whipped, and then he showed me the Debtor's Door, out of which culprits came to be hanged: heightening the interest of that dreadful portal by giving me to understand that 'four on 'em' would come out at that door the day after tomorrow to be killed in a row. This was horrible, and gave me a sickening idea of London, the more so as the Lord Chief Justice's proprietor wore (from his hat down to his boots and up again to his pocket-handkerchief exclusive) mildewed clothes which had evidently not belonged to him originally, and which, I took it into my head, he had bought cheap of the executioner. Under these circumstances, I thought myself well rid of him for a shilling.

I dropped into the office to ask if Mr Jaggers had come in yet, and I found he had not, and I strolled out again. This time I made the tour of Little Britain, and turned into Bartholomew Close. 2.1.165–66

I · SMITHFIELD

Four settings are implied in this passage from *Great Expectations*, which focus Pip's impressions when he first arrives in London to become a 'gentleman': Little Britain, Smithfield, St Paul's, Newgate. Pip has come up from Kent, and the coach has put him down at the Cross Keys Inn, in Wood Street, Cheapside.[1] Cheapside was the main market street of the old medieval city, also, in medieval times, a place of execution. A hackney-coach, 'like a straw-yard' and 'like a rag-shop' takes him the short distance to Little Britain, to Mr Jaggers' office.

This has no window but a skylight, making Pip feel that he is under surveillance from above, as well as from the death-masks of the figures 'peculiarly swollen and twitchy about the nose' who look down accusingly from the shelf above Mr Jaggers' chair. As with *Oliver Twist*, this is claustrophobic London. After sitting and 'wondering' about what is in the office, Pip walks out of it into Little Britain, a street named for the Dukes of Brittany, who owned a house here in the sixteenth century. Its name makes it a microcosm of England: at its heart is Mr Jaggers, who can say, 'I am pretty well known' (1.18.137). But perhaps 'Little Britain' is even more a name for London.

As Bedlam had statues of madness allegorically represented outside it, so there is something equivalently minatory and teasing in the death-masks of hanged criminals above Mr Jaggers' desk, 'with the twitchy leer' that Wemmick so jauntily cleans up, talking about the one who murdered his master. This suggests Courvoisier here, subject of Thackeray's essay 'Going to See a Man Hanged' (1840); Courvoisier blamed Ainsworth's novel *Jack Sheppard* for his crime. The other, 'with the genuine [hanged] look [. . .] as if one nostril was caught up with a horsehair and a little fish-hook', Wemmick says 'forged wills' and perhaps 'put the supposed testators to sleep too' (2.5.200–201).[2] 'A Visit to Newgate' had noticed casts of the heads and faces of 'the two notorious murderers, Bishop and Williams', who were hanged at Newgate in 1831 (*SB* 236). These are allegorical witnesses to Mr Jaggers, like Allegory to Mr Tulkinghorn: masks being, of course, forms of allegory.[3]

We examine the 'great criminal', the subject of *Oliver Twist*, in detail with the chapter on *Our Mutual Friend*, but these death-masks, which imply that everything has become a commodity, even dead bodies, indicate how the past continues its power over the present, even after the state has had its way by hanging people. They suggest what Mr Jaggers' power means more openly than he can say: power to hang, since hanging is 'quite the natural end here' (2.5.201). The masks can but recall the convicts of the first part of the novel, Magwitch and Compeyson, the first of whom seems like the pirate who has been hung by chains, and the latter of whom can never be seen properly, because 'he had a badly bruised face' (1.3.21), and when Pip sees him next time, his face 'had a white terror on it that I shall never forget' (3.15.444) and when his body is found his face is unrecognisable, 'horribly disfigured' (3.16.448).

The office, as if because empty of Jaggers, is a death-mask too (the skylight is patched 'like a broken head'), and Pip leaves it for Smithfield, north of St Bartholomew's hospital, which dates back to Rahere (1123), courtier of Henry the First, who founded a priory and hospital together. After the dissolution of the priory, in 1546, St Bartholomew's, with Bedlam, St Thomas' and Bridewell, became a Royal Hospital administered by the City of London: here Jack Hopkins worked in the casualty ward (*PP* 32.421). Today, its only medieval building is the fifteenth-century tower of the church of St Bartholomew the

Kensal Green cemetery: Thackeray, who died at the end of 1863, is buried in the tomb with the iron surround to the left; his friend from Charterhouse days, John Leech (1817–64), illustrator for *Punch* and for *A Christmas Carol*, is buried nearby.

Night-time: Graveyard, St Bartholomew the Great (fragment of a Priory), Smithfield.

Night-time: Shop in Cloth Court, Smithfield.

Less; other older buildings are eighteenth century (James Gibbs) and later, by Philip Hardwick.

Bartholomew Fair was authorised by Henry the First in 1133, in the priory, for three days, around 24 August, which lengthened to a fortnight. Closed in 1855, it was the only fair within the City, and is recalled in Cloth Fair and Hosier Lane. Like Smithfield, which Oliver Twist passes twice, Bartholomew Fair is mentioned in *Oliver Twist*, for Sikes tells Nancy he was 'shopped' at 'Bartlemy time' (1.16.125). This associates with other brutish crowd scenes: the chasing of Oliver Twist (1.10) and the hounding of Sikes at Jacob's Island; occasions when lynch-law seems likely, when people become scapegoats and the riotous carnival Fair establishes the rule of order. The Fair was visited by Wordsworth and his sister in September 1802, taken there by Lamb, and *The Prelude* (1850) makes it an imminent threat:

> when half the city shall break out
> Full of one passion, vengeance, rage, or fear?
> To executions, to a street on fire,
> Mobs, riots, or rejoicings? (7.672–75)

Wordsworth wants to see and show the Fair from a panoramic position 'upon some showman's platform'. From that imaginary vantage-point, he describes the Fair as a 'phantasma' – like a hideous dream, or as a 'phantasmagoria':

> a shock
> For eyes and ears! what anarchy and din,
> Barbarian and infernal, – a phantasma,
> Monstrous in colour, motion, shape, sight, sound! (7.685–88)

A long account follows of the varieties of people making up the Fair, suggesting comparisons with Hogarth's *Southwark Fair* (1733):

> All out-o' the way, far-fetched, perverted things,
> All freaks of nature; all Promethean thoughts
> Of man, his dullness, madness, and their feats
> All jumbled up together, to compose
> A Parliament of Monsters, Tents, and Booths
> Meanwhile, as if the whole were one vast mill,
> Are vomiting, receiving on all sides,
> Men, Women, three-years' Children, Babes in arms. (7.714–21)

There is an emphasis on the monstrous, and on the Fair as a microcosm of London, as both carnivalesque and monstrous, and mechanical:

> Oh blank confusion! true epitome
> Of what the mighty city is herself
> To thousands upon thousands of her sons,
> Living amid the same perpetual whirl
> Of trivial objects, melted and reduced
> To one identity, by differences
> That have no law, no meaning, and no end –
> Oppression, under which even highest minds
> Must labour, whence the strongest are not free. (7.722–30)

Wordsworth makes the Fair typical of London, reducing souls 'to one identity'. He rejects its 'riot' and carnival, which Jonson seizes on, however equivocally, in his play *Bartholomew Fair* (1614).[4] As with Dickens writing about Sikes' capture, Bartholomew Fair, inextricably linked with Smithfield, is associated with execution: the Fair is 'holden where martyrs suffered in past time' (*The Prelude* 7.677). If that was not enough to link the Fair with the prison, in *Pickwick Papers*, the worst areas of the Fleet Prison are called 'the Fair', meaning Bartholomew Fair (*PP* 40.544). Carnival and imprisonment have been identified.

The images of violence come from several sources. Smithfield and Bartholomew Fair are violent on their own, and united. St Bartholomew's Day was associated with St Bartholomew's Day massacre at Paris, in 1572, when tens of thousands of Huguenots were killed in a carnival of violence, starting with their leader, Coligny, as ordered by Catherine of Medici, mother of Charles the Ninth. It is the theme of Marlowe's play, *The Massacre at Paris*, of Meyerbeer's opera *Les Huguenots*, of Dumas' novel *La Reine Margot* (1845) and Millais' painting *The Huguenot* (1852). Smithfield, apart from Bartholomew Fair, has two forms of violence, animal-directed and human-directed. William Wallace, in 1305, died there, Wat Tyler, Sir Leicester Dedlock's *bête noire*, was executed there in 1381 during the Peasants' Revolt, which came up from the eastern parts of London and Essex. Dickens knew that, and the name of the man who killed him: Mayor Walworth, from the Fishmongers' Livery Company; Walworth as a place-name has uneasy resonances in his writings, as will be seen. And others died before the place of execution was moved to Tyburn, at the beginning of the fifteenth century. During Mary's reign (1553–58), over 200 martyrs were burned at Smithfield. The memory of the Protestant martyrdoms appears in *Barnaby Rudge* (37.305). Excavations in March 1849 outside the doorway of the priory church of St Bartholomew the Great in West Smithfield uncovered charred bones.

Smithfield means 'smooth field', but its name recalls Pip as the blacksmith: the place is appropriate to him. North-west of the City walls, and to the west of Aldersgate, Smithfield was a horse-fair, and a market for sheep, pigs and cattle, as well as a place for tournaments. The cattle market was established in 1638, by the City of London corporation, and not moved till 1855. A new market, designed by Horace Jones, opened in 1866, and another followed in 1963. For an account of what Smithfield looked like, set near the time Pip would have known Smithfield, we may take Thomas Carlyle, arrived in London in December 1824, and writing from 'these dingy streets' of Pentonville to his brother, about London – 'this enormous Babel of a place':

> Paris scarcely occupies a quarter of the ground, and does not seem to have the twentieth part of the business. O that our father saw Holborn in a fog! with the black vapour brooding over it, absolutely like fluid ink; and coaches and wains and sheep and oxen and wild people rushing on with bellowings and shrieks and thundering din, as if the earth in general were gone distracted. Today I chanced to pass through Smithfield, when the market was three-fourths over. I mounted the steps of a door, and looked upon the area, an irregular space of perhaps thirty acres in extent, encircled with old dingy brick-built houses, and intersected with wooden pens for the cattle. What a scene! Innumerable herds of fat oxen, tied in long rows, or passing at a trot to their several shambles; and thousands of graziers, drovers, butchers, cattle-brokers with their quilted frocks and long goads pushing on the hapless beasts; hurrying to and fro in confused parties, shouting, jostling, cursing, in the midst of rain and *shairn* [dung of cattle], and braying discord such as the imagination cannot figure.[5]

That Pip should be revolted by Smithfield recalls Wordsworth's reaction in *The Prelude*. No Dickens novel is as full of the thought of execution as *Great Expectations*, though no execution happens in it. Wordsworth thinks of crowds reduced 'to one identity'; here, too, the fear is of identity-loss, through being contaminated by Smithfield's overwhelming identity, threatening to 'stick' to Pip as filth, all that is left from killing and devouring life.

Smithfield recalls earlier images of being devoured. Pip, terrorised by the thought of the young man eating his heart and his liver, is compared, by Pumblechook, when eating 'out-of-the-way No Thoroughfares of Pork' (1.19.154), at the Christmas dinner, to a pig. Pumblechook reflects how he would be killed by 'Dunstable the butcher' (1.4.27). The convict on the marshes is 'terrible good sauce for a dinner' (1.5.33). The sense of animal-killing as related to cannibalism – Miss Havisham speaks about her relations coming to the table when she is laid out on it, to 'feast on me' (1.11.88), and Pip the pig – returns with Smithfield. Oliver Twist's vulnerability, passing through it, becomes Pip's, who is about to be 'done very brown' at 'Lunnon town' (1.15.109) ('done' (cooked) meaning also 'undone', with all the Shakespearian sexual senses of that latter word, and with a pun on 'dun' (brown) as in *Dun*stable, and dunned). The cattle market as the place where all forms of flesh and life are traded, affects everything: the two one-pound notes that Pip gets from the convict, delivered by 'the strange man taking aim at me with his invisible gun' (as if being shot and being given a gift are the same) are 'two fat sweltering one-pound notes that seemed to have been on terms of the warmest intimacy with all the cattle-markets in the country' (1.10.78–79). The notes remain as a nightmare to Pip 'many and many a night and day'. They evoke exchange as the swapping of money for lives. Orlick confirms the idea of violence to the human being equivalent to violence to the animal when he says that he 'dropped' Mrs Joe with the leg-iron that had been fixed on Magwitch, 'like a bullock' (3.14.428). 'Dropped' means 'made to drop', and the image evokes hanging.

For Pip, Smithfield's visibility makes it the 'shameful' place: similarly Pip said that he felt 'ashamed of home' (1.14.106), because it makes visible what he has become. He repeats the point at the end of that chapter, this time after describing how he imagines Estella looking in upon him working 'at my grimiest and commonest . . . with a black face and hands, doing the coarsest part of my work'. If shame, in the Bible, is associated with nakedness (as in Genesis 2.25: 'and they were both naked . . . and were not ashamed'), so that Adam and Eve must hide when they know they are naked, shame attaches itself to sexual fear, and to the dread of being looked at. Pip's assessment of Smithfield as 'shameful' has to do with the body being put on display, in the form of the bodies of animals. Smithfield is 'asmear' with contaminating 'filth' and 'fat' and 'blood' and 'foam'. The two first words imply the solids of London waste, the last two, its liquids. They reappear throughout *Great Expectations*, where filth takes numerous forms (in this chapter: 'odd litter', flies' excreta, 'dust and grit', mildew in clothes, even as 'a black eye in the green stage of recovery, which was painted over'). Fat recalls the pork that Pip eats while hearing it praised as plump and juicy, and the wall opposite Mr Jaggers' chair which is 'greasy with shoulders'. Magwitch, the first convict, has an old chafe upon his leg, which he is filing at, increasing its bloodiness (1.3.21); the man has been reduced by punishment to the point where he treats his own body as an object. The other convict (Compeyson) shakes with fear when he is standing next to Magwitch, and 'there broke out upon his lips, curious white flakes, like thin snow' (1.5.38), marks of foam. Perhaps foam as a figure for waste liquids recalls Mike in Mr Jaggers' office wiping his nose on his sleeve.

II · ST PAUL'S AND NEWGATE

The third site, St Paul's, appears as Pip reaches Newgate, presumably by walking away from Smithfield down Giltspur Street (earlier Knightrider Street, because it was a way to the tournament). This had at its east end, where it meets Newgate Street, the Giltspur Street Compter, a debtors' prison of the end of the eighteenth century (destroyed 1855). Opposite is St Sepulchre-without-Newgate, a medieval church rebuilt by Wren, outside the City walls, which started at Newgate (demolished, as an entry-point to the City, in 1767). Newgate stood on a corner with a front running down Old Bailey towards Ludgate, and a wall running back along present Newgate Street. Defoe (1661–1731) in *A Journal of the Plague Year* (1722), refers to Newgate market. Before the Fire (1666) it did not exist, but:

> in the Middle of the Street, which is now call'd *Blow-bladder Street*, and which had its Name from the Butchers, who us'd to kill and dress their Sheep there; (and who it seems had a Custom to blow up their Meat with Pipes to make it look thicker and

Church of the Holy Sepulchre without Newgate, whose bell tolled for prisoners going to execution, much changed (see *BR* 64.534, 77.641). Samuel Gurney's Metropolitan Drinking Fountain and Cattle Trough Association began in 1859 (for humans), 1867 (for dogs and horses); this fountain was its first example.

fatter than it was, and were punish'd there for it by the Lord Mayor) I say, that from the End of the Street towards *Newgate*, there stood two long Rows of Shambles for the selling Meat.[6]

In terms of a remembered history of London, Pip has not left the 'shambles' (butchers' benches) behind. He sees, behind Newgate, and as if sanctioning it with its authority, the alienating 'great black dome of Saint Paul's' which is said to be 'bulging', aloof and inflated with self-importance, and swollen up by the flesh which is served up at both Smithfield and Newgate. Its dome-nature makes it a centre, pulling London towards it. The brevity of description shows a development from *Master Humphrey's Clock*, which saw St Paul's clock as the killing heart of London (*MHC* 135), but the spirit is the same.

Behind St Sepulchre's, the road fell away into Snow Hill, which had, immediately on the right, and behind St Saviour's, a coaching inn, the Saracen's Head. The area Pip enters is the subject of *Nicholas Nickleby* chapter 4, which poses a question asked by the traveller from the north: what is Snow Hill and the Saracen's Inn like? The shock is to find them associated with Newgate hangings:

> There, at the very core of London, in the heart of its business and animation, in the midst of a whirl of noise and motion: stemming as it were the giant currents of life that flow ceaselessly on from different quarters, and meet beneath its walls, stands Newgate; and in that crowded street on which it frowns so darkly – within a few feet of the squalid tottering houses – upon the very spot on which the vendors of soup and fish and damaged fruit are now plying their trades – scores of human beings, amidst a roar of sounds to which even the tumult of a great city is as nothing, four, six or eight strong men at a time, have been hurried violently and swiftly from the world, when the scene has been rendered frightful with excess of human life; when curious eyes have glared from casement, and house-top, and wall and pillar, and when, in the mass of white and upturned faces, the dying wretch, in his all-comprehensive look of agony, has met not one – not one – that bore the impress of pity or compassion.
>
> Near to the jail, and by consequence, near to Smithfield also, and the Compter, and the bustle and noise of the city, and just on that particular part of Snow Hill . . . is the coachyard of the Saracen's Head Inn . . .
>
> . . . when you walk up this yard [of the Inn], you will see the booking-office on your left, and the tower of Saint Sepulchre's church darting abruptly into the sky on your right . . . Just before you, you will observe a long window with the words 'coffee-room' legibly painted above it . . . (*NN* 4.33)

The coffee room seems a movement towards civilisation, but it is where Squeers waits for the boys condemned to Dotheboys Hall, and where Nickleby meets him, before the coach goes off to Yorkshire via the Peacock in Islington for the hero to receive his initiation into reality.[7] The Coffee Room of the decapitated Saracen's Head would only further the primitiveness implied (however ideologically) in the MOOR of MOOR EEFFOC: the coffee-room is a sign ready to reverse into something traumatising.

This area accumulates significances: it is near Fagin's den; it links Oliver Twist, Nicholas Nickleby and Pip. Newgate links Fagin, and Pip, who rewrites the experience of Nicholas Nickleby in the sense that this is where both start life, one by leaving London, having arrived from Devonshire, one by coming. In both, initiation is adjacent to execution at Newgate. *Great Expectations*, noting the association of Newgate with the Old Bailey Sessions House (1834: the Central Criminal Court, until it was pulled down and rebuilt in 1907), makes justice, and the machinery for punishment and revenge indistinguishable. Newgate, symbolising court *and* execution follows the novel's early references to the Hulks.[8] These, as a mode of imprisonment, began in 1776, when the War of Independence ended transportation to America, a mode of punishment which needed no prison-building. Transportation to Australia began in 1787. Prisoners in the Hulks often served first a period of hard labour in the naval dockyards: hence the convicts (always in twos in this novel) with whom Pip travels to Kent go from Newgate to the dockyards, presumably at Chatham (2.9). This labour associated with the Hulks was seen as a way of improving the Thames, by dredging it; in this way, the prison and the river come together in this novel. The last Hulks ship was burned at Woolwich in 1857.[9] Transportation did not end completely until 1867, a few months before the end of public hanging.[10]

The 'exceedingly dirty' minister of justice, representative of the drunken crowd waiting because 'the trials are on', will show Pip the judge as though he was a waxwork. This evokes an earlier reference to waxworks, when Pip thought of Miss Havisham as not only an exhumed skeleton, but 'some ghastly waxwork at the Fair' (1.8.58). He also takes Pip to see where the gallows are kept – as an object of pride, as inanimate a form of justice as the judge – and where people were publicly whipped (another carnival of violence). Whipping did not cease for women until 1817; for men, not till the 1830s. He also shows him the Debtor's Door (to be discussed in chapter ten), where four people, like Smithfield animals, would be brought out to be hanged later. The straw around Newgate, which recalls the hackney-coach, adds to the filth, increases the analogy with the meat market: Dunstable (a stable is a place for straw) would come up to Pip the pig 'as you lay in your straw . . . and he would have shed your blood and had your life' (1.4.27). Pip reflects on these hangings, and their casualness: 'This was horrible, and gave me a sickening sense of London': making the shame visceral. Everything that has happened implies his diminution under a sense of London as a place scarcely more than primitive, accepting a level of violence quite routinely. Dickens has so mapped London as to associate these four sites with violence. It is an alternative mapping to the representations of space that would make St Paul's the centre of a London for tourists. He omits to say that Smithfield had closed in 1855; this London is conceptual, not literal.

Smithfield was London's carnival; it can be compared with another. Three years after its closure, Frith displayed at the Royal Academy his massive canvas, *Derby Day*, a record of the annual horse-race first held in June 1779 at Epsom, eighteen miles south of London, on the North Downs. By the 1850s this 'English carnival', as Hippolyte Taine and Ruskin called it, reviewing Frith, had become established.[11] For Blanchard Jerrold, it was the occasion where 'it is Dickens' children you meet, rather than Thackeray's. All the company of Pickwick – Sam Weller and his father, a hundred times: Mr Pickwick, benevolent and bibulous: Jingle on the top of many a coach and omnibus. Pushing through the crowd, nimble, silent and unquiet-eyed, Mr Fagin's pupils are shadows moving in all directions. The brothers Cheeryble pass in a handsome barouche . . .' (*A London Pilgrimage* 69–70). Jerrold's account of Dickens' 'London on the Downs' concludes, interestingly, with noticing, when going through Petticoat Lane one Sunday, that 'the Lane clothes thousands at Epsom' (*A London Pilgrimage* 77). The central episode of the picture, which does not have the freaks of Smithfield, being more bourgeois and petit-bourgeois altogether, is the child acrobat being disturbed from his act by seeing a footman lay out a picnic on the grass. Right of this, a kept woman is sitting in a carriage, with a gypsy trying to tell her her fortune, while her lover, cigar in mouth, gloved hands in pockets, leans against the carriage, looking at a barefoot flower-girl, whose presence seems a response to Dickens' Nell. Beneath the carriage, a thief picks up a bottle. At the left, a young man, also with hands in pockets, has been 'done very brown' by three sharpers playing at a table.

This carnival detail is within the novel. Miss Havisham met Compeyson 'at the races, or the public balls', and Magwitch, too, says he met Compeyson 'at Epsom races', 'the night afore the great race, when I found him on the heath, in a booth that I know'd on'. Perhaps Frith's man leaning against the carriage is a Compeyson in so far as he is a standard figure of a gentleman who is obviously a fraud; it is a feature of *Great Expectations* that it makes little allusions to sporting activities: the rowing on the river, the tumbling pigeons, Drummle and Estella riding being other instances, but the suggestions of Derby Day imply, as with Frith, the revelation of London at its most carnival, where it can also be seen to be London displaying its violence, fraudulence, and general skill in sharp practice.

III · NEWGATE AND WALWORTH

London's different spaces produce self-division, as with Wemmick, who, unlike Pancks in *Little Dorrit*, divides his state of mind between two geographical spaces, and is as if he was 'twins'. Pip goes with Wemmick to his home at Walworth, south of the river. They must cross either Blackfriars or Southwark Bridge, and walk to Elephant and Castle, where Walworth begins, between the New Kent Road (then called Greenwich Road) and the Old Kent Road, and Walworth Road. Crossing by Southwark Bridge, they would reach Newington Causeway, with Newington to the east, north of the New Kent Road, and the marshland of St George's Fields to the west. Getting onto Newington Causeway would mean passing Horsemonger Jail.

Wemmick's 'castle' at Walworth contrasts with the 'grim stone building' which is Newgate, once part of a fortress. The name – the Castle – and its Gothicism, are significant; Newgate produces a corresponding reaction in Wemmick, in militarising his home. Perhaps Walworth echoes 'The Black Veil' in *Sketches by Boz*. Between the Walworth Road, which runs from Elephant and Castle to Camberwell, and the New and the Old Kent Road, Walworth had a period of prosperity, signalled by the presence of St Peter's (architect: Sir John Soane, 1825). But in the story 'The Black Veil', it is 'little better than a dreary waste, inhabited by a few scattered people of most questionable character'. The surgeon who has been directed there, goes 'across a marshy common, through irregular lanes, with here and there a ruinous and dismantled cottage . . . [and] a stunted tree, or pool of stagnant water . . . and now and then a miserable patch of garden-ground, with a few old boards knocked together for a summer-house, and old palings imperfectly mended with stakes pilfered from the neighbouring hedges . . . [and] a filthy looking woman' who would 'make her appearance from the door of a dirty house, to empty the contents of some cooking utensil into the gutter in front, or to scream after a little slipshod girl, who had contrived to stagger a few yards from the door under the weight of a sallow infant almost as big as herself' (*SB* 432). The body that the surgeon has come to see, and revive if possible, was hanged that morning, and is dead; he was the son of the woman who came to find the surgeon, and who goes mad.[12]

The Castle is 'a little wooden cottage in the midst of plots of gardens, and the top of it was cut out and painted like a battery full of guns': Pip calls it 'the smallest house I ever saw, with the queerest gothic windows (by far the greater part of them sham), and a gothic door, almost too small to get in at' (2.6.206). For Wemmick, 'it brushes the Newgate cobwebs away'. These cobwebs are not unique to Newgate: they characterise Satis House, and Miss Havisham's wedding-cake (1.11.84). Wemmick goes out further still from Little Britain when he gets married, and goes with Pip towards Camberwell Green, where the wedding takes place, with a fishing-rod to increase the pastoralism (as if he will fish in the Surrey Canal, as if saying that he is a man with nothing to do with his time), and then has the wedding-breakfast 'at a pleasant little tavern, a mile or so away upon the rising ground beyond the Green' (3.16.453–54).

This escape from the city recalls George Barnwell's uncle, killed by his nephew, in George Lillo's play *The London Merchant* (1731). As performed by Mr Wopsle, he 'dies amiably at Camberwell' (1.15.119; compare *J2* 145). The church may be the medieval parish church of St Giles which burned down in 1842, replaced by Gilbert Scott's design of 1844. The 'rising ground' to its south must be Denmark Hill, named for Prince George of Denmark, husband of Queen Anne, who had a residence there, and ascending to Herne Hill, or Camberwell Grove, where Joseph Chamberlain was born in 1836. Ruskin's parents moved in 1823 to Herne Hill from Hunter Street, Brunswick Square. Ruskin describes the hill having Dulwich on the east, Cold Harbour Lane

Croydon Canal, a fragment, Betts' Park, Anerley, South London.

on the west, the 'dale of the Effra' on the south, and north, going towards Champion Hill, 'the plains of Peckham, and the rural barbarism of Goose Green'.[13] He calls the accumulation of fruits at Herne Hill Edenic and describes with contempt the coming of the railways (1861 to Camberwell), and of the Crystal Palace, which, 'without ever itself attaining any true aspect of size, and possessing no more sublimity than a cucumber frame between two chimneys, yet by its stupidity of hollow bulk, dwarfs the [Norwood] hills at once; so that now one thinks of them no more but as three long lumps of clay, on lease for building' (*Praeterita* 38). Present-day Walworth and Camberwell indicate the impossibility of making an escape such as Wemmick attempted in the 1820s, but even then, as now, the existence of 'the Castle' depends on a disavowal of the real urban conditions in which it takes root.

As with the opposition of places in 'The Black Veil', Little Britain and Walworth are opposed. Perhaps the Castle, which Wemmick has taken freehold, evokes Gad's Hill in Kent, Dickens' escape from London, whose purchase was so significant to him.[14] Wemmick was once a stranger to London; Walworth is his gesture towards getting out of it. The writing suggests that Wemmick's condition, that of a cultural schizophrenia, and a disavowed inability to tolerate the city, is also the novelist's condition. In contrast, Mr Jaggers' house, which has Molly as housekeeper, mother of Estella, and her supposed murderer, is in the centre of London, in eighteenth-century Gerrard Street, Soho: 'rather a stately house of its kind, but dolefully in want of painting, and with dirty windows . . . we all went into a stone hall, bare, gloomy, and little used. So, up a dark brown staircase into a series of three dark brown rooms on the first floor. There were carved garlands on the panelled walls . . . and I knew what kinds of loops I thought they looked like' (2.7.211). The last detail is Pip's obsessionalism, or Mr Jaggers', who is not as much at his ease as his reputation allows, or is more self-divided: Wemmick said Jaggers did not lock his house at night (2.6.205) but he certainly gets into his house by a key.

IV · HANGING FANTASIES

The draft titles for *David Copperfield*, which Dickens reread for *Great Expectations*, include those which make the novel 'the last living speech and confession' of David Copperfield, 'who was never executed at the Old Bailey' (*DC* 941). The humour does not quite disguise the anxiety about being hanged, and the relief that he has not been recalls the predictions of the gentleman in the white waistcoat about Oliver Twist, 'I know that boy will be hung' (*OT* 1.2.15). *Great Expectations*, Dickens' last completed novel to use a prison, Newgate, repeatedly evokes hanging, starting from when Pip must identify himself with a poor version of George Barnwell, apprentice to the 'London merchant', who is 'happily hanged' at Newgate (1.15.117). Lillo's play suggests in turn Hogarth's *The Idle 'Prentice Executed at Tyburn* (1747), also behind *Great Expectations*.

But more than the threat of Pip being hanged is the threat to Magwitch which is directed as a threat to Pip – "Ware Compeyson, Magwitch, and the gallows!' (3.14.428). Dead parents are strangely resurrected and made what the son must protect: Pip is threatened via what will happen to Magwitch. The fear is that Pip will see his surrogate father hanged, as at the beginning, where Pip sees 'a gibbet with some chains hanging to it which had once held a pirate' and says, 'The man was limping on towards this latter as if he were the pirate come to life, and come down, and going back to hook himself up again' (1.1.7).[15] The 'chains' are an iron frame acting as a manacle around the entire body. But the symbolism of this is presented differently. Magwitch is 'hunted near death and dunghill' and dies at Newgate, but images of hanging are, strangely, even more associated with the woman, with Miss Havisham. This appears in what Pip sees when he first goes to Satis House, and walks in the brewery, and sees Estella before him:

> I saw her pass among the extinguished fires, and ascend some light iron stairs, and go out by a gallery high overhead, as if she were going out into the sky.
> It was in this place, and at this moment, that a strange thing happened to my fancy. I thought it a strange thing then, and I thought it a strange thing long afterwards. I turned my eyes . . . towards a great wooden beam in a low nook of the building

near me on my right hand, and I saw a figure hanging there by the neck. A figure all in yellow white, with but one shoe to the feet; and it hung so, that I could see that the faded trimmings of the dress were like earthy paper, and that the face was Miss Havisham's, with a movement going over the whole countenance as if she were trying to call to me. In the terror of seeing the figure, and in the terror of being certain that it had not been there a moment before, I at first ran from it, and then ran towards it. And my terror was greatest of all, when I found no figure there. (1.8.64)

Estella and Miss Havisham are contrasted in this moment, though both seem to come before Pip as ghosts. But the sense of hanging as a suspension between life and death is unique to Miss Havisham; how she appears here dramatises her existence.

This episode is recalled in the second part of the novel, when Pip and Estella are standing in the same place, and Pip asks himself 'what *was* it that was borne in upon my mind when she stood still and looked attentively at me?' (2.10.237). Estella has just said she has no heart; she has virtually pronounced herself dead, in another alignment of herself with Miss Havisham as ghost. The sense of *déjà vu* then reappears:

In another moment we were in the brewery so long disused, and she pointed to the high gallery where I had seen her going out on that same first day, and told me she remembered to have been up there, and to have seen me standing scared below. As my eyes followed her white hand, again the same dim suggestion that I could not possibly grasp, crossed me. My involuntary start occasioned her to lay her hand upon my arm. Instantly the ghost passed once more and was gone.

What *was* it? (2.10.238)

The 'ghost', which can be called no more than a 'suggestion' of something in Estella that is known but unattributable, is associated with the other memory of Miss Havisham hanging. It is not stated as a memory; nor stated at all; but it belongs to the allusiveness of this text, part of Pip's being a 'visionary boy' (3.5.364). It is recalled in the next visit Pip makes to Newgate, when he waits for Estella in Wood Street, Cheapside, and, being too early, meets Wemmick on his way to Newgate to see a client in prison about a case of fraud (a counterfeit parcel was substituted for a real one (2.13.259–62)). Pip then visits Newgate: being too early produces an 'accidental' detour for him, a 'going astray' which is itself significant.

V · NEWGATE AND ESTELLA

Newgate is seen at 'visiting time'. Pip compares Wemmick walking among the prisoners to a gardener surveying his plants in a greenhouse: the irony being that Wemmick is a keen gardener at Walworth. The gardener-image emphasises his mere professionalism and dissociation at both Newgate and Walworth (he is still alienated there because of his detachment from his professional life). He signs off with one condemned prisoner by shaking his hand, calling him

'Colonel' – 'a portly upright man (whom I can see now, as I write), in a well-worn olive-coloured frock coat, with a peculiar pallor overspreading the red in his complexion, and eyes that went wandering about when he tried to fix them'. The text memorialises the man, more than death-masks could. He puts his hand to his hat 'which had a greasy spotty surface, like cold broth' (recalling the dirt of Smithfield) 'with a half-serious and half-jocose military salute'. The man is composed of contradictions, in complexion, eyes, salute and status, and plural ironies associated with him and Wemmick subtend their brief conversation. He is unwilling to free Wemmick's hand, and, in what he says, wants more reality from Wemmick than he will give him. He also would have wanted him to have another ring, 'in acknowledgement of your intentions': but the ring is also so that he will be mourned; Wemmick has already explained that his brooch, representing a lady and a weeping willow at the tomb with an urn on it is a memorial which was made by the hanged man whose cast is in Little Britain (2.5.200). So that unknown man is remembered in these two ways. Wemmick says he takes the mourning rings from those who are about to die, and never refuses: 'They're curiosities' (2.5.201), like the casts. The interview with the Colonel seems to be typical of others; and association with Little Britain contributes to being turned into a relic in a curiosity shop.

Wemmick says in a moment which betrays his insincerity, because he uses the past tense for him – 'you were quite a pigeon-fancier'. The man looks up at the sky, a detail which, understated, and poignant in its sense of lost freedom, recalls Estella 'going out into the sky'. The pigeons are tumblers: 'a variety of domestic pigeon characterized by the habit or faculty of turning over and over backwards during its flight' (OED, giving 1678 for the first citation). Wemmick wants the pigeons, and adds, 'if you've no further use for 'em', which again shows an insincerity (losing his professionalism, since he refused to admit the case was over). Such a self-division has already been noted by the text. The self-division in the Colonel which makes him both a domestic figure and 'a Coiner, a very good [sic] workman', is also noted. Both men are full of contradictions, but the text sides, at this point, with the man with whom Wemmick twice shakes hands; shaking hands being a gesture of the sincerity that he lacks, as well as a way of indicating that this is the end of the man: this is as far as human sympathy, in this London, can go.

At the end of the visit, Pip wishes that 'I might not have had Newgate in my breath and on my clothes. I beat the prison dust off my feet as I sauntered to and fro, and I shook it out of my dress, and I exhaled its air from my lungs'. The gestures repeat his earlier repudiation of Smithfield and Newgate. Then he sees Estella, and asks, 'What *was* the nameless shadow which again in that one instant had passed?' (2.13.264). It is a potentially traumatic moment: he has just missed an encounter with something, which is nothing, because it is ghostly, but which, had it not eluded him, would have enabled for him a revaluation of all his values.

After a meal in the coaching inn, and a carriage journey towards Richmond, 'turning up Cheapside and rattling up Newgate-street, we were soon under the walls of which I was so ashamed'. The word recalls Smithfield as 'shameful'; Estella uses the word 'wretches' about the Newgate prisoners – which, oddly sympathetic as a comment, indicates that unlike Pip she feels no alienation from them – and then conversation follows about Jaggers, whom it is clear she recoils from. And then there is another of those curious passages of which *Great Expectations* is so full:

> I should have . . . describe[d] the dinner in Gerrard-street, if we had not then come into a sudden glare of gas. It seemed, while it lasted, to be all alight and alive with that inexplicable feeling I had before; and when we were out of it, I was as much dazed for a few moments as if I had been in Lightning. (2.14.269)

The epiphanic moment, which is traumatic, is a knowledge which Pip cannot quite attain to; that this dinner cannot be described, because if it was it would include Molly, Estella's mother, in it. And it is the sight of her, as a woman who was nearly hung for killing a woman at Hounslow Heath, which has provided the 'suggestion' that Pip has seen in Estella. This is the traumatic moment which Lacan describes: a 'missed encounter' with 'the real', which cannot be symbolised, represented. Pip thinks of an encounter with a flash of gas as giving this indescribable moment: gas has no form (its etymology is the Greek 'chaos'). When the figure of Molly was seen at Mr Jaggers', Pip says that 'I had been to see Macbeth at the theatre . . . and that her face looked to me as if it were all disturbed by fiery air, like the faces I had seen rise out of the Witches' caldron'. He adds:

> . . . she set on every dish; and I always saw in her face, a face rising out of the caldron. Years afterwards, I made a dreadful likeness of that woman, by causing a face that had no other natural resemblance to it than it derived from flowing hair, to pass behind a bowl of flaming spirits in a dark room. (2.7.212)

This is extraordinary writing, which breaks the novel's chronology to give a much older Pip – presumably the solitary Pip of the novel's first ending – who fantasises in some way Molly's flowing hair as if linking her with Estella (in the chronology of the text he was unaware, when at Gerrard Street, that the housekeeper is Estella's mother). Has this Pip become a drug-addict, or is he holding a séance? The image of the woman cannot be contained within the text's chronology; it becomes another traumatic moment, whose effects cannot be absorbed. As if emphasising self-division and division of perception, Pip associates the two women, Molly and Miss Havisham, with two different Shakespeare tragedies in which he is the two heroes. Molly associates with *Macbeth*, Miss Havisham with *Hamlet*, since in a dream Pip has seen the image of her as the Ghost in Hamlet (2.12.258). As Hamlet, Pip is affronted by the ghost of Miss Havisham, hanging herself. It may be added that Arthur's nightmares of Miss Havisham, his sister, make her Ophelia: 'she's all in white

... with white flowers in her hair' (3.3.348–49). She is the Ghost of Hamlet's father, and the ghost of Ophelia – as Ophelia, when mad, is her own ghost. But as a Macbeth figure, Pip invokes – not over a caldron but over a bowl of flaming spirits – this other mother, the passional Molly and Estella, from a play where the woman, Lady Macbeth, says that she would dash the brains out of her sucking child. But both Miss Havisham (*Hamlet*) and Molly (*Macbeth*) are also Estella, and not her, and the 'it' which Pip associates with Estella and misses at the same moment, is so powerful because all the women are ghosts of each other.

In a later episode, Pip has another missed encounter. He has been rowing down the river, and has left the boat near the Custom House, and gone to the theatre (perhaps the theatre of 'Gone Astray'). He sees Wopsle performing; afterwards, Wopsle tells him that someone – one of the two convicts, whom Pip can identify from what Wopsle says as Compeyson, was sitting behind Pip 'like a ghost' (3.8.385). This figure is significant, in watching Pip's every move- ment, but it has other associations, which appear in a later passage, which give him a shocking perception of the 'identity of things' (1.1.3), when he again sees Molly at Jaggers' home, after Estella has been mentioned:

> I looked at those hands, I looked at those eyes, I looked at that flowing hair; and I compared them with other hands, other eyes, other hair, that I knew of, and with what those might be after twenty years of a brutal husband and a stormy life. I looked again at those hands and eyes of the housekeeper, and thought of the inexplicable feeling that had come over me when I last walked – not alone – in the ruined garden, and through the deserted brewery. I thought how the same feeling had come back when I saw a face looking at me, and a hand waving to me, from a stage-coach window; and how it had come back again and had flashed about me like Lightning, when I had passed in a carriage – not alone – through a sudden glare of light in a dark street. I thought how one link of association had helped that identification in the theatre, and how such a link, wanting before, had been riveted for me now, when I had passed by a chance swift from Estella's name to the fingers with their knitting action, and the attentive eyes. And I felt absolutely certain that this woman was Estella's mother. (3.9.390–91)

The writing is full of recognitions, not the least of which is the possibility it allows for that if Estella will be a beaten figure twenty years hence, Molly has been a figure beaten over the past twenty years by Mr Jaggers, which would explain why he likes Bentley Drummle: one man does for the mother what the other does for the daughter. But there is a further traumatic discovery, which can only be named now, though it has been held as a traumatic knowledge already. It associates a ghostly Miss Havisham as the hanged mother as an other of the Molly who could have been hanged. It associates Estella with Miss Havisham as one ghostly figure, and with Molly as another. The figures of Compeyson in the theatre and of Molly are associated, as they are for Magwitch in his narration of his life in a moment which he cannot speak of;

but which is associated for him with both of them (3.3.350). It seems that Molly was the revengeful woman (like Miss Havisham) who is supposed to have murdered her child, which Magwitch has kept quiet about, while Compeyson has blackmailed Magwitch over his silence (3.11.407). The 'ghost' is Magwitch returning to see Pip, answering to what Joe says: 'If the ghost of a man's own father cannot be allowed to claim his attention, what can?' (2.8.220). The ghost is also Compeyson, there and not there, as he is throughout the novel, and also Miss Havisham, and Estella and Molly, as an apparition. What this ghost 'is', who moves across both sexes, cannot be said. The connections between the figures Magwitch/Compeyson/Miss Havisham/Estella/Molly are close: Magwitch and Compeyson are both potential husbands to Miss Havisham (because Magwitch is Estella's father). The three women are bound to each other. Magwitch and Molly were both parents of Estella. Compeyson, destructive to both Magwitch and Miss Havisham, seems a bisexual figure between them, fascinated by both men he attempts to destroy (using Orlick against both Magwitch and Pip) and by the woman he abandons.[16] Estella, caught between two vengeful mother-figures, represents the woman designed to wreak vengeance on males, in substitution for Compeyson (Miss Havisham) and Magwitch (Molly), but caught by a wife-beater in her turn. The women who try to destroy do so in a form of masochism. Each of these five ghosts is a figure of pain, each scarred: Magwitch by the leg-iron, Compeyson facially, Miss Havisham by the jilting, Estella by the absence of heart and by being beaten, Molly by scarred wrists. The three women help to show that the men are also feminine. How they overlap with each other suggests that they may stand in for the absent, dead parents over whose grave Pip weeps at the beginning; but as ghosts, they remain shadowy, on the edge.

VI · THE RIVER

Great Expectations begins with 'the marsh country, down by the river', with the view from the churchyard across to the Thames; it mirrors Dickens' own living at Gad's Hill, which is nearby to these sites. The novel moves to London, and upstream on the north side of the Thames as far as Hammersmith and, in allusion, to Compeyson's house at Brentford. On the south side, it moves to Kingston jail – where Magwitch was: it is a prison alluded to in *Oliver Twist* (2.8.254), with whose geography *Great Expectations* has some resemblances – and to Richmond. When Magwitch returns from Australia to find Pip in the Temple:

> It was wretched weather; stormy and wet, stormy and wet, and mud, mud, mud, deep in all the streets. Day after day, a vast heavy veil had been driving over London from the East [the place of the marshes, straight up the river], and it drove still, as if in the East there were an Eternity of cloud and wind. So furious had been the gusts, that high buildings had had the lead stripped off their roofs; and in the country, trees had

Lawyers' gardens, The Temple, where the Embankment has pushed the river back; beforehand, the river came up to where the steps are now. 'Alterations have been made in that part of the Temple since that time, and it has now not so lonely a character as it had then, nor is it so exposed to the river', *GE* 2.20.313.

been torn up, and sails of windmills carried away; and gloomy accounts had come in from the coast, of shipwreck and death. Violent blasts of rain had accompanied these rages of wind, and the day just closed as I sat down to read had been the worst of all. (2.20.313)

This insistent recall of the East implies the poor end of the town; at the end of the novel Pip haunts the 'weary western streets of London . . . with their ranges of stern shut-up mansions' (3.17.458–9) – so both streets and private houses are prisons – pursuing a government pardon for Magwitch. It replays the East wind of *Bleak House*, and the 'tempest' that drowns Steerforth. The 'wind rushing up the river' recalls 'the distant savage lair from which the wind was rushing, was the sea' (1.1.4). The chapter ends with Pip waking as:

the clocks of the Eastward churches were striking five, the candles were wasted out, the fire was dead, and the wind and rain intensified the thick black darkness. (2.20.324)

What is described is the severest attack on settled identity in an upheaval which associates Magwitch with the most elemental forces; identity so lost is a theme which runs throughout the novel's third 'stage'.

Magwitch is trapped in London through the agencies of Compeyson and Orlick: in such a moment, Wemmick must send Pip a note, 'DON'T GO HOME' (3.5.366), so making Pip go back to Fleet Street and take a hackney chariot to the Hummuns, a hotel in Covent Garden which closed in 1865 (another is the meeting place for the Finches of the Grove (2.15.273)). It is described with less romanticism here than in 'Where We Stopped Growing'.[17] The fake Orientalism of the place (named because it stood on the site of former, eighteenth-century, Turkish baths) enforces Pip's alienation from London, yet Wemmick advises that 'under existing circumstances there is no place like a great city when you are once in it' (3.6.371). The city becomes the prison itself, and both Magwitch and Pip the hunted down criminals in it. Magwitch must be hidden 'down river', between Limehouse (north of the river) and Greenwich (south). Pip finds his way to the hiding-place 'Mill Pond Bank, Chink's Basin, Old Green Copper Rope Walk' (3.7.373), which, it is assumed, must be beyond the West India Docks.

Pip's and Wemmick's intention involves taking Magwitch by boat to the long reaches below Gravesend, to pick up a steamer coming down the Thames that will get them to the Continent, perhaps Rotterdam. Pip practises rowing from Garden-court, at Temple Stairs, to Blackfriars to London Bridge, and then to Erith, fourteen miles downstream of London, below Woolwich, and passing Mill Pond Bank. (An article on people 'shooting' old London Bridge in boats and drowning appeared in *All the Year Round* 4 May 1861.) On the day itself: 'Old London Bridge was soon passed, and old Billingsgate market with its oyster-boats and Dutchmen, and the White Tower, and Traitors' Gate, and we were in among the tiers of shipping' (3.15.435). Billingsgate is Smithfield's equivalent, for fish. Virtually the last sight of London is of its prime prison; the Tower of London's White Tower (1078), and its water-gate of the 1270s, which accrued such a reputation as the place for traitors. They pick up Magwitch, and reach Gravesend, and put up for the night at a public-house and see that customs men are indeed interested in their boat, as it is hauled up on the causeway for the night; but they 'struck across the marsh in the direction of the Nore' (3.15.442).

This journey downstream is linked with the first part of the novel; the river there, and the progress from London out to sea means that the locales are not two, but one, and the marsh country is not different from London, but its expression. The Custom House, based at Gravesend (in a new building of 1816) but linked to London, also associates the areas. The next morning, as the escapees are out in the water, and looking for the Hamburg steamer to come down with the tide, a galley reaches them, presumably manned by the Thames River Police (founded 1798), but including Compeyson as the informer.[18] In a moment of reversal, followed by another, Magwitch is arrested and arrests Compeyson; the boat goes down and Pip is in the water, giving him another of those epiphanic moments characteristic of this text and showing a struggle with death: 'It was but for an instant that I seemed to struggle with a thousand mill-weirs and a thousand flashes of light' (3.15.444–45).

Magwitch and Compeyson fight under water, Compeyson being drowned, in a display of violence paralleling the fight at the bottom of the ditch (1.5.36), not just in replaying it, but in that it takes place, geographically speaking, almost due north of the earlier fight, only in the Thames, not in the water and marsh and mud of the book's first part. As if completing the symmetry of these places with London, the Jack at the Ship – 'who was as slimy and smeary as if he had been low-water mark' (3.14.440) is instructed to look for Compeyson's body. It becomes apparent that he dresses himself from drowned men's clothes, as the minister of justice in clothes from the gallows (3.15.446). The journey down the river, and which Pip has travelled on by road on the coach, is also one Pip has walked, as Dickens walked it, all thirty miles, in October 1857.

If Pip's second visit to Newgate, with Wemmick, showed him disavowing the place, his third encounter does not, for he now identifies with Magwitch in Newgate and its infirmary, and with the death-sentence on Magwitch, one of thirty-two condemned together, while 'the sheriffs with their great chains and nosegays, other civic gewgaws and monsters, criers, ushers, a great gallery full of people – a large theatrical audience – looked on, as the two-and-thirty and the Judge were solemnly confronted' (3.17.457). 'Gewgaws' mean baubles, toys and trifles, and fit with the chains and nosegays that the sheriffs carry (to prevent the smells that are more than implicit in Smithfield London). Or they refer to civic dignitaries themselves (the passage is satire against the City of London, in which case they pair with 'monsters' as the fullest expression of what people who administer justice actually are, as well as what they may carry with them. The theatrical audience turns the trial's ceremony into theatre. The thirty-two confront the Judge as much as he them, and the writing links the condemned and the Judge through the broad shaft of light. The chapter ends with Magwitch's death in the prison, and Pip's memory of those who went up to the Temple to pray (Luke 18.10–13), where the Temple certainly acquires another meaning, of the place for lawyers, where Pip himself lived.

After Magwitch's death, Pip is in the situation where he is likely to become a John Dickens figure, arrested by bailiffs for debt. It is preceded by an account of a night of 'great duration', 'which teemed with anxiety and horror':

Whether I really had been down in Garden-court in the dead of the night, groping about for the boat that I supposed to be there; whether I had two or three times come to myself on the staircase with great terror, not knowing how I had got out of bed; whether I had found myself lighting the lamp, possessed by the idea that he was coming up the stairs, and that the lights were blown out; whether I had been inexpressibly harassed by the distracted talking, laughing, and groaning, of some one, and had half suspected those sounds to be of my own making; whether there had been a closed iron furnace in a dark corner of the room, and a voice had called out over and over again that Miss Havisham was consuming within it; these were things that I tried to settle with myself and get into some order, as I lay that morning on my bed. But the vapour of a limekiln would come between me and them, disordering them all, and it was through the vapour at last that I saw two men looking at me. (3.18.461)

The language characteristically confuses identity; 'come to myself' implies self-recognition, or recognition of another. On the night when Magwitch returned, he was encountered coming up the stairs, and when Pip descended the stairs in the dark the next morning, it was to fall over a man on the stairs (3.1.327), who turns out to be Orlick (3.14.427). So 'come to myself' includes the idea of stumbling over the self on the staircase, an other self who is Orlick; and this is followed by the idea of another self coming up the stairs.

Like the earlier dream of the file 'coming at me out of a door, without seeing who held it' (1.10), the identity of the 'he' coming up the stairs is ambiguous, whether Magwitch, or Orlick, or Compeyson ('like a ghost'). And when Magwitch's footsteps were heard, Pip had associated them with his 'dead sister' (the sister as a ghost). This 'he' and the strange 'it', both there and not there in Estella, is the something which is also nothing which is coming at Pip, as he feels feverishly in the day before the attempt to get Magwitch out of London, and says: 'Now it has come and I am turning delirious' (3.14.433).

Delirium affects the text: the idea of Pip hearing voices is almost a classic description of schizophrenia, especially when the voice calls out that Miss Havisham is 'consuming' within the furnace. This calling out repeats the vision of Miss Havisham as ghost. The 'vapour' – which is also ghostly – of the limekiln further disorders thoughts; and recalls the encounter with Orlick when he wanted to put Pip's body in the limekiln, and said that he wanted to do that with his sister too (3.14.425, 426). That passage suggests, then, the obliteration of identity, in a burning more complete than that of Miss Havisham, in rescuing whom, Pip is 'done very brown'. Miss Havisham is virtually killed; Pip is burned. That associates with what the threat of the limekiln represents: the absolute loss of identity. But that is threatened already by Orlick's words, in an extraordinary speech which marks him out as schizophrenic. He names himself as 'Old Orlick', so that he assumes a different, other, identity, as if he was defending someone else, not 'I', and declares to Pip that:

it warn't Old Orlick as did it [attacked Mrs Joe]; it was you. You was favoured and he was bullied and beat. Old Orlick bullied and beat, eh? Now you pays for it. You done it; now you pays for it. (3.14.426)

While calling this other self 'Old', he infantilises himself through what he says, like a beaten child. The last two uses of 'it' allow for a shift from 'it' being the attack on Mrs Joe to meaning 'being an accomplice to Orlick's being bullied and beat'. It is both these: Orlick, who bullied and beat Mrs Joe, projects himself onto Pip and so sees himself as the victim, since Pip was bullied and beat. A favoured Pip is made to have 'beat' his sister, and to have aided in Orlick being beaten (as he was by Joe). Grammatically, Orlick makes Pip to disappear in an elision of himself as a fantasised Old Orlick and Pip together. The logic of 'you done it; now you pays for it' means that the 'it' which was done is simultaneously the beating of Mrs Joe and the beating of Orlick. Not only does he identify with Pip, he identifies with his sister, as though 'bullied and beat' applies to what he did to Mrs Joe, as if he was Mrs Joe. Pip is accused of beating Orlick and beating his sister, as though these two were the same thing. Pip's being 'done very brown' (passive) has been turned into an active: 'you done it'. Orlick's language – you done it, now you pays – creates a cause and effect of an action done, and a payment to be exacted, but there is no such logic possible, and in *Great Expectations* people pay for what they have not done.

In the trauma of the night, Pip has been made to do two impossible things: there is the pressure to help a surrogate father get off (by water, by the boat) and a surrogate mother to be freed (Miss Havisham, burning). The father must be saved for the second time; once on the marshes, now, out from London, as if out of prison. Miss Havisham, the only person named here, has been fantasised as imprisoned in an iron furnace, like the gibbet which had once held a pirate, as if the furnace was a more intense form of Satis House. Whereas her burning up expresses her passion, her existence in the furnace is different, in that it suggests the blacksmith's forge, as though Miss Havisham is like the 'red-hot bar' that is pulled out of the fire (1.15.113). As such, the image marks out her masochism. Conflictual impulses to save the father and the mother stress contradictory demands upon Pip which he cannot satisfy; so that he cannot row the boat when Magwitch is taken down river; his arms are too badly burned. Both forms of attempted release are connected through the links between Miss Havisham and Magwitch. Trying to save the father, he must first save the mother, making him anable to save the father.

VII · ESTELLA AND THE CITY

When Joe comes to London with Mr Wopsle, their act of tourism is to go to look at the 'Blacking Ware'us' but they decide that it didn't 'come up to its likeness in the red bills at the shop doors' because it is 'there drawd too architectooralooral' (2.8.221–22) which word of baroque excess Pip thinks is 'mightily expressive of some architecture that I know'. This gives a sense of architecture's designs as façadal, hypocritical (like Pecksniff the architect) and covering over what is pretentious, as in the description of Bentley Drummle – the parallel to Compeyson – as 'an old-looking young man, of a heavy order of architecture' (2.4.190). Perhaps Drummle is well-built, or thick-headed (his head a Corinthian capital: compare Eqan's 'Corinthian Tom'). There seems no complimentary sense that Dickens gives to architecture, which implies an opposition to the architecture of London. The other sense that could be derived from what Joe says is that architecture covers over shame, the warehouse being an autobiographical reminder in an autobiographical text of the blacking-factory as a memory that no architecture can cover over. We have already discussed Dickens' experiences in Warren's blacking-factory.[19]

London's buildings in *Great Expectations* are always oppressive. Pip's delirium when he is 'a brick in the house-wall, and yet entreating to be released from the giddy place where the builders had set me' (3.18.462) is part of that alienation from architecture. When Pip bids farewell to Estella before she marries, he says:

> The stones of which the strongest London buildings are made, are not more real, or more impossible to be displaced by your hands, than your presence and influence have been to me, there and everywhere, and will be. Estella, to the last hour of my life, you cannot choose but remain part of my character, part of the little good in me, part of the evil. (3.5.364)

The strongest London buildings are no doubt, and logically, its prisons, its strongholds, especially Newgate, stony in every sense (recalling Blake's *Proverb of Hell*, 'Prisons are built with stones of law, brothels with bricks of religion').[20] Pip's sentence is strange. It first reverses a fantasy by saying that Estella cannot move the stones of London buildings, while it also implies that Estella's being is a match for any London prison – and second, it associates their alienating effect (they should be moved) with Estella's presence and influence. She is, strangely, aligned with Newgate; the comparison is odd, though not entirely so, because she has an association with Newgate, through her parents, however much Pip wanted to dissociate her from it as a figure of ideal beauty.

Further, Pip's next sentence also sanctions the comparison with the prison since Estella is part of the 'evil' in Pip's character. It is not necessary to argue how much guilt Pip should carry with him (no more than anyone else) to see that the passage first opposes London's buildings to Estella, and then associates them with her. London, too, Pip says, is 'part of the little good in me, part of the evil'. That sense of the indistinguishability of these things, the good and the evil, and the city outside and the city inside, aligns the woman in her beauty and her mechanical quality with the city. Knowledge of that cannot be separate, in this novel, from the awareness that London is the place for killing people. But that association of Estella with Newgate, as someone both on the inside of it, in terms of her birth, and outside of it in having power over Pip, is part of what makes London so ambiguous. Discussing *David Copperfield*, it was argued that London is not seen as a woman; this is not the case with *Great Expectations*, but the result is less to eroticise the city in an obvious sense, as to render it delirious, like the mad White Woman of Berners Street, in anticipation of Miss Havisham, in 'Where We Stopped Growing'.

CHAPTER TEN

'CITY FULL OF DREAMS'
The Uncommercial Traveller

> The river had an awful look, the buildings on the banks were muffled in black shrouds, and the reflected lights seemed to originate deep in the water, as if the spectres of suicides were holding them to show where they went down. The wild moon and clouds were as restless as an evil conscience in a tumbled bed, and the very shadow of the immensity of London seemed to lie oppressively upon the river. 'Night Walks', *J4* 151

The Uncommercial Traveller collects essays, some of which preceded *Great Expectations* in date, and which appeared in book-form in 1860. After that novel, more essays appeared in 1863, resulting in another volume contemporary with the single complete novel written in the 1860s, *Our Mutual Friend* (1865). Further essays followed after that, in 1868–69.[1] All these pieces, many of them London-based, were first published in Dickens' weekly *All the Year Round*.[2] In them, the Uncommercial presents himself an unattached *flâneur*, living in Covent Garden, describing experiences some of which go back before 1860. Some have been mentioned already; this chapter concentrates on those which are directly about London. They include, from the first collection, 'Two Views of a Cheap Theatre', 'City of London Churches', 'Shy Neighbourhoods' and 'Night Walks' and 'Arcadian London'; I add for discussion from the first series, 'Travelling Abroad', though this is not about London. From the second series, I look at 'Some Recollections of Mortality', 'The Short-Timers', 'The City of the Absent', 'The Boiled Beef of New England' and 'Titbull's Almshouses'. From the third series comes 'The Ruffian', 'A Small Star in the East', and 'On an Amateur Beat'.

I · MELANCHOLY

If 'Chambers' opened with Gray's Inn as a 'stronghold of Melancholy' (*J4* 159), that is the keynote for London in *The Uncommercial Traveller*. Melancholy has taken over the amusements of the people. For example, the very last essay notes, wryly, the power of the total abstinence movement: 'A Plea for Total Abstinence' (5 June 1869) (*J4* 391) describes a procession advertising the temperance movement, witnessed from Covent Garden. The essay becomes a plea for total abstinence from using horses in such processions, on the grounds that they are overloaded. One form of abuse (alcohol) is only to be driven out through another form (abusing the horses). Alcoholism and temperance was a sub-text in 'Two Views of a Cheap Theatre' (25 February 1860) (*J4* 52). It starts with the Uncommercial going up Bow Street in January, past the 'FOUND DEAD' notice on the police-station blackboard, which he says refers to the contemporary state of the theatre. Having eaten a steak at the Cock in Fleet Street at 4.30, with Wilkie Collins and Edmund Yates (see *Letters* 9.202, a detail not in the essay), he goes to the Britannia theatre at Hoxton, 'a mile north of St Luke's hospital in the Old-street-road', near Shoreditch Church. It is a theatre he admires as much as opera-houses in Milan, Naples or Paris. What distinguishes Dickens' London from a usual perception of Paris is that in his work, London is decentred, as here, where the centre is not Covent Garden but Hoxton. He has gone to look at the audience, over 2,000: 'besides prowlers and idlers, we were small clerks, milliners, stay-makers, shoe-binders, slop-workers, poor workers'. He describes going back on the Sunday evening, when a religious meeting was being put on, to some 4,000, except that 'the lowest part of the audience of the previous night *was not there*'. While conceding that these religious meetings are valuable, he suggests that preachers should not 'disparage the places in which they speak, or the intelligence of their hearers' nor 'set themselves in antagonism to the natural inborn desire of the mass of mankind to recreate themselves and be amused'.[3]

The tone recalls 'The Amusements of the People', which had appeared in two parts in *Household Words*, 30 March 1850 and 13 April 1850 (*J3* 179, 193). The first part of that visited the Royal Victoria theatre; the second discussed going to an earlier version of the Britannia 'cheap' theatre, the Britannia Saloon (i.e. a theatre entered through a tavern), subtitled 'The People's Theatre'. Built in 1841, it reopened in 1843, after the Theatre Regulations Act had allowed all theatres to perform plays, under the control of the Lord Chamberlain. But they could not sell drink (the alternative was that premises could be licensed, but not perform plays). A letter of 1848 (*Letters* 5.429) proposes going to a performance there which included a man with a wooden leg dancing the Highland Fling. The Britannia was rebuilt in 1858 by the owner, Samuel Lane (1804–71), and Dickens notes the absence of alcohol during the interval. (Saloons which offered drink became Music Halls.)

'The Amusements of the People' distinguished the Britannia Saloon from the Eagle in the City Road, through the different entertainment offered there. The Eagle, also called the Grecian Saloon, opened in the City Road in 1832 as a music hall. *Sketches by Boz* features it, in 'Miss Evans and the Eagle' (4 October 1835, *SB* 266–72), when Samuel Wilkins and Miss Evans visit it from Camden Town. They come down St Pancras Road, so past St Pancras Old Church, and the churchyard where Mary Wollstonecraft was buried (the body was later removed to Bournemouth), and Sir John Soane also, and into the Pentonville Road, which leads into City Road. Stopping *en route* at the Crown, another tavern, with two other friends, the men get drunk and when they arrive at the Eagle, an affray follows. The sketch contrasts the genteel drinking of expensive Chinese green tea, and the ending, when the two men disgrace themselves by getting into a brawl with the men with whom the women are flirting, their charms being preferable to those of Samuel Wilkins.

Drink, and abstinence, also underlies 'The Boiled Beef of New England' (15 August 1863, *J4* 277), which discusses the 'shabbiness' and 'second-hand' nature of London in comparison with other capitals or large cities, whether in Europe, or America, or even other parts of Britain. It produces one of Dickens' few references to Trafalgar Square, laid out to Nash's design by Sir Charles Barry in the 1830s. After saying that 'there is nothing shabbier than Drury-lane, in Rome itself', the Uncommercial continues, 'the meanness of Regent-street, set against the great line of Boulevards in Paris, is as striking as the abortive ugliness of Trafalgar-square, set against the gallant beauty of the Place de la Concorde'. Trafalgar Square was not universally admired: John Timbs, in *Curiosities of London* (1855), reports that it was seen as 'an artificial stone-quarry'.[4]

In 'The Boiled Beef of New England', clothes have a 'second-hand' look. The image is of fashions descending from one class to another; this produces the conceit of manners descending from one class to another, and one class communicating to another through 'patronage'. The particular example of patronage comes from an experience off Commercial Street, Whitechapel, in Flower and Dean Streets, between Commercial Street and Brick Lane, near what would become Toynbee Hall (1884). It is of eating at a cheap-dining hall in a newly-built warehouse. The Uncommercial comments on it with interest, with only two criticisms, the lack of variety of food, and the absence of beer, which he regards as symptomatic of a patronising attitude, since 'the drunken man does not get drunk when he goes to eat and drink, but where he goes to drink – expressly to drink'. Patronage is a kind of shabbiness; noting its presence is part of a perception of London.

II · THE CITY

If London is shabby, and patronising, it has regions which cannot renew themselves: 'City of London Churches' (5 May 1860) (*J4* 105) describes visiting some fifty churches over the course of a year; but not knowing their names, apart from St Giles Cripplegate (for Milton) and St Peter upon Cornhill. It is surmised that the first church described is St James Garlickhythe, on Garlick Hill, Wren's church (1682). The surname Dowgate is mentioned: Dowgate (?Downgate) runs down south from Walbrook to Thames Street, a little to the east of Garlick Hill. If it is this church, that may give point to the sense of smell that is noted, from 'the decay of dead citizens in the vaults below', and the sense of the decay of death being in the atmosphere. The second church is Queen Anne in date (Wren is not mentioned), and includes four boys and two girls from a charity school, and gives a sense of 'exhaustion'. The church is said to be in Huggin Lane, west of Garlick Hill, and the name, originally to do with hogs, is punned on, because the anecdote told about it relates to lovers. In a third, a 'City Personage', who has a small girl with him, is the subject; he is deduced to be an old bookkeeper, or a trader who had kept his own books, but nothing else can be said about him or his house in the City 'behind a pump'. He feels that the man is waiting for the return of the citizens of the City to it. One church is mentioned for having got up a theatrical performance in it, 'but in other cases, rot and mildew and dead citizens formed the uppermost scent', or 'the staple character of the neighbourhood':

> In the churches about Mark-lane, for example, there was a dry whiff of wheat; and I accidentally struck an airy sample of barley out of an aged hassock in one of them. From Rood-lane to Tower-street, and thereabouts, there was often a subtle flavour of wine; sometimes of tea. One church near Mincing Lane smelt like a druggist's drawer. Behind the Monument the service had a flavour of damaged oranges, which, a little further down towards the river, tempered into herrings, and gradually toned into a cosmopolitan blast of fish. In one church, the exact counterpart of the church in the Rake's Progress where the hero is being married to the horrible old lady, there was no speciality of atmosphere, until the organ shook a perfume of hides all over us from some adjacent warehouse.

Rood Lane, Mincing Lane and Mark (mart, or market) Lane, where the Corn Exchange used to be, lead south out of Fenchurch Street; the church which Hogarth depicts, where the Rake marries the old and ugly, one-eyed bride in *The Rake's Progress* (1735) is Marylebone Old Church; as Paulson says, 'almost out in the country, and therefore popular as a place for secret or hasty weddings' (Paulson, Hogarth's Graphic Works 95). The piece, which recalls *Little Dorrit* 1.3, closes with a reminder of how the documents of these churches have now lost their meaning:

> So with the tomb of the old Master of the old Company on which [the tree in the churchyard] drips. His son restored it, and died, his daughter restored it and died, and then he had been remembered long enough and the tree took possession of him, and his name cracked out.

The parallel between the lost names and the lost identities of the churches is plain; these churches hold smells and fragments which suggest the past, but there is no bringing them back to life again by working out their identities. The piece concludes by saying they have died 'a slow death'. The same year saw the Union of Benefices Act, which closed and demolished some twenty-two City churches between 1870 and 1907.[5]

The City is dead and ghostly in 'The City of the Absent' in the second series (18 July 1863, *J4* 260). It begins discussing his 'haunting' of City Churchyards, ones sometimes wholly detached from their churches. One, near Fenchurch Street Station (probably St Olave's, Hart Street) has an 'attraction of repulsion', on account of its stone skulls pierced with spikes.

Gateway to St Olave's, Hart Street, associated with Pepys, usually thought of to be 'Saint Ghastly Grim' because of the skulls over the churchyard, associated with plague-warnings.

An encounter with an old couple making hay, 'gravely among the graves', he thinks of as Time and his wife. They are contrasted with two Charity School figures whom he sees on three occasions in another churchyard making love. The piece turns to discussion of how to work out that a churchyard may be down some court or alley, and becomes openly speculative, as it describes wandering past businesses which are closed on Sunday. Particularly he thinks of money in the city ('yellow earth') and notes being counted out, called 'the rustling of that south-cash wind'. Thinking about the possibilities of robbing the 'money cellars' of banks, he speculates on 'reverses' happening to people, whether 'some shoeless boy in rags' is on his way to become a Banker:

> much as I also want to know whether the next man to be hanged at Newgate yonder, had any suspicion upon him that he was moving steadily towards that fate, when he talked so much about the last man who paid the same great debt at the same small Debtor's door.

That Newgate had a debtor's door recalls the point that it included debtors amongst its prisoners until 1815, when Whitecross prison was built. Talk of money has concluded with this ironic note of another enclosed space

Some of the oldest houses in Newington Green, from 1650s onwards.

Unitarian Chapel, Newington Green, which still has houses going back to 1658, and was the birthplace of Samuel Rogers (1763–1855); a dissenting area, in the eighteenth century: this chapel was built on the green in plain classical style.

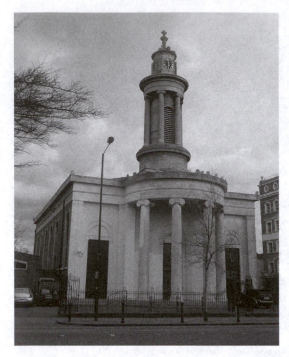

(*left*) Church Greek Revival architecture: All Saints', originally called Camden Chapel; William and Henry Inwood, between 1822 and 1827: close to Bayham Street and other Dickens homes in Camden Town. It was built after St Pancras New Church, Euston Road with its caryatids, based on those in the temple of the Erechtheum, Athens.

(*below left*) Whitecross Street, between Old Street and the Barbican, and formerly containing the Whitecross Street Prison, intersects with Fortune Street, site of Philip Henslowe's Fortune theatre (1600), managed by him and Edward Alleyn.
(*below right*) Sheperdess Place, City Road. The Eagle Tavern is on the other side of the courtyard. An inscription of 1864 on the back of the house announces it is the parish boundary of St Luke's, Middlesex.

in the City: Newgate, which is identified with it. The passage recalls *Great Expectations* 2.1.166, and the four prisoners who will come out of the door to be hanged. It also emphasises a point in *Little Dorrit* about debt: it is ironic that it is that door which is used for the person to be hanged, because being in debt is not criminal; but to be in debt is to be made to feel guilty. Hanging enforces the sense of a debt to be paid; it creates a continuum between being in debt financially, being guilty, and being deserving of death. This is the narrative imposed by the City upon those who live in it; it flatters with the dream of money, but it exacts punishment. The passage concludes wondering where the people have gone. He stands outside Garraway's, thinking of those who wait for people there, and of the point that every working person in the City goes clean away on a Sunday. 'This characteristic of London City greatly helps its being the quaint place it is in the weekly pause of business, and greatly helps my Sunday sensation in it of being the Last Man'.[6]

Melancholic humour characterises 'Shy Neighbourhoods' (26 May 1860, *J4* 117) which recalls a 'vagabond course of shy metropolitan neighbourhoods and small shops', and discusses 'the moral effects upon fowls of life in a London slum'.[7] OED cites Dickens for the use of 'shy' meaning 'of questionable character, disreputable, "shady"'. The piece concerns not humans – postponed for another piece – but 'the lower animals of back streets and byeways', including 'the bad company birds keep', for instance, around St Giles. There is the description of a donkey 'over on the Surrey side of London-bridge, among the fastnesses of Jacob's Island and Dockhead', to the east of Jacob's Island, who is seen as like a 'blackguard', caught trapped in a narrow alley, 'a picture of disgrace and obduracy'. When the dogs of shy neighbourhoods are brought in, it becomes clear that 'shy' includes 'work-shy'; there is the discussion of a Newfoundland dog in a back street of Walworth, who appears in the drama, but who has too much honesty to become a successful actor, as Dickens shows in a passage of wonderful comic drama. This is followed by two dogs 'in a shy street, behind Long-acre' (the Seven Dials rookery), who act in Punch, much to the astonishment of a country dog. A dog in a 'shy corner of Hammersmith' who keeps a man follows, a mongrel in Somerstown, another in Southwark who keeps a blind man, described in relation to Piccadilly; another shy one in Notting-hill who keeps a drover. From dogs, we move to cats 'about the Obelisk in St George's Fields, and also in the vicinity of Clerkenwell-green, and also in the back settlements of Drury-lane', who are compared to women, especially pregnant women. The last section turns to fowls, including 'a reduced Bantam family of my acquaintance in the Hackney-road, who are incessantly at the pawnbroker's'. Other geographical locations include a disorderly tavern near the Haymarket, the other side of Waterloo Bridge, and the densest part of Bethnal Green, and a wonderful conceit appears as it is said that the fowls think of the moment of the public-house shutters being taken down as sunrise.

III · FASHIONABLE LONDON

Dickens on London contrasts with the journalist George Augustus Sala (1828–95), in *Twice Round the Clock* (1859), articles first published in serial form in a weekly edited by Henry Vizetelly (1820–94), *The Welcome Guest: A Magazine of Recreative Reading for All*.[8] (The title echoes the sense of the bourgeois home that had been established in *Household Words*.) Sala starts at 4 am at Billingsgate, when the market opens. In twenty-four chapters, he goes to Printing House Square, in the City, for the publication of the *Times*, Covent Garden at six o'clock, looks at London waking up at seven, and particularly waiting at Euston Square terminus, and discussing Parliamentary Trains (trains that followed the legislation of 1844 which insisted on third-class carriages being both covered, and affordable). At eight he is at St James and the Mall. At nine, looking at the clerks at the bank and at the boats on the river. At ten, at Westminster Hall. At eleven, trooping the guard, and looking at a wedding in Piccadilly. At twelve, at the Mansion House police-court, and dining at the Bay Tree, down a narrow lane in the City, he is not sure which. At one, he is watching dockers eating. At two, he is in Regent Street, which, unlike Dickens, he speaks of with pride, as 'the most fashionable street in the whole world' (155), 'an avenue of superfluities – a great trunk-road in Vanity Fair' (157). He follows one lady going from Regent Street to meet her husband at the Royal Exchange, and thinks of the City, like the West End, as embodying worship of Mammon. At three, he is at the auction-room of Debenham and Storr in King Street, Covent Garden, and at the Pantheon, between Oxford Street, and Great Marlborough Street; this comprised assembly rooms (1772) which were rebuilt after fire (1795), but which became a bazaar (1814) until demolition in 1937. At four, he has gone over to Hyde Park Corner, where he approves of the way that the area has been brought out by the battle of Waterloo, and says 'London grows handsomer every day':

> I grant the smoke – in the city – and I confess that the Thames is anything but odiferous in sultry weather [Sala writes a year after the 'Great Stink' which notoriously prompted the construction of sewers and the Embankment], and is neither as blue nor so clear as the Neva [Sala had been to St Petersburg in 1856, and wrote on Russia for *Household Words*]; but I say that London has dozens and scores of splendid streets and mansions, such as I defy Paris, Vienna, Berlin, or St Petersburg – I know their architectural glories by heart – to produce. I say that Pall Mall beats the Grand Canal at Venice, that Regent Street, with a little more altitude in its buildings, would put the Boulevard des Italiens to shame; and that Cannon Street makes the Nevskoi Perspective hide its diminished head. (188)

The chapter is a treatment of Tattersall's, auctioneering rooms for horses, which were opposite Hyde Park, on a site later taken over by St George's Hospital (1865). The hospital moved to Tooting, Tattersall's to Newmarket.

At five, Sala discusses clubs, and then moves to Bow Street, to discuss the Prisoners' Van. At six, omnibuses, and a Charity Dinner at the London Tavern in the City, at seven, theatres and their green-rooms. Eight discusses Her Majesty's theatre in the Haymarket, whose Italian Opera contrasts favourably with Milan (La Scala Opera House), Paris and Berlin. (But he makes an exception with the Italian Opera House in Moscow.) And he refers to Mr Turveydrop's 'Fops' Alley' (258). The chapter ends with leaving the opera-house, wearied of Verdi's 'figments' (264), to visit a pawnbroker's between St Giles and the Strand. At nine, he goes to the 'Vic' – the Coburg theatre in the Waterloo Road – and discusses the New Cut, which he pronounces 'low' (274). At ten, he walks towards Pentonville, which was spoiled when 'they pulled down that outrageously comic statue of George IV, at Battle Bridge [in 1845]. Then they built the Great Northern Railway Terminal' [King's Cross] (286). He is going to the Belvidere, a tavern which has every Saturday a meeting for political discussion. He then discusses oratorio at Exeter Hall in the Strand, as supplying the place of the opera for the 'seriously-inclined middle-classes' (293). At eleven, he discusses the 'conversazione world of London' (304), at twelve, the Haymarket, and newspaper offices in the Strand. At one, he dines at Evans' in Covent Garden, and discusses a fire at St Giles. At two, a late debate in Parliament, and Waterloo Bridge, nicknamed, after Thomas Hood's poem, the 'Bridge of Sighs' because of its suicides. Three describes a masked ball for dissolute 'swells' in some area like Haymarket, Panton Street, Soho or Leicester Square, and finishes at Bow Street.

Sala's London is superior to other cities, and is treated optimistically. This associates with a sense of the city working as a harmonious whole, to be seen and summed up in its entirety. His prolixity exhibits no resistance to or alienation from London; his images of London show him hardly moving out of areas which are public and tourist-conscious, whereas Dickens on London is, especially in *The Uncommercial Traveller*, the reverse, searching out what in London does not confirm those signs which define London as 'London', or finding things that could be the source of shame, or which work beneath the gaze of the usual journalist. Everything Sala sees implies company and group activity and denies solitude. This is true of his night scenes, in contrast to Dickens, who avoids such sociality, even in essays which are witty, whose alternative London is neither threatening nor obscene. In 'Arcadian London' (29 September 1860) Dickens' topic is solitude in London, noting, ironically, that this exists in the daytime in the West End in September. As in 'Night Walks', to be discussed later, the Uncommercial notes an alternative London, of houselessness, and solitude. 'Arcadian London' gives a vignette of life between Bond Street and Regent Street, and between Piccadilly and Conduit Street, that area which began to be laid out in the 1680s (for instance, St James Piccadilly was commissioned from Wren by Henry Jermyn, Earl of St Albans, in 1684, and completed in the year of Jermyn's death). The area expanded in the eighteenth century, becoming more class-conscious, as with, in the mid-nineteenth century, Savile Row for tailoring, giving the alternative to shabby London.

In 'Arcadian London', all depends on the pun: Arcadia and Arcade. If the Uncommercial becomes a *flâneur* in the Burlington Arcade, the place of 'ultra civilisation', he notes that the Beadles of the area 'might turn their heavy maces into crooks, and tend sheep in the Arcade, to the purling of the water-carts as they give the thirsty streets much more to drink than they can carry'. He has taken temporary lodgings in Bond Street, named for the financier, Sir Thomas Bond, who built Old Bond Street (1684); New Bond Street (1720) followed. Everyone is out of town; the hatter, where he lodges, is holidaying with his family on the Isle of Thanet. Milkwomen are selling cow's milk, and not bothering to adulterate it, thus increasing the sense of London as Arcadia. The Mayfair butler is reading a newspaper in 'the pleasant open landscape of Regent-street'. The life of people living an alternative existence in this part of London is noted, people of apparently no fixed abode, who 'creep about with beds and go to bed in miles of deserted houses', the houses of 'the awful perspectives of Wimpole-street and Harley-street, and similar frowning regions' on the other side of Oxford Street. In a few areas he notes things which are still happening; that it is still necessary to have boots cleaned, to eat a penny ice, and to be photographed. In metropolitan Arcadia, the absence of Talk is noted. In such areas as Savile Row, Clifford Street, Old Burlington Street and Burlington Gardens, he notes the servants of the respectable classes are now 'making love' and this is associated with a 'chaste simplicity . . . in the domestic habits of Arcadia'. Unlike Sala, Dickens' sense of what makes a city is not to be found in its publicly describable spaces or architecture: hence this essay, however slight it seems, is of a journalism harder to write than Sala in his cheerful inclusiveness.

IV · INSTITUTIONS

'The Short-timers' (20 June 1863, *J4* 237) opens with the Uncommercial reflecting, as he is taken down river, and 'looking – not inappropriately – at the drags that were hanging up at certain dirty stairs to hook the drowned out, and at the numerous conveniences provided to facilitate their tumbling in'.[9] The 'reflection' is given in the first paragraph, before the setting is announced, so that it draws attention to itself as a special meditation, which the reader must consider before getting any context for the statement. The essay's subject is the presence of outcast and neglected children, since, as he says, that in going around the city, 'I can find – *must* find, whether I will or no – shameful instances of neglect of children'. He writes, 'I can slip out at my door, in the small hours after any midnight, and in one circuit of the purlieus of Covent-garden Market' find all forms of oppression, where the state intervenes to no purpose.

The sentence's diction is strange. '*Must* find' could imply a compulsion on him to find something, whether he wants to or not. Desire to go out after midnight, familiar in *The Uncommercial Traveller*, is the sign of a non-bourgeois compulsion to find something that he already knows intellectually to be there. But if he knows it is there, why 'must' he find it? The question impinges on what is fascinating in these essays: the need to look at that which is obscene, a source of 'shame' (a word used twice in the paragraph), or put out of sight. The desire to see is to be shamed; it is a wish for the abject, for what disturbs, and for what returns a look.

This opening 'reflection' – a mind going astray – contrasts with what else is in this essay, an account of going downstream, and then taking the train to the Stepney Union, where the 'the half-time system' is practised at Limehouse Hole. Workhouse children are being educated for half the day, so that they can also go out to work.[10] The essay records the good work taking place here, but perhaps too heartily, and idealistically, and ends reflecting that what one Board of Guardians can do in education, so can others, and this would 'clear London streets of the most terrible objects they smite the sight with – myriads of children who awfully reverse Our Saviour's words, and are not of the Kingdom of Heaven, but of the Kingdom of Hell. Clear the public streets of such shame and the public conscience of such reproach?' The tone has partly changed from the opening, and the rhetoric is strained, as with the phrase 'Kingdom of Hell', as a characterisation of London, as if it was like Dante's Inferno. Clearing the streets sounds more like a modernising and authoritarian response to the 'shame' that has been identified than the opening has allowed for; indeed, 'clearing' sounds more like a repression of the issue. In such an essay, self-division is apparent; the self that is attracted into the streets after midnight (streets not exactly the same as the 'public streets') is not the self that can admire what is done in Limehouse. The journalism shows internal splits, and these are inherent to its interest.

'Titbull's Alms-Houses' (24 October 1863, *J4* 315) reflects on the architecture of almshouses, and their pretensions, and on those of the founders, and trustees, and the occupants, people whose receipt of charity, which is deemed insufficient, leaves them 'in a state of chronic injury and resentment', while they attempt to maintain gentility and social difference, as with the widow who says that her son was 'cast away in China' 'with a modest sense of its reflecting a certain geographical distinction on his mother'. The essay reviews 'journeys made among those common-place smoky-fronted London Alms-Houses, with a little paved court-yard in front enclosed by iron railings, which have got snowed up, as it were, by bricks and mortar; which were once in a suburb, but are now in the densely populated town; gaps in the busy life around them, parentheses in the close and blotted texts of the streets'. The particular almshouse is in East London, usually thought to be based on the Vintners' Company Almshouses in the Mile End Road, built at the beginning of the nineteenth century for twelve women. It has a 'grim stone, very difficult to read, let into the front of the the centre house' saying that the almshouses were

Trinity Almshouses, Whitechapel Road. The houses run back at right-angles to the road from the gates, and a chapel is at the back, facing the road. The inscription within a cartouche reads: 'This Almshouse, wherein 28 decayed Masters and Commanders of Ships and the widows of such are maintained by the Corporation of Trinity House Anno 1695. The Ground was given by Captain Henry Mudd and Elder Brother whose company did also contribute'. Trinity House, established by 1514, was the company controlling lighthouses. Rebuilt after 1941 bombing.

built by Sampson Titbull (d. 1723) who left almshouses for six men and nine women. But 'the establishment is a picture of many' almshouses (*J4* 317). The essay moves between life and death: the latter, since the courtyard before the almshouses is likened to a graveyard for the inhabitants, and details of funerals follow, and the almshouse could be regarded as a grave, but it ends with the visit from outside of two maimed Greenwich Pensioners, and Mrs Mitts' marriage to one of them, so leaving the almshouse; this episode suggests that the almshouse is not simply a 'gap', or a 'parenthesis' within the East End, but integral to the streets' 'close and blotted text'.

'The Ruffian' (10 October 1868, *J4* 334) discusses thieves ('ruffians') practising in the Waterloo Road, particularly against women, and the laxness of the police in pursuing them. It discusses particularly 'habitual criminals' – those who regularly committed minor crimes and went often to prison; these were the subject of the 'Habitual Criminals' Act (1869), which, in the wake of the end of transportation in 1857, and a wave of garrotting in 1862, attempted to put ex-convicts on a national register, and further enforce the declaration, or admission, of identity to the police.[11] The article is in favour of virtual 'perpetual imprisonment', but its subject is the inadequacy of law-enforcement. Its second half, relating to Dickens' time living in Devonshire Terrace, near Regent's Park, turns on the Uncommercial's demand to have a woman arrested for foul language. Here it is obvious that the Uncommercial is identifiable as Dickens, since he gives his name to the police-officer; the text in that way is policing itself. The police know that nothing else can be expected from the woman who comes from 'Charles Street, Drury Lane'. The emphasis is placed on 'the streets', and on policing as ineffectual, and magistrates too lenient, and it is easy to see the text as fearful of what the city yields in the way of 'ruffians'.

The ruffian is also a subject of 'On an Amateur Beat' (27 February 1869, *J4* 377), an essay which recalls two others, 'Wapping Workhouse' (18 February 1860, *J4* 41), and 'A Small Star in the East' (*All the Year Round* 19 December 1868, *J4* 352). 'On an Amateur Beat' implies the Uncommercial becoming the policeman, in going from Covent Garden to Limehouse, going through Drury Lane, then an area which no Uncommercial could, supposedly, travel; he reflects on how modernisation has happened, and on the possibilities of surveillance, but concludes that: 'a costly police-service . . . has left in London, in the days of steam and gas and photographs of thieves and electric telegraphs, the sanctuaries and stews of the Stuarts'. He notes, near some demolished buildings near Temple Bar, the 'public savagery of neglected children'. He passes Newgate and Smithfield and St Paul's, and the City, till he comes to Houndsditch Church (St Botolph, Aldgate), noticing there a woman completely bent over, as by osteoporosis (a type he says he sees often around the Strand). He then travels down the Commercial Road.

The journey repeats one made nine years earlier, described in 'Wapping Workhouse'. There, he left Covent Garden to go eastwards to inspect a workhouse, passing the 'India House', and later, two old coaching-inns, the Saracen's Head (gone by 1868), and 'the Black, or Blue, Bull, or Boar', belonging to the time before 'the age of railways', and then Whitechapel Church, before reaching the 'abundant mud' of the Commercial Road. Reaching the docks at Wapping, he has one of those strange encounters of which *The Uncommercial Traveller* has many, with a creature who suddenly appears, and vanishes, like a Dantean lost soul, and 'who may have been the youngest son of his filthy old father, Thames, or the drowned man about whom there was a placard on the granite post'. This figure talks about the women who attempt suicide at that particular spot, a swing-bridge over some locks (identified with a bridge in Old Gravel Lane, in the London docks), and speaks with a 'gurgle in his throat', as if the river was inside him. 'On an Amateur Beat' is less jaunty than this, and reacts against the *laissez-faire* attitude which permits suicide with another which, driven by a sense of shabbiness in the streets, desires to police it.

'A Small Star in the East' is recollected in the essay: this had visited Ratcliff and the 'impure river', to see an Irish woman, and another woman in the same house, sick from the poison of the Lead Mills. He sees also an unemployed boiler-maker, a wife who does slop-work (slop = rough clothes for seamen), making pea-jackets (overcoats formerly worn by seamen). At another house, he comes across a coal porter. He discusses the reluctance of people to enter the workhouse. About to return to Fenchurch Street by catching a train at the Stepney Railway Station, he sees the 'East London Children's Hospital', which gives him the meaning of the essay's Christmas title.[12] The hospital, created by Dr Nathanael Heckford (1842–71) opened in 1868, after Heckford had observed a cholera epidemic in Wapping in 1866. The hospital began in a warehouse in Narrow Street, and in 1875, moved to Glamis Road, Shadwell, to the north of the Highway: Heckford showed Dickens round, and around the houses that he described.[13]

'On an Amateur Beat', whose preoccupation with death shows in its opening reference to looking through the 'Dance of Death' illustrations, revisits this Children's Hospital, seeing a girl there whose leg has been amputated because of cancer of the bone. The destination is, however, Limehouse Church, and the Lead Mills of 'A Small Star in the East', in Burdett Road (1862), a thoroughfare connecting with Hackney from the West India Docks, so joining Victoria Park to Limehouse. The road itself was a philanthropic gesture of Angela Burdett-Coutts, after whom it was named. The Lead Mills employ women like the Irish woman in 'A Small Star in the East', and the process of turning pig-lead into white-lead produces lead-poisoning in the women, so that this essay reads as

St Paul's Shadwell, The Highway, originally 1656, rebuilt 1717 to 1720 by John Walters, added to by Butterfield, in 1848. The chief expense here was the tower and spire.

St Anne's Church, Limehouse, Hawksmoor, 1730; the Commercial Road to its north, railways and the river south.

a series of ways in which the disadvantaged are destroyed: neglected children, the woman bent double, the children in the hospital, and the women in the Lead Mills; even if the report, which is 'policing' the factory-owners, does exonerate them of any individual blame.

V · DEATH

The Uncommercial Traveller's interest in deaths and corpses has been often commented on.[14] The essays open with a shipwreck, and the deaths resulting from it. Another early essay, 'Refreshments for Travellers' (24 March 1860) – on travelling by railroad – discusses suicides in the Surrey Canal. We have seen the preoccupation with death in 'City of London Churches', 'Chambers', 'The Short-timers', 'The City of the Absent', and 'A Small Star in the East'. 'Medicine Men of Civilization' (26 September 1863) discusses English funerals. 'A Fly-Leaf in a Life' (22 May 1869), which post-dates the Staplehurst railway accident, discusses the nervous pressure on Dickens, which virtually killed him.

Fascination with death, which also links London with death, goes back much further, and crystallises around the interest in the Morgue. A connection was noted in chapter two, discussing 'Railway Dreaming' (*Household Words* 10 May 1856, *J3* 369), a piece about how ideas associate in a state of distraction while travelling by rail, for 'I am never sure of time or place upon a Railroad, I can't read, I can't think, I can't sleep, I can only dream' (370). In such a state, the Morgue wanders into Dickens' thoughts.[15] And before writing that, 'Lying Awake' (30 October 1852, *J3* 88) had considered the Morgue. The piece is about wandering thoughts, where he is testing 'the theory of the Duality of the Brain', where 'one part of my brain, being wakeful, sat up to watch the other part which was sleepy', and also about the impossibility of sleep. Those phrases imply everything of self-division. He meditates on the line from *Macbeth* (2.2.36) that sleep is 'the death of each day's life', which makes him think how dreams break the individual life. Considering sleep, he wanders off into different associations of ideas, one of which is about how the Queen, he himself, and a prisoner in jail, surely not accidentally called 'Winking Charley', may all have the same experiences in sleep, since dreams do not respect people, or places. Wandering in the city, and wandering in thought at night become the same thing; contrasted people share similar dreams and they cut across identities. 'Drawn by no links that are visible to me' (a line which may recall the dagger which leads Macbeth to Duncan), he finds himself remembering the Great St Bernard Pass, theme of *Little Dorrit* 2.1. His thoughts portray the Pass and the convent, and its Morgue (first seen in September 1846).[16] The Paris Morgue then comes into his thought as one of many fantasies, 'strange images of death' (*Macbeth* 1.3.95). Recalling it, he comments on his revulsion. The dream-Morgue repeats the historical Morgue: Forster says of Dickens' visits to Paris in 1846: 'he went at first rather frequently to the Morgue, until shocked by something so repulsive [the word recalls "the attraction of repulsion"] that he had not courage for a long time to go back' (*Life* 5.7.445). Forster adds: 'on the day that closed the old year he had gone into the Morgue and seen an old man with grey head lying there' and records Dickens' sense of the man as an allegory: 'it was just dusk when I went in; the place was empty, and he lay there, all alone, like an impersonation of the wintry eighteen hundred and forty-six' (5.7.449).[17] Though this was Dickens' first visit to Paris, yet the image of the drowned body taken from the Seine had already been alluded to in 'Chapter the Last' of *The Old Curiosity Shop* (553), where it seems that Frederick Trent has been either a suicide or murder-victim. Dickens reached the Morgue in imagination before he arrived there.

As 'Lying Awake' presents one fantasy after another of destruction, he resolves to 'awake no more', punning on the voice that says Macbeth shall 'sleep no more' (2.1.33). Each ghost and fantasy that has come – or has it been his imagination? – has brought him more and more into association with Macbeth, made him more like the 'criminal' that the essay says he regards as lower than a 'mad wolf'. It is a disavowal that he must make, like the later hatred of the 'ruffian', for lying awake is a state which deterritorialises, and destroys a sense of identity. The essay ends with going for a 'night walk', another act whose nomadicism threatens identity, like the city.

The Uncommercial Traveller has two essays developing further the Morgue. There is 'Travelling Abroad' (7 April 1860, *J4* 83), a title which perhaps prompts the overall title for the series, and which develops ideas from 'Lying Awake', since dreaming, and travelling, whether across countries, or across the city, and the centrality of the Morgue within dreams, go together. 'Travelling Abroad' tricks the reader, since the journey, London to Switzerland via Paris and Strasbourg, is a day-dream, the fantasy of someone remembering previous journeys.

The first encounter on the road gives it away, because it is with a 'very queer small boy': the nine-years-old Dickens of the years living in Chatham, who knows all about Gad's Hill and its Shakespearian associations with Falstaff. 'Very queer' recalls the 'odd' boy and 'odd' man of 'Gone Astray', and 'small' is the property of many Dickens 'children' who confront the great city: Tiny Tim, Little Dorrit, Pip, confronting the city morally, and 'undersized for my years' (*GE* 1.1.4). Or that London product, the Artful Dodger, 'one of the queerest-looking boys . . . a snub-nosed, flat-browed, common-faced boy . . . and as dirty a juvenile as one would wish to see, but he had got about him all the airs and manners of a man. He was short of his age . . .' (*OT* 1.8.60). The Uncommercial's encounter suggests the idea of Dickens as a divided subject, for it is with his alter-ego, and it is with his memory, for it comes from the standpoint of some-one who has achieved his ambition and lives at Gad's Hill. He is looking down, and looking back, and also having an intimation of mortality, for the boy tells the dreamer that his father told him that if he was to be very persevering and was to work hard, he might some day come to live at Gad's Hill. This recollec-tion of early childhood allows for consideration of what success means: to live in the house significantly placed at the top of the hill would mean that there was no other place to go but down, no other place to go but astray: achieve-ment would equal death, ambition could go no further.

'Travelling Abroad' says that the Paris Morgue draws him into it whenever he goes to Paris, including one Christmas Day. He says that one New Year's Day he was attracted in to see a boy of eighteen with a bullet wound and his hands cut with a knife, and found in the river. 'This time I was forced into the same dread place, to see a large dark man whose disfigurement by water was, in a frightful manner, comic'. The figure causes a deep revulsion and returns in fantasy several times over – a fantasy within a fantasy journey, or a memory which cannot be kept back within memories of going abroad. He says that the image lasted with him for a week, gradually obtruding itself on him less frequently.

The attraction returns in 'Some Versions of Mortality' (16 May 1863, *J4* 218). The Uncommercial in Paris strays to Notre Dame, to see 'the obscene little Morgue' on the river's brink, compared to a coach-house, plus a London tailor's or linen-drapers' plate-glass window, where are hung the clothes of the dead. Death is a subject for tourism, while its shows are compared to the commodities in shops (compare, above, p. 55). There is a crowd wanting to see an anonymous man who has been killed by a stone falling on him from one of Paris' new buildings; the Custodian of the Morgue tells the impatient viewers to see 'the other curiosities' while waiting for this man to be 'exposed': 'Fortunately the Museum is not empty today'.

The description turns upon looking at the people who are looking at the old man, noticing the 'wolfish stare' and the 'much more general, purposeless, vacant staring . . . like looking at waxwork, without a catalogue, and not knowing what to make of it. But all these expressions concurred in possessing the one underlying expression of *looking at something that could not return a look*'. To look at something but not be looked back at confirms a sense of subjectivity, and superiority, because a clear distinction has been maintained between the self as subject and the object which is stared at. However, such a stability is thrown into doubt here, since looking at the dead body is like looking at a waxwork, that which mimics the human, and is modelled on the human (like the death-masks of Madame Tussaud (1761–1850); these went on permanent display in the Baker Street Bazaar in 1835). It might be truer to say that in so far as the Uncommercial is looking at the body, he is looking at something he hopes could not return a look, but this is not possible. And his look is divided, because it is both towards the body and the onlookers, who, if they are a mirror of himself, show his fascination with the idea that the self is always under the gaze, is always looked at. He is not just looking at something that could not, ideally, return a look.

In Lacan's psychoanalysis, the subject is not complete, because it receives its identity from outside; identity comes from an identification with what is outside, and the subject starts to look in the mirror in 'the mirror stage' because he is already in the field of vision, already looked at, already under the gaze. Dickens, in being drawn to the dead body, just as he was drawn to the memory of the hanging bodies of the Mannings at Horsemonger Jail ('Lying Awake', *J4* 92), shows an attraction to what he calls 'obscene', and to that which in its very uncanniness (is it waxwork or dead body?) questions his identity. If the thing looked at could not return a look, that would mean the annihilation of the self that looks. Further, the dead body is what the subject must keep away from, as the 'abject', as Julia Kristeva calls it. The 'abject' threatens the subject's difference, its identity, yet it is what fascinates, even with the power of disgust, so that the subject cannot keep separate, or move away. The point applies to Dickens, evidenced in the intense writing of night walks and night thoughts, which take him in directions he is attracted to in spite of everything; insomnia indicating his dependence on the 'other'. Attraction to London at night and towards the dead body may hold in them both a desire for that which is normally out of sight (obscene), that which is other, and which he cannot be sure does not return a look. Certainly he cannot dominate it, cannot objectify it.[18]

'Some Recollections of Mortality' then recalls, from the vantage-point of walking across Paris, an experience of death in London, in the hard winter of 1861. Saying it 'seemed as strange to me . . . as if I had found it in China' makes London, very little described in these papers, 'other', unknown. He remembers coming in to London at the north part of Regent's Park, and encountering a dead woman who had been pulled out of the Regent's Canal. Her body lay dead on the towpath near the Canal Bridge, 'near the cross-path to Chalk Farm', drowned, like the people in the Morgue. The costermonger who helped the policeman get her out was staring at the body 'with that stare which I have likened to being at a waxwork exhibition without a catalogue'. The image is striking: no identification can be made; even the costermonger cannot have his own identity confirmed for him from any form of writing. This mournful experience, its melancholia supplemented by the passing bargewoman ignoring the dead woman, is followed by another memory, given from walking via the Boulevard de Sebastapol towards the 'brighter scenes' of Paris. One city, one scene, evokes another, as if one city typified another, just as Sebastapol has now been made, as a result of French victory in the Crimea, part of the new Paris.

Crossing the Boulevard connects, in memory, with Dickens and London, and his old days at Doughty Street. The writing suggests that memory has no point of anchorage; it is unbound, astray. It creates Baudelaire's state, where 'everything becomes allegory'; one non-real place-name evokes, uncontrollably, a disconnected memory; in this case, of being summoned by the Beadle as a juryman to a coroner's inquest. The object is to discover whether a woman has killed her newborn child, or merely concealed it, because it was stillborn. The jury must see the child's body and eventually decide that the woman had only concealed the birth. Everything in the inquest isolates the 'friendless orphan girl', who had been working as a servant-of-all-work, especially from the nurse and her employer. He concludes that the woman's face and voice came to him in his sleep that night, as a recollection of mortality. Dreams work in the same unfixed way as memory.

VI · 'NIGHT WALKS'

At the heart of *The Uncommercial Traveller* is an essay written a little before beginning *Great Expectations*: 'Night Walks' (21 July 1860, *J4* 148). The subject recalls 'Little Dorrit's Party' (*LD* 1.14); indeed, perhaps that episode was prompted by an experience narrated in 'A Nightly Scene in London' (*Household Words*, 26 January 1856, *J3* 346), which is about straying into Whitechapel, and seeing five (Forster's *Life* says there were seven) women outside the workhouse in the rain, 'five awful Sphinxes by the wayside'.[19] In *Confessions of an English Opium Eater*, the record of Thomas de Quincey's opium-driven wanderings in London after 1804, he speaks of coming suddenly 'upon such knotty problems of alleys, such enigmatical entries, and such sphynx's riddles of streets without thoroughfares'.[20] London is the sphinx, as Oxford Street is the 'stony-hearted step-mother' (*Confessions* 34); or even, in his fantasy, the castrating mother, who separates him from Ann, the child-prostitute who befriended him the first time he came to London in 1802. London as a sphinx challenges his ability to pass through its 'mighty labyrinths' (34). The city is the expression of a drugged state, and its existence is to question the subject. In Dickens, these women are not so personally challenging as they are for De Quincey, the question they pose is not so much to him, or, at least, he takes action by trying to give relief to the women.

But 'Night Walks' is a piece where the subject is under question. It gives the Uncommercial a lesson in 'houselessness'. The word and idea derive from *King Lear*.[21] The mad and sleepless Lear has sent his Fool in to sleep in the shelter (this is apparent in the second line of the quotation) and then thinks of his subjects:

> You houseless poverty –
> Nay, get thee in. I'll pray, and then I'll sleep.
> Poor naked wretches, whereso'er you are,
> That bide the pelting of this pitiless storm,
> How shall your houseless heads and unfed sides,
> Your looped and windowed raggedness, defend you
> From seasons such as these? (3.4.27–33)

'Houseless' recurs in Dickens' essay some seventeen times: London is Lear's heath, deserted, exposed. 'Houselessness' becomes an allegorical term for the Uncommercial to describe himself, pluralising identity, so that he is 'I', and 'we', and 'Houselessness'. Following Blanchot on where and what writing leads to, Houselessness implies the space of 'solitude', and the destiny of all writing. This figure, the Uncommercial as King Lear, is also the Traveller, not just outside his house, but a tramp, a down-and-out, like the one met with in 'Tramps' (16 June 1860), who wants to get to Dover (a *King Lear* and a *David Copperfield* theme) to find a relative who will help him to get back to 'a *ouseless* family awaiting with beating hearts the return of a husband and father from Dover upon the cold stone seats of London-bridge' (*J4* 131, my emphasis). The threat in the piece is the loss of identity: this is hinted at in the title, for 'night' may be either an adjective, or a noun: if the latter, it is night that 'walks', like a spectre haunting London. The figure that walks is not so much an entity as the space of night.

'Night Walks' thinks of the Haymarket, Kent Street in the Borough, and the Old Kent Road for instances of drunkenness, and Waterloo Bridge, recalling 'a chopped-up murdered man' whose body was found there on 9 October 1857. It recalls Sadler's Wells at night, when everyone has gone and in the dark, the orchestra pit looked like 'a great grave dug for a time of pestilence'. There is discussion of Newgate where he lingers 'by that wicked little Debtor's Door –

shutting tighter than any other door one ever saw – which has been Death's door to so many'. The pun: debt/death will be noticed, as will the prison as a form of houselessness, so will the idea that to come out of the prison door is to come out to death; the door is shut that would lead back to the prison's safety; the space outside is houseless. He moves to the Bank, and to Billingsgate, then across London Bridge, to the brewery in Southwark, and then on to the King's Bench prison in Southwark, and onto a meditation on 'dry rot' in men, saying that this begins with:

> a tendency to lurk and lounge; to be at street-corners without intelligible reason; to be going anywhere when met; to be about many places rather than at any; to do nothing tangible, but to have an intention of performing a variety of intangible duties tomorrow or the day after.

This will-lessness, with its death-drive, suggests another form of houselessness.

From the prison he moves to Lambeth, to Bedlam, which prompts another 'night fancy', to be pursued in sight of its walls and dome:

> Are not the sane and insane equal at night as the sane lie a dreaming? Are not all of us outside this hospital who dream [this includes the Uncommercial who is not asleep, but whose thinking is a form of dreaming] more or less in the condition of those inside it, every night of our lives? [. . .] I wonder that the great master who knew everything, when he called Sleep the death of each day's life, did not call Dreams the insanity of each day's sanity.

Again, the quotation from *Macbeth*: sleep as 'the death of each day's life' (2.2.36). To be sleepless is, on that basis, to be unable to die. If the grave is 'the house appointed for all living' (Job 30.23), having no power to die is an extreme form of houselessness. The movement from sleep to dreams, which is Hamlet-like (*Hamlet* 3.1.68), goes towards a Hamlet-like will-lessness, and Lear-like insanity, like that of Cibber's statues. Dreams, madness and houselessness, 'unsettled, dissipated, wandering', the state he calls 'nomadic' (*J3* 245), merge. Over Westminster Bridge, he passes around Parliament, Westminster Hall, and Westminster Abbey and thinks 'what enormous hosts of dead belong to one old great city'. The meditation is succeeded by an encounter at St Martin-in-the-Fields at three in the morning, similar to one with a damned soul from Dante's *Inferno*, or with one of the figures of 'raggedness' from *King Lear*, like Poor Tom, a Bedlam figure:

> Suddenly, a thing that in a moment more I should have trod upon without seeing, rose at my feet with a cry of loneliness and houselessness, struck out of it by the bell, the like of which I never heard. We then stood face to face looking at one another, frightened by one another. The creature was like a beetle-browed hare-lipped youth of twenty, and it had a loose bundle of rags on, which it held together by its hands. It shivered from head to foot, and its teeth chattered [note the anticipation of Magwitch: 'who limped, and shivered, and glared and growled, and whose teeth chattered in his head' – *Great Expectations* 1.1.4, written later the same year], and as it stared at me

– persecutor, devil, ghost, whatever it thought me – it made with its whining mouth as if it were snapping at me, like a worried dog. [Again, the echo of Magwitch.] Intending to give this ugly object, money, I put out my hand to stay it – for it recoiled as it whined and snapped – and laid my hand upon its shoulder. Instantly, it twisted out of its garment, like the young man in the New Testament [Mark 14.51, 52], and left me standing alone with its rags in my hand. [Compare Pip's gesture with 'the young man', and Compeyson's response, *GE* 1.3.17–18.]

The 'thing' which night can walk on, is like De Quincey's or Dickens' sphinx, only not a woman, but a youth, or even genderless ('it'). But more unnerving than the sphinx, who has a question. The words 'loneliness' and 'houselessness' fuse the image of Tom-All-Alone's with Tom o' Bedlam (*King Lear* 1.2.124), the Bedlam beggar that Edgar fashions himself like, so much that when he appears as a madman, he is virtually naked (2.3.13–21, 3.4.61–63). The loneliness of *Bleak House* and the poverty and madness of *King Lear* fuse.[22] The earlier meditation on dreams in Bedlam has been intensified by seeing this Tom o'Bedlam, Tom-All-Alone. As Pip calls himself a 'small bundle of shivers', before encountering Magwitch, so Lear speaks of 'the wind [coming] to make me chatter' (*Lear* 4.6.99). This encounter with the other, where the self which thought itself houseless ends holding the very house that the other destitute 'thing' has vacated, echoes Lear with the Fool and with Tom, and Pip with Magwitch and Compeyson. As with all those encounters, the question of who has power and who has not flashes up: perhaps no-one has power. With much less spirit than the Artful Dodger, who in a spat with Fagin leaves him holding his coat (*OT* 1.13.97), this figure leaves the Uncommercial like a fool with nothing but rags. If Lear tears his own clothes off, that gesture, which implies loss of identity and self-consciousness, becomes another learning of the meaning of houselessness, but here the 'I' of the narrative is left with rags to remind him of his own identity.

From this passage where 'looped and windowed raggedness' has appeared insufficient to even attempt to clothe the body, the Uncommercial passes to Covent Garden market, to see children with naked feet (unhoused feet) who sleep in baskets, and he looks at the man – 'the most spectral person my houselessness encountered', which makes him another Dantean figure – who eats a cold meat pudding taken out of his hat, and who is red-faced, and thus accounts for his redness: '"My mother", said the spectre, "was a red-faced woman that liked drink, and I looked at her hard when she was laid in her coffin, and I took the complexion"'. The narrator says that 'the pudding seemed an unwholesome pudding after that, and I put myself in its way no more'. It is as if he has gone further down in the circles of *Inferno*, and is hearing the dead talk in a way which suggests that the dead affect each other, and could affect him.

The last place is a railway terminus, the last sight cattle coming in to London to be killed. And with the day he can sleep, sleep being sanity, and reflects as he goes home, that it is not the least wonderful thing about London that 'in the real desert region of the night, the houseless wanderer is alone there. I knew well enough where to find Vice and Misfortune of all kinds, if I had chosen, but they were put out of sight, and my houselessness had many miles upon miles of streets in which it could, and did, have its own solitary way'. The ending recalls the conclusion of *Paradise Lost*, when Adam and Eve 'through Eden took their solitary way'; 'solitary' links with 'loneliness', the word used about the spectral figure seen at three in the morning.

These have been houseless words; for to be houseless not only suggests how far this text has gone beyond the assumptions of domesticity in the title of *Household Words*, it is to have lost all familiar markers, to be in the sphere of what Freud calls the *unheimlich*, the unfamiliar (the 'uncanny' in the English translation of his essay *Das Unheimlich*). If London in the small hours is unfamiliar, uncanny, this accords with what Georg Lukács (1885–1971) described in *The Theory of the Novel*: 'transcendental homelessness'.[23] The state of homelessness is what Lukács associates with people in the novel as an art-form, people like Oliver Twist, David Copperfield, Nemo, Arthur Clennam, Pip: those with no home or relationship either to their world or to any reality around them. Three things come together in 'Night Walks': London as a dream-place with no resting-place for the walker in it; the city as a space which awakens the idea of houselessness; the novelist/essayist as the person who realises that his subject is being houseless, exposed to random dreams and random encounters which expose his madness, and who must write in relation to that. 'Traveller' puns not just on being an imitation of the salesman, the commercial traveller, who travels and lives on the road, but on life as travel, or travail (the words are the same) because there is nothing else.

CHAPTER ELEVEN

'THE SCENE OF MY DEATH'
Our Mutual Friend

... we cannot have gone a mile from that shop before we came to the wall, the dark doorway, the flight of stairs, and the room ... The room overlooked the river, or a dock, or a creek, and the tide was out. Being possessed of the time down to that point, I know by the hour that it must have been about low water; but while the coffee was getting ready, I drew back the curtain (a dark brown curtain), and, looking out, knew by the kind of reflection below, of the neighbouring lights, that they were reflected in tidal mud ...

Now I pass to sick and deranged impressions; they are so strong, that I rely upon them, but there are spaces between them that I know nothing about, and they are not pervaded by any sense of time.

I had drank some coffee, when to my sense of sight he began to swell immensely, and something urged me to rush at him. We had a struggle near the door. He got from me, through my not knowing where to strike, in the whirling round of the room, and the flashing of flames of fire between us. I dropped down. Lying helpless on the ground, I was turned over by a foot. I was dragged by the neck into a corner ... The figure like myself was assailed, and my valise was in its hand. I was trodden down and fallen over. I heard a noise of blows, [. . .] I could not have said that my name was John Harmon – I could not have thought it – I didn't know it – [. . .]

That is still correct? Still correct, with the exception that I cannot possibly express it to myself without using the word I. But it was not I. There was no such thing as I, within my knowledge.

It was only after a downward slide through something like a tube, and then a great noise and a sparkling and crackling as of fires, that the consciousness came upon me, 'This is John Harmon drowning! John Harmon, struggle for your life. John Harmon, call on Heaven and save yourself!' I think I cried it out aloud in a great agony, and then a heavy horrid unintelligible something vanished, and it was I who was struggling there alone in the water.

I was very weak and faint, frightfully oppressed with drowsiness, and driving fast with the tide. Looking over the black water, I saw the lights racing past me on the two banks of the river, as if they were eager to be gone and leave me dying in the dark. The tide was running down, but I knew nothing of up or down then. When, guiding myself safely with Heaven's assistance before the fierce set of the water, I at last caught at a boat moored, one of a tier of boats at a causeway, I was sucked under her, and came up, only just alive, on the other side ...

As to this hour I cannot understand that side of the river where I recovered the shore, being the opposite side to that on which I was ensnared, I shall never understand it now. Even at this moment, while I leave the river behind me, going home, I cannot conceive that it rolls between me and that spot, or that the sea is where it is.   *Our Mutual Friend* 2.13.362–65[1]

The Thames, first discussed by Dickens in 'The River' (*SB* 122), opens three Dickens novels: *Bleak House*, where it is inseparable from fog, and invisible to those on the bridges, *Great Expectations*, where the north Kent marshes are 'down by the river, within, as the river wound, twenty miles of the sea' and *Our Mutual Friend*. This has a boat going downstream 'between Southwark Bridge, which is of iron, and London Bridge, which is of stone' (1.1.13). John Rennie designed both bridges, and the materials make it look as though London is regressing in time from iron to stone age. Over 200 miles long, from Gloucestershire to the North Sea, the Thames reappears incessantly in this novel from Oxfordshire down to where it flows between Essex and Kent. Where it ceases being tidal, three miles up from Richmond, is noted (4.1.619). Characters move between the towns and villages which it touches: Lizzie Hexam between the poverty of East End Limehouse and Henley, thirty miles west of London, Bradley Headstone between Bermondsey and Hurley Lock, following Wrayburn from Temple Stairs, or Hampton, to Henley; Riderhood between Limehouse and Hurley Lock, Betty Higden between Brentford and Henley.

In the passage quoted above, the river at Limehouse was seen at low tide, then running full towards the sea. John Harmon describes being shot into the river at Limehouse and, carried downstream, coming ashore somewhere towards Deptford.

The Thames: Southwark Bridge in the distance. Taken later than the 'autumn evening' that was 'closing in' (*OMF*, 1.1), but the same part of the water.

Limehouse: combination of old wharves and warehouses and modern 'Docklands' apartments; as much rubbish as in *Our Mutual Friend*.

The Thames: Limehouse.

Harmon is analysing what happened to him. He has gone, in Book 2 chapter 12, to find Riderhood in Limehouse Hole, and his daughter, Pleasant, an unlicensed pawnbroker. He appears at Riderhood's door, to reveal that he knows that the idea that Hexam murdered the body that was found in the water at the beginning of the novel, was false. Riderhood was involved in Harmon's attempted murder, having supplied the drug that 'stupefied' him. Harmon comes out of the door, recognising that he has been in it before, but all he can remember of the night of 'the scene of my death' is 'a wall, a dark doorway, a flight of stairs, and a room'.

He recalls his journey back to England, where he was to inherit his dead father's money on the condition of marrying Bella Wilfer, whom he does not know. Determined to become incognito to be able to see her, he quit the ship early, arranged with another sailor, George Radford, to change clothes with him, and was enticed into a room in Limehouse Hole. Drugged, he was attacked, and shot into the river, like refuse, or out of the womb into a new birth. Loss of his senses means that he cannot quite know that Radford was also attacked and killed. Inside the river, he struggles for life and emerges, as the illustration-title says, 'More dead than alive'.[2] Since then, he has stayed incognito, first as Julius Handford, then as Mr Rokesmith, working for Mr Boffin, who, since the heir was 'murdered', has inherited the Harmon money. Mr Boffin, a dust-contractor, has adopted Bella Wilfer, since coming into this unexpected fortune, and Rokesmith/Harmon is in love with her.

He has come out of Limehouse Hole past St Anne's Limehouse, Hawksmoor's church, looks in at its graveyard and at the church's 'high tower spectrally resisting the wind'. It was where he had met Radfoot, having disembarked from the ship at Limehouse, watched by two witnesses, Job Potterson and Jacob Kibble. They then went to Riderhood's, which he remembers, and then to another room, less than a mile away, where Harmon changed his clothes: he remembers a black man with him, like a ship's steward. Thinking through his experience in the water, Harmon walks back to the City, to the Boffins' house. Having failed when telling Bella Wilfer he loves her, he goes out again, and wanders around London all night, in the task of subduing his old identity, burying it, as much as the river had buried it. I will discuss the river's symbolic force, as a margin, an other space, but will first note how it borders on places on shore, making them marginal.

I · THE RIVER

The wheels rolled on, and rolled down by the Monument and by the Tower, and by the Docks, down by Ratcliffe, and by Rotherhithe; down to where accumulated scum of humanity seemed to be washed from higher grounds, like so much moral sewage, and to be pausing until its own weight forced it over the bank and sunk it in the river. (1.3.30)

Our Mutual Friend almost completely ignores the West End, where Twemlow lives in Duke Street, St James (1.2.17), Podsnap in 'a shady angle adjoining Portman Square' (1.11.134), and Lady Tippins 'over a staymaker's, in Belgravian borders' (2.3.248). Silas Wegg's stall is at a corner house 'not far from Cavendish Square' (1.5.52): Marcus Stone illustrates it in 'The Evil Genius of the House of Boffin'. The Lammles, who marry at Wren's church, St James in Piccadilly, live at Sackville Street in Piccadilly, neighbouring street to the Albany, where Fascination Fledgeby lives (1.10.121, 2.4.255, 2.5.266).

In chapter 3, Mortimer Lightwood and Eugene Wrayburn have crossed London from 'Stucconia' (1.10.121), which is usually assumed to be Tyburnia (the Hyde Park Estate), the part of Bayswater where the Veneerings live. Going 'down', they pass Wren's Monument, the Tower of London, and St Katherine's Docks. Rotherhithe, the last place mentioned in the passage, on the south side of the river, held the Surrey Commercial Docks. Ratcliff Highway, on the north side, was a Roman road to Limehouse, through Shadwell, and the place of the Ratcliff murders (December 1811), when seven people were killed in two separate violent incidents: John Williams, caught for the murders, hanged himself.

The Uncommercial Traveller shows how Dickens often discussed the East End. Earlier, 'On Duty with Inspector Field' (*Household Words* 14 June 1851), calls Ratcliff Highway the place where 'the sailors dance', and alludes to Field's confidence in this part of London, as though he had been born there:

> *He* does not trouble his head, as I do, about the river at night. *He* does not care for its creeping, black and silent, on our right there, rushing through sluice gates, lapping at piles and posts and iron rings, hiding strange things in its mud, running away with suicides and accidentally drowned bodies faster than a midnight funeral should, and acquiring such various experience between its cradle and its grave. (*J2* 367)

'Down with the Tide' (*Household Words* 5 February 1853), describes Southwark and Waterloo Bridges, and the Thames Police, 'whose district extends from Battersea to Barking Creek'. Going downstream, into the area that Lightwood and Wrayburn traverse by land, 'tiers of shipping' rise out of the water, like 'black streets':

> Here and there, a Scotch, an Irish, or a foreign steamer, getting up her steam as the tide made, looked, with her great chimney and high sides, like a quiet factory among the common buildings. Now, the streets opened into clearer spaces, now contracted into alleys; but the tiers were so like houses, in the dark, that I could almost have believed myself in the narrower bye-ways of Venice. (*J3* 121)

The conceit is of the river creating its own town, like Venice: it further aligns the city with the river. The journey ends at Wapping, at the old Thames Police office. Shadwell, a little further east of Wapping, may be the setting for the opening of the last novel, *The Mystery of Edwin Drood*. Jasper, the Chinese and the Lascar, and the old woman, are all lying across the same bed, drugged, and the old woman refers to 'Jack Chinaman' on the other side of the court, who cannot mix opium as well as she.[3] The novel follows on from the John Harmon narrative, since in both, a man has been drugged, and in the East End, and both Harmon and Jasper must return to consciousness out of a state of not knowing who, or where, or what, they are; in both cases, the drug is opium. Jasper returns to the area; he is as double in his being as Bradley Headstone is, and incidentally, the same age, twenty-six (also the age of Monks in *Oliver Twist*). Jasper has gone first to a hotel behind Aldersgate Street, near the General Post Office. Then, 'eastward and still eastward through the stale streets he takes his way, until he reaches his destination: a miserable court, specially miserable among many such' (23.256).[4]

Lightwood and Wrayburn go further east to Limehouse, with its disused windmill, where Hexam lives, its police-station, and The Six Jolly Fellowship Porters tavern, described in chapter 6, and usually identified as in Narrow Street, Limehouse, either the Bunch of Grapes (now The Grapes), or another, now destroyed pub, The Two Brewers. In chapter 6, the owner, Abbey Potterson, bars the pub to Rogue Riderhood and Gaffer Hexam, suspicious that they may have murdered the corpse that was found. In chapter 12, Riderhood appears at Lightwood's office, and Mortimer and Eugene, who share a bachelor cottage near Hampton, on the brink of the Thames, and work together, follow him 'round by the Temple Church, across the Temple, into Whitefriars, and so on by the waterside streets' until they arrive at the police-station in Limehouse. Going into the Six Jolly Fellowship Porters, the Inspector tells them to represent themselves as 'interested in some lime works . . . about Northfleet', and as fearful whether some of the lime doesn't get 'into bad company, as it comes up in barges'. The Limehouse episode ends with Hexam drowned.

A different water-scene opens 'Book the Second', recalling the Ragged school (so called in the number-plans for instalment no. 6) where Charley Hexam learned to read with 'unwieldy young dredgers and hulking mudlarks'.[5] Charley becomes a pupil-teacher at the Church of England National School where Bradley Headstone – product of the teacher training college set up in Battersea by James Kay-Shuttleworth (1804–77) – is schoolmaster. Headstone is like Mr M'Choakumchild in *Hard Times*, and his 'criminality' underlines the implications of the chapter-title 'Murdering the Innocents', which is about Gradgrind's school. And 'stone' recalls the 'hard' of *Hard Times*, just as the ruined landscape where the school is situated also recalls Coketown. Its suburbs are ruined; they are called 'the neutral ground upon the outskirts of the town, which is neither town nor country, and yet was either spoiled' (*HT* 1.3.17). The new schools are 'down in that district of the flat country tending to the Thames [the language echoes the second paragraph of *Great Expectations*], where Kent and Surrey meet, and where the railways still bestride the market gardens that will soon die under them':

Railway viaduct at Spa Road, Bermondsey; illustrating the railway's destruction of previous local neighbourhoods. Left is the modern Neckinger Estate, a reminder of the river that runs to Jacob's Island.

> They were in a neighbourhood which looked like a toy neighbourhood taken in blocks out of a box by a child of a particularly incoherent mind, and set up anyhow; here, one side of a new street; there, a large solitary public-house facing nowhere; here another unfinished street already in ruins; there, a church; here an immense new warehouse; there a dilapidated old country villa; then, a medley of black ditch, sparkling cucumber-frame, rank field, richly cultivated kitchen-garden, brick viaduct, arch-spanned canal, and disorder of frowziness and fog. (2.1.219)

This is Bermondsey, Rotherhithe, New Cross, and Deptford. The Surrey Canal is referred to, like the railway into London Bridge Station. As 'bestride' implies, (Cassius of Caesar: 'he doth bestride the narrow world/Like a colossus', *Julius Caesar* 1.2.136–37), the Greenwich line ran on a brick-arched viaduct, suggesting the lingering death that railway-order in its monotony delivers the landscape; this is a dead atmosphere whose effect is felt in Headstone. (In *Edwin Drood* (20.222), Rosa's 'train came into London over the housetops, and down below lay the gritty lamps with their yet un-needed lamps aglow, on a hot light summer night'.) Railway-order is imposed on disorder, so that the landscape suggests a split state, rigidity, control, and an incoherent mind.

'A Flight' (*Household Words* 30 August 1851), discusses an eleven-hour journey from London Bridge to Paris on the new South Eastern Railway's 'Double Special Express Service'. The 'very hot roof of the Terminus at London Bridge', is like a gardener's forcing frame, while the wind blows:

Railway tunnel, Spa Road, Bermondsey (station opened 1836, closed 1915).

over these interminable streets, and scatter[s] the smoke of this vast wilderness of chimneys. Here we are . . . in Bermondsey where the tanners live. Flash! The distant shipping in the Thames is gone. Whirr! The little streets of new brick and red tile, with here and there a flagstaff growing like a tall weed out of the scarlet beans, and every-where, plenty of open sewer and ditch for the promotion of the public health, have been fired off in a volley. Whizz! Dustheaps, market-gardens, and waste-grounds. Rattle! New Cross Station. Shock! There we were at Croydon. (*J3* 28–29)

Further places noted beyond Croydon, a then small Surrey market town, ten miles south of central London, and a London borough in 1886, are Reigate and Tunbridge, then Folkestone and Boulogne, before arriving at Paris, and noting everything pleasant within it, and finishing with a comparison of the cult of Napoleon with the cult of Wellington, both examples of their respective cities' 'monomania'. 'A Flight' recalls one of the primary industries of Bermondsey: leather-working, as well as processing imported foodstuffs. New Cross, suc-ceeding Bermondsey in the article, was named for a coaching inn, the Golden Cross (New Cross Gate refers to a toll gate established on the road in 1718). Deptford (the 'deep ford' across the Ravensbourne River, which meets the Thames at Deptford Creek), became in the eighteenth century a ship-building town with two parishes, St Nicholas and St Paul.

Bermondsey United Charity School for Girls, 1830: like 'the schools' at the opening of Book 2 of *Our Mutual Friend*, except that those were Ragged Schools.

Statue of Wellington (1844) in front of the Royal Exchange, architect William Tite, pediment designed by Richard Westmacott, showing the triumph of Commerce.

Section of Wilton Square, north of Regent's Canal.

Hexam and Headstone walk from the schools to 'the Surrey side of Westminster Bridge', cross it, and go along 'the Middlesex shore towards Millbank', with its prison. The house where Lizzy Hexam stays is in Church Street (present-day Dean Stanley Street), off Smith Square, laid out around 1726, around a Roman Baroque church, which World War Two gutted, like parts of the Square. Like St Paul's in Deptford, it was designed by Thomas Archer, as one of the fifty new churches commissioned by Parliament after 1710. It was altered during the eighteenth century, and by William Inwood, in 1824–25. The text calls it 'very hideous', with 'four towers at the corners, generally resembling some petrified monster, frightful and gigantic, on its back with its legs in the air' (2.2.1). The sarcasm yields the sense of this part of London resembling something both monstrous and primitive – like *Bleak House*'s Megalosaurus – that is out of place, and dead.

Charley is angry with his sister that she should still live near the river, and with Jenny Wren's drunken grandfather, acts which, for Lizzy, recall her past, and her sense of her father's possible guilt, something Charley would forget, as he would the river. For both Charley and Lizzie, Millbank is aligned with Limehouse. The men return over Vauxhall Bridge, and encounter Eugene Wrayburn, whose *flânerie* it seems has brought him from Lambeth. The bridge becomes the place of suspension of social identities, and a point of tension between safety and death by water. And negotiations of the river by bridges in the text are suggestive for either being a *flâneur* who uses them to cross and recross idly, or for being someone who needs to use space economically; as later Mr Riah leaves St Mary Axe in the City one fog-bound evening, going over London Bridge, and across the Surrey side of London to recross the Thames at Westminster Bridge, to reach Church Street.

Other parts of the Thames are named. In Book 2 chapter 8, Bella Wilfer and her father leave London for Greenwich, on the south bank, downstream from Limehouse. They sit in a tavern overlooking the water, and muse on the shipping: collier ships going to Newcastle, and three-masted ships going to China, 'to bring back opium' (2.8.315), which it seems, is Veneering's trade: drug-dealing. The chapter contrasts with the next, set upstream at Brentford, on the north side. It had been introduced earlier (1.16), when the Milveys were searching for an orphan for the Boffins to adopt, and discovering one in 'muddy' Brentford, looked after by his grandmother, Betty Higden. The squalor of London is both upstream and downstream.[6] The orphan dies in a children's hospital.

In 3.1 Riah and Jenny visit Limehouse and go to the Six Jolly Fellowship Porters. The episode, whose action is intended to rectify Hexam's reputation, leads to the episode of Riderhood being virtually drowned, when a steamer runs down his wherry. In the river, his 'spark of life' is 'in abeyance' (3.3.442), but as it returns, he forgets how the river is an *arrêt du mort*, an arrest of death: both a suspension of death, and a suspension of life, a death sentence.[7] And the river invites towards another death sentence, in 3.8.497, when Betty Higden runs away from Brentford, going upstream to the 'pleasant towns' of Chertsey, Walton, Kingston, and Staines:

> In these pleasant little towns on Thames, you may hear the fall of the water over the weirs, or even, in still weather, the rustle of the rushes; and from the bridge you may see the river, dimpled like a young child playfully gliding away among the trees, unpolluted by the defilements that lie in wait for it on its course, and as yet out of hearing of the deep summons of the sea ... [Betty Higden] heard the tender river whispering to many like herself, 'Come to me ... When the cruel shame and terror you have so long fled from, most beset you, come to me!'

The bridge incites suicide. The chapter interweaves fear of dying and being sent to the parish workhouse, with the death-drive induced by the river, for any woman on the bridge. Death, and the river, comprises the 'mutual friend' within the text, affecting Harmon, Hexam, Riderhood, and Betty Higden. After running away from a riverside town (identifiable with Hampton), she is found by the Deputy Lockkeeper: Riderhood, in his new job, at Plashwater Weir Mill Lock (Hurley Lock, in Berkshire). Riderhood extorts money from her. She collapses near a paper-mill (Marsh Mill, a little upstream from Henley); dying, she is found by Lizzie Hexam, who has escaped from Bradley Headstone's

THE SCENE OF MY DEATH

attentions by coming upstream to the borders of Oxfordshire. Betty Higden has also escaped, and her 'ashes' are buried near the river.

Headstone comes into contact with Riderhood at the Temple where Lightwood and Wrayburn have their offices. He and Riderhood walk through the night along the Strand, Pall Mall, and towards Hyde Park Corner, and further westward until they reach a country road, separating after drinking at an early-opening public-house. Riderhood goes off to Plashwater Weir Lock on a carter's wagon; Headstone walks back to Bermondsey. The relationship is sealed, however; in Book 4 chapter 1, Headstone dresses as a bargeman, as if becoming Riderhood, to murder Wrayburn.

Book 4 chapter 4, returns to Greenwich, via steamboat from London. Looked on by a Greenwich pensioner, Bella and John Harmon are married at Greenwich church, and have a wedding-breakfast at Blackheath.[8] Later, they walk to Greenwich from central London; Harmon now works in the City at a 'China House'). The action goes upstream, with Headstone's attempted murder of Wrayburn, and the subsequent marriage of Lizzie and Wrayburn (chapter 11). Henley must be reached from London by train, when Bella, Lightwood and the Milveys go there via Reading, from Waterloo:

> Then, the train rattled among the housetops, and among the ragged sides of houses torn down to make way for it and over the swarming streets, and under the fruitful earth, until it shot across the river: bursting over the quiet surface like a bomb-shell, and gone again as if it had exploded in the rush of smoke and steam and glare. A little more, and again it roared across the river, a great rocket, spurning the watery turnings and doublings with ineffable contempt, and going straight to its end, as Father Time goes straight to his. (4.11.731)

The railway thinks nothing of the houses, nor of hills, nor of the river, which it bridges twice. It goes 'straight' to its end, as 'Father Time' goes towards its end; but Time puns with Thames, going downstream towards the sea; in that sense railway-order looks superior, but cannot compete with the river.

The last sense of the river is in 4.15, when Riderhood walks into the schoolroom in Bermondsey to blackmail Headstone, who follows him back to Plashwater Weir Lock. Headstone starts back, walking towards London in the snow, but Riderhood follows him, so that Headstone must turn back again, as if with the indecision that marked Bill Sikes. Suicidal and murderous, he seizes Riderhood in an iron grip, pushing him into the 'ooze and scum' of the temporarily dry lock. The bodies are found behind its 'rotting gates', Riderhood underneath Headstone.

Death and the river have been associated. John Harmon's passage of self-reflection on being nearly killed makes the river an 'other' force, heterogeneous, threatening death, and, strangely, sustaining life. Flowing to the sea, the river in more intense form, it is the source of both life and death, and also the heart of London. It evokes something that we may call, following Derrida,

'life death', neither one nor the other singly, but the reminder that every con-
cept contains its other. The river attracts people to it. But there is another
possibility: 'Come up and be dead' (2.5.280). Jenny Wren says this, sitting with
Lizzie Hexam on the rooftop of the offices and house of Pubsey and Co. in St
Mary Axe. She addresses the exploited Jewish Mr Riah, agent to the financier
Fascination Fledgeby. He, who misuses Mr Riah, cannot be part of this world:
Jenny says he is not dead, adding: 'Get down to life!' (2.5.279). Death is the
'mutual friend' Fledgeby does not know in his confined sense of life.

In *Growing Up Poor in London*, Louis Heren, born in Shadwell in 1919
says that the watermen called the Thames 'The London River'. As such, and as
London's privileged symbol, the river is inside people when they drown, and
outside them, sustaining them and that from which they emerge. So Wrayburn,
virtually dying, is described, after his attack, as going in and out of conscious-
nessness: 'the frequent rising of a drowning man from the deep, to sink again,
was fearful to the beholders' (4.10.721). The expression of London, the river
forms London identities. As Rogue Riderhood is recalled to life from drowning: 'the low, bad, unimpressible face is coming up from the surface, or from
whatever depths, to the surface again' (3.3.441). Death, or unconsciousness
is mirrored by the river, and emerging out of that river of unconsciousness
is painful:

> like us all, when we swoon – like us all, every day of our lives when we wake –
> [Riderhood] is instinctively unwilling to be restored to the consciousness of this
> existence, and would remain dormant, if he could. (3.3.440)

Later, Riderhood tries to discover if Bradley Headstone has dressed as a
bargeman to look like him:

> this was the subject-matter in his thoughts; in which, too, there came lumbering up,
> by times, like any half floating and half sinking rubbish in the river the question, Was
> it done by accident? (4.1.622)

The course of thinking and the river, which contains and throws up rubbish,
are images for each other. Or, before Eugene's attack:

> The rippling of the water seemed to cause a correspondent stir in his uneasy
> reflections. He would have laid them asleep if he could, but they were in movement,
> like the stream, and all tending one way with a strong current. As the ripple under the
> moon broke unexpectedly now and then, and palely flashed in a new shape and with
> a new sound, so parts of his thoughts started, unbidden, from the rest, and revealed
> their wickedness. (4.6.682)[9]

Thought, and what the river produces, its rubbish, are identified with each
other. If the river expresses London, what appears in these last two quotations
is the sense of rubbish as heterogeneous to the river, as much as 'wickedness'
may be heterogeneous within thought. As rubbish appears in the river, so
thoughts are stirred. The river contains 'rubbish' and suggests the other

dominant image in this novel: waste, symbolised by the dustheaps that have made Harmon's fortune. The river receives waste, carries it, and absorbs it, and, as with those humans who come out of it alive, returns it in a form that could be purified, while dustheaps, which are also London, pile up waste to the sky. River and waste echo each other.[10] John Harmon is shot like rubbish into the river which must absorb his body.

But the river is heterogeneous in itself. Flowing out to the sea, it suggests surplus and excess, in which sense it is waste already, before it receives anything of extra, dead matter. Georges Bataille sees waste matter as 'heterogeneous' – other – to any system.[11] It 'is opposed to any homogeneous representation of the world, in other words, to any philosophical system'. It is the 'formless', singular. Waste, and the excremental, cannot be slotted into a system of thought; cannot be appropriated. Bataille calls 'heterology' the study, or 'science of what is completely other', saying that 'scatology' (the science of excrement) would serve well as its doublet. When, in *Little Dorrit*, 'through the heart of the town, a deadly sewer ebbed and flowed in the place of a fine fresh river' (1.3.41), both aspects of the heterogeneous – waste and excess – are stressed, and exhibited.

But Bataille goes further in speaking of the 'identical nature . . . of God and excrement', adding that 'the cadaver is not much more repugnant than shit, and the spectre that projects its horror is *sacred* even in the eyes of modern theologians'. The sacred and the filthy – whether that means excrement or the dead body – are associated in religions, both forms of taboo, and both, the sacred and the filthy, are heterogeneous to systems of thought. The river as heterogeneous makes the city which it symbolises also heterogeneous. Thoughts that are stirred into consciousness through the river, image how the city creates consciousness.

II · WASTE

His home was in the Holloway region north of London, and then divided from it by fields and trees. Between Battle Bridge and that part of the Holloway district in which he dwelt, was a tract of suburban Sahara, where tiles and bricks were burnt, bones were boiled, carpets were beat, rubbish was shot, dogs were fought, and dust was heaped by contractors. Skirting the border of this desert, by the way he took, when the light of its kiln-fires made lurid smears on the fog, R. Wilfer shook his head. (1.4.41–42)

Our Mutual Friend never lets up on London's filth. Mr Wilfer, Bella's father, is a clerk for Chicksey, Veneering and Stobbles in Mincing Lane. He goes home from the City to City Road, to Pentonville Road, and then to Battle Bridge (perhaps 'Broad Bridge'), which crossed the Fleet River, north of present-day King's Cross Station. Or, he must cross to Holborn, up Gray's Inn Road, to join the Caledonian Road (1826) and go over the Regent's Canal, past Thornhill Square (1832), past Pentonville Prison, beyond which comes Lower Holloway and the Holloway Road, which runs up towards Highgate.[12] Wilfer's way is parallel to Mr Boffin's, the dustman, living in the vicinity of Maiden Lane, Battle Bridge. Maiden Lane currently survives as a name for a bridge crossing the Regent's Canal; the road was in what is now York Way, northbound to Camden Road from near King's Cross.[13] Here the dustheaps, epitome of Victorian waste, are to be found.[14]

The Lacanian psychoanalyst and Foucaultian historian, Dominique Laporte, in his *The History of Shit*, which focuses its history on Paris, sees an edict issued by Francois I in 1539 in Paris as a beginning point for writing the history of subjectivity. Perhaps playfully, he suggests that the 'modern subject' is born when a person's excrement was to be seen as proper to that person, and therefore not to be thrown into the public space of the street. Privacy and the private subject are commanded into being.[15] And at that moment, too, the city and the country are divided, the latter seen as the place of excrement in the form of dung on the ground, the former the place of money-making, of gold, as the denial of shit, or its sublimation. This recalls the opening of *Bleak House*, and Mr Merdle, in *Little Dorrit*, fusing money and excrement in his being.

The place of the state, the state itself, and the city, are to be linked with clean money: 'money has no smell' (77), but Laporte writes, remembering Bataille, and Freud's *Civilization and its Discontents*: 'civilization does not distance itself unequivocally from waste, but betrays its fundamental ambivalence in act after act' (32). 'Ambivalence' suggests the fascination civilisation has with, even when trying to deny, the existence of the excremental. This happens with Jeremy Bentham's Panopticon, his dream for dealing with the criminal as the waste product of society. The Panopticon creates an homogeneous space, where:

> everything must be usable, must work toward a result . . . The panoptic ideal is to achieve the integral subjection of nature to the useful. Some way must be found to fit even the most basic needs into the profit system. One day Bentham said the following to his editor, Bowring, who has passed it on to us, 'Remember we do not exercise, or ought not to exercise, even a *besoin* ("need", Bentham genteelly used the French word) in vain. It should serve for manure'.[16]

The Lacanian psychoanalyst Jacques-Alain Miller comments: 'Bentham has conceived a world without waste, a world in which anything left over is immediately reused, a superusable world' (8). Waste has been euphemistically described by Bentham as the body's 'need', and not acknowledged as waste; in this Utilitarianism, anything of 'need' is recyclable. Dominique Laporte also comments on this Benthamite passage:

> the imperative of profit is not entirely driven by the imperative of utility, which subjugates even physiological functions. It also marks the return of a repressed fantasy of which utility is merely the displaced reversal, that is, the dream of satisfying all need and thus liberating the subject from lack. (History 119)

The unconscious desire of capitalism on this basis is a world without 'need', where waste is intolerable because it might mean that there was a surplus need beyond what can be supplied in material terms. Capitalism, Laporte argues, cannot allow for the idea of 'need' because it cannot acknowledge the idea of what psychoanalysis calls the 'lost object' (123), which suggests that, psychically, desire may be, definitionally, that which cannot be satisfied.[17]

The impulse towards hygiene, in the drive to eliminate waste, aims for a self-contained and self-sufficient ego (an ego without waste). Such an ego, which can deny that it has waste, would have no heterogeneous elements. The ambivalence towards shit that Laporte notes in civilisation, though it evokes Freud, also connects Laporte with Foucault, for whom sexuality was not repressed by the Victorians, but rather was created by the power of a 'normalising' discourse, with power to make people think of themselves as marked by particular forms of sexuality. As Laporte writes, in a way equivalent to Foucault, 'we dare not speak about shit. But . . . no other subject – not even sex – has caused us to speak so much' (112). The subject constructs discourse, just as Laporte shows that Francois I's edict, which attempted to expel excretion from public life, also was one that tried to clean up language, in this way, introducing a repression into language, but which makes the language speak that which it has excluded.

For Laporte, the odour of excrement affects all smells and dictates a removal of these from the public place. It requires a new attention to personal hygiene, and a relegation of smell which the historian Alain Corbin sees taking place in France c.1750 to 1880.[18] Expelled from the public space in the sixteenth century, excrement is legislated against in nineteenth-century Britain and France. Similarly, the Manchester-born Edwin Chadwick (1800–90) produced the *Report on the Sanitary Conditions of the Labouring Population of Great Britain* in 1842, with the aim of producing a working-class with middle-class habits; sanitation would have moral effects, and would make the home – not the street, nor the public house – the centre of working-class life. Chadwick restricted public health to this measure, inspiring the Public Health Act of 1848, which set up the General Board of Health.[19] Dickens was enlisted into movements to promote public health, and a turn in his writing towards this is discernible in *Dombey and Son* chapter 47.[20] In the second half of the nineteenth century, in the city, new sewers were laid to remove smells. The earlier part of the nineteenth century had laid stress on the power of miasmas and mephitic smells, and in London, a 'great stink' (June 1858) gave an incentive to the Metropolitan Board of Works (1855) to begin Sir Joseph Bazalgette's new system of sewage building. Completed in 1875, his system imposed concrete embankments along the Thames, and Dickens writes approvingly, in 1869:

The Thames embankment is (faults of ugliness in detail, apart) the finest public work yet done. From Westminster Bridge to near Waterloo, it is now lighted up at night, and has a fine effect. They have begun to plant it with trees; and the footway (not the road) is already open to the Temple. Besides its beauty, and its usefulness in relieving the crowded streets, it will greatly quicken and deepen what is known as the 'scour' of the river. (*Letters* 12.268)

In Paris, though the fear that smells caused infection had been replaced by another discourse, which made microbes a more potent and invisible cause of contagion than open sewers, hidden sewage pipes were laid down after 1880.[21]

Alexandre-Jean-Baptiste Parent-Duchâtelet (1790–1835), who trained as a doctor, wrote both on Parisian hygiene – finding sewers and sewermen fascinating – and on prostitution. The alignment between these as two public and visible sources of 'disease' was apparent to him.[22] Success in cleaning up towards the end of the nineteenth century becomes so pronounced as to make David Trotter argue that 'mess', as a discrete subject, became a forceful preoccupation in European art and fiction after 1860, discussing it in relation to waste, and littering.[23]

Corbin argues that in Paris, the combination of sanitation and removal of smells was resisted by the poor, especially the rag-pickers. OED associates this word with Mayhew in 1851, and dates the equivalent, 'chiffonier', to 1856, though Dickens uses 'chiffonier' in 1851, in 'A Monument of French Folly' (*Household Words* 8 March 1851, *J2* 332). In 1832, out of what Corbin calls a 'loyalty to filth' (213), rag-pickers rioted against attempts to remove it.[24] Walter Benjamin quotes Baudelaire on the rag-picker as a hero of modern life:

> The most provocative figure of human misery. Ragtag [*Lumpenproletarier* in a double sense: clothed in rags and occupied with rags]. 'Here we have a man whose job it is to pick up the day's rubbish in the capital. He collects and catalogues everything that the great city has cast off, everything it has lost, and discarded, and broken. He goes through the archives of debauchery, and the jumbled array of refuse [stockpile of waste]. He makes a selection, an intelligent choice; like a miser hoarding treasure, he collects the garbage that will become objects of utility or pleasure when refurbished by Industrial magic'.

Benjamin adds: 'Baudelaire recognizes himself in the figure of the ragman' (*Arcades* 349–50). Rag-picker and poet are aligned:

> the refuse concerns both, and both go about their business in solitude at times when the citizens indulge in sleeping; even the gesture is the same with both. Nadar speaks of Baudelaire's 'jerky gait'. This is the gait of the poet who roams the city in search of rhyme-booty; it must also be the gait of the rag-picker who stops on his path every few moments to pick up the refuse he encounters.[25]

A difference between the rag-picker and the poet is that the first puts what he has salvaged back into the capitalist economy while the poet tries to abstract them.[26] Yet the rag-picker's drunkenness affirms that he is not part of the capitalist system; this appears in Baudelaire's *Le Vin des chiffoniers* (*The Rag-Pickers' Wine*). The poem makes the chiffonier waste and a reject, and drunk, but a figure of revolutionary excess. *Pictures from Italy* notes that 'there were, outside the Post-office Yard in Paris, before daybreak, extraordinary adventurers in heaps of rags, groping in the snowy streets with little rakes, in search of odds and ends'.[27] *Our Mutual Friend*, thinking of the dust in London winds, and air-borne paper, notes the rag-pickers' absence:

that mysterious paper currency which circulates in London when the wind blows, gyrated here, there and everywhere. Whence can it come, whither can it go? It hangs on every bush, flutters in every tree, is caught flying by the electric wires, haunts every enclosure, drinks at every pump, cowers at every grating, shudders upon every plot of grass, seeks rest in vain behind the legions of iron rails. In Paris, where nothing is wasted, costly and luxurious city though it be, but where wonderful human ants creep out of holes and pick up every scrap, there is no such thing. There it blows nothing but dust. There, sharp eyes and sharp stomachs reap even the east wind, and get something out of it. (1.12.147)

An absence of revolutionary politics in London shows in the absence of rag-pickers. London's economy makes the heterogeneous homogeneous as much as possible, as with the dustheaps, which are sifted and sold. Similarly with the bones and fragments of bodies in the shop of Mr Venus, 'Preserver of Animals and Birds' and 'Articulator of human bones' (1.7.89). Dead bodies' clothes and contents of pockets are rifled, money comes from dustheaps and bones, and the doll's dressmaker Jenny Wren makes pincushions and penwipers 'to use up my waste' (2.1.223). 'Dust' indicates and includes the excremental (since excrement is like gold in this novel), whether or not the dustmounds literally contain excrement. And, as Hillis Miller says, 'dustmounds' suggests 'burial mounds'.[28] Evidence for associating dust with dung and money appears in the historical account of a miser, Daniel Dancer (1716–94), one of whose 'richest escritoires was found to be a dung-heap in the cowhouse; a sum but little short of two thousand five hundred pounds was contained in this rich piece of manure' (3.6.476). Dancer, described in 1850 by his biographer Merryweather, as 'a walking dunghill', made, with his sister, clothing from rags 'collected from the streets or raked from out the dustheaps'.[29] Men as walking rubbish are symbols of the Thames, flowing with rubbish. These are rag-pickers, heterogeneous forces, but as misers, they produce no surplus energy; they illustrate London's acquisitive economy, not challenge it. The opposition between homogeneity and heterogeneity, receives, however, in Bradley Headstone, a more powerful expression.

III · HEADSTONE/HETEROGENEITY

The state of the man was murderous, and he knew it. More, he irritated it with the perverse pleasure akin to that which a sick man sometimes has in irritating a wound upon his body. Tied up all day with his disciplined show upon him . . . he broke loose at night like an ill-tamed wild animal. Under his daily restraint, it was his compensation . . . to give a glance towards his state at night, and to the freedom of its being indulged. If great criminals told the truth – which being great criminals they do not – they would very rarely tell of their struggles against the crime. Their struggles are towards it. They buffet with opposing waves, to reach the bloody shore, not to recede from it. (3.11.535–36)

This reference to the 'great criminal' parallels another passage from *All the Year Round* discussing the portrait of Richard the Third by an unknown artist, in the Carlyle-inspired National Portrait Gallery, housed, then, at Great George Street. (The Gallery had been agreed on in 1856 but building was delayed until 1890). The article discusses physiognomy, recognising Richard's as a 'painful picture', where the face, not the body, seems 'deformed':

> The picture may or may not be genuine. The internal evidence is strong in favour of its authenticity. The restless misery of this face of Richard absolutely excites a feeling of pity. There is almost deformity in the features of this great criminal; the eye and the mouth are drawn up on the left side, all the parts of the face are contracted in an excess of peevish irritability, which is also expressed with remarkable force in the very peculiar action of the small woman-like hands – tell-tale extremities always. The king has screwed the ring nearly off his right little finger, working the trinket backwards and forwards in nervous anguish with the forefinger and thumb of his left hand.[30]

(Bradley Headstone, first seen, is biting his finger (2.1.217).) Shakespeare's Richard, having in his solipsism dispensed with his 'other self', the Duke of Buckingham, says:

> but I am in
> So far in blood that sin will pluck on sin.
> Tear-falling pity dwells not in this eye. (*Richard the Third* 4.2.65–67)

The lines are echoed by Macbeth, another 'great criminal':

> I am in blood
> Stepped in so far that, should I wade no more,
> Returning were as tedious as go o'er. (*Macbeth* 3.4.135–37)

The lines evoke the criminal buffeting with opposing waves in the river. Headstone as criminal suggests the power of heterogeneity, though what he has learned, and teaches, is absolute homogeneity. Such heterogeneity also marks John Jasper, bored with his work as cathedral organist (another form of homogeneity, productive of what the text calls the 'average'), and incomprehensible to Rosa:

> for what could she know of the criminal intellect, which its own professed students perpetually misread, because they persist in trying to reconcile it with the average intellect of average men, instead of identifying it as a horrible wonder apart... (*Edwin Drood* 20.220)

Our Mutual Friend shows fascination throughout with the heterogeneous – with waste, the river, the criminal. Headstone is self-divided, living in an alienating and degraded part of London. That part of his life – his railway-like order imposed on his chaos – reflects a sado-masochism. His other life is fed by his tortures in London streets, when Wrayburn makes him go astray nightly, saying he 'tempts him all over London':

> I study and get up abstruse No Thoroughfares in the course of the day. With Venetian mystery I seek those No Thoroughfares at night, glide into them by means of dark courts, tempt the schoolmaster to follow, turn suddenly, and catch him before he can retreat. Then we face one another, and I pass him as unaware of his existence, and he undergoes grinding torments. (3.10.533)

The labyrinthine structure of London complements the school environment in inciting Headstone towards murder. The city's 'No Thoroughfare' character incites him towards the river, looking at it 'as if the place had a gloomy fascination for him' (4.1.623). That is said immediately after a nose-bleed; it suggests that the river is in him and breaking out in him, an insight also derivable from what Harmon has noticed in him:

> [Rokesmith] thought, as he glanced at the schoolmaster's face, that he had opened a channel here indeed, and that it was an unexpectedly dark, and deep, and stormy one, and difficult to sound. All at once, in the midst of his turbulent emotions, Bradley stopped and seemed to challenge his look. Much as though he suddenly asked him, 'What do you see in me?' (2.14.381)

The man with the river in him drives Wrayburn into the river, and, in his form of 'going astray', 'struggles towards' the riverbank and its suffocating mud (his 'no thoroughfare'), to die with Riderhood.

Calling Headstone a 'great criminal' is problematic; it seems to take the deeds that the man works towards as evidence of a pre-driven, pre-set, given character. But urban identity cannot be so fixed, as it is not with the strangely bisexual image of Richard the Third, where a great criminal is not 'beyond good and evil', but held by guilt, outside the guilt-free narcissism that Freud thought characterised 'great criminals'.[31] There is an ambivalence in Dickens, who would have a 'great criminal' in his fiction, and yet recognise that the conditions which make the criminal make him not great, unable to sustain the violent character that Walter Benjamin discussed, when noting:

> how often the figure of the 'great' criminal, however repellent his ends may have been, has aroused the secret admiration of the public. This cannot result from his deed, but only from the violence to which it bears witness.[32]

For Benjamin, the great criminal testifies to the law's violence, against which he reacts violently. But Headstone speaks for the law in his professional life, his 'official' existence, which makes him conformist, like his pupil, Charley, who finally repudiates him to develop his petit-bourgeois respectability. Yet Headstone and Charley begin with a strange, heterogeneous attraction, which is followed by Headstone and Wrayburn together, and by the doubling between

Headstone and Riderhood.[33] In making Wrayburn and Headstone confront each other, there is a development from *David Copperfield*, which does not bring together Steerforth and Uriah Heep, both figures of a strange attraction to DC: it encourages a rereading of that earlier text.

The no doubt unconsciously homosexual series of doublings echoes Harmon's changing of clothes with Radfoot, which is repeated when Headstone tries on clothes similar to those of Riderhood. Ratcliff – Radfoot – Riderhood; place-name and people's names seem connected, as identities flow into each other. Foucault says that the word 'homosexual' came into discourse at the end of the 1860s; homosexual attraction, inseparable from Headstone's awareness of class and his criminality, persists into the last novel, in the Jasper/Drood relationship.[34] Wrayburn shifts his attention from Charley (which has attracted him to Charley's sister Lizzie), to Headstone in the interview which he and Charley have with Wrayburn when the 'schoolmaster' is snubbed by Wrayburn on Charley's account:

> Very remarkably, neither Eugene Wrayburn nor Bradley Headstone looked at all at the boy. Through the ensuing dialogue, those two, no matter who spoke, or who was addressed, looked at each other. There was some secret, sure perception between them, which set them against one another in all ways. (2.6.285)

Wrayburn seems to need Headstone; the anonymity of those London 'No Thoroughfares' brings that out. The mute mutuality between these two appears in Headstone's proposal of marriage to Lizzie in the city churchyard, usually identified with Wren's St Peter's, Cornhill. Headstone says that his words are 'different from what I want to say' (2.15.388); Lizzie's words evoke his knowledge of a river within:

> 'No man knows, till the time comes, what depths are within him. To some men it never comes; let them rest and be thankful! To me, you brought it; on me, you forced it; and the bottom of this raging sea,' striking himself upon the breast, 'has been heaved up ever since'. (2.15.389)

We note the repeated rhythms of thought in the wave-like sentence which gives: 'you brought it' and 'you forced it'. The sea-image ironically recalls the point that Headstone would have made a good sailor (2.1.218); as if that implies a spontaneous kind of negotiation of elemental powers different from the rigid repression he has exercised, like a railway viaduct over the countryside. Headstone's accusation of Lizzie represents himself as passive, and as subject, but the union of sadism and masochism in relation to Wrayburn, which is more relevant, appears in his reaction to her refusal of him:

> 'Then,' said he, suddenly changing his tone and turning to her, and bringing his clenched hand down upon the stone with a force that laid the knuckles raw and bleeding; 'then I hope that I may never kill him!' (2.15.390)

This, which anticipates his nose-bleed, reveals the undercurrent of his thought; attraction to Lizzie is now on account of Wrayburn. The sadism, which is also masochism, takes the form of hoping that he may not kill his rival, since he has the unconscious knowledge that murder is a suicide-note; he needs the Other for his own survival. After 'killing' Wrayburn, he is repudiated by Charley, as though the latter was the symbol of both Wrayburn and Lizzie, two elements of Headstone's bisexuality. Headstone turns on Riderhood who becomes his double, and stalks him as he had followed Wrayburn. The two die together in a way which echoes the Limehouse experience, when both Harmon and Radfoot went into the water together. But mud, unlike water, does not dissolve the men's identities.

In Harmon's narration to himself of his experiences, he cannot say that what has happened has happened to him. In the plurality of identities which have been assumed, what happened, happened also to Radfoot, attacked and killed, as his double.[35] Any knowledge of identity is a 'dead idea'. He says, 'I cannot possibly express it to myself without using the word I. But it was not I. There was no such thing as I within my knowledge'. Only after going into the river 'the consciousness came upon me, "This is John Harmon drowning! John Harmon, struggle for your life . . . I think I cried it out aloud in a great agony, and then a heavy horrid unintelligible something vanished, and it was I who was struggling there alone in the water' (2.13.363). Out of the filth of the river another identity emerges, after the disappearance of 'a heavy horrid unintelligible something' – what Bataille would call 'the formless'. There is a fantasy of waste, as 'unintelligible', disappearing, but the words 'it was I who was struggling' shows that the self can never be without waste, for the 'I' speaking is separate from, is additional to, and supplements, the 'I' who is spoken of. The self always has that which is other to it.

Harmon speaks about when he was drugged, of having 'sick and deranged impressions', but adds 'there are spaces between them that I know nothing about, and they are not pervaded by any idea of time' (2.13.362). These heterogeneous moments figure a gap in identity. If the city compels the sense of time, it is significant that time is lost. So it is for Wrayburn, who, near to death, has the sense on reviving of 'wandering away', in his delirium, and speaks of the 'harassing anxiety that gnaws and wears me when I am wandering in those places – where are those endless places, . . . ? They must be at an immense distance' (4.10.719). Similarly, Harmon knows that the water where he nearly drowned is gone, has moved on: 'The sea is where it is' (2.13.365). The sea is the nowhere which ends identity, and, in that, only the apparent opposite of London. Time and space become, for Harmon and Wrayburn, waste material, evidence of the self's otherness to itself. Perhaps, when Harmon is attacked, the language of fires, by anticipating the 'flames [that] shot jaggedly across the air' when Wrayburn is attacked (4.6.682) makes Wrayburn's experience

Harmon's, and Harmon's Wrayburn's. Identities are dissolved across time and space. If London comprises places which define people, those places are not mappable but 'endless'; their 'immense distance' functions like the changes of size that Harmon observes in the person who attacks him. London, as a space that defines, also undefines.

It is contradictory to say that Headstone is a 'great criminal', because it implies an attempt to stabilise schizophrenia into a single identity. There can be such an identity least of all in this schizoid character, who is not a 'great' criminal, nor a criminal at all, but driven from one mode of being to another by the city and its suburbs, and never free of the river. His madness appears in his knowing this.

CHAPTER TWELVE

DICKENS AND GISSING

London of that time differed a good deal from the London of today [1901]; it was still more unlike the town in which Dickens lived when writing his earlier books; but the localities which he made familiar to his readers were, on the whole, those which had undergone least change. If Jacob's Island and Folly Ditch could no longer be seen, the river side showed many a spot sufficiently akin to them, and was everywhere suggestive of Dickens; I had but to lean, at night, over one of the City bridges, and the broad flood spoke to me in the very tones of the master. The City itself, Clerkenwell, Gray's-Inn Road, the Inns of Court – these places remained much as of old. To this day, they would bear for me something of that old associ-ation; but four and twenty years ago, when I had no London memories of my own, they were simply the scenes of Dickens' novels, with all remoter history enriching their effect on the great writer's page. The very atmosphere declared him; if I gasped in a fog, was it not Mr Guppy's 'London particular'? – if the wind pierced me under a black sky, did I not see Scrooge's clerk trotting off to his Christmas Eve in Somers Town? We bookish people have our consolations for the life we do not live. In time I came to see London with my own eyes, but how much better when I saw it with those of Dickens!   Gissing, 'Dickens in Memory'[1]

I · LONDON AFTER DICKENS

Dickens died in 1870, leaving a legacy of ways of thinking about the London he described and constructed. Representations of nineteenth-century London after him are much in his shadow, as with George Gissing (1857–1903), author of remarkable novels which use London freely, and of some of the most gen-erous estimates of Dickens, which show him working within an archive of knowledge set up by Dickens.[2] Before Gissing, there had appeared *London: A Pilgrimage* (1872), 180 engravings from drawings by the book-illustrator Gustave Doré (1832–83), with an essay by Blanchard Jerrold (1826–84), son of the radical journalist Douglas Jerrold (1803–57). His daughter, Jane (1825–80), married Henry Mayhew (1812–87).[3] Doré, who had illustrated Dante between 1861 and 1868, and visited London from Paris every year, produced, starting in 1869, romanticised and celebratory versions of London. Some have become definitional: such as *Ludgate Hill in Traffic* (29), *Wentworth Street, Whitechapel* (26), and *The Opium-den* (12), which enlarges on knowledge made accessible by *The Mystery of Edwin Drood*. Another is *River-side Street in Dockland* (42), and *Over London by Rail* (56), which looks down at rooftops and chimneys and a row of houses from above, and shows them through the arch of a viaduct; another viaduct is seen in the distance with a train crossing it; its smoke g to the 'frowsiness' of the night scene. Others are *Bishopsgate Street* (81), *der the Arches* (103), *Dudley Street, Seven Dials* (104), *Houndsditch* (107), *Coffee Stall – Early Morning* (116), *The Barrel-Organ in the Court* (191) and *Newgate Gaol* (159), which Van Gogh painted from Doré's print in 1889. This gives confined space, a view downwards towards the floor of the prison. De-individualised prisoners – some thirty-two – move around in a ring out of darkness and back into it. London's medievalism is suggested by the Romanesque, fortress-like windows high in the wall.

Doré's London relies on people, particularly children; on contrasts between dark and light, often aroused by night-scenes; on crowded scenes, whether these are with houses, in *Over London by Rail*, or traffic in *Ludgate Hill*. The sense of London as like Dante's *Inferno*, which is also strong, requires that often there is no skyline, but that the view looks downwards, and, several times, on the picture being framed by an arch, to increase its theatricality, and allow for light to shine on the theatrical space within the enframed space. The pictures depend on vertiginous contrasts in height, and on Piranesi-like bridges, which make the pictures studies in confined spaces.

By 1889, London had become a separate County with its own Council (the GLC from 1965 to 1986), and twenty-eight boroughs formed ten years later. The LCC replaced the Metropolitan Board of Works (1855–88), whose functions were building sewers and streets. At the same time, Charles Booth (1840–1916) brought out *Life and Labour of the People in London* (1892–97, 9 volumes). Using information derived from the Visitors for the London School Board, set up after 1870 and in charge of elementary schooling within London, this showed that 1.4 million, a third of London's population, lived below the poverty line. The principal areas of poverty were declared to be along both banks of the Thames, Wapping, Shadwell and the Isle of Dogs, and from Battersea to Greenwich. The City was almost surrounded by very poor districts, and there was extreme poverty in parts of Pimlico, Notting Dale, Paddington, Barnsbury, Holloway, and Peckham.

Booth's mapping of London in terms of poverty built on work which was already implicit, mid-century, through Mayhew. He is often romanticised as a sketch-writer portraying fraudulent beggars and picturesque street-wise children and vagrants working in sewers rather than as a social analyst of London with an interest in classification and marking social divisions. A founder of *Punch*, Mayhew worked on the *Morning Chronicle*, between 1849 and 1850 – one year after Chartism and in a year of cholera – writing eighty-two letters on the condition of the poor in London, on those who *will* work, those who *can't* work (the disabled) and those who *won't* work (Thompson and Yeo, *The Unknown Mayhew* 120). Poverty was definable in terms of the gap between what workers could earn, and what living costs meant: Mayhew talked to people who worked but could not afford to eat, like the 'distressed gentlewoman' who worked with her needle (*The Unknown Mayhew* 183–90). Mayhew continued with his journal, *London Labour and the London Poor* (1851–1852); later work followed throughout the 1850s, but he was almost forgotten by the time of his death, five years before Booth's work began to appear, the year of Gissing's novel of Lambeth, *Thyrza*.[4] But not wholly so: in 1877 John Thomson (1837–1921) brought out *Street Life in London*, a collection of photographs of London street life with a text by the journalist Aldophe Smith, who was well aware of Mayhew. There are no views of London here; the photographs concentrate on the lives of the London poor, especially around Lambeth, where it becomes apparent that the embanking of the Thames that had taken place in the 1860s had still allowed Lambeth to be prone to flooding, the water going to a height of four feet in ground floor dwellings.[5]

Mayhew wanted a comprehensive social survey of London, and in this he compares with Dickens. He noted that few manufacturing crafts were localised in London, except for the silk-weavers of Spitalfields and 'the tanners of Bermondsey – the watchmakers of Clerkenwell – the coachmakers of Long-acre – the marine store dealers of Saffron-hill – the old clothes men of Holywell-street and Rosemary-lane – the potters of Lambeth – the hatters of the Borough' (*The Unknown Mayhew* 122). He looked at seasonal and casual labour, at slop-workers and workers at the docks, at street-pedlars and street-traders, and prostitutes.[6] He studied sweated labour, where production was subdivided among many workshops into repetitive tasks, using unskilled labour. And he let the worker speak. Yet for him labour was an absolute good; criminality was associated with the work-shy. He accepted the view of the 'constabulary commissioners' that 'crime proceeds from a desire to acquire the good things of this world with a less degree of industry than ordinary labour' (Binny and Mayhew, *Criminal Prisons* 302). Ideal prison-discipline would involve not useless labour, but returning to 'those natural laws which the Almighty has laid down for the regulation of human life, and making a man's food and enjoyments, while in prison, depend upon the amount of work he does, as is the case with the rest of the world *out* of prison' (302). The same attitude to work affected his response to prostitutes, the number of whom in London, in the 1850s – decade of William Acton's *Prostitution Considered in its Moral, Social and Sanitary Aspects* (1857) – was estimated at 80,000.[7] Women were 'considerably less criminal than men': they did not belong to the criminal classes, those to whom crime was naturally habitual. Prostitution was explicable:

> What theft is to the evil-disposed among men, street-walking is to the same class among women – an easy mode of living; so that those females, among the poorer classes of society, who are born to labour for their bread, but who find work inordinately irksome to their natures, and pleasure as inordinately agreeable to them, have no necessity to resort to the more daring career of theft to supply their wants, but have only to trade upon their personal charms in order to secure the apparent luxury of an idle life. (*Criminal Prisons* 454)

Dickens contrasts with Mayhew in this reading of city-poverty. He neither accepts the existence of a criminal class, nor is so unaware of women that he thinks of prostitution as a way for the lazy to make money, nor is dismissive of the view that poverty creates prostitution; nor so unequivocal about the place that should be given to work.[8] Perhaps he is not so affirmative about London either.

II · GISSING IN LONDON

In 1876, George Gissing, born in Wakefield, was expelled from Owens College, Manchester, after a month's hard labour in prison, for stealing to support the prostitute Nell Harrison (1858–88), with whom he was in love. In 1877 he moved to London. A favourite book, which he abridged, was Forster's *Life of Charles Dickens* (1872–74). He used it for parallels between Dickens' upbringing and his. In an essay, 'Dickens in Memory' (1901), he parallels Dickens' death in 1870 with his father's death, the same year, and says that he came to London seven years later:

> what I chiefly thought of was that now at length I could go hither and thither in London's immensity, seeking for the places which had been made known to me by Dickens.[9]

The Private Papers of Henry Ryecroft (1903) recalls this time in London, not mentioning Nell Harrison (married in 1879, separated from in 1882). Thinking of the contrast between London and Paris, he says that London could not be like Paris because it 'has no *pays latin*', though beginners in literature may have comrades, who are 'garreteers in Tottenham Court Road district' or in 'unredeemed Chelsea'.[10] Henry Ryecroft thinks back twenty-five years ago to that London, virtually quoting *David Copperfield*'s experiences of London as a boy:

> I see the winding way by which I went from Oxford Street, at the foot of Tottenham Court Road, to Leicester Square, and, somewhere in the labyrinth (I think of it as always foggy and gas-lit) was a shop which had pies and puddings in the window . . . How many a time have I stood there, raging with hunger, unable to purchase even one pennyworth of food . . . I see that alley hidden on the west side of Tottenham Court Road, where, after living in a back bedroom on the top floor, I had to exchange for the front cellar . . . The front cellar was stone-floored; its furniture was a table, a chair, a wash-stand, and a bed; the window, which of course had never been cleaned since it was put in, received light through a flat grating in the alley above. Here I lived; here *I wrote* . . . At night, as I lay in bed, I used to hear the tramp, tramp of a *posse* of policemen who passed along the alley on their way to relieve guard; their heavy feet sometimes sounded on the grating above my bed. (25)

The setting is recalled from *New Grub Street*, which compares the old Grub Street of the eighteenth century (now Milton Street, in Moorfields), with the modern, placeless Grub Street in a world of 'telegraphic communication' (1.39).

New Grub Street places Edwin Reardon in a garret off Tottenham Court Road (5.88), and makes the British Museum Reading Room the hub of London's wheel. *Henry Ryecroft* recalls the notice in the lavatories in the British Museum, prescribing the basins as only to be used 'for casual ablutions'. He thinks of those who were working 'under the great dome', recalling Dickens on the 'shabby genteel' man working in the Reading Room, then with no dome (*SB* 305). If the law in Dickens is the state of Dante's *Inferno*, that idea has been transferred, via the fusions of Inferno and London in Doré, to the British Museum. Marian Yule:

> discerned an official walking along the upper gallery, and . . . her mocking misery . . . likened him to a black, lost soul, doomed to wander in an eternity of vain research along endless shelves. Or again, the readers who sat here at these radiating lines of desks, what were they but hapless flies caught in a huge web, its nucleus the great circle of the Catalogue? Darker, darker. From the towering wall of volumes seemed to emanate visible motes, intensifying the obscurity; in a moment, the book-lined circumference of the room would be but a featureless prison-limit. (8.138)

This wittily changes the Decalogue (the Law) into the Catalogue, and writes in the shadow of Dante, Milton, Piranesi, *Bleak House*, and *Little Dorrit*, the Dickens novel Gissing most admired (*Charles Dickens* 81). And it is melancholic, as Marian Yule leaves the British Museum for an omnibus 'that would take her to the remoter part of Camden Town', and then walks ten minutes to 'a quiet by-way called St Paul's Crescent [off Agar Grove, between St Pancras Way and York Way] consisting of small, decent houses' (7.115).

If Gissing is more district-bound than Dickens in his perception of the city, that recalls the increasing size of London. It suggests that Gissing notes the different grades of living that were possible in its suburbs. We can trace Gissing's residences, variously single, or two rooms, in London houses: finding lodgings is a constant preoccupation in Gissing's novels, London embodying rootlessness. In 1878 he is at 22 Colville Place by Goodge Street, off Tottenham Court Road, then 31 Gower Place, in Gower Street, near Euston Square Station, then 70 Huntley Street, Bedford Square (then at no. 35); in 1879 at 38 Edward Street, Hampstead Road, then 5 Hanover Street, Islington. In 1881, 55 Wornington Road, Westbourne Park, north of Notting Hill, a 'wretched workman's suburb'. Then back to 15 Gower Place, then in 1882 to 29 Dorchester Place, Blandford Square, then to 17 Oakley Crescent, Chelsea (now no. 33). In 1884, 62 Milton Street, Regent's Park, and then 18 Rutland Street, Hampstead Road. (These lodgings appear in *The Odd Women* 7.76–79.) Then to 7K Cornwall Residences, Clarence Gate, Regent's Park, saying, 'I used to have a prejudice against flats, but I see that it came of insufficient knowledge, like most prejudices. In a wilderness like London, it is vastly better even than a house of one's own'.[11] He adds that 'they are building flats now all over London': flat-dwelling differentiating Gissing's from Dickens' Londoners. That was the longest period of living in one address. In 1888, he left London, returning from 1893 to 1894 to live at 76 Burton Road, Brixton, his last London home, and the only one south of the river (Nell Harrison died in lodgings at 16 Lucretia Street, Lower Marsh, in Lambeth). Gissing's homes in London were as near to the Reading Room at the British Museum as possible, and many addresses were near where Dickens had lived in his poverty.

The novels begin with *Workers in the Dawn* (1880), *The Unclassed* (1884), and *Demos* (1886), written after the Trafalgar Square riot (8 February 1886), when William Morris was arrested:

> On the dun borderland of Islington and Hoxton, in a corner made by the intersection of the New North Road and the Regent's Canal, is discoverable an irregular triangle of small dwelling houses, bearing the name of Wilton Square. In the midst stands an amorphous structure, which on examination proves to be a very ugly house and a still uglier Baptist chapel built back to back. The pair are enclosed within iron railings, and more strangely, a circle of trees, which in due season do verily put forth green leaves. One side of the square shows a second place of worship, the resort, as an inscription declares, of 'Welsh Calvinistic Methodists'. The houses are of one storey, with kitchen windows looking upon small areas; the front door is reached by an ascent of five steps.
>
> The canal – *maladetta e sventurata fossa* – stagnating in utter foulness between coal-wharfs and builders' yards, at this point divides two neighbourhoods of different aspects. On the south is Hoxton, a region of malodorous market streets . . . Walking northwards, the explorer finds himself in freer air, amid broader ways, in a district of dwelling-houses only; the roads seem abandoned to milkmen, cat's meat vendors, and costermongers. Here will be found streets in which every window has its card advertising lodgings; others claim a higher respectability, the houses retreating behind patches of garden-ground and, occasionally showing plastered pillars and a balcony. The change is from undisguised struggle for subsistence to mean and spirit-broken leisure . . . (3.25–26)

The setting reappears in *Henry Ryecroft* (26). Wilton Square (see p. 245) is north of the Regent's Canal, which Booth (who referred to *Demos*), called 'a girdle of poverty, the banks of the canal being, along nearly its whole length, occupied by a very poor population' (Fried and Elman, *Charles Booth's London* 51). The New North Road, noted in discussing Sikes' flight (*OT*), runs from City Road (Shoreditch), to Canonbury Road, and into Holloway Road. Wilton Square was an 1850s development.

Another set piece marks the funeral of Jane Vine, who lived off the New North Road south of the canal, in a street of four-storeyed houses. She is taken from Hoxton to Manor Park Cemetery (opened 1874), where 'the regions around were then being built upon for the first time; the familiar streets of pale, damp brick were stretching here and there, continuing London, much like the spreading of a disease. Epping Forest is near at hand, and nearer the dreary expanse of Wanstead Flats' (*Demos* 16.220): Wanstead being an area which developed after the railway (1856).

In 1887 came *Thyrza*, set in Lambeth, but the masterpiece of the 'slum' novels was *The Nether World* (1889), set in Clerkenwell. Chapter 12, describing a Bank holiday Monday in August, shows the rush of people at Holborn Viaduct going by train to Crystal Palace, described mockingly by contrasting the scene with the Roman Saturnalia. The train speeds off 'over the roofs of South London'.[12] Pennyloaf, the new bride, knows, by the chapter's end, that she will have to pawn her wedding-ring.[13] Gissing in the 1890s turned to more middle-class topics, with *The Emancipated* (1890), *New Grub Street* (1891), and *Born in Exile* (1892). In 1893, there appeared *The Odd Women*, and at the end of 1894, *In the Year of Jubilee*, which opens in Camberwell. Later novels included *The Whirlpool* (1897), and *Will Warburton*, written in France while he was dying, appeared posthumously (1905). He died in France, living with a new woman, Gabrielle Fleury.

III · REALISM AND IDEALISM

Charles Dickens: A Critical Study says that 'had the word been in use, [Dickens] must necessarily have called himself a Realist' (69). It finds Dickens' realism limited: for instance, with Dostoyevsky, 'the magnificent scene in which Raskolnikov makes confession to Sonia is beyond Dickens as we know him; it would not have been so but for the defects of education and the social prejudices which forbade his gifts to develop' (214). Deficiencies in Dickens show in comparison to the French (Balzac, Hugo, Daudet) and the Russians; but also with Hogarth:

> Try to imagine a volume of fiction produced by the artist of *Gin Lane*, of *The Harlot's Progress*, and put it beside the books which from Pickwick onwards, have been the delight of English homes. Puritans both of them, Hogarth shows his religion on the sterner side, Dickens, in a gentle avoidance of whatsoever may give offence to the pure of heart, the very essence of his artistic conscience being that compromise which the other scorned. In truth, as artists they saw differently, Dickens was no self-deceiver; at any moment his steps would guide him to parts of London where he could behold, and had often beheld, scenes as terrible as any that the artist struck into black and white; he looked steadily at such things, and, at the proper time, could speak of them. But when he took up the pen of the story-teller, his genius constrained him to such use, such interpretation, of bitter fact as made him beloved, not dreaded, by readers asking, before all else, to be soothingly entertained. (26)

Gissing's contemporaries called him a realist, like Zola, whom Harold Biffen discusses in *New Grub Street* (10.173). While saying he lacked Zola's 'prurience', they implied that his realism was problematic since it illustrated poverty. Gissing wrote:

> the most characteristic, the most important part of my work is that which deals with a class of men distinctive of our time – well educated, well bred, but *without money*. It is this fact . . . of the poverty of my people which tells against their recognition as civilised beings.[14]

Ryecroft's sense that he can 'remember spots in London where I have stood, savage with misery, looking at the prosperous folk who passed' (119) divides him from the very poor, and makes him 'unclassed', since he says that he preserved a sense of the 'ideal' which they could not desire. 'What they at heart desired, was to me barren; what I coveted, was to them for ever incomprehensible' (120).

Yet things in Gissing contrast with this sense of alienation. He describes standing hungry one evening in 1883 on Battersea Bridge, and writing 'On Battersea Bridge', published the following day in the *Pall Mall Gazette* (see *Ryecroft* 129–30). The first paragraph is about pedestrians, but the second, with the view presented as a picture, such as a Whistler 'Nocturne', opens:

> But stand and gaze awhile. The water here, broadening in its sweep to the south, is rich with the reflection of dusky gold . . . A mist lurks about the river, vapour which thickens, obscuring the objects on either bank. Obscuring, but not hiding; blotting out all meaner details, shading off the harsher intermediate lines, leaving only the broad features of buildings massed darkly against the grey background . . . [N]ow the eye loves to dwell on what would offend it in the clearer light; the rude blocks of new houses on the north bank show only a glimmering window here and there on the surface of what looks like a lordly pile; to the left, the group of factory chimneys does not lack its suggestive beauty in the murkier air which hangs about it; the brief spire of St Mary's of Battersea has lost its commonplace ugliness; the railway bridge which remotely spans the river is only a faint vision of arches, bounding the prospect not ungracefully. Then the foreground is ideal . . . Over the river there, in the shadow of the factories, is crowded together a flotilla of steamboats, moored for the night; you can just discern their shapes, but nothing of the wharfage behind them, nothing of walls and sheds and work-yards. Night has fallen upon that unsightly confusion, blending all in the rich shadow of the etcher. Here, however, on the nearer side, the broader mass of black outline is relieved by a few gas-lamps: their light burns strangely of a pale green, the effect of contrast with the sky above.

The third paragraph describes what movement there is on the river, barges behind a tug with a 'red light in its front'. The fourth paragraph gives the sunset, the 'fire in the west', so that:

> All above pales; the softer tints grow dusky; but, as if in compensation, the bands of fire which lie across the limit of vision glow with a deeper and sterner red. The tops of the houses come out before them now, and the impression of lordly mansions grows stronger yet. On the banks everything is dimmer: the mist seems borne this way by the south-west wind, which begins to moan out of the distance; the lamps flicker, and their clear emerald changes to something between yellow and red. Now the cloud-bank is hard at work rebuilding itself; the distance is lost; presently the shapes on the little strand hard by lose their pleasant suggestiveness and become mere phantoms. From the old tower of Chelsea Church, just at hand, there is struck out the hour of five.

The last paragraph returns to the pedestrians on the bridge.[15]

The visual sense recalls Whistler (1834–1903), who had exhibited at the Grosvenor Gallery (1877–90), created by the Scottish landowner Sir Coutts Lindsay as an alternative space to the Royal Academy. Ruskin attacked Whistler in 'Fors Clavigera' Letter 79 (July 1877): 'I have seen, and heard, much of Cockney impudence before now; but never expected to hear a coxcomb ask two hundred guineas for flinging a pot of paint in the public's face'.[16] This view contrasts with Holbrook Jackson, saying that Whistler 'taught the modern world how to appreciate the beauty and wizardry of cities'.[17] If Ruskin's critique draws attention to how paint is used rather than to the object represented, that may signal a new sense that art is presentation, rather than giving an access to a pre-given truth, something which, in terms of novel-writing, Dickens certainly knew. But, in addition, Whistler's *Nocturnes* implied a new way of seeing the city by night. In Dickens, the night is an alternative space; in Whistler it brings out the city in different colours: and Gissing responds to this.

Monet (1840–1926) came first to England in 1870, staying at 11 Arundel Street, Piccadilly, and then at Bath Place, Kensington. He painted *The Thames at Westminster*, and the London Parks, and the Pool of London; returned in 1887 as the guest of Whistler, and stayed at the Savoy for three winter visits, from 1899 to 1901, and painting London's bridges from the hotel. And Pissaro (1830–1903) came in 1870 for a year, staying at 2 Chatham Terrace, Palace Road, Upper Norwood, and painting the suburb. In 1890 and 1892, he lodged at Kew Green; in 1897, he stayed at Bedford Park. Sisley (1839–1899), too, visited in 1874 and painted the Thames and the area around Hampton Court.[18]

Gissing's word 'impression' in his description of Battersea Bridge is suggestive, as is 'ideal', that word which he contrasted with 'realism'. So did an anonymous critic in *The Spectator*, about *In the Year of Jubilee*:

> the realist endeavours to present all the facts, and to preserve in his presentation, their true proportionate values; while the idealist, consciously or instinctively, selects the facts, and confers upon them a value of his own for the sake of achieving a certain effect or impression. Generally, no doubt, the idealist will strive after an effect of beauty, simply because to the majority beauty is more admirable than ugliness; but this choice is not inevitable. (*Gissing: Critical Heritage* 240)

For the critic, 'idealism' bears two meanings: it is capturing an essence, what is most typical in a person or class of people, and it means picking out the ideal, the beautiful, the spiritual. The implicit contradiction structures all Gissing's work, since idealism can imply the strictest fidelity to realism, or the opposite of that. *On Battersea Bridge* holds these two senses in play; sees that the moment of sunset permits the ideal to appear in both ways, not negating the real, only being its temporary occlusion. It fits that such a moment is published in a newspaper; the momentary medium holds something momentary (the perception) within itself.

The extent to which far Gissing finds the ideal in this London landscape differentiates his London from that of Dickens. The contrasts show up what is particular about Dickens' London. In Gissing, London is a series of environments, Lambeth, or Camberwell. Lambeth is the other life from Westminster and Parliament, and politics, and so has a symbolic value. Camberwell houses stifling conformity, but once the locales have been presented, nothing can be added about them; they do not develop; there are no discoveries which indicate that they possess secrets that their first description could not unpack, though it might hint at them. There is no uncanny in Gissing's London. The point may be put another way. Gissing was shocked by the idea that *The Mystery of Edwin Drood* was to do with murder: 'it is unfortunate that the last work of a great writer should have for its theme nothing more human than a trivial mystery woven about a vulgar deed of blood' (*Charles Dickens* 56). There is comparatively little violence in Gissing: the idea of secrecy which explodes into something else, basic to Dickens' London, is absent for him, and confines his realism. His London is not traumatic, does not hide the past, has nothing not pre-given in the environment's flatness. The major difference to be noted in his London is the moment when the landscape looks ideal.

A second point relates: Dickens' descriptions of London are always narrated; the presence of the narrator is as vivid and subjective as what is represented; the realism is never neutral, so that it is not, strictly, realist, nor is there an opposition of realism and idealism. The narrator's presence constructs each scene; the reader must note both the scene and its presentation. Seeing London doubly is characteristic of each Dickens novel, less in Gissing. I illustrate this from *Thyrza*; first when Gilbert Grail goes towards Lambeth Bridge, past Lambeth Walk, place of the Christmas Eve market, and hears a street-organ, which sets children dancing:

> Do you know that music of the obscure ways, to which children dance? . . . To hear it aright you must stand in the darkness of such a by-street as this, and for the moment be at one with those who dwell around, in the blear-eyed houses, in the dim burrows of poverty, in the unmapped haunts of the semi-human. Then you will know the significance of that vulgar clanging of melody . . . and therein the secret of hidden London will be half revealed. The life of men who toil without hope, yet with the hunger of an unshaped desire; of women in whom the sweetness of their sex is perishing under labour and misery; the laugh, the song of the girl who strives to enjoy her year or two of youthful vigour, knowing the darkness of the years to come; the careless defiance of the youth who feels his blood and revolts against the lot which would tame it; all that is purely human in these darkened multitudes speaks to you as you listen. It is the half-conscious striving of a nature which knows not what it would attain . . . (9.111–12)

What is 'hidden' here has not the force of repression, or of something in the past which will come out in the present, as in Dickens. The secret is that there is poverty, which conceals 'all that is purely human', i.e. the ideal, that which

King's Cross Station, built Lewis Cubitt, 1852 for the Great Northern Railway; St Pancras, which cut through Agar Town, is to the far right (1868). Twin arches visible, with clock-tower just visible behind.

is partly unknown to the people themselves, but not a secret to the realist narrator, who, speaking from an outside position, makes the secret generalisable.

Second, a set-piece in *Thyrza* giving the sense of ugliness which can hold no secrets. It discusses the Caledonian Road, which was named after the Caledonian Asylum, an orphanage which opened in 1828, for the children of Scots killed in service:

> Caledonian Road is a great channel of traffic running directly north from King's Cross to Holloway. It is doubtful whether London can show any thoroughfare of importance more offensive to eye and ear and nostril. You stand at the entrance to it, and gaze into a region of supreme ugliness; every house front is marked with meanness and inveterate grime; every shop seems breaking forth with mould or dry-rot, the people who walk here appear one and all to be employed in labour that soils body and spirit. Journey on the top of a tram-car from King's Cross to Holloway, and civilization has taught you its ultimate achievement in ignoble hideousness. You look off into narrow side-channels where unconscious degradation has made its inexpugnable home, and sits veiled with refuse. You pass above lines of railway, which cleave the region with black-breathing fissure. You see the pavements half occupied with the paltriest and most sordid wares; the sign of the pawnbroker is on every hand; the public-houses look and reek more intolerably than in other places . . . (27.319)

This is the area between Camden Town and Islington, 'its public monument a cyclopean prison' (Pentonville), a 'desert' round 'the Great Northern Goods

Mausoleum for Sir John Soane (1753–1837), architect, in Old St Pancras Churchyard: here Jerry Cruncher was a resurrection-man (*TTC* 2.14.162). Angela Burdett-Coutts constructed a monument in 1879 for those bodies disinterred when St Pancras railway, parallel to King's Cross, cut through the churchyard.

Depot', its only open ground 'a malodorous cattle-market', Smithfield's successor. (It opened in 1855 as the Metropolitan Cattle Market and Caledonian Market, on Copenhagen Fields, closing in World War Two.) The passage compares with the journey home of Mr Wilfer (*OMF* 1.4), across the same territory, but that is conveyed with an irony and sense that something is to be learned from the language's excess. The space described is in movement and history: when Dickens wrote, it was with a sense of the place as in change. A narrative and a history is less present in Dickens' city than Gissing's. Dickens' city is medieval and modern and changing; but in Gissing, older buildings in Lambeth do not fold into them any other life: the medieval 'Archbishop's Palace' (Lambeth Palace), is, for Gilbert Grail, simply 'dark, lifeless' (113); nothing is to be learned from it; it stands as alienated from him.

IV · SUBURBAN LONDON

Gissing as noted moves to more bourgeois themes in the 1890s, and his London becomes more commercial and modern. There are often dates in his novels, and they are always of his time: his London is on the move. With *In the Year of Jubilee*, Luckworth Crewe, the advertising agent, the man of the new age, knows the city, but not its history: he has stories to tell of the success or failure of firms: 'to him the streets of London were so many chapters of romance, but a romance always of today, for he neither knew nor cared about historic associations' (2.3.89). The city contains crowds, so that, as Crewe says about the traffic near Oxford Street and Tottenham Court Road, 'these big crossings are like whirlpools, you might go round and round and never get anywhere' (1.8.60). The image makes London the 'whirlpool', title of his next novel. One of its new spaces is the underground, place of the whirlpool and the new world of advertising:

> They [Samuel Barmby and Jessica Morgan] descended and stood together upon the platform, among hurrying crowds, in black fumes that poisoned the palate with sulphur. This way and that sped the demon engines, whirling lighted waggons full of people. Shrill whistles, the hiss and roar of steam, the bang, clap, bang of carriage doors, the clatter of feet on wood and stone – all echoed and reverberated from a huge cloudy vault above them. High and low, on every available yard of wall, advertisements clamoured to the eye: theatres, journals, soaps, medicines, concerts, furniture, wines, prayer-meetings – all the produce and refuse of civilisation announced in staring letters, in the daubed effigies, base, paltry, grotesque. A battle-ground of advertisements, fitly chosen amid subterranean din and reek; a symbol to the gaze of that relentless warfare which ceases not, night and day, in the world above. (*In the Year of Jubilee* 5.2.259)

In the Year of Jubilee shows 'suburban London', as is announced on the first page of that book. The LCC encouraged the building of new estates further out which connected with London by cheap fares, which began creating the distinction between London as a place with huge areas of poverty, as in Dickens, and a city now with new areas of poverty moved out into outer suburbs, thus intensifying differentations amongst the suburbs. *In the Year of Jubilee* describes De Cresigny Park, between Denmark Hill and Grove Lane, where the houses seem to announce that 'in this locality, lodgings are *not* to let' (1.1.5), in contrast to Wilton Square in *Demos*. Camberwell 'in the second half of the nineteenth century [was] almost a symbol of social uniformity, its social structure a kind of lowest common multiple of suburbs everywhere, as the lower middle-class poured into them'.[19] But in announcing that houses are not to let, the suggestion that they might be let is raised: this is suburbia needing to keep respectable. This is Camberwell, where Denmark Hill runs up to Herne Hill, where Ruskin lived. Here Mr Widdowson lives, in what is carefully called a 'villa', keeping the appearance of a pastoral retreat. So Monica Madden lives there after marrying him (*The Odd Women* 15). Perhaps the place was chosen to suggest that Widdowson was as authoritarian as Ruskin. Suburban London is identified by Lionel Tarrant with 'provincialism', or with 'Camberwellism' (2.6.152); this is in the context of Nancy's demurrals at visiting him in his rooms at Staple Inn. They have made love together at Teignmouth: holidays at the coast appear frequently in Gissing, and make seaside resorts extensions of London.

Further out from inner suburbs are others. Harrow is where Nancy Lord lives 'in a byway which has no charm but that of quietness', in one of 'a row of small plain houses' each of which 'contains six rooms' and 'has a little strip of garden at the rear'. Its advantage is 'lying beyond the great smoke-area' of London (6.3.334, 335). It represents genteel poverty. Pinner in *The Whirlpool*, 'only about half an hour from Baker Street' on the Metropolitan Railway (extended to Pinner in 1885), is, as Alma, the violinist, says, 'on the outer edge of the whirlpool' (2.5.175). Later, Alma and Rolfe move to Gunnersbury, north of Kew Bridge, but Rolfe feels 'hardly more sense of vital connection with this suburb' than with his place of business (3.6.354–55). As for Alma, she must forget everything that lies east of Gunnersbury, condemned to 'a small house' and 'a baffled ambition' to be a musician and to 'house-ruling' (3.9.383, 388, 389).

The suburb becomes the wife's sphere, creating a stronger gender-division, and division between work and home, than appeared in Dickens. Spaces in Gissing are now differently owned; for instance, Gissing wishes to discuss in *The Odd Women* (chapter 4) the new, qualified freedom of walking in London on Sundays that Monica Madden enjoys, while she works at a draper's shop in the Walworth Road. Her sister, Virginia, walks from lodgings on Lavender Hill in Battersea, 'past Battersea Park, over Chelsea Bridge, then the weary stretch to Victoria Station and the upward labour to Charing Cross' – which is five miles – to buy a book, and then stops in the refreshment room at Charing Cross Station for a brandy (2.19–20). The passage suggests poverty (she cannot afford the omnibus and the drink), and rootlessness (the station), but shows the woman as being of the city, of having to know 'London transit' (5.51). And Nancy Lord travels in by tram-car from Camberwell to the West End to see the celebrations of the Queen's Jubilee (*In the Year of Jubilee*).

Or take the use of flats. Will Warburton, who walks from Whitechapel to Chelsea, lives on 'the fourth floor of the many-tenanted building hard by Chelsea Bridge' (1.5), flats built in 1878 by the Improved Industrial Dwellings Co. *In the Year of Jubilee* makes Nancy Lord move through South London to find Beatrice French, who has set up the South London Fashionable Dress Supply Association (4.4.200), and now lives in a 'bachelor flat' (4.5.212), with electricity supplied (noted in the bell, which contrasts with Dickens' door-knockers):

> Another cab conveyed her to Brixton, and set her down before a block of recently built flats. She ascended to the second floor, pressed the button of a bell, and was speedily confronted by a girl of the natty parlour-maid species. This time she began by giving her name, and had only a moment to wait before she was admitted to a small drawing-room, furnished with semblance of luxury. A glowing fire and the light of an amber-shaded lamp showed as much much fashionable upholstery and bric-à-

St Luke's Chelsea, James
Savage, 1824: Gothic revival,
where Dickens married.

brac as could be squeezed into the narrow space. Something else was perceptible
which might perhaps have been dispensed with; to wit, the odour of a very savoury
meal, a meal in which fried onions had no insignificant part. Before the visitor could
comment to herself upon this disadvantage of flats, Beatrice joined her. (5.4.274–75)

Beatrice gives Nancy a job as a 'shop-girl', a description which her estranged
husband, Lionel Tarrant, regards as a euphemism (5.8.304), not understanding
her consumer-culture. Though it comprises 'artificial necessities' (*The Whirlpool*
2.7.201), it gives her apparent liberty. Flats suggest new possibilities for women's
independent space in London, which, however, are also frustrated.

Gissing's fascination is increasingly with money; 'All London speaks to
him in the language of money; streets, clubs, theatres, lodgings, restaurants,
suggest to him the human fight and fret and fume over money' (review
of *The Whirlpool* in *Academy, Gissing: Critical Heritage* 282). Middle-class
suburbia's spread is money-dictated: a representative new suburb, described
as half-built, is accounted for in the following way:

A year or two ago, the site had been an enclosed meadow, a portion of the land
attached to what was once a country mansion; London, devourer of rural limits, of a
sudden made hideous encroachment upon the same estate, now held by a speculative
builder; . . . on this rising locality had been bestowed the title of 'Park'. (4.2.183–84)

It is a history that has been seen many times, considering nineteenth-century
London in this book.

CONCLUSION
No Thoroughfare

'. . . It's no thoroughfare, Sammy, no thoroughfare.'   *Pickwick Papers* 43.577

'I enter in this little book the names of the streets that I can't go down while the shops are open. This dinner today closes Long Acre. I bought a pair of shoes in Great Queen Street last week and made that no thoroughfare, too. There's only one avenue to the Strand left open now, and I shall have to stop up that to-night with a pair of gloves.'   *Old Curiosity Shop* 8. 67–68

the [blind] court had no thoroughfare, and was not that kind of place in which many people were likely to take the air, or to frequent as an agreeable promenade.   *Barnaby Rudge* 8.80

In the throats and maws of dark no-thoroughfares near Todgers's, individual wine-merchants and wholesale dealers in grocery-ware had perfect little towns of their own . . .   *Martin Chuzzlewit* 9.132

. . . no thoroughfare in any direction . . .   *Bleak House* 19.309.

. . . the streets of Cloisterham city are little more than one narrow street by which you get into it and get out of it, the rest being mostly disappointing yards with pumps in them and no thoroughfare . . .   *Edwin Drood* 3.23

This book has attempted four things. It has been as empirical as possible in reading Dickens by comparing the topography in the texts with the topography which is still on the ground. It worked on the basis of thinking that out of the eighteenth-century and city-based visual art of Hogarth, there emerges a new urban art within Dickens, which makes London not just a background, but a subject of the text. Dickens is not unique in writing the great city; we have discussed Wordsworth, Thackeray, Baudelaire, Dostoyevsky; we could add in Blake, Gogol, Balzac, Flaubert, Galdos, Zola, and James.[1] Nonetheless, half the writers named here have been fascinated by the city at least in part through the eyes of Dickens, and with none of them is there such intense identification of the subject with the city, or the subject-matter of the text with the city. The intensity is in the writings. So is the knowledge of what London meant biographically to Dickens. And the impression, which remains valid beyond the general sense that we see London through Dickens, is that London has accrued something from having had Dickens write about it.

Dickens makes locales symbolic, and uses them personally and autobio-graphically, in a way that suggests that the texts are returning to discover more fully only half-disclosed meanings. Sites are what Wordsworth calls 'the hiding places of my power' (*The Prelude* 11.336), but when approached, their significance resists naming; an empirical approach fails; places have unconscious and repressed significance. It is not that there is any essential quality of places (this is not an exercise in 'psychogeography'), rather, it is to say that places accrue significance because of their names, their associations, and because of unconscious factors that come out in what Freud in 'Beyond the Pleasure Principle' calls 'the compulsion to repeat'.[2] As the critical theorist Michel de Certeau writes about places in everyday life, locales which contest being squeezed into being the thoroughly knowable spaces of the Panoptical gaze, 'Places are fragmentary and inward-turning histories, pasts that others are not allowed to read, accumulated times that can be unfolded but like stories held in reserve, remaining in an enigmatical state, symbolizations encysted in the pain or pleasure of the body'.[3] The last phrase suggests – like Proust – that places are associated with memories possessed by the body. Accretions of suggestion accumulate around places in Dickens: the Golden Cross, Camden Town, Furnival's Inn, Newgate, the Monument, Putney or Richmond, St Giles, Seven Dials, Southwark. There are similar scenes of trauma: Smike and Florence Dombey are both kidnapped around the same area of Somers Town. And similar haunts: Bill Sikes and Bradley Headstone both go upstream. Places return from novel to novel, as though possessing an attraction like the river drawing Martha, or Amy Dorrit seeing the Marshalsea (now gone) everywhere else. The novels juxtapose places apparently different to affirm repressed connections, as in *Oliver Twist* and *Bleak House*.

London's bulk and reality not only produces character-types – secret, traumatised, nomadic, schizoid or paranoid – but constructs a context for events, framing them within a local history: bringing out their significance by situating them within the history of an area. *David Copperfield* shows this throughout, looking back from a more modern to an older London. The filth and waste which characterise London's streets and rivers figure the city both as excess, heterogeneous beyond all imagination, and as constructing extreme states of disgust and requiring new ways of thinking about what has been classed as obscene. London produces new forms of subjectivity, sometimes going beyond all forms that realism could describe, leaving Dickens open to the charge that he caricatures reality (he often does deliberately, but that is not what is meant) or that his art exaggerates, which it does, but in the precise sense that Adorno meant when he said that 'in psychoanalysis, nothing is true except the exaggerations'.[4] The same may be said of Dickens, as of psychoanalysis. The modern city goes beyond all ways of representing it; it requires, and produces, a writing which works by excess.

There are several Londons in Dickens, and characters get caught between them. Bradley Headstone is absolutely of the split world of Bermondsey and Deptford, trapped between the order of the railway and the incoherence of the

Fragment of the Marshalsea wall, with distant view of the church of St George the Martyr through the gateway.

world beneath it, which it in part constructs. The city is a molar structure of power, as glimpsed at in those figures of power like Tulkinghorn, or Bucket, but it also comprises discontinuous spaces, which are perceived differently because they are seen in different speeds: walking, in the coach, or in the train, that which implied a new thing: that cities go with speed. Hence the tempo of Sam Weller's wit, as sudden and discontinuous and changing as the streets of London. Hence the name the Artful Dodger, and his smartness, and the way he builds into his name a way of moving round its spaces. It recalls how Michel de Certeau discusses the 'practices of everyday life', which show people's resistance to the Panoptic tendency inscribed in city planning and architecture. Certeau says that 'the walking of passers-by offers a series of turns and detours that can be compared to "turns of phrase" or "stylistic features"' (*The Practice of Everyday Life* 100). Walking in the streets, like poetry, relies on 'turns' that evade all arrest or fixing. In *Oliver Twist* the dodger twists. There emerges an affinity between Dickens' comedy, speed, the discontinuity of the streets, and resistance to the molar structures of London. But London builds into itself resistance to molar structures, as with its folds and labyrinths, as seen in legal London, or in the thieves' world, while the secrecy which is so much inherent in 'the modern Babylon' both concentrates power and makes it frightening (Mrs Clennam's house) and disperses it endlessly.

Dickens' fascination is with those parts of London which bring out unrepressed forms of life, less than *Dombey and Son*'s 'better parts of the town'. The better parts are marked out by monotony, like Mayfair in *Little Dorrit*. The others require movement, knowing that the city can never be got out of. This vastness accords with the size of the nineteenth-century novel, and poses questions about the relation between the city and narrative. Dickens' narratives are plural, with multiple destinies, like London's dispersed places, yet the city pulls its separate parts together, makes them relate, or connect, sometimes oppressively. But as the name for several sites of power, London has no centre; what pulls separate people or narratives together turns out to be nothing, like the emptiness in the Jarndyce versus Jarndyce case, or Merdle's bankruptcy. Being in the city is being in a labyrinth, which definitionally has no centre, nor any point at which it is left, as the lawyer who commits suicide in the 1860 essay 'Chambers' (*The Uncommercial Traveller*) knows (see p. 148). He says that London is so small. Going west (towards death) means coming to Hounslow, east is to Bow (to bow can mean to crush), south is to Brixton or Norwood (going south you get north) and north 'you can't get rid of Barnet' (*J4* 164), as if beginning a joke with Barnet/Bar/and Barnacle (*Little Dorrit*). These places, continuations of London, its 'net', make it too big, inescapable: by 1860, its bigness was becoming truly apparent through the railways, which pushed London outwards.

As labyrinthine, London implies the unsettling of identity, and the non-destiny of what has 'gone astray', which can never reappear in the form it had before, as John Harmon knows after being in the river. One phrase dominating in Dickens is 'No Thoroughfare', title of a story co-written with Wilkie Collins in 1867.[5] It is a recurring motif, suggestive of the prison, or of the traumatic experience which compels repetition, appearing not only in the quotations given above, but in other novels, such as *Dombey and Son*, *Little Dorrit*, *Great Expectations* and *Our Mutual Friend*, where its use was quoted.[6] With *Little Dorrit*, it seems as if 'No Thoroughfare', along with 'Nobody's Fault', was a draft title (*Life* 9.7.757 and 760), and perhaps a clue for that appears in one of the Memoranda notes:

> Bed-ridden (or room-ridden) twenty – five and twenty – years [the number Tattycoram must count to]; any length of time. As to most things, kept at a standstill all the while [cp. 'deadlock']. Thinking of altered streets as the old streets – changed things as the unchanged things – the youth or girl I quarrelled with all those years ago, as the same youth or girl now. Brought out of doors by an unexpected exercise of my latent strength of character, and then how strange! (*Life* 9.7.748).

Being frozen in time relates to Betsy Trotwood, Mr Dick, and Miss Flite, or to Mrs Clennam, to whom Forster applies the passage in Dickens' Memoranda, or Flora Finching, or Mr Dorrit, or Dr Manette, before he is 'recalled to life', or Miss Havisham. Everything here is suggestive of the power of repression, with the difference that the Memoranda assumes the possibility of change, whereas the novels are much more equivocal. In Baudelaire's 'Le Cygne', discussed in chapter two, 'altered streets' are still the 'old streets', and though street clearances and modernisations take place in Dickens, they do not have the power of making altered streets suggestive of altered lives. 'No thoroughfare' keeps a person in a state of repression, and makes the self unknown to itself. Mrs Gamp's constant use of Mrs Harris represents a 'no thoroughfare' in her existence; she cannot break through the barrier which allows her not to know this other is fictional. In the Christmas story, 'No Thoroughfare', Obenreizer and Vendale are linked to each other, virtual doubles, yet they are unknown to each other; the self knowing neither the self, nor the history of the self, nor what is other to the self.

Dickens' text has an interest in thoroughfares, as may be seen with the fascination with the potentialities of the railroad. *The Uncommercial Traveller* as a title suggests thoroughfares: the pleasant wallowing in the abundant mud of the Commercial Road as a thoroughfare (*J4* 43), or, as a sign of hope, there is the 'external thoroughfare' which runs past Titbull's Almshouses, which suggests another life than that which exists inside its confines (*J4* 325). There is the 'straight, broad, public thoroughfare of immense resort' that the Waterloo Road is described as being, 'traversed by two popular cross thoroughfares of considerable traffic' (*J4* 336). But a thoroughfare in Dickens can also be a point which resists passage through it, a space in itself containing its own other space. 'The gin-shops in and near Drury-lane, Holborn, St Giles', Covent-garden and Clare-market, are the handsomest in London. There is more of filth and squalid misery near those great thoroughfares than in any part of this mighty city' (*SB* 217). These 'thoroughfares' are 'no thoroughfares'. They make problematic the idea of narrative moving on, as Joe must 'move on' in *Bleak House* but cannot, or like the warning, 'For God's sake clear the way' in 'The Signalman' (*CS* 536), which freezes the signalman, as if under the power of a death-drive. 'Gin Shops' implies that thoroughfares are no thoroughfares because spaces in London are simultaneously handsome and filthy, or handsome because filthy. In such a space, where everything is double, ordered progress becomes impossible; there is 'no thoroughfare' because of the power of fascination with disgust, that which causes going astray. London is the unbounded, heterogeneous, containing potentialities that defeat organisation into different categories. It is unbounded and no thoroughfare at the same time. 'No thoroughfare' implies the reserve, the secret, within London, however much it is probed; 'Gone astray' the state the secret impels: constant digressiveness, being drawn further and further into the configuration of places, fascinated out of all thinking which assumes the self's identity to itself.

'No thoroughfare' implies a halt, or deadlock, disrupting narrative as this is based on ongoing chains of causes followed by effects. Gissing criticised Dickens for what he called his 'abuse' of coincidence (*Charles Dickens* 51), finding this supreme in *Bleak House*, but against this we may put Tim Linkinwater saying: 'I don't believe now that there's such a place in all the world for coincidences as London is!' (*NN* 43.530). Dickens' London creates the aporia which makes movement impossible, and it haunts the self with the dread of repetition. But it permits or creates coincidence, working against 'melancholy-madness' and stasis. For OED, when 'coincidence' means 'a notable concurrence of events or circumstances having no apparent causal connexion', it is usually qualified by such words as 'strange', 'singular', 'unexpected', as if suggesting that coincidence is not the norm. In Dickens, coincidence *is* the norm, partly because the city gives the sense that there is something other than causality structuring events, partly because London is uncanny, strange and singular to itself: odd. Its nooks are archives which are always surprising. Because coincidence is another way of seeing how the city exists, rich cheek by jowl with poor, contrasted people living on different floors of apartments. Coincidence gives London meaning in an alternative mode from how meanings in the city are created in sociology or social or cultural history. These commentaries rely on the developmental logic of cause and effect (where coincidence cannot rule). And coincidence confuses distinctions between inside and outside; it disallows the possibility of representing it from a single point outside, because coincidence implies more than one time-scale, and it affects the person who thinks they are outside it. No maps for the city, no way of reading it. Dickens' symbols for the city – fog, or the river – are those which cannot be a finite image of the city. Nor can the prison; who can say where prison walls start? Or who is inside, who outside? When am I out of the city? In Dickens, nothing can be an image of London, save the city itself, because nothing can represent it, nor sum it up and its possibilities.

DICKENS' LONDON: A GAZETTEER

The Gazetteer has four sections. The first, the City and the East End, comprises sites east of the Fleet River, London's hidden seam. The second, the West End and west London, comprises Holborn, Westminster, Kensington and Chelsea, and everything further west than that. The third is everything south of the River Thames, the fourth, everything else north, including Islington and Hackney.

THE CITY AND THE EAST END

Austin Friars. *MC* 39.573, off Old Broad Street; the Augustinian monastery of 1253, between London Wall and Throgmorton Street, north of Threadneedle Street. It became the house of Thomas Cromwell, being taken over by the Draper's Company for their hall. The Augustinian Friars were founded by Humphrey de Bohun, Constable of England, after a Crusade, c.1225. Other foundations for Friars in the medieval City: **Greyfriars** (1225, Franciscan, between Newgate Street and the City wall). The monastery buildings became Christ's Hospital, the school founded by Edward the Sixth (1553); Coleridge, Lamb and Leigh Hunt were pupils. It moved out of London in 1902. Christ Church became a parish church. **Whitefriars** (Carmelites, mid-thirteenth century) is memorialised in Whitefriars Street and Carmelite Street, from Fleet Street to the river, including Hanging Sword Alley (*BH* 27.438, *TTC* 2.1.57). It acquired a theatre, the Salisbury Court, 1629. **Blackfriars** (Dominican), east of present Blackfriars Bridge. After the dissolution, the new parish church was St Ann Blackfriars, destroyed in the Fire. The monks' refectory became a Blackfriars playhouse, starting in 1576, and used by a boys' company, 1600–1608. Ireland Yard, off St Andrew's Hill, contains stones from Blackfriars; Shakespeare bought a house here in 1613. East of Blackfriars was the Norman Castle Baynard, built on the Roman wall running alongside the river, destroyed in the Fire.

Bevis Marks, north-west from Aldgate, via Duke's Place, had a synagogue for Portuguese and Spanish (Sephardic) Jews (1701). Name perhaps from Bury St Edmunds, whose monastery owned land here until the 1530s; the land was given to Sir Thomas Heneage (hence Heneage Lane). **Houndsditch** runs parallel to Bevis Marks, up to Bishopsgate, and corresponds to a Roman ditch outside the wall. Jerry Cruncher comes from Houndsditch (*TTC* 2.1.57), he would have been baptised at St Botolph without Bishopsgate (like Keats). Duke's Place was named for Thomas Howard, Duke of Norfolk, who had a house here, sold to the City after his execution in 1572. Earlier it was the site of Holy Trinity Priory, and the parish church was St Katherine Cree [Christ]. Bentham was born on the corner of Creechurch Lane and Duke's Place in 1748. For the Jewish population of Houndsditch and Whitechapel, see *Barnaby Rudge* (63.521).

Billingsgate. A water gate onto the Thames, with 'Billing' a personal name; a medieval wharf, alongside Dowgate (where the Walbrook, which bisected the City, reached the Thames), Queenhithe (for St Paul's) and the mouth of the Fleet at Blackfriars; established as a fish-market in 1698, rebuilt in the 1850s, and again by Sir Horace Jones (1877): the new Billingsgate opened on the Isle of Dogs in 1982.

Bow, where the Nicklebys live courtesy of the Cheeryble brothers (*NN* 35.436), was part of Stepney, becoming a separate parish in 1719. St Mary was first built in the fourteenth century as a chapel of ease on an island site in the middle of the highway. Its name recalls a medieval bowed bridge over the River Lea, the border with Essex; on the other side was Stratford Langthorne Abbey, a Cistercian foundation of the 1130s. The bridge replaced a crossing at Old Ford, a Roman settlement. North of present-day Bow is Victoria Park (Pennethorne, 1845), south, the Mile End Road, and then Bromley by Bow, around the northern approach to the Blackwall Tunnel (opened 1897). Location of Bryant and May's match factory, and the matchworkers' strike (1888), also of Bow cemetery, one of seven licensed in the 1830s.

Bucklersbury, between Poultry and Walbrook, in the City, with cheap eating-houses, belonged to the Buckerel family in the twelfth century. It later became a place for groceries and herbs and spices: Falstaff speaks of men smelling like Bucklersbury (*The Merry Wives of Windsor* 3.3.66), contrasting that city-smell with 'walking by the Counter-gate' – a debtor's prison. Bucklersbury was cut through by Queen Victoria Street (1865–71), part of the creation of Victoria Embankment. The Roman temple of Mithras was excavated in 1954 under the 1950s Bucklersbury House.

Charterhouse Street runs from Holborn Circus, over Farringdon Road, behind Smithfield, to Charterhouse Square (south of Clerkenwell Green, between St John Street and Aldersgate). Used as a burial ground by the City for the Black Death (1348), it became a Carthusian monastery. Thackeray attended the school founded, along with the hospital, by Thomas Sutton (1532–1611: often considered a source for Jonson's *Volpone*) between 1822 and 1828. The school moved out of London in 1872.

Cheapside. The sense of commodities for sale in the medieval city shows in Cheapside, and Poultry, its continuation on the east, and Cornhill, further still, and Gracechurch (Grasschurch) Street; i.e. the church by the medieval haymarket. Other trades are signalled in Goldsmith Street, Bread Street, Wood Street and Milk Street, and further east, Ironmonger street, Threadneedle Street and Lime Street (lime for mortar). Cannon Street's name comes from Candlewick Street; it was continued beyond Walbrook and Dow Hill to St Paul's in the 1840s by City Surveyor J.B. Bunning. Fish Hill and Eastcheap are also significant names. Coleman Street, north of Poultry, is named for charcoal burners, or coalmen.

City Road, home of Micawber; bypass constructed in the 1760s, carrying traffic from the Angel to the built-up area around Bunhill Fields and Old Street, so connecting the City with the New Road. Shepherdess Walk runs north towards Islington, and the Regent's Canal.

Docks. Pitt laid the foundation stone for the West India Docks in the Isle of Dogs (Stebenhithe [= Stepney] Marsh) in 1800: they inaugurate London's nineteenth century. Opening in 1802, the **Commercial Road** was built to take its traffic, carrying sugar for refining in Back Church Lane, Whitechapel, and in Leman Street. The East India Docks, for the East India Company, were opened in 1806 in Blackwall, downstream of the Isle of Dogs, and amalgamated with the West India Docks in 1838. Both closed in 1980. Blackwall, like Blackheath south of the river, seems to have been named for the colour of its shrubs; it was the port from which the Virginian colonists sailed in 1606. The London Docks opened at Wapping in 1805, bringing all the tobacco, rice, wine and brandy to London that did not come from the West and East India Docks. After Surrey Docks (eighteenth century) and St Katherine's Docks (1828), came the Royal Victoria (1855), Millwall (1868) and Albert Dock at West Ham (1880), and Tilbury (1886), twenty-six miles downstream in Essex. After financial losses, all came under the Port of London Authority (1908).

Doctors' Commons. A plaque on the Faraday Building on the north side of Queen Victoria Street marks the site of Doctors' Commons, demolished in 1867, discussed in *SB* 109, *PP* 10.132, and central to *DC* (chapter 23 especially). It was the hall which comprised lawyers dealing with admiralty and ecclesiastical courts, the latter called 'Court of Arches', being the ecclesiastical court of appeal for the province of Canterbury, formerly held at the church of St Mary-le-Bow (or 'of the Arches') in Cheapside, named, probably, from the arches in the crypt. Doctors' Commons had offices dealing with marriage licences and divorces, and registration of wills. Thus its scope was ecclesiastical and civil law; it ended with changes to divorce law in 1857. South of St Paul's churchyard, between Great Knightrider Street and Queen Victoria Street (which replaced Thames Street). North of Wren's St Benet's [Benedict], which was on the wharfside (see *Twelfth Night* 5.1.35), and near the College of Arms (seventeenth century: rebuilt after World War Two).

Exchange (Dickens' 'Change) as a meeting place for merchants, on the lines of a bourse seen in Antwerp; called 'Royal' in 1570. The Victorian building opened in 1844, its open courtyard roofed over 1880, its portico designed like the Pantheon in Rome with allegories of Commerce in the roof-pediment; it ceased functioning in 1939. (The previous building of 1669 burned down 1838.) Gresham left money in his will for Gresham College, which led to the development of the Royal Society. (Gresham College is now at Barnard's Inn, Holborn, but had its own buildings in Gresham Street in the 1840s.)

Fleet market. Opened 1737, designed by George Dance for the Stock Market previously outside the Mansion House: cleared between 1826 and 1830 to make way for Farringdon Street (see *PP* 41.548). In 1733, the Fleet was covered from Holborn Bridge (see *BR* 67.559) to Fleet Bridge (linking Ludgate Hill to Fleet Street), creating Farringdon Street. The river, rising in Hampstead and flowing to the Thames, was covered over by 1765. The **Fleet prison** stood at present-day no. 15 Caronne House. Built in 1197, it was variously destroyed in the Peasants' Revolt, the Great Fire, and the Gordon Riots, and closed in 1842.

Garraway's, opened in the 1660s, and closed in 1866, was in Exchange Alley; it sold tea, organised the fur trade with the Hudson Bay Company; is called in *MC* 27.425 'a business coffee-room'. *UT* no. 23 refers to its 'old monastery-crypt'.

Jerusalem Coffee House, demolished 1872, was a newsroom, and associated with the China trade, and the East Indies and Australia. It was in Cowper's Court, Cornhill, between Change Alley and Birkin Lane. Both closed when telegraphic messages replaced their old news services.

Gresham Street. Created 1845, in a road-widening which removed the Swan-with-two-Necks, terminus for the northern mail-coaches, which went out of town on the present A1; the Cross Keys in Wood Street (closed 1865) was for mails to Rochester (*GE* 2.1.163). Sir Thomas Gresham (1519–79) founded the **Royal**.

Guildhall. Scene of Pickwick's trial; built 1411 for civic government by the merchant guilds of the city, reconstructed after the Great Fire (1671), with revisions by George Dance the Younger in 1789, and by Sir Horace Jones (1819–87), in 1866, rebuilt after bombing in 1940.

Leadenhall Street. Named for a leaden-roofed mansion of the fourteenth century which was sold to the City of London corporation in 1411, leading to the area becoming a general market, Leadenhall market, rebuilt after the Fire, and again in 1881 as the present-day Leadenhall Market (architect: Sir Horace Jones), based on the Milan covered market.

Limehouse. Lime kilns gave Limehouse its name in the fourteenth century, though the area grew through its links with the sea and with shipping. Limehouse Basin opened in 1820, as the end of the Regent's Canal. Another canal, Limehouse Cut (1770) connected the Thames and the Lea River. Limehouse Hole was probably so called from a deep section of the river, not from anything inland.

Little Britain. Street for booksellers and publishers in the seventeenth and eighteenth centuries, Milton lodged here (1662), and Johnson as a child (1712), and Benjamin Franklin (1724). Charles Wesley was converted in the house of John Bray (adjacent to no. 13) in 1738, as John Wesley was converted the same year in **Aldersgate** Street. Little Britain starts from the north from West Smithfield, passes St Bartholomew's hospital, continues south to King Edward Street, crosses it, and goes east, into Aldersgate Street (Aldersgate: Roman gate, but Saxon name: Gate of Ealdred). Robert Smirke's Post Office (see *NN* 39.476) was built on the site of St Mary-le-Grand nearby in 1829, destroyed 1912.

Lombard Street. Named for northern Italian bankers who settled in the street in the twelfth century, who gave it its tradition of banking; it runs into the Bank area from the east, with Threadneedle Street and Cornhill to its north. That area, including Mansion House, the Bank of England and the Royal Exchange, constitutes the highest hill within the City. Construction of King William Street made Hawksmoor's St Mary Woolnoth (1717), between Lombard Street and King William Street, more visible on its south wall. Pope was born, the son of a linen-draper, in Lombard Street, in 1688.

London Bridge, in Dickens' time, was the five-arch span of Dartmoor granite completed in 1831, by John Rennie, and his son, and replaced by a new bridge in 1973. The Bridge goes back to Roman times; Rennie's bridge was 180 feet upriver from the thirteenth century one, causing strong redevelopments north and south of the river (see *DC* 59.825).

Ludgate Hill rises towards the City and St Paul's from Ludgate Circus (1875) Ludgate, demolished 1770, with its statue of Elizabeth now outside St Dunstan's. On the north side is St Martin within Ludgate (rebuilt by Wren) and the London coffee house (destroyed 1867), see *LD*. 1.3.44, and the Bel Savage, once a theatre (1583) attached to an inn (destroyed 1873). A railway station was built 1865 (closed 1929), and a railway bridge crossed Ludgate Hill taking trains towards Farringdon.

Mansion House. Built on the site of the thirteenth-century stocks (cattle) market, and on part of the churchyard of St Mary Woolchurch (rebuilt after the Fire by Hawksmoor, as St Mary Woolnoth). The work of George Dance, between 1739 and 59, in Palladian style; the building's central courtyard was roofed over by Dance's son in 1795 who also removed another storey behind the courtyard. The building opposite, on Cornhill, is the **Bank of England**; created 1694, architects: George Sampson (till 1734), Robert Taylor (1765); Sir John Soane (1788), modified by Herbert Baker (1862–1946).

Mincing Lane. Named, according to John Stowe, after the nuns (mynchen) of St Helen's, Bishopsgate; the church, for a Benedictine nunnery (1204–1538) survives between Bishopsgate and St Mary Axe. Between Great Tower Street and Fenchurch Street, it was the spice-trading centre of London, after the East India Company took over all trading ports from the Dutch East India Company in 1799: Bella thinks of it as a 'drug-flavoured region', as if she has 'just opened a drawer in a chemist's shop' (*OMF* 3.16.589).

Norton Folgate. Off Bishopsgate, which begins the Roman road north out of London; and outside the City. Old spelling: Falgate. One of the 'liberties' outside the jurisdiction of the City of London, which had contained the medieval priory St Mary Spital, i.e. Spitalfields. Portsoken was the liberty to the south, site of Matilda's Priory of Holy Trinity (1107), and one of the City's twenty-five wards.

Old Street. Given that name in medieval times, Old Street suggests a Roman road running north of the City, and north of Finsbury, from Goswell Street to Shoreditch, a continuation of Clerkenwell Road. Contains St Luke's church (1733), designed by John James and Hawksmoor, and St Luke's hospital for the poor (George Dance and his son).

Rag Fair. Second-hand clothes market, Rosemary Lane near Tower Hill, where stolen clothes could be bought and sold: for the poorest. Since 1850, called Royal Mint Street, leading into **Cable Street** (site of the Battle of Cable Street with Mosley's Fascists on 5 October 1936), the eighteenth-century place of manufacture of ropes and cables. **The Mint** moved out of the Tower of London in 1810, into a building designed by Robert Smirke (and moved to Wales in 1968). Rag Fair appears in Pope's 1728 *The Dunciad* (1.27). Run by Jewish and Irish settlers, it declined in the early twentieth century.

Ratcliff Highway (Radcliffe). Ratcliff began as a hamlet in Stepney, and as a landing-place on the Thames. The Highway extends a mile from the Royal Mint to Limehouse. In the early nineteenth century it catered for sailors on shore-leave; in 1797, it was estimated that thefts from ships there amounted to half a million pounds annually, prompting calls for the River Police and for the creation of the

Docks. The area attracted journalistic attention up to the 1860s, when attention switched northwards of the street, towards the East End. Contains Hawksmoor's church, St George in the East (1729).

St Katherine's. Docks designed by Thomas Telford, opened 1828. Becoming part of the London Docks in Wapping in 1864; closed 1968. Built on a site of houses, and a brewery, and the Royal Foundation of St Katherine, including a twelfth-century church (St Katherine), founded in 1148 by Queen Matilda, for the maintenance of thirteen poor persons on land next to the Tower of London. This belonged to the Holy Trinity Augustinian priory at Aldgate and survived the dissolution of the monasteries; it gave refuge to foreigners in the seventeenth and eighteenth centuries.

St Mary Axe. Site of an early medieval church, suppressed in 1560 and made a warehouse, supposed to contain an axe with which eleven thousand virgins were beheaded by Attila the Hun. Residential in the eighteenth and nineteenth centuries, associated with shipbrokers, and marine insurance companies. The Baltic Exchange of 1903, which was there, has been replaced (after bomb damage in 1992) by Norman Foster's 'Gherkin'. Mr Podsnap, who works in marine insurance (*OMF* 1.11.131), would have had his offices in St Mary Axe. It is 'the heart of the City'; and 'not a very lively spot' (*OMF* 3.1.417).

St Paul's Cathedral. Wren's masterwork (1708) replaced, after the Fire of London, the medieval cathedral, with its St Paul's Cross, an exterior pulpit near the east end on the northern side, and its 'walks' inside which allowed for business (see Act 3 of Jonson's *Every Man Out of His Humour*) and its booksellers and stationers' shops in St Paul's Churchyard. Bobadill, in Jonson's *Every Man in His Humour* (the part Dickens played) was a 'Paul's Man', i.e. a loiterer dressed as a soldier, associated with 'Duke Humphrey' whose tomb was erroneously thought to be in the Cathedral. W.H. Ainsworth (1805–1882)'s *Old Saint Paul's* (1841) discusses London between the Plague and the Great Fire. The Cathedral clock (see *Master Humphrey's Clock*) was by Richard Phelps, 1716. Though Nelson had expected a Westminster Abbey internment, his state funeral was at St Paul's in 1806, like Wellington in 1852. The top of St Paul's (*Little Dorrit* 2.25.742) is 404 feet from the pavement.

Shadwell. Developed in the seventeenth century, becoming a parish in 1699. Its church, St Paul's, had been built in 1656 as a chapel of ease to St Dunstan's, Stepney, and was rebuilt by John Walters (1820). Dickens describes visiting the opium-den at Shadwell, *Letters* 12.520 n., perhaps twice in 1869. Birthplace of Water Pater (1839–94) whose father was a doctor there.

Shoreditch has as its centre St Leonard's, Shoreditch Church (George Dance, 1740), where Old Street meets Shoreditch High Street. Running south from Old Street is Curtain Road, which crosses Great Eastern Street; beyond, where Curtain Road continues, is Holywell Lane and Hewett Street. Here were the sites of the Theatre (1576) and the Curtain theatre, both run by James Burbage, who had kept horses at livery in Smithfield, and his son Richard Burbage. Shoreditch, which as a parish included the hamlets of Hoxton (Hogsden in Jonson's *Every Man in His Humour*) and Haggerston, began its modern development with Hoxton Square, place of a Dissenting Academy, in the 1680s. Charles Square, to the east, and similarly north of City Road, followed. Hoxton and Haggerston became separate parishes in the 1820s. Marie Lloyd (1870–1922) was born in Hoxton, making her music-hall *début* at the Eagle tavern in the City Road. Old Nichol Street (see *A Child of the Jago*), is behind St Leonard's. East of Shoreditch is **Bethnal Green**; Columbia Road here marks Angela Burdett-Coutts' Nova Scotia scheme, which Dickens assisted with, building flats (1859–62); see *Letters* 6.626 n.

Southwark Bridge. Completed 1819 by John Rennie; replaced 1921 (architect: Ernest George). Present-day Southwark Bridge is flanked by the pedestrian-only London Millennium Bridge (Norman Foster) and, downstream, by Cannon Street Railway Bridge. This, built between 1863 and 1866 for Sir John Hawkshaw's Cannon Street Station, which opened in 1866 (only its redbrick towers remain of the original design), was the work of Hawkshaw and John Wolfe-Barry. The station was built for the London, Chatham and Dover line, which till then had used the Elephant and Castle for its terminus. The Cannon Street hotel (see *The Waste Land*) was by E.M. Barry; it was replaced in the 1960s in a rebuilding of the station by John Poulson. Hawkshaw carried the bridge into the station over a viaduct spanning Upper Thames Street. Cannon Street Railway Bridge was revised in design in 1886–93 (Francis Brady) and again between 1979 and 1982. Dickens omits reference to the building of the Cannon Street Bridge in *OMF* 1.1.

Spitalfields was associated with Flemings as immigrants (beer brewing), and after 1685, and the Revocation of the Edict of Nantes, with silk-weaving from Huguenot French: this industry spread from Bishopsgate, Spitalfields, Shoreditch, to Bethnal Green. Spitalfields became a separate parish from St Dunstan's, Stepney, in 1728, with Hawksmoor's Christ Church, whose grandeur, with Hawksmoor's sole spire, exceeded Wren's churches in the previous generation. It was one of the fifty churches planned by the Church Commissioners as part of Tory legislation in 1711: twelve were built (others: John James' St George's, Hanover Square, St John's Horselydown, destroyed 1970, Hawksmoor's St George's in the east, St George's Bloomsbury, St Anne's Limehouse, St Luke's, Old Street, St Mary Woolnoth, St Alphege's, Greenwich, Thomas Archer's St Paul's Deptford and St John's Smith Square, John Gibbs, St Mary le Strand). In 1824, legislation allowed for import of foreign goods, which ruined Spitalfields' weaving industry, impoverishing the area.

Stepney, part of Tower Hamlets, originally comprised the area from the City of London to the River Lea, and from Hackney to the Thames. It contained the medieval church of St Dunstan's (where the humanist John Colet (1466–1519) was the cleric), and the Red Lion as a temporary theatre in 1567. Ratcliff, port for Stepney, grew to its south because of ship-building and the fitting out of ships. By the end of the nineteenth century, some sixty-seven daughter parishes had been created out of Stepney. Development began in the seventeenth century with increased dockside work, and the expansion from the City into suburbs. **Wapping**, south of Shadwell, became a parish in the seventeenth century (1694). **Poplar**, including Blackwall and the Isle of Dogs, became a separate parish in 1817, as a result of the East and West India Docks.

Stock Exchange. Since 2004 in Paternoster Square, north of St Paul's. The first Stock Exchange building, in Capel Court, was of 1773, the next, designed by James Peacock, 1802, a year after the Stock Exchange was set up on a formal member-subscription basis. Another building replaced this in 1854, designed by Thomas Allason (father and son). Replaced in 1888, and again in 1972.

Theobald's Road. Named for James the First's route to Theobald's Palace, near Cheshunt in Hertfordshire, where he died in 1625, and built up in the eighteenth century. **Clerkenwell Road** (1874–78), which joins Old Road to reach Shoreditch, connected, via Theobald's Road, with New Oxford Street. As it cut across Farringdon Road, the Fleet valley and St John's Street, new warehouses and factories followed. Clerkenwell had two theatres: the Fortune, in the parish of St Giles-without-Cripplegate (1600), and the Red Bull (St John's Street, Clerkenwell, 1604).

Whitechapel. Named from a thirteenth-century chapel; an overspill area for the City and for City trades, especially in metalwork, and an area of poverty by the seventeenth century. A temporary theatre stood outside Aldgate, which runs into Whitechapel, in 1557: the Boar's Head Inn; it became a permanent theatre in 1599. The London Hospital, dating to 1740, moved to the Whitechapel Road in 1757. The second-hand clothes trade moved to Whitechapel, becoming dominated by Jews: hence **Petticoat Lane** (1832: called Middlesex Street)'s importance. It had been a market since the beginning of the seventeenth century. The 'East End' was not so named until the 1840s, nor opened up until William Booth – author of *In Darkest England and the Way Out* (1890) – set up the Salvation Army headquarters in Whitechapel Road in 1867. Walter Besant (1836–1901) says 'East London' had a population of two million, and neither hotels nor restaurants. The decisive decade which constructed the East End as distinctive, and polarised it and the City, as had not happened in Dickens, was the 1880s, which saw new Jewish immigrants from eastern Europe and Russia. 1883 saw the publication of the Baptist minister Andrew Mearns' pamphlet, *The Bitter Cry of Outcast London*; 1884, Rev. Samuel Barnett's opening of Toynbee Hall in Commercial Street, for adult education. Victoria opened the People's Palace, Mile End Road in her Jubilee year, 1887, after the publication of Walter Besant's *All Sorts and Conditions of Men* (1882). Six women were killed in the Whitechapel murders of 1888, the same year as the matchworkers' strike at the factory of Bryant and May, at Bow, led by Annie Besant (1847–1933), Walter Besant's sister-in-law. It was succeeded by the Dock strike, led by Ben Tillett (1859–1943) in 1889. Margaret Harkness (1847–1921), under the name John Law, wrote *Out of Work* (1888), about 'Bloody Sunday' in Trafalgar Square (13 November 1887), and *Captain Lobe, A Story of the Salvation Army*, republished as *In Darkest London* (1889).

THE WEST END, AND WEST LONDON

Bloomsbury Square. Originally Southampton Square, laid out as virtually the first London square to be so called, in the 1660s for Thomas Wriothesley, Fourth Earl of Southampton, who acquired it after the Dissolution of the Monasteries; before, it belonged to the London Charterhouse. Southampton House, destroyed 1800, stood at the north of the square. Lord Chief Justice Mansfield's house was on the east side. For the hangings there of two of the rioters, Charles King and John Gray, see *Barnaby Rudge* 77. **Kenwood House** built in 1616 in Hampstead, and rebuilt several times, was bought by Mansfield in 1754, and remodelled by Robert Adam (1728–92); later developments were by George Saunders (1762–1839), for Mansfield's nephew.

Bow Street formed a curve (bow) from Floral Street to Tavistock Street when it was built in the seventeenth century; it later extended to Long Acre (originally the name of a field (Elm Close, or Elm Field) built over by 1650), and the Strand. Covent Garden theatre was built in 1732; the Magistrates' Court in 1740. Henry Fielding lived in Bow Street from 1749 to 1753, becoming a magistrate in 1749, the year he set up the 'Bow Street Runners', disbanded in 1839; the courts closed in 2006.

Brompton (Broom Farm). Rural area of market-gardens, a hospital and a cemetery (1839); developed in the late nineteenth century, with the Brompton Oratory (Herbert Gribble, 1884) and the Victoria and Albert Museum (Aston Webb, 1909) on the site of Brompton Park House; this was acquired by the Commissioners for the Great Exhibition in 1851, and used for the South Kensington Museum of Ornamental Art (1857; called the 'Brompton Boiler' for its looks, *J3* 486). The Brompton Boiler, with a remodelled façade by James Wild (1814–92) moved to Bethnal Green (1872) as the present Museum of Childhood. Site of the Exhibition of 1861. Expansion of the 'South Kensington' area included the Albert Hall (1871), the Natural History Museum (Alfred Waterhouse, 1881), the Albert Memorial (1882).

Buckingham Palace. The Queen's house, built 1705 for the first Duke of Buckingham (John Sheffield); bought by George III in 1762 for Sophia of Mecklenburg-Strelitz (1744–1818), rebuilt for George IV by John Nash, and after 1830, by Edward Blore, in improvements incomplete until 1855. See *BR* 67.557.

Burlington House. 1660s, was developed by the third Earl, Richard Boyle, in Palladian style, with the architect Colen Campbell (1676–1729), who lived at 76 Brook Street, a house he designed. (Handel lived at no. 25.) The Government bought Burlington House in 1854. Boyle's wife, Lady Dorothy Savile, gave her name to Savile Row, laid out in the 1730s; his great grandmother, Elizabeth Clifford, gave her name to Clifford Street (begun 1719). For Burlington Arcade, see Johann Friedrich Geist, *Arcades: The History of a Building Type*, 318–27, pointing out that Samuel Ware (1781–1860) designed the Arcade as a 'walk', or 'piazza' or 'row' for Lord George Cavendish, who had bought Burlington House in 1815, and had been in Paris and seen the Passage des Panoramas (1800) on Boulevard Montmartre: see Geist 464–75. The Arcade opened in 1819.

Charing Cross Station. 1864, designed by John Hawkshaw, with a hotel by E.M. Barry. Hawkshaw's Hungerford Bridge, incorporating a footbridge, carried the railway from London Bridge and Waterloo, replacing Brunel's Hungerford Bridge (1845). A westwards expansion from London Bridge Station, it opened after five years' lobbying and building. Charing was the hamlet at the point where the road from the west turned to meet the Strand. For a view of Charing Cross, Northumberland House and the Strand in 1746, see the view by the artist Joseph Nickolls (c.1726–1755, Tate Britain).

Covent Garden. Between St Martin's Lane and Drury Lane west and east, and Acre Lane and the Strand, north and south. The land belonged to Westminster Abbey; after the Dissolution of the monasteries, it went to John Russell, First Earl of Bedford, Marquess of Tavistock. Bedford House, first built in the 1580s, was pulled down in 1705 when the Duke moved to Southampton House in Bloomsbury; that house is the site of Southampton Street, named for the Earl of Southampton (related to the Earl of Bedford). The Fourth Earl of Bedford, Francis Russell, commissioned Inigo Jones to build a square with arcading around: it was actually longer in its east–west direction, and the arcading only was built to the north and east. It included St Paul's church (1638), designed to face **Russell Street** with its famous eighteenth-century eating houses to the east, also laid out at the time. This symmetry accounts for the church's orientation, which places the façade behind the west, not the east end. The church is visible in e.g. Hogarth's *The Times of the Day: Morning*, and in Balthasar Nebot (1685–1766)'s view of the market (Tate Britain, 1737). Building developments on the south side came when the now second Duke of Bedford vacated Bedford House and destroyed the gardens, whose wall backed onto the market. The market, which opened in 1671, was given a permanent structure after the building of Waterloo Bridge made it increasingly popular for produce coming from Kent and Surrey. The market moved out in 1974. Covent Garden's first theatre opened in 1732 for John Rich, the second 1809; it became the Italian Opera in 1847, under Giuseppe Persiani, and was rebuilt by E.M. Barry in 1858.

Drury Lane, like Chancery Lane, a link between Holborn and the Strand, and named for Sir Thomas Drury's house in Elizabeth's reign, home of the Cockpit theatre (1616), ceased being fashionable in the eighteenth century (it is the setting for the third plate of *The Harlot's Progress*, when Madam Hackabout is being arrested). The present theatre, the fourth on the site, is of 1812. The slum area around, including Holywell Street (*SB* 96), was partially cleared away by the building of the Aldwych and Kingsway (1905). Holywell Street, a place for booksellers, ran north of St Mary-le-Strand, to St Clement Danes; the south side of St Mary-le-Strand comprised the Strand. Drury Lane met Holywell Street on the west side. Wych Street ran diagonally as a side-turn from Drury Lane, to come out facing St Clement Danes, just north of Holywell Street.

Eaton Square, bisected by the King's Road, going westward to Chelsea, takes its name from the Grosvenors, who owned the land from 1677 onwards, and whose house was Eaton Hall, Cheshire. The King's Road was Charles the Second's route to Hampton Court, and, for George the Third, to Kew. It was a private road till 1830, but Eaton Square was laid out between 1826 and 1855 by Thomas Cubitt (1788–1855), who also laid out Belgravia, with Belgrave Square at its centre, and Pimlico: these three areas belonged to the Grosvenor Estate.

Ely Place. Site of the Bishops of Ely's London Palace, from the thirteenth century until 1772, and where the Waterbrooks live (*DC* 25). The land had been acquired by John Kirkby, Treasurer of the realm, in 1272: he later became Bishop of Ely. Saffron Hill was on the dilapidated estate of Ely Place, which stood between Hatton Garden (west) and Field Lane (east); thieves' rookeries developed from neglect of the area at the end of the eighteenth century.

Fetter Lane. Stow called this 'Fewter Lane' (348), fewters being idle people; east of Chancery Lane, it runs from Holborn to Fleet Street, and, like many other streets in London, was used for capital punishment. Widened 1841.

Foundling Hospital. Referred to in *Little Dorrit* and in 'No Thoroughfare': built on Lamb's Conduit Fields, a dam on a tributary of the Fleet River, made active by William Lamb in 1577; he also provided 120 buckets for poor women. The hospital, founded 1739, added Brunswick Square, named for Caroline of Brunswick (1768–1821), wife of the future George the Fourth, and Mecklenburgh Square, named for Queen Charlotte, Princess of Mecklenburgh-Strelitz (1744–1818) in speculative building, designed by Samuel Pepys Cockerell. The hospital moved out in 1926, eventually to Berkhamsted, and the buildings were demolished. The area behind Coram Fields, St George's Gardens, was a burial-ground which, opening 1715, became a public space 1885.

Fulham. Site of the old manor-house of the Bishops of London, until 1973, and of several settlements, such as Parsons Green and Waltham Green, set amongst market-gardens; treated as a single area towards the end of the nineteenth century. **Hammersmith** became a separate parish from Fulham in 1834; its riverside houses are eighteenth century (e.g. Kelmscott House (1780), home of George MacDonald (1824–1905) from 1868–77, was then rented to William Morris, who died there in 1896). The Pockets' house, reached by coach, may be assumed to be one of these (*GE* 2.3.186). Mentioned several times as a place for private schools for the genteel, e.g. 'Sentiment' in *SB*; *NN* 17.212; compare Chiswick, *Vanity Fair* chapter 1.

Harley Street. Named for Edward Harley, the Second Earl of Oxford (1689–1741); (Harley's father, a politician in Anne's reign, had been given the title in 1711). He had **Cavendish Square** laid out after 1717 and named for his wife, Henrietta Cavendish Holles, daughter and heir to the Duke of Newcastle. (Probably Gaunt Square, home of Lord Steyne in *Vanity Fair* 47.) Harley Street followed by 1753, becoming identified with doctors after the 1840s (compare Physician in *Little Dorrit*), when Sir William Jenner (1815–98), who worked on typhus and typhoid, moved to no. 8 in 1851.

Hatton Garden. Hatton House was built c.1576 by Sir Christopher Hatton (1540–91), Elizabeth's Lord Chancellor, on lands acquired when he possessed Ely House. Hatton Garden, originally Hatton Street, was the name for the lands from Leather Lane to Saffron Hill. A home for gentry till the nineteenth century, it became the home for jewellers in Victorian times.

Inns of Chancery. These were: **Furnival's** Inn (1383), part of Lincoln's Inn after 1548; **Thavie's** (from thirty years earlier: John Thavie was an armourer; abolished after 1769), **Barnard's** Inn (1435) and **Staple** Inn – the only one surviving (both part of Gray's Inn). Staple Inn was previously called Staple Hall, a meeting place for wool-merchants (staplers). Also **Clifford's** Inn (1344) – the gatehouse remains by St Dunstan's church in Fleet Street; it did not cease use till 1903; **Lyon's** Inn, on the site of the present Aldwych, and **Clement's** Inn to the west of the present Royal Courts of Justice (Inner Temple), near St Clement Danes' Church (see *2 Henry IV* 3.2.12); hence 'we have heard the chimes at midnight, Master Shallow'

(*2 Henry IV* 3.2.197), cf. *The Chimes*. Also the **Strand** Inn (1294), opposite St Mary-le-Strand church, also known as Chester Inn, after the Bishop of Chester who had owned it. Demolished in 1549, to become part of the site of Somerset House. **New** Inn (1485) replaced another which had fallen into disuse: St George's. These belonged to Middle Temple. The education system whereby barristers from the Inns of Court taught in the Inns of Chancery finished after 1642, and with the beginning of the Law Society (1825, incorporated by royal charter in 1831, amended in 1903) the profession of solicitor was reorganised, and the Inns of Chancery disappeared, and were sold off during the later part of the nineteenth century. (The Law Society buildings, designed by Lewis Vulliamy (1831), are in Chancery Lane.)

Inns of Court. Four legal societies, called Inns of Court: **Lincoln's** Inn (1422), the **Inner Temple** (1505) and the **Middle Temple** (1501), and **Gray's** Inn (1569). Lincoln's Inn takes its name from Henry de Lacy, Third Earl of Lincoln, who died in 1311, who acted as the Inn's protector. The Temple, and Temple Bridge, giving on to the Thames, comes from the Templar church, consecrated in 1185. Lord Gray of Wilton owned the manor of Portpoole which was sold off, first to the priory and convent at East Sheen, so that the land reverted to the Crown at the Dissolution. It was acquired by lawyers. It comprises: South Square (previously Holborn Court), Gray's Inn Square, including Chapel Court, Coney Court and Field Court. Much of this was damaged in World War Two. **Gray's Inn Road** (Lane, until 1862) was an old route from the north, via Hampstead.

Kensal Town. Developed in the 1840s with the railway; associated with Kensal Green Cemetery (1833), burial-place of Mary Hogarth, Thomas Hood, Brunel, Leigh Hunt, Thackeray (see *Letters* 10.332 n.), Leech (*Letters* 10.447), Trollope, Wilkie Collins and Cruikshank (who was moved to St Paul's). The manor of Chelsea became the nearby estate, Queen's Park (1881).

Lisson Grove. North of the Marylebone Road, first named 1783, one of the homes of Leigh Hunt, after 1815. The Yorkshire Stingo, in Lisson Green, was south of the Marylebone Road, and a place for giving relief to Indians and Africans in London, as well as the place from where Shillibeer started the omnibus service in 1829. OED gives 1756 for 'the best Yorkshire stingo' (= beer).

Long Acre. Part of the gardens belonging to the monks of Westminster Abbey, and developed after the Dissolution. In the seventeenth century, a place for coach-building, in the eighteenth, for cabinet-making. In 1859 Dickens gave his first public reading at St Martin's Hall, towards its west end.

Marylebone (St Mary's by the Bourne – i.e. Tyburn river). Comprised manors which passed to the Crown with the Dissolution of the monasteries. The eastern side became the Portman estate, the north a royal hunting park, the west passed to John Holles, Duke of Newcastle. After Regent's Park, the north part was developed as **St John's Wood**: a place for artists: e.g. Landseer (1824). Gordon MacKenzie, following Taine, thinks that Napoleon III's period in St John's Wood prompted his development of Paris (*Marylebone: Great City North of Oxford Street* (London: Macmillan 1972), 16–17). Suburb for kept women, and political émigrés; home of Fosco in *The Woman in White*.

Mayfair. Between Oxford Street and Piccadilly, site of a fair from 1686 till the middle of the eighteenth century, which had moved from being in front of the Haymarket. It includes Hanover Square, and to the west, Bond Street, and Berkeley and Grosvenor Squares. **Grosvenor Square**, the second largest square in London (after Lincoln's Inn Fields) was laid out by Sir Richard Grosvenor, between 1725 and 1731. Flanked by Brook Street (north) and Grosvenor Street (south), the only streets which connect Park Lane and Bond Street. Audley Street connects Oxford Street and Curzon Street, named for Nathaniel Curzon (1675–1758), a Derbyshire baronet from Kedleston Hall. Curzon Street was built on Great Brookfield Street, the fair's site, along with Shepherd Market. The latter was named after Edward Shepherd (d.1747), architect of much of Mayfair, as of Covent Garden theatre. He lived at no. 72 (formerly 25) Brook Street; this street, where Mr Dorrit stays, is named for the Tyburn River, which flowed beneath it.

Northumberland House. The Earls of Northumberland had a mansion near to the present Fenchurch Street Station (in Northumberland Alley); from there they moved to a Jacobean palace at Charing Cross, demolished 1874 to make way for Northumberland Avenue. The house was built on the site of the medieval hospital of St Mary Rouncivall (c.1230), shelter for pilgrims coming to the shrine of Edward the Confessor, memorialised in Chaucer, *Prologue* 669. 'Gone Astray' discusses going to see the leaden Percy Lion, above the Strand façade of the palace, looking westwards. It was removed to Syon House, Isleworth, the Duke of Northumberland's country house; the house, redesigned by Robert Adam, was built on a monastery-site, named for Mount Zion.

Park Lane. From Tyburn – site of Nash's Marble Arch (1827, for Buckingham Palace, but moved in 1851) – to Piccadilly. Built up in the mid-eighteenth century, and became fashionable in the 1820s with the opening up of Hyde Park, when iron railings replaced the brick wall, set up by Charles the Second in 1660. Then, Decimus Burton (1800–81), who worked with Nash, set up lodges for entry into Hyde Park, at Hyde Park Corner, Grosvenor Gate, Stanhope Gate and Cumberland Gate, up the east side of Hyde Park, and created the triumphal arch for Wellington which originally (1846) had a statue of Wellington, designed by Matthew Cotes Wyatt surmounting it (the monthly wrapper designs for *Vanity Fair* show the Duke above his arch). In front of Apsley House, it was moved to the top of Constitution Hill in 1883. At the same time (1822), the statue of Achilles, by the Canova-trained Richard Westmacott (1775–1856) was set up, cast in cannon from various Wellington victories. This coincided with the restructuring of Apsley House for Wellington, by Benjamin Dean Wyatt (between 1825 and 1829): it fitted with the screen that Burton erected to the west of Aspley House. The railings to Hyde Park were torn down on 23 July 1866 in a demonstration urging the passing of the Second Reform Bill. Park Lane was widened by eating into Hyde Park after World War Two, forming a dual carriageway.

Regent Street. The work of John Nash (1752–1835), part of the project for the Prince Regent, George, to link crown lands in Marylebone with Westminster, specifically Carlton House; named Regent Street (earlier, New Street) in 1819, and with three axes: Piccadilly Circus, Oxford Circus, Regent's Circus. A frontier between Mayfair and Soho. The 'Quadrant', between Piccadilly and Oxford Street, was for shops, other parts were to be residential. Above Oxford Circus, Regent Street continues to Langham Place (Langham House, belonging to Sir James Langham at the beginning of the nineteenth century). All Souls (1824), surmounted by a Greek peristyle and steeple, completed the vista before the road became Portland Place, laid out by the Adam brothers in 1778, and named after the Duke of Portland. Carlton House was pulled down in 1820 when George the Fourth became King, and partly replaced by Carlton House Terrace (Nash, 1827–32) and Carlton Gardens. At the northern end, Portland Place becomes Park Crescent (rebuilt post-1945).

Royal Courts of Justice. Neo-Gothic Law Courts, commissioned 1865, begun in 1871. The architect was G.E. Street. The Court comprises: the Court of Appeal, the High Court (King's Bench, Chancery, and the Family Division), and the Crown Court (for criminal trials). Clearances for it are happening in 'On an Amatur Beat' (*J4* 381).

Royal Opera Arcade. Built 1818, adjacent to the **Haymarket**, which had been a market for straw and hay since Elizabeth the First's reign, and became a street in the mid-seventeenth century; the market closing in 1830. The Colonnade is near Nash's Regent Street. Nash wanted the street a boundary between the nobility and gentry (west side), and the lower-class area to its east. The Royal Opera Arcade runs from Pall Mall to Charles the Second Street, and was called, by the Victorians, 'Fop's Walk'. Nash rebuilt the Haymarket theatre in 1820–21 (it had been first built a hundred years before), and also designed Suffolk Street as part of a development of the area from Carlton Terrace up to Regent's Park. George Repton (1786–1858), Nash's assistant, wanted the Colonnade to be part of a larger design behind the opera-house (originally built by Vanburgh (1704); today partly occupied by Her Majesty's theatre).

Russell Square, in *Vanity Fair*, is the home of the Sedleys (stockbrokers) and the Osbornes (Mr Osborne has prospered through the tallow trade: see *VF* 13). Named after the Russells, who were Dukes of Bedford, and owners of the land, the square, which comprises ten acres, was laid out in 1800 by Humphry Repton; only the houses left on the west side are original. Sir Thomas Lawrence (1769–1830) moved to Russell Square from Greek Street in 1814.

St Andrew's, Holborn. Phiz's illustration of Tom-All-Alone's shows St Andrew's, according to John Lehmann (123). Medieval, rebuilt by Wren as his largest parish church, bombed 1941, reconsecrated 1961. Peffer, Snagsby's partner, is buried in the church (*BH* 10.155), as is the Thomas Coram of the Foundling Hospital. Chatterton, who died at 39 Brooke Street in 1770, was buried there, but the graveyard was dispersed with the building of Holborn Viaduct.

St Dunstan's. Fleet Street; the medieval church was demolished in 1828, for widening of Fleet Street, and rebuilt by John Shaw in 1831. The clock, of 1671, with figures of Gog and Magog, was removed to Regent's Park, and returned in 1935; it was the first in London to have the minutes marked on the dial.

St Giles' Fields and Rookery. The area between Great Russell Street and Long Acre, and Charing Cross Road and Drury Lane to the east, and bisected by Shaftesbury Avenue. The church of St Giles in the Fields was founded c.1116 by Matilda of Boulogne, wife of Henry the First, to accompany a leper hospital. In 1299, it was granted to the Hospital of Burton Lazars, Leicestershire. In 1414, Sir John Oldcastle, (Lord Cobham) was executed for Lollardy there; according to Stow, it was where a drink was offered to prisoners Tyburn-bound. This, where the Great Plague started, had its present church (1733), designed by Henry Flitcroft (1697–1769). Hogarth shows its spire in *The Times of the Day: Noon* (1738). In Hogarth's *Four Stages of Cruelty* (1), Tom Nero bears a badge marked SG: he comes from this parish. St Giles marked the boundary between Westminster and Holborn. By 1847, Sir James Pennethorne's New Oxford Street was driven through this slum area.

St Martin-in-the-Fields. Probably a religious site from Roman times since a Roman burial was discovered there in 2006, far outside the Roman city of London. A medieval church is recorded in the 1220s; Henry VIII had the church rebuilt as an alternative parish to St Margaret's, Westminster; rebuilt again by James Gibbs (1721). **St Martin's Lane** is the setting for Hogarth's *The Enraged Musician* (1741); the church interior for *The Industrious 'Prentice Performing the Duty of a Christian* (1747). The workhouse, on the site of the National Portrait Gallery, was pulled down in 1871.

St Mary-le-Strand. (James Gibbs, 1717.) Dickens' parents were married here 13 June 1809. On the site of a medieval church, demolished in 1549, to make way for Somerset House; still called the New Church in *SB* 255. Further, in the Strand, to the East beyond Aldwych, is Wren's **St Clement Danes**: based on a medieval stone church which in its turn replaced a wooden church. The area was where Alfred the Great permitted the Danes to live, between Westminster and Ludgate. Gutted in 1941, reconstructed.

Seven Dials. Laid out as a building development in the 1690s by Thomas Neale (who also developed Shadwell during the Commonwealth period), on St Giles' Fields, also known as Marshland, and Cock and Pye Fields. The sundial at the centre of the star formation (which meant that, unlike putting a square at the centre, Neale could maximise the amount of houses in the approach-roads), was made by Edward Pierce (removed 1773, set up in Weybridge in 1820, a replica replacement set up 1989). The houses were single-fronted, a contrast is the double-fronted house at 78 Neale Street. Seven Dials' degeneration into a slum, which included St Giles, was modified by the eastern part of Shaftesbury Avenue, to its north, and Charing Cross Road to its west (1889), where Monmouth Street used to be. Timbs calls Seven Dials 'Little Dublin' (329–30); Flora Tristan equally describes St Giles' Rookery as Irish (155–67). Present Monmouth Street (once Great St Andrew's Street and Little St Andrew's Street) gained its name in the 1930s. Short's Gardens are named after William Short, who acquired land here in the 1590s. Mercer Street recalls previous ownership of the land by the Mercers' Company in the City: mercers deal in fine fabrics, such as silks.

Soho, south of Oxford Street, its name first appearing in 1632, began to be laid out after the Restoration and specifically after the Great Fire: Soho Square after 1660, containing Monmouth House, for the bastard son of Charles the Second, was begun in 1682, destroyed in 1773. Frith Street (after developer Richard Frith) followed after 1670. Here, at no. 6, Hazlitt died in 1830 of cholera; Mozart, aged nine, lived at no. 20 from 1764 to 1765, William Charles Macready, Dickens' actor-friend, at no. 64 from 1843 to 1851. Greek Street housed Greek refugees from the Turks in the 1670s. Gerrard Street was of the 1670s. St Anne's Soho, in Wardour Street, was a Wren church (1680s); Wardour Street was begun in 1689 (by Edward Wardour). Earlier, as Colman Hedge Lane, it was a boundary: hence it connects Oxford Street and Shaftesbury Avenue, the only street to do so, and continues south into Whitcomb Street towards Whitehall. Dean Street, where Marx lived between 1851 and 1856 (no. 28) and wrote *The Eighteenth Brumaire of Louis Bonaparte*, was created by Henry Compton, Bishop of London and Dean of the Chapel Royal (hence Dean Street, east of Wardour Street). Berwick Street (1688–89), west of Wardour Street, was named for the Duke of Berwick, bastard son of James the Second, fighting for his father's lost throne; it continues south into Rupert Street (1676) named for Prince Rupert of the Rhine. Poland Street (1689), west of Berwick Street, was named for John Sobieski, ruler of Poland, who fought at the siege of Vienna in 1683: Blake lived there from 1785 to 1790. For the Manettes to live off Soho Square responds to the Huguenots arriving at Soho in the eighteenth century (see the French Protestant church of the end of the nineteenth century on the square). Golden Square (earlier Gelding Close), begun in 1674, with a present-day statue of George the Second, has north of it Broadwick Street, which, as Broad Street (the name changed in 1936), and broad because it was intended for a hay-market, was the birthplace of Blake (corner of Broad Street and Marshall Street). North of Broad Street, Great Marlborough Street was named after the hero of Blenheim (1704). South of Broadwick Street is Beak Street (old Silver Street), where Newman Noggs says he stayed at the Crown Inn (*NN* 93). The laying out of Regent's Street (1819) and of Charing Cross Road and Shaftesbury Avenue (both 1886), both bisect Soho, and have confined the area, one to the east (so that it no longer runs to St Martin's Lane) and one to the south. Charing Cross Road replaced Crown Street (earlier Hog Lane) and Castle Street. South of Shaftesbury Avenue, Gerrard Street, which Dean Street runs into, derives from Charles, Baron Gerard of Brandon: Dryden lived there from 1686 till his death in 1700. Meard Street is off Dean Street. Newport Street, site of the seventeenth-century Newport House, had a meat market (*PP* 49.656), cleared for Charing Cross Road: see Dickens' essay, 'A Monument of French Folly' (*Household Words*, 8 March 1851, *J2* 330). ('A Detective Police Party', *Household Words*, 10 August 1850, *J2* 277, mentions the following markets: Newgate, Newport, Clare and Carnaby.)

Somerset House. At the eastern end of the Strand, overlooking the Thames, a royal palace, built 1547–50 for the Lord Protector, the Duke of Somerset. Demolished 1775, rebuilt for government offices (architect: Sir William Chambers, the Surveyor-General). Additions by Robert Smirke and James Pennethorne. The new building included the Royal Academy, and the Royal Society and the Society of Antiquaries, and the Naval Office, where John Dickens worked.

Tottenham Court Road, from St Giles' Circus at Oxford Street to the Euston Road, led to a manor house north of this. George Whitefield built his tabernacle in 1756 in this road, after splitting with Wesley's Methodists. The Dominion theatre (1928) stands on the site of an eighteenth-century brewery (Meux's brewery after 1809). Hogarth's *The March to Finchley* (1750) shows the turnpike on the site of the New Road: the soldiers are marching north to Finchley to guard the capital against the Jacobites in 1746. Highgate village is in the background.

Westminster. Perhaps a trading-centre in Anglo-Saxon England, along the Thames foreshore by the Strand; the Benedictine abbey of St Peter at Westminster was founded c.960, to which a palace was added by Edward the Confessor a century later; c.1200, Henry the Second made Westminster his chief court. Henry the Eighth began rebuilding the palace, as Whitehall Palace after 1530. Inigo Jones' Banqueting House (1622) survives from this. Tothill Street runs from the west end of the Abbey (whose two West Towers were built by Hawksmoor) into Petty France, which was officially named York Street, after the Duke of York, in the French Revolution. Milton lived there during the Commonwealth, facing St James' Park, Bentham owned it and Hazlitt rented it from 1813 to 1819 (house demolished in 1875). Bentham's house adjoined in Queen Square Place (now Queen Anne's Gate), leading into Birdcage Walk. South of Petty France was a Rookery reaching to Old Pye Street (south) and to Great Smith Street, almost to Westminster Abbey: legislation for building Victoria Street (1845) would end this, but not before Hollingshead wrote about slums 'Near Westminster Abbey' in 1861. Parliament Square (Barry, 1868) also cleared slum areas. (Barry's House of Lords opened 1847, his House of Commons 1851, the clock-tower 1858.) Pye Street remembers Sir Robert Pye, a courtier in Charles the First's court, who had a house there. Tothill Fields Prison (Middlesex House of Correction) opened in 1834, and closed in 1883, to be replaced by Westminster Cathedral (Early Christian Byzantine style; architect John Francis Bentley, opened 1903). Manchester Buildings (*SB* 189, *NN* 16.189) as premises for MPs from outside London (along with others in Millbank Street), was between Canon Row and the Thames.

SOUTH LONDON, SURREY AND KENT

Astley's. Where Upper Marsh, Westminster Bridge Road and Lambeth Palace Road met, at Stangate, in Lambeth. As a theatre, and circus, it opened in 1770, and after several lives, including William Batty's rebuilding in 1843, closed finally in 1893. See *SB* 128, *OCS* chapter 39, and *BH* chapter 31, when Mr George visits; see also Thackeray's *The Newcomes* chapter 16.

Battersea. An Anglo-Saxon settlement, with a church, St Mary's (1067) replaced in 1777 by another, where Blake married Catherine Boucher, daughter of a market-gardener. Became industrial when the London to Southampton Railway (1838) made its terminus at Nine Elms, creating goods yards and works (replaced in 1974 by the New Covent Garden Market). The first Chelsea Bridge (1851–58) was replaced by another in 1934, the wooden Battersea Bridge (1771–72) replaced in 1890. Battersea Park, agreed on in 1845, was designed by Sir James Pennethorne, following Victoria Park in Hackney; opened 1857. The Albert Bridge is of 1873. Battersea Park replaced the Red House (*SB* 122), a resort for pigeon-shooters. New factories, such as Price's Candle Factory, and the Nine Elms Gasworks followed, Clapham Junction in 1863; the first Arding and Hobbs department store (Lavender Hill and St John's Road) in 1885. Clapham is a genteel (and Evangelical) area in 'Mrs Joseph Porter' (*SB* 482), its name punned on in 'calm as Clapham' (*J2* 343); the same applies to Wandsworth. Wandsworth Road, joining Vauxhall and Battersea, an old road out of Westminster, with a few Regency houses, attracted suburban development after the railway in 1864.

Bermondsey began as a sand and gravel island above the marsh by the Thames, with a Cluniac Abbey founded in the eleventh century, dissolved at the Reformation. Its site was along Abbey Street, Long Lane, and Tower Bridge Road. (Tower Bridge opened 1894.) 'A Flight' discusses Bermondsey's industries: processing foods (as at Butler's Wharf, built between 1871 and 1873), tanning and leatherworking. A leatherwork market north of Long Lane, in Weston Street, opened in 1833. Tanning happened where the **Neckinger** River reaches the Thames, and west of St Saviour's Dock. East of that dock was Jacob's Island. A municipal park for Bermondsey, Southwark Park, opened in 1868. The river rose in St George's Fields, passing by Elephant and Castle, to Abbey Street and Jamaica Road, reaching the Thames at Dockhead, and St Saviour's Dock.

Brixton grew after the building of Vauxhall Bridge (1816); St Matthew was constructed in 1824 as one of the Waterloo churches (architect C.F. Porden), to the east of the Effra river. 'Brixton Surrey' is the home of Wilkins Flasher of the Stock Exchange (*PP* 54.733). On Brixton Hill, a windmill was built, and a prison (1819 – Surrey House of Correction); the big development came with the railways, in the 1870s.

Crystal Palace. After the Great Exhibition closed in 1851, the buildings were moved, at the inspiration of the directors of the London, Brighton and South Coast Railway Company who wanted to encourage visitors out of central London to the country in Sydenham for the day. The railway opened in 1856, two years after the Crystal Palace (so named by *Punch*) opened on 1 June 1854, on the area so renamed. It burned down in 1936. Sydenham's population grew from 4,500 to 10,500 between 1851 and 1861.

Dartford. Sixteen miles south of London, on the River Darent, a market town on the London to Dover road, and where Wat Tyler's Peasants' Revolt began in 1381 (moving to Blackheath, from which point the peasants descended on London); developed paper-milling as an industry, as well as other engineering industries.

Dulwich, to whose village Mr Pickwick retires, belonged to the Priory at Bermondsey till the Dissolution (1538); was sold by Henry the Eighth into private hands, and eventually bought by Edward Alleyn, who founded a college (1619) for twelve poor pupils, and an almshouse for twelve (present buildings 1870). The Gallery, designed by Sir John Soane, opened in 1817: Hazlitt wrote of it in *Sketches of the Principal Picture Galleries* (1824), commenting on the Village and the school standing 'just on the verge of the metropolis, and in the midst of modern improvements'. East Dulwich became a suburb through the railways, created as such after 1865. For Dickens' speech to actors on the subject of the endowments for Dulwich College (18 March 1856), see *Speeches*, 215–20.

The Elephant and Castle. Site of an old coaching inn, meeting-point for the A3 road to Kennington, and the A215 through Walworth, while the Old Kent Road (A2) branches off to meet it via the New Kent Road. The road to Lambeth (A3203), the Waterloo Road (A30), the Blackfriars Road (A201) and Newington Causeway, leading to Borough High Street and London Bridge, go north into central London from it. The area is in the southern part of **Newington**, in Newington Butts; it had a theatre in 1576 on a site near the present Metropolitan Tabernacle (1861), built for Charles Haddon Spurgeon (1834–92)'s preaching.

Greenwich Hospital. Founded by Mary the Second in 1694; Wren began work in 1696. It followed the Chelsea Hospital for veteran soldiers, founded by Charles the Second, completed by Wren in 1692. The model for both was Les Invalides in Paris designed by Libéral Bruant, which Louis XIV commissioned (1675), with a church designed by Jules Hardoin-Mansart. Greenwich Hospital closed in 1869, remaining as the Royal Naval College until 1998. It was built on the site of the fifteenth-century Palace of Placentia, constructed under the authority of Duke Humphrey of Gloucester. Hawksmoor and Vanburgh also worked on it. There are two principal buildings: the King Charles Court, designed by John Webb for Charles the Second in 1664, and Queen Mary's Court, completed in 1742. A third building is Queen Anne Court, a fourth, King William Court. Dickens first writes on Greenwich in 'Greenwich Fair', *SB* 135; also *OMF*.

Horsemonger Jail. The Surrey Detentional Prison, Horsemonger Jail, built in 1799 as a model prison by George Gwilt (1746–1809), closed 1878. The Mannings were hanged at Horsemonger Jail (1849); Horsemonger Lane is now Harper Road. Horse-trading and execution seem to be connected.

Isle of Thanet. The most easterly point of Kent, on a peninsula going into the north sea, and a seaside resort; with Margate and Northgate on the north side, and Broadstairs on the east and Ramsgate on the south. Broadstairs was a holiday resort for Dickens. Before the railway, these sites were reached by steamboat from London. Dickens describes Londoners at Ramsgate, *SB* 386; Frith painted *Life at the Seaside: (Ramsgate Sands)* (1854). Ruskin in *Praeterita* 2.12 records Turner saying that the most beautiful skies in the world known to him were those of the Isle of Thanet.

Jacob's Island. See chapter three. The church of St Mary's, designed by John James and built in 1716, with a tower added later, abuts here onto the Thames. The church is near the entrance to Rotherhithe Tunnel (1908), crossing the Thames.

Kennington, with a Waterloo church (St Mark's, designed by D.R. Roper, between 1822 and 1824), built on the site of Surrey's place of public execution before the building of Horsemonger Jail (and the place of hanging for some Jacobites), saw the birthplace of Phiz (K. Halbot Browne, Dickens' illustrator). Kennington Common, scene of the Chartists' meeting in 1848, was enclosed in 1852 and became a park. The Oval became a cricket ground in 1846; 'Kennington Oval' (*J2* 206) is described in genteel terms.

Lambeth. Marshland till the nineteenth century, but with the Archbishop of Canterbury's Palace, on land owned by the See of Canterbury since 1197, its Tudor brick gatehouse built by one 'Morton' after 1486. Nearby Kennington had a manor which, since James the First, belongs to the Duchy of Cornwall. Lambeth Bridge was built in 1862, replaced in 1932. Lambeth Walk, which in the eighteenth century included a spa, Lambeth Wells, was, and is, a market. William Blake lived at Hercules Buildings, Hercules Road (1793 to 1802). Lambeth also contains St George's Roman Catholic Church designed by Pugin (1812–52), who had converted to Catholicism, opened in July 1848 (bombed, reopened 1958), with Cardinal (then Bishop) Wiseman (1802–65), becoming a Cathedral in 1850 when Pius IX created the diocese of Southwark.

Lant Street runs between Borough High Street and Southwark Bridge Road, just south of St George's. Named for a London merchant of the seventeenth century, who possessed land there. See *PP* 31.417.

London Bridge Station. Trains ran from Deptford to Spa Road, Bermondsey in 1836; the London and Croydon railway followed in 1839, the London to Brighton line in 1841. London Bridge Station (1844) was rebuilt in 1849 by Samuel Beazley, with one section for the Greenwich railway, and another for the railway companies which in 1846 formed the London, Brighton, and South Coast Railway. Spa Road Station closed in 1915. The South Eastern, or Dover, line opened in 1842, and a line to Gravesend in 1849. The London and Croydon, and the South Eastern, opened another terminus just north of the Old Kent Road, at the Bricklayers' Arms in 1844, which continued, for passengers, till 1852, but was afterwards used for freight.

The Marshalsea. One of five debtors' prisons (with the Fleet, the King's Bench, and Whitecross Street and Horsemonger Lane). It is marked by a fragment of wall – the prison's southernmost wall – just north of St George's, Southwark, in Angel Place. An earlier version stood where the Mermaid Court is found, and was attacked by Wat Tyler's men in 1381. The name means 'court (seat) of the Marshal' of the King's household, and was the place for judging disputes amongst servants of the King's household; its jurisdiction was twelve miles, excluding the City of London. The court moved to Scotland Yard in 1801; the prison, merged with other debtors' prisons, closed 1849.

Northfleet. London side of Gravesend, in Kent, part of *Great Expectations*' 'marsh country, down by the river'. Medieval town, with dockyard, closed 1860. When steamboats started coming from London to Gravesend, in 1815, the area became smarter, with Jerome Rosher's laying out of what was intended to be a smart new town, Rosherville, and the opening of the Kent Zoological and Botanical Gardens in 1837, Rosherville Gardens, on the site of an old chalk-pit. This Victorian pleasure ground closed 1901.

Norwood. Upper Norwood, where Mr Spenlow lives, runs from Crystal Palace and Anerley Hill in the east to Beulah Hill, and on to Crown Point. The hills' height here imposes a natural southern barrier to south London. West Norwood (Lower Norwood till 1885) runs down northwards from Beulah Hill, following the course of the underground Effra River (which reaches the Thames near Vauxhall Bridge). The church of St Luke (1822–25), designed by Francis Bedford, was one of the 500 planned Waterloo churches. North of West Norwood is Tulse Hill (named after the family who owned a farm during the period of the Commonwealth) and Brockwell Park, where there was a large hall, built for a glass merchant, John Blades, in 1813. Mrs Beeton (1836–65) is buried in the cemetery (1837) at West Norwood. South Norwood, below Upper Norwood, and on the way to Croydon, was more industrial than Upper Norwood (brickfields).

Old Vic. Built in 1818 as the Royal Coburg, and so named for Prince Leopold of Saxe-Coburg and Princess Charlotte, daughter of the future George the Fourth by Caroline of Brunswick, who married in 1816, died in 1817. They laid the foundation-stone in 1816. The architect was Rudolph Cabanel of Aachen. Construction materials came from the Savoy Palace, demolished to make way for John Rennie's Waterloo Bridge (1817), originally to be called The Strand Bridge. The theatre became the Royal Victoria theatre in 1833. 'The Amusements of the People', *Household Words*, 30 March 1850, discusses the theatre enjoyed by 'Joe Whelks of the New Cut, Lambeth'. The New Cut (1820) continued Lower Marsh Road across Waterloo Road to Blackfriars, across the Lambeth Marsh.

St George the Martyr. Norman foundation first mentioned in 1122, as part of Bermondsey Priory. The church's previous tower was painted by Hogarth in *Southwark Fair* (1733), the present, Little Dorrit's church, designed in 1734 by John Price (d.1736).

Southwark means the old medieval borough (= fortification), and the modern borough which includes Bermondsey, Rotherhithe, Newington, Elephant and Castle, Walworth, Camberwell, Peckham, Nunhead (with its cemetery, 1840), and Dulwich. Southwark is also the local area: the Roman settlement south of the first London Bridge. This area was famous for, first, its inns, e.g. the George (preserved; *LD* 1.22.269), the White Hart (see *PP* 10) and the Tabard (Chaucer: *The Canterbury Tales*). Second, for the playhouses built on Bankside: the Bear Garden and the Bull Ring (both 1576, the former replaced by the Hope, 1614), Rose (1587), the Swan (1595), the Globe (1599). Third, for St Mary Overey church, housing the tomb of the poet Gower (*J4* 108). Part of a priory after the Reformation it became St Saviour's Church, and Southwark Cathedral in 1905. By then, its population (Southwark plus Bermondsey plus Camberwell) was over half a million. Fourth, for the town house of the Bishops of Winchester; the Winchester geese (*Troilus and Cresssida* 5.10.53) were the prostitutes in the stews. Fifth, for its prisons: the Clink, the Marshalsea, the King's Bench, Horsemonger Jail, which replaced Surrey County Jail in Borough High Street, the Compter in Tooley Street, the New Bridewell. Sixth, for its Fair, pictured by Hogarth (1733). The right to hold a Fair in Southwark was granted by the City of London in 1462; it ended in 1763. Seventh, Borough Market, now in Rochester Yard (land belonging to the Bishop of Rochester's town house), and built in 1851. The market has a longer, medieval history. Southwark also had hospitals: St Thomas', named after Beckett, was part of the Priory of

St Mary Overey. Another, outside, was called the Lock, which was for lepers, before they could arrive into the city. (There is still a road called Lockfield; the Lock seems to have been a stream flowing towards the Thames.) St Thomas' moved to Lambeth in 1871, after its land had been acquired by the Charing Cross Railway Company. Thomas Guy, a benefactor of St Thomas', had Guy's Hospital built in 1721, opening in 1726. The brewery, Barclay and Perkins, which had belonged to Henry Thrale (d.1781), husband of Mrs Thrale (later Piozzi) (1740–1821) who lived at Streatham Park (demolished in 1863), was in Park Street. It is marked by Perkins Square; the company merged with Courage in 1955; the brewery closed 1962.

Surrey Docks. Rotherhithe, developed in the nineteenth century, beginning with the Howland Great Dock of 1697 (Greenland Dock) and attempting to link itself with a hinterland, through the Grand Surrey Canal, dug after 1801. Intended to reach Epsom, the canal only managed Walworth, with another arm to Peckham, and ceased to be used after 1836. The Port of London authority closed it in 1971 and drained it. It joined up with the Croydon Canal at New Cross; this ended at a basin which is now the site of West Croydon Station: the London to Croydon railway, which killed off the canal's financial viability, opened in 1839, largely built on the canal, a fragment of which is visible at Bett's Park, Anerley.

Surrey theatre, in Blackfriars Road, opened for equestrian entertainment in 1782, first by Charles Dibdin (1745–1814), actor and song-writer, then by his son Thomas Dibdin (1771–1841): the venture bankrupted him in 1822. Rebuilt 1803 after a fire, by Thomas Cabanel, who built the Royal Coburg, it became the Surrey theatre in 1809. Rebuilt after fire in 1865, demolished 1934.

Tooting Corner became Tooting Broadway, and the underground was built in 1926. The farm for orphans was at Surrey Hall, an area of fifty-two acres in Tooting Graveney, behind the present Tooting Broadway underground. (The name of Tooting's other underground station, Tooting Bec, comes from the Benedictine Abbey of Le Bec-Hellouin in Normandy.) Graveney records the name of Hamo de Gravenell, a twelfth-century feudal lord. The river which flows through to join the Wandle is named after the parish. Part of Streatham, Tooting began to be developed in the eighteenth century. Tooting Bec and Tooting Graveney Commons and Streatham Common were all common land stretching to Mitcham, and protected by the Metropolian Commons Act (1866), but by then the areas had been split up by roads and railways: the West End and Crystal Palace line in the north (1855) and the London to Brighton line in the south (1861).

Vauxhall Gardens, called the New Spring Garden in 1660, when it opened, and then Vauxhall Gardens in 1728, and the Royal Gardens (by George IV, in 1822), closed 1859. The springs recall the point that there was a Lambeth Wells in the early eighteenth century, and a Spa Field at the Dog and Duck (where Bedlam was built, 1815). Vauxhall Bridge was London's first iron bridge (1816), built the same year as Vauxhall Bridge Road.

Walcot Square (actually a triangle) is off Kennington Road, two streets to the back of the old Bedlam (present-day Imperial War Museum); laid out between 1837 and

1839. Seventeen acres in Lambeth had been donated to the poor by the haber-dasher Edmund Walcott, in 1667.

Walworth and Camberwell. The division between Walworth and Camberwell is at Albany Road and the modern Burgess Park, which includes the end of the Surrey Canal, which ran up to the Surrey Docks. (The Park was created out of the 1943 Abercrombie recommendation for more open spaces in London.) Browning was born in Southampton Street, Camberwell, and is commemorated by a plaque at 179 Southampton Way; he was baptised at a Congrgational chapel in Walworth, which is recalled in Browning Road. Camberwell is a smart area in 'Horatio Sparkins', *SB* 412, and in *MC* 9.137, where there is the mansion of a brass and copper founder, and it had a fair (*SB* 143), but its decline begins with its availability to London: when Vauxhall Bridge was opened in 1816, Camberwell New Road linked it directly to Camberwell and Denmark Hill.

Waterloo Bridge Station. Opened 1848; the present station reconstructed 1900–22 (and bombed). The London and South-Western railway ran trains to Nine Elms (1838); a viaduct of 290 arches continued the line to Waterloo. The route taken by the train in *OMF* 4.11 is across that viaduct, towards Clapham Junction. The train crosses the Thames between Richmond and Twickenham (whose bridge was built in 1848) and again after Staines.

Woolwich. In 1694 the Royal Laboratory was built on Woolwich Warren: the begin-ning of Woolwich Arsenal, though the arsenal itself dates from Tudor times. The main government foundry moved there from Moorfields in 1715–17: it was then called the Warren. George III renamed it the Royal Arsenal (1805). In *Barnaby Rudge*, the Warren resonates with the haunted house, the Warren, burned in chap-ter 55 (and with Warren's factory). **Shooters Hill**, South London's highest hill, and associates with archery and highwaymen, where Weller senior retires, is beyond Blackheath, place of David Copperfield's school and that of Mr F. (*LD* 2.17.648) on the way to Woolwich: see *TTC* 1.2.8.

NORTH LONDON, MIDDLESEX AND ESSEX

The A1. The Great North Road, which started to be named as such at the end of the seventeenth century, comes to Highgate, and continues through Archway, dividing then into Holloway Road, and the road to Kentish Town. A tollhouse was at Lidyard Road, just before this junction, till 1871. The Holloway Road splits, its left fork becoming Upper Street. Archway memorialises a tunnel built through Highgate Hill, which collapsed in construction (1812). It was followed by a deep cutting into the hill, but the arch was left to carry Hornsey Lane traffic to Highgate: Nash designed the Archway (1813); it was replaced in 1897. The Archway toll in *BH* 57 is where Bucket learned that Lady Dedlock was travelling towards Barnet and St Albans.

Barking Creek. The mouth of the Roding River in Essex, seven miles east of the City of London. Barking, to the east of the river, once a fishing village, contained England's largest Benedictine Abbey (666–1539). Industry came with the railway (1854): it is now part of the London borough of Barking and Dagenham, as the west side of the river became part of the borough of Newham.

Barnet. A medieval town halfway between London and St Albans (see *Bleak House*), just inside the London orbital M25, had a turnpike established in 1712, and a cattle and horse market; but its character changed after 1850, with the railway, which made it look more towards London. Whereas the Romans used the present A10 to go north from London, following the Lea valley, the Great North Road was medieval.

Brentford ('the ford over the River Brent', into which the Grand Union Canal flows, old county town of Middlesex) is on the main road out of London (now the M4), on the river side, and opposite Kew, whose bridge over the Thames was finished in 1759. In *OMF* 1.16, Betty Higden includes amongst the children she minds Sloppy, who was brought up in the Poor House. This was at Isleworth, further upstream, but still opposite Kew Gardens, on the east side of the Twickenham Road; rebuilt, it survives in a mental health hospital site.

Exmouth Street. Islington, named for the Exmouth Arms (c.1816), commemorating Admiral Edward Pellew, First Viscount Exmouth (1757–1833); Exmouth Market belongs to the 1890s. Spa Field Street, nearby, recalls a spa in the district, compare the names Cold Bath Fields, Sadler's Wells, and Bagnigge Wells, the latter a spa, between 1758 and 1841, off the present King's Cross Road (an inscribed head and stone at nos 61 and 63 marks the place).

Finchley, south of Barnet and north of Highgate and Hampstead, developed with the Great North Road, but in the eighteenth century was agricultural, supplying milk to London, and hay for horses. Its growth came with the railway in 1867.

Hackney. East of Bethnal Green on the far side of Kingsland Road: Clapton is further north-east, towards the River Lea. The borough includes Stoke Newington, where Defoe lived (note the cemetery of 1840 at Abney Park), and Stamford Hill, which during the nineteenth century became a Jewish community. Hackney was built round a coaching road from Mile End, via Cambridge Heath, which joined the main North Road at Stamford Hill. Its high street was Mare Street ('mere', pond). It saw steady growth during the Georgian period, with a new church between 1791 and 1779, St John at Hackney, designed by J. Spiller. See its use in *SB* 117. Its nearness to the River Lea produced industrial development, e.g. around the Lea Bridge Mills, rebuilt after 1791: tile kilns, brick kilns, calico-grounds. Hackney became further industrialised in the nineteenth century, e.g. at Hackney Wick, between Victoria Park and the Lea Marshes.

Hampstead. Known for its spas, became in the mid-eighteenth century a summer resort, and, like Highgate, was never developed fully because its topography did not allow for building squares and terraces. Early residents included Akenside, Romney, Constable, Leigh Hunt, Keats, and William Collins, father of Wilkie Collins. Its Heath, associated with Pickwick's early researches, was not enclosed, despite Sir Thomas Maryon Wilson's six Bills wanting this, from 1829 on. Reached from Camden Town via Chalk Farm and Haverstock Hill. Dickens' associations with Hampstead included staying after Mary Hogarth's death at Collins Farm, north of the Heath, which had been rented by John Linnell, 1824–29, and where Blake visited.

Hampton, a mile upstream from Wolsey's Hampton Court Palace, built after 1514, which is fifteen miles south-west of central London, is identified in *OMF* by the sign of the Red Lion Inn and the 'old grey church' of St Mary. Scene of horseracing *NN* 50, producing a duel downstream, across the river by the seventeenth-century Ham House, opposite Twickenham.

Highgate. Dickens lodged here in 1832, Pickwick researched here. In *DC*, Mrs Steerforth's house was supposed to be at Church House, in South Grove, above Highgate Cemetery (opened 1839) where Dickens' parents are buried. Dr Strong lives away from there, but *DC* notes also St Michael's church in South Grove, consecrated in 1832, designed by Lewis Vulliamy (1791–1871). The cemetery opened in 1839, the result of legislation to move burials out of the centre of London.

Holloway. North of Camden Town and Kentish Town, setting for George and Weedon Grossmith's *Diary of a Nobody* (1892). Holloway Prison, on Camden Road before reaching Holloway Road, was built in 1852, rebuilt 1970. Seven Sisters Road continues on towards Finsbury Park (a municipal park of 1869, north of Highbury) and runs up to the A10 at **Tottenham**, a village in 1800, but built over as a result of industry and the building of the Enfield to Liverpool Street railway line (1872).

Hounslow was on the Great West Road (the present A4), ten miles out, on the way to Bath, with the road towards Exeter and Cornwall forking from it. The Heath was associated with highwaymen (e.g. Claude Duval, pictured in Frith's 1860 picture with that name; see also *PP* 42.580). Until the railway between London and Bristol, the town gained much of its work from servicing transport going through towards the west.

Islington, a mile from the City walls, relied on milk production for London in the eighteenth century; becoming important after the building of the New Road (1757), which intersects with traffic going north on the Great North Road. This produced development of new squares (Canonbury, Lonsdale, Myddleton). The **Angel Inn** at Islington derived its name from its sign, which showed the Annunciation. It was a coaching inn, rebuilt in 1819, and a Lyons' Corner House in 1921, in new buildings of 1899. Closed as such in 1960. **Newington Green**, on the Essex Road from Islington to Stoke Newington, past **Canonbury**, whose manor belonged to the Canons at St Bartholomew's Priory, was a seventeenth- and eighteenth-century Dissenting centre.

Kilburn. *SB* 118 refers to the Kilburn Road, a Roman road, which, as the A5, starts as the Edgware Road, becomes Maida Vale (Maida after the battle in the Napoleonic Wars in 1806), then Kilburn High Road. Kilburn was a village on the Roman road, and the site of a priory; its name implying a cold stream (Kyle bourne) flowing down from Hampstead.

New River Head. Behind Sadler's Wells theatre was the New River Head, terminus of the New River, cut from the Lea river to bring water to London, in 1613: its architect was Sir Hugh Myddleton (1560–1631), who is remembered in street-names nearby. Uriah Heep stays at a 'sort of private hotel and boarding house' by the New River Head (*DC* 25.390). *BR* 4.38 evokes the area, as does Hogarth in *The Four*

Times of the Day: Evening (1738). George Cruikshank lived at Myddleton Terrace (named 22 Amwell Street in 1825) in 1824, moving next door ten years later.

Pentonville, east of King's Cross Station, in the parish of St James, Clerkenwell, was built up between 1780 and 1820. The name derived from the owner of the estate, Captain Henry Penton, MP for Winchester and a Lord of the Admiralty; Penton Place was where the first houses were built, in the 1770s.

Regent's Canal. Built 1812–20, an extension of the Grand Junction Canal from Brainston (Northamptonshire) to Brentford and to Paddington; a Nash project, it circled the boundary separating Regent's Park from Primrose Hill, and going to Islington, Hackney, Stepney, and the Thames at Limehouse, linking it with the Midlands and Lancashire.

Sadler's Wells. Richard Sadler built the first theatre as a 'musick house' to accompany cures at a medicinal well on the site in 1683. Mrs Jenkins, in *Humphrey Clinker* (140), comments on the 'tumbling and dancing upon ropes and wires' in the entertainments in Sadler's Wells (after the Licensing Act of 1737 forbade theatres to put on plays with dialogue, apart from the Royal Patent theatres (Drury Lane and Covent Garden, and, after 1776, the Haymarket); the ban continued till 1843). Dickens refers to the theatre in 'Private Theatres', *SB* (147), and in 'The Pantomime of Life', a 'stray chapter by Boz' in *Bentley's Miscellany* (March 1837) (*J1* 506). Between 1844 and 1862, the theatre was managed by Samuel Phelps (1804–78), who staged thirty-four of Shakespeare's plays.

Twickenham, in Middlesex, gained a new parish church in 1715 (John James), and was associated with Pope's house (after 1719), with Marble Hill House (1720s) and with Horace Walpole's Gothic Strawberry Hill, a cottage made into a sham Gothic castle after 1750, and a source for Wemmick's 'Castle' in conditions the opposite of Walpole's; at ten miles out from London far enough to be a place to take a summer cottage, as Dickens did in the later 1830s; Eel-pie Island, an 'ait' on the Thames was reached by steamer from Westminster Bridge (*NN* 52.642–3). Home of Mr Meagles in *LD*.

NOTES

INTRODUCTION
Going Astray: Dickens and London

1. Quoted, *James McNeill Whistler*, ed. Richard Dorment and Margaret F. MacDonald (London: Tate Gallery 1994), 106. For recent readings of John Gay's poem, *Trivia* (1716), on walking London streets, see Clare Brant and Susan E. Whyman, *Walking the Streets of Eighteenth-Century London: John Gay's Trivia (1716)* (Oxford: Oxford University Press 2007).

2. Julian Wolfreys, *Writing London: The Trace of the Urban Text from Blake to Dickens* (London: Macmillan 1998) applies the term 'writing London' to consider London not as an object, nor 'history' or 'reality', but to discuss 'rhetoric and the architecture of nineteenth-century writing about the city' (228). Discussing Dickensian 'architextures', he sees in Dickens' writing a 'textual randomness' which has 'the desire to shake the solidity of the monumental' (148). It is an interesting application of Derrida, but perhaps omits to discuss that which in London requires writers to contest it.

3. Walter Bagehot, 'Charles Dickens', *National Review*, 7 October 1858, 458–86, see Michael Hollington, *Charles Dickens: Critical Assessments* (London: Croom Helm 1995), 4 vols, 1.171.

4. J.-K. Huysmans, *Against Nature*, trans. Robert Baldick (Harmondsworth: Penguin 1959), 138.

5. Henry James, 'London', *Collected Travel Writings: Great Britain and America* (New York: The Library of America 1993), 37.

6. For Dickens and London, see, for example, E. Beresford Chancellor, *The London of Charles Dickens* (New York: George H. Doran Co. 1924) and Walter Dexter, *The London of Dickens* (New York: E.P. Dutton 1923), Piers Dudgeon, *Dickens' London*, introduction Peter Ackroyd (London: Headline 1987). See also Alexander Welsh, *The City of Dickens* (Cambridge, Mass.: Harvard University Press), and Philip Collins in H.J. Dyos and Michael Wolff (eds), *The Victorian City: Images and Realities* (London: Routledge and Kegan Paul 1973), 2 vols, 2.537–58, and F.S. Schwarzbach, *Dickens and the City* (London: Athlone 1979). See also David Trotter, *Circulation: Defoe, Dickens and the Economics of the Novel* (London: Macmillan 1988), 77–136. On London, see Asa Briggs, *Victorian Cities* (London: Harmondsworth 1963), and amongst recent treatments, Ben Weinreb and Christopher Hibbert (eds), *The London Encyclopaedia* (London: Macmillan 1992), Roy Porter, *London: A Social History* (Harmondsworth: Penguin 1996), Michael Hebbert, *London: More by Fortune than Design* (Chichester: John Wiley 1998), Francis Sheppard, *London: A History* (Oxford: Oxford University Press 1998), Jerry White, *London in the Twentieth Century* (London: Viking 2001), and *London in the Nineteenth Century* (London: Jonathan Cape 2007). Still useful: Henry Harben, *A Dictionary of London: Being Notes Topographical and Historical Relating to the Streets and Principal Buildings in the City of London* (London: H. Jenkins 1918), and Steen Eiler Rasmussen, *London: The Unique City* (1934; Harmondsworth: Penguin 1960).

7. For these statistics and details, see Doreen Massey, *World City* (Cambridge: Polity Press 2007), especially 27–72.

8. Henri Lefebvre, *The Production of Space*, trans. Donald Nicholson-Smith (Oxford: Blackwell 1991), 39, see also 33 and 38–39. On Lefebvre, see Stuart Elden, *Understanding Henri Lefebvre: Theory and the Possible* (London: Continuum 2004), 181–92.

9. David Kynaston, *The City of London, vol. 1: A World of its Own, 1815–1890* (London: Chatto and Windus 1994) discusses how insurance companies changed the face of the City, 'erecting a series of grandiose headquarters, usually in the grand Italian manner'. He refers to the building, 'between 1836 and 1843, [of] the Atlas in Cheapside . . . the Globe, the Alliance, the Sun', adding that the building of the Royal Exchange (1844) 'altered the very hub of the City . . . prompting not only a widening of Threadneedle Street, but also the construction of one of the City's first office blocks, the Royal Exchange Buildings directly opposite' (139). The implications of this new separation of work and living space are significant.

10. For the *Arcades Project*, see Rolf Tiedemann, 'Dialectics at a Standstill: Approaches to the *Passagen-Werk*' in Gary Smith (ed.), *On Walter Benjamin: Critical Essays and Recollections* (Cambridge, Mass.: MIT Press 1988), 260–91, and Susan Buck-Morss, *The Dialectics of Seeing: Walter Benjamin and the Arcades Project* (Cambridge, Mass.: MIT Press 1991).

11. Criticism of Dickens becomes urgent after Edmund Wilson, 'Dickens: The Two Scrooges' in *The Wound and the Bow*; the essay first appeared in 1939. Criticism in the 1940s takes its best forms in Humphry House, *The Dickens World*, R.C. Churchill in *Scrutiny*, and F.R. Leavis on *Hard Times* in *The Great Tradition* (1948): his work, with Q.D. Leavis, continued up to *Dickens the Novelist* (1970). Scholarly attention to Dickens, following from House, produces John Butt and Kathleen Tillotson's *Dickens at Work* in the 1950s, and results in the Clarendon editions of Dickens' novels, and the Pilgrim edition of the Letters. Lionel Trilling's essay on *Little Dorrit* appeared in 1953; Hillis Miller's work on Dickens in 1958; his essay on *Bleak House* appeared in 1971. In the 1960s, criticism centres on the work of Philip Collins and Steven Marcus. To all these pioneering critics, obviously not all in agreement with each other, all subsequent work on Dickens must be indebted.

12. On the *flâneur*, see *Arcades* 416–55 and *Charles Baudelaire: A Lyric Poet in the Era of High Capitalism* (London: Verso 1973), 35–66, and Robert L. Herbert, *Impressionism: Art, Leisure and Parisian Society* (New Haven: Yale University Press 1988) 33–57. Baudelaire's essay discussing the *flâneur* is 'The Painter of Modern Life', see *My Heart Laid Bare and Other Prose Writings*, trans. Norman Cameron (London: Soho Book Company 1986), 21–72.

13. Forster reprints sections of Dickens' autobiographical fragment (written some time after 1845, and before the writing of *David Copperfield*, see *Life* 1.1.13–14, 1.2.24–35. I reprint the extracts in my edition of *David Copperfield*, and cite references from that.

14. Erich Auerbach, 'Figura', *Scenes from the Drama* 'Figura' in *Scenes from the Drama of European Literature: Six Essays* (New York: Meridian Books 1959), discusses the medieval sense of 'figural' reality as one allegorical understanding of history laid over another, which it illuminates. 'Figure' also means 'face', and implies Dickens' interest in physiognomy.

15. Disraeli, *Tancred* (London: Bodley Head 1905), 174.

CHAPTER ONE
The *Eidometropolis*: A View of London

1. For London after the Fire, see Craig Spence, *London in the 1690s: A Social Atlas* (University of London Institute for Historical Research: Centre for Metropolitan

History 2000), and for the eighteenth century, see George Rudé, *Hanoverian England 1714–1808* (London: Secker and Warburg 1971), drawing on Daniel Defoe, *A Tour Through the Whole Island of Great Britain* (1724–26), see Letter 5 (Harmondsworth: Penguin 1971), 286–336. See also Dorothy George, *London Life in the Eighteenth Century* (1925; Harmondsworth: Penguin 1966), Sheila O'Connell, *London 1753* (London: British Museum Press 2003), John Summerson, *Georgian London* (3rd edition, Harmondsworth: Penguin 1978), and for later, Robert Furneaux Jordan, *Victorian Architecture* (Harmondsworth: Penguin 1966) and Donald J. Olsen, *The Growth of Victorian London* (Harmondsworth: Penguin 1979).

2. See Roy Porter, 'Visitors' Visions: Travellers' Tales of Georgian London', in Chloe Chard and Helen Langdon, *Transports: Travel, Pleasure, and Imaginative Geography, 1600–1830* (New Haven: Yale University Press 1996), 31–47. See also Celina Fox (ed.), *London – World City 1800–1840* (New Haven: Yale University Press 1992). On gas-lighting in homes (after 1840) see *Letters* 3.206.

3. Carl Philip Moritz, *Journals of a German in England in 1782*, trans. Reginald Nettel (London: Jonathan Cape 1965).

4. Stephen Gill, *William Wordsworth: A Life* (Oxford: Oxford University Press 1989) says that the experiences of Book 7 come from visits made in 1793, 1795 and 1802 (50). See Gill 53, for 1791, 90 for 1795, 104 for 1796, when he met Lamb, and 210, where Gill quotes Lamb's letter to Wordsworth of 30 January 1801: 'I have passed all my days in London, until I have formed as many and intense local attachments as any of you *Mountaineers* can have done with dead nature. The Lighted shops of the Strand and Fleet Street, the innumerable trades, tradesmen and customers, coaches, waggons, play houses, all the bustle and wickedness round about Covent Garden, the very women of the Town, the Watchmen, drunken scenes, rattles . . . coffee houses, steams of soups from kitchens, the pantomimes, London itself, a pantomime and a masquerade, . . . The wonder of these sights impels me into night-walks about her crowded streets, and I often shed tears in the motley Strand from fullness of joy at so much **Life** –'.

5. See Lucy Newlyn, '"In City pent": Echo and Allusion in Wordsworth, Coleridge and Lamb, 1797–1801', *Review of English Studies* 32 (1981), 408–28. One suggested source for Wordsworth's interest in London is Charles Lloyd (1775–1839), in his poems written with Lamb, particularly 'London' (1798) in a volume called *Blank Verse*.

6. Quotations from William Wordsworth, *The Prelude, 1799, 1805, 1850*, ed. Jonathan Wordsworth, M.H. Abrams and Stephen Gill (New York: W.W. Norton 1979).

7. Jonathan Andrews, Asa Briggs, Roy Porter, Penny Tucker and Keir Waddington, *The History of Bethlem* (London: Routledge 1997), 153, 238–39. Sydney Smirke (1798–1877) designed the British Musum Reading Room; his brother, Robert Smirke (1781–1867), the British Museum's façade (1847) and Covent Garden. Bedlam moved from Moorfields to Lambeth because of insanitary conditions, and to Beckenham in 1930. Much of the building was destroyed by Lord Rothermere, who bought the site and the park, before the Imperial War Museum moved in (1935).

8. See articles by A.C.N. Borg, 'The Museum: The History of the Armouries as a Showplace', and 'The Royal Menagerie', and 'The Record Office', and by M.R. Holmes, 'The Crown Jewels' in John Charlton (ed.), *The Tower of London: Its Buildings and Institutions* (London: Department of the Environment, HMSO 1978), especially 69–71 (70 reprints Rowlandson's version of the 'Line of Kings'), 23, 103, 105. See also Raphael Samuel, *Theatres of Memory: Island Stories vol. 2: Unravelling Britain*, ed. Alison Light, Sally Alexander and Gareth Stedman-Jones (London:

Verso 1998) 101–24. Vol. 1 of *Theatres of Memory: Past and Present* (1994), 401–25, has interesting comments on Dickens as part of 'heritage' London, discussing Christine Edzard's (two-part) film of *Little Dorrit* (1987).

9. An example of the proliferation of playbills, and advertisements covering an outer wall giving onto a street appears in John Orlando Parry's picture, *A London Street Scene* (1835). Parry (1810–79), a musician, has a playbill advertising himself in the centre. The street-scene in front of these playbills is full of interest: a pickpocket robbing a policeman talking to a soldier; a sweep watching a billsticker posting a playbill. To the left of the building, in the rear of the picture, is St Paul's – see reproduction and discussion in Raymond Lister, *Victorian Narrative Paintings* (London: Museum Press 1966), 31.

10. Christopher Rivers, *Face Value: Physiognomical Thought and the Legible Body in Marivaux, Lavater, Balzac, Gautier, and Zola* (Madison: University of Wisconsin Press 1994), 93.

11. For the Panorama, see Benjamin, *Arcades*, 527–36; and Robert Altick, *The Shows of London* (Cambridge, Mass.: Harvard University Press 1978). Stephan Oetterman, *The Panorama: History of a Mass Medium*, trans. Deborah Lucas Schneider (New York: Zone Books 1997), Jonathan Crary, *Techniques of the Observer: On Vision and Modernity in the 19th Century* (Cambridge, Mass.: MIT Press 1990), Jonathan Arac, *Commissioned Spirits: The Shaping of Social Motion in Dickens, Carlyle, Melville, and Hawthorne* (New Brunswick, NJ: Rutgers University Press 1979), James Chandler and Kevin Gilmartin (eds), *Romantic Metropolis: The Urban Scene of British Culture, 1780–1840* (Cambridge: Cambridge University Press 2005), 5–13. For Wordsworth and the Panoramas, see Ross King, 'Wordsworth, Panoramas, and the Prospect of London', *Studies in Romanticism* 32 (1933), 57–73.

12. See references to the Panorama in *J2*, 134–37 and 201–12; and to the Colosseum, built by Decimus Burton in Regent's Park in 1827, and run by Thomas Hornor, *J2*, 14–18. The latter was to show a Panorama of London from St Paul's, an effect used in Dickens; see the end of *LD* 2.25.742–43.

13. On these locales, see Michael Allen, *Charles Dickens' Childhood* (London: Macmillan 1988), and Frederic G. Kitton, *The Dickens Country* (London: Adam and Charles Black 1905).

14. A contemporary print of this Bazaar forms the Frontispiece to *MP* vol. 2.

15. E.V. Lucas (ed.), *The Works of Charles and Mary Lamb, vol. 1, Miscellaneous Prose 1798–1834* (London: Methuen 1903), 39.

16. See Lamb's 'The Old Benchers of the Inner Temple', *Essays of Elia*, in E.V. Lucas, *The Works of Charles and Mary Lamb*, 2.82–91; Lamb lived in the Inner Temple till 1782, when he went to Christ's Hospital School in 1782 (where he knew Coleridge), and effectively until 1792, when Salt, the Lambs' patron, died. Later addresses were Holborn, and a period in a madhouse at Hoxton (1795–96), Pentonville and Islington (1823–27), and Enfield Chase and Church Street, Edmonton, where he died.

17. For these theatres, see Millicent Rose, *The East End of London* (London: Cresset Press 1951), 95–100, 224.

18. Ruskin calls Gower Street a 'desert of Ugliness' in *Modern Painters* vol. 3, 'Of Many Things' (1856) 4.16: *Modern Painters* (London: George Allen 1897), 270.

19. See Claire Tomalin, *The Invisible Woman: The Story of Nelly Ternan and Charles Dickens* (Harmondsworth: Penguin 1991), 129; she discusses the houses for Ellen Ternan: Ampthill Square (2 Houghton Place, near Mornington Crescent), the High Street in Slough (1866), and Linden Grove at Peckham Rye. The offices for *Household Words* were at 16 Wellington Street, and Dickens lodged in a suite of rooms above;

those for *All the Year Round* were at no. 11 (renumbered 76). Kitton, 76–78, discusses the London houses Dickens took for his family each year: Hanover Terrace, Regent's Park, and addresses south and north of Hyde Park; the last, 5 Hyde Park Place.

20. For these details, see Vivien Knight, 'The Private Life of William Powell Frith' in Mark Bills and Vivien Knight, *William Powell Frith: Painting the Victorian Age* (New Haven: Yale University Press 2006), 1–27.

21. See E. Beresford Chancellor, *The London of Thackeray* (London: Grant Richards 1923). Trollope's interest in an 'other' London appears in the stories collected in *An Editor's Tales*; see *Anthony Trollope: The Complete Short Stories* vol. 2 (London: The Trollope Society, n.d.).

22. In *English Hours* (1905), James – first in London in 1855, by himself in 1869, and settling in London in 1876 (Piccadilly, then Kensington; he died in Chelsea) – gathered essays on 'London' (1888), on 'Browning in Westminster Abbey' (1890), and 'London in Midsummer' (1877). Uncollected essays include 'London Sights' (1875), which discusses the Albert Memorial, unveiled in 1874 'opposite the great red-and-yellow rotunda of Albert Hall' which he calls 'a sort of utilitarian Colosseum' (269), 'The Oxford-Cambridge Boat-Race' (1877), discussing the dead heat result of an event inaugurated in 1829, which he viewed from the railway bridge at Barnes. Also, 'The Suburbs of London' (1877), which discusses Kensington Palace, and other palaces, and says that 'the term "suburban" has always seemed to me to have a peculiarly English meaning' (276), and 'London in the Dead Season' (1878). See John Kimmey, *Henry James and London: The City in his Fiction* (New York: Peter Lang 1991).

23. On social realities in the nineteenth-century novel, see Richard Altick, *The Presence of the Present: Topics of the Day in the Victorian Novel* (Columbus, Ohio: Ohio University Press 1991).

24. Compare, for the sense of the city as kaleidoscopic, the sense of a new consciousness which responds to the new culture of the city: 'A man may be very sober – or at least firmly set upon his legs on that neutral ground which lies between the confines of perfect sobriety and slight tipsiness – and yet feel a strong tendency to mingle up present circumstances with others which have no manner of connection with them; to confound all consideration of persons, things, times, and places; and to jumble his disjointed thoughts together in a kind of mental kaleidoscope, producing combinations as unexpected as they are transitory'. *(BR 3. 32–33)*

25. Edward Bulwer (Lord Lytton), *Eugene Aram* (1832, London: Collins, n.d.), 316–17.

26. Georg Simmel, *On Individuality and Social Forms: Selected Writings*, edited and with an introduction by Donald N. Levine (Chicago: University of Chicago Press 1971), 324–39.

27. See Friedrich Engels, *The Condition of the Working Class in England*, ed. Victor Kiernan (Harmondsworth: Penguin 2005), 69.

28. Maurice Blanchot, 'The Essential Solitude', trans. Lydia Davis in *The Gaze of Orpheus and Other Literary Essays* (Barrytown, NY: Station Hill Press 1981), 69.

CHAPTER TWO
Street-Scenes: *Sketches by Boz*, with *Pickwick Papers* and *Nicholas Nickleby*

1. Cancelled passage beginning 'The Prisoner's Van', *SB*, originally published November 1835, quoted, John Butt and Kathleen Tillotson, *Dickens at Work* (London: Methuen 1957), 44. 'The amusements of the people' appears as the title for an essay in *Household Words*, 30 March 1850. Note its tone of acceptance of the non-genteel character of the

streets. On *Sketches by Boz*, see J. Hillis Miller and David Borowitz, *George Cruikshank* (Los Angeles: William Andrews Clark Memorial Library 1971). Hillis Miller discusses the interrelationship between Dickens' writing and Cruikshank's illustration, showing that neither can be said to be originating material; the *Sketches* cannot be taken as an empiricist account of what has been observed in London. See also Kathyrn Chittick, *Dickens and the 1830s* (Cambridge: Cambridge University Press 1990).

2. Michael Hollington, *Dickens and the Grotesque*, (London: Croom Helm 1984), 19, quotes Una Pope-Hennessy for the view that the knocker derives from knowledge of Hoffman's fairytale, *The Golden Pot* (1814), mediated through Carlyle.

3. Cancelled passage, which as a draft beginning 'Scotland-yard', published October 1836. Quoted, Butt and Tillotson, 55, and also in Duane DeVries, *Dickens' Apprentice Years: The Making of a Novelist* (Brighton: Harvester Press 1976). I discuss 'Scotland-yard' in *Blake's Night Thoughts* (London: Macmillan, 2004), 109–10.

4. For *Life in London* see John Marriott, with Masaie Matsumura and Judith R. Walkowitz, *Unknown London: Early Modernist Visions of the Metropolis, 1815–45* (London: Pickering and Chatto, 2000), 6 vols, vol. 2.

5. On Egan, and comparisons between him and Wordsworth, and Lamb, and De Quincey, and Dickens in writing 1820s London, see Deborah Epstein Nord, 'The City as Theater: From Georgian to Early Victorian London', *Victorian Studies* 31.2 (1988), 159–88. See also Gregory Dart, '"Flash Style": Pierce Egan and Literary London 1820–1828', *History Workshop Journal* 51 (2001), 181–205, and Roger Sales, 'Pierce Egan and the Representation of London', in *Reviewing Romanticism*, ed. Philip W. Martin and Robin Jarvis (London: Macmillan 1992).

6. 'The South-Sea House' (Lamb 2.1) refers to Lamb's middle-class reader walking from the Bank where he works to 'the Flower Pot' – an inn in Bishopsgate – 'to secure a place for Dalston or Shacklewell, or some other thy suburban retreat northerly'. Both these places are off the A10, here called the Stoke Newington road, to the east; both Lamb and Dickens are interested in deriving a poetry from the names, e.g. Shacklewell. In 'The Old and New Schoolmaster', Lamb refers to his daily jaunts between the City and 14 Kingsland Road, Dalston, where in 1816 he was doing his literary work uninterrupted: Lucas notes that 'at that time Dalston was the country, and Kingsland Green an open space opposite Lamb's lodging' (Lamb 2.50, 346). Dalston, Kingsland, Shacklewell and Hackney were four villages transformed by railway developments. The journey out north includes 'Norton Falgate', past George Dance's St Leonard's, Shoreditch (1736); and ends at Kingsland turnpike. The Flowerpot also appears in *SB* 367, when Mr Minns must visit his cousins, the Buddens, at Poplar-walk, Stamford Hill. They have moved out from London having made 'a moderate fortune by exercising the trade or calling of a corn-chandler, and having a great predilection for the country' (*SB* 363): hence their cottage: Budden walks to Minns in Tavistock Street from there, and Minns must get to his home from the cottage the same way.

7. Sharon Marcus, *Apartment Stories: City and Home in Nineteenth-Century Paris and London* (Berkeley: University of California Press 1999), 83–132 for London.

8. See W.J. Carlton, 'The Third Man at Newgate', *The Review of English Studies*, 8 (1957), 406; Philip Collins, *Dickens and Crime* (London: Macmillan 1962), 39.

9. Quoted, H.G. Cocks, *Nameless Offences: Homosexual Desire in the Nineteenth Century* (London: I.B. Tauris 2003), 38.

10. For figures for hanging, see Graham Robb, *Strangers: Homosexual Love in the Nineteenth Century* (London: Picador 2003), 22–25; Cocks, *Nameless Offences*, 23; and for the eighteenth century and Regency context, Louis Crompton, *Byron and*

Greek Love (London: Gay Men's Press 1998), 12–62 and Matt Cook, *London and the Culture of Homosexuality, 1885–1914* (Cambridge: Cambridge University Press 2003), 7–14.

11. *The Works in Prose and Verse of Charles and Mary Lamb* 2 vols, ed. Thomas Hutchinson (Oxford: Oxford University Press 1908) 1.96. Lamb's essay, 'On the Genius and Character of Hogarth' (1811), evokes Wordsworth's Sonnet 'Composed Upon Westminster Bridge' – 'the very houses seem asleep'.

12. On Whitecross prison, see Margot Finn, 'Being in Debt in Dickens's London: Fact, Fictional Representation and the Nineteenth Century Prison', *Journal of Victorian Culture*, vols 1 and 2, 1996–97, 203–26.

13. See the introductions by Robert L. Patten to the Penguin edition of 1971 (quotation p. 13), and the Clarendon edition (James Kinsley, 1986). Kinsley (xx) quotes from Dickens' advertisement of 26 March 1836, for the serial, that the Club of 1822 was renowned 'in the annals of Huggin Lane, and so closely entwined with the thousand interesting associations connected with Lothury and Cateaton Street' (Gresham Street, 1845). (The old and new Penguin editions differ in chapter-numberings, and I follow the old Penguin, as more familiar, while retaining the pagination.) This makes it a City text.

14. Dostoyevsky, letter of January 1868, quoted, W.J. Leatherbarrow, introduction to *The Idiot*, trans. Alan Myers (Oxford: Oxford University Press 1992), xv.

15. See especially 'The Stroller's Tale' (3), 'A Madman's Manuscript' (in chapter 11), and the stories narrated in chapter 21 (see chapters 7 and 10 below for discussion of these). In suggesting that Pickwick represents a radical form of innocence, there may be support in the title *The Posthumous Papers of the Pickwick Club*. As David Copperfield is a posthumous child (see my *Becoming Posthumous: Life and Death in Literary and Cultural Studies* (Edinburgh: Edinburgh University Press 2001)), that implies a certain freedom from the law of the Father; posthumous papers free the novel's events from conscious authority, make them independent, like 'The Madman's Manuscript'.

16. Dostoyevsky, *Crime and Punishment* 6.3, trans. David Magarshack (Harmondsworth: Penguin 1966), 478–79. It would be expected that discussion of the climate in St Petersburg would of the cold and snow, as it often is, but in *Crime and Punishment*, it is hot, mid-summer, enforcing the sense of unbearable heat in Raskolnikov's room, and in the streets. Compare Dickens' treatment of the effects of the heat in *BH* 19.

17. See the comparisons made by H.M. Daleski between Pickwick and Parson Adams, in *Dickens and the Art of Analogy* (London: Faber 1970).

18. See H.J. Dyos, 'The Slums of Victorian London', in David Cannadine and David Reeder (eds), *Exploring the Urban Past: Essays in Urban History by H.J. Dyos* (Cambridge: Cambridge University Press), 129–53; see also John Hollingshead, *Ragged London in 1861*, ed. Anthony Wohl (London: Everyman 1986), 53 and 200, indicating that the word was popularised by Cardinal Wiseman in 1850, describing the area around Westminster Abbey. On slum clearance, and overcrowding in London, see Anthony Wohl, *The Eternal Slum: Housing and Social Policy in Victorian London* (London: Edward Arnold 1977).

19. E. Beresford Chancellor, *The Romance of Soho* (London: Country Life 1931) 229 suggests Carnaby Street (laid out in the 1680s, and originally largely Huguenot) as the setting for the Kenwigs, similarly the setting for the discovery of Emily (*DC* 50.721–72).

20. Marx, *Capital*, in David McLellan (ed.), *Karl Marx: Selected Writings* (Oxford: Oxford University Press 2000), 473–74.

21. For the phantasmagoria, see Lutz Koepnick, *Walter Benjamin and the Aesthetics of Power* (Lincoln: University of Nebraska Press 1999), 141–63.

22. Walter Benjamin, *The Origin of German Tragic Drama*, trans. John Osborne (London: Verso 1973), 218.

23. Baudelaire, *Les Fleurs du Mal et autres poèmes*, ed. Henri Lemaître (Paris: Garnier-Flammarion 1964), 108, my translation.

CHAPTER THREE
Newgate London: *Oliver Twist*

1. For Holywell Street, see Lynda Nead, *Victorian Babylon: People, Streets and Images in Nineteenth-Century London* (New Haven: Yale University Press 2000), 161–203.

2. For a reproduction, see Walter S. Gibson, *Bruegel* (London: Thames and Hudson 1977), 184.

3. See *Master Humphrey's Clock and Other Stories*, ed. Peter Mudford (London: Dent 1997), 21.

4. For this prison, see Philip Collins, *Dickens and Crime*, 52–56.

5. John Gay, *The Beggar's Opera*, ed. Bryan Loughrey and T.O. Treadwell (Harmondsworth: Penguin 1986) 1.6. (52).

6. Defoe's *Moll Flanders* (1722) and *Colonel Jack* (1722) both use Newgate, like Gay and Hogarth. For *Jack Sheppard* and the 'mania' it caused, see Kathyrn Chittick, *Dickens and the 1830s* (Cambridge: Cambridge University Press 1990), 152–77.

7. Examples of its radicalism: John Wilkes speaking against his expulsion from the House of Commons, 1764, Cobbett attacking the Corn Laws in 1826, the crowds cheering Lovett, Watson and Benbow, leaders of the National Union of the Working Class after they had been acquitted of sedition; and Chartist activity in 1842 and 1848. *BR* chapter 4 opens with the 'venerable suburb' of Clerkenwell, adding that it was a suburb once, and alluding to the Charter House. In *OMF* 1.7 it is home to Mr Venus' shop, associating him with precision-work, like clock-making, for which Clerkenwell was famous. Home of Mr Jarvis Lorry (*TTC* 1.6).

8. Brick Lane appears in *PP* 33.439 as housing a branch of the United Grand Junction Ebenezer Temperance Association.

9. Arthur Morrison, *A Child of the Jago*, 1896. Its subject is the Rev. A. Osborne Jay, who worked in 'this Shoreditch parish of 8,000 people, with a death rate four times that of the rest of London, with 17 public houses, and no church of any kind at all, a parish with a record of criminality which none could surpass or even equal, a parish which was described in the newspaper, as 'the sink of London' . . . worse than barbarian' – quoted W.J. Fishman, *East End 1888: A Year in a London Borough Among the Labouring Poor* (London: Duckworth 1988), 7. Arthur Morrison (1863–1945) also produced *Tales of Mean Streets* (1894); here, and in *A Child of a Jago* (1896), unlike Dickens, the East End is portrayed as an inherently different space from the City: 'But who knows the East End? It is down through Cornhill and out beyond Leadenhall Street and Aldgate Pump, one will say: a shocking place where he once went with a curate: an evil plexus of slums that hide human creeping things . . . the East End is a place, says another, which is given over to the Unemployed' (*Tales of Mean Streets*, 19). The Jago is declared to be worse than either Seven Dials or Ratcliff Highway (*Jago*, 45): it is Ratcliff Highway without the policing that Dickens describes in 'On Duty with Inspector Field'.

10. Robert Tracy, ' "The Old Story" and Inside Stories: Modish Fiction and Fictional Modes in *Oliver Twist*', *Dickens Studies Annual* 18 (1988), 20.

11. The significance of the ditch – though not these ditches – is discussed by Catherine Robson, 'Down Ditches, on Doorsteps, in Rivers: *Oliver Twist*'s Journey to Respectability', *Dickens Studies Annual* 29 (2000), 61–81.

12. For the M25 as a girdle round London, see Ian Sinclair, *The London Orbital: A Walk Round the M25* (Cambridge: Granta 2002).

13. Frederic G. Kitton, *Dickens and his Illustrators* (1899, Amsterdam: S. Emmering 1972), 12, quotes Cruikshank in 1872 saying that the landscape here represented the old Pentonville fields, north of London.

14. The death-drive is Freud's speculation in *Beyond the Pleasure Principle* (1920), when asking what, if anything, lies 'beyond' the conservative powers of the 'pleasure principle', that which in the self tries to minimise its expenditure of energy, the extent to which it permits excitation to break through. Freud thinks of the pleasure principle working by repetition, keeping to the bounds of known experience, but he also thinks of repetition as caused by trauma, as out of the conscious control of the psyche, and as activated by a masochism which leads the organism to death. The sexual drives, in Freud, are not separable from the death-drive, and he speculates on masochism as primary; see *Beyond the Pleasure Principle*, in *The Penguin Freud 11: On Metapsychology* (Harmondsworth: Penguin 1977), 328.

15. See Robert L. Patten, *George Cruikshank's Life, Times and Art, vol. 2: 1835–1878* (Cambridge: Lutterworth Press 1996), 77.

16. Quoted, Richard Maxwell, *The Mysteries of Paris and London* (Charlottesville: University Press of Virginia 1992), 91. See his accounts of *Oliver Twist* for the trope of hanging throughout, and of allegory in *The Old Curiosity Shop* (96–125).

17. 'Part of life's difficulty for most people most of the time is that they fail to see the ego as a dog. Aphorism 312 of *Gay Science* reads: "*My dog* – I have given a name to my pain and call it 'dog'. It is just as faithful, just as obtrusive and shameless, just as entertaining, just as clever as any other dog – and I can scold it and vent my bad mood on it, as others do with their dogs, servants, and wives." How liberating it would be if we could see our "pain" – the sum of our resentments and frustrations, for example – as a dog that frequently amuses us but needs to be kept in its place and can serve as an outlet for our bad temper. This would be far superior to seeing ourselves as identical with the pain, and the same holds true for our relation to the ego, which follows us about like a dog': Gary Shapiro, 'Dogs, Domestication, and the Ego' in Christa Davis Acampora and Ralph R. Acampora (eds), *A Nietzschean Bestiary: Becoming Animal Beyond Docile and Brutal* (Lanham, Md.: Rowman and Littlefield 2004), 55.

18. Steven Marcus' argument, in 'Who is Fagin?' in *Dickens from Pickwick to Dombey* dramatises that: the boy Bob Fagin, however poor, could not be shown where Dickens lived; the destitute Dickens had to hide it from him. See also Jim Barloon, 'The Black Hole of London: Rescuing Oliver Twist', *Dickens Studies Annual* 28 (1999), 1–12.

CHAPTER FOUR
London as Ruin: Tales from *Master Humphrey's Clock*

1. Scott, *The Antiquary*, ed. David Hewitt (Harmondsworth: Penguin 1998), 28–29. A fuller reference to Scott's *The Antiquary* (1816) follows in *PP* 11.157 when 'Bill Stumps, his mark' becomes the subject of the Royal Antiquarian Society (i.e. the Society of Antiquaries, founded 1707). The equivalent passage from Scott (chapter 4) comes when Jonathan Oldbuck, the Antiquary, thinks he has discovered the

battlefield between Agricola and the Caledonians, having found an inscription with the letters A.D.L.L.

2. Nietzsche, 'On the Uses and Disadvantages of History for Life', *Untimely Meditations*, trans. R.J. Hollingdale (Cambridge: Cambridge University Press 1983), 75.

3. Walter Benjamin, *The Origin of German Tragic Drama*, 166.

4. *MHC* was published also in book-form; the first volume dated 1840, two others 1841; for these volumes, Cattermole produced a frontispiece. In this chapter, apart from the new Penguins, I use the Penguin *OCS*, ed. Malcolm Andrews and Angus Easson (1972) and of *BR*, ed. Gordon Spence, and the Oxford *OCS*, ed. Elizabeth M. Brennan (1997) (based on her Clarendon edition, 1992). On Gordon, see Jeffrey L. Spear, 'Of Jews and Ships and Mob Attacks, Of Catholics and Kings: The Curious Career of Lord George Gordon', *Dickens Studies Annual* 32 (2002), 65–106; on the background to *MHC* see Paul Schlicke, 'Embracing the New Spirit of the Age: Dickens and the Evolution of *The Old Curiosity Shop*', *DSA* 32 (2002), 1–36; Robert Tracy, 'Clock Work: *The Old Curiosity Shop* and *Barnaby Rudge*', *DSA* 30 (2001), 23–43. Avron Fleishman, *The English Historical Novel: Walter Scott to Virginia Woolf* (Baltimore: Johns Hopkins University Press 1971) sees antiquarianism in *BR* (108), and links the novel to Carlyle via Gabriel Verden as a Carlylean 'hero of labour'. See also Juliet MacMaster, '"Better to be Silly": From Vision to Reality in *Barnaby Rudge*', *DSA* 13 (1984), 1–17. A bibliography for *Barnaby Rudge* appears in the Oxford edition, ed. Clive Hurst, Iain McCalman and Jon Mee (2003).

5. William Morris formed the Society for the Protection of Ancient Buildings in 1877.

6. Elizabeth Brennan, in the Clarendon edition of the novel (1992), assigns all to Browne, apart from the second (Samuel Williams), and nos 6 (chapter 5, the warehouse), 10 (opening of chapter 9, in the shop), 13 (the old man and Nell leaving the shop, 16 (chapter 15, the view back to London), 19 (chapter 18, the landlord with the cauldron), 21 (chapter 19, Nell and her grandfather), 49 (the church, chapter 46), 54 (the vaulted chamber, chapter 52) and 55 (Nell among the tombs, chapter 53). All these are Cattermole's, like the last four. No. 57, Nell and the Sexton (chapter 55), is by Maclise.

7. The editors of *Save the City: A Conservation Study of the City of London* (David Lloyd, Jennifer Freeman, Jane Fawcett) (London: Society for the Protection of Ancient Buildings 1984), 8, note the decline in the City's population, 128,000 in 1801, 123,000 in 1851, 9,000 in 1939. One factor in this was clearance of populations for the building of railway stations, especially Liverpool Street.

8. W.H. Ainsworth, *The Tower of London* (1840) 1.2 (London: Everyman 1909), 21.

9. In *MC* 39 and 40, where Tom Pinch works. It was laid out by Wren in 1681; the pumps were to fight Temple fires. The character in the initial seems to be leaning on a pump, while another shines a torch into his face.

10. See William Kent, *London for Dickens Lovers* (London: Methuen 1935), 105.

11. Robert L. Patten, *George Cruikshank's Life, Times and Art: vol. 1: 1792–1835* (London: Lutterworth Press 1992), 313.

12. William Hazlitt, *Lectures on the English Poets* (London: Everyman 1910), 97.

13. Quoted, Yoon Sun Lee, 'A Divided Inheritance: Scott's Antiquarian Novel and the British Nation', *English Literary History* 64 (1997), 571–601, **562**.

14. Quoted, John Hervey, *Victorian Novelists and their Illustrators* (London: Sidgwick and Jackson 1970), 122–23: all of Harvey's discussion of *MHC*, 116–29, is relevant.

15. Steven Marcus, *Dickens from Pickwick to Dombey* (New York: Norton 1965), 145.

16. See Humphry House, *The Dickens World* (Oxford: Oxford University Press 1942), 179–80; Kathleeen Tillotson, Introduction to the Oxford Illustrated edition of *Barnaby Rudge* (1954), and with John Butt, *Dickens at Work*, 76–89. See Patrick Brantlinger, *The Spirit of Reform: British Literature and Politics 1832–1867* (Cambridge, Mass.: Harvard University Press 1977), 81–96, who discusses both Chartism, and, in Sim Tappertit's Apprentice Knights, Dickens' negativity about Trades Unions. On the Gordon Riots, see George Rudé, *Hanoverian London, 1714–1808* (London: Secker and Warburg 1971), 220–27.

17. The Captain Swing Riots are alluded to in *PP* 1.17: 'The praise of mankind was his Swing; philanthropy was his insurance office'.

18. See Jennifer Bennett, 'The London Democratic Association 1837–1841: A Study in London Radicalism', in James Epstein and Dorothy Thompson (eds), *The Chartist Experience: Studies in Working Class Radicalism and Culture, 1830–1860* (London: Macmillan 1982), 87–119.

19. Thomas Carlyle, *Selected Writings*, ed. Alan Shelston (Harmondsworth: Penguin 1971), 152.

20. See David Large, 'London in the Year of Revolutions', in John Stevenson (ed.), *London in the Age of Reform* (Oxford: Basil Blackwell 1977), 177–212. On London in 1848, see Malcolm Chase, *Chartism: A History* (Manchester: Manchester University Press 2007), 294–303.

21. E.P. Thompson, *The Making of the English Working Class* (Harmondsworth: Penguin 1968), 804.

22. Quoted, Edward Royle, *Chartism* (2nd edition, London: Longman 1986), 99.

23. See George Rudé, *Wilkes and Liberty: A Social Study* (London: Lawrence and Wishart 1983), 48–50.

24. See Philip Collins, *Dickens and Crime*, 27–51. The Sessions House (65.544) refers to the Old Bailey Sessions House, rebuilt in 1774, 'beyond the main walls of the prison though connected to it': they were replaced by the Central Criminal Court in 1834. See also the reference to Surgeons' Hall (75.622) in the Old Bailey, which was used for the dissection of corpses of felons (1752–1832).

25. 'Piccadilly' refers to the then new Apsley House (1771–78), built by Robert Adam, and the residence of Henry, Lord Bathurst (1714–94), the Lord Chancellor; later, Wellington's house. Lambeth Palace was the home of Frederick Cornwallis (1713–83), Archbishop of Canterbury. The Lord Chancellor, Edward Thurlow (1731–1806), lived at 45 Great Ormond Street, named after the Duke of Ormonde, James Butler, Royalist commander in Ireland (1610–88). The reference to Rockingham is to Charles Watson-Wentworth (1730–82), who headed the Whigs and spoke for the Catholic Relief Bill in the House of Lords.

26. The Borough Clink in Tooley Street (the name a corruption of St Olave's Street, from the Flitcroft church that stood there) is given by Gordon Spence as 'the Borough Compter, re-erected in Tooley Street early in the eighteenth century', and not the Clink (cp. the Oxford edition, 698). Of the other prisons, the New Bridewell was the Surrey Bridewell, east side of Glasshill Street (then St George's Fields).

27. The first chapel belonged to the Sardinian Ambassador (from 1720 to 1798): demolished 1910. Fanny Burney married here in 1793. The Bavarian Chapel was in Golden Square, which in the eighteenth century had many foreign legations. Moorfields was a poor area for Irish weavers; the chapel in Ropemaker Alley.

28. Jerome H. Buckley, '"Quoth the Raven": The Role of Grip in *Barnaby Rudge*', *Dickens Studies Annual* 21 (1992), 27–35 (35).

CHAPTER FIVE
Camden Town: *Dombey and Son*

1. *Dombey and Son* appeared in monthly parts between October 1846 and April 1848, and then in book-form: Alan Horsman's edition for Clarendon (1974) appears with notes and an excellent introduction and bibliography by Dennis Walder (Oxford: Oxford University Press 2001). The old Penguin edition (1970) had an introduction by Raymond Williams, who also discusses the novel in *The English Novel from Dickens to Lawrence* (London: Chatto and Windus 1970).

2. On these two periods of mania, see David Kynaston's narrative account of the City, *The City of London: vol. 1: A World of its Own, 1815–1890*, 102–3, 151–53. Kynaston defines 'stagging', a practice relevant for the putative origins of the name Staggs' Gardens – 'applying heavily for the shares in new companies with a view to selling them immediately at a premium', adding that *Punch* in 1845 satirised 'Stag-hunting in Capel Court' (152).

3. See T.C. Barker, 'Urban Transport' in Michael J. Freeman and Derek H. Aldcroft (eds), *Transport in Victorian Britain* (Manchester: Manchester University Press 1988), 134–70, for forms of transport in the nineteenth century. He records the dockers at Liverpool in the 1830s who were estimated to walk 43 miles making 750 trips per day from warehouse to vessel, carrying sacks of oats (135).

4. On this, see W. Schivelbusch, *The Railway Journey: The Industrialisation of Time and Space in the Nineteenth Century* (Berkeley: University of California Press 1986).

5. For information on railways, see Hamilton Ellis, *British Railway History* 2 vols, 1830–76 and 1877–1947 (London: George Allen and Unwin 1954), Francis Sheppard, *London 1808–1870: The Infernal Wen* (London: Secker and Warburg 1971), 117–57, John R. Kellett, *Railways and Victorian Cities* (London: Routledge and Kegan Paul 1969). On the railway in Dickens, see Humphry House, *The Dickens World*, 136–52, and Murray Baumgarten, 'Railway/Reading/Time: *Dombey & Son* and the Industrial World', *Dickens Studies Annual* (1990), 65–89.

6. Michael Freeman, *Railways and the Victorian Imagination* (New Haven: Yale University Press 1999), 176.

7. Two pictures are reproduced in Terry Coleman, *The Railway Navvies* (Harmondsworth: Penguin 1968), see illustrations 8 and 9. See also John Cooke Bourne, *Drawings of the London and Birmingham Railway with History and Description by John Britton* (London 1839). Britton compares the work to the sensation Gibbon felt on looking at the Eternal City. He gives a summary of the growth of transport: 1564 for the first use of coaches, 1754 for the first stage-coach from London to Edinburgh, tolls after 1764, a letter-office in the time of Charles the First, and a weekly post in 1649 and special mail-coaches in 1784; 1756 for the first navigable canal (Worsley to Manchester, seven miles), steam-vessels after 1812, iron rails first used in 1767. The arch at Euston 'connects the British metropolis with the most important towns of the kingdom' (13). Britton says that he remembers when there was no development north of Bloomsbury Square, adding that there is now a continuity of houses from Highgate Hill to Tavistock Square (12). On Bourne, see Francis D. Klingender, *Art and the Industrial Revolution*, revised by Arthur Elton (London: Paladin 1968), 133–42. Nos 83–88 of the illustrations are examples of Bourne's work on the London to Birmingham railway. See also *MP* 1.490 for a reprint of Bourne's 'Building the Stationary Engine House, Camden Town'.

8. On this picture, see Caroline Arscott, 'William Powell Frith's *The Railway Station*: Classification and the Crowd', in Mark Bills and Vivien Knight (eds), *William*

Powell Frith: Painting the Victorian Age (New Haven: Yale University Press 2006), 79–94.

9. For reproductions, see Anthony Farrington, *Trading Places: The East India Company and Asia 1600–1834* (London: The British Library 2002), 111.

10. The passage coincides with Dickens' interest in Urania Cottage, between Shepherds' Bush and Notting Hill ('between Acton Road (now Uxbridge Road) and New Road (now Goldhawk Road), to the east side of the connecting turnpike (now Lime Grove' – *Letters* 5.63 n.) which he bought on behalf of Angela Burdett-Coutts (1814–1906). It opened November 1847. Dickens discusses plans for the asylum in a letter of 26 May 1846 (*Letters* 4.552). It was for former prostitutes, eighteen in all, arranging to send them to Cape Town or Australia. Hence the characters of Martha and Emily in *David Copperfield*. See Clara Burdett Patterson, *Angela Burdett-Coutts and the Victorians* (London: John Murray 1953), 142–77. On the differential way men and women possess the streets, discussing *Sketches by Boz, Pickwick Papers, Dombey and Son* and *Bleak House* see Deborah Epstein Nord, *Walking the Victorian Streets: Women, Representation, and the City* (Ithaca: Cornell University Press 1995), 19–111. See also Judith Walkowitz, *Prostitution and Victorian Society: Women, Class, and the State* (Cambridge: Cambridge University Press 1980) and *City of Dreadful Delight* (Chicago: Chicago University Press 1992).

11. See Iwan Rhys Morus, 'The Electric Telegraph and Commercial Culture in Early Victorian England', *Victorian Studies* (1996), 339–78.

12. Quoted, Kenneth Clark (ed.), *Ruskin Today* (Harmondsworth: Penguin 1964), 63. For Ruskin on the city, see Phillip Mallett, 'The City and the Self' in Michael Wheeler (ed.), *Ruskin and Environment* (Manchester: Manchester University Press 1995), 38–57. The same volume contains Jeffrey Richards, on 'The Role of the Railways', 123–43.

13. The number-plans for no.3 of *Dombey and Son* identify Mrs Pipchin with Mrs Roylance, but a Mrs Pipchin appears in 'New Year's Day', 1 January 1859, *Household Words* (J3.492) as a woman who took the boy to the bazaar (see *Letters* 4.635 n.5). Chronologically, she must pre-date Mrs Roylance. Perhaps the name is to be considered generic, or the association went further back than 1824.

14. W.M. Thomas published 'A Suburban Connemara', a short story about a Manchester man settling his family in Agar Town, *Household Words* 8 March 1851.

15. For the image, compare: 'the historian [here, Dickens] takes the friendly reader by the hand, and springing with him into the air, and cleaving the same at a greater rate than ever Don Cleophas Leandro Perez Zambulo and his familiar travelled through that pleasant region in company, alights with him upon the pavements of Bevis Marks. The intrepid aeronauts alight before a small dark house, once the residence of Mr Sampson Brass' (*OCS* 33.250). The reference is to Alain René Le Sage (1668–1747)'s romance, *Le Diable boiteux* [*The Devil on Two Sticks* 1707], where the familiar, on two crutches, is Asmodée: he reveals what is going on in the houses below as they go through the air. 'Aeronaut' derives from the French first balloon ascents, of 1783.

16. 'Monotony' becomes a leitmotif of the novel; note its recurrence in Carker's flight towards England, 55.835.

17. See my discussion of Carker's death: 'Carlyle Through Nietzsche: Reading *Sartor Resartus*', *Modern Language Review* 102 (2007), 326–40. For Paddock Wood, see *Letters* 5. 415.

18. Freud, 'Moses and Monotheism', *The Penguin Freud 13: The Origins of Religion* (Harmondsworth: Penguin 1985), 309–10.

19. Cathy Caruth, *Unclaimed Experience: Trauma, Narrative and History* (Baltimore: Johns Hopkins University Press 1996), 17.
20. Freud, 'From the History of an Infantile Neurosis,' *The Penguin Freud 9: Case Histories II* (Harmondsworth: Penguin 1979), 269, 278.
21. Jacques Lacan, *The Four Fundamental Concepts of Psychoanalysis*, trans. Alan Sheridan (Harmondsworth: Penguin 1977), 55.
22. Benjamin reads city-experience as involving, inherently, shock. 'Moving through this traffic involves the individual in a series of shocks and collisions. At dangerous crossings, nervous energies flow through him in rapid succession [. . .] Baudelaire speaks of a man who plunges into the crowds as into a reservoir of electric energy. Circumscribing the experience of the shock, he calls this man "a kaleidoscope equipped with consciousness"'. Walter Benjamin, *Charles Baudelaire: A Lyric Poet in the Era of High Capitalism*, trans. Harry Zohn (London: Verso 1973), 132.
23. For repetition, see Helmut Bonheim, 'The Principle of Cyclicity in Charles Dickens' "The Signalman"' in Michael Hollington (ed.), *Charles Dickens: Critical Assessments* 4 vols, 3. 811–21.

CHAPTER SIX
Modernising London: *David Copperfield*

1. *David Copperfield* appeared in monthly parts between May 1849 and November 1850, and then in book-form. It shows signs of including within it an autobiographical fragment, which Forster also included in the second chapter of his *Life of Dickens*. Dickens seems to have discussed such writing in November 1846; Forster records seeing something of the fragment in January 1849.
2. Quoted, Ken Young and Patricia L. Garside, *Metropolitan London: Politics and Urban Change 1837–1881* (London: Edward Arnold 1982), 14.
3. On the building of Trafalgar Square on the site of the King's Mews, which had been established by the fourteenth century, and which, in 1830, was to be named after William the Fourth, see Rodney Mace, *Trafalgar Square: Emblem of Empire* (London: Lawrence and Wishart 2005), and Richard L. Stein, *Victoria's Year: English Literature and Culture 1837–1838* (Oxford: Oxford University Press 1987). See *Letters* 5. 549–50 for a letter to Sir Edwin Landseer (1802–73), congratulating him on his lions (1867) at the base of William Railton's monument to Nelson, which have been 'subdued' by his 'genius'. Nelson was put in place in 1843.
4. The Boar Yard was between 29 and 31 Whitechapel, north side (Chancellor, 184). Pickwick leaves for Ipswich from the Bull inn, Whitechapel (*PP* 22.290).
5. The Marchioness herself, an 'old-fashioned child' (*OCS* 34.261), like Paul Dombey, was supposed, in a draft of chapter 66, to be the daughter of Sally Brass, possibly by Quilp (see the dialogue between her and Quilp, 51.383–84). See the comments by Angus Easson in the old Penguin edition, 699 and 715–16.
6. Henry James, recalling a visit to Europe between 1869 and 1870, says that Craven Street 'absolutely reeked, to my fond fancy, with associations born of the particular ancient piety embodied in one's private altar to Dickens . . . the whole Dickens world looked out of its queer, quite sinister windows – for it was the socially sinister Dickens, I am afraid, rather than the socially encouraging or confoundingly comic who still at that moment was most apt to meet me with his reasons. Such a reason was just the look of the inscrutable riverward street, packed to blackness with accumulations of suffered experience, these, indescribably, disavowed and confessed at one and the same time, and with the fact of its blocked old Thames-side

termination, a mere fact of more oppressive enclosure now, telling all sorts of vague loose stories about it' – *The Middle Years* in James, *Autobiography*, ed. Frederick W. Dupee (Princeton: Princeton University Press 1983), 572.

7. Disraeli, *Tancred*, 155. On the Strand as the centre for publishing (Dickens' publishers, Chapman and Hall, opened at 130 Strand in 1830), see Rosemary Ashton on John Chapman, resident there between 1847 and 1854, *142 Strand: A Radical Address in London* (London: Chatto and Windus 2006), 1–13. Also popular for middle-class entertainment: Thackeray refers in *Pendennis* chapter 30 to the Back Kitchen, which Sutherland thinks was an amalgam of the Cider Cellars (Maiden Lane), the Coal Hole (the Strand) and Evans' (Covent Garden) (*Pendennis* 1035). The Cider Cellars, an underground tavern, also appears in *PP* 31.402. Ronald Paulson brings out Hogarth's attitude to the law (incidentally putting it into the context of Hogarth's father being imprisoned in the Fleet when Hogarth was eleven) in *Book and Painting: Shakespeare, Milton and the Bible* (Knoxville: University of Tennessee Press 1982), 82–98.

8. William Kent, *London For Dickens Lovers* 47; his pages are full of first and last happenings, such as public whipping in 1817, and the first traffic lights by 1868.

9. There are excellent illustrations by George Scharf (1788–1860) of St Martin's Lane, and the old Charing Cross area, and of the shops in the Strand; see Peter Jackson, *George Scharf's London: Sketches and Watercolours of a Changing City, 1820–1850* (London: John Murray 1987), 19–32.

10. See David King, *The Complete Works of Robert and James Adam* (Oxford: Butterworth Architecture 1991), 77–82.

11. On heterotopias, see Michel Foucault, 'Of Other Spaces' in *Aesthetics: Method, and Epistemology*, ed. James Faubion, trans. Robert Hurley (Harmondsworth: Penguin 2000), 175–85.

12. On the Savoy, see Robert Somerville, *The Savoy: Manor: Hospital: Chapel* (London: The Savoy 1960).

13. See G.E. Bentley, Jr., *The Stranger from Paradise: A Biography of William Blake* (New Haven: Yale University Press 2001), 392–94.

14. See Johann Friedrich Geist, *Arcades: The History of a Building Type* (Cambridge, Mass.: MIT Press 1983), 336–38.

15. Quoted, Christopher Prendergast, *Paris and the Nineteenth Century* (Oxford: Blackwell 1992), 136. See also T.J. Clark, *The Painting of Modern Life: Paris in the Art of Manet and his Followers* (London: Thames and Hudson 1984), 108.

16. On rebuilding London Bridge, see Dana Arnold, *Re-Presenting the Metropolis: Architecture, Urban Experience and Social Life in London 1800–1940* (Aldershot: Ashgate 2000), 19–24. For visual representation of the destruction of houses in Fish Street, and of Wren's St Michael, Crooked Lane, and Great Eastcheap, and the demolition of 318 houses, see Peter Jackson, *George Scharf's London*, 110–19.

17. I have discussed the trauma implied in chapter 55, 'Tempest' in my *Becoming Posthumous*, 59–87.

CHAPTER SEVEN
Bleak House: London Before the Law

1. *Bleak House* was written at Dickens' house in Tavistock Square, which the family began occupying in November 1851, the month of beginning the novel. It began publication in twenty instalments (March 1852 to August 1853) then came out in book-form.

2. OED gives Maria Edgeworth, writing in 1830, for the first reference to a 'London fog'. See also *Letters* 3.273.

3. Harold Bloom (ed.) *The Literary Criticism of John Ruskin* (New York: Doubleday 1965), 360.

4 See Shatto, 91, 111, 253, for the Irish influence in the novel. The Banshee appears in *OCS* 67.507, in preparation for Quilp's death.

5. On the Gothic elements of the text, and for the idea that Gothic novels were fascinated by places, see Allan Pritchard, 'The Urban Gothic of *Bleak House*', *Nineteenth-Century Literature* 45 (1991), 432–52.

6. For Dickens and Holborn, see John Lehmann, *Holborn: An Historical Portrait of a London Borough* (London: Macmillan 1970), 109–25.

7. Ronald Paulson (ed.), *Hogarth's Graphic Works* (London: The Print Room 1989), 154.

8. For Lincoln's Inn Fields, see Elizabeth McKellar, *The Birth of Modern London: The Development and Design of the City 1660–1720* (Manchester: Manchester University Press 1999), 193–97. This considers the view of Jules Lubbock, that Moorfields could be regarded as the first, but arguing that since there 'houses were not built around the fields in direct relation to the space' (195) that puts it in a different category.

9. The most famous representation of Westminster Hall, showing its stationery shops and business activities, was the popular print by Hubert Gravelot (1699–1773) which was used by C. Mosley to accompany a satirical poem about the law of 1797, *The First Day of Term*, often reproduced. See the illustration of it by Cattermole, *BR* 43, and Dickens' description of it as a meeting-place.

10. OED7 'chancery' gives another meaning: 'a slang term for the position of the head when held under the opponent's left arm to be pommelled severely, the victim meanwhile being unable to retaliate effectively; hence sometimes figuratively used of an awkward fix or predicament': OED gives 1832 for the first use in this sense.

11. See Turner's 1835 oil-painting, viewing from Lambeth: 'The Burning of the House of Lords and Commons, 16th of October 1834', Martin Butlin and Andrew Wilton, *Turner 1775–1851* (London: Tate Gallery 1974), 128, 142. (Philadelphia Museum of Art)

12. Jacques Derrida, *Archive Fever: A Freudian Impression*, trans. Eric Prenowitz (Chicago: University of Chicago Press 1995), 10.

13. Sir Walter Besant and G.E. Mitton, *The Fascination of London: Holborn and Bloomsbury* (London: Adam and Charles Black 1903), 4.

14. David Paroissien's edition annotates this: PJT is Principal John Thompson, President of Staple Inn in 1747. The new buildings were of 1843, for the Taxing Masters, and later for the Patent Office and the Land Registry Office.

15. Slater writes that this 'was brought from Italy in 1700, but removed to the Inner Temple on the construction of the Aldwych . . . it now faces the King's Bench walk' (*J4* 158).

16. For Temple Bar in *TTC* see 1.3. and 2.1. The passages describe Tellson's Bank, hard by 'the heavy shadow of Temple Bar'. The entrance is two steps down from the road, so that the windows 'were always under a shower-bath of mud from Fleet Street'. Sanders (55) discusses the exposing of heads on Temple Bar, saying that the last were Townley and Fletcher, Jacobite rebels, beheaded in 1746, but gone by 1772. (England's last beheading took place in 1747, at Tower Hill, of a Jacobite, Lord Lovat.) Note the phrase 'as comfortable as Temple Bar in a Scotch mist', *SB* 7.260.

17. Andrew Goodman, *The Walking Guide to Lawyers' London* (London: Blackstone Press 2000), 160–61. Goodman (131–32, 149–50) also gives details about Serjeants' Inn, which occupied the site from 1415 to 1910, and was so called by 1484. The Order of Serjeants at Law (Latin: serviens ad legem: one who serves the King in matters of law) was that of Servitors of the Knights Templar: the order was a brotherhood: members addressed each other as brothers. Until 1873, all Common Law judges were selected from this order, which was abolished in 1880.

18. OED8 citation of 1591: 'the House of the Rolls . . . hath been of long time, as it were, the College of the Chancery Men'. The Rolls Chapel was given to the Keeper of the Rolls of Chancery in 1377, but older, in date, and rebuilt in 1617 (Inigo Jones) and in 1734, and demolished in 1895.

19. See A.W.C. Brice and K.J. Fielding, 'Dickens and the Tooting Disaster', *Victorian Studies* 12 (1968), 235–39. See Dickens on the scandal: 'The Paradise at Tooting', 20 January 1849, 'The Tooting Farm', 27 January, 'A Recorder's Charge', 3 March, 'The Verdict for Drouet', 21 April, as well as an article in *Household Words*, 'Home for Homeless Women', 23 April 1853, which discusses Urania Cottage, and a girl like Guster who was sent there: 'she had been brought up in the establishment of that amiable victim of popular prejudice, the late Mr Drouet, of Tooting. It did not appear that she was naturally stupid, but her intellect had been so dulled by neglect that she was in the Home many many months before she could be imbued with a thorough understanding that Christmas Day was so called as the birthday of Jesus Christ'. See for three of these articles, and for the *Household Words* piece, Charles Dickens, *MP* 1.404; 1.152 reprints a contemporary print of the asylum.

20. Based on Sloman's House, 4 Cursitor Street, where John Dickens was held in 1834; see 'A Passage in the Life of Mr Watkins Tottle' in *SB*, and *PP* 40.534, where the officer is Namby of Bell Alley, Coleman Street (in the City, south of Moorgate, home of the poet Robert Bloomfield (1766–1823)): see also *Vanity Fair* chapter 51, and *The Newcomes* chapter 25.

21. Snagsby has been reading John Stow (c.1525–1605), author of *The Survey of London* (1598; London: Dent 1945), 15: 'Oldborne, or Hillborn, was the like water, breaking out about the place where now the bars do stand, and it ran down the whole street till Odborne bridge, and into the river of the Wells, or Turnemill brook'. Turnmill Street is in Clerkenwell, the other side of the old Fleet.

22. Norman O. Brown, *Life Against Death: The Psychoanalytic Meaning of History* (London: Routledge 1959), 247.

23. Bucket was associated with Inspector Charles Field (?1805–74). Articles on detective work appeared in *Household Words*: W.H. Wills' 'The Modern Science of Thief-Taking' (13 July 1850), 'A Detective Police Party' (27 July, 10 August), 'Three "Detective" Anecdotes' (14 September), 'On Duty with Inspector Field' (14 June 1851) – the last three appearing also in *Reprinted Pieces*. Field, a former Bow Street Runner (see *Letters* 10.72), retired from the Metropolitan detective police in 1851, but continued to work for the police at Great Scotland Yard and as a private inquiry agent (see *Letters* 6.689 n.). See Dickens' denial of use of Fields' experiences in *Letters* 7.149, and a critique by Dickens in *Letters* 7.151. Field escorted Dickens round the East End in 1869 (see *Letters* 12.359).

24. See 'Market Gardens', *Household Words*, 2 July 1853, 409–14, which mentions a Mr Myatt, as the first gardener in Deptford, forty years previously, cultivating rhubarb for commercial sale.

25. On Dickens and sanitation, see K.J. Fielding and A.W. Brice, '*Bleak House* and the Graveyard' in Robert B. Partlow, Jr, *Dickens the Craftsman: Strategies of*

Presentation (Carbondale: Southern Illinois University Press 1970), 117–39, and F. S. Schwarzbach, '*Bleak House*: The Social Pathology of Everyday Life' in Peter W. Graham and Elizabeth Sewell, *Literature and Medicine* vol. 9 (Baltimore: Johns Hopkins University Press 1990), 93–104.

26. See Richard Tames, *Soho Past* (London: Historical Publications 1994), 26 for a reproduction of Savile House; the top floor was Green's Shooting Gallery, the first floor a Gun and Pistol Repository, and the ground floor Miss Linwood's Exhibition. The house burnt down in 1865, and is the site of a cinema. Dickens does not refer to James Wyld, geographer and MP, and his Great Globe in the centre of Leicester Square, a huge building and tourist attraction operating from 1851 to 1862 (Tames, 114–15), nor the Royal Panopticon of Science and Art built in massive 'Saracenic' style on the east side of the square (1854–58) which became the Alhambra music hall until 1936 (Tames, 118–19).

27. Flora Tristran, *The London Journal of Flora Tristan 1842, Or, The Aristocracy and the Working Class of England*, trans. Jean Hawkes (London: Virago 1982), 31. Hawkes' note adds that the 1851 census had a total of 26,000 foreigners in London, 5,900 French.

28. The story is analysed by Jacques Derrida in 'Before the Law' in *Acts of Literature*, ed. Derek Attridge (London: Routledge), and the following discussion, which takes in Freud's 'Totem and Taboo', uses this commentary.

29. Kafka, *The Trial*, trans. Breon Mitchell (New York: Schocken Books 1998), 213.

30. For Dickens' antipathy to the Great Exhibition, and for *Bleak House* in relation to it, see two articles in *Dickens Studies Annual* 33 (2003): Robert Tracy, 'Lighthousekeeping: *Bleak House* and the Crystal Palace' (25–53), and Katherine Williams, 'Glass Windows: The View from *Bleak House*' (55–85). *LD* refers to 'the great social Exhibition', which includes a reference to Royal Academy exhibitions (*LD* 1.13.164).

31. Freud, 'Civilization and Its Discontents', in *Civilization, Society and Religion: The Penguin Freud 12* (Harmondsworth: Penguin 1985), 327.

32. George Gissing, *The Immortal Dickens* (London: Cecil Palmer 1925), 241 uses the word 'rotting' to describe London. He also quotes from *I Henry IV* 1.2.63, 'old Father antic, the law' (226): if Miss Flite is mad, so is the law, the father. The law is both the father of guilt, and produced by it.

CHAPTER EIGHT
London and Taboo: *Little Dorrit*

1. The novel ran from December 1855 to June 1857. See the Oxford Clarendon edition, ed. Harvey Peter Sucksmith (1979) and the edition by Angus Easson for the Dent Everyman edition (1999) whose annotations supplement the John Holloway Penguin edition (1967); see also Trey Philpotts, *The Companion to Little Dorrit* (London: Croom Helm 2003). On the novel: see Lionel Trilling, *Introduction to the Oxford Illustrated Dickens* (1853), F.R. Leavis in *Dickens the Novelist* (London: Chatto and Windus 1970). On its London locales, see Nancy Aycock Metz, '*Little Dorrit*'s London: Babylon Revisited', *Victorian Studies* 34 (1990), 465–86.

2. Dickens' account of London on a Sunday may be compared with Lamb's essay, 'The Superannuated Man' (1825), a fictional account of his time as a clerk with the East India Company (1792–1825); changing the place of work to Mincing Lane, and describing the gloom of 'a city Sunday' – 'those eternal bells depress me. The closed shops repel me' (Lamb, 2.193).

3. See Christopher Herbert on the taboo: 'Rat Worship in Taboo in Mayhew's London', *Representations* 23 (1988), 1–24, and 'Filthy Lucre: Victorian Ideas of Money', *Victorian Studies* 44 (2002), 185–213: the latter discusses *LD*. Captain Cook's sea-voyages are referred to by Mr Meagles (1.2.35); the attempts of the 'savages' to teach him are mentioned in 1.25.323.

4. Freud, in *The Origins of Religion: The Penguin Freud 13* (Harmondsworth: Penguin 1985), 71.

5. Benjamin (*Arcades* 209–10) associates the taboo with property: because 'to appropriate to oneself an object is to render it sacred and redoubtable to others'. Tabooed objects in the museum speak of the acquisitive mentality of the colonialists.

6. For Dickens and Sundays, and *Little Dorrit*, see Dennis Walder, *Dickens and Religion* (London: Allen and Unwin 1981), 170–94.

7. Sally Ledger links the poster to 'the story of Arthur's mother that guiltily haunts the home he is about to return to', *Dickens and the Popular Radical Imagination* (Cambridge: Cambridge University Press 2007), 229. Compare the picture by George Frederic Watts (1817–1904), *Found Drowned* (c.1850), showing the body of a female suicide under the Adelphi arches; the Patent Shot Manufactory appears on the other side of the water.

8. See, for instance, the doorways in Andrew Byrne, *London's Georgian Houses* (London: The Georgian Press 1986), 140–41.

9. Robert Mighall, *A Geography of Victorian Gothic Fiction: Mapping History's Nightmares* (Oxford: Oxford University Press 1999), 116, quotes this passage to bring out London's 'Gothicism'; his approach is interesting, but confines attention to the House of Clennam as a thing in itself, omitting the sense in which there is also a critique of the City implicit throughout.

10. Dickens describes its inhabitants: 'a few clear-starchers, a sprinkling of journeymen bookbinders, one or two prison agents for the Insolvent Courts [with whom Dickens lodged], several small housekeepers who are employed in the Docks, a handful of mantua-makers [dress-makers], and a seasoning of jobbing tailors. The majority of the inhabitants either direct their energies to the letting of furnished apartments, or devote themselves to the healthful and invigorating pursuit of mangling. The chief features in the still life of the street, are green shutters, lodging-bills, brass door-plates, and bell-handles; the principal specimens of animated nature, the pot-boy, the muffin-youth and the baked-potato man. The population is migratory, usually disappearing on the verge of quarter-day, and generally by night. His Majesty's revenues are seldom collected in this happy valley, the rents are dubious, and the water communication is very frequently cut off' (*PP* 417). Bob Sawyer works at Guy's Hospital.

11. Turn-up bedsteads are discussed in 'Brokers and Marine-Store Shops': 'A turn-up bedstead is a blunt, honest piece of furniture; it may be slightly disguised with a sham drawer, and sometimes a mad attempt is made to pass it off for a bookcase: ornament it as you will, however, the turn-up bedstead seems to defy disguise' – whereas a sofa-bedstead 'strives to appear an article of luxury and gentility . . . it has neither the respectability of a sofa, nor the virtues of a bed' (*SB* 210). Dick Swiveller's 'apartments' near Drury Lane have a turn-up bedstead disguised as a bookcase (*OCS* 7.101).

12. J. Hillis Miller, *Charles Dickens: The World of his Novels* (Bloomington: Indiana University Press 1958), 242.

13. Nietzsche, *Thus Spoke Zarathustra*, trans. Graham Parkes (Oxford: Oxford University Press 2005), 86.

14. Rugg wishes Clennam to go to the King's Bench prison (2.26) as more roomy than the Marshalsea; similarly Perker wished Pickwick not to go to Whitecross Street debtors' prison since 'there are sixty beds in a ward, and the bolt's on, sixteen hours out of the four-and-twenty' (*PP* 39.537). Whitecross prison, opened in 1815, closed 1870, had no private apartments.

15. Nietzsche, *The Genealogy of Morals*, trans. Douglas Smith (Oxford: Oxford University Press 1996), 44.

16. William Blake, *Complete Writings*, ed. Geoffrey Keynes (Oxford: Oxford University Press 1966), 451.

17. In 'On Duty with Inspector Field', 14 June 1850, *Household Words* (*J3* 356), Dickens refers to Field patrolling the British Museum, including 'the Parrot Gods of the South Sea Islands' (so described because of their feathers). If the gods are figures of the taboo, Mrs Merdle's parrot may have that function, of embodying the taboo.

18. Thorstein Veblen, *The Theory of the Leisure Class* (1899), the theory of 'conspicuous consumption': how American businessmen need wives so that these can display the extent of a man's wealth.

19. On Merdle's relationship to the John Sadleir scandal, and others which Dickens refers to in the Preface, see Norman Russell, *The Novelist and Mammon: Literary Responses to the World of Commerce in the Nineteenth Century* (Oxford: Clarendon 1986), 131–48, and Barbara Weiss, *The Hell of the English: Bankruptcy in the Victorian Novel* (Lewisburg: Bucknell University Press 1986), 148–59.

20. See Edmund Bergler, '*Little Dorrit* and Dickens' Intuitive Knowledge of Psychic Masochism', *American Imago* 14 (1957), 371–88. I discuss Miss Wade in *Confession: Sexuality, Sin, the Subject* (Manchester: Manchester University Press 1990), 141–48, and in my *Dickens, Violence and the Modern State: Dreams of the Scaffold* (London: Macmillan 1996), 207–10, and see the chapter on *LD*, 98–128.

21. As Freud writes in *Civilization and its Discontents*, the superego, in the form of 'conscience' is aggressive towards the ego: 'the tension between the harsh superego and the ego that is subjected to it is called by us the sense of guilt; it expresses itself as a need for punishment. Civilization . . . obtains mastery over the individual's dangerous desire for aggression by weakening and disarming it, and by setting up an agency within him to watch over it, like a garrison in a conquered city' (315–16).

22. Edward H. Gibson III, 'Baths and Washhouses in the English Public Health Agitation 1839–1848', *Journal of the History of Medicine* (1954), 391–406. See also Trollope's short story, 'The Turkish Bath' (in Jermyn Street), *Anthony Trollope: The Complete Short Stories* vol. 2 (London: The Trollope Society 1991), 1–24.

CHAPTER NINE
Traumatic London: *Great Expectations*

1. Compare 'Dullborough Town' in *The Uncommercial Traveller* (*All the Year Round* 30 June 1860), *J4* 140, where Dickens describes leaving Dullborough (Chatham – in 1823) and arriving at the Cross Keys, packed in the stage-coach, in 'damp straw'. Jerome Meckier, 'Dating the Action in *Great Expectations*', *Dickens Society Annual* 21 (1992), 157–94, puts the events opening the second stage of Pip's expectations as 1823.

2. Simon Joyce, *Capital Offenses: Geographies of Class and Crime in Victorian London* (Charlottesville: University of Virginia Press 2003), 95–96.

3. Other examples of interest in the criminal appear with James Blomfield Rush (1800–49) who shot the owner of Stanfield Hall on 28 November 1848 and hanged

for it at Norwich the following 21 April (*Letters* 5. 473). This produced four articles in *The Examiner* on prison and prison discipline: 'Prisons and Convict Discipline', 10 March 1849, 'Rush's Conviction', 7 April 1849, 'Capital Punishment', 5 May 1849, and 'False Reliance', 2 June 1849; and mention of Rush in Dickens' second letter to the *Times* on capital punishment, and again in the article 'The Demeanour of Murderers', *Household Words*, 14 June 1856, discussing the trial of William Palmer in 1856, hanged for poisoning, and reminding readers of John Thurtell, 'one of the murderers best remembered in England' hanged in 1824 and also, of Mr Manning (*J3* 377–83).

4. For Wordsworth and Jonson, see Anne Barton, *Ben Jonson, Dramatist* (Cambridge: Cambridge University Press 1984), 194–218.

5. *Early Letters of Thomas Carlyle*, ed. Charles Eliot Norton, vol. 2 1821–1826 (London: Macmillan 1886), 285–86.

6. Daniel Defoe, *Journal of the Plague Year*, ed. Paula R. Backscheider (New York: W.W. Norton 1992), 187–88.

7. The site of this inn is 11 Islington High Street; it changed from being a coaching inn in 1857. It is mentioned in a trip to Yorkshire in 'The Holly Tree', *CS* 99.

8. See on the prison-ships, Jonathan Schneer, *The Thames* (New Haven: Yale University Press 2005), 136–43.

9. Henry Mayhew and John Binny, *The Criminal Prisons of London and Scenes of Prison Life* (1862; London: Frank Cass 1968), 197–231.

10. Martin J. Wiener, *Reconstructing the Criminal: Culture, Law and Policy in England, 1830–1914* (Cambridge: Cambridge University Press, 1990), 100.

11. Ruskin is quoted in Lionel Lambourne, *Victorian Painting* (London: Phaidon 1999), 261, see the reproduction 262–63.

12. De Quincey gives an example of a Lancashire highwayman who was cut down from the gallows 'within the legal time, and instantly put into a chaise and four; so that when he reached Cruikshank [a famous anatomist] he was positively not dead. Mr — , a young student at the time, had the honour of giving him the *coup de grâce* – and finishing the sentence of the law' – 'On Murder Considered as One of the Fine Arts', *The Works of Thomas de Quincey* vol. 6, ed. David Groves and Grevel Lindop (London: Pickering and Chatto 2000), 126. Dickens also cites a woman who went mad after her brother was hanged for forgery, in 'Where We Stopped Growing', *Household Words* 1 January 1853 (*J3* 111). Another instance in this article, of a memory which cannot be transcended, is relevant for *GE*: it is a 'White Woman' who haunts Berners Street, Oxford Street, who is in her bridal dress, 'no doubt because a wealthy Quaker wouldn't marry her'. The passage intuits that she would have led the Quaker 'a sharp life'. See Malcolm Andrews, *Dickens and the Grown-up Child* (London: Macmillan 1994), 57–70.

13. John Ruskin, *Praeterita: Outlines of Scenes and Thoughts Perhaps Worthy of Memory in My Past Life* (London: Rupert Hart-Davis, 1948), 25–26.

14. See 'Travelling Abroad' in *The Uncommercial Traveller* (from *All the Year Round* 7 April 1860), *J4* 86; compare the letter to M. de Cerjat, January 1857, *Letters* 8. 265–66. Dickens bought Gad's Hill in 1856.

15. Dickens associates the North Kent Marshes with Execution Dock, situated at Wapping Old Stairs, off Wapping High Street, and used by the Admiralty until 1830 to hang pirates in chains. In *OCS* 67, Quilp is drowned and his body is carried downstream, like that of Compeyson, and 'flung on a swamp – a dismal place where pirates had swung in chains through many a wintry night – and left . . . there to bleach'. Drowning and hanging are associated. It is usually assumed that this is

Execution Dock, but the illustration does not look built-up enough for that; there may be an association between the Kentish marshes and the place of the dead body of Quilp.

16. David Holbrook, in *Charles Dickens and the Image of Women* (New York: New York University Press 1993), 127, suggests that Miss Havisham may evoke Catherine Hogarth, whom Dickens separated from in 1858: in this case, Compeyson ghosts Dickens.

17. 'We have a general idea that the passages at the Old Hummuns lead to groves of gorgeous bed-rooms, eating out the whole of the adjacent houses, where Chamberlains who have never been in bed themselves for fifty years, show any country gentleman who rings at the bell, at any hour of the night, to luxurious repose in palatial apartments fitted up after the Eastern manner. (We have slept there in our time, but that makes no difference.)' (*J3* 110). Pip in this moment is a 'country gentleman'. 'Don't go home' resonates from *BH* 48.747.

18. The Thames River Police, to protect customs on imports, was formed by John Harriott (an Essex JP) and Patrick Colquhoun, a Westminster magistrate, who wrote a *Treatise on the Police of the Metropolis*. Its offices were in Wapping High Street. It was incorporated into the Metropolitan Police in 1839. The importance of Dickens writing on the other side of the law, as it were, away from the tone and approval in 'Down with the Tide', *Household Words* 3 February 1853, a piece about the Thames River Police, is obvious.

19. The bills presumably have their poetry (in acrostic form) set by Mr Slum, who has just written an acrostic for Warren's, *OCS* 28.218: writing poetry for Warren's is a prevalent theme, see *SB* 95.

20. Blake, '*The Marriage of Heaven and Hell*', *Complete Writings* 151.

CHAPTER TEN
'City Full of Dreams': *The Uncommercial Traveller*

1. The first seventeen essays of *The Uncommercial Traveller*, the title giving a new persona, the 'Uncommercial', started 28 January 1860. Finishing on 13 October 1860, they preceded serialisation of *GE* (1 December 1860). *The Uncommercial Traveller* was published 13 December 1860. The second batch of essays, beginning with 'The Calais Night Mail', were written between 2 May 1863 and 24 October 1863; they appeared in the Cheap Edition of Dickens' works, published in 1865, while *OMF* was being serialised. In 1875, the posthumously produced Illustrated Edition added eight more, beginning with 'The Ruffian' (10 October 1868), previously published as an occasional paper. The third series actually began, technically, with 'Aboard Ship' (5 December 1868) when the weekly became a 'new series' and ran on to 5 June 1869. The Gad's Hill Edition (1890) added 'A Fly-Leaf in a Life' (from 22 May 1869) which had belonged to that third batch. There are thus thirty-seven essays. The 1860 volume had no pictures, the 1865 had a frontispiece, by G.J. Pinwell, and the Illustrated Library edition of 1868, four pictures by Pinwell and four by W.M., surmised to be W. Maddox. On the period of *All The Year Round*, see Lynn Pykett, *Charles Dickens: Critical Issues* (London: Macmillan 2002), 156–60. On Dickens' journalism, see John M.L. Drew, *Dickens the Journalist* (London: Palgrave Macmillan 2003); on the text see Philip Drew, 'Dickens and the Real World: A Reading of *The Uncommercial Traveller*', *Essays and Studies* 1985, 66–82; Geoffrey Hemstedt, 'Dickens' Later Journalism' in Kate Campbell (ed.), *Journalism,*

Literature and Modernity: From Hazlitt to Modernism (Edinburgh: Edinburgh University Press 2000).

2. The month after *OMF* appeared saw a second edition of *The Uncommercial Traveller*, succeeding the first of 1860, and supplemented by eleven esssays from 1863. After *OMF*, Dickens' writing was mainly for *All the Year Round*. Christmas numbers appeared in 1862 ('Somebody's Luggage'), 1863–64 ('Mrs Lirriper's Lodgings' and 'Mrs Lirriper's Legacy'), 1865 ('Doctor Marigold's Prescriptions'), 1866 ('Mugby Junction'), 1867 ('No Thoroughfare,' with Wilkie Collins). Eight more essays were included in *The Uncommercial Traveller* in 1875. For Dickens' reading-tours, subsequent to this, see Malcolm Andrews, *Charles Dickens and his Performing Selves: Dickens and the Public* Readings (Oxford: Oxford University Press 2006). Plans for the next – final – novel began in July 1869; its writing that October. Twelve farewell readings took place in London between January and March 1870, before *ED* began appearing for the first of its monthly parts.

3. For the context, see Norris Pope, *Dickens and Charity* (London: Macmillan 1978), 142–51.

4. John Timbs, *Curiosities of London: Exhibiting the Most Rare and Remarkable Objects of Interest in the Metropolis, With Nearly Fifty Years' Personal Recollections* (London: Daniel Bogue 1855), 681. For another reference to Trafalgar Square in Dickens, see *J2* 348.

5. See Kynaston, 287–88; he records that the population of the City in 1871 was 75,000, while 200,000 people worked there.

6. See on 'The City of the Absent', David L. Pike, *Subterranean Cities: The World Beneath Paris and London, 1800–1945* (Ithaca: Cornell University Press 2005), 132–34.

7. George Gissing, *The Immortal Dickens*, 182. I discuss Dickens' interest in the non-human in 'Sameness and Otherness: Versions of Authority in *Hard Times*', *Textus* 19 (2006), 439–60.

8. George Augustus Sala, *Twice Round the Clock: Or, The Hours of the Day and Night in London*, introduction by Philip Collins (Leicester: Leicester University Press 1971). On Sala, see P.D. Edwards, *Dickens' 'Young Men': George Augustus Sala, Edmund Yates, and the World of Victorian Journalism* (Aldershot: Ashgate 1997).

9. The 'drags' recall Esther being taken through London with Inspector Bucket to find Lady Dedlock, and going into the East End, and to a morgue there: 'Against the mouldering wall by which they stood, there was a bill, on which I could discern the words 'FOUND DROWNED'; and this, and an inscription about Drags, possessed me with the awful suspicion shadowed forth in our visit to that place' (*BH* 57). When Lady Dedlock is found, the description evokes drowning: 'I lifted the heavy head, put the long dank hair aside, and turned the face' (*BH* 59). See Ron M. Brown, *The Art of Suicide* (London: Reaktion 2001), 146–93 for representations of women's suicides by drowning.

10. See Philip Collins, *Dickens and Education* (London: Macmillan 1965), 81–83.

11. For garrotting, see Trollope, *Phineas Finn* (1869), chapter 30. For the 1869 Act, see Leon Radzinowicz and Roger Hood, 'Incapacitating the Habitual Criminal: The English Experience', *The Michigan Law Review* 78 (1980), 1305–89.

12. Trey Philpotts in *The Companion to Little Dorrit* (London: Croom Helm 2003), 129–30 says Maggy in *LD* has been to the Children's Hospital at Great Ormond Street, founded by Charles West (1816–98), which opened in 1852. He shows Dickens noting in 'Drooping Buds', *Household Words* 3 April 1852, that whereas

continental cities had children's hospitals, this was the first in England. See also *Speeches* 151–53.

13. See Letter to James and Annie Fields of 16 December 1868. Dickens took the Fields to see the hospital again in 1869, and Annie Fields noted 'Dickens was perfectly at home in this part of London' (quoted, Michael Slater, *J4* 353).

14. F.S. Schwarzbach, *Dickens and the City*, 180 (see 178–84 for an account of *UT*).

15. The Morgue in Paris appears in several illustrations in Harry Stone, *The Night Side of Dickens: Cannibalism, Passion, Necessity* (Columbus: Ohio State University Press 1994), 86–100, see also 564–66. I find Stone's insistence on cannibalism as the guiding trope in Dickens' writing overstated, as well as the attempt to root the cannibalism in feelings towards the mother (106); his approach does not draw on psychoanalytic work on 'cannibalism' nor attitudes to the mother, and he makes Dickens' approach to the Morgue overly aggressive.

16. See the letter to Forster, 6 September 1846, *Letters* 4.619 for this. Philpotts, *The Companion to Little Dorrit*, 348, sees the collection of dead bodies in the Morgue as a version of the novel's intention 'to show people people coming together, in a chance way, as fellow-travellers, and being in the same place, ignorant of one another, as happens in life; and to connect them afterwards, amd to make the waiting for that connection a part of the interest' (from *Letters* 7.692–93). In Part 1, chapter 2, 'Fellow Travellers', the characters are unknown to each other; in Part 2, they know each other but pretend not to, and the dead souls are an addition to this: as if a version of a third meeting. This chance meeting applies, of course, to social existence in London.

17. Compare Collins' use of the 'the terrible dead-house of Paris – the Morgue', *The Woman in White*, ed. John Sutherland (Oxford: Oxford University Press 1996), 639–40. Sutherland's note (701) recalls Collins' visit to the Morgue in 1844, where he saw 'a dead soldier laid out naked . . . like an unsaleable codfish all by himself on the slab'. The difference between Dickens and Collins is in Dickens' 'obscene' against Collins' 'terrible'.

18. The abject is the subject of Julia Kristeva, *Powers of Horror: An Essay on Abjection*, trans. Leon Roudiez (New York: Columbia University Press 1982), 2–4; for Lacan, see the discussion of the gaze in *Four Fundamental Concepts of Psychoanalysis*, trans. Alan Sheridan (Harmondsworth: Penguin 1977), 73.

19. Luke Fildes' engraving for the *Graphic* magazine, in 1869, was 'Houseless and Hungry', revised for the painting, *Applicants for Admission to a Casual Ward*, which uses St Martin-in-the-Fields as background. The picture uses words from Forster's account, 'Dumb, wet, silent horrors! Sphinxes set up against that dead wall, and none likely to be at the pains of solving them until the general overthrow' (*Life* 7.2.576). See E.D.H. Johnson, 'Victorian Artists and the Urban Milieu' in H.J. Dyos and Michael Wolff (eds), *The Victorian City* vol. 2, 2, 459.

20. Thomas de Quincey, *Confessions of an English Opium-Eater*, ed. Grevel Lindop (Oxford: Oxford University Press 1998), 47. See my 'No Thoroughfare: Charting De Quincey's Confessions', in Laurent Bury (ed.), *Confessions of an English Opium-Eater: Thomas De Quincey* (Paris: Ellipses 2003), 59–72.

21. Adrian Poole, 'The Shadow of Lear's "Houseless" in Dickens', *Shakespeare Survey* 53 (2006), 103–13.

22. See Alexander Welsh, *Dickens Redressed: The Art of Bleak House and Hard Times* (New Haven: Yale University Press 2000), 104.

23. Georg Lukács, *The Theory of the Novel*, trans. Anna Bostock (London: Merlin Press 1978), 41.

CHAPTER ELEVEN
'The Scene of My Death': *Our Mutual Friend*

1. *Our Mutual Friend* appeared in twenty parts between May 1864 and November 1865, then in two-volume form. Illustrations were by Marcus Stone (1840–1921), son of Dickens' friend Frank Stone. On *Our Mutual Friend* see Catherine Gallagher, 'The Bioeconomics of *Our Mutual Friend*' in David Simpson (ed.), *Subject to History: Ideology, Class, Gender* (Ithaca: Cornell University Press 1991), 47–64. (Also in that volume, Mary Poovey, 'Domesticity and Class Formation: Chadwick's 1842 *Sanitary Report*, 65–83.) Also on *OMF*, Pamela K. Gilbert, 'Medical Mapping: The Thames, the Body and *Our Mutual Friend*', in William A. Cohen and Ryan Johnson (eds), *Filth: Dirt, Disgust and Modern Life* (Minneapolis: University of Minnesota Press 2005), 78–102.

2. See discussion by Lawrence Frank, *Dickens and the Romantic Self* (Lincoln: University of Nebraska Press 1984), 243–47.

3. David Paroissien (*ED* 313–14) suggests as a possible site Bluegate Fields (by St George's in the East); another possibility is Whitechapel. He notes that Dickens made visits to Shadwell on 31 May 1869, perhaps on consecutive nights (see *Letters* 12.520).

4. Dickens describes Shadwell's docks, and mentions its church, in 'Bound for the Great Salt Lake' (*Uncommercial Traveller*), first published in *All the Year Round* 4 July 1863. The piece, discussing 800 Mormons emigrating, refers to Jews, and Malays, and Chinese in the area.

5. On Ragged Schools, see Philip Collins, *Dickens and Education* (London: Macmillan 1964), 86–93, and Pope, 152–99. Dickens discussed Field Lane Ragged School in 'A Sleep to Startle Us', *Household Words* 13 March 1852, after visiting it first in September 1843 (see *Letters* 3.562–64), again in 1846, which resulted in a letter to the *Daily News* (4 February 1846) – see also letter to Kay-Shuttleworth, 28 March 1846 (*Letters* 4.526). He revisited in November 1849 and February 1852, by which time it was in Farringdon Street.

6. Another view of the river appears in *ED*: Rosa goes up the river from the Temple stairs to dine in 'some everlastingly green garden' (22.247). Luke Fildes (1844–1927)'s illustration shows Putney Church (1836, with a medieval tower), and the old wooden bridge (1729), replaced by Bazalgette's stone bridge in 1884. Tartar, who rows, keeps a yacht at Greenhithe, near Dartford, Kent.

7. The title of a short story by Maurice Blanchot, translated as 'Death Sentence': see *The Blanchot Reader*, ed. George Quasha (Barrytown, NY: Station Hill Press 1999): Blanchot and Derrida have developed much on the double-meaning of life and death. For Derrida on 'life death', see 'Freud and the Scene of Writing' in *Writing and Difference*, trans. Alan Bass (London: Routledge 1977), 203.

8. The wedding at Greenwich must take place at Hawksmoor's St Alfege's church (1719), facing Wren's Greenwich Royal Hospital. Two other Hawksmoor (1661–1736) churches appear in this chapter: one implicitly, St George in the East, off Ratcliff Highway (1729), and St Anne's Limehouse (1730). These churches, and Christ Church Spitalfields (1729), were carved out of the original St Dunstan's parish of Stepney.

9. The interest in the river by moonlight (compare 'Night Walks', *J4* 151) suggests a visual theme taken up by Atkinson Grimshaw (1836–93) in his picture of *Heath Street by Night* (1882) and pictures of the Thames by moonlight: see Alexander Robinson, *Atkinson Grimshaw* (London: Phaidon 1988), 73–103.

10. On the rubbish, see Humphry House, *The Dickens World* (Oxford: Oxford University Press 1942), 166–68, and Michael Cotsell, *The Companion to Our Mutual Friend* (London: Allen and Unwin 1986) 30–34. See the article by R.H. Horne, 'Dust, or Ugliness Redeemed', *Household Words* 1, 13 July 1850, 379–84, on London dustheaps, which contained, primarily, cinders and ashes, and vegetable and animal matter, and bits of metal. All could be reused; the poorest people sorted through these heaps and sold things on: mainly for brick-making. The article discusses the banker's cheque found in a dustheap in 1847, and considers how much previously could be made from buying the dustheaps from the London parishes which accumulated them.

11. Georges Bataille, 'The Use Value of D.A.F. de Sade: An Open Letter to My Current Comrades', *Visions of Excess* 97.

12. On Holloway's history, see Jerry White, *The Worst Street in North London: Campbell Bunk, Islington, Between the Wars* (London: Routledge 1976).

13. If Wilfer's journey seems long, Mayhew and Binny describe walking from Tottenham Court Road, along Euston Road, up Pentonville Road, to the Angel, Islington, and up Upper Street to Highbury Park, before taking an omnibus to the prison at Holloway ('built on a rising ground . . . originally purchased by the City Corporation to be used as a cemetery at the time of the cholera in 1832'). See Henry Mayhew and John Binny, *The Criminal Prisons of London and Scenes of Prison Life* (1862, London: Frank Cass 1968), 533–35.

14. Compare the description of Boz walking in 1836 as far as Copenhagen House, and then down Maiden Lane 'with the intention of passing through the extensive colony lying between it and battle-bridge, which is inhabited by proprietors of donkey-carts, boilers of horseflesh, makers of tiles, and sifters of cinders' (*SB* 207). Copenhagen House, a seventeenth-century house, demolished in 1853, was built for Danish dignitaries, but became a tea-garden and place for radical meetings, and was replaced by the Cattle Market (Caledonian Market) which replaced Smithfield in 1855.

15. See Dominique Laporte, *History of Shit*, trans. Nadia Benabid and Rodolphe El-Khoury (Cambridge, Mass.: MIT Press 2000). See also Jeff Persels and Russell Ganim, *Fecal Matters in Early Modern Literature and Art: Studies in Scatology* (Basingstoke: Ashgate 2004).

16. Jacques-Alain Miller, 'Jeremy Bentham's Panoptic Device', trans. Richard Miller, *October* 41 (1987), 3–29, **7**.

17. The 'lost object' is Lacan's theme in *The Ethics of Psychoanalysis 1959–1960: Seminar 7*, trans. Dennis Porter (London: Routledge 1992), 52. It implies that every search to find something is to retrieve something that has been lost, which is 'always already lost', and unregainable.

18. Alain Corbin, *The Foul and the Fragrant: Odour and the Social Imagination*, trans. M. Koshan (1982, London: Picador 1994), 229.

19. On the narrowness of Chadwick, focusing on filth and water and sewers, in a form of social control that avoided questions of poverty and destitution, see Christopher Hamlin, *Public Health and Social Justice in the Age of Chadwick* (Cambridge: Cambridge University Press 1998). London was excluded from the terms of the Public Health Act; a cholera epidemic followed in 1848–49. Dickens spoke on behalf of the Metropolitan Sanitary Association, 6 February 1850, to create a new movement for action, see *Speeches* 104–10.

20. See Norris Pope, *Dickens and Charity* (London: Macmillan 1978), 200–42. See an article in *Household Words*, 'The Registrar-General on "Life" in London', 29 June

1850, 330–32. Examining the 1841 census figures, and considering that a thousand die each week in London, it records which parishes are healthiest, thinking about density of population per acre in each, access to good water, and freedom from flooding, and relation to cholera. Most healthy is Lewisham, including 'the hamlet of Sydenham'. Then, in descending order: St George's, Hanover Square, Hampstead, Hackney, Camberwell, Wandsworth, 'Merry Islington', Kensington (including Chelsea, Brompton, Hammersmith and Fulham), the City around Mansion House, St James, St Pancras, Marylebone, Newington, Lambeth, Greenwich and St Martin-in-the-Fields, which is criticised for having no rural character; 'Trafalgar Square, with its fountains, is almost its only enjoyable open space'. Then comes Stepney. Below the limits come: Clerkenwell, Bethnal Green, Strand, Shoreditch, Westminster, Bermondsey, Rotherhithe, St Giles', St George's (Southwark), the two parts of the City, to the East (round the Fleet area) and the West (Leadenhall Street), Holborn, St George's in the East, St Saviour's and St Olaves', St Luke's and, last, Whitechapel. The variants from the present will be noticed; also how London divided into local communities, and the greater extent of population in the centre, and the intense interest in being above the water-level.

21. See David S. Barnes, 'Confronting Sensory Crisis in the Great Stinks of London and Paris', in Cohen and Johnson (eds), *Filth*, 103–129.

22. See Donald Reid, *Paris Sewers and Sewermen: Realities and Representations* (Cambridge, Mass.: Harvard University Press 1991), 74–77, 95–106.

23. David Trotter, *Cooking with Mud: The Idea of Mess in Nineteenth-Century Art and Fiction* (Oxford: Oxford University Press 2000), 20–21. Trotter uses Ruskin's comparison of Giorgione and Turner in 'The Two Boyhoods', *Modern Painters* 5.9. Turner was born in Maiden Lane, Covent Garden, so he painted litter as if it were like that in Covent Garden, and ugliness: 'Dead brick walls, blank square windows, old clothes, market-womanly types of humanity – anything fishy and muddy, like Billingsgate or Hungerford Market, had attraction for him; black barges, patched sails, and every possible condition of fog', and 'that mysterious forest [of ships] below London Bridge' (*Modern Painters* 5, (1860, London: George Allen 1997), 317–19).

24. In *Bohemian Paris*, Jerrold Seigel refers to Alexandre Privat d'Anglemont (1815–59)'s *Paris inconnu* (1861) which discusses those who live in Paris like the peasant gleaners of fields; the rag-pickers. See *Bohemian Paris: Culture, Politics and the Boundaries of Bourgeois Life, 1830–1930* (Harmondsworth: Penguin 1986), 140–42.

25. Benjamin, *Charles Baudelaire: A Lyric Poet in the Age of High Capitalism*, trans. Harry Zohn (London: New Left Books 1973), 79–80.

26. See Irving Wohlfarth, 'Et Cetera? The Historian as Chiffonier', *New German Critique* 39 (1986), 142–68.

27. *Pictures from Italy* 383. See Marcus Stone's Chiffonier for the 1862 Library Edition of *PI*, Everyman 505.

28. J. Hillis Miller, *Charles Dickens: The World of his Novels* 316.

29. Quoted, Michael Cotsell, *The Companion to Our Mutual Friend* (London: Allen and Unwin 1986), 207. For Merryweather, see Wilfred P. Dvorak, 'Charles Dickens' *Our Mutual Friend* and Frederick Somner Merryweather's *Lives and Anecdotes of Misers*', *Dickens Studies Annual* 9 (1981), 117–41.

30. Dickens, 'National Portraits', *All the Year Round*, 7 November 1863, 252–56, **253**.

31. Freud, 'On Narcissism: An Introduction', *The Penguin Freud vol. 11: On Metapsychology* (Harmondsworth: Penguin 1977), 83.

32. Walter Benjamin, 'Critique of Violence', *One Way Street and Other Writings*, trans. Edmund Jephcott and Kingsley Shorter (London: Verso 1979), 136.

33. This doubling, which means there is something 'mutually' present in two men, is the subject of J. Hillis Miller, 'The Topography of Jealousy in *Our Mutual Friend*', in John Schad (ed.), *Dickens Refigured: Bodies, Desires and Other Histories* (Manchester: Manchester University Press 1996), 218–35.

34. Michel Foucault, *The History of Sexuality*, trans. Richard Hurley (Harmondsworth: Penguin 1978), 43.

35. See Lacan, discussing 'transitivism': 'A child who beats another child says that he himself was beaten; a child who sees another child fall, cries' – 'Aggressiveness in Psychoanalysis', *Ecrits*, trans. Bruce Fink (New York: W.W. Norton 2002), 92.

CHAPTER TWELVE
Dickens and Gissing

1. George Gissing, *The Immortal Dickens* (London: Cecil Palmer 1925), 9–10.

2. Quotations from Gissing come from: *Demos: A Story of English Socialism* (London: Smith, Elder and Co. 1888), *Thyrza: A Tale*, ed. Jakob Borg (Brighton: Harvester Press 1974), *The Nether World*, ed. Stephen Gill (Oxford: Oxford University Press 1992), *New Grub Street*, ed. Bernard Bergonzi (Harmondsworth: Penguin 1968), *The Odd Women*, with introduction by Elaine Showalter (Harmondsworth: Penguin 1993), *In the Year of Jubilee*, ed. Paul Delany and John Paul Henry (London: Everyman 1994), *The Whirlpool*, ed. William Greenslade (London: Everyman 1997), *Will Warburton*, ed. John Halperin (London: Chatto and Windus 1985), *The Private Papers of Henry Ryecraft*, ed. Mark Storey (Oxford: Oxford University Press 1987).

3. See Eric de Maré, *Victorian London Revealed: Gustave Doré's Metropolis* (1973: Harmondsworth: Penguin 2001), for a classic 'celebration' of Victorian London.

4. *The Great World of London*, another serialisation, appeared in 1856, and was developed and reprinted as another volume, *The Criminal Prisons of London*, which appeared in 1862. In 1861 *London Labour and the London Poor* was reissued in three volumes, with a fourth added in 1862, discussing prostitutes (often needle-workers who needed to supplement their income) and crime, much of it not written by Mayhew. Writings in the *Morning Chronicle* have been edited in E.P. Thompson and Eileen Yeo, *The Unknown Mayhew: Selections from the Morning Chronicle, 1849–1850* (Hamondsworth: Penguin 1973). Bertrand Taithe, *The Essential Mayhew: Representing and Communicating the Poor* (London: Rivers Oram Press 1996) presents the public correspondence on and in the journal *London Life and the London Poor* (1851–52), revealing how Mayhew was attempting a scientific sociology. Peter Quennell edited *London's Underworld* from volume 4 of *London Labour and the London Poor* (1862) (London: Spring Books 1950), and *Mayhew's London* from volumes 1 to 3 in 1951, and also *Mayhew's Characters* (further selections from 1 to 3, in 1951). *London Labour and the London Poor* was reprinted in four volumes (London: Frank Cass 1967), and *The Criminal Prisons of London* (co-written with John Binny) in 1968. See Victor Neuburg (ed.), *London Labour and the London Poor* (Harmondsworth: Penguin 1985) for selections from the four volumes. On Mayhew, see Anne Humpherys, *Travels into the Poor Man's Country: The Work of Henry Mayhew* (Athens: University of Georgia Press 1977).

5. John Thomson, *Victorian London Street Life in Historic Photographs* (New York: Dover Publications 1994), 15–19 for Lambeth flooding.

6. On casual labour in London, see Gareth Stedman-Jones, *Outcast London: A Study in the Relationships between Classes in Victorian Society* (1971: Harmondsworth: Penguin 1984): this makes frequent use of Mayhew.

7. On prostitution, see Kellow Chesney, *The Victorian Underworld* (Harmondsworth: Penguin 1972), 363–433. Chesney discusses the Contagious Diseases Act, passed in 1869, repealed in 1883, which made prostitutes liable to be stopped and inspected for evidence of sexually acquired diseases. Bracebridge Hemyng, collaborating with Mayhew on *London Life and the London Poor* vol. 4, and discussing prostitution, (Neuburg 473–91) is responsible for the figure of 80,000.

8. On Mayhew and Betty Higden and Gaffer Hexam in *Our Mutual Friend*, see Harland S. Nelson, 'Dickens's "Our Mutual Friend" and Henry Mayhew's "London Labour and the London Poor"', *Nineteenth-Century Fiction* 20 (1965), 207–22. Neuburg, 209–49, reprints Mayhew's vol. 2 interviews with mudlarks and dustmen. Also see Brian Maidment, *Dusty Bob: A Cultural History of Dustmen, 1780–1870* (Manchester: Manchester University Press 2007): this also discusses *Our Mutual Friend*.

9. Gissing, *The Immortal Dickens*, 7. Gissing brought out *Charles Dickens: A Critical Study* in 1898 (London: Blackie 1929), and followed it with introductions to an edition of Dickens: those nine extant became *The Immortal Dickens*. For Gissing on Dickens, see John Goode, *George Gissing: Ideology and Fiction* (London: Vision Press 1978), 13–40; Simon J. James, *Unsettled Accounts: Money and Narrative in the Novels of George Gissing* (London: Anthem Press 2003), 36–62; Barbara Rawlinson, *A Man of Many Parts: Gissing's Short Stories, Essays and Other Works* (Amsterdam: Rodopi 2006), 193–211; Michael Cronin, 'Gissing's Criticism of Dickens', in Bouve Postmus (ed.), *A Garland for Gissing* (Amsterdam: Rodopi 2001), 23–32. Other accounts of Gissing appear in Martin Ryle and Jenny Bourne Taylor (eds), *George Gissing: Voices of the Unclassed* (Aldershot: Ashgate 2005); a good earlier critique is Gillian Tindall, *The Born Exile: George Gissing* (London: Temple Smith 1974).

10. Gissing, *The Private Papers of Henry Ryecraft*, ed. Mark Storey (Oxford: Oxford University Press 1987), 21.

11. Quotations from *George Gissing: Collected Letters* 9 vols, ed. Paul F. Matthiesen, Arthur C. Young and Pierre Coustillas (Athens: Ohio University Press 1990–97), 2.54 and 2.279.

12. George Gissing, *The Nether World*, ed. Stephen Gill (Oxford: Oxford University Press 1992), 106.

13. 'It is a familiar fact that many of [Gissing's] best descriptions are actuated by dislike. Morley Roberts has given us his memories of Gissing's experiences in writing the Crystal Palace chapter in *The Nether World*. He states that Gissing spent a bank holiday there for the express purpose of writing this chapter and arrived home tired, worn out and disgusted with all that he had seen'. Samuel Vogt Gap, 'Influence of the Classics on Gissing's Novels of Modern Life' in Pierre Coustillas (ed.), *Collected Articles on George Gissing* (London: Frank Cass 1968), 88–89.

14. Gissing to Morley Roberts, 10 February 1895, quoted, Pierre Coustillas and Colin Partridge (eds), *Gissing: The Critical Heritage* (London: Routledge and Kegan Paul 1972), 244.

15. George Gissing, *Selections Autobiographical and Imaginative from the Works of George Gissing, With Biographical and Critical Notes by his Son* (London: Jonathan Cape 1929), 54–58.

16. John Ruskin, 'Fors Clavigera', *Collected Works of John Ruskin*, 39 vols, ed. E.T. Cook and Alexander Wedderburn (London: George Allen 1904), 29.160.

17. Quoted, Adrian Poole, *Gissing in Context* (London: Macmillan 1995), 51. Whistler's painting was the *Nocturne in Black and Gold: The Falling Rocket*, derived from fireworks at the Cremorne Gardens. These pleasure gardens, at the west end of Cheyne Walk, now covered by Lots Road power station, were open between 1832 and 1877. Ruskin's critique was probably related to Cremorne Gardens' night-time reputation: earlier in the century, Chelsea had been far enough away from respectable London for this not to matter, but now no longer. See Whistler's depictions of Battersea and Chelsea, and Cremorne Gardens, and of Wapping, Rotherhithe and of Black Lion Wharf (1859) – the latter virtually a view from Mrs Clennam's back-window: see Richard Dorment and Margaret F. MacDonald, *James McNeill Whistler*, 98–108, 120–39, 238–40.

18. Alan Bowness, *The Impressionists in London* (London: Hayward Gallery Exhibition Catalogue, Arts Council, 1973); for Pissarro's interest in cityscapes in France, see Richard R. Brettel and Joachim Pissarro, *The Impressionist and the City: Pissarro's Series Paintings* (London: Royal Academy of Arts Exhibition Catalogue, 1993).

19. H.J. Dyos, *A Victorian Suburb: A Study of the Growth of Camberwell* (Leicester: Leicester University Press 1961), 192.

CONCLUSION
No Thoroughfare

1. On the European dimensions of Dickens, see Donald Fanger, *Dostoyevsky and Romantic Realism: A Study of Dostoyevsky in Relation to Balzac, Dickens and Gogol* (Cambridge, Mass.: Harvard University Press 1965), and Robert Alter, *Imagined Cities: Urban Experience and the Language of the Novel* (New Haven: Yale University Press 2005).

2. Freud, Sigmund, 'Beyond the Pleasure Principle', in *On Metapsychology: The Penguin Freud 11*, ed. Angela Richards (Harmondsworth: Penguin 1977), 292.

3. Michel de Certeau, *The Practice of Everyday Life*, trans. Steven Rendall (Berkeley: University of California Press 1984), 108.

4. Theodor Adorno, *Minima Moralia*, trans. E.F.N. Jephcott (London: Verso 1974), 49.

5. See Deborah Thomas, *Dickens and the Short Story* (London, Batsford 1982) for Dickens' collaborations, for instance with Collins.

6. See Ned Lukacher, *Primal Scenes: Literature, Philosophy, Psychoanaysis* (Ithaca: Cornell University Press 1988), 275–331: a section on 'Benjamin, Dickens, Freud' has a fine analysis of the meaning of 'No Thoroughfare', which he contrasts with the title of Benjamin's *Arcades* project, the *Passagen-Werk*.

BIBLIOGRAPHY

Ackroyd, Peter, *London: The Biography* (London: Chatto and Windus), 2000.

_____, *Thames, Sacred River* (London: Chatto and Windus 2007).

Adorno, Theodor, *Minima Moralia*. Trans. E.F.N. Jephcott (London: Verso 1974).

Ainsworth, W.H., *The Tower of London* (1840: London: Everyman 1909).

Alber, Jan, *Narrating the Prison: Role and Representation in Charles Dickens' Novels, Twentieth-Century Fiction and Film* (New York: Cambria Press 2007).

_____, (ed.) *Stones of Law: Bricks of Shame* (Toronto: University of Toronto Press 2008).

Allen, Michael, *Charles Dickens' Childhood* (London: Macmillan 1988).

Alter, Robert, *Imagined Cities: Urban Experience and the Language of the Novel* (New Haven: Yale University Press 2005).

Altick, Robert, *The Shows of London* (Cambridge, Mass.: Harvard University Press 1978).

_____, *The Presence of the Present: Topics of the Day in the Victorian Novel* (Columbus, Ohio: Ohio State University Press 1991).

Andrews, Jonathan, Asa Briggs, Roy Porter, Penny Tucker and Keir Waddington, *The History of Bethlem* (London: Routledge 1997).

Andrews, Malcolm, *Dickens and the Grown-up Child* (London: Macmillan 1994).

_____, *Charles Dickens and his Performing Selves: Dickens and the Public Readings* (Oxford: Oxford University Press 2006).

Arac, Jonathan, *Commissioned Spirits: The Shaping of Social Motion in Dickens, Carlyle, Melville, and Hawthorne* (New Brunswick, NJ: Rutgers University Press 1979).

Arnold, Dana, *Re-Presenting the Metropolis: Architecture, Urban Experience and Social Life in London 1800–1940* (Aldershot: Ashgate 2000).

Ashton, Rosemary, *142 Strand: A Radical Address in London* (London: Chatto and Windus 2006).

Auerbach, Erich, *Scenes from the Drama of European Literature: Six Essays* (New York: Meridian 1949).

Bagehot, Walter, 'Charles Dickens', *National Review*, 7 October 1858, 458–86.

Barker, T.C., 'Urban Transport' in Michael J. Freeman and Derek H. Aldcroft (eds), *Transport in Victorian Britain* (Manchester: Manchester University Press 1988), 134–70.

Barloon, Jim, 'The Black Hole of London: Rescuing Oliver Twist', *Dickens Studies Annual* 28 (1999), 1–12.

Barnes, David S., 'Confronting Sensory Crisis in the Great Stinks of London and Paris', in William A. Cohen and Ryan Johnson (eds), *Filth: Dirt, Disgust and Modern Life* (Minneapolis: University of Minnesota Press 2005), 103–29.

Bataille, Georges, 'The Use Value of D.A.F. de Sade: An Open Letter to My Current Comrades', *Visions of Excess: Selected Writings, 1927–1939* (Minneapolis: University of Minnesota Press 1985).

Barton, Anne, *Ben Jonson, Dramatist* (Cambridge: Cambridge University Press 1984).

Baudelaire, Charles, *Les Fleurs du Mal et autres poèmes*, ed. Henri Lemaître (Paris: Garnier-Flammarion 1964).

_____, *My Heart Laid Bare and Other Prose Writings*, trans. Norman Cameron (London: Soho Book Company 1986).

Baumgarten, Murray, 'Railway/Reading/Time: *Dombey and Son* and the Industrial World', *Dickens Studies Annual* (1990), 65–89.

Benjamin, Walter, *Charles Baudelaire: A Lyric Poet in the Age of High Capitalism*, trans. Harry Zohn (London: New Left Books 1973).

_____, *The Origin of German Tragic Drama*, trans. John Osborne (London: Verso 1977).

_____, 'Critique of Violence', *One Way Street and Other Writings*, trans. Edmund Jephcott and Kingsley Shorter (London: Verso 1979).

_____, *The Arcades Project*, trans. Howard Eiland and Kevin McLaughlin (Cambridge, Mass.: Harvard University Press 1999).

Bennett, Jennifer, 'The London Democratic Association 1837–1841: A Study in London Radicalism', in James Epstein and Dorothy Thompson (eds), *The Chartist Experience: Studies in Working Class Radicalism and Culture, 1830–1860* (London: Macmillan 1982), 87–119.

Bentley, G.E., Jr, *The Stranger from Paradise: A Biography of William Blake* (New Haven: Yale University Press 2001).

Bergler, Edmund, '*Little Dorrit* and Dickens's Intuitive Knowledge of Psychic Masochism', *American Imago* 14 (1957), 371–88.

Besant, Sir Walter and G.E. Mitton, *East London* (London: Chatto and Windus 1901).

_____, *The Fascination of London: Holborn and Bloomsbury* (London: Adam and Charles Black 1903).

Binny, John and Henry Mayhew, *The Criminal Prisons of London and Scenes of Prison Life* (1862: London: Frank Cass 1968).

Blake, William, *Complete Writings*, ed. Geoffrey Keynes (Oxford: Oxford University Press 1966).

Blanchot, Maurice, 'The Essential Solitude', trans. Lydia Davis in *The Gaze of Orpheus and Other Literary Essays* (Barrytown, NY: Station Hill Press 1981).

Bloom, Harold (ed.) *The Literary Criticism of John Ruskin* (New York: Doubleday 1965).

Bonheim, Helmut, 'The Principle of Cyclicity in Charles Dickens' 'The Signalman', in Michael Hollington (ed.), *Charles Dickens: Critical Assessments* (London: Helm Information 1995), vol. 3, 811–21.

Bourne, John Cooke, *Drawings of the London and Birmingham Railway with History and Description by John Britton* (London: J.C. Bourne 1839).

Bowness, Alan, *The Impressionists in London* (London: Hayward Gallery Exhibition Catalogue, Arts Council 1973).

Brant, Clare and Susan E. Whyman, *Walking the Streets of Eighteenth-Century London: John Gay's Trivia (1716)* (Oxford: Oxford University Press 2007).

Brantlinger, Patrick, *The Spirit of Reform: British Literature and Politics 1832–1867* (Cambridge, Mass.: Harvard University Press 1977).

Brettel, Richard R. and Joachim Pissarro, *The Impressionist and the City: Pissarro's Series Paintings* (London: Royal Academy of Arts Exhibition Catalogue 1993).

Brice, A.W.C. and K.J. Fielding, 'Dickens and the Tooting Disaster', *Victorian Studies* 12 (1968), 235–39.

_____, '*Bleak House* and the Graveyard' in Robert B. Partlow, Jr, *Dickens the Craftsman: Strategies of Presentation* (Carbondale: Southern Illinois University Press 1970), 117–39.

Briggs, Asa, *Victorian* Cities (London: Harmondsworth 1963).

Brown, Norman O., *Life Against Death: The Psychoanalytic Meaning of History* (London: Routledge 1959).

Brown, Ron M., *The Art of Suicide* (London: Reaktion 2001).

Buckley, Jerome H., '"Quoth the Raven": The Role of Grip in *Barnaby Rudge*', *Dickens Studies Annual* 21 (1992), 27–35, **35**.

Buck-Morss, Susan, *The Dialectics of Seeing: Walter Benjamin and the Arcades Project* (Cambridge, Mass.: MIT Press 1991).

Bulwer, Edward (Lord Lytton), *Eugene Aram* (1832: London: Collins n.d.).

Butlin, Martin and Andrew Wilton, *Turner 1775–1851* (London: Tate Gallery 1974).

Butt, John and Kathleen Tillotson, *Dickens at Work* (London: Methuen 1957).

Byrne, Andrew, *London's Georgian Houses* (London: The Georgian Press 1986).

Cannadine, David and David Reeder, *Exploring the Urban Past: Essays In Urban History by H.J. Dyos* (Cambridge: Cambridge University Press 1982).

Carlton, W.J., 'The Third Man at Newgate', *The Review of English Studies* 8 (1957), 406.

Carlyle, Thomas, *Selected Writings*, ed. Alan Shelston (Harmondsworth: Penguin 1971).

Caruth, Cathy, *Unclaimed Experience: Trauma, Narrative and History* (Baltimore: Johns Hopkins University Press 1996).

Chancellor, E. Beresford, *The London of Thackeray* (London: Grant Richards 1923).

_____, *The London of Charles Dickens* (New York: George H. Doran Co. 1924).

_____, *The Romance of Soho* (London: Country Life Co. 1931).

Chandler, James and Kevin Gilmartin (eds), *Romantic Metropolis: The Urban Scene of British Culture, 1780–1840* (Cambridge: Cambridge University Press 2005).

Charlton, John (ed.), *The Tower of London: Its Buildings and Institutions* (London: Department of the Environment, HMSO 1978).

Chesney, Kellow, *The Victorian Underworld* (Harmondsworth: Penguin 1972).

Chittick, Kathyrn, *Dickens and the 1830s* (Cambridge: Cambridge University Press 1990).

Clark, Kenneth (ed.), *Ruskin Today* (Harmondsworth: Penguin 1964).

Clark, T.J., *The Painting of Modern Life: Paris in the Art of Manet and his Followers*, (London: Thames and Hudson 1984).

Cocks, H.G., *Nameless Offences: Homosexual Desire in the Nineteenth Century* (London: I.B. Tauris 2003).

Coleman, Terry, *The Railway Navvies* (Harmondsworth: Penguin 1968).

Collins, Philip, *Dickens and Crime* (London: Macmillan 1962).

_____, *Dickens and Education* (London: Macmillan 1965).

Collins, Wilkie, *The Woman in White*, ed. John Sutherland (Oxford: Oxford University Press 1996).

Corbin, Alain, *The Foul and the Fragrant: Odour and the Social Imagination*, trans. M. Koshan (1982) (London: Picador 1994).

Cotsell, Michael, *The Companion to Our Mutual Friend* (London: Allen and Unwin 1986).

Coustillas, Pierre and Colin Partridge (eds), *Gissing: The Critical Heritage* (London: Routledge and Kegan Paul 1972).

Crary, Jonathan, *Techniques of the Observer: On Vision and Modernity in the 19th Century* (Cambridge, Mass.: MIT Press 1990).

Cronin, Michael, 'Gissing's Criticism of Dickens', in Bouve Postmus (ed.), *A Garland for Gissing* (Amsterdam: Rodopi 2001), 23–32.

Daleski, H.M., *Dickens and the Art of Analogy* (London: Faber 1970).

Dart, Gregory, '"Flash Style": Pierce Egan and Literary London 1820–1828', *History Workshop Journal* 51 (2001), 181–205.

De Certeau, Michel, *The Practice of Everyday Life*, trans. Steven Rendall (Berkeley: University of California Press 1984).

Defoe, Daniel, *A Tour Through the Whole Island of Great Britain*. (1724–26: Harmondsworth: Penguin 1971).

_____, *Journal of the Plague Year*, ed. Paula R. Backscheider (New York: W.W. Norton 1992).

De Quincey, Thomas, *Confessions of an English Opium-Eater*, ed. Grevel Lindop (Oxford: Oxford University Press 1998).

_____, 'On Murder Considered as One of the Fine Arts', *The Works of Thomas de Quincey*, vol. 6, ed. David Groves and Grevel Lindop (London: Pickering and Chatto 2000).

Derrida, Jacques, *Archive Fever: A Freudian Impression*, trans. Eric Prenowitz (Chicago: University of Chicago Press, 1995).

_____, 'Freud and the Scene of Writing' in *Writing and Difference*, trans. Alan Bass (London: Routledge 1977).

_____, 'Before the Law' in *Acts of Literature*, ed. Derek Attridge (London: Routledge 1992), 181–211.

DeVries, Duane, *Dickens' Apprentice Years: The Making of a Novelist* (Brighton: Harvester Press 1976).

Dexter, Walter, *The London of Dickens* (New York: E.P. Dutton 1923).

Dickens, Charles, *Barnaby Rudge*, ed. Gordon Spence (Harmondsworth: Penguin 1986).

_____, *Barnaby Rudge*, ed. Jon Mee (Oxford University Press 2003).

_____, *Dombey and Son*, ed. Alan Horsman and Dennis Walder (Oxford: Oxford University Press 2001).

_____, *Little Dorrit*, ed. John Holloway (Harmondsworth: Penguin 1967).

_____, *Little Dorrit*, ed. Angus Easson (London: Everyman 1999).

_____, *The Old Curiosity Shop*, ed. Elizabeth M. Brennan (Oxford: Oxford University Press 1998).

_____, *The Old Curiosity Shop*, ed. Malcolm Andrews and Angus Easson (Harmondsworth: Penguin 1972).

_____, *Oliver Twist*, ed. Kathleen Tillotson and Stephen Gill (Oxford: Oxford University Press 1999).

_____, *Our Mutual Friend*, ed. Stephen Gill (Harmondsworth: Penguin 1971).

_____, *The Pickwick Papers*, ed. Robert L. Patten (Harmondsworth: Penguin 1971).

_____, *The Pickwick Papers*, ed. James Kinsley (Oxford: Clarendon Press 1986).

Disraeli, B., *Tancred, Or The New Crusade* (1847: London: Bodley Head 1905).

Dorment, Richard, and Margaret F. MacDonald, *James McNeill Whistler* (London: Tate Gallery 1994).

Dostoyevksy, Fyodor, *Crime and Punishment*, trans. David Magarshack (Harmondsworth: Penguin 1966).

_____, *The Idiot*, trans. Alan Myers, introduction by W.J. Leatherbarrow (Oxford: Oxford University Press 1992).

Drew, John M.L., *Dickens the Journalist* (London: Palgrave Macmillan 2003).

Drew, Philip, 'Dickens and the Real World: A Reading of *The Uncommercial Traveller*', *Essays and Studies*, 1985, 66–82.

Dudgeon, Piers, *Dickens' London* (London: Headline 1987).

Dvorak, Wilfred P., 'Charles Dickens' *Our Mutual Friend* and Frederick Somner Merryweather's *Lives and Anecdotes of Misers*', *Dickens Studies Annual* 9 (1981), 117–41.

Dyos, H.J., *A Victorian Suburb: A Study of the Growth of Camberwell* (Leicester: Leicester University Press 1961).

Dyos, H.J., and Michael Wolff (eds), *The Victorian City: Images and Realities* (London: Routledge and Kegan Paul), 2 vols, 1973.

Edwards, P.D., *Dickens' 'Young Men': George Augustus Sala, Edmund Yates, and the World of Victorian Journalism* (Aldershot: Ashgate 1997).

Eigner, Edwin M., *The Dickens Pantomime* (Berkeley: University of California Press 1989).

Elden, Stuart, *Understanding Henri Lefebvre: Theory and the Possible* (London: Continuum 2004).

Ellis, Hamilton, *British Railway History*, 2 vols, 1830–1876 and 1877–1947 (London: George Allen and Unwin 1954).

Engels, Friedrich, *The Condition of the Working Class in England*, ed. Victor Kiernan (Harmondsworth: Penguin 2005).

Fanger, Donald, *Dostoyevsky and Romantic Realism: A Study of Dostoyevsky in Relation to Balzac, Dickens and Gogol* (Cambridge, Mass.: Harvard University Press 1965).

Farrington, Anthony, *Trading Places: The East India Company and Asia 1600–1834* (London: The British Library 2002).

Fawcett, Jane, Jennifer Freeman and David Lloyd, *Save the City: A Conservation Study of the City of London* (London: Society for the Protection of Ancient Buildings 1984).

Finn, Margot, 'Being in Debt in Dickens' London: Fact, Fictional Representation and the Nineteenth Century Prison', *Journal of Victorian Culture*, vols 1 and 2, 1996–97, 203–26.

Fishman, W.J., *East End 1888: A Year in a London Borough Among the Labouring Poor* (London: Duckworth 1988).

Fleishman, Avron, *The English Historical Novel: Walter Scott to Virginia Woolf* (Baltimore: Johns Hopkins University Press 1971).

Forster, John, *The Life of Charles Dickens*, ed. J.W.T. Ley (London: Cecil Palmer 1928).

Foucault, Michel, *The History of Sexuality*, trans. Richard Hurley (Harmondsworth: Penguin 1978).

_____, *Discipline and Punish: The Birth of the Prison*, trans. Alan Sheridan (Harmondsworth: Penguin 1979).

_____, 'Of Other Spaces' in *Aesthetics: Method, and Epistemology*, ed. James Faubion, trans. Robert Hurley (Harmondsworth: Penguin 2000), 175–85.

Fox, Celina (ed.), *London – World City 1800–1840* (New Haven: Yale University Press 1992).

Frank, Lawrence, *Dickens and the Romantic Self* (Lincoln: University of Nebraska Press 1984), 243–47.

Freeman, Michael, *Railways and the Victorian Imagination* (New Haven: Yale University Press 1999).

Freud, Sigmund, 'Beyond the Pleasure Principle', *On Metapsychology: The Penguin Freud 11* (Harmondsworth: Penguin 1977), 292.

_____, 'On Narcissism: An Introduction', ibid.

_____, 'From the History of an Infantile Neurosis', *Case Histories II: The Penguin Freud 9* (Harmondsworth: Penguin 1979).

_____, 'Moses and Monotheism', *The Origins of Religion: The Penguin Freud 13* (Harmondsworth: Penguin 1985).

_____, 'Civilization and Its Discontents', *Civilization, Society and Religion: The Penguin Freud 12* (Harmondsworth: Penguin 1985).

Fried, Albert, and Richard M. Elman (eds), *Charles Booth's London: A Portrait of the Poor at the Turn of the Century, Drawn from his Life and Labour of the People in London* (London: Hutchinson 1969).

Gallagher, Catherine, 'The Bioeconomics of "Our Mutual Friend"' in David Simpson (ed.), *Subject to History: Ideology, Class, Gender* (Ithaca: Cornell University Press 1991), 47–64.

Ganim, Russell and Jeff Persels, *Fecal Matters in Early Modern Literature and Art: Studies in Scatology* (Basingstoke: Ashgate 2004).

Gap, Samuel Vogt, 'Influence of the Classics on Gissing's Novels of Modern Life' in Pierre Coustillas (ed.), *Collected Articles on George Gissing* (London: Frank Cass 1968), 88–89.

Garside, Patricia L. and Ken Young, *Metropolitan London: Politics and Urban Change 1837–1881* (London: Edward Arnold 1982).

Gay, John, *The Beggar's Opera*, ed. Bryan Loughrey and T.O. Treadwell (Harmondsworth: Penguin 1986).

Geist, Johann Friedrich, *Arcades: The History of a Building Type* (Cambridge, Mass.: MIT Press 1983).

George, Dorothy, *London Life in the Eighteenth Century* (1925: Harmondsworth: Penguin 1966).

Gibson III, Edward H., 'Baths and Washhouses in the English Public Health Agitation 1839–1848', *Journal of the History of Medicine* 1954, 391–406.

Gibson, Walter S., *Bruegel* (London: Thames and Hudson 1977).

Gilbert, Pamela K., 'Medical Mapping: The Thames, the Body and *Our Mutual Friend*', in William A. Cohen and Ryan Johnson (eds), *Filth: Dirt, Disgust and Modern Life* (Minneapolis: University of Minnesota Press 2005), 78–102.

Gill, Stephen, *William Wordsworth: A Life* (Oxford: Oxford University Press 1989).

Gissing, George, *Demos: A Story of English Socialism* (London: Smith, Elder and Co. 1888).

_____, *The Immortal Dickens* (London: Cecil Palmer, 1925).

_____, *Charles Dickens: A Critical Study* (1898: London: Blackie 1929).

_____, *Selections Autobiographical and Imaginative from the Works of George Gissing, With Biographical and Critical Notes by his Son* (London: Jonathan Cape 1929), 54–58.

_____, *New Grub Street*, ed. Bernard Bergonzi (Harmondsworth: Penguin 1968).

_____, *Thyrza: A Tale*, ed. Jakob Borg (Brighton: Harvester Press 1974).

_____, *Will Warburton*, ed. John Halperin (London: Chatto and Windus 1985).

_____, *The Private Papers of Henry Ryecroft*, ed. Mark Storey (Oxford: Oxford University Press 1987).

_____, *The Nether World*, ed. Stephen Gill (Oxford: Oxford University Press 1992).

_____, *The Odd Women* (Harmondsworth: Penguin 1993).

_____, *In the Year of Jubilee*, ed. Paul Delany and John Paul Henry (London: Everyman 1994).

_____, *The Whirlpool*, ed. William Greenslade (London: Everyman 1997).

_____, *George Gissing: Collected Letters*, 9 vols, ed. Paul F. Matthiesen, Arthur C. Young and Pierre Coustillas (Athens: Ohio University Press 1990–97).

Goode, John, *George Gissing: Ideology and Fiction* (London: Vision Press 1978).

Goodman, Andrew, *The Walking Guide to Lawyers' London* (London: Blackstone Press 2000).

Greenblatt, Stephen (ed.), *The Norton Shakespeare: Based on the Oxford Edition* (W.W. Norton & Co. 1997).

Hamlin, Christopher, *Public Health and Social Justice in the Age of Chadwick: Britain 1800–1854* (Cambridge: Cambridge University Press 1998).

Harben, Henry, *A Dictionary of London: Being Notes Topographical and Historical Relating to the Streets and Principal Buildings in the City of London* (London: H. Jenkins 1918).

Hazlitt, William, *Lectures on the English Poets* (London: Everyman 1910).

Hebbert, Michael, *London: More by Fortune than Design* (Chichester: John Wiley 1998).

Hemstedt, Geoffrey, 'Dickens' Later Journalism' in Kate Campbell (ed.), *Journalism, Literature and Modernity: From Hazlitt to Modernism* (Edinburgh: Edinburgh University Press 2000).

Herbert, Christopher, 'Rat Worship in Taboo in Mayhew's London', *Representations* 23, 1–24, 1988.

Herbert, Robert L., *Impressionism: Art, Leisure and Parisian Society* (New Haven: Yale University Press 1988).

Heren, Louis, *Growing Up Poor in London* (London: Hamilton 1973).

Hervey, John, *Victorian Novelists and their Illustrators* (London: Sidgwick and Jackson 1970).

Holbrook, David, *Charles Dickens and the Image of Women* (New York: New York University Press 1993).

Hollington, Michael, *Dickens and the Grotesque* (London: Croom Helm 1984).

_____, *Charles Dickens: Critical Assessments* (London: Croom Helm 1995).

Horne, R.H., 'Dust, or Ugliness Redeemed' *(Household Words* 1, 13 July 1850, 379–84) (Athens: University of Georgia Press 1977).

House, Humphry, *The Dickens World* (Oxford: Oxford University Press 1942).

Hutchinson, Thomas (ed.), *The Works in Prose and Verse of Charles and Mary Lamb* 2 vols (Oxford: Oxford University Press 1908).

Huysmans, J.-K. *Against Nature,* trans. Robert Baldick (Harmondsworth: Penguin 1959).

Jackson, Peter, *George Scharf's London: Sketches and Watercolours of a Changing City, 1820–1850* (London: John Murray 1987).

Jacobson, Wendy, *The Companion to 'The Mystery of Edwin Drood'* (London: Allen and Unwin 1986).

James, Henry, *Autobiography; A Small Boy and Others, Notes of a Son and Brother, The Middle Years,* ed. Frederick W. Dupee (New Jersey: Princeton University Press 1983).

_____, *Collected Travel Writings: Great Britain and America (English Hours, The American Scene, Other Travels)* (New York: The Library of America 1993).

James, Simon J., *Unsettled Accounts: Money and Narrative in the Novels of George Gissing* (London: Anthem Press 2003).

Jerrold, Blanchard, and Gustave Doré, *A London Pilgrimage,* 1872 (New York: Dover, 1970).

Jordan, Robert Furneaux, *Victorian Architecture* (Harmondsworth: Penguin 1966).

Joyce, Simon, *Capital Offenses: Geographies of Class and Crime in Victorian London* (Charlottesville: University of Virginia Press 2003).

Kafka, Franz, *The Trial,* trans. Breon Mitchell (New York: Schocken Books 1998).

Kellett, John R., *Railways and Victorian Cities* (London: Routledge and Kegan Paul 1969).

Kent, William, *London for Dickens Lovers* (London: Methuen 1935).

King, David, *The Complete Works of Robert and James Adam* (Oxford: Butterworth Architecture 1991).

King, Ross, 'Wordsworth, Panoramas, and the Prospect of London', *Studies in Romanticism* 32 (1933), 57–73.

Kingsford, Charles Lethbridge, *The Early History of Piccadilly, Leicester Square, Soho and their Neighbourhood, Based on a Plan Drawn in 1585 and Published by the London Topographical Society in 1925* (Cambridge: Cambridge University Press 1925).

Kimmey, John, *Henry James in London: The City in his Fiction* (New York: Peter Lang 1991).

Kitton, Frederic G., *Dickens and his Illustrators* (1899: Amsterdam: S. Emmering 1972).

_____, *The Dickens Country* (London: Adam and Charles Black 1905).

Klingender, Francis D., *Art and the Industrial Revolution*, revised by Arthur Elton (London: Paladin 1968).

Koepnick, Lutz, *Walter Benjamin and the Aesthetics of Power* (Lincoln: University of Nebraska Press 1999).

Kristeva, Julia, *Powers of Horror: An Essay on Abjection*, trans. Leon Roudiez (New York: Columbia University Press 1982).

Kynaston, David, *The City of London: vol 1: A World of its Own, 1815–1890* (London: Chatto and Windus 1994).

Lacan, Jacques, *The Four Fundamental Concepts of Psychoanalysis*, trans. Alan Sheridan (Harmondsworth: Penguin 1977).

_____, *The Ethics of Psychoanalysis 1959–1960: Seminar 7*, trans. Dennis Porter (London: Routledge 1992).

_____, 'Aggressiveness in Psychoanalysis', *Ecrits*, trans. Bruce Fink (New York: W.W. Norton 2002).

Lamb, Charles, *The Works of Charles and Mary Lamb*, ed. E.V. Lucas, 3 vols (London: Methuen 1903).

Lambourne, Lionel, *Victorian Painting* (London: Phaidon 1999).

Laporte, Dominique, *History of Shit*, trans. Nadia Benabid and Rodolphe El-Khoury (Cambridge, Mass.: MIT Press 2000).

Leavis, F.R., *The Great Tradition: George Eliot, Henry James, Joseph Conrad* (1948: Penguin 1993).

_____, *Dickens the Novelist* (London: Chatto and Windus 1970).

Ledger, Sally, *Dickens and the Popular Radical Imagination* (Cambridge: Cambridge University Press 2007).

Lee, Yoon Sun, 'A Divided Inheritance: Scott's Antiquarian Novel and the British Nation', *English Literary History* 64 (1997) 571–601, **562**

Lefebvre, Henri, *The Production of Space*, trans. Donald Nicholson-Smith (Oxford: Blackwell 1991).

Lehmann, John, *Holborn: An Historical Portrait of a London Borough* (London: Macmillan 1970).

Lister, Raymond, *Victorian Narrative Painting* (London: London Museum Press 1966).

Lukacher, Ned, *Primal Scenes: Literature, Philosophy, Psychoanalysis* (Ithaca: Cornell University Press 1988).

Lukács, Georg, *The Theory of the Novel*, trans. Anna Bostock (London: Merlin Press 1978).

Mace, Rodney, *Trafalgar Square: Emblem of Empire* (London: Lawrence and Wishart 2005).

MacMaster, Juliet, '"Better to be Silly": From Vision to Reality in *Barnaby Rudge*', *Dickens Studies Annual* 13 (1984), 1–17.

Maidment, Brian, *Dusty Bob: A Cultural History of Dustmen, 1780–1870* (Manchester: Manchester University Press 2007).

Mallett, Phillip, 'The City and the Self' in Michael Wheeler (ed.), *Ruskin and Environment* (Manchester: Manchester University Press 1995), 38–57.

Marcus, Sharon, *Apartment Stories: City and Home in Nineteenth-Century Paris and London* (Berkeley: University of California Press 1999).

Marcus, Steven, *Dickens from Pickwick to Dombey* (New York: Norton 1965).

Maré, Eric de, *Victorian London Revealed: Gustave Doré's Metropolis* (Harmondsworth: Penguin 2001).

Marriott, John (ed.), with Masaie Matsumura and Judith R. Walkowitz, *Unknown London: Early Modernist Visions of the Metropolis, 1815–45* (London: Pickering and Chatto), 6 vols, 2000.

Massey, Doreen, *World City* (Cambridge: Polity Press 2007).

Mayhew, H., *London Labour and the London Poor* (London: Frank Cass 1967).

Maxwell, Richard, *The Mysteries of Paris and London* (Charlottesville: University Press of Virginia 1992).

McKellar, Elizabeth, *The Birth of Modern London: The Development and Design of the City 1660–1720* (Manchester: Manchester University Press 1999), 193–97.

McLellan, David (ed.), *Karl Marx: Selected Writings* (Oxford: Oxford University Press 2000), 473–74.

Meckier, Jerome, 'Dating the Action in *Great Expectations*', *Dickens Studies Annual* 21 (1992), 157–94.

Merritt, J.F. (ed.). *Imagining Modern London: Perceptions and Portrayals of the City from Stow to Strype, 1598–1720* (Cambridge: Cambridge University Press 2001).

Metz, Nancy Aycock, '*Little Dorrit*'s London: Baylon Revisited', *Victorian Studies* 34 (1990), 465–86.

Mighall, Robert, *A Geography of Victorian Gothic Fiction: Mapping History's Nightmares* (Oxford: Oxford University Press 1999).

Miller, Jacques-Alain, 'Jeremy Bentham's Panoptic Device', trans. Richard Miller *October* 41 (1987), 3–29.

Miller, J. Hillis, *Charles Dickens: The World of his Novels* (Bloomington: Indiana University Press 1958).

———, 'The Topography of Jealousy in *Our Mutual Friend*', in John Schad (ed.), *Dickens Refigured: Bodies, Desires and Other Histories* (Manchester: Manchester University Press 1996), 218–35.

Miller, J. Hillis and David Borowitz, *George Cruikshank* (Los Angeles: William Andrews Clark Memorial Library 1971).

Moritz, Carl Philip, *Journals of a German in England in 1782*, trans. Reginald Nettel (London: Jonathan Cape 1965).

Morrison, Arthur, *A Child of the Jago* (1896: Woodbridge: Boydell Press 1982).

———, *Tales of Mean Streets* (1894: Woodbridge: Boydell Press 1983).

Morus, Iwan Rhys, 'The Electric Telegraph and Commercial Culture in Early Victorian England', *Victorian Studies* (1996), 339–78.

Mudford, Peter (ed.), *Master Humphrey's Clock* (London: Everyman: Dent 1997).

Nead, Lynda, *Victorian Babylon: People, Streets and Images in Nineteenth-Century London* (New Haven: Yale University Press 2000).

Nelson, Harland S., 'Dickens' *Our Mutual Friend* and Henry Mayhew's *London Labour and the London Poor*', *Nineteenth-Century Fiction* 20 (1965), 207–22.

Neuburg, Victor (ed.), *London Labour and the London Poor* (Harmondsworth: Penguin 1985).

Newlyn, Lucy, '"In City Pent": Echo and Allusion in Wordsworth, Coleridge and Lamb, 1797–1801', *Review of English Studies* 32 (1981).

Nietzsche, Friedrich, 'On the Uses and Disadvantages of History for Life', *Untimely Meditations*, trans. R.J. Hollingdale (Cambridge: Cambridge University Press 1983).

_____, *The Genealogy of Morals*, trans. Douglas Smith (Oxford: Oxford University Press 1996).

_____, *Thus Spoke Zarathustra*, trans. Graham Parkes (Oxford: Oxford University Press 2005).

Nord, Deborah Epstein, 'The City as Theater: From Georgian to Early Victorian London', *Victorian Studies* 31.2 (1988), 159–88.

_____, *Walking the Victorian Streets: Women, Representation, and the City* (Ithaca: Cornell University Press 1995).

Norton, Charles Eliot (ed.), *Early Letters of Thomas Carlyle*, vol. 2 1821–1826 (London: Macmillan 1886).

O'Connell, Sheila, *London 1753* (London: British Museum Press 2003).

Oetterman, Stephan, *The Panorama: History of a Mass Medium*, trans. Deborah Lucas Schneider (New York: Zone Books 1997).

Olsen, Donald J., *The Growth of Victorian London* (Harmondsworth: Penguin 1979).

Paroissien, David, *The Companion to 'Oliver Twist'* (Edinburgh: Edinburgh University Press 1992).

Patten, Robert L., *George Cruikshank's Life, Times and Art*, vol. 2: 1835–1878 (Cambridge: Lutterworth Press 1996).

Patterson, Clara Burdett, *Angela Burdett-Coutts and the Victorians* (London: John Murray 1953).

Paulson, Ronald, *Book and Painting: Shakespeare, Milton and the Bible* (Knoxville: University of Tennessee Press 1982), 82–98.

_____, (ed.), *Hogarth's Graphic Works* (London: The Print Room 1989).

Pevsner, Nikolaus, *The Buildings of England: London, Except the Cities of London and Westminster*, and *London I: The Cities of London and Westminster* (Harmondsworth: Penguin 1952 and 1957).

Philpotts, Trey, *The Companion to Little Dorrit* (London: Croom Helm 2003).

Pike, David L., *Subterranean Cities: The World Beneath Paris and London, 1800–1945* (Ithaca: Cornell University Press 2005).

Poole, Adrian, *Gissing in Context* (London: Macmillan 1995).

_____, 'The Shadow of Lear's "Houseless" in Dickens', *Shakespeare Survey* 53 (2006), 103–13.

Pope, Norris, *Dickens and Charity* (London: Macmillan 1978).

Porter, Roy, *London: A Social History* (Harmondsworth: Penguin 1996).

_____, 'Visitors' Visions: Travellers' Tales of Georgian London', in C. Chard and H. Langdon, *Transports: Travel, Pleasure, and Imaginative Geography, 1600–1830* (New Haven: Yale University Press 1996), 31–47.

Prendergast, Christopher, *Paris and the Nineteenth Century* (Oxford: Blackwell 1992).

Pritchard, Allan, 'The Urban Gothic of *Bleak House*', *Nineteenth-Century Literature* 45 (1991), 432–52.

Pykett, Lynn, *Charles Dickens: Critical Issues* (London: Macmillan 2002).

Quasha, George (ed.), *The Blanchot Reader* (Barrytown, NY: Station Hill 1999).

Quennell, Peter (ed.), *London's Underworld* (London: Spring Books 1950).

Radzinowicz, Leon and Roger Hood, 'Incapacitating the Habitual Criminal: The English Experience', *The Michigan Law Review* 78 (1980), 1305–89.

Rasmussen, Steen Eiler, *London: The Unique City* (1934: Harmondsworth: Penguin 1960).

Rawlinson, Barbara, *A Man of Many Parts: Gissing's Short Stories, Essays and Other Works* (Amsterdam: Rodopi 2006), 193–211.

Reid, Donald, *Paris Sewers and Sewermen: Realities and Representations* (Cambridge, Mass.: Harvard University Press 1991), 74–77, 95–106.

Rivers, Christopher, *Face Value: Physiognomical Thought and the Legible Body in Marivaux, Lavater, Balzac, Gautier, and Zola* (Madison: University of Wisconsin Press 1994).

Robb, Graham, *Strangers: Homosexual Love in the Nineteenth Century* (London: Picador 2003).

Robert, Somerville, *The Savoy: Manor: Hospital: Chapel* (London: The Savoy 1960).

Robertson, Alexander, *Atkinson Grimshaw*, (London: Phaidon 1988).

Robinson, Alan, *Imagining London, 1770–1900* (London: Palgrave 2004).

Robson, Catherine, 'Down Ditches, on Doorsteps, in Rivers: *Oliver Twist*'s Journey to Respectability', *Dickens Studies Annual* 29 (2000), 61–81.

Rose, Millicent, *The East End of London* (London: Cresset Press 1951).

Rosser, Gervase, *Medieval Westminster 1200–1540* (Oxford: Clarendon Press 1989).

Roundell, James, *Thomas Shotter Boys, 1803–1874* (London: Octopus 1974).

Royle, Edward, *Chartism*, 2nd edition (London: Longman 1986).

Rudé, George, *Hanoverian London, 1714–1808* (London: Secker and Warburg 1971).

_____, *Wilkes and Liberty: A Social Study* (London: Lawrence and Wishart 1983).

Ruskin, John, *Modern Painters*, 6 vols (London: George Allen 1897).

_____, *Praeterita: Outlines of Scenes and Thoughts Perhaps Worthy of Memory in My Past Life* (London: Rupert Hart-Davis 1948).

_____, 'Fors Clavigera', *Collected Works of John Ruskin*, 39 vols, ed. E.T. Cook and Alexander Wedderburn (London: George Allen 1904), 29.106.

Russell, Norman, *The Novelist and Mammon: Literary Responses to the World of Commerce in the Nineteenth Century* (Oxford: Clarendon 1986).

Ryle, Martin and Jenny Bourne Taylor (eds), *George Gissing: Voices of the Unclassed* (Aldershot: Ashgate 2005).

Sala, George Augustus, *Twice Round the Clock: Or, The Hours of the Day and Night in London* (Leicester: Leciester University Press 1971).

Sales, Roger, 'Pierce Egan and the Representation of London', in *Reviewing Romanticism*, ed. Philip W. Martin and Robin Jarvis (London: Macmillan 1992).

Samuel, Raphael, *Theatres of Memory, vol. 1: Past and Present in Contemporary Culture*, and *vol. 2: Island Stories: Unravelling Britain*, ed. Alison Light, Sally Alexander and Gareth Stedman-Jones (London: Verso 1994 and 1998).

Sanders, Andrew, *The Companion to 'A Tale of Two Cities'* (London: Unwin Hyman 1988).

Schivelbusch, W., *The Railway Journey: The Industrialisation of Time and Space in the Nineteenth Century* (Berkeley: University of California Press 1986).

Schlicke, Paul, 'Embracing the New Spirit of the Age: Dickens and the Evolution of *The Old Curiosity Shop*', *Dickens Studies Annual* 32 (2002), 1–36.

Schneer, Jonathan, *The Thames* (New Haven: Yale University Press 2005).

Schwarzbach, F.S., *Dickens and the City* (London: Althlone Press 1979).

_____, '*Bleak House*: The Social Pathology of Everyday Life' in Peter W. Graham and Elizabeth Sewell, *Literature and Medicine*, vol. 9 (Baltimore: Johns Hopkins University Press 1990), 93–104.

Scott, Walter, *The Antiquary*, ed. David Hewitt (Harmondsworth: Penguin 1998).

Seigel, Jerrold, *Bohemian Paris: Culture, Politics and the Boundaries of Bourgeois Life, 1830–1930* (Harmondsworth: Penguin 1986).

Shapiro, Gary, 'Dogs, Domestication, and the Ego' in Christa Davis Acampora and Ralph R. Acampora (eds), *A Nietzschean Bestiary: Becoming Animal Beyond Docile and Brutal* (Lanham, Md.: Rowman and Littlefield 2004).

Shatto, Susan, *A Companion to Bleak House* (London: Unwin Hyman 1988).

Sheppard, Francis, *London 1808–1870: The Infernal Wen* (London: Secker and Warburg, 1971).

_____, *London: A History* (Oxford: Oxford University Press 1998).

Sicher, Efraim, *Rereading the City, Rereading Dickens: Representation, the Novel, and Urban Realism* (Brooklyn, NY: AMS Press Inc. 2003).

Simmel, Georg, *On Individuality and Social Forms: Selected Writings*, ed. Donald N. Levine (Chicago: University of Chicago Press 1971).

Sinclair, Ian, *The London Orbital: A Walk Round the M25* (Cambridge: Granta 2002).

Smollett, Tobias, *The Expedition of Humphrey Clinker*, ed. Angus Ross (Harmondsworth: Penguin 1967).

Spear, Jeffrey L., 'Of Jews and Ships and Mob Attacks, Of Catholics and Kings: The Curious Career of Lord George Gordon', *Dickens Studies Annual* 32 (2002), 65–106.

Spence, Craig, *London in the 1690s: A Social Atlas* (University of London Institute for Historical Research: Centre for Metropolitan History 2000).

Stedman-Jones, Gareth, *Outcast London: A Study in the Relationships between Classes in Victorian Society* (1971: Harmondsworth: Penguin 1984).

Stein, Richard L., *Victoria's Year: English Literature and Culture 1837–1838* (Oxford: Oxford University Press 1987).

Stevenson, John (ed.), *London in the Age of Reform* (Oxford: Basil Blackwell 1977).

Stone, Harry, *The Night Side of Dickens: Cannibalism, Passion, Necessity* (Columbus: Ohio State University Press 1994).

Stow, John, *The Survey of London* (1598: London: Dent, 1945).

Summerson, John, *Georgian London*, 3rd edition (Harmondsworth: Penguin 1978).

Taithe, Bertrand, *The Essential Mayhew: Representing and Communicating the Poor* (London: Rivers Oram Press 1996).

Tallis, John, *London Street Views 1838–1840*, revised and enlarged 1847, ed. Peter Jackson (London: London Topographical Society 2002).

Tambling, Jeremy, *Confession: Sexuality, Sin, the Subject* (Manchester: Manchester University Press 1990).

_____, *Dickens, Violence and the Modern State: Dreams of the Scaffold* (London: Macmillan 1995).

_____, *Henry James: Critical Issues* (London: Palgrave Macmillan 2000).

_____, *Becoming Posthumous: Life and Death in Literary and Cultural Studies* (Edinburgh: Edinburgh University Press 2001).

_____, *Lost in the American City: Dickens, James, Kafka* (London: Palgrave 2001).

_____, 'No Thoroughfare: Charting De Quincey's *Confessions*' in Laurent Bury (ed.), *Confessions of an English Opium-Eater* (Paris: Ellipses 2003), 59–72.

_____, *Blake's Night Thoughts* (London: Macmillan 2004).

_____, 'Sameness and Otherness: Versions of Authority in *Hard Times*', *Textus* 19 (2006), 439–60.

_____, 'Carlyle Through Nietzsche: Reading *Sartor Resartus*', *Modern Language Review* 102 (2007), 326–40.

Thackeray, William Makepeace, *The History of Pendennis: His Fortunes and Misfortunes, His Friends and His Greatest Enemy*, ed. John Sutherland (Oxford: Oxford University Press 1999).

_____, *The Newcomes: Memoirs of a Most Respectable Family*, ed. David Pascoe (Harmondsworth: Penguin 1996).

_____, *Vanity Fair: A Novel without a Hero*, ed. John Sutherland (Oxford: Oxford University Press 1999).

Thompson, E.P., *The Making of the English Working Class* (Harmondsworth: Penguin 1968).

Thompson, E.P. and Eileen Yeo, *The Unknown Mayhew: Selections from the Morning Chronicle, 1849–1850* (Hamondsworth: Penguin 1973).

Tiedemann, Rolf, 'Dialectics at a Standstill: Approaches to the *Passagen-Werk*' in Gary Smith (ed.), *On Walter Benjamin: Critical Essays and Recollections* (Cambridge, Mass.: MIT Press 1988).

Timbs, John, *Curiosities of London: Exhibiting the Most Rare and Remarkable Objects of Interest in the Metropolis, With Nearly Fifty Years' Personal Recollections* (London: Daniel Bogue 1855).

Tindall, Gillian, *The Born Exile: George Gissing* (London: Temple Smith 1974).

Tomalin, Claire, *The Invisible Woman: The Story of Nelly Ternan and Charles Dickens* (Harmondsworth: Penguin 1991).

Tracy, Robert, '"The Old Story" and Inside Stories: Modish Fiction and Fictional Modes in *Oliver Twist*', *Dickens Studies Annual* 18 (1988), 20.

_____, 'Clock Work: *The Old Curiosity Shop* and *Barnaby Rudge*', *Dickens Studies Annual* 30 (2001), 23–43.

_____, 'Lighthousekeeping: *Bleak House* and the Crystal Palace', *Dickens Studies Annual* 33 (2003), 25–53.

Trench, Richard, and Ellis Hillman, *London Under London: A Subterranean Guide* (London: John Murray 1993).

Trilling, Lionel, *The Opposing Self* (Oxford: Oxford University Press 1980).

Tristan, Flora, *The London Journal of Flora Tristan 1842, Or, The Aristocracy and the Working Class of England*, trans. Jean Hawkes (London: Virago 1982).

Trollope, Anthony, *Anthony Trollope: The Complete Short Stories*, vol. 2 (London: The Trollope Society 1991).

Trotter, David, *Circulation: Defoe, Dickens and the Economics of the Novel* (London: Macmillan 1988).

_____, *Cooking with Mud: The Idea of Mess in Nineteenth-Century Art and Fiction* (Oxford: Oxford University Press 2000).

Veblen, Thorstein, *The Theory of the Leisure Class*, ed. Alan Wolfe and James Danly (New York: Modern Library 2001).

Walder, Dennis, *Dickens and Religion* (London: Allen and Unwin 1981).

Walkowitz, Judith, *Prostitution and Victorian Society: Women, Class, and the State* (Cambridge: Cambridge University Press 1980).

_____, *City of Dreadful Delight* (Chicago: Chicago University Press 1992).

Weinreb, Ben, and Christopher Hibbert (eds), *The London Encyclopaedia* (London: Macmillan 1992).

Weiss, Barbara, *The Hell of the English: Bankruptcy in the Victorian Novel* (Lewisburg: Bucknell University Press 1986).

Welsh, Alexander, *The City of Dickens* (Cambridge, Mass.: Harvard University Press 1986).

_____, *Dickens Redressed: The Art of Bleak House and Hard Times* (New Haven: Yale University Press 2000).

White, Jerry, *The Worst Street in North London: Campbell Bunk, Islington, Between the Wars* (London: Routledge 1976).

_____, *London in the Twentieth Century* (London: Viking 2001).

_____, *London in the Nineteenth Century* (London: Jonathan Cape 2007).

Wiener, Martin J., *Reconstructing the Criminal: Culture, Law and Policy in England, 1830–1914* (Cambridge: Cambridge University Press 1990).

Williams, Katherine, 'Glass Windows: The View from *Bleak House*', *Dickens Studies Annual* 33 (2003), 55–85.

Williams, Raymond, *The English Novel from Dickens to Lawrence* (London: Chatto and Windus 1970).

Wohl, Anthony, *The Eternal Slum: Housing and Social Policy in Victorian London* (London: Edward Arnold 1977).

Wohlfarth, Irving, 'Et Cetera? The Historian as Chiffonier', *New German Critique* 39 (1986), 142–68.

Wolff, Janet, 'The Invisible Flâneuse' in *Feminine Sentences: Essays on Women and Culture* (Polity Press: Cambridge 1990), 34–50.

Wolfreys, Julian, *Writing London: The Trace of the Urban Text from Blake to Dickens* (London: Macmillan 1998).

Wordsworth, William, *The Prelude, 1799, 1805, 1850*, ed. Jonathan Wordsworth, M.H Abrams and Stephen Gill (New York: W.W. Norton 1979).

INDEX

This is principally an index of names, though some topics are included. Names appearing solely in the Bibliography do not appear here, while names from the Endnotes appear when the notes contain additional information about them. Numbers in bold refer to photographs.

INDEX OF LONDON SITES

The Index gives places named in the text and in the Gazetteer, but cannot be quite exhaustive (it is sometimes not even possible to decide whether we are considering two streets or one, or how to designate some areas). Nor is it possible to ensure complete consistency regarding the accidentals in names, whether in spelling, or in how compound words combine to form a name (St Martin-in-the-Fields / Saint Martin in the Fields, with or without a possessive (St Martin's): the differences involved here are only some of the inconsistencies which must be worked with. Numbers in bold refer to photographs.